Ius Gentium: Comparative Perspectives on Law and Justice

Volume 106

Ius Gentium is a book series which discusses the central questions of law and justice from a comparative perspective. The books in this series collect the contrasting and overlapping perspectives of lawyers, judges, philosophers and scholars of law from the world's many different jurisdictions for the purposes of comparison, harmonisation, and the progressive development of law and legal institutions. Each volume makes a new comparative study of an important area of law. This book series continues the work of the well-known journal of the same name and provides the basis for a better understanding of all areas of legal science.

The *Ius Gentium* series provides a valuable resource for lawyers, judges, legislators, scholars, and both graduate students and researchers in globalisation, comparative law, legal theory and legal practice. The series has a special focus on the development of international legal standards and transnational legal cooperation.

Howard Chitimira • Tapiwa Victor Warikandwa

Editors

Financial Inclusion and Digital Transformation Regulatory Practices in Selected SADC Countries

South Africa, Namibia, Botswana and Zimbabwe

 Springer

Editors
Howard Chitimira
Faculty of Law
North-West University
Mmabatho, South Africa

Tapiwa Victor Warikandwa
School of Law
University of Namibia
Windhoek, Namibia

ISSN 1534-6781   ISSN 2214-9902   (electronic)
Ius Gentium: Comparative Perspectives on Law and Justice
ISBN 978-3-031-23865-9   ISBN 978-3-031-23863-5   (eBook)
https://doi.org/10.1007/978-3-031-23863-5

This Springer imprint is published by the registered company Springer Nature Switzerland AG
The registered company address is: Gewerbestrasse 11, 6330 Cham, Switzerland

Preface

In order to examine the progress made toward achieving financial inclusion in the Southern Africa Development Community (SADC) region and to offer guidance on the topic to the rest of Africa and other regional blocs around the world, this book project was deemed necessary by the editors. The premise of the book is the knowledge that, generally speaking, financial inclusion in the SADC area is low and varies greatly between nations. 41.9 million people (34%) still do not have access to official or informal financial services or products, despite the fact that more than half of adults (66%) in the SADC region are financially included, which is 12% higher than the continent-wide average. In addition, there are significant differences among the region's nations in terms of access levels and the standard of financial inclusion.

The central premise of the book project is the recognition that financial inclusion is a key enabler of the Sustainable Development Goals (SDGs) of the United Nations, which include the eradication of poverty and ensuring economic development, among other goals. The book project's central thesis is to argue for more policies and laws to be adopted in order to expand the space of financial inclusion in the region. When interpreting this, it is important to keep in mind that when SADC Member States signed the SADC Treaty in 1992, they agreed to collaborate in order to: (1) achieve development and economic growth; (2) reduce poverty; (3) raise the standard of living for Southern Africans; and (4) support the socially disadvantaged through regional integration. The SADC Treaty serves as the foundation for a number of initiatives aimed at eradicating poverty via collaborative, sustainable development in a number of crucial sectors, including financial services. In order to speed up financial inclusion programs in all SADC Member States, the SADC Council of Ministers approved the SADC Strategy on Financial Inclusion and Small and Medium Enterprises Access to Finance in September 2016.

The 16 authors of this book, who are all authorities in fields related to law and economics, will make the case that in order to ensure inclusivity, equal access to opportunities, and regional economic growth and development, people and businesses need to have access to a variety of financial institutions and products in a stable competitive market. The SADC region will experience sustainable growth and development once all economic sectors and the entire population have access to and are proficient users of relevant financial services to meet their needs. The SDGs will also be realized. Thus, the book emphasizes the adoption of strategies to promote financial inclusion in SADC (and beyond) and reduce the costs of cross-border payments using, among other mechanisms, digital financial inclusion.

Thus, the approach for SADC's financial inclusion is discussed in this book. In a few SADC member states, the authors analyse stakeholder involvement, policy and regulatory alignment, and strategy creation. The authors also attempt to address the particular difficulties, demands, and conditions present in the selected jurisdictions. In addition, the authors propose that SADC member states coordinate their policy and regulatory measures to address regional concerns and promote regional financial integration.

The various concerns relating to financial inclusion in the SADC area will be examined in this book. Financial inclusion refers to the availability to both individuals and businesses of useful and cost-effective financial goods and services, including payments, transactions, savings, credit, and insurance, that are provided in a sustainable and ethical manner. Financial inclusion has received attention since it is associated with both economic expansion and the reduction of poverty. This is why one of the main goals of this book project is to align financial inclusion as a policy and regulatory tool in addressing the difficulties in achieving the Sustainable Development Goals (SDGs). Seven of the 17 Sustainable Development Goals are made possible by financial inclusion, according to this goal. The relationship between financial inclusion and the macroeconomic sphere is becoming more prominent, and this report uses data on personal, business, and governmental payments to relate observed financial inclusion metrics to potential implications for macroeconomic factors like economic growth, employment, wages, and poverty.

It will be argued that financial inclusion makes it possible for individuals and organizations within SADC to engage in economic activity and, consequently, trade. The importance of financial inclusion in transforming the informal to the formal business sector will be emphasized as well as its necessity for company growth. The growth engines for intra-African trade will be small firms, which are more likely to lack access to capital, for example, especially in the digital age (particularly in the context of the recently launched Africa Continental Free Trade Area Agreement).

However, the book will make the case that people and enterprises must be financially included in order for such a purpose to be realized. Thus, ensuring economic transformation and progress in the SADC area requires financial inclusion. The concerns of digital financial inclusion are one of the main theme areas that will be covered in the book. Some authors in the book will discuss how the concepts of digital financial inclusion must be adopted in the SADC region if financial inclusion is to be fully realized. The ongoing COVID-19 crisis and the associated economic shocks have impacted the book's discussion of the need for digital financial inclusion.

Digital financial inclusion entails the use of cost-effective digital means to provide populations that are currently underserved and financially excluded with a variety of formal financial services that are responsibly delivered at a cost that is affordable for customers and sustainable for providers. The World Bank Group views financial inclusion as a critical facilitator to reduce extreme poverty and increase shared prosperity, hence this is one of the project's main goals.

Daily life is made easier by having access to money, which also helps families and businesses prepare for everything from long-term objectives to unanticipated emergencies. Since a transaction account enables people to keep money and send and receive payments, having access to one is a first step toward greater financial inclusion. Account holders are more likely to use additional financial services like credit and insurance to launch and grow enterprises, make investments in their children's or own health or education, manage risk, and recover from financial setbacks, all of which can enhance their overall quality of life.

A transaction account acts as a portal to other financial services, therefore ensuring that people in SADC can access one remains a priority for the region, particularly when it comes to intra-African trade. Most significantly, the completion of the 2020 World Bank Group's Universal Financial Access effort will increase the emphasis on financial inclusion in this book. The benefits of financial inclusion as well as possible and current obstacles to realizing it in SADC will also be covered in the book.

Therefore, in general, the book covers topics relating to financial inclusion and the progress made in the region toward achieving financial inclusion. Implicit in this strategy is the notion that previously underserved and excluded poor clients are shown to advance towards financial inclusion. To help marginalized people transition from only utilizing cash for transactions to formal financial services that can be accessed using a mobile phone or other digital technologies, financial education-related issues will also be covered. The discussions in the book may be instructional to other economic blocs around the world. These advancements will contribute to sustainable development in the SADC.

This book's chapters have each undergone a double-blind peer review by reviewers to ascertain their academic rigour and suitability for publication.

Mmabatho, South Africa   Howard Chitimira
Windhoek, Namibia   Tapiwa Victor Warikandwa

Contents

Contributors

Howard Chitimira Faculty of Law, North-West University, Potchefstroom, South Africa

Tinashe Chuchu Marketing Division, University of Witwatersrand, Johannesburg, South Africa

Sharon Handongwe Cheshire Homes Society of Zambia National Office, Lusaka, Zambia

Martha N. Jonas Department of Higher Education and Lifelong Learning, University of Namibia, Windhoek, Namibia

Alex T. Kanyimba Department of Higher Education and Lifelong Learning, University of Namibia, Windhoek, Namibia

Herbert Kawadza School of Law, University of the Witwatersrand, Johannesburg, South Africa

Tinashe Kondo Department of Mercantile and Labour Law, University of the Western Cape, Cape Town, South Africa

Vivienne A. Lawack Department of Mercantile and Labour Law, University of the Western Cape, Cape Town, South Africa

Eugene L. Libebe School of Law, Faculty of Commerce, Management and Law, University of Namibia, Windhoek, Namibia

Nombulelo Lubisi Faculty of Law, University of Fort Hare, East London, South Africa

Charles Makanyeza Namibia Business School, University of Namibia, Windhoek, Namibia

Clement Marumoagae School of Law, University of the Witwatersrand, Johannesburg, South Africa
Faculty of Law, University of Lesotho, Maseru, Lesotho

Tshepo H. Mongalo School of Law, University of the Witwatersrand, Johannesburg, South Africa

Shelton T. Mota Makore Faculty of Law, University of Fort Hare, East London, South Africa

Dumisani R. Muzira Department of Agribusiness & Management, Marondera University of Agricultural Sciences and Technology, Marondera, Zimbabwe

Menelisi Ncube Faculty of Law, North-West University, Potchefstroom, South Africa

Emmanuel Ndhlovu Vaal University of Technology, Vanderbijlpark, South Africa

Brighton Nyagadza Department of Marketing, Marondera University of Agricultural Sciences and Technology, Marondera, Zimbabwe

Patrick C. Osode Faculty of Law, University of Fort Hare, East London, South Africa

Clemence Rusenga School for Policy Studies, University of Bristol, Bristol, United Kingdom

Elize Shakalela School of Law, Faculty of Commerce, Management and Law, University of Namibia, Windhoek, Namibia

Tendai Douglas Svotwa Department of Graduate Studies, Botho University, Gaborone, Botswana

Maphuti D. Tuba Department of Mercantile Law, University of South Africa, Johannesburg, South Africa

Tapiwa Victor Warikandwa School of Law, University of Namibia, Windhoek, Namibia

Eukeria Wealth School of Law, Faculty of Commerce, Management and Law, University of Namibia, Windhoek, Namibia

Financial Inclusion as an Enabler of United Nations Sustainable Development Goals in the Twenty-First Century: An Introduction

Howard Chitimira and Tapiwa Victor Warikandwa

Abstract Financial inclusion attempts to provide digital financial solutions to a country's economically disadvantaged citizens. It also plans to introduce mobile banking or financial services to reach the poorest individuals living in the country's most distant places. The process of providing appropriate financial services to the "unbanked" (individuals or businesses) in a cheap, sustainable, and ethical manner is referred to as financial inclusion. This can include traditional credit through banking and insurance products, as well as saving mechanisms for healthcare or education, as well as investment items, allowing citizens to benefit even more from their economy's rapid growth. Increased financial inclusion has been found to boost economic development, potentially raising GDP by up to 14% in emerging markets and 30% in frontier nations. According to World Bank statistics, 1.7 billion individuals worldwide, or 31% of the adult population, do not have access to financial services. Asia accounts for half of the unbanked population, with Africa accounting for 25% and Latin America accounting for 10%. Women make up a large share of the unbanked population. As a result, more financial inclusion can lead to greater gender equality. Financial inclusion, according to this chapter, is a crucial enabler of the United Nations Sustainable Development Goals (SDGs), which will be a key driver of poverty reduction and shared global economic success. This is significant for investors because economic growth is a key long-term driver of company sales and earnings, which in turn helps to underpin asset prices. Financial inclusion's importance is underlined by being an aim in no fewer than seven of the 17 SDGs. The chapter will also serve as a synopsis of the book's 16 chapters, all of which were authored by specialists in the field.

H. Chitimira
Faculty of Law, North West University, Potchefstroom, South Africa
e-mail: Howard.Chitimira@nwu.ac.za

T. V. Warikandwa (✉)
School of Law, University of Namibia, Windhoek, Namibia
e-mail: twarikandwa@unam.na

H. Chitimira, T. V. Warikandwa (eds.), *Financial Inclusion and Digital Transformation Regulatory Practices in Selected SADC Countries*, Ius Gentium: Comparative Perspectives on Law and Justice 106, https://doi.org/10.1007/978-3-031-23863-5_1

1 Introduction

The United Nations (UN) 2030 Sustainable Development Goals (SDGs) place a high priority on financial inclusion, with eight of the 17 goals including it as a primary aim.[1] These include SDG 1, which focuses on eliminating poverty, SDG 2, which aims to end hunger, achieve food security, and promote sustainable agriculture, SDG 3, which prioritizes health and well-being, SDG 5, which aims to achieve gender equality and give women economic empowerment, SDG 8, which encourages economic growth and jobs, SDG 9, which supports industry, innovation, and infrastructure, and SDG 10, which focuses on reducing inequality.[2] SDG 17 on improving the means of implementation, which focuses on increasing savings mobilization for investment and consumption that can spur growth, also acknowledges the implicit role for broader financial inclusion.[3]

The 17 SDGs of the UN do not explicitly mention financial inclusion, but it may be deduced that it is one of the primary enablers of developmental goals.[4] It is simple to identify goals like inclusive growth and more equality among others, but there is no explicit mention of goals like ensuring that everyone has access to savings accounts, loans, insurance, and other financial services.[5] We do not think that those who formulated the plausible SDGs intended to explicitly exclude direct mention of issues related to financial inclusion. Instead, we will demonstrate in this chapter how the SDGs might advance issues relating to financial inclusion. The views put forward by various contributors in this book will be guided by amongst other issues, the conceptual framework on SDGs and financial inclusion that is laid forth in this chapter.

The accomplishment of more broad development goals as well as overall economic growth can be supported by financial inclusion. In a 2016 study by the McKinsey Global Institute, it was shown that digital finance alone may benefit billions of people by promoting inclusive growth and raising the Gross Domestic Product of emerging countries by \$3.7 trillion over the course of 10 years.[6] According to the results of a long-term impact study on the M-PESA mobile money service in Kenya, mobile money has successfully improved the economic well-being of low-income women and members of households headed by women, as well as helped an estimated 200,000 households, or an equivalent of 2% of the country's population, escape poverty.[7] Moreover, there is growing evidence that financial inclusion promotes domestic savings, boosts tax collection, and improves economic and financial stability.

---

[1] United Nations (n.d.) https://sdgs.un.org/2030agenda. Accessed 10 July 2022.

[2] United Nations (n.d.) https://sdgs.un.org/2030agenda. Accessed 10 July 2022.

[3] United Nations Capital Development Fund (n.d.-a).

[4] Klapper et al. (2016), p. 1, para. 2.

[5] Klapper (2016).

[6] McKinsey Global Institute (2016), p. 2.

[7] Kuzmina (2018).

The last mile financing strategies used by the UN Capital Development Fund (UNCDF) help banks, cooperatives, microfinance organizations, money transfer businesses, and mobile network providers expand the reach of financial markets where they would not otherwise go.[8] The UNCDF makes sure that appropriate financial products (savings, credit, insurance, payments, and remittances) are accessible to people, particularly the excluded and underbanked, as well as micro, small, and medium-sized businesses, at a fair price and in a sustainable manner.[9] The UNCDF focuses on women in particular because there is emerging evidence that having access to savings leads to better economic outcomes for women, including higher productivity, earnings, and investments in their companies.[10] Savings also reduces the likelihood that women may sell assets to pay for medical crises, stabilizes their earnings during economic shocks, and gives them more financial autonomy.

The Southern African Development Community (SADC) and the rest of Africa should view financial inclusion as a top priority. By broadening financial inclusion, the population's economic potential to fight poverty and promote income distribution is developed. The goal of this study is to examine how financial inclusion relates to the SADC region's progress toward achieving the SDGs in terms of reducing poverty. This chapter introduces the ideological and contextual framework to this book project. It also provides an outline of the chapters to be presented in the book.

2   Contextual Background to Financial Inclusion

Financial inclusion, according to the World Bank, is the availability to people and businesses of useful and reasonably priced financial products and services that satisfy their needs for transactions, payments, savings, credit, and insurance that are provided in a sustainable and responsible manner.[11] Financial inclusion involves not only the availability and use of financial services by people and enterprises, but also the aspect of product and service delivery quality. It is also essential for responsible financial growth and well-being, both for an individual and the economy as a whole. To achieve the worldwide objective of Universal Financial Access (UFA) by 2020, a comprehensive strategy that considers both the supply side and the demand side must be used, according to the World Bank.[12]

---

[8] United Nations Capital Development Fund (n.d.-b).
[9] UNCDF (2020).
[10] UNCDF (n.d.).
[11] The World Bank (2022).
[12] The World Bank (2020).

2.1 Important Signs of Financial Inclusion

Having access to a transaction account that enables people to exchange and save money is the first and most important step towards greater financial inclusion. Therefore, the most important aspect of financial inclusion is to make sure that everyone has transaction accounts.[13] Financial access opens the door to a variety of financial services, including managing short-term financial needs, long-term planning, and even making plans for unforeseeable future events. However, the goal of financial inclusion cannot be attained by merely having an account. The use of these financial services, which is the second dimension of financial inclusion, must therefore get equal attention.[14]

The Global Findex database estimates that between 2014 and 2017, 515 million adults worldwide created an account at a financial institution or through a mobile money provider. In comparison to 62% in 2014 and 51% in 2011, approximately 69% of adults currently have an account. Adult women make up about 65% of the population. Adults make or receive payments in the amount of 52%. A formal financial institution has accounts with about 87% of SME's. Around 30% of people globally have received government transfers or wages that were paid straight into their accounts.[15] By adhering to the G20 High-Level Principles for Digital Financial Inclusion, UFA by 2020, the Sustainable Development Goals, national financial inclusion strategies, financial consumer protection and literacy, and many other initiatives already taken in this direction, the economies around the world are moving closer to the goal of financial inclusion, as shown by the facts above.

2.2 Sustainable Development Goals and Financial Inclusion

The UN General Assembly adopted a new set of development objectives in September 2015 known as the SDGs, for the year 2030. The agenda for these goals was established after years of discussion and debate, and it has received the support of 193 of the General Assembly's members, including both developed and developing states. The SDGs are a group of 17 objectives.[16] The accomplishment of sustainable development objectives is aided by financial inclusion. It provides a wide range of advantages, including higher earning potential, increased female entrepreneurship, lower transaction costs, simple capital accumulation, increased usage of digital platforms, amongst other things. Increasing access to financial services has cleared the path for the accomplishment of a number of sustainable development

---

[13] Maas (2018).

[14] Global Partnership for Financial Inclusion (n.d.).

[15] The World Bank (2021).

[16] UN Department of Economic and Social Affairs: Sustainable Development. https://sustainabledevelopment.un.org/sdgs. Accessed 7 July 2022.

objectives, even though financial inclusion does not specifically aim to achieve the SDGs.[17] According to the World Bank, some of the 17 SDGs have been highlighted as being enabled by financial inclusion.

Enhanced financial inclusion can help accomplish some SDGs. For example, people in SADC countries or any country can have better access to money and other associated financial services if they have better access to financial services, especially in the remote areas.[18] This makes it possible for individuals to escape poverty, enabling the achievement of SDG 1, which places emphasis on eradicating extreme poverty. Persons employed in primary sectors such as agriculture and fisheries sector can manage their finances during the planting or fishing season and produce larger yields thanks to better and enhanced access to avenues for raising cash, access to insurance, and improved credit facilities.[19] This not only improves food production in the country but also generates food security in the economy, which is SDG 2 relating to reducing hunger and promoting food security. Increased planting season investments can result from farmers' financial inclusion. Higher yields and progress toward better food security are the results as envisaged in SDG 2. Malawian farmers boosted their spending on equipment by 13% and their crop output's worth by 21% after having their revenues transferred into a new bank account.[20]

In pursuit of SDG 2 as well, small-scale fisheries households and their enterprises are likely to have few choices for financing and managing cash flow for personal necessities or business investments due to the marginalized coastal and inland communities' restricted access to financial institutions in nations like Namibia.[21] Informal lenders, who may also be the main consumers of fish or the boat owners, fill the access gap. Financial inclusion can boost a household's financial resilience in rural and marginalized coastal fishing communities.[22] Therefore, it is necessary to remove the current obstacles to financial inclusion of SSF households in the SADC region. These obstacles include low financial capability and literacy, a lack of assets for collateral, physical distance from a financial institution, and a lack of formal identification. Financial literacy, de-risking financial institutions, financial data collection, the provision of a range of financial services other than credit, and client understanding are some of the solutions to these problems that must be offered in order to allow fishing households to maintain control over their earnings and savings.[23] Particularly among the SSF sector in nations like Namibia, financial inclusion can assist minimize the various vulnerabilities of low-income inland and coastal fishing households and rural communities and boost economic resilience.[24]

---

[17] United Nations Conference on Trade and Development (2015).

[18] Hope (2018).

[19] Oxford Business Group (2017).

[20] Klapper (2016).

[21] Food and Agriculture Organisation of the UN (2020).

[22] Prathap (2011), pp. 79–105.

[23] Pomeroy et al. (2020). See also Stopler and Walter (2017), p. 581.

[24] Matongela (2014), p. 171.

When people are able to come out of the poverty line, are ensured of their food security, have access to various insurance facilities there is greater likelihood that SDG 3 relating to achieving good health and well-being, is bound to fall in place.[25] Financial inclusion can promote health in the context of SDG 3. Parents can use a savings account to pay for their children's clinic visits. One of the main factors keeping individuals in poverty is the cost of health care out of pocket.[26] Giving them a secure place to put money, for instance, increased health spending by 66%, according to a Kenyan research.[27] It has been noted in Jordan that insurance can assist women in managing health-related shocks and covering treatment expenditures that might otherwise disrupt their economic activity and cause them to lose income.[28]

The availability of more funding options has removed the obstacle of financial constraints that restrict people from pursuing higher education. The SDG 4, which focuses on fostering high-quality education, is achieved with the aid of parents investing in their children's education.[29] Financial inclusion has also inspired women business owners to pursue endeavours that were previously out of reach for them. Promoting gender equality (SDG 5), requires increased women's empowerment.[30] The connection between smaller aims and bigger socio-economic goals becomes weaker when there is financial exclusivity. These five SDGs provide as a solid foundation for accomplishing other, more general socioeconomic objectives like SDG 8's aim of "Promoting shared economic growth" and SDG 9's goal of "Promoting innovation and sustainable industrialization".[31]

Given the correlation between financial inclusion and overall economic growth, it can be inferred that financial inclusivity merits further attention as will be done in this book project. Without financial inclusion, achieving the SDGs will probably be a more difficult goal for SADC and the rest of Africa.[32] Due to the connection between financial inclusion and development, many more individuals need to be included in the banking system or have access to financial services. The role that financial inclusion may play in achieving numerous SDGs, among other concerns, will be highlighted in this book project by academics with a wide spectrum of experience in the discourse. As already alluded to in this chapter, most of the objectives of the SDGs such as eradicating poverty, generating jobs, enhancing gender equality, and promoting good health are directly related to financial inclusion. Because those who can use financial services have greater protection and privacy over their money, financial inclusion is a crucial method for assuring

---

[25] The World Bank (2013).

[26] The World Bank (2014).

[27] The World Bank (2019).

[28] Avitsian (2020).

[29] United Nations International Children's Emergency Fund (2018).

[30] Robino et al. (2020).

[31] Ahmed (2019), pp. 1–17.

[32] Lipper and Benton (2020).

economic growth and development in SADC. For example, savings accounts make it simpler for people to save, which encourages more saving and increased income. This was observed in Nepal where offering women a straightforward bank account raised their assets by 16%.[33] In India, a government initiative to establish banks in rural areas assisted in reducing rural poverty by as much as 17 percentage points.[34]

Increasing account ownership would support SDG 5's goal of gender equality. Consider that the majority of those who are financially excluded—1.1 billion adults—are impoverished women.[35] Female market vendors in Kenya who received savings accounts saw a 37% increase in daily spending compared to a similar group of women who did not.[36] Digital technology can also promote financial inclusion and assist realize important SDG goals.[37] Digital financial payment solutions, such as a mobile phone connected to a bank account, enable people to borrow money from distant family and friends during a time of need, lowering the likelihood that they would become impoverished.[38] Users of Kenya's M-Pesa mobile phone-based money platform are more likely to receive remittances when confronted with a financial shock, such as a job loss, according to a study of the program.[39]

There is mounting evidence that digitizing payments for health, education, and other social safety nets not only increases efficiency for governments and aid organizations by lowering transaction costs and leakage, but also benefits individuals greatly. In India, automating government transfers reduced the need for bribes by 47% and increased beneficiary payouts by omitting middlemen who stole money.[40] Further, there are still differences in how digital financial services are used across areas, despite more access to them. Compared to 9% of individuals in the Middle East, 46% of adults in Europe and Central Asia use at least one sort of digital payment.[41] Mobile devices contribute to the expansion of financial services, particularly for those who live in rural areas that are underserved by conventional banks. Adults in sub-Saharan Africa use mobile money accounts to make 12% of phone-based payments, with Kenya having the highest percentage at 55%.[42]

Governments should continue pushing for greater access to and usage of financial services, according to the core thesis of this book, given the connection between financial inclusion and development. Putting financial services first does not deprive other SDG goals of resources. The evidence obtained so far actually makes a compelling case that financial inclusion contributes to the conditions that make

---

[33] Salman and Nowacka (2020), p. 3.

[34] Government of India (2020).

[35] Klapper (2016).

[36] Klapper (2016).

[37] Tay et al. (2022), pp. 1–10.

[38] Klapper (2016). See also Ozili (2018), pp. 329–340.

[39] Donovan (2012), pp. 2647–2669.

[40] Adam and Fazekas (2021), pp. 2–14.

[41] Khera et al. (2021), p. 6.

[42] Ahmad (2020), pp. 753–792.

several of the SDGs attainable. The UN has set out to mobilize the roughly $3 trillion in financing required to achieve the SDGs of the 2030 Agenda by utilizing global resources in partnership with significant financing partners like global, multilateral institutions, regional development banks, member countries, and the private sector.[43] The current effects of extreme weather events, the water crisis, the loss of biodiversity, and the ensuing unintended consequences, such as illegal migration resulting from global inequalities, are symptoms of a crystallization of the climate crisis, even though some people may view extreme climate risks as longer-term.

According to a research by the UN, the world could generate at least US$12 trillion in market opportunities and 380 million new employment by meeting the SDGs, and by 2030, efforts to combat climate change could have saved at least US$26 trillion.[44] Big finance has re-invigorated calls for a financial green revolution supported by international multilaterals acting as first-loss absorbers or insurers to support poor economies' transition to sustainability rather than waiting for new loans or debt write-offs. The payment systems that will be used as the foundation for transaction settlement are a crucial step in accomplishing the funding of the SDGs. For instance, diaspora remittances generated 9% of GDP in 2015, and in many countries, they are equivalent to or more than official development assistance, which offers more regularity as compared to portfolio loan and equity flows.[45] The United Nations has set a goal to lower the costs of remittances made through formal channels from an average of 6.5% in 2020 (the lowest in history) to 3% by 2030 as part of the SDGs.[46] Thus, there is a critical need for more efficient, less expensive, and secure ways for these remittances to reach the micro-beneficiaries in order to promote greater cash flow, increased activity, and economic redistribution. Sustainable development still requires financial access.

The world's poorest people, especially women who own an increasing number of Micro, Small, and Medium-Sized Enterprises, but have a relatively lesser part of the world's wealth, could benefit from global efforts to increase financial inclusion. Due to the systemic risks they pose, payments systems are frequently highly regulated globally. As a result, entry hurdles are substantially greater, and international cooperation is required to align objectives and make real progress. Over the past 10,000 years, the use of money as a medium of exchange has changed from barter, commodity money, and coins to paper money.[47] The sole practical development by banks in the previous 20 years, according to Paul Volcker in 2009, was the Automated Teller Machines (ATM).[48] Despite ATMs, credit cards, and even

---

[43] Economic Commission for Latin America and the Caribbean [ECLAC] (2018).
[44] United Nations Development Programme (2019).
[45] Barne and Pirlea (2019).
[46] UN (2022).
[47] Peneder (2022), pp. 175–203.
[48] The Wall Street Journal (2009).

check books having a substantial impact on the payments system, smart phones have resulted in the widespread use of mobile money and e-wallets.[49]

Cryptography and Distributed Ledger Technology are continuing to drive a boom in the use of bitcoin and stable coins.[50] Even the idea of using cryptocurrencies as a second national currency has been studied by some nations. The global payments system would be significantly impacted by the emergence of dematerialized payments. The SDGs' financial architecture serves as the "blood arteries" that make infrastructure projects financially viable. For instance, digital collection methods improve tax collection and the payment of public goods. Aid, financial transfers, and remittances would enable additional benefits to the micro-population through the SDG financing as well.[51]

Consideration in the past has been given by other scholars to the approach adopted in the spectrum or a maturity model[52] for Environmental, social, and corporate governance (ESG) and Impact commitment outlines the advancements occurring across payment systems in connection to the SDGs.[53] The model starts with the conventional bank investor, who makes investments in search of the most advantageous risk-return frontier while attempting to maximize shareholder value.[54] Without regulation (such as carbon taxes), the typical investor would engage in regulatory arbitrage and harm the environment since they do not really care about internalizing the external or social costs of doing business. Further, the significance of it is increased, in the context of blended finance, which is a crucial tool for financing the SDGs and uses a combination of private and concessional capital to pursue early-stage, venture-capital, or private equity projects with a mix of social and financial returns.

To implement sustainable projects on a large scale and keep global temperature rise to 1.5 °C over pre-industrial levels, enormous sums of money would need to be invested, revolutionizing current systems, and impact investment projects with ESG prospects would be considered.[55] Fintech firms, which are still working to digitize money and its associated impact model of TechFin firms following a strategy of monetizing data, play this role. Impact investments will undoubtedly be the type of investments required in the payments sector to ignite SDG benefits for citizens.[56] Central banks would need to adopt a hybrid digital currency model that offers backups for intermediaries in order to achieve the goals of financial inclusion, cost reduction, and improved affordability of remittances. This would prevent a

---

[49] Lei et al. (2022), pp. 1071–1087.

[50] Arner et al. (2020), pp. 2–28.

[51] Akanle et al. (2022).

[52] Saskia et al. (2016), pp. 312–323.

[53] Mohabbati-Kalejahi et al. (2022), p. 1222.

[54] Saskia et al. (2016), p. 312.

[55] Tiefenbacher (n.d.).

[56] ECLAC (2018).

crowding-out of financial intermediaries and enable the infrastructure for interoperability with financial systems around the world.

In order to attract private capital through a combination of seigniorage and philanthropy, a reasonable return would need to be paid. The Bill and Melinda Gates Foundation, the Rockefeller Foundation, and the Mastercard Foundation, for instance, would offer catalytic funding to finance financial inclusion goals in a sustainable way so that costs are not passed down to the ultimate consumers.[57] These first-loss investments would be backed by public finance and political risk protection from multilaterals like The World Bank Multilateral Investment Guarantee Agency.[58] These projects could be funded for expansion with the help of private money while still producing a respectable return for owners. As a result, a variety of initiatives have the potential to address the problems with financial inclusion that are particular to developing nations, include small business owners and entrepreneurs in the economic tax system, and increase long-term tax collections. Through these activities, financial inclusion will be improved, investments in fragile economies will be encouraged, and the contradictions and denials of greenwashing at some companies in the established capital markets will be addressed.

SDG 17, "Partnership for the Goals," will play a crucial role as all stakeholders work as collaborators rather than competitors towards a common goal in the race towards greener, digital, cleantech assets, an end to poverty, eradication of hunger, good health for all, clean energy, clean water, zero hunger, and other SDG targets.[59] In order to sustain the central issuance of currency, the COVID-19 pandemic has hastened the digital transformation, leading to a rapid progress and global wave of central banks adopting digital money.[60] These retail Central Bank Digital Currencies have the potential to be more advantageous for both customers and the payments system. Instead of a direct model, a hybrid model assisted by financial intermediaries would limit anonymity through initial identification and eventual expiration, minimize privacy issues, promote private sector engagement, and increase system trust.[61]

Realising the UN SDGs of eradicating poverty, enhancing health and education, and reducing inequality may be directly impacted by access to finance.[62] Some contributors to this book project will methodically evaluate the growing body of empirical data to determine whether or not a person's socioeconomic status and demographic traits, such as income and education, have an impact on their capacity to get credit. Additionally, it will be argued in some chapters that having more education and/or financial literacy makes it easier for households and business owners to acquire financing. Less wealthy and lower-income people are less likely to be granted credit by traditional financial organizations. Women are more likely to

---

[57] Sklair and Gilbert (2022), pp. 51–77.

[58] Matsukawa and Habeck (2007), pp. 1–88.

[59] Emebinah (2021).

[60] Wang et al. (2022).

[61] Soderberg (2022).

[62] Vorisek and Yu (2020), pp. 1–29.

be rejected, denied access to formal loans, and charged higher prices in developing nations. Immigrants, persons of colour, members of racial and ethnic minorities, and those with disabilities are more likely to be shut out of the official credit markets. We discover that the aforementioned credit-challenged groups in society frequently turn to expensive pawnbrokers or payday lenders. These results are strikingly comparable in industrialized and developing nations. Finally, by pointing out several flaws in the existing literature and empirical data, we offer guidance for future research on achieving SDGs through financial inclusion and access to credit.

This book is divided into 16 chapters. In this chapter, Howard Chitimira and Tapiwa Victor Warikandwa argue that financial inclusion is a critical enabler of the UN SDGs, which will be a fundamental driver of poverty reduction and shared global economic prosperity. To this end, Chitimira and Warikandwa emphasize that governments and investors should take note of the significance of financial inclusion to realising SDGs since economic growth is a crucial long-term driver of business sales and profitability, which in turn supports asset prices. The fact that financial inclusion is an enabler of some of the 17 SDGs highlights how important it is. The chapter will also provide a summary of the 16 chapters of the book, all of which were written by experts in the discourse of financial inclusion.

Vivienne A. Lawack and Maphuti D. Tuba provide a critical analysis of the existing international policy framework on financial inclusion in the chapter "Towards an International Financial Inclusion Strategy, Institutional Frameworks and Enforcement: Setting Regulatory Benchmarks for the SADC Countries". They assess whether imposing responsibilities on nations to advance financial inclusion is effective, concentrating on establishing policy and regulatory benchmarks for SADC nations. The framework and guiding principles outlined in the National Financial Inclusion Strategy Reference Framework and the Template for the Design of National Financial Inclusion Strategy from the World Bank and the Alliance for Financial Inclusion are also covered by Tuba and Lawack. The chapter addressed how to create a responsive international financial inclusion strategy with institutional and enforcement frameworks that function, as well as how national financial inclusion frameworks, particularly those in the SADC nations, may be implemented and enforced. It also covered the prospect of establishing an integrated framework for financial inclusion based on the inclusion-stability-integrity-protection paradigm as a global norm. According to this theory, national policymakers in the SADC region should actively pursue and maximize the connections between financial inclusion and all of the key goals of financial stability, financial integrity, and financial consumer protection. In order to benchmark the regulatory, institutional, and enforcement frameworks for promoting global financial inclusion, it also drew insights from important enforcement mechanisms used by the Financial Action Task Force to combat money laundering and counter terrorism financing.

In the chapter "Facilitating Financial Inclusion Through the Development of a Decentralised Cryptocurrencies' Regulatory Regime in South Africa, Zimbabwe and Botswana", Shelton T. Mota Makore, Patrick C. Osode, and Nombulelo Lubisi argue that since their introduction, cryptocurrencies have gained popularity in the financial industry all over the world. Countries like South Africa, Zimbabwe, and

Botswana in the sub-Saharan region have the potential to achieve financial inclusion through the use of cryptocurrencies. Mota Makore, Osode and Lubisi further point out that due to attitudes sparked by chrematophobia and other hazards connected with using banks, unbanked people in these emerging market nations may be drawn to cryptocurrencies. They further argue that the technology of cryptocurrencies could be deployed as sui generis instruments of payment, asset accumulation and investment, thereby challenging and dislodging conventional financial tools for transacting, storing and transferring economic value. More importantly, cryptocurrencies can drive financial inclusion by enlarging the space for monetary innovations in South Africa, Zimbabwe and Botswana, lowering the cost of trans-actions, making the countries less dependent on the use of cash, and promoting the transnational mobility of money. More pointedly, the authors emphasise that South Africa, Zimbabwe and Botswana seem behind in tapping into the financial inclusion opportunities presented by this new technology. In principle, the chapter argues that South Africa, Botswana and Zimbabwe need to adopt a responsive regulatory regime in order to reap the financial inclusion benefits derivable from the adoption of cryptocurrency technology.

In the chapter "The Role of Corporate Directorship in Financial Inclusion Within Selected SADC Countries", Tshepo H. Mongalo notes that the majority of the SADC countries' corporate statutes are comparable to the relevant United States of America (USA) federal legislation and USA state corporate laws in that they forbid the appointment of legal entities (including partnerships and close corporations) as corporate directors. However, a handful of other SADC nations, mostly those with a civil law system, permit corporate directors. The chapter argues that objections to the usage of corporate directors, as put out in the two largest industrialized nations, the USA and the United Kingdom, are exaggerated. Due to the broad prohibition on corporate directors, available resources in corporate entities that may possibly be utilized in corporate boards are barred from doing so because of the clearly defined role of the board in SADC nations' corporations. According to Mongalo, this unjustifiably hinders legitimate corporate governance actors from profiting adequately from the efficient operation of those firms. The likelihood of averting corporate governance disasters in a few SADC nations is further diminished by the blanket prohibition on corporate directors. Thus, Mongalo makes the case for the development of a board service business, which is backed by some of the country's top critics.

Herbert Kawadza and Sharon Handongwe argue in the chapter "Financial Inclusion and Persons Living with Disabilities in Zambia: Reality Versus Rhetoric" that while Zambia has made progress in creating legislative and institutional procedures intended to improve the lives of people with disabilities, these by themselves are insufficient. More specifically, the authors contend that while these good intentions are admirable, they will not be very effective if there are no systems in place to support the financial independence of the disabled. Kawadza and Handongwe go on to discuss the problem of financial exclusion of people with disabilities in Zambia as it relates to civil justice. They argue that because they cannot participate in wealth creation due to lack of access to financial services, their capacity to change their way of life is hampered. Kawadza and Handongwe's chapter is essential in creating a foundation for future research on social-economic justice in Zambia because it reveals these barriers.

In the chapter "The Prospects and Challenges for Mobile Money Regulation and the Promotion of Financial Inclusion in Zimbabwe", Howard Chitimira and Menelisi Ncube make the case that mobile money services have been helpful for the majority of informal employees, who make up about 85% of the workers in Zimbabwe without conventional bank accounts. They point out that nearly 90% of adult Zimbabweans use Ecocash, a cutting-edge mobile payment system that enables users to complete financial transactions directly from their mobile phone, for mobile money transfers and for urban to rural money remittances for family support, as well as payment for goods and services in retail settings. Apart from Ecocash, which offers a variety of savings, investment, and loan provision services, Chitimira and Ncube note that it is clear that other mobile money services in Zimbabwe, such as Telecash, Mycash, and Onemoney, do not encourage savings in the same way that traditional banking institutions would. They add that there has been widespread money laundering and other exploitation of mobile money services in Zimbabwe. Chitimira and Ncube assert that this situation is thought to be caused by Zimbabwe's lack of a regulatory framework for mobile money services. As of now, the Statutory Instrument Banking (Money Transmission, Mobile Banking and Mobile Money Interoperability) Regulations, which were put into place to regulate mobile money operations in Zimbabwe, are overseen by the Reserve Bank of Zimbabwe (RBZ) and the Postal and Telecommunications Regulatory Authority of Zimbabwe (POTRAZ). In an effort to advance financial inclusion in Zimbabwe, Chitimira and Ncube studied the difficulties associated with mobile money services in Zimbabwe.

In the chapter "Land Reform and Financial Inclusion Challenges in South Africa", Rusenga and Ndlovu discuss the financial inclusion/exclusion experiences of South African land reform recipients. They draw attention to the fact that beneficiaries of the South African government's land reform program are primarily forced to engage in agricultural production under an expensive agribusiness model without having adequate access to financial and material resources. Rusenga and Ndlovu also point out that black farmers still encounter barriers to accessing financial services, even from government organizations in charge of promoting agricultural growth. The authors make a compelling case that both public and private organizations favour large-scale commercial producers when allocating funding and other forms of assistance. As a result, the production of land beneficiaries is significantly impacted by a lack of resources, which also affects their access to more lucrative markets and their revenue. The Rusenga and Ndlovu give empirical evidence indicating how financial exclusion severely effects the livelihoods of land beneficiaries using a case study from the Limpopo area of South Africa. They contend that the output and livelihoods of land beneficiaries have been negatively impacted by a combination of financial exclusion and the costly agribusiness model that has been imposed and encourages large-scale development.

Tendai Douglas Svotwa, Charles Makanyeza and Eukeria Wealth explore digital financial inclusion strategies for rural and urban communities in Botswana, Namibia,

South Africa, and Zimbabwe, in the chapter "Exploring Digital Financial Inclusion Strategies for Urban and Rural Communities in Botswana, Namibia, South Africa and Zimbabwe". The authors contend that the importance of financial inclusion in advancing socioeconomic development has propelled it to the forefront of scholarly discussions. Financial services that are accessible online and through mobile devices are referred to as digital financial services. Svotwa, Makanyeza, and Wealth cite data from The World Bank showing that families in developing nations own more mobile phones than those who have access to water and electricity, highlighting the high mobile penetration rates in these nations. The authors argue that by integrating the formerly excluded into the formal financial system, digital financial services are essential for improving financial inclusion. More than 60% of the world's population now has access to digital financial services, according to statistics, therefore regulators and policymakers need to concentrate on this growing problem. The marginalization of rural people and their depressed spending patterns are the main causes of the stark differences in the levels of digital financial inclusion between rural and urban communities in the nations under consideration. Svotwa, Makanyeza and Wealth thus conclude that proposed digital financial strategies should, therefore, address this anomaly and include the rural communities into the manifold of digital services to ameliorate the vagaries of poverty rampant in rural communities.

In the chapter "A 'Social Justice' Movement in the Banking Industry? Banking, Competition and Financial Inclusion in South Africa with Insights from Zimbabwe", Tinashe Kondo makes the case that even if social justice discussions have appeared to be waning in philosophical circles during the past 10 years, there are still good reasons to keep them going. Social justice discussions in law have typically only occurred in human rights contexts. Kondo adamantly maintains that social justice is concerned with how society is set up and the realization of equality in material circumstances. These goals cannot be achieved if society's members are constrained by "markets" and "financial institutions." Kondo contends that social justice has a place in the banking industry and, more broadly, in other economic domains (including their regulation too). Kondo suggests the idea of financial inclusion as a means of advancing this cause. Financial inclusion aims to increase the accessibility of banking products for all people. It is safe to state that when it comes to banking goods, financial inclusion is about (social) justice. Kondo also explores the impact of competition in the banking industry in South Africa on financial inclusion. Kondo concludes from a review of the literature and current secondary data from empirical studies that there is a clear link between increased industry rivalry and better access and product selection for consumers as firms compete for new customers and markets. Oddly enough, while having a shared interest in transformation, competition law and financial inclusion are seen to make unusual bedfellows. Then, Kondo suggests that more intentional legal and legislative measures be implemented to promote greater financial inclusion and enforce competition within the banking industry.

Tapiwa V. Warikandwa, in the chapter "Intra-African Trade and the AFCFTA: A Law and Economics Perspective", observes that because financial inclusion in Africa is low and trade is largely supported by the unofficial financial system, it is challenging to calculate the value of Sub-Saharan Africa's contribution to world trade. Although access to more affordable and effective formal financial services can help boost intra-African trade, small traders in Africa cannot afford to use official financial channels for cross-border transactions. Almost no official trade is conducted between African nations. Through the interchange of agricultural products, informal trade can help communities living close to borders by generating income, assisting in the creation of jobs, and maintaining food security. However, this is done at the expense of tax revenue and undermines efforts to make policy. Financial inclusion, according to Warikandwa, should be a top priority in Africa in light of the launch of the African Continental Free Trade Agreement on January 1, 2021, which aims to create a single African market by removing 90% of tariffs and allowing free movement of goods, services, and capital. Warikandwa also notes that the high cost of moving money across Africa is a barrier to success, despite the World Bank projecting $292 billion in revenue gains from increased trade facilitation, such as cheaper cross-border transfers. Money transfers to Sub-Saharan Africa (SSA) are more expensive than money transfers to any other part of the world. Sending money to SSA costs 8.9% of the total cost, which is more than the global average of 6.8%, per World Bank data. In 2019, the average cost of sending money from South Africa to China was 25.1%, compared to 15.5% for sending money from Cameroon to Nigeria. Warikandwa contends that lowering the cost of cross-border payments, among other difficulties, depends on the financial inclusion of players in the informal sector using mobile money.

In the chapter "Retirement Funding and Financial Inclusion in South Africa: A Contrary Policy Approach", Clement Marumoagae illustrates that the South African government has narrowly approached the financial inclusion debate by failing to include retirement funding in its understanding of this concept. It argues that failure to identify retirement funding as one of the priority financial inclusion products, prevented the government from creating a platform that will enable those currently excluded from retirement funding to access important financial products offered by retirement funds. Marumoagae further argues that there is a need to establish a national retirement fund that would focus on those who are currently excluded from retirement funding. Further, Marumoagae argues that the membership of this retirement fund should be voluntary for those who currently have retirement funding but compulsory for those who earn a living but not currently saving for their retirement through retirement funds. This will prevent financial dependence on the state when people reach retirement age. Marumoagae concludes by arguing that this initiative must be accompanied by efforts to eradicate retirement financial illiteracy through provision of dedicated retirement funding education to all retirement fund members and future members.

In the chapter "Mobile Fin-Tech Ecosystem Shaping Financial Inclusion in Zimbabwean Banking and Financial Services Markets", Brighton Nyagadza, Dumisani R. Muzira and Tinashe Chuchu explore the mobile financial technology ecosystem shaping financial inclusion in Zimbabwean banking and financial services markets. Nyagadza, Muzira and Chuchu base their arguments on a narrative approach of secondary data sources, mainly peer reviewed reputable journal articles.

The purpose of this approach by the authors is to draw conclusions and identify the research gaps that exist within the banking and financial services markets in Zimbabwe. The chapter is based on a structural analysis methodology to frame the categories of the major analysis in combination with scientific rigour to a broad and complex problem. Research results proved that the mobile financial technology ecosystem shaping financial inclusion in Zimbabwean banking and financial services markets is a necessity for sustainable economic growth and development. Implications to contemporary banking and financial services industry business leaders include bringing-in present day digital financial technologies, incubating survival plans of actions or strategies so as to fully operationalise mobile financial technology seamlessly. In addition to this, establishing technological innovation appetite is meant to address, respond and navigate within the associated financial digital disruptive complexities for the sustenance of banking and financial services markets in Zimbabwe. The study results underscore the necessity of understanding mobile financial technology ecosystem so as to design relevant strategies in a bid to carve financial inclusion in Zimbabwean banking and financial services markets. Nyagadza, Muzira and Chuchu thus conceptually examined how mobile financial technology ecosystem can shape financial inclusion in Zimbabwean banking and financial services markets. Their chapter contributes to literature and theoretical novel introspections into the depth and breadth of how mobile financial technology can contribute to the development of financial inclusion in the Zimbabwean banking and financial markets.

In the chapter "Financial Inclusion Challenges and Prospects during the COVID-19 Pandemic: Insights from Botswana, Namibia, South Africa and Zimbabwe", authors Charles Makanyeza, Eukeria Wealth, and Tendai Douglas Svotwa examine the difficulties and opportunities associated with financial inclusion in the COVID-19 pandemic era using data from Botswana, Namibia, South Africa, and Zimbabwe as examples. According to the authors, financial inclusion is a process that makes it possible for all participants in an economy to easily access, find, and use formal financial services. They further note that financial inclusion is a key objective of the United Nations Sustainable Develop Goals earmarked to alleviate poverty and income inequality. As a result, financial inclusion has caught the interest of numerous researchers and decision-makers. The COVID-19 pandemic outbreak, however, has paralyzed the whole planet. The economy has been impacted in many different ways. The financial services industry has been altered by the pandemic. One aspect of the economy that the epidemic has had a mixed impact on is financial inclusion. Thus, Makanyeza, Wealth, and Svotwa investigate the literature on financial inclusion and the potential and problems brought on by COVID-19. They go into further detail in the chapter about the difficulties and opportunities presented by the COVID-19 epidemic for financial inclusion. They give some suggestions for future research in their conclusion.

In the chapter "Financial Inclusion and the Small-Scale Fisheries Sector in Namibia: A Contemporary Legal Perspective", Tapiwa V. Warikandwa, Elize Shakalela, and Eugene L. Libebe make the case that Namibia's small-scale fisheries (SSF) industry has been largely left out of the financial system and is primarily characterized by limited access to financial services and a lack of funding for investment fishing projects. The majority of the fishermen that make up Namibia's SSF sector, according to the authors, come from marginalized coastal communities since they have limited or restricted access to marine resources. These groups include some of the most disenfranchised, including the Topnaar. They are exploited by intermediaries and merchants, which contributes to their low social status. The power that middlemen have over finance and fish marketing sucks away the surplus produced and frequently leaves them in debt. The economics of fishing and jobs associated to fishing are unpredictable due to a variety of factors, including catch variability, technological advancements, excess capitalization, growing expenses, aggressive fishing practices, and overcrowding, among others. Although the overall output is almost unchanged, the investment and operating expenditures have increased significantly. As a result, fishermen are becoming more and more reliant on loans to cover their expenses and as a coping technique. There is a common misconception that Namibia has no artisanal marine fisheries. The law on fisheries allows for both recreational fishing and commercial fishing, which is controlled by a sizable industrial fleet (from which the sale of catches is prohibited.) However, there are a few people who work in a fashion that would be considered artisanal elsewhere in the globe on the periphery of both of these fisheries. In order to empower the SSF sector in Namibia, Warikandwa, Shakalela, and Libebe argue in favour of using financial inclusion techniques.

In the chapter "Barriers to Integrating Financial Inclusion for Coastal Small-Scale Fishermen into Namibian Fisheries Policies and Regulatory Frameworks", Alex T. Kanyimba and Martha N. Jonas point out that the Ministry of Fisheries and Marine Resources has been applauded intercontinentally for laying the groundwork to develop the Namibian fisheries sector since the dawn of the country's independence in 1990. However, there are no financial inclusion policies for small scale artisanal fishermen. This paper aims to report on barriers to integrating financial inclusion for coastal small-scale fishermen into the Namibian fisheries policies and regulatory frameworks. Kanyimba and Jonas's chapter reviews the understanding of financial inclusion, the elements of financial inclusion such bank inclusion and financial credit schemes breaks for the economically marginalized small-scale fishermen and access to fish markets for the small-scale fishermen. It offers an analysis of several international policies and regulatory frameworks that ought to direct small-scale fishermen's financial inclusion. The authors argue that the Food and Agriculture Organisation guidelines for securing sustainable small-scale fisheries in the context of food security, as well as SDG targets 14b and 17 have the potential to improve and advance financial inclusion for small-scale fishermen among international policies. The rules and regulatory frameworks at the national level do not specifically mention small-scale fisherman.

The authors further contend that although the issue of financial inclusion is still up in the air, the creation of Namibia's National Plan of Action for Small-Scale Fishers will present a possibility for small-scale fisherman inclusion in Namibian policies and regulatory frameworks. Financial institutions are hesitant to do business with small-scale fishermen because the majority of them lack bank accounts and collateral, have limited capacity for production, lack education, training, and capacity, and have no access to markets for their catch. These factors all contribute to the barriers to financial inclusion. There is also the false belief that, if small-scale fishermen's ability to catch more fish is increased, this will lead to overexploitation of marine resources. Kanyimba and Jonas propose that the establishment of support organizations by small-scale fishers is encouraged in order to advance representative participation in policy making and assistance for financial inclusion. They further call on the Namibian government to establish programs that will offer small-scale fisherman financial credit guarantees. Finally, they advise that small-scale fishermen build their capacity in order to give knowledge in the post-harvest management, preservation, processing, and marketing of marine goods as well as a crucial connection to markets.

In the final chapter, Tendai Douglas Svotwa, Eukeria Wealth and Charles Makanyeza interrogate the policy and regulatory frameworks for financial inclusion in the SADC region, focusing on South Africa, Botswana, Namibia and Zimbabwe. Financial inclusion plays a pivotal role in the economic development and inclusive growth of a country, as well as a critical role in the alleviation of poverty, reduction of gender inequalities and improvement in the standards of living for societies. The authors point out that notwithstanding these benefits, constraints to financial inclusion in the countries under study include lack of trust in the financial services sector, financial illiteracy, high costs of setting up banks in remote rural areas and poor infrastructure. Generally, to some extent, the sampled countries have instituted country specific policies and regulations that are geared towards the enhancement of financial inclusion in their respective countries which has resulted in positive outcomes. However, Svotwa, Wealth and Makanyeza observe that in some instances, there is no coordination between financial policies and other legislation to realise countrywide financial inclusion. They recommend that there should be common financial inclusion legislation that is effectively and homogeneously applied in the SADC region, that must be upheld by all member states for uniformity to realise greater financial inclusion.

3 Conclusion

Some policy documents have promoted financial inclusion as a tool for reducing poverty in emerging countries. In order to take advantage of attractive investment opportunities in their economies, it offers to improve impoverished families' capacity to reduce financial shocks, make human capital investments in health and education, and/or engage in modest asset accumulation. However, it has been discovered that the financial sectors in the majority of SSA nations are either incapable or unwilling to serve the lowest sections of the population. As a result, SSA continues to face significant challenges in promoting growth and reducing poverty. As a result, this chapter has outlined the various contexts in which academics will explore the various ways that financial inclusion might contribute to the

UN's SDGs of eradicating poverty, preserving the environment, and providing prosperity for all by 2030. The discussions also highlight some of the issues that require attention. One important takeaway is that financial inclusion might not be enough to give the poorest SADC people the knowledge and abilities they need to discover routes out of poverty. In order to help SADC's masses and other people in other regions of the world to escape poverty, financial inclusion must work to increase their sense of control over their circumstances and to enhance their faith in that ability.

Bibliography

Adam I, Fazekas M (2021) Are emerging technologies helping win the fight against corruption? A review of the state of evidence. Inf Econ Policy 57:2–14

Ahmad AH (2020) Mobile money, financial inclusion and development: a review with reference to African experience. J Econ Surv 34(4):753–792

Ahmed SM, Jassim J, Basharat A, Malik W (2019) Microfinance poised to play a vital role in achieving developmental objectives of the Government. MicroNote 38:1–17

Akanle O, Kayode D, Abolade I (2022) Sustainable Development Goals (SDGs) and remittances in Africa. Cogent Soc Sci 8(1):2037811. https://doi.org/10.1080/23311886.2022.2037811

Arner D, Auer R, Frost J (2020) Stablecoins: risks, potential and regulation. Bank for International Settlements working papers no 905, pp 2–28

Avitsian, T (2020) The healthcare system in Jordan https://borgenproject.org/the-healthcare-system-in-jordan/. Accessed 6 July 2022

Barne D, Pirlea F (2019) Money sent home by workers now largest source of external financing in low- and middle-income countries (excluding China). https://blogs.worldbank.org/opendata/money-sent-home-workers-now-largest-source-external-financing-low-and-middle-income. Accessed 6 July 2022

Donovan KP (2012) Mobile money, more freedom? The impact of M-PESA's network power on development as freedom. Int J Commun 6:2647–2669

ECLAC (2018) Data, algorithms and policies: redefining the digital world. https://repositorio.cepal.org/bitstream/handle/11362/43515/4/S1800052_en.pdf. Accessed 8 July 2022

Economic Commission for Latin America and the Caribbean [ECLAC] (2018) The 2030 Agenda and the Sustainable Development Goals: an opportunity for Latin America and the Caribbean. https://repositorio.cepal.org/bitstream/handle/11362/40156/25/S1801140_en.pdf.   Accessed 10 July 2022

Emebinah C (2021) Enhancing financial inclusion toward the SDGs. https://impactentrepreneur.com/enhancing-financial-inclusion-toward-the-sdgs/. Accessed 4 July 2022

Food and Agriculture Organisation of the UN (2020) Voluntary guidelines for securing sustainable small-scale fisheries in the context of food security and poverty eradication. https://www.fao.org/voluntary-guidelines-small-scale-fisheries/news-and-events/detail/en/c/1333232/. Accessed 10 July 2022

Global Partnership for Financial Inclusion (n.d.). G20 financial inclusion indicators. https://databank.worldbank.org/data/download/g20fidata/G20_Financial_Inclusion_Indicators.pdf. Accessed 6 July 2022

Government of India (2020) Poverty alleviation in rural India - strategy and programmes. https://niti.gov.in/planningcommission.gov.in/docs/plans/planrel/fiveyr/10th/volume2/v2_ch3_2.pdf. Accessed 7 July 2022

Hope A (2018) Women, trade and financial inclusion. Tralac, 30 August 2018 https://www.tralac.org/blog/article/13422-women-trade-and-financial-inclusion-in-sadc.html.   Accessed 7 July 2022

Khera P, Ng S, Ogawa S, Sahay R (2021) Measuring digital financial inclusion in emerging market and developing economies: a new index. IMF working paper on Monetary and Capital Markets Department, March 2021, WP/21/90, p 6

Klapper L (2016) Financial inclusion has a big role to play in reaching the SDGs. https://blogs.worldbank.org/developmenttalk/financial-inclusion-has-big-role-play-reaching-sdgs. Accessed 10 July 2022

Klapper L, El-Zoghbi M, Hess J (2016) Achieving the Sustainable Development Goals: the role of financial inclusion. United Nations Secretary General's Special Advocate for Inclusive Finance for Development, p 1, para 2

Kuzmina A (2018) Kenya case study part II: M-PESA vs The Market. https://medium.com/what-the-money/kenya-case-study-part-ii-m-pesa-vs-the-market-107ef4559497. Accessed 11 July 2022

Lei H, Lan J, Sleiman K (2022) An empirical study on investigating mobile payment effect on automated teller machine use. Open J Bus Manag 10:1071–1087. https://doi.org/10.4236/ojbm.2022.103057

Lipper L, Benton TG (2020) Mega-trends in the Southern African Region. SADC Futures: Developing Foresight Capacity for Climate Resilient Agricultural Development Knowledge Series. CCAFS Report. Wageningen, the Netherlands: CGIAR Research Program on Climate Change, Agriculture and Food Security (CCAFS)

Maas T (2018) The importance of financial inclusion in socio-economic development. https://hollandfintech.com/2018/07/the-importance-of-financial-inclusion-in-socio-economical-development/. Accessed 7 July 2022

Matongela AM (2014) Understanding the state of financial inclusion in Namibia. Res J Financ Acc 5(23):171–175

Matsukawa T, Habeck O (2007) Review of risk mitigation instruments for infrastructure financing and recent trends and developments, trends and policy options no 4, pp 1–88

McKinsey Global Institute (2016) Digital finance for all: powering inclusive growth in emerging economies. McKinsey & Company, p 2

Mohabbati-Kalejahi N, Alavi S, Zahed MA (2022) Sustainable Development Goals (SDGs) as a Framework for Corporate Social Responsibility (CSR). Sustainability 14:1222. https://doi.org/10.3390/su14031222

Oxford Business Group (2017) The Report: The Philippines 2017 https://oxfordbusinessgroup.com/philippines-2017/country-profile. Accessed 10 July 2022

Ozili PK (2018) Impact of digital finance on financial inclusion and stability. Borsa Istanbul Rev 18(4):329–340

Peneder M (2022) Digitisation and the evolution of money as a social technology of account. J Evol Econ 32:175–203

Pomeroy R, Arango C, Lomboy CG, Box S (2020) Financial inclusion to build economic resilience in small-scale fisheries. Mar Policy 118(2):103982

Prathap SK (2011) Financial inclusion of fisher households in coastal Kerala - role of micro-finance. Doctor of Philosophy degree, Cochin University of Science and Technology, pp 79–105

Robino C, Trivelli C, Villanueva C, Sachetti FC, Walbey H, Martinez L (2020) Financial inclusion for women: a way forward. https://www.g20-insights.org/policy_briefs/financial-inclusion-for-women-a-way-forward/. Accessed 5 July 2022

Salman A, Nowacka K (2020) Innovative financial products and services for women in Asia and the Pacific. Asian Development Bank Sustainable Development working paper series no. 67, April 2020, p 3

Saskia B, Schneider S, WeBels D (2016) The Kiel maturity model as a future-oriented mindset for sustainable knowledge management processes. Int J Sustain Econ 8(4):312–323

Sklair J, Gilbert P (2022) Giving as "De-Risking": philanthropy, impact investment and the pandemic response, public. Anthropologist 4:51–77

Soderberg G (2022) Behind the scenes of central bank digital currency: emerging trends, insights, and policy lessons, FinTech Note/2022/004, International Monetary Fund, Publication Services

Stopler OA, Walter A (2017) Financial literacy, financial advice, and financial behaviour. J Bus Econ 87:581–643

Tay L, Tai H, Tan G (2022) Digital financial inclusion: a gateway to sustainable development. Heliyon 8:1–10

The Wall Street Journal (2009) Paul Volker: think more boldly. https://www.wsj.com/articles/SB10001424052748704825504574586330960597134. Accessed 5 July 2022

The World Bank (2013) Poverty reduction in practice: how and where we work. https://www.worldbank.org/en/news/feature/2013/02/05/poverty-reduction-in-practice.   Accessed 6 July 2022

The World Bank (2014) Poverty and health. https://www.worldbank.org/en/topic/health/brief/poverty-health. Accessed 6 July 2022

The World Bank (2019) In Kenya, uplifting the poor and vulnerable through a Harmonised National Safety Net System. https://www.worldbank.org/en/results/2019/04/18/in-kenya-uplifting-the-poor-and-vulnerable-through-a-harmonized-national-safety-net-system. Accessed 6 July 2022

The World Bank (2020) UFA2020 Overview: Universal Financial Access by 2020. https://www.worldbank.org/en/topic/financialinclusion/brief/achieving-universal-financial-access-by-2020. Accessed 7 July 2022

The World Bank (2021) The Global Findex Database 2021: financial inclusion, digital payments, and resilience in the age of Covid-19. https://globalfindex.worldbank.org/basic-page-overview. Accessed 6 July 2022

The World Bank (2022) Financial inclusion: financial inclusion is a key enabler to reducing poverty and boosting prosperity. https://www.worldbank.org/en/topic/financialinclusion/overview. Accessed 8 July 2022

Tiefenbacher JP (ed) (n.d.) Environmental management – pollution, habitat, ecology, and sustainability. https://www.intechopen.com/books/10765. Accessed 13 July 2022

UN (2022) Remittances and the SDGs https://www.un.org/en/observances/remittances-day/SDGs. Accessed 6 July 2022

UN Department of Economic and Social Affairs: Sustainable Development. https://sustainabledevelopment.un.org/sdgs. Accessed 7 July 2022

UNCDF (2020) Financial inclusion for what? https://www.financedigitalafrica.org/2020/03/02/financial-inclusion-for-what/. Accessed 10 July 2022

UNCDF (n.d.) Women's empowerment to strengthen food security. https://www.uncdf.org/f4f/womens-empowerment. Accessed 8 July 2022

United Nations (n.d.) Transforming our world: the 2030 Agenda for Sustainable Development. https://sdgs.un.org/2030agenda. Accessed 10 July 2022

United Nations Capital Development Fund (n.d.-a) Financial inclusion and the SDGs. https://www.uncdf.org/financial-inclusion-and-the-sdgs. Accessed 11 July 2022

United Nations Capital Development Fund (n.d.-b) What is the Last Mile Finance Trust Fund - UN Capital Development Fund (UNCDF). https://www.uncdf.org/lmftf/what-is-the-last-mile-finance-trust-fund. Accessed 11 July 2022

United Nations Conference on Trade and Development (2015) Access to financial services as a driver for the Post-2015 Development Agenda. Policy brief no. 35, September 2015. Access to Financial Services as a Driver for the Post-2015 Development Agenda (unctad.org). Accessed 8 July 2022

United Nations Development Programme (2019) Corporate, investment leaders review SDG impact plans. https://www.undp.org/stories/corporate-investment-leaders-review-sdg-impact-plans. Accessed 10 July 2022

United Nations International Children's Emergency Fund (2018) Goal 4: quality education. https://data.unicef.org/sdgs/goal-4-quality-education/. Accessed 6 July 2022

Vorisek D, Yu S (2020) Understanding the cost of achieving the Sustainable Development Goals. Policy research working paper no 9146, pp 1–29

Wang Y, Lucey BM, Vigne SA, Yarovaya L (2022) The effects of central bank digital currencies news on financial markets. Technol Forecast Soc Chang 180:121715. https://doi.org/10.1016/j. techfore.2022.121715

Howard Chitimira (co-editor of the book)—Howard Chitimira is a full Professor of Law and Research Professor at the Faculty of Law, North-West University. He is also an advocate of the High Court of South Africa and a National Research Foundation (NRF) rated legal scholar. Prof Chitimira holds the degrees Bachelor of Laws (LLB) (Cum Laude) from the University of Fort Hare (UFH); Master of Laws (LLM) from UFH and Doctor of Laws (LLD) from the Nelson Mandela Metropolitan University (NMMU). For his doctorate, he specialised in securities and financial markets law. To date, he has published three books and over 50 journal articles in this field. Prof Chitimira is a reviewer and editorial board member of several law journals in South Africa and elsewhere, as well as an external examiner for LLB, LLM and LLD degrees at several universities. He serves on editorial boards of journals and a member of several academic and related associations. For instance, Prof Chitimira is an assistant editor of the Potchefstroom Electronic Law Journal and an editorial board member of the Journal of Corporate & Commercial Law & Practice. He has acted a guest editor for the Interdisciplinary Journal of Economics and Business Law and the Namibia Law Journal. He was appointed by the Academy of Science of South Africa (ASSAF) on behalf of the Department of Higher Education and Training (DHET) to serve on an ad hoc ASSAF Consensus Panel to peer review new applications and re-applications of journals for DHET accreditation on 11 October 2019. To date, he has delivered numerous keynote speeches on Securities and Financial Markets Law in South Africa and elsewhere. Prof Chitimira was invited to comment on the Financial Action Task Force's Recommendation 1 on Risk-Based Measures to Proliferation Financing in August 2020. He successfully launched the annual Corporate and Financial Markets Law Conference in 2019.

Tapiwa Victor Warikandwa (co-editor of the book)—Tapiwa Victor Warikandwa holds a Doctor of Laws in International Trade Law. He is a Senior Lecturer and former Head of Department in the Faculty of Law at the University of Namibia. He specialises in International Trade Law, Labour Law, Indigenisation Laws, Mining Law and Constitutional Law amongst other disciplines. Prior to coming to Namibia, Dr. Warikandwa worked as a legal officer and later legal advisor in the Ministry of Public Service Labour and Social Welfare in Zimbabwe. Key amongst his duties was legal drafting. Dr Warikandwa worked with the law reviser of the Ministry of Justice in Zimbabwe in reviewing laws administered by the Ministry of Public Service Labour and Social Welfare. Dr Warikandwa also completed an ordinary and advanced training in Labour Law Making at the International Labour Organization's International Training Centre in Turin Italy. On numerous occasions, Dr. Warikandwa was actively involved in the activities of the Cabinet Committee on Legislation on behalf of the Ministry of Public Service Labour and Social Welfare. Dr. Warikandwa has since written books on labour law and women's rights in South Africa and Namibia amongst others, as well as publishing articles in accredited peer reviewed journals such as Law, Development and Democracy, Speculum Juris, Journal for Black Studies, Potchefstroom Electronic Law Journal, Comparative International Law Journal for Southern Africa and the African Journal of International and Comparative Law, Juridical Tribune, amongst others. He was also a Post-doctoral Fellow and has also worked as a senior lecturer at the University of Fort Hare in South Africa. Dr Warikandwa studied for his Bachelor of Laws, Master's degree and Doctoral degree at the University of Fort Hare in South Africa. He currently is the Chief Editor of the Namibian Law Journal.

Towards an International Financial Inclusion Strategy, Institutional Frameworks and Enforcement: Setting Regulatory Benchmarks for the SADC Countries

Maphuti D. Tuba and Vivienne A. Lawack

Abstract Financial Inclusion has been on the global policy agenda, including in the Southern African Development Community (SADC), for many years. Global standards-setting bodies, such as the United Nations, the Group of 20 countries, the Alliance for Financial Inclusion, the Financial Action Task Force (FATF), and the World Bank have committed to various financial inclusion policy initiatives. These bodies have recently introduced financial inclusion as part of their traditional policy and regulatory objectives, such as financial stability, integrity and consumer protection. Due to their varying mandates, these bodies often recommend conflicting approaches on the same objective when they pursue these objectives together with financial inclusion. Also, the international policy and regulatory framework on financial inclusion remains fragmented due to the haphazard policy and regulatory approach of these bodies. The Alliance for Financial Inclusion (AFI) and the Work Bank have developed policies and principles on how to develop national financial inclusion strategies. Various countries in Africa and in the SADC region have adopted different types of financial inclusion strategies based on the recommendations of these standards setting bodies. However, the AFI and the World Bank policies and principles are in the form of an international soft law. They are not effectively applied and implemented at regional and national level. These policies and principles do not impose specific national FI frameworks. This chapter critically analyses the current international policy framework on financial inclusion. It determines whether it is effective to impose obligations on countries to promote financial

M. D. Tuba
Department of Mercantile Law, University of South Africa, Johannesburg, South Africa
e-mail: Tubamd@unisa.ac.za

V. A. Lawack (✉)
Department of Mercantile and Labour Law, University of the Western Cape, Cape Town, South Africa
e-mail: Vlawack@uwc.ac.za

© The Author(s), under exclusive license to Springer Nature Switzerland AG 2023
H. Chitimira, T. V. Warikandwa (eds.), *Financial Inclusion and Digital Transformation Regulatory Practices in Selected SADC Countries*, Ius Gentium: Comparative Perspectives on Law and Justice 106,
https://doi.org/10.1007/978-3-031-23863-5_2

inclusion, focusing on setting policy and regulatory benchmarks for SADC countries. It discusses the framework and the principles introduced in the AFI and the World Bank's National Financial Inclusion Strategy Reference Framework and the Template for the Design of National Financial Inclusion Strategy. The main aim of this chapter is to determine ways to formulate a responsive International Financial Inclusion Strategy with effective enforcement and institutional frameworks and how national financial inclusion frameworks, including in the SADC countries may implement and effectively enforce their financial inclusion frameworks. It further discusses a possible introduction of an Integrated Framework for Financial Inclusion that adopts an Inclusion-Stability, Integrity and Protection theory ('I-SIP theory') as an international standard. This theory requires national policy makers in the SADC region to pursue and optimise the linkage of financial inclusion with all the core objectives of financial stability, financial integrity and financial consumer protection. It also draws lessons of key enforcement mechanisms from the FATF's anti-money laundering and countering of terror financing enforcement mechanisms to benchmark the regulatory, institutional and enforcement frameworks to promote global financial inclusion.

1 Introduction

Financial inclusion (FI)—defined generally as access and usage of financial services—has become one of the important policy initiatives to alleviate poverty and for economic growth[1] Despite being on the global policy agenda for a number of years, 70% of the global adult population still lacks access to formal financial services.[2] There is also still no coordinated and comprehensive international FI policy and regulatory framework that is enforceable by some of the recognised traditional international policy and regulatory organisations, such as the United Nations.[3] Various global standards-setting bodies (GSSBs) adopt a haphazard approach to FI policies that focuses on providing different financial services and products, creating co-operative banking and microfinance institutions, enforcing civil rights to prevent discriminatory practices, and lately, by innovating financial technology(fintech) and virtual currency.[4] In 2010, The Group of 20 (G20)

---

[1] United Nations Development Programme (2016), p. 43. For the significance of financial inclusion policies as poverty alleviation strategies, see Zahanogo (2017), p. 212; see also Demirgüç-Kunt et al. (2017), See a detailed definition of financial inclusion in Sect. 2 below.

[2] Global Partnership for Financial Inclusion (2020).

[3] An example of a policy framework that focuses on the main objectives of the relevant GSSB is the Basel Committee on Banking Supervision (2016).

[4] A reference to financial inclusion/exclusion in this discussion relates to where these words are used interchangeably in the literature, either to define financial inclusion or exclusion. Such interchangeable use is applied where it illustrates similar references or definitions in both policy and academic discussions. Examples of civil rights legislation are the Community Reinvestment Act 1977, and the Home Mortgage Disclosure Act 1975 that regulate the prevention of redlining practices in the USA.

established the Financial Inclusion Expert Group that comprises of the G20 Global Partnership for Financial Inclusion (GPFI), the Alliance for Financial Inclusion (AFI),[5] and the World Bank to embrace FI through proper policy, regulatory and supervisory frameworks.[6] As a result, these GSSBs have emerged as important transnational FI policy and regulatory institutions to promote the development of a comprehensive and coordinated global FI policy and regulatory framework. There is currently no comprehensive regulatory framework to promote FI that have been adopted by SADC. A number of countries however, as discussed below,[7] have adopted NFISs with the relevant guidance from the AFI, the GPIF and the World Bank's guidelines and principles on national financial inclusion strategies. The purpose of this chapter is, therefore, to analyse policy documents that the AFI, the GIPF and the World Bank developed and to determine whether these policy frameworks and guidelines are effective to impose the relevant obligations on SADC countries to promote FI. These policy documents are the AFI's *Maya Declaration*,[8] the World Bank's *National Financial Inclusion Strategy Reference Framework*,[9] and the G20 *Principles for Innovative Financial Inclusion*.[10] Together they provide for the formats and approaches of developing national financial inclusion strategies (NFIS), and guide for countries to develop regulatory frameworks to promote FI and prevent financial exclusion (FE). The chapter focuses on the components of the international regulatory framework to guide the development and implementation of national frameworks to promote FI in the SADC region.

This chapter begins with the definition of FI practices. This is followed by the discussion current FI and financial exclusion (FE) position in the SADC region. The current international policy and regulatory framework follows and focuses on key FI instruments that have been developed by the AFI, and the World Bank. The chapter thereafter focuses on key aspects of the current FI policy documents that help to distinguish them as either soft international law or hard law and how they are enforced. The chapter also discusses FI framework in the SADC regions. It further introduces the Financial Action Task Force (FATF)'s international anti-money laundering and the combating the financing of terrorism (AML/CFT) standards. It discusses the specific enforcement mechanisms applied by the FATF to benchmark possible enforcement for FI policies as soft international law that may be adopted internationally and in SADC countries. The chapter concludes with the authors'

---

[5] Visit <https://www.afi-global.org/about/> accessed on 21 July 2021. See Shah and Shah (2014), pp. 51–52, for the discussion of its origin.

[6] See Soederberg (2013), p. 593. See also de Sousa (2015), for other GSSBs that embrace FI objectives.

[7] See Sect. 5.2 below.

[8] Alliance for Financial Inclusion (2012).

[9] The World Bank (2012) ('*NFIS Reference Framework*'). See also World Bank Group (2016) ('*NFIS Template*'), World Bank (2018) ('*World Bank NFIS Toolkit*'). The latter two policy documents are similar to the NFIS Reference Framework and is only referred to where necessary.

[10] Group of 20 Global Partnership for Financial Inclusion 'G20 Principles for Innovative Financial Inclusion' (2011) ('*G20 FI Principles*').

remarks on the character, components and the sources of international FI regulatory framework, the enforcement mechanisms, as well as a number of recommendations on how to improve the effectiveness of the global and the SADC FI regulatory frameworks.

2   The Definition of Financial Inclusion

There is no universal definition of financial inclusion or its antithesis 'financial exclusion'. It has also been defined differently and many of the definitions relate to the challenges of financial exclusion and the circumstances of a particular country. Financial Inclusion generally refers to the promotion of access to and use of financial services and products.[11] FI concept originally evolved from a narrow and restrictive definition focusing on the geographical aspects and 'access' to financial services as the main indicators of inclusion.[12] Lately, various additional dimensions, namely, accessibility, availability, and usage have been identified as other important dimensions of FI.[13] Other dimensions include the quality, appropriateness, availability and safety of financial services and products.[14] The latest addition to these dimensions is welfare, which questions the impact of FI on the welfare of the communities.[15] This literature also widely agrees that these concepts are multidimensional, involving a variety of possible financial services that must be available to the society, as well as different dimensions, components, and indicators of such availability.[16]

Price and costs related dimensions that focus on the affordability of financial services and products are also some of the key elements that form part of the FI definition.[17] The latest addition to these dimensions is welfare, which questions the impact of FI on the welfare of the communities.[18] The literature widely agrees that FI

---

[11] See Howell and Wilson (2005), p. 148. See Sarma and Pais (2011), p. 614.

[12] Leyshon and Thrift (1995), p. 315. See also Shetty and Pinto (2015), p. 1606. The geographical aspects of financial inclusion derive from the period of restricted physical access of banking services because of closure of bank branches in The United Kingdom.

[13] Sarma and Pais (2011), p. 614, See also Prahalad (2005), p. 18, who identify affordability, access and availability as the three basic principles upon which creating the capacity to consume is based on and describe them as the 'Three As', See also Mehta et al. (2015), p. 2, the authors identified access, usage, affordability and quality as the key areas that must be addressed for achieving financial inclusion objectives.

[14] CGAP (2017), p. 55. See also Bank of Papua New Guinea (n.d.), p. 11; Howell and Wilson (2005), p. 129; Cheston et al. (2016), p. 12.

[15] Alliance for Financial Inclusion (2017), p. 4; Honohan and King (2009), p. 3. See further CGAP (2017), p. 10; Regan and Paxton (2003), pp. 1 and 24.

[16] World Bank (2014), p. 15. See also Roa (2015), p. 6; Alliance for Financial Inclusion (2010), p. 4; Sarma and Pais (2011), p. 614.

[17] Prahalad (2005), p. 18.

[18] AFI (2017), p. 4, See also Honohan and King (2009), p. 3; Regan and Paxton (2017), pp. 1 and 24.

is multidimensional, and involving a variety of possible financial services that must be available to the society, as well as different dimensions, components, and indicators of such availability.[19]

According to the Consultative Group to Assist the Poor's (CGAP) *Guideline Statements*, a 'clear definitional framework for financial inclusion that includes definitions at the national, policy and product levels is needed to establish priorities, to avoid both irresponsible and misguided inclusion, and to measure progress'.[20] AFI has established a correlation between defining and setting appropriate policies and regulations to promote FI.[21] AFI provides key elements that assist to define FI, and that guide to formulate national policy and regulatory frameworks. They include the relevant dimensions to measure it;[22] the types of financial services that should be under the inclusion banner;[23] and the types of institutions that should provide these services.[24] The multi-dimensional patterns of FI and FE create uncertainties regarding universally adopted definitions of these concepts. Nonetheless, their definitions are important to guide the regulatory framework suitable to address the challenges of FE internationally and in the SADC region. The definition also helps to guide policy and regulatory frameworks reforms, and to measure the progress and outcomes of such reforms.[25]

3 Financial Inclusion and Exclusion in the SADC

Like many countries globally and in Africa, SADC member states are not spared from the challenges associated with financial exclusion. The overall FI of adults—covering both access and use of formal and informal financial products and services—in the SADC region according to the latest reports is at 68%.[26] This leaves 32% of the adult population in the region financially excluded. The number of the population who are financially included differs in different SADC member states.[27] FI statistics in SADC countries ranges from the high percent of 96 in

---

[19] World Bank (2014), p. 15; See also Roa (2015), p. 6; Alliance for Financial Inclusion (2010), p. 04; Sarma and Pais (2014), p. 614.

[20] CGAP (2012), p. 6.

[21] Alliance for Financial Inclusion (2010), p. 4.

[22] This includes access, use, and the quality of financial service.

[23] Such as credit, savings insurances and pensions.

[24] Alliance for Financial Inclusion (2010), p. 4. See also The World Bank (n.d.). This includes institutions such as banks, formal or semi-formal microfinance institutions, or informal institutions such as moneylenders.

[25] Alliance for Financial Inclusion (2013), p. 32. See also Aduda and Kalunda (2012), p. 99.

[26] SADC (2021). See also SADC (14 October 2021); FinMark Trust (2019).

[27] FinMark Trust (2016). See this chapter of this book on different percentages of FI in different SADC countries.

Seychelles to the lowest of 40% in Mozambique.[28] The levels of FI in different countries raise a concern with regard to the progress made to promote FI. The majority of the SADC countries have adopted national FI strategies that are aligned with the international guidelines and policy principles.[29] However, limitations and challenges that FinMark Trust has identified with the current data on FI and progress include lack of translating the enactments of these strategies and regulatory frameworks into effective FI data by financial services provider.[30]

4 International Regulatory Frameworks to Promote Financial Inclusion

4.1 Current International Financial Inclusion Regulation

There is no international instrument that specifically regulates access to financial services and FI in general. The absence of an international regulatory framework on FI results in a haphazard approach for regulating FI at domestic levels.[31] As Neves correctly posited about the regulation of FI in the relevant context, '[w]here the discourse of FI does surface in South Africa is in attempts, exercised by moral suasion and regulatory fiat'.[32] Except for the United Nations Convention on the Elimination of All Forms of Discrimination against Women (CEDAW),[33] access to financial services has also not been recognised as an international human right.[34] Few countries globally, such as Cambodia and Brazil, specifically provides for access to finance or FI in their Constitutions.[35] Except for South Africa, no

---

[28] See the latest coordinated statistics provided in the FinMark Trust (2018), for financial inclusion statistics of each countries and their breakdown into different types of products and the demographics factors that contribute to financial exclusion and inclusion percentages.

[29] See Sect. 5.2 below for the discussion of the SADC NFIS and some of the SADC countries that have adopted NFISs.

[30] Kettle (2019).

[31] See, for instance, Chitimira and Ncube (2020), p. 354.

[32] Neves (2018), p. 96.

[33] See Article 13(b) of 1979 United Nations Convention on the Elimination of All Forms of Discrimination Against Women (CEDAW), that provides to eliminate discrimination against women in the areas of economic and social life including bank loans. See Khan and Akther (2017), p. 15; Tully (2006), p. 68.

[34] See Tully (2006), pp. 67–68; Hudon (2009), p. 17; Bayulgen (2013), p. 491; Kumar (2014); Wade (2014); Gersham and Mudorch (2015), pp. 23–24; Bremer and Krain (2015), p. 377; Meyer (2018), p. 304.

[35] See Article 192 of The Constitution of the Federal Republic of Brazil 1988 (national financial systems to development credit cooperatives). See also Article 62 of the Constitution of the Kingdom of Cambodia 1993 (state to promote economic development. and 'to begin with the remotest areas, with concern for credit system'), See the Financial Inclusion in Banking Act of 2021, that was introduced recently as part of the Consumer Financial Protection Act of 2010 (12 U.S.C. 5493(b)

legislation in the SADC region specifically refers to FI.[36] Many SADC countries have legislation that only impact on promoting FI.[37] The FI international policy and regulatory frameworks are still developing and are currently fragmented. The GSSBs have taken the initiatives to develop these frameworks.[38] The policy documents and guidelines discussed in this chapter provide guidance on how to regulate FI at the national level, including SADC countries. The chapter also outlines the main elements that the NFIS must incorporate. The chapter will further outline key international role players, that are responsible to develop and implement these frameworks and strategies.

4.2 The AFI and FI Commitments

The AFI was established in 2008[39] to advance the development of FI policies in developing and emerging economies.[40] In 2011, members of the AFI committed their efforts to promote FI in developing countries by creating an enabling environment for access to financial services through signing the Maya Declaration.[41] The

---

(2)), This Act requires among others, the Office of Community Affairs to submit a report to Congress, within 2 years that identifies any factors impeding the ability of, or limiting the option for, individuals or households to have access to fair, on-going, and sustainable relationships with depository institutions to meet their financial needs, discusses any regulatory, legal, or structural barriers to enhancing participation of under-banked, un-banked, and underserved consumers with depository institutions.

[36] See ss 7(1)(f), 34(1)(e) 58(1)(e), 177(1)(i) Financial Sector Regulation Act 9 of 2017, See also the Conduct of Financial Institutions Bills, that requires financial institutions to promote financial inclusion.

[37] See Central Bank of Nigeria 'National Financial Inclusion Strategy' (n.d.), See for example the Namibian Payment System Management Act 2010. S 2 (d) provides that this is to ensure that the fees or charges payable by a user are in line with public interest, promote competition, efficiency and cost-effectiveness in the National Payment System, See Matongela (2014), p. 71. Different aspects that impacts on financial inclusion are microfinance, usury regulations, capping of interest rates, and consumer protection.

[38] See note 1 above.

[39] Alliance for Financial Inclusion (n.d.-a, n.d.-b). AFI is a network of financial inclusion policymakers comprising of central banks and other financial regulatory institutions from developing countries, visit <https://www.afi-global.org/about-us> accessed on 06 April 2021. Its members comprise of central banks and other financial regulatory institutions in more than 90 developing countries, including South Africa. AFI organises annual Global Policy Forums that serve as platforms for leaders of different member institutions to discuss and exchange ideas on how to develop and improve their national financial strategies and policies. South Africa is a member of AFI through the National Treasury and South African Reserve Bank, as principal member and associate member, respectively, visit <https://www.afiglobal.org/sites/default/files/inlinefiles/AFI%20Official%20Members_9%20April%202018.pdf> accessed on 06 April 2021.

[40] Alliance for Financial Inclusion (n.d.-a, n.d.-b).

[41] The Maya Declaration.

Maya Declaration represents the world's first set of commitments by central banks, supervisors and other financial regulatory authorities to prioritise FI through policy and regulatory frameworks.[42] Signatories to the Maya Declaration made a number of commitments relating to the promotion of FI. These include adopting FI policy to cost effective access to financial services, implementing proportional framework to achieve the complementary goals of financial inclusion, financial stability, and financial integrity, and recognising consumer protection and empowerment as a key pillar of FI.[43] The Maya Declaration is not a mandatory regulation but a set of voluntary guidelines to promote FI.[44] It is important to note that the majority of SADC member states are also member of the AFI.[45] They have also made commitments to develop policies and regulatory frameworks to promote FI under the Maya Declaration.[46]

4.3   The World Bank NFIS Reference Framework and the NFIS Template

The specific commitments made in the Maya Declaration are outlined in the *NFIS Reference Framework* and the *NFIS Template*.[47] Notably, these documents adopt a bottom-up approach and draw lessons from existing regulatory models from national regulatory frameworks, instead of a top-down approach that seeks to impose the formulation of a specific regulatory framework for FI.[48] The *NFIS Reference Framework* identifies and recommends six components for each country's FI actions.[49] These are:

---

[42] Alliance for Financial Inclusion 'A Quick Guide to the Maya Declaration on Financial Inclusion' (n.d.-a).

[43] The Maya Declaration Commitment (a)–(e). Other commitments are evidence-based FI data collection and supporting FI for SMMEs.

[44] Soederberg (2013), p. 599.

[45] See Alliance for Financial Inclusion 'Members' (n.d.-b). See also Alliance for Financial Inclusion '2020 Maya Declaration Progress Report – Approaching a Decade of Maya Declaration' (2020). They include Angola, Democratic Republic of Congo Eswatini, Seychelles, Namibia, Mozambique, Madagascar Lesotho, South Africa, Tanzania, Zambia, Zimbabwe.

[46] Alliance for Financial Inclusion (note 45 above).

[47] See also World Bank (June 2018), that provides for similar principles and framework to develop NFIS.

[48] Staschen and Nelson (2013), p. 78. See also Stein et al. (2011), p. 442, See the authors views on the adoption of a bottom-up approach in Sect. 8 below.

[49] NFIS Reference Framework 6.

(1) Stocktaking: data and diagnostics[50]
(2) Targets and objectives.[51]
(3) Strategy-Building or Revision.
(4) Public Sector Actions: Policies, Regulation, and Financial Infrastructure
(5) Progress-Monitoring.
(6) Private Sector Actions.

These components are complementary and each important as the other. We discuss components (3), (4) and (5) and (6) below. We focus specifically on these components as they determine specific regulatory actions and measures that are key to the formulation a national FI regulatory framework.

4.3.1 The NFIS Format and Approaches

The *NFIS Reference Framework* defines an NFIS as a roadmap of actions that is agreed and defined at national and subnational levels which all stakeholders can follow to achieve and improve FI objectives using effective and efficient measures and tools.[52] This framework aims to bring various stakeholders from both public and private sectors to improve FI.[53] The framework recommends countries to develop NFISs as accessible references for regulators and policymakers to reflect on existing FI approaches. As discussed in detail in Sect. 5.2 below a number of SADC countries have developed NFIS in line with the NFIS Reference Framework.

The *strategy-building and revision* component in the *NFIS Reference Framework* identifies the actual format on how an NFIS must be developed. It also outlines how an existing one may be revised or adapted. An NFIS is not required to be an all-inclusive policy document incorporating all key aspects to enhance FI.[54] It may be developed in 'whatever form'.[55] This implies that each country has the discretion to adopt a NFIS that suits her own circumstances. The *NFIS Reference Framework* identifies three different approaches for developing a NFIS. These are (1) standalone NFIS, (2) one that forms part of an overall financial sector development strategy, and (3) one that focuses on specific aspects of FI.[56]

---

[50]This requires a collection of relevant data, which outlines the state of financial inclusion or exclusion in a country.

[51]This generally requires countries to set specific targets and objectives in their NFISs, with regard to space and time to achieve certain level of FI or products.

[52]*NFIS Reference Framework* 6.

[53]Mdasha et al. (2018), p. 52.

[54]See the authors views on the adoption of this approach in Sect. 8 below.

[55]NFIS Reference Framework 11.

[56]NFIS Reference Framework 11. See also Alliance for Financial Inclusion 'Strategy Development Organizing for Financial Inclusion Supporting Strategic Approaches in the AFI Network' (2012). See further Prochaska 'Financial Inclusion Strategies: Global Trends and Lessons Learnt for the AFI Network' (2014), who identifies traditional two approaches as the stand-alone FIS and the broader financial sector strategy.

A *standalone NFIS* is published as a detailed strategic document that specifies action plans and targets to promote FI. It may focus on one or more areas where action that focuses on promoting FI is required.[57] This type of an NFIS may incorporate one of existing policies that interrelate with the promotion of FI. These generally include financial stability, financial integrity, market conduct, or financial capability.[58] The *NFIS Reference Framework* recommends an NFIS with a specific focus on one of these objectives but prioritises the promotion of FI.[59]

A country's NFIS may form part of the overall national financial sector strategy identified FI as an ancillary and complementary objective. A relevant example is a national financial strategic document that focuses on financial stability, integrity, market conduct and financial capability of consumers, or financial consumer protection and small-and-medium enterprise finance (SME) and outlines these strategic plans as the main objectives, with FI elevated to a status of simply one other important target.[60] It may also be part of other national strategic documents such as national poverty reduction strategy or national development plan.[61]

National policymakers and regulators could consider adopting NFISs that specifically focus on specific areas where there are identified needs for actions.[62] For instance, an NFIS may specifically focus on the lack of financial education as a key barrier towards FI,[63] on addressing barriers to microfinance,[64] or access, usage, affordability, and availability to low-income retail banking, or prioritise micro lending. The Indian *Master Circular - Lending to Priority Sector* that stimulates the provision of microcredits to the priority sectors such as agriculture, is a good example of this type of NFIS.[65]

The *NFIS Reference Framework* largely favours an NFIS that specifically targets one or more barriers towards FI. However, it takes cognisance of the interrelation between the FI policy objective with other long-standing policy objectives outlined above.[66] These policy objectives may be prioritised according to their relative importance for achieving the vision of the NFIS. The NFIS should however, not rank one or more of each objective as more important than the other to achieve FI.[67]

---

[57] NFIS Reference Framework 11.

[58] NFIS Reference Framework 11.

[59] NFIS Reference Framework 11–12. See also NFIS Template 8.

[60] See for instance National Treasury (2011). This policy document was developed following the global financial crisis to address financial sector instability provided in the United Nations (2006) ('United Nations Bluebook'), and provides that the NFIS may also be part of other national strategic documents such as the national poverty reduction strategy or the national development plan.

[61] United Nations Bluebook (2006) 3. See also Mdasha et al. (2018), p. 52.

[62] NFIS Reference Framework 11.

[63] See for instance, Reserve Bank of India (2021). On the main objectives of this document see Das (2021), p. 1.

[64] Alliance for Financial Inclusion (n.d.-a, n.d.-b), p. 2.

[65] Reserve Bank of India (2008) *RBI/2008-09/69*.

[66] NFIS Reference Framework 11. See also NFIS Template 8.

[67] NFIS Template 8.

4.3.2 Policy Framework and Infrastructure

The *NFIS Reference Framework* also addresses the provision of infrastructure and the relevant national policies and regulations. This framework recommends a coordinated partnership among different government agencies to implement policies and regulations, and for effective formulation and execution of the *NFIS*.[68] The *NFIS Reference Framework* recommends governments and regulators to implement reforms that promote financial sector activities and innovations in accordance with their NFISs' targets.[69] Possible actions that governments may implement include regulatory reforms to remove barriers to FI and bottlenecks that impede private sector actions.[70] An example of possible reforms is to remove possible barriers to financial service innovations and deliveries.[71] The *NFIS Reference Framework* requires reform to be proportional and flexible to allow new business models and innovations to enhance FI, while also ensuring financial stability and the soundness of financial institutions and agents, financial integrity, and to strengthen the protection of consumers and depositors.[72] This must proportionately enhance the regulatory role of designing and implementing an enabling environment for FI.[73]

The *NFIS Reference Framework* also requires government, regulators and other relevant stakeholders to put financial infrastructures in place that complement regulatory reforms and to lower financial products costs and others that may be incurred by the service providers.[74] Such infrastructures are necessary for regulatory reforms to introduce new financial innovations such as channelling payment through bank accounts and the introduction of low-cost products and delivery models.[75]

4.3.3 Private Sector Actions and Commitments

From the analysis of the *NFIS Reference Framework,* it is evident that the private sector also plays a major role to advance the financial growth of the poor. Private financial sector helps to develop and deliver financial products and services. The *NFIS Reference Framework* also recommends their active participation to design FI strategies, to set FI target, and to monitoring FI progress.[76] This framework identifies two possible actions that the private sectors can take to implement the NFIS. The first

---

[68]NFIS Reference Framework 13. See also Alliance for Financial Inclusion (2013), p. 1, on the importance of effective coordination, Mdasha et al. (2018), p. 68.
[69]NFIS Reference Framework 13.
[70]NFIS Reference Framework 13.
[71]NFIS Reference Framework 13.
[72]NFIS Reference Framework 13.
[73]NFIS Reference Framework 29.
[74]NFIS Reference Framework 13.
[75]NFIS Reference Framework 13.
[76]NFIS Reference Framework 40.

involves financial infrastructure development. The financial sector can help to achieve national FI targets by introducing products, and delivery mechanisms that respond to the needs of the excluded.[77] The second action that the *NFIS Reference Framework* recommends the private sector to introduce a voluntary self-regulatory model as a voluntary private commitments to promote FI.[78] The framework encourages banks and other financial institutions to cooperate with relevant government departments and take a leading role to achieve FI.[79] This framework specifically recommends them to set up task forces and coordinating bodies to identify barriers and to develop shared objectives towards FI.[80] As an example of a voluntary commitment, the *NFIS Reference Framework* recommends financial institutions to develop their FI targets and actions through a charter.[81] This will provide them with the opportunity to take the ownership of their achievements towards enhancing FI. They will therefore avoid external impositions of FI regulations from the regulator.[82]

4.3.4 NFIS Monitoring and Enforcement Mechanism

The last component of the *NFIS Reference Framework* deals with monitoring and implementing the NFIS.[83] It requires monitoring and evaluation of the progress made, and to assess the level that a country is achieving FI targets and objectives outlined in a NFIS. Importantly, the *NFIS Reference Framework* also requires countries to assesses 'the effectiveness of the reforms, products, or delivery mechanisms that have been introduced.[84] A country must further assess possible risks that may affect the implementation of the strategies. The *NFIS Reference Framework* encourages continuous monitoring of the NFIS to achieve FI.[85] Such monitoring involves global cross-country data from national surveys.[86] The framework further requires the establishment of relevant institutional mechanisms.[87]

---

[77] NFIS Reference Framework 10. Examples of these products include mobile phone banking, electronic money, microinsurance and accessible low-income savings accounts and credits.

[78] NFIS Template 13.

[79] NFIS Template 13.

[80] NFIS Reference Framework 40, See also NFIS Template 13.

[81] NFIS Reference Framework 40.

[82] NFIS Reference Framework 40.

[83] NFIS Reference Framework 13.

[84] NFIS Reference Framework 13.

[85] NFIS Reference Framework 13.

[86] NFIS Reference Framework 19.

[87] Adeyemi (2021).

4.3.5   The G20 FI Principles and Specific Contents of the FI Framework

The *G20 FI Principles* form a set of innovations that the G20 adopted to enhance FI. In 2010, leaders of the G20 committed to provide practical recommendations and conditions for policymakers to spur innovations for FI.[88] The G20 adopted them against the backdrop of the global financial crisis and emphasised the safe adoption of delivery models and extending financial services to the poor 'while safeguarding financial stability and protecting consumers'.[89] A number of these principles resemble many components of the *NFIS Reference Framework* and the commitments made in the Maya Declaration.[90] We discuss Principles 4, 5, 8, 9, as they add key policy and regulatory objectives that support or compete with the FI policy. These principles also address continuing debates relating to trade-offs and synergies between FI policy and other traditional policy frameworks that focus on financial stability, integrity and consumer protection.[91]

Principle 4 deals with consumer protection. It recognises the prevention of possible risks of fraud and abuse that result from human or technical errors in providing financial services as a vital part of a broader FI framework.[92] It encourages governments, service providers and consumers to adopt a comprehensive approach to consumer protection to prevent their impact on consumers' access to financial services.[93] Principle 5 focuses on the demand-side of FI and the knowledge that consumers require 'to make the most of new financial services'.[94] It recommends national financial literacy and capability frameworks that form the integral part of consumer protection regulation.[95]

Principles 8 and 9 consider existing policy objectives that may either promote or hamper the FI progress. Principle 8 takes stock of the need to protect the financial system and institutions and proposes a policy and regulatory framework that is proportionate to the risks in innovative products and services and that understands gaps and barriers in existing regulation. Principle 9 provides key components of what must be included in a FI regulatory framework. Principle 9 draws together many of the principles in the *G20 FI Principles* and outlines components that form an effective regulatory framework to promote FI.[96] This principle recommends such framework to consider components that reflect international standards; support for a

---

[88] Global Partner for Financial Inclusion (2011).

[89] G20 FI Principles (see the overview).

[90] These include government commitments and institutional cooperation (P1 and 6); products, provider and delivery methods diversity (P2); technological and institutional innovation (P3); and data and knowledge management of FI (P7).

[91] Aduda and Kalunda (2012), p. 109; Lawack (2013), p. 317; de Koker and Jentzsch (2013), p. 267; Dema (2014); de Sousa (2015); Morgan and Pontines (2018), p. 111.

[92] GPFI (2011), p. 3.

[93] G20 FI Principle 4. See also GPFI (2011), p. 3.

[94] GPFI (2011), p. 3.

[95] G20 FI Principle 4. See also GPFI (2011), p. 3.

[96] GPFI (2011), p. 5.

competitive landscape; and an appropriate, flexible, and a risk-based approach to AML/CFT regime. Principle 9 further recommends a framework to include the use of agents as a customer interface, a regulatory regime for electronically stored value, and market-based incentives to achieve the long-term goal of broad interoperability and interconnection.[97] Principally, the *G20 FI Principles* complement both the Maya Declaration and the World Bank *NFIS Reference Framework* by guiding regulators and policymakers on key considerations and the main components that form an effective FI regulatory framework.

5   SADC Financial Inclusion Framework

5.1   SADC Financial Inclusion Strategies

Prior to 2016, SADC did not have a specific regional policy framework to promote FI. The SADC Committee of Ministers of Finance and Investment in first presented a draft *SADC Financial Inclusion Strategy* (draft SADCFIS) at the SADC Financial Inclusion Strategy Workshop in 2016.[98] The draft SADCFIS was developed in line with World Bank's *NFIS Reference Framework.*[99] The main purpose of the draft SADCFIS is to outline the FI strategy and to align isolated and uncoordinated FI policies to support a regional financial integration.[100] This FI strategy identifies a number of FI barriers. They include barriers to new entrants to provide financial services, physical infrastructure to address the distance gap, mobile connectivity challenges in the region that may create a barrier for the provision of these services, and lack of documentation and the effect of applying stringent KYC.[101] Another key barrier is the lack of appropriate products such as savings and credits, which are relatively inflexible to meet the needs of the majority of the low-income population.[102]

   The draft SADCFIS proposes five categories of interventions to promote FI in the SADC. These interventions are funding, advocacy, research and development, capacity building, and technical assistance. These interventions generally seek to establish funding, create FI awareness among various stakeholders and regulators, and to capacitate both states and non-government actors to drive FI nationally and

---

[97]GPFI (2011), p. 5. On interoperability and financial inclusion, see Arabehety et al. (2016).

[98]FinMark Trust (2016), See also SADC 'SADC Financial Inclusion Strategy' (2016-2021).

[99]Although the document does not refer to the *NFIS Reference Framework* or *Template*, it acknowledges the existing international efforts on financial inclusion, including AFI's Maya Declaration, see SADCFIS 51 and 52.

[100]SADCFIS 5.

[101]SADCFIS 36–40.

[102]SADCFIS 38. See also other barriers such as limited financial capability and education and negative perception about financial institution only providing services to the elite.

the regional level.[103] These interventions are however not regulatory in nature or promoting FI through a legal framework.

The draft SADCFIS seeks to coordinate variety of existing national activities and policies to promote FI. However, it is not its objective to elevate FI framework to a regional level and to side-line the existing national FI strategies. It also does not replace these strategies or to prescribe what they must cover, but targets to complement and support them.[104] The draft SADCFIS was developed to align national and regional strategies, and to address regional FI issues that support regional integration.[105] Such issues include the 'regulatory harmonisation and alignment' of FI strategies.[106] From the reading of the draft SADCFIS, it is quite clear that it does not propose the form that the regulatory strategy for FI in the SADC must follow.

The SADFIS remains in a draft form and has not fully been implemented as a regional policy or regulatory framework.[107] Identified deficiencies that delayed its implementation include lack of specific reference to the impact of FI on poverty alleviation, and not covering a wide range of FI dimensions, products and target group.[108] In its current form, it does not provide for enforcement mechanisms that will be applied to ensure that SADC countries effectively implement the FI policies and regulations locally. The draft SADCFIS only outlines monitoring frameworks that use indicators to measure progresses and to suggest new NFIS targets.[109] It intends to use these indicators to determine how the 'implementation of national financial inclusion strategies within SADC will be used to assess how regional efforts are spurring legislative change at the national level'.[110]

5.2 National Financial Inclusion Strategies in SADC Countries

A number of SADC countries have developed NFIS in line with the AFI and World Bank FI policy documents. Some countries have NFISs under development,[111]

---

[103] SADCFIS 43–50.

[104] SADCFIS 5.

[105] SADCFIS 5, See also FinMark Trust (2016).

[106] SADCFIS 5.

[107] See FinMark Trust (2016).

[108] FinMark Trust (2016), which refer to the implementation of the SADC Financial Inclusion Strategy and SME Access to Finance (2016–2020), which was approved in 2016, as 'ongoing'. However, the SADFIS that is available of FinMark Trust website is still in its draft form. Visit <https://finmark.org.za/system/documents/files/000/000/207/original/FI-strategy-SADC.pdf?1601 978334#:~:text=The%20SADC%20Council%20of%20Ministers,Indicative%20Strategic%20 Development%20Plan%20(RISDP> accessed on 19 October 2021.

[109] SADCFIS 5.

[110] SADCFIS 63.

[111] See National Treasury: South Africa 'An Inclusive Financial Sector For All' (n.d.), the document is still in draft form for consultations.

whereas others have not developed them yet.[112] Existing NFISs range from stand-alone NFIS,[113] those that include FI within the overall financial sector strategies,[114] and those that focus on one specific area of needs that is related to the promotion of FI.[115] Examples of stand-alone NFISs focus on FI as a key priority such as access cost bank account and credit, but include other related financial sector policy objectives to enhance FI.[116] The NFIS of Botswana, for instance, focuses on access to low-cost saving products and access to credit for consumption smoothing, but include consumer protection and tied know your customer measures as other priorities.[117] Zambia's NFIS focuses specifically on a wide variety of financial products such as savings, credit, pensions and insurance, but also include consumer protection and financial education.[118] Namibia's Financial Sector Strategy prioritises both financial stability and FI (that include access and use of financial services and consumer protection and education) equally,[119] whereas Lesotho's Financial Sector Development Strategy prioritises FI, promoting savings culture (by among others, consumer protection measures), financial stability and soundness, and ensuring efficient payment system.[120] Seychelles Financial Education Strategy focuses on financial education and literacy and only refers to how they enhance FI, stability and consumer protection.[121]

The stand-alone NFISs in SADC countries show a disparities in terms of the issues that are included in the relevant policy. A NFIS of Zimbabwe outlines key steps to balance FI and financial integrity.[122] Zambia and Mozambique NFISs only refer to a complementary value of FI policy to other financial sector initiatives such

---

[112] See in the case of Angola, World Bank (2020), where the World Bank recommends the government of Angola to develop NFIS that will enhance financial inclusion.

[113] Ministry of Finance and Economic Development: Government of Botswana (2015), Minister of Finance and Budget (2018) (NFIS Madagascar), National Financial Inclusion Council: Tanzania (2018), Ministry of Finance: Malawi (2010) (NFIS Malawi), Bank of Mozambique (2016) (NFIS Mozambique). Ministere Des Finances: Comores (2011), Ministry of Finance: Eswatini (2017) (NFIS Eswatini), Ministry of Finance: Zambia (2017–2022) (NFIS Zambia), Reserve Bank of Zimbabwe (2016) ('NFIS Zimbabwe').

[114] Ministry of Finance (2011–2021) (Namibia FSS), Central Bank of Lesotho (2013) (Lesotho FSDS).

[115] Central Bank of Seychelles (2017).

[116] See NFIS Botswana 25–27 and 56.

[117] See NFIS Botswana 25–27 and 56.

[118] See NFIS Zambia 19–20, See also NFIS Madagascar that focuses on the access and use of various products, together with financial education and protection.

[119] It set financial safety that ensures financial stability, financial inclusion, and financial literacy and protection as they main outcome that it seeks to achieve 2030. See NFSS Namibia 22–54.

[120] Lesotho FSDS Part I–V.

[121] NFES Seychelles 1, where it says "FinEd is therefore relevant in the context of financial inclusion as well as financial market stability. It also holds a close relationship with consumer financial protection and it is through FinEd that individuals are informed of their rights, recourse mechanisms and responsibilities."

[122] NFIS Zimbabwe 35.

as financial stability, financial integrity, and consumer protection.[123] The majority of NFIS in the SADC include consumer protection as part of their FI objectives.[124] However, they do not address the impact of financial stability and integrity on enhancing FI.[125] For instance, Botswana, Eswatini, Malawi, and Mozambique's NFISs only refer to the importance of promoting FI while ensuring financial stability.[126] They, however, do not provide key steps to balance these competing policy objectives. The overall financial sector strategies in Namibia and Lesotho cover and make specific commitments to align FI and other competing financial policy objectives.[127] A significant similarity between all the NFISs in the SADC is the application of monitoring and evaluation as the implementation mechanisms to ensure their effectiveness and to determine FI progress.[128]

6 Hard Law and Soft Law: International Financial Inclusion Regulatory Best Practices

Effective international and SADC policy and regulatory frameworks to promote FI requires policy makers and regulators to make a decisive choice relating to the form of regulation that they must adopt. Over the years, regulation has taken the form of hard law or soft law. The guidelines and principles discussed in this chapter still

---

[123] NFIS Zambia 2, Mozambique viii.

[124] See NFIS Botswana 29, Lesotho 37–38, NFIF Tanzania 6, NFIS Zambia 2, NFIS Mozambique 17–18, NFIS Madagascar 17, NFIS Seychelles 9–10, NFIS Zimbabwe 19. NFIS Malawi 21, FSS Namibia 25–26.

[125] Cf NFIF Tanzania 13 ('maintaining an appropriate balance between financial inclusion objectives and other policies, such as financial stability and consumer protection').

[126] NFIS Mozambique 22 ('financial inclusion should be accomplished in a responsible manner which does not impact negatively on the stability of the financial system')and NFIS Botswana 33 ('from a stability perspective financial stability risks can increase when access to credit is expanded without proper supervision'), NFIS Malawi 14–15 (referring to its formulation based on internationally accepted inclusive finance guiding principles and paradigm that ensure effective oversight on the activities of inclusive finance providers, adoption of best practices and stability of the financial system), NFIS Eswatini ('Ensure a balance between the implementation of the strategy and the financial stability').

[127] FSS Namibia 33 ('The inherent conflict between financial integrity and financial access shall be guarded to ensure a good balance') FSDS Namibia viii ('regulatory constraints on expansion of financial services will be minimized to the extent consistent with consumer protection and financial stability'), Lesotho para 253–261, See further draft NFIS South Africa 73 ('The pursuit of these objectives and any resulting trade-offs must be balanced and proportionate, an approach referred to as I-SIP. The pursuit of the balanced (or I-SIP) approach encapsulated in this principle highlights that financial inclusion efforts should not be to the detriment of the other components (and vice versa)').

[128] NFIS Botswana 35–37, Lesotho paras 253–261, NFIS Malawi 24–25, NFIS Mozambique 38, NFIS Madagascar 23–24, FSS Namibia 38, NFIF Tanzania 33, NFIS Zambia 25–26, NFIS Zimbabwe 46, See also draft NFIS South Africa 89–90.

lacks important components that provide for effective regulation of FI. A brief discussion of these types of law is necessary to determine the types of regulation that policymakers and regulators should adopt to effectively promote FI.

International law lacks an 'official global legislature' similar to domestic laws.[129] Article 38 of the Statute of the International Court of Justice (SICJ) outlines recognised sources of international law.[130] These include international conventions, international customs, and the general principles of law recognised by civilised nations.[131] These are traditionally classified as hard law, as distinguished from 'soft law'. Three key features characterise an instrument as an international hard law. These are precision, obligation and delegation.[132] It also requires certain procedural formalities to give the rules a specific legal status.[133] On the other hand, soft law denotes international standards that lack key tenants of international law such as formalities for its legitimacy, precise normative content, enforceability, and formal legal status. Examples are general principles, guidelines, policy statements, recommendations and other provisional international legal frameworks.[134]

Soft law is generally not recognised by Article 38 of SICJ.[135] Contrary to hard law, its contents are less precise and it does not impose binding obligations.[136] It includes non-binding principles and voluntary standards that depend on consent and consensus for their adoption and implementation.[137] Many of these standards and principles serve 'norm-creating' and progressive law-making roles in the area where there is absence of binding international standards to influence the development of the law or in anticipation of themselves becoming laws that are enforceable.[138] For instance, soft law may serve as a template for hard law and subsequently result in becoming a model treaty.[139] However, soft law promulgation can also serve to

---

[129] Goldbarsht (2020), p. 4.

[130] See Hirsch (2012), p. 9.

[131] Bjorklund and Reinisch (2012), p. 52. See also Ebikakev (2016), p. 351.

[132] Abbott and Snidal (2000), pp. 421–422, See also Dostov et al. (2019), pp. 477 and 423. 'Delegation' in this context connotes simply that soft law does not allow for delegation of sovereignty from states to supranational bodies, nor does it delegate authority for interpreting and implementing the law.

[133] Weber (2012), pp. 11–13; CF at page 11 where the author indicates that '[t]he notion that legalization entails a specific form of discourse, requiring justification and persuasion in terms of applicable rules and pertinent facts is not only an element of hard law, but also of soft law'.

[134] Johansson and Donner (2015), p. 93. See also Dostov et al. (2019), p. 477. Others include non-binding decisions of international organisations and bodies, programmes, declarations, directives, opinions, plans of action, and programmes of action. See Blutman (2010), p. 607.

[135] Blutman (2010), pp. 606–608.

[136] Dostov et al. (2019), p. 477.

[137] Johansson and Donner (2015), p. 93.

[138] Blutman (2010), pp. 617–618. See also Bjorklund and Reinisch (2012), pp. 51 and 53–54. According to this author, '[t]he concept of soft law is effective in alerting users 'to the possibility of different levels [and] components of any legal formulation', See further Weber (2012), p. 12.

[139] Bjorklund and Reinisch (2012), pp. 55 and 73, The author however, identifies one goal of soft law 'promulgation to forestall formal regulation that would likely be more cumbersome and intrusive and thus less welcome'.

forestall formal regulation that would likely be more cumbersome and intrusive and thus less welcome'.[140]

Additional distinguishing character of the two is the language used in each instrument. Soft law signifies unspecific, vague, and informal principles that are not rules.[141] It consists of 'law-like promises or statements that fall short of hard law' and uses the language that is merely 'hortatory, aspirational or promotional in character'.[142] Where it takes the form of principles, they are formulated with a high level of abstraction. Such vagueness precludes objective verification. Therefore, members can choose to comply with these voluntary standards.[143]

One feature that distinguishes hard law from soft law is the type of institutions that formulate and implement international standards. Generally, many of the traditional international regulatory institutions and organisations traditionally establish international instruments and agreements between states, such as treaties and charters that impose international legal obligations.[144] International soft law norms are generally developed by informal institutions, such as standards-setting transnational and intergovernmental bodies that also adopt various compliance mechanisms.[145] These institutions are established by either informal by-laws, agreements, or declarations that do not have formal international obligations or existence, unlike most traditional international regulatory institutions such as the United Nations.[146] In many instances, they lack effective enforcement and dispute settlement mechanisms. Their available enforcement mechanisms include the disciplining of members when they fail to comply with their obligations as members of the organisation.[147]

7 The FATF Standards and Enforcement Mechanisms

7.1 The FATF and the International AML/CFT Standards

The FATF is one of the influential GSSBs that promotes FI. The main objectives of the FAFT include setting standards on anti-money laundering and combating the

---

[140] Bjorklund and Reinisch (2012), pp. 73 and 74.

[141] Guzman and Meyer (2010), p. 205.

[142] Guzman and Meyer (2010), p. 188.

[143] Bjorklund and Reinisch (2012), p. 58.

[144] Brummer (2012), p. 64.

[145] See Borlini and Montanaro (2017), p. 1024. See also Andonova and Elsig (2012), pp. 64–65. Examples of these standards setting bodies in the financial sector include the Bank for International Settlement (BIS), the International Organisation of Securities Commissions (IOSCO), the International Association of Insurance Supervisors (IAIS), the Financial Stability Board (FSB) and the Organisation for Economic Co-operation and Development (OECD).

[146] Brummer (2012), pp. 64–65.

[147] Brummer (2012).

financing of terrorism (AML/CFT), known as the 'Recommendations'.[148] The Recommendations, as Dasser correctly observed 'are prime example of the force of soft law: although non-binding'.[149] They are lauded as 'the most successful and ambitious international standards' and have been endorsed by the United Nations as comprehensive international AML/CFT standards.[150] The current revised 2012 Recommendations[151] require countries to have measures that include the identification of risks of money laundering and terrorism financing posed to the financial sector.[152]

In 2011, the FATF developed the *FATF Financial Inclusion Guidance* to balance its AML/CFT measures with the new FI policy objective.[153] The guidance establishes possible solutions to address challenges that regulators and financial institutions encounter in their efforts to meet the needs of the financially excluded and complying with the FATF's AML/CFT measures.[154] It proposes a risk-based approach (RBA) that countries must comply with by building their AML/CFT regimes in a way 'that addresses the most pressing money laundering and terror financing risks while taking into account the importance of financial inclusion'.[155] First introduced in the FATF 2012 Recommendations, a RBA requires countries to apply lower-risk assessment to financial products or services that provide limited services to certain types of customers to increase access to FI.[156]

---

[148] Financial Action Task Force (n.d.-c) 'Who We Are' <http://www.fatf-gafi.org/fr/aproposdugafi/> accessed on 15 March 2021. See also Pieth and Aiolfi (2004), pp. 3–35, de Koker *South African Money Laundering and Terror Financing Law* (2013a), p. 9, Goldbarsht (2020), p. 58, on the ancient history of the FATF.

[149] Dasser (2021), p. 49. See also Ryder (2011), pp. 16–18, They have also been endorsed by the United Nations Security Council.

[150] Bachus (2004), pp. 859–860. See also Martuscello (2011), p. 365; Brummer (2012), p. 86. See the United Nations Security Council Resolution 1617 (2005) S/RES/1617, adopted by the Security Council at its 5244th meeting on 29 July 2005.

[151] The Recommendations were revised in 1996, 2003 to address the challenges of the September 11, 2001 terror attacks, and recently revisited in 2012 to include the Know Your Customer and Customer Due Diligence procedures in relation to new technologies among other.

[152] See page 6 of the 2012 Recommendations.

[153] Asia/Pacific Group on Money Laundering, The World Bank Group and FATF (2011) ('FATF *Financial Inclusion Guidance* 2011'), Guidelines were revised in 2012 as FATF, Asia/Pacific Group on Money Laundering and The World Banking (2013) ('FATF *Financial Inclusion Guidance* 2013').

[154] FATF Financial Inclusion Guidance 2011 16.

[155] FATF Financial Inclusion Guidance 2011 17. See also FATF Financial Inclusion Guidance 2013 9. Other measures include reading customer due diligence (CDD) measures in light of financial inclusion, by introducing simplified CDD; introducing alternative identification processes that do not create new barriers that further undermine financial inclusion; and the integration of financial inclusion into the mutual evaluation methodology and process.

[156] See the Interpretive Note to Recommendation 10(17) (b) of the FATF 2012 Recommendations.

7.2 The FATF's Enforcement Mechanisms

The FATF is a 'policy making body' and its purpose is to generate the relevant political will for relevant legislative and regulatory reforms.[157] As Mugarura correctly asserted;[158]

> it is a voluntary task force and not a treaty organization: its 40 recommendations do not constitute a binding national convention but provide a guideline framework for combating money laundering.

The FATF's *Financial Inclusion Guidance* is also non-binding.[159] This guidance also does not override national measures on FI.[160] The FATF's *Financial Inclusion Guidance* provides simple guidelines to assist countries to develop AML/CFT measures that meet the goals of FI.[161] Likewise, the FATF Recommendations seem to mean just 'recommendations'. Many of them are phrased in voluntary terms and are not mandatory.[162] A number of them refer to the phrase 'should consider', and provide countries with choices to apply or reject its approaches.[163] The FATF Recommendations have, however, contributed to the adoption of AML/CFT measures by many countries. The FATF achieves its objectives by applying mutual evaluations (ME) and naming and shaming 'Higher Risk Jurisdictions Subject to Call for Action' (HRJSCA) as effective measures to implement, enforce and monitor national compliance with AML/CFT standards.[164] It is important to note that African countries including those in the SADC have been on the list of NCCT, HRJSCA, or simply as countries having strategic AML/CFT deficiencies.[165] Currently, the FATF has identified Zimbabwe as one of the countries with strategic deficiencies to counter terror financing and money laundering.[166]

---

[157] FATF (n.d.-a) 'About the FATF' <http://www.fatf-gafi.org/about/> accessed on 02 April 2021, see also Hayes (2012), p. 14.

[158] Mugarura (2012), pp. 79–80.

[159] FATF Financial Inclusion Guidance 2011 6 and 10, FATF Financial Inclusion Guidance 2013 5.

[160] FATF Financial Inclusion Guidance 2013 5.

[161] *Ibid.*

[162] Png (2010), p. 91, on the deliberate choice not to cast the recommendations in the form of a treaty. See further Ryder (2011), p. 15; Ghoshray (2014), p. 521; Shami (2015), p. 21.

[163] See FATF 2012 Recommendations Rec 4 ('Countries should consider adopting measures'); Rec 10 (Financial institutions...should consider making a suspicious transactions report'), See also Recs 24 and 25, See further Broome (2005), p. 555.

[164] Another mechanism that it applies is the 'Annual Self-Assessment Exercise' in terms of which it sends questionnaire to countries to record progresses of their AML/CFT measures and how they meet the criteria for each Recommendation. See FATF (1997), See also the FATF (2018a) amended 2020 ('FATF *Effectiveness Assessment Methodology* 2013'); Koh (2006), p. 162; Tuba (2012), p. 106; Roberger (2011), p. 46.

[165] Nigeria on the NCCT list, See FATF (2003), Ethiopia Ghana, Nigeria, and Tanzania in 2012, See FATF (2012) Nigeria on the list of NCCT. Currently, only Democratic Republic of Korea and Iran are on the HRJSCA list. See FATF (2020a, b, c).

[166] FATF (2020).

7.2.1 Mutual Evaluations

The FATF's ME involves a peer-review and the assessment of a country's compliance with its Recommendations.[167] Importantly, FI is now one of the core issues that the assessors must focus on.[168] They must determine how countries apply the AML/CFT measures to prevent the legitimate use of formal financial systems.[169] It currently assesses countries' levels of promoting FI and 'the manner in which they avoid applying AML/CFT to prevent the legitimate use of the formal financial system.[170] For instance, during the fourth ME in 2018, the FATF found Mauritius to have a high percentage of FI and not posing a high risk of money laundering and terror financing.[171] In 2021, South Africa was found to have progressed to make financial services accessible. However, the FATF was concerned with failure to limit the use of cash that may pose AML/CFT risk to pose such risks due to higher percentage of consumers that use products in the informal financial sector.[172]

7.2.2 High Risk Jurisdiction Subject to Call for Action[173]

During the ME, countries that have ineffective AML/CFT measures, are given an opportunity to improve and deliver a progress report.[174] For countries that do not comply or show progress following their assessments, the FATF relies on coercive enforcement methods that identify a country as HRJSCA and requires financial institutions to apply enhanced due diligence measures to business relationships and financial transactions with anyone in that country.[175]

---

[167] FATF (2018a, b, c) ('FATF *Mutual Evaluation Procedure* 2018'); See FATF (2009).

[168] FATF (2013), p. 103. Cf FATF Financial Inclusion Guidance 2013 9. According to this guidance paper, it 'does not explore how financial inclusion should be integrated into the mutual evaluation methodology and process. However, it highlights the need to better inform the assessors and the assessed countries based on the principle that financial exclusion could undermine the effectiveness of an AML/CFT regime given'.

[169] FATF Effectiveness Assessment Methodology 2013 103.

[170] FATF Effectiveness Assessment Methodology 2013 103.

[171] Eastern and Southern Africa Anti-Money Laundering Group (2018), para 58. See also Eastern and Southern Africa Anti-Money Laundering Group (2021), para 121, where the FATF indicates South Africa's progress with ensuring access to financial services, but highlighted the need for steps to cap the use of cash to prevent money laundering and terror financing.

[172] FATF (2021), para 54. For other countries elsewhere see for instance, the FATF and El Grupo de Acción Financiera de Latinoamérica (GAFILAT) (2018), para 53, where the FATF found AML/CFT in Mexico to pose such risks due to higher percentage of consumers that use products in the informal financial sector.

[173] FATF (n.d.-a, n.d.-b, n.d.-c). For the history of the new methods and the participation of the ICRG see Nance (2018), p. 131.

[174] FATF Effectiveness Assessment Methodology 2013 5. See also FATF Mutual Evaluation Procedure 2018, See also Damais (2007), pp. 75–76, Jensen and Png (2011), p. 113.

[175] FATF 2012 Recommendations Rec 19 and Rec 21.

In the past, the FAFT used the non-co-operative countries and territories (NCCT) method,[176] to name and shame identified countries. The HRJSCA is a slightly revised approach to the 'NCCT', that indicated major success to coerce countries to adopt and comply with the FATF standards.[177] The procedure resembles the defunct NCCT and relies on ME results to conduct reviews and assists with action plans to meet the FATF standards. The FATF continues to enforce the NCCT-style of listing by publishing names of countries with deficiencies through the HRJSCA. Importantly, and as with the NCCT, the revised method also appeals to both its members and non-members to consider risks of AML/CFT and to apply counter-measures to protect the international financial system from risks emanating from these jurisdictions.[178] The ME and the identification of HRJSCA remain the FATF's effective mechanisms to enforce the AML/CFT measures.[179]

8 Analysis and Concluding Remarks

The efforts and commitments of the AFI, the G20, and the World Bank to provide guidelines, principles and a template to develop national financial inclusion strategies are commendable. As indicated above,[180] the majority of the SADC member' states are also members of the AFI. Therefore, the developments of effective policy and regulatory frameworks at international level will assist similar steps in the SADC to promote FI. These policy documents have provided the necessary guidelines on important aspects for the promotion of FI globally and in the SADC. In the SADC in particular, the adoption of NFIS by the majority of members states is a clear indication that an effectively enforced international and SADC FI regulation will increase FI in the SADC region. These guidelines and principles include the format that both the regulatory and institutional framework must take, outlining specific contents of the relevant instrument, and the relation between the promotion of FI and other competing policy and regulatory objectives such as financial integrity, financial stability, and consumer protection. Whether the aspiration to promote FI is achievable in the foreseeable future depends on a number of issues. Firstly, as policy measures to promote FI, these guidelines and principles indicate a lack of consistent approach to NFIS resulting from the adoption of the bottom-up approach, rather than commanding a clear top-down approach. Benchmarking possible

---

[176] FATF (n.d.), See also Nance (2018), pp. 141–142.

[177] FATF (2007), for the countries listed and delisted since between 200–2006, A total of 47 countries that were reviewed between 2000–2001, 23 were identified as NCCT. See further Koh (2006), p. 162; Shahin et al. (2012), p. 64; Tsingou (2010), p. 619; Hardouin (2010), p. 154. See also Ryder (2011), pp. 16–17 for the criticisms against the NCCT process. See further Broome (2005), p. 556.

[178] FATF (2018), the statement list Korea Republic and Iran on the list.

[179] See the FATF 'Annual Report 2019-2020' (2020) listing Iran.

[180] See Sect. 5.2 above.

approaches to NFIS is a good start. A challenge is to determine the actual approach that must be adopted at an international level. In particular, these guidelines and principles do not specifically propose a specific approach that countries, including those in the SADC region, must adopt to implement effective FI regulatory frameworks. Secondly, each of the approaches or formats of NFISs that the *NFIS Reference Network* and *NFIS Template* propose has its own drawbacks. For instance, and as discussed further below, a FI framework must balance the FI objective against competing policy objectives such as financial stability and financial integrity. FI regulation and policy objective should certainly be an independent and a standalone objective of financial regulation. Other financial regulatory objectives such as financial stability, integrity and consumer protection, are undoubtedly integral parts towards promoting FI. However, a *Standalone NFIS* that focuses on one or some of these objectives may undermine evitable trade-offs to FI. If all of these objectives are not included in an NFIS that focuses only on FI policy objective, such NFIS may become ineffective. The reason is that, it does not recognise the importance of these traditional financial regulation objectives for enhancing equally important FI policy objective. Similarly, a NFIS that forms part of the overall national financial sector strategy and identifies FI as an ancillary objective will arguably not prioritise it when other traditional financial regulatory objectives, such as financial stability do not complement this objective. Also, FI is now an important policy objective that cannot be promoted under the wing of a policy instrument that addresses one of its barriers such as financial education. Although this policy guideline rejects a blanket approach to a comprehensive NFIS that incorporates all key components to promote FI and prevent FE, such an approach is essential to put FI at the same level with other longstanding financial policy and regulatory objectives. Such a comprehensive NFIS must include various components of the AFI definition. These components must include the types of financial services and products, institutions that help to promote FI, and identify barriers to FI. The NFIS must also create a space for the development of new innovations such as agent banking, mobile phone money transfer services, virtual currency and fintech generally. Such NFIS must also ensure that existing policies and regulations do not hamper these innovations.

As discussed above,[181] many national and international frameworks deal with important financial policy objectives separately. A comprehensive NFIS proposed in this chapter must cross-reference these existing frameworks and objectives, and how they must be applied to promote FI.[182] It must outline how to minimise possible trade-offs and to maximise synergies between competing objectives. For instance, improving FI through tailored rules that allow for the establishment of small financial markets and tailor-made products may create financial instability resulting in market failure. A comprehensive NFIS that must be introduces in SADC countries

---

[181] See Sect. 1 above.

[182] The FATF's Financial Inclusion Guidance is one good example of how the AML/CFT policy objective balances itself with FI objective, See Sect. 5.2 above.

should take cognisance of the benefits of FI. It must appreciate how access to bank accounts and deposits and payment systems to the majority facilitate and advance profitability and financial stability.[183] Likewise, a strict know your customer enforcement of AML/CFT measures to protect financial integrity may hamper FI by relegating the unserved majority to the informal financial systems. However, measures that ensure that more clients use formal financial services increase the reach and effectiveness of the AML/CFT controls.[184] A country's NFIS and the relevant regulatory frameworks must therefore adopt the proportionality principle and focus not only on the risks of financial instability and lack of integrity and consumer protection, but also on the benefits of FI.[185]

A further important issue that determines the effectiveness of the current FI framework globally and in the SADC relates to the power and the legitimacy of the current GSSBs to develop binding legal instruments. Notably, the FI guidelines, principles and template discussed in this chapter are not established through binding international legal instruments, but by agreements between member states and declarations. As discussed above,[186] the AFI is member-driven peer learning framework that is founded on a declaration between members states including SADC countries.[187] Likewise, the G20 was formed as an informal *ad hoc* grouping of government and central banks comprising of 19 countries and the European Union to coordinate and drive policy and regulations after the 2008 financial crisis.[188] It lacks structural and legal resemblance to formal international organisations such as the United Nations. As with the AFI, these institutions lack legitimacy as international law-making bodies. The World Bank's influence on international, national and regional policies and regulation of financial institutions does not go unnoticed. It also is not a formal international organisation with the power to specifically regulate.[189] These bodies lack formal legal mandates or consents by their non-members who are also subjects to their policy standards.[190]

The formality of the institution or organisation has not remained the sole determinant of the effectiveness of all international and regional policy and legal frameworks. Another main issue to determine the effectiveness of these frameworks has largely focused on the character of the current FI policy frameworks. Arguably, the FI frameworks discussed in this chapter do not constitute international hard law. The AFI's Maya Declaration, the G20 and the World Bank's FI frameworks are not international conventions or treaties recognised as laws that bind both their members

---

[183] See Lawack (2013), p. 329; Alexandre and Eisenhart (2013), p. 301; de Koker (2013b), p. 165, on possible trade-offs between widening of access in the payment system and systemic risk.

[184] Bester et al. (2008), p. vi, See also de Koker and Jentzsch (2013), p. 269.

[185] de Sousa (2015).

[186] See Sect. 5.2 above.

[187] Mehrotra and Nadhandel (2016), p. 96.

[188] See G20 (n.d.), South Africa is the only member of the G20 form Africa and in the SADC.

[189] Donnelly (2012), p. 188.

[190] Choo and Kelly (2012), p. 491; Alexander et al. (2014), p. 2.

and contesting states.[191] They are not yet evidenced by consistent practices in national laws nor constitute general principles recognised by civilised nations and 'accepted as law' in terms of Article 38 of SICJ.[192]

The current FI framework has the character of an international soft law. The language of the *G20 FI Principles* and the World Bank *FI Reference Framework* is suggestive and recommends relevant issues and components of a FI policy and regulatory framework.[193] They nonetheless do not impose binding obligations on states as they are not rigid FI requirements.[194] The reliance on monitoring and continuous data collection without effective enforcement mechanisms is also one factor that renders them non-binding. If the collected data indicates low percentages of FI and lack of commitments, effective enforcement of these soft law standards will become essential. This leaves a question whether FI internationally and in the SADC must be promoted through strict and binding hard law rules or quasi-legal soft instruments that only have a direct influence on the practices of states to promote FI.

Various factors that are discussed in this chapter do not support an early adoption of a binding hard law international instrument. Such an approach is preconditioned on identifying a legitimate institution that will focus on the promotion of FI through policies and regulatory frameworks. Also, as this framework is benchmarked through a bottom-up approach that considers national contexts and approaches, it is clear that FI has not developed into an exact science that requires off-the-shelf solutions. It still lacks precision relating to the types of products and issues that must be included in the regulatory instrument. Although the proportionality principle to balance competing financial regulatory objectives is proposed, there is still no consensus on the linkage between financial regulation and other traditional financial policy objectives, and how policy makers can optimise the linkage that minimise trade-offs and maximise synergies.[195] Such linkage and balancing must be established. The CGAP has proposed an Integrated Framework for Financial Inclusion that adopts an I-SIP theory to achieve this balance.[196] This theory requires national policy makers to pursue all the core objectives of financial stability (S), financial integrity (I) and financial consumer protection (P) to optimise their linkage.[197] This will specifically require policy makers to adapt policies and regulations

---

[191] *Norway v Denmark* [1933] P.C.I.J. Ser. A/B, No. 53, 71.

[192] Dumbwerry (2016), p. 293.

[193] See G20 FI Principles indicating that it aims to bring experiences from different countries together to produce a set of recommendations for policymakers, The World Bank NFIS Reference Framework refer to itself as a 'resource' for policymakers and regulators.

[194] See G20 FI Principles.

[195] See CGAP (2017), p. 1. See also García (2016), p. 81; Elsayed (2020).

[196] CGAP (2017), p. 1, See also Nader (2019); Louis and Chartier (2017), p. 170, for proposing a similar approach that only focuses on modifying financial existing regulation in South Africa through a Twin-Peak South African Financial Inclusion Model.

[197] Nader (2019), p. 2.

over time in light of the collected evidence on each objective.[198] Therefore, we propose a comprehensive international soft law regulatory framework that will adapt to the changing needs to cater for evolving financial services and products and institutions from continental and regions such as SADC into account. Rather than adopting a haphazard approach from different institutions, the AFI should be recognised as a legitimate GSSB that will develop FI international standards. Continental and regional regulatory bodies such as SADC must form part of tits policymaking and regulatory structures. We further propose that, rather than taking a completely top-down regulatory approach, AFI should adopt relevant standards over time in the form of *International Financial Inclusion Regulatory Strategy* (IFIRS) with specific measures to influence FI practices of various states. The IFIRS must outline stakeholders and their different roles, key FI objectives, and cross-reference key components of the I-SIP objectives, as outlined in Principles 8 and 9 of the *NFIS Reference Framework*, to establish a linkage between FI and other longstanding financial policy objectives. It must further outline the roles that continental and regional structures such as the SADC must play to develop FI frameworks and to implement them effectively. It must also provide enforcement mechanisms that will assist these continental and regional structures to coerce countries to implement the relevant FI standards and to increase the likelihood of compliance. Such measures can begin with continuous monitoring and evaluations of each country's progress to improve FI. The AFI may gradually adopt similar FATF measures such as continuous mutual evaluation and monitoring to ensure the implementation of its FI standards. Similar to the FATF's global network of FATF-Style regional bodies such as Eastern and Southern Africa Anti-Money Laundering Group (ESAAMLG) and Task Force on Money Laundering in Central Africa, SADC and others related bodies should serve as specific regional bodies to implement international measures on FI.[199] The ME processes that they apply must focus both on the technical compliance with each IFIRS standard, as well as testing the effectiveness of each nationally adopted standard, based on the FI or FE data collected. Reputational sanctions such as the FATF's naming and shaming HRJSCA mechanism must be applied to both recalcitrant AFI members and non-members as a sanction of last resort. A universal adoption of these standards will determine whether the IFIRS serves norm-creating and progressive law-making roles towards an international instrument, such as CEDAW. An increase adoption of the IFIRS will also determine whether AFI should adopt a more effective instrument that binds all countries, including those in SADC, and that would likely be more cumbersome and intrusive or will forestall such a formal hard law regulation.

---

[198] Nader (2019), p. 2.

[199] Visit <https://www.fatf-gafi.org/countries/> accessed on 18 October 2021 for the nine global network of FATF-Style regional bodies.

Bibliography

Abbott KW, Snidal D (2000) Hard and soft law in international governance. Int Organ 54:421

Adeyemi PO (2021) How to Implement a National Financial Inclusion Strategy (March 2021). https://www.afi-global.org/newsroom/blogs/how-to-implement-a-national-financial-inclusion-strategy/. Accessed 21 July 2021

Aduda J, Kalunda E (2012) Financial inclusion and financial sector stability with reference to Kenya: a review of literature. J Appl Financ Bank 2:95

AFI (2011) Maya Declaration: The AFI Network commitment to financial inclusion. https://www.afi-global.org/publications/879/Maya-Declaration-The-AFI-network-commitment-to-financial-inclusion. Accessed 16 May 2021

Alexander K, Lorez K, Zobl M, Thürer D (2014) The legitimacy of the G20 – a critique under international law (April 2014). https://ssrn.com/abstract=2431164. Accessed 26 July 2021

Alexandre C, Eisenhart LC (2013) Mobile money as an engine of financial inclusion and lynchpin of financial integrity. Washington J Law Technol Arts 8:285

Alliance for Financial Inclusion (2010) Financial inclusion measurement for regulators: survey design and implementation (February 2010). https://www.afi-global.org/sites/default/files/afi_policypaper_datameasurement_en.pdf. Accessed 06 Apr 2021

Alliance for Financial Inclusion (2012) Strategy development organizing for financial inclusion supporting strategic approaches in the AFI Network (2012). https://www.afiglobal.org/sites/default/files/publications/AFI_Strategy%20development_AW_low%20res.pdf.   Accessed 18 May 2021

Alliance for Financial Inclusion (2017) Defining Financial Inclusion (July 2017) *Guideline Note No. 28*. https://www.afi-global.org/sites/default/files/publications/2017-07/FIS_GN_28_AW_digital.pdf. Accessed 06 Apr 2021

Alliance for Financial Inclusion (n.d.-a) A quick guide to the Maya Declaration on financial inclusion

Alliance for Financial Inclusion (n.d.-b) Official members. https://www.afi-global.org/sites/default/files/inline-files/AFI%20Official%20Members.pdf. Accessed 16 May 2021

Arabehety PG, Chen G, Cook W, McKay C (2016) Digital Finance Interoperability & Financial Inclusion (December 2016) CGAP Working Paper. https://www.cgap.org/sites/default/files/researches/documents/interoperability.pdf. Accessed 18 Mar 2021

Asia/Pacific Group on Money Laundering, The World Bank Group and FATF (2011) FATF Guidance: Anti-Money Laundering and Terrorist Financing Measures and Financial Inclusion (June 2011). https://www.fatfgafi.org/media/fatf/content/images/AML%20CFT%20measures%20and%20financial%20inclusion.pdf. Accessed 21 July 2021

Bank of Mozambique (2016) National Financial Inclusion Strategy 2016–2022. https://thedocs.worldbank.org/en/doc/469371468274738363-0010022016/original/MozambiqueNationalFinancialInclusionStrategy20162022.pdf. Accessed 22 Oct 2021

Bank of Papua New Guinea (n.d.) National Financial Inclusion Strategy 2016–2020 Papua New Guinea. http://www.thecefi.org/images/2nd%20NFIS%20-%20CEFI%20PNG.pdf. Accessed 19 Oct 2021

Basel Committee on Banking Supervision (2016) Guidance on the application of the core principles for effective banking supervision to the regulation and supervision of institutions relevant to financial inclusion (September 2016)

Bayulgen O (2013) Giving credit where credit is due: can access to credit be justified as a new economic right? J Hum Rights 12:491

Bester H, Chamberlain D, de Koker L, Hougaard C, Short R, Smith A, Walker R (2008) Implementing FATF standards in developing countries and financial inclusion: findings and guidelines (May 2008). https://cenfri.org/wp-content/uploads/2009/12/Implementing-FATF-standards-in-developing-countries-and-finacial-inclusion-final-report_Genesis_May-2008.pdf. Accessed 04 July 2021

Bjorklund AK, Reinisch A (eds) (2012) International investment law and soft law. Edward Elgar, Cheltenham

Blair W, Brent R, Grant T (eds) (2010) Banks and financial crime - the international law of tainted money. Oxford University Press, Oxford

Blutman L (2010) In the trap of a legal metaphor: international soft law. Int Comp Law Q 59:606

Borlini L, Montanaro F (2017) The evolution of the EU law against criminal finance: the hardening of FATF standard within the EU. Georgetown J Int Law 48:1009

Bremer EC, Krain M (2015) The effects of human rights on the success of microcredit lending institutions. J Hum Rights 14:377

Broome J (2005) Anti-money laundering: international practice and Policies. Thomson, Hong Kong

Brummer C (2012) Soft law and the global financial system, 2nd edn. Cambridge University Press, New York

Central Bank of Lesotho (2013) Lesotho: Financial Sector Development Strategy. https://www.centralbank.org.ls/images/Financial_Stability/Financial_Inclusion/Lesotho%20FSDS%20%20-%20Nov%202013.pdf. Accessed 22 Oct 2021

Central Bank of Nigeria (n.d.) National Financial Inclusion Strategy. https://www.cbn.gov.ng/out/2013/ccd/nfis.pdf. Accessed 18 Oct 2021

Central Bank of Seychelles (2017) Seychelles National Financial Education Strategy. https://www.cbs.sc/Downloads/publications/psd/National%20Financial%20Education%20Strategy.pdf. Accessed 22 Oct 2021

CGAP (2012) Financial inclusion and the linkage to stability, integrity and protection: insights from South Africa perspective (November 2012). https://www.cgap.org/sites/default/files/Working-Paper-Insights-from-the-South-African-Experience-Nov-2012_0.pdf. Accessed 07 Apr 2021

Cheston S, Conde T, Bykere A, Rhyne E (2016) The Business of Financial Inclusion (July 2016) IIF & CFI. https://responsiblefinanceforum.org/wp-content/uploads/2016/07/iif_cfi_report.pdf. Accessed 19 Oct 2021

Chitimira H, Ncube M (2020) Legislative and other selected challenges affecting financial inclusion for the poor and low-income earners in South Africa. J Afr Law 64:337

Choo S, Kelly CR (2012) Promises and perils of new global governance: a case of the G20. Chic J Int Law 12:491

Community Reinvestment Act 1977

Constitution of the Federal Republic of Brazil 1988

Constitution of the Kingdom of Cambodia 1993

Das S (2021) National Strategy on Financial Education 2020–25. *Reserve Bank of India (RBI) Bulletin* (January 2021)

Dasser F (2021) "Soft Law" in International Commercial Arbitration. Brill, Nijhoff

de Koker L (2013a) South African money laundering and terror financing law. LexisNexis, Durban

de Koker L (2013b) The 2012 Revised FATF Recommendations: assessing and mitigating mobile money integrity risks within the New Standards Framework. Wash J Law Technol Arts 8:165

de Koker L, Jentzsch N (2013) Financial inclusion and financial integrity: aligned incentives? World Dev 44:267

de Sousa MM (2015) Financial Inclusion and Global Regulatory Standards (March 2015). *Centre for International Governance Innovation New Thinking and the New G20 Series Paper No. 7.* https://www.cigionline.org/sites/default/files/new_thinking_g20_no7.pdf.   Accessed 16 May 2021

Dema E (2014) Managing the twin responsibilities of financial inclusion and financial stability. In: ASEAN Financial Inclusion Conference, Yangon, 29–30 October 2014

Demirgüç-Kunt A, Klapper L, Ansar S, Jagati A (2017) Making it easier to apply for a bank account: a study of the Indian Market (September 2017). *World Bank Group Policy Research Working Paper 8205.* http://documents.worldbank.org/curated/en/504741506452393306/pdf/WPS8205.pdf. Accessed 03 Apr 2021

Dostov V, Shust P, Leonova A, Krivoruchko S (2019) "Soft Law" and innovations: empirical analysis of ICO-related statements, digital policy. Regul Gov 21:476

Dumbwerry P (2016) The formation and identification of rules of customary international law in international investment law. Cambridge University Press, Cambridge

Eastern and Southern Africa Anti-Money Laundering Group (ESAAMLG) (2018) Anti-money laundering and counter-terrorist financing measures: Mauritius, Mutual Evaluation Report (July 2018). https://www.fatf-gafi.org/media/fatf/documents/reports/mer-fsrb/ESAAMLG-MER-Mauritius 2018.pdf. Accessed 18 Apr 2021

Ebikakev E (2016) Money laundering an assessment of soft law as a technique for repressive and preventive anti-money laundering control. J Money Laundering Control 19:346

Elsayed A (2020) The interrelationship between financial inclusion, financial stability, financial integrity and consumer protection (I-SIP Theory) (December 2020). https://ssrn.com/abstract=3 745874. Accessed 21 July 2021

Fardoust S, Kim Y, Sepúlveda C (eds) (2011) Postcrisis growth and development. World Bank, Washington DC

FATF (1997) Financial Action Task Force on Money Laundering Annual Report 1996–1997 (June 1997). http://www.fatf-gafi.org/media/fatf/documents/reports/1996%201997%20ENG.pdf. Accessed 25 June 2021

FATF (2007) Annual Review of Non-Cooperative Countries and Territories 2006–2007: Eighth NCCT Review (October 2007). http://www.fatf-gafi.org/media/fatf/documents/reports/2006%202007%20NCCT%20ENG.pdf. Accessed 04 July 2021

FATF (2009) Mutual Evaluation Report, anti-money laundering and combating the financing of terrorism: South Africa (February 2009). http://www.fatfgafi.org/media/fatf/documents/reports/mer/MER%20South%20Africa%20full.pdf. Accessed 18 Apr 2021

FATF (2012) FATF Public Statement - 16 February 2012 (February 2012). http://www.fatf-gafi.org/publications/high-riskandnon-cooperativejurisdictions/documents/fatfpublicstatement-1 6february2012.html. Accessed 26 Oct 2021

FATF (2018a) Methodology for assessing technical compliance with the FATF recommendations and the effectiveness of AML/CFT systems (February 2018) amended 2020. https://www.fatf-gafi.org/publications/mutualevaluations/documents/fatf-methodology.html. Accessed 25 June 2021

FATF (2018b) Procedures for the FATF Fourth Round of AML/CFT mutual evaluations (June 2018). http://www.fatf-gafi.org/media/fatf/content/images/FATF-4th-Round-Procedures.pdf. Accessed 18 Apr 2021

FATF (2018c) Public statements (29 June 2018). http://www.fatf-gafi.org/publications/high-riskandnon-cooperativejurisdictions/documents/public-statement-june-2018.html. Accessed 09 July 2021

FATF (2020a) Annual Report 2019–2020. https://www.fatf-gafi.org/media/fatf/documents/brochuresannualreports/FATF-annual-report-2019-2020.pdf. Accessed 09 July 2021

FATF (2020b) High-risk jurisdictions subject to a call for action – 21 February 2020 (21 February 2020). http://www.fatf-gafi.org/publications/high-risk-and-other-monitored-jurisdictions/documents/call-for-action-february-2020.html. Accessed 26 Oct 2021

FATF (2020c) Jurisdictions under increased monitoring – 21 February 2020 (21 February 2020). http://www.fatf-gafi.org/publications/high-risk-and-other-monitored-jurisdictions/documents/increased-monitoring-february-2020.html. Accessed 26 Oct 2021

FATF (n.d.-a) About the FATF. http://www.fatf-gafi.org/about/. Accessed 02 Apr 2021

FATF (n.d.-b) About the Non-Cooperative Countries and Territories (NCCT) Initiative. https://www.fatf-gafi.org/publications/high-riskandnoncooperativejurisdictions/more/aboutthenon-cooperativecountriesandterritoriesncctinitiative.html?hf=10&b=0&s=desc(fatf_releasedate). Accessed 05 July 2021

FATF (n.d.-c) Who we are. http://www.fatf-gafi.org/fr/aproposdugafi/. Accessed 15 Mar 2021

FATF and El Grupo de Acción Financiera de Latinoamérica (GAFILAT) (2018) Anti-money laundering and counter-terrorist financing measures: Mexico Mutual Evaluation Report (January 2018). http://www.fatf-gafi.org/media/fatf/documents/reports/mer4/MER-Mexico-2018.pdf. Accessed 06 May 2021

FATF, Asia/Pacific Group on Money Laundering and The World Banking (2013) FATF guidance: anti-money laundering and terrorist financing measures and financial inclusion (February 2013). https://www.fatfgafi.org/media/fatf/documents/reports/AML_CFT_Measures_and_Financial_ Inclusion_2013.pdf. Accessed 21 July 2021

Financial Inclusion in Banking Act of 2021

Financial Sector Regulation Act 9 of 2017

FinMark Trust (2016) An excluded society? Financial inclusion in SADC through FinScope lenses. FinMark Trust, Johannesburg

G20 (n.d.) About the G20. https://www.g20.org/about-the-g20.html. Accessed 26 Oct 2021

G20 Global Partnership for Financial Inclusion (2011) G20 Principles for Innovative Financial Inclusion (April 2011). https://www.gpfi.org/sites/gpfi/files/documents/G20%20Principles%20 for%20Innovative%20Financial%20Inclusion_Bringing%20the%20Principles%20to%20Life. pdf. Accessed 30 July 2021

García MJR (2016) Can financial inclusion and financial stability go hand in hand? Econ Issues 21: 81

Ghoshray S (2014) Compliance convergence in FATF rulemaking: the conflict between agency capture and soft law. N Y Law Sch Law Rev 59:521

Goldbarsht D (2020) Global counter-terrorist financing and soft law: multi-layered approaches. Edward Elgar, Cheltenham

Gopalan S, Kikuchi T (eds) (2016) Financial inclusion in Asia: issues and policy concerns. Palgrave, London

Guzman AT, Meyer TL (2010) International soft law. J Leg Anal 2:174

Hale T, Held D (eds) (2011) The handbook of transnational governance: institutions and innova-tions. Polity Press, Cambridge

Hardouin P (2010) The aftermath of the financial crisis: poor compliance and new risks for the integrity of the financial sector. J Financ Crime 18:148

Hayes B (2012) Counter-terrorism, policy laundering, and the FATF: legalizing surveillance, regulating civil society. Int J Not-for-Profit Law 14:5

Home Mortgage Disclosure Act 1975

Howell N, Wilson T (2005) Access to consumer credit: the problem of financial exclusion in Australia and the Current Regulatory Framework. Macquarie Law J 5:127

Hudon M (2009) Should access to credit be a right? J Bus Ethics 84:17

Jensen N, Png C (2011) Implementation of the FATF 40+ recommendations: a perspective from developing countries. J Money Laundering Control 14(2):110

Johansson T, Donner P (2015) The shipping industry, ocean governance and environmental law in the paradigm shift. Springer, Cham

Kashyap AK (ed) (2014) Indian Banking: contemporary issues in law and challenges. Allied Publishers, New Delhi

Kettle N (2019) SADC Financial Inclusion – Measuring Progress (14 August 2019)

Khan MH, Akther R (2017) Microfinance for promoting human rights in Bangladesh: a right-based assessment. J Humanit Soc Sci 12:12

Koh J (2006) Suppressing terrorist financing and money laundering. Springer, Heidelberg

Kumar BP (2014) Access to finance and human rights. *Munich Personal RePEc Archive Paper 80336*. https://mpra.ub.uni-muenchen.dc/80336/1/MPRA_paper_80336.pdf. Accessed 23 July 2021

Lawack VA (2013) Mobile money, financial inclusion and financial integrity: The South African Case. Wash J Law Technol Arts 8:317

Ledgerwood J, Earne J, Nelson C (eds) (2013) The new microfinance handbook. The World Bank, Washington DC

Leyshon A, Thrift N (1995) Geographies of financial exclusion: financial abandonment in Britain and the United States. Trans Inst Br Geogr 20:315

Martuscello M (2011) The FATF's nine special recommendations: a too soft approach to combating terrorism. Touro Int Law Rev 14:363

Matongela AM (2014) Understanding the state of financial inclusion in Namibia. Comput Eng Intell Syst 5:71

Mdasha Z, Irungu D, Wachira Z (2018) Effect of financial inclusion strategy on performance of small and medium enterprises: a case of selected SMEs in Dar es Salaam, Tanzania. J Strateg Manag 2:5152

Mehta L, Jindal S, Singh S (2015) Financial inclusion in India: shifting the base towards crowning glory. Arabian J Bus Manag Rev 5:2

Meyer M (2018) The right to credit. J Polit Philos 26:304

Minister of Finance and Budget (2018) National Financial Inclusion Strategy of Madagascar

Ministere Des Finances: Comores (2011) De Finance Inclusive Aux Comores (SD-FIC) 2011–2013. https://www.findevgateway.org/sites/default/files/publications/files/mfg-fr-etudes-de-cas-schema-directeur-finance-inclusive-comores-2011-2013-09-2011.pdf. Accessed 22 Oct 2021

Ministry of Finance (2011–2021) Namibia Financial Sector Strategy 2011–2021

Ministry of Finance and Economic Development: Government of Botswana (2015) Botswana Financial Inclusion Roadmap and Strategy 2015–2021. https://www.finance.gov.bw/index.php?option=com_content&view=article&id=249&catid=36&Itemid=116. Accessed 22 Oct 2022

Ministry of Finance: Eswatini (2017) National Financial Inclusion Strategy for Swaziland 2017–2022. https://www.afi-global.org/publications/national-financial-inclusion-strategy-for-swaziland-2017-2022/. Accessed 22 Oct 2021

Ministry of Finance: Malawi (2010) The Malawi National Strategy for Financial Inclusion (2010–2014). https://dfsobservatory.com/sites/default/files/Malawi%20National%20Strategy%20for%20Financial%20Inclusion.pdf. Accessed 22 Oct 2021

Ministry of Finance: Zambia (2017–2022) National Financial Inclusion Strategy 2017-2022. https://www.boz.zm/National-Financial-Inclusion-Strategy-2017-2022.pdf. Accessed 22 Oct 2021

Morgan PJ, Pontines V (2018) Financial stability and financial inclusion: the case of SME lending. Singapore Econ Rev 63:111

Mugarura N (2012) The global anti-money laundering regulatory landscape in less developed countries. Ashgate, Farnham

Nader A (2019) Financial Inclusion, Stability, Integrity and Protection (I-SIP) (February 2019). https://ssrn.com/abstract=3335904. Accessed 21 July 2021

Nance MT (2018) Re-thinking FATF: an experimentalist interpretation of the Financial Action Task Force. Crime Law Soc Change 69:131

National Financial Inclusion Council: Tanzania (2018) National Financial Inclusion Framework 2018-2022. https://www.afi-global.org/wp-content/uploads/publications/2017-12/NFIF%202018-2022.pdf. Accessed 22 Oct 2021

National Treasury (2011) A safer financial sector to serve South Africa better. *National Treasury Policy Document.* http://www.treasury.gov.za/twinpeaks/20131211%20-%20Item%202%20A%20safer%20financial%20sector%20to%20serve%20South%20Africa%20better.pdf. Accessed 18 May 2021

Norway v Denmark [1933] P.C.I.J. Ser. A/B, No. 53, 71

Pauwelyn J, Wessel R, Wouters J (2012) Informal international lawmaking. Oxford University Press, Oxford

Pieth M, Aiolfi G (eds) (2004) A comparative guide to anti-money laundering. Edwards Elgar, Northampton

Pillay D, Khadiagala GM, Southall R, Mosoetsa S, Kariuk S (2018) New South African Review 6: the crisis of inequality. Wits University Press, Johannesburg

Prahalad CK (2005) The fortune at the bottom of the Pyramid: eradicating poverty through profit. Wharton, Upper Saddle River

Prochaska K (2014) Financial inclusion strategies: global trends and lessons learnt for the AFI Network (3 June 2014). https://www.worldbank.org/content/dam/Worldbank/Event/ECA/Turkey/tr-fin-incl-confer-klaus-prochaska.pdf. Accessed 17 May 2021

Regan S, Paxton W (2003) Beyond bank accounts: full financial inclusion. Institute for Public Policy Research London. https://www.ippr.org/research/publications/beyond-bank-accountsfull-financial-inclusion. Accessed 19 Oct 2021

Reserve Bank of India (2021) National Strategy on Financial Education 2020-2025 (March 2021). https://rbidocs.rbi.org.in/rdocs/PublicationReport/Pdfs/NSFE202020251BD2A32E39F74D32 8239740D4C93980D.PDF. Accessed 21 July 2021

Reserve Bank of Zimbabwe (2016) National Financial Inclusion Strategy 2016–2020

Roa MJ (2015) Financial inclusion in Latin America and The Caribbean: access, usage and quality (April 2015). *Center For Latin American Monetary Studies Research Paper 19.* https://www.cemla.org/PDF/investigacion/inv-2015-04-19.pdf. Accessed 19 Oct 2021

Ryder N (2011) Financial crime in the 21st century. Edward Elgar, Cheltenham

Sarma M, Pais J (2011) Financial inclusion and development. J Int Dev 23:613

Shami H (2015) *The impact of economic, governance and terrorist activity on compliance with FATF recommendations.* Unpublished PhD Dissertation, The State University of New Jersey 2015

Soederberg S (2013) Universalising financial inclusion and the securitisation of development. Third World Q 34:593

Sorrel T, Cabrera L (eds) (2015) Microfinance, rights and global justice. Cambridge University Press, Cambridge

Triki T, Faye I (eds) (2013) Financial inclusion in Africa. African Development Bank, Tunis

Tsingou E (2010) Global financial governance and the developing anti-money laundering regime: what lessons for international political economy? Int Polit 47:617

Tuba M (2012) Prosecuting money laundering the FATF way: an analysis of gaps and challenges in South African Legislation from a comparative perspective. Acta Criminologica: 2011 Conference Special Edition No 2: 103

Tully S (2006) The exclusion of women from financial services and the prospects of a human rights solution under Australian law. Aust J Hum Rights 12:53

United Nations (2006) Building Inclusive Financial Sectors for Development (May 2006)

United Nations Convention on the Elimination of All Forms of Discrimination Against Women 1997

United Nations Development Programme (2016) Human development for everyone: Human Development Report 2016. http://hdr.undp.org/sites/default/files/2016_human_development_report.pdf

United Nations Security Council Resolution 1617 (2005) S/RES/1617, adopted by the Security Council at its 5244th meeting on 29 July 2005

Wade M (2014) Access to credit a 'Human Right', says the father of microfinance. *The Sydney Morning Herald,* 9 October 2014

Weber RH (2012) Overcoming the hard law/soft law dichotomy in times of (financial) crises. J Gov Regul 1:8

World Bank (2012) Financial Inclusion Strategies Reference Framework (August 2012). https://siteresources.worldbank.org/EXTFINANCIALSECTOR/Resources/2828841339624653091/8703882-1339624678024/8703850-1339624695396/FI-Strategies-ReferenceFramework-FINAL Aug2012.pdf. Accessed 17 May 2021

World Bank (2014) Global Financial Development Report Financial Inclusion. http://Siteresources.Worldbank.Org/Extglobalfinreport/Resources/8816096-1361888425203/9062080-1364927957721/Gfdr-2014_Complete_Report.Pdf. Accessed 19 Oct 2021

World Bank (2016) Template for the design of a National Financial Inclusion Strategy (January 2016). http://pubdocs.worldbank.org/en/379031452203008464/WBG-FMGP-Template-for-Designing-a-NFIS-Jan-2016-FINAL.pdf. Accessed 17 May 2021

World Bank (2018) Toolkit: developing and operationalizing a National Financial Inclusion Strategy (June 2018). http://documents.worldbank.org/curated/en/201761530163552405/pdf/127712-REVISED-WP-PUBLIC.pdf
World Bank (2020) Enhancing Financial Capability and Inclusion in Angola: a demand-side survey (October 2020). https://www.bna.ao/uploads/%7B36a2ae06-5517-41f4-a907-979fd625c8ea%7D.pdf. Accessed 22 Oct 2021
World Bank (n.d.) Indicators of financial access household-level surveys. http://siteresources.worldbank.org/FINANCIALSECTOR/5399141118439900885/20700929/Indicators_of_Financial_Access_Household_Level_Surveys.pdf. Accessed 06 Apr 2021
Zahanogo P (2017) Financial development and poverty in developing countries: evidence for sub-Saharan Africa. Int J Econ Financ 9:211

Maphuti D. Tuba Advocate Maphuti David Tuba is a senior lecturer in the Department of Mercantile law in the College of Law at the University of South Africa (Unisa). He completed his LLB from the University of the Witwatersrand (Wits) in 2006, and LLM in Banking Law at Unisa in 2014. He also completed a Diploma in Compliance Management at the University of Johannesburg in 2016. He teaches modules in Commercial law, and Banking and Finance Law, and supervises LLM students in these areas, and property law. His research areas are banking and finance law, and property law, focus on land registration, and he has presented research papers at national and international conferences and has published widely in these areas. He served on both the Compliance and Education and Training Committees of the Compliance Institute of Southern Africa. He also served as the assistant editor of the Athens Institute of Educational and Research, based in Greece, Athens, and currently the assistant editor of the South African Mercantile Law Journal housed in the Department of Mercantile at Unisa. He is currently registered for a PhD in Law at Unisa and his research is on the effectiveness of the regulatory framework in South Africa, with specific focus on access to basic bank account.

Vivienne A. Lawack Professor Lawack began and advanced her legal career by spending a number of years at the South African Reserve Bank in various capacities, including senior payment system analyst, senior legal consultant and legal consultant and as Senior Legal Counsel for Strate Limited, South Africa's central securities depository. In 2008, she moved to the Nelson Mandela University in Port Elizabeth where she served as the Executive Dean of the Faculty of Law. Professor Lawack joined the University of Western Cape (UWC) on 1 April 2015 and in her capacity as Deputy Vice-Chancellor at UWC, she is currently leading UWC's academic project in relation to its learning and teaching activities at both undergraduate and postgraduate levels. She is an expert in law, economics and the intersection of the two fields, both at an international level and in the South African context. She also has contract, policy and legislative drafting experience. As regards her academic career, Professor Lawack has published extensively, including numerous articles, reports and contributions to chapters in books. She has also delivered papers at conferences, both locally and internationally. Professor Lawack has also supervised a number of masters and doctoral candidates and continues to do so. Her field of academic research is in the legal and regulatory frameworks pertaining to the payment system, banking system and financial markets in South Africa. Professor Lawack is highly engaged in her community, regularly chairing and/or participating in various committees in the legal, financial and education sectors, leveraging her expertise to add value and push her community to greater heights.

Facilitating Financial Inclusion Through the Development of a Decentralised Cryptocurrencies' Regulatory Regime in South Africa, Zimbabwe and Botswana

Shelton T. Mota Makore, Patrick C. Osode, and Nombulelo Lubisi

Abstract Since their emergence, cryptocurrencies are increasingly gaining uptake in the financial sector across the globe. In the sub-Saharan region, countries such as South Africa, Zimbabwe and Botswana have the potential to achieve financial inclusion through the use of cryptocurrencies. More specifically, unbanked individuals in these emerging market economies could be attracted to cryptocurrencies due to sentiments spawned by chrematophobia and other risks associated with the use of banks. The technology of cryptocurrencies could be deployed as sui generis instruments of payment, asset accumulation and investment, thereby challenging and dislodging conventional financial tools for transacting, storing and transferring economic value. More importantly, cryptocurrencies can drive financial inclusion by enlarging the space for monetary innovations in South Africa, Zimbabwe and Botswana, lowering the cost of transactions, making the countries less dependent on the use of cash, and promoting the transnational mobility of money. However, South Africa, Zimbabwe and Botswana seem behind in tapping into the financial inclusion opportunities presented by this new technology. This chapter argues that South Africa, Botswana and Zimbabwe need to adopt a responsive regulatory regime in order to reap the financial inclusion benefits derivable from the adoption of cryptocurrency technology.

S. T. Mota Makore · P. C. Osode (✉) · N. Lubisi
Faculty of Law, University of Fort Hare, East London, South Africa
e-mail: smotamakore@ufh.ac.za; posode@ufh.ac.za; nlubisi@ufh.ac.za

© The Author(s), under exclusive license to Springer Nature Switzerland AG 2023
H. Chitimira, T. V. Warikandwa (eds.), *Financial Inclusion and Digital Transformation Regulatory Practices in Selected SADC Countries*, Ius Gentium: Comparative Perspectives on Law and Justice 106,
https://doi.org/10.1007/978-3-031-23863-5_3

1 Introduction

The idea that cryptocurrencies could be instrumental for the successful pursuit of financial inclusion has attracted the attention of government officials, investors, scholars and financial services regulators across the world.[1] However, cryptocurrencies can indeed be a vehicle for promoting financial inclusion because of their intrinsic nature which enables them to perform multiple functions as a medium of exchange, assets and investment instruments.[2] Accordingly, in sub-Saharan African countries such as South Africa, Zimbabwe and Botswana where there are many unbanked and under-banked persons, cryptocurrencies can drive financial inclusion by enlarging the room for monetary innovations, making these countries less dependent on the use of cash and promoting the transnational mobility of money.[3] Nonetheless, critics opine that cryptocurrencies can also be a drawback for financial inclusion due to the problems of cybersecurity and speculative risks associated with their use.[4] Despite these divergent viewpoints, the argument that cryptocurrencies can facilitate financial inclusion remains compelling.[5] Countries across the world have, therefore, embarked on a search for an appropriate and effective model for regulating cryptocurrencies in pursuit of *inter alia*, the goals of eliminating financial exclusion and promoting financial inclusion, especially in developing countries.[6]

Cryptocurrencies are a form of denationalised virtual currency and a representation of value endowed with cryptographic features protecting them against counterfeiting or double-spend.[7] From the global regulators' perspective, the fascination and interest in cryptocurrency is largely predicated on the premise that cryptocurrencies present prospects for creating a unique international financial system that wrestles financial control from conventional third parties, such as banks and governments, while avoiding the issue of double-spending prevalent in electronic transactions.[8] Double-spending refers to the use of the same asset for two or more transactions. Indeed, cryptocurrencies address the problem of double spending by preventing currency duplication by making payment to two or more parties using the same asset impossible. Crudely put, it is almost impossible to "copy and paste" cryptocurrency transactions and thereby, theoretically, making duplicate versions of them for use.[9] In spite of these unique characteristics which make cryptocurrencies suitable for advancing financial inclusion, South Africa, Zimbabwe

[1]Lim (2015), p. 361.
[2]Matshane (2021), pp. 1 2; Scott (2016), p. 4.
[3]Chuen and Deng (2017), p. 8.
[4]Raymaekers (2015), pp. 30 37.
[5]World Economic Forum (2021a).
[6]Cvetkova (2018), p. 150.
[7]Ozturk and Sulungur (2021), p. 4.
[8]Christopher (2016), p. 140.
[9]Roestoff (2016), pp. 248–303.

and Botswana seem very slow in tapping into the financial inclusion opportunities presented by this new technology.[10]

This chapter argues that Zimbabwe, Botswana and South Africa need to adopt a responsive regulatory regime to reap the financial inclusion benefits derivable from cryptocurrencies' technology. It achieves this by exploring possible cryptocurrencies' regulatory models that can be deployed by regulators in South Africa, Zimbabwe and Botswana to facilitate financial inclusion through widespread adoption of cryptocurrencies. The chapter proceeds as follows. The first part examines the meaning of the term 'cryptocurrencies' laying the foundation for exploring the relationship between cryptocurrencies and financial inclusion. In the second part, the contribution presents a brief overview of the regulatory challenge thrown up by the emergence and increasing use of cryptocurrencies. Part three discusses the origin, nature and definition of cryptocurrencies which is immediately followed by an examination of the conceptual linkage between cryptocurrencies and financial inclusion in part 4. The objective is to demonstrate how cryptocurrencies facilitate financial inclusion. Part five then presents a proposal for a decentralised model for the regulation of cryptocurrencies in South Africa, Zimbabwe and Botswana in order to quicken the achievement of financial inclusion. The chapter briefly examines the theoretical, practical and policy implications of the adoption of such a regulatory model in the penultimate part six before the conclusion.

2 An Overview of the Regulatory Challenge

Since their creation, cryptocurrencies are increasingly gaining uptake in the financial sector across the globe.[11] They arguably provide a paradigm shift in the way people create, store and transfer economic value.[12] Equally, cryptocurrencies have the capacity to promote financial inclusion by providing an investment and transaction option to people irrespective of barriers such as geography, nationality, ethnicity, race, gender, or socio-economic class.[13] Some countries have, therefore, taken significant steps towards the adoption of cryptocurrencies as a means of storing value and as an instrument of payment.[14] For example, El Salvador has enacted the first comprehensive Blockchain and Cryptocurrencies Regulation 2021, which declares Bitcoin as legal tender in that country.[15] As it stands, more than three million people in El Salvador have downloaded the cryptocurrencies application,

---

[10]Grinberg (2012), p. 160.

[11]Peters et al. (2015), p. 1.

[12]Hofman (2014).

[13]OECD (2020).

[14]Renteria and Esposito (2021).

[15]CNB (2021).

Chivo wallet.[16] This means about 46% of the total population of El Salvador have access to cryptocurrency facilities which surpasses the users of traditional banking currently standing at 26 percent.[17] Remarkably, the number of Salvadorans with bitcoin wallets exceeds those who are holders of traditional bank accounts.[18]

Further, the Central Bank of Nigeria recently launched the e-Naira digital currency on the 25th of October 2021, joining a growing list of countries who have introduced a digital currency which can potentially reduce transaction costs and increase the participation of their people in the formal financial system.[19] The issuing of the eNaira came after the Nigerian central bank earlier prohibited banks and other financial institutions from dealing in cryptocurrencies based on the view that they are a significant threat to the current financial system.[20] As opposed to cryptocurrencies, the value of Central Bank Digital Currencies (CBDCs) is in part derived from fiat currency.[21] Since its launch, the uptake of the eNaira has been low largely due to the unmitigated risk associated with its use.[22] Many people in Nigeria have developed a wait and see approach because of the financial risks associate with the eNaira. For one to transact in eNaira, one should be in possession of a smartphone which makes the whole eNaira transition more prone to cyber related risks including fraud and data privacy problems.[23] The situation is exacerbated by the fact that the role out of the eNaira has not been buttressed by the legislative and policy support instruments necessary for strengthening the currency.[24] Another drawback relates to the Nigerian government's failure to furnish potential users with adequate information that is critical for them to make informed decisions relating to the use of the eNaira.[25]

The aforementioned shortcomings show that there is a need to develop an efficient and effective mechanism and approach for regulating cryptocurrencies to boost financial inclusion.[26] The lack of cryptocurrencies' regulations and the absence of a uniform and international regulation remain a significant drawback to the promotion of financial inclusion through the use of cryptocurrencies.[27] This lack of regulation has a negative bearing on the adoption of cryptocurrencies and by extension financial inclusion.[28] Potential cryptocurrencies' users are often

---

[16] Roy (2021).

[17] Roy (2021).

[18] Hernandez (2021).

[19] Diphoko (2021).

[20] Salami (2021).

[21] Bech and Garratt (2017).

[22] Ajifowoke (2021).

[23] Abdulbaseet (2021).

[24] Benson (2021).

[25] Obiezu (2021).

[26] Girasa (2018), p. 7.

[27] Blemus (2017), p. 4.

[28] Cermeño (2016).

discouraged from using the instrument due to the absence of cryptocurrency regulation.[29] This is the regulatory problem that this chapter addresses.[30] It provides valuable insights to government officials, investors, and civil society, among others, on the appropriate model for the regulation of cryptocurrencies to facilitate financial inclusion.[31]

3   Origin, Nature and Definition of Cryptocurrencies

In order to ascertain the distinction between cryptocurrencies and other instruments as well as highlight how they can be used to facilitate financial inclusion, we need to explore the origins of cryptocurrencies and uncover the rationales and mischiefs which underpin the development of such instruments.[32] The precise point of cryptocurrencies' origin is unclear. This is because the histography of cryptocurrencies has been underexplored and largely undocumented.[33] According to the scarce literature available, the origins of cryptocurrencies may be traced back to the 1980s, when an American software expert and cryptographer, David Lee Chaum, created the first known cryptographic system named eCash.[34] In 1992 he then invented another system called DigiCash designed to make economic transactions confidential by using a cryptographic system.[35] Nonetheless, the term cryptocurrencies as understood today was not known until 1998 when Wei Dai began exploring the idea of creating a new decentralised cryptographic method of payment.[36]

However, it was the pseudo character Satoshi Nakamoto who popularised cryptocurrencies' usage by creating the first known cryptocurrency in 2009 as a counter to the global financial crisis of that period.[37] It must be accepted that he was not the first person to originate the idea of cryptocurrencies.[38] The rationale for cryptocurrencies are manifold, but the main one is to create a distinctive international decentralised financial payment system based on cryptography, functioning with minimum involvement of the existing financial institutions.[39] The system of cryptocurrencies creates new forms of financial intermediaries distinct from the

---

[29] Guégan and Sotiropoulou (2017), p. 479.

[30] Congressional Research (2015).

[31] World Economic Forum (2021a).

[32] Granot (2018).

[33] Aziz (2019), p. 31.

[34] Nahorniak et al. (2016), p. 113.

[35] Rueckert (2019), p. 2.

[36] Bernadette et al. (2019).

[37] Congressional Research Service (2020).

[38] European Parliament (2018).

[39] South African Parliament (2021).

currently existing ones.[40] It is this feature of cryptocurrencies, among others, which is a 'game changer' for the instrument's users and is potentially supportive of financial inclusion.[41]

Further, while cryptography is a distinctive feature which makes cryptocurrencies distinguishable from other instruments such as digital and fiat currencies, an attempt to determine the nature and definition of the term cryptocurrencies and the digital elements categorised as such, remains elusive and is fraught with challenges.[42] This is due to several reasons. First, the concept of cryptocurrencies is a relatively recent phenomenon and a constantly evolving one in sync with the dynamism of our modern digital era and technological developments.[43] Therefore, what constitutes and qualifies as a cryptocurrency is indeterminable and highly contested.[44] Secondly, what worsens the situation is that there is confusion regarding which terminology should be used when one is referring to cryptographic instruments such as bitcoins and other digital assets.[45] A reading of the literature on the subject shows that legal scholars and technology experts make use of different terminology.[46] Some prefer to use the terms cryptocurrencies, virtual currency, crypto assets, digital tokens, digital assets while others use the term blockchain technology loosely.[47] All the terms carry similarities and differences in terms of their import and meaning. The primary difference between the terms is that blockchain technology generally refers to the parent technology that enables the existence of cryptocurrencies.[48] Cryptocurrencies and crypto assets can potentially function as a medium of exchange, and as financial products, with some (dis)similar attributes to the South African rand, Zimbabwean dollar or Botswana pula.[49] The distinction between cryptocurrencies and national currencies is that the latter are widely recognised and accepted as legal tender whilst the former are merely digital currencies whose regulatory status is still controversial, evolving and unclear depending on the country in question.[50]

Cryptocurrencies are based on a decentralised distributed ledger system which operates without much involvement of traditional third parties or middlemen, making the system exceptional from the extant traditional banking system.[51] They are a

---

[40] Cai (2018), p. 966.

[41] Mike (2016), p. 154.

[42] Ly (2014), p. 590.

[43] Liang (2018), p. 8.

[44] Bierer (2016), p. 81.

[45] Omarova (2019), p. 736.

[46] Omarova (2019), p. 736.

[47] Fatás (2019), p. 8.

[48] Shannon (2014).

[49] Islam et al. (2018).

[50] Islam et al. (2018).

[51] Johnson (2021), p. 978.

unique form of abstract electronic currencies exchangeable between peers.[52] Examples of such cryptocurrencies include: (a) Bitcoin (BTC); (b) Litecoin (LTC); (c) Ethereum (ETH); (d) Bitcoin Cash (BCH); (e) Ethereum Classic (ETC); (f) Zcash (ZEC); (g) Stellar Lumen (XLM); and (h) the Bitcoin Satoshi's Vision (BSV).[53] These cryptocurrencies constitute a self-enforcing representation of computer based information and numbers.[54] They are a form of immaterial property which gives the owners exclusive rights of use over the abstract instrument.[55] Cryptocurrencies function as an instrument of payment not only capable of replacing conventional cash payments and bank transfers, but also electronic cash payments.[56] Legally speaking, cryptocurrencies create cambial obligations as well as property rights since they are both an instrument of payment and a commodity.[57] Cryptocurrencies are created through a 'mining' process and are not backed by gold or other common assets of intrinsic value; their value emanates from trust, acceptance and a degree of speculative interest generated from their uniqueness.[58]

The mining of cryptocurrencies refers to the process of creating new cryptocurrencies by solving cryptographic equations using highly charged super-ended computers.[59] The production process consists of the 'verification of data blocks and placing the transaction records onto a public record (ledger) system called blockchain.'[60] The ledger is secured by complex encryption techniques. In order to create new currencies on the ledger, the system demands solving complicated mathematical puzzles that assist in verifying virtual currency transactions and then updating them on the blockchain ledger system.[61] The miners are rewarded by retaining ownership of the cryptocurrencies.[62] This process brings new currencies into circulation.[63] Block chain technology and cryptocurrencies mining require high energy consumption, and generate environmental waste when the computer hardware becomes obsolete.[64] Cryptocurrencies are a form of disruptive virtual currency endowed with the potential to fundamentally change the payment system in South Africa, Zimbabwe and Botswana by providing an alternative that is faster and safer.[65]

---

[52] Blemus (2017).

[53] Härdle (2019).

[54] Nabilou and Prüm (2019), p. 5.

[55] Chason (2018), p. 134.

[56] Kozak (2019), p. 35.

[57] Sari and Pujiyono (2019), p. 369.

[58] Alonso (2021), p. 14.

[59] Boehm and Pesch (2014).

[60] Goldenfein and Hunter (2017), p. 7.

[61] Lee (2016), p. 84.

[62] Ankalkoti and Santhosh (2017), p. 1363.

[63] Varadarajan (2017).

[64] Robberson and McCoy (2018), p. 6. See also Noack (2018).

[65] Ammous (2017).

4 Facilitating Financial Inclusion Through Cryptocurrencies' Use: A Paradigm for Dismantling Financial Hegemony

Before discussing whether and how cryptocurrencies facilitate financial inclusion, an ancillary, yet necessary inquiry which should be addressed relates to the exact meaning of the term 'financial inclusion'.[66] Upon ascertaining the meaning of the concept of financial inclusion, the discussion will proceed to determine whether cryptocurrencies are instrumental for the elimination of financial exclusion and the promotion of financial inclusion.[67] Lastly, if the answer to the latter question is in the affirmative, then a determination should be made on how cryptocurrencies can be strategically deployed and regulated in pursuit of financial inclusion.[68] The concept of financial inclusion is an anti-thesis to the notion of financial exclusion.[69] It is premised on the perspective that people, especially those who are impoverished or living on low income, should have access to a plethora of financial services, such as banking, credit, savings, insurance and money transfers, so that they can manage their money effectively, which would enable them to meet their long- and short-term economic needs.[70]

Financial inclusion provides a much needed lifeline and conduit for people living in poverty to lift themselves out of poverty and improve their livelihoods through savings, and the opportunity to initiate and participate in income generating activities.[71] Financial inclusion laws and policy interventions promoted by governments in South Africa, Botswana, Zimbabwe and other countries are mainly based on the premise that affordable and available financial services are indispensable for the realisation of pivotal sustainable development goals such as access to clean water, adequate health care services, and poverty reduction.[72] Nonetheless, most of the interventions do not always explicitly address the economic inequalities that cause financial exclusion. It can be argued that only interventions which address the root causes of socio-economic inequality, which in turn leads to financial exclusion, qualify as adequate responses to the pursuit of financial inclusiveness and egalitarianism.[73]

Financial inclusion has, since the 1980s, been accepted as a developmental stratagem, especially in developing countries such as South Africa, Botswana and Zimbabwe, operationalised mainly in the forms of access to an assortment of

---

[66]The AFI Financial Inclusion Strategy Peer Learning Group (2017).

[67]Blockchain Africa (2019).

[68]Freund (2017), p. 20.

[69]World Bank (2015).

[70]Kshetri (2017), p. 1732.

[71]Omar and Inaba (2020), p. 3.

[72]Zheng et al. (2018), p. 356.

[73]Sarma and Pais (2011), p. 614.

financial products and services as well as microcredit programmes.[74] A further catalyst to the discussion on financial inclusion was the 2007–2009 financial crisis.[75] What is clear from the bourgeoning literature on the histology of financial inclusion is that legal scholars and other researchers on microfinance in developing countries have long questioned the ability of financial inclusion to extricate poor people out of abject poverty due to the so called "poverty" finances offered by an increasingly lucrative financial services industry.[76] For the poor and low income earners, efforts towards financial inclusion have largely resulted in a debt trap, reckless lending and over-indebtedness.[77] Furthermore, scholars have pointed out that stratagems for financial inclusion as a development strategy in countries such as South Africa, Botswana and Zimbabwe have not properly responded to the complex challenges posed by the neo-colonial and neo-liberal financial architecture.[78] This includes other policies which reinforce the socio-economic relations informing the extant financial inclusion gap between developed and developing countries.[79]

The aforementioned concerns are particularly relevant because global leaders at the United Nations (UN) level and other international forums have re-affirmed the international liberal agenda for promoting universal financial inclusion as a policy instrument for attaining financial stability, economic growth and the realisation of other social goals, in response to the financial crisis emanating from Covid-19 and other socio-economic challenges.[80] This commitment to financial inclusion has also been backed by the Financial Inclusion Experts Group (FIEG), various non-governmental organisations including the Alliance for Financial Inclusion, Better than Cash Alliance, Groupe Spéciale Mobile Association and other non-profit making foundations.[81]

Aside from the above, the FIEG has developed Principles for Innovative Financial Inclusion, a non-binding regulatory framework premised on the World Bank (WB) concept termed 'Finance for all'.[82] This non-binding instrument encourages governments to improve access to finance by creating an enabling environment for the provision of new types of financial services.[83] The Principles, which have been endorsed by the G20, African Development Bank, and the Central Bank of the Republic of China, support, at least in theory, the use of digital technology to reach the financially excluded via mobile phones.[84] Cryptocurrencies have become an

---

[74]Isakul and Tantua (2021).

[75]Dullien et al. (2010), p. 18; Kasradze (2020), p. 70.

[76]Carletti et al. (2014), p. 640.

[77]Wazvaremhaka and Osode (2018), p. 2.

[78]Soederberg (2013), p. 610.

[79]Das and Espinoza (2020), p. 4.

[80]Kasradze (2020), p. 74.

[81]Bill and Melinda Gates Foundation (2012).

[82]WB (2020).

[83]GPFI (2010).

[84]G20 Leaders Statement (2010).

example of digital financial innovation that extends financial services to those locked out of the mainstream financial systems.[85]

There is compelling empirical evidence and scholarly opinion in support of the view that cryptocurrencies should be embraced and recognised as powerful drivers of financial inclusion.[86] For instance, on 31 May 2021, the Organisation for Economic Co-operation and Development (OECD) held a virtual meeting, attended by many finance experts, non-governmental organisations, United Nations (UN) agencies and central bank representatives, which acknowledged the crucial role that cryptocurrencies can play in advancing financial inclusion and economic reconstruction.[87] Further, the WB has held various symposiums whose thematic focus was on how to harness financial technologies such as cryptocurrencies in support of economic development and the reduction of extreme poverty in poor countries.[88]

It is noteworthy that the facilitation of financial inclusion is one of the most significant benefits derivable from cryptocurrencies for people living in developing and least developed countries.[89] Importantly, many people in South Africa, Botswana and Zimbabwe have access to mobile phones which gives them the capacity to engage in cryptocurrency transactions by plugging in to an internet outlet or sending and receiving SMS through their mobile phones.[90] Whilst internet coverage and access is still low in some remote areas of South Africa, Zimbabwe and Botswana, many people in the urban and peri-urban areas have good internet connectivity and penetration which supports the use of cryptocurrencies.[91] This means that as long as there is access to a mobile phone with SMS functions or internet connection even when available intermittently, cryptocurrencies' use will provide an opportunity for ordinary people to engage in diverse commercial transactions and investments.[92] Cryptocurrencies, such as Bitcoin, only require a mobile phone for people to exchange the currency, thereby minimising the need for banks as people will eventually become their own banks.[93] The capacity for cryptocurrencies to replace orthodox forms of payment remains the greatest promise of these currencies.[94]

The transactional costs incurred for using the conventional or orthodox payment systems remain very high in South Africa, Botswana and Zimbabwe.[95] This has the

---

[85] Chen (2021), p. 5.

[86] Das (2016).

[87] OECD (2021).

[88] WB (2019).

[89] Bourreau and Valletti (2015).

[90] Silver and Johnson (2018).

[91] Abrahams (2017), p. 16.

[92] World Economic Forum (2021b).

[93] Vincent and Evans (2019), p. 3.

[94] Congressional Research Service (2020).

[95] Chitimira and Ncube (2020), p. 355.

effect of dis-incentivising many people who become hesitant to use traditional financial services due to the envisaged diminished gains.[96] Cryptocurrencies provide a unique alternative by removing some traditional intermediaries, substantially decreasing concomitant transaction fees.[97] Transaction costs in cryptocurrencies' transfer systems are close to nil and even where platform fees are charged for maintaining cryptographic security standards, such charges remain comparatively lower than what the current financial intermediaries, such as banks, demand for similar transactions.[98]

Additionally, the majority of people in South Africa, Botswana and Zimbabwe do not have a digital identity, which substantially limits their ability to have access to digital financial services offered by many financial institutions.[99] In conjunction with other technologies offering digital identity tools, blockchain technology, which is the technology driving cryptocurrencies, can be of assistance in the establishment of a decentralised digital identity management data system which will enhance access to financial institutions and products for individuals.[100] Already the fintech company, Ethereum, is a leading light, having designed an application which has an algorithm capable of capturing people's facial profile and voice recognition.[101] Unbanked persons in South Africa, Botswana and Zimbabwe can potentially benefit from using this digital identity technology as they will then not be required to always have a physical identity document, a passport or an email account for them to participate in financial transactions.[102] For South Africa, digital identity may provide a solution to the current problem of identity theft, which results in unauthorised transactions arising from the unlawful use of a person's identity document.[103]

Further, many unbanked or under-banked persons in South Africa, Botswana and Zimbabwe have chrometophobia.[104] This is especially so in Zimbabwe, which once experienced a near collapse of its banking system at the height of the hyper-inflation era.[105] The financial woes currently faced by Zimbabweans, due mainly to economic sanctions imposed by western countries, de-industrialisation, capital flight and political instability, have resulted in many individuals doing without bank accounts because they distrust their financial institutions, which they perceive as fragile and

---

[96] World Bank Group (2018).

[97] Erdina et al. (2020), p. 1017.

[98] Kasahara and Kawahara (2016).

[99] Bankable Frontier Associates (2018).

[100] Abrahams (2017), p. 3.

[101] International Monetary Fund (2018).

[102] Ncube (2020).

[103] Ana (2018).

[104] This term chrometophobia refers to an abnormal and persistent fear of spending money or access to financial services such as credit, among others. People with chrometophobia fear that they might mismanage their financial affairs. Okeahalam (1998), p. 45.

[105] Dzomira (2014), p. 76.

untrustworthy.[106] Ideally, when the client-bank relationship has broken down due to mistrust, there is a need for to rebuild it or alternatively introducing new facilitators and guarantors in the client-bank relationship.[107] Cryptocurrencies satisfy this need by offering an alternative to the traditional financial intermediaries, thereby attracting the unbanked.[108]

The use of cryptocurrencies also allows people in South Africa, Botswana and Zimbabwe to store their money through instruments they have control over, making trust obligations easier among transacting parties and drastically reducing the information imbalance prevalent in the traditional payment system and related transactions.[109] The blockchain technology underlying cryptocurrencies substitutes trust in the traditional intermediaries with computer generated codes and rules which define how transactions are concluded, thereby providing a highly independent and autonomous technology-based currency and value exchange while avoiding system abuses from financial managers or employees.[110] This reduction of information asymmetries also results in the reduction of costs. The need for the replacement of financial intermediaries is greater in South Africa, Botswana and Zimbabwe where trust in these intermediaries is lower than in developed countries such as the US. France and Britain, which supports the uptake of cryptocurrencies.[111]

However, the aforementioned envisaged financial inclusion gains derivable from cryptocurrencies will largely remain a pipe dream if South Africa, Botswana and Zimbabwe fail to develop and adopt a robust legal framework capable of effectively dealing with digital fraud, illicit money flows and money laundering, in addition to strengthening the present cybersecurity accountability mechanism.[112] The absence of an adequate cyber related accountability mechanism and response laws has resulted in the greatest and now famous 2021 cryptocurrency heist in South Africa.[113] Regarding the essential details, two South African brothers who operated a cryptocurrencies platform collected more than 3.6 billion US dollars or 50 billion rands worth of cryptocurrencies and vanished. The regulator, the Financial Services Conduct Authority (FSCA), has stated that the two brothers were operating their cryptocurrencies platform outside the scope of the FSCA's regulatory jurisdiction.[114] This case of the South African brothers is illustrative of the need and imperative to develop strong domestic cyber security related policies and regulation in the three selected countries.[115]

---

[106] Chidochashe (2009), p. 112.

[107] Global Legal Research Center (2018).

[108] Harwick (2016), p. 580.

[109] Griffin and Shams (2020), p. 4.

[110] Global Commission on Internet Governance (2017).

[111] Carstens (2021).

[112] Carstens (2021).

[113] Quach (2021).

[114] Quach (2021).

[115] Henderson and Prinsloo (2021).

5 Developing a Decentralised Cryptocurrencies' Regulatory Architecture for South Africa, Botswana and Zimbabwe

The preceding discussion demonstrates that South Africa, Zimbabwe and Botswana can potentially benefit from the financial inclusion benefits and potential offered by the increased usage of cryptocurrencies.[116] This necessitates a shift in the debate from whether cryptocurrencies should be adopted and regulated to a more nuanced pragmatic position of how cryptocurrencies can be regulated in a manner that addresses the challenges associated with their use while simultaneously maximising on their financial inclusion benefits.[117] Nonetheless, their official acceptance and legal status differs substantially across the globe with varied implications.[118] Already some countries, such as the United States of America (US), Canada, Australia, Germany, Switzerland, France and Japan, are in the process of developing a pro-cryptocurrency financial regulatory framework or environment.[119] As mentioned earlier, El Salvador has been a leading light by enacting the first comprehensive Blockchain and Cryptocurrencies Regulation 2021, which declares Bitcoin as legal tender in the country.[120] Given these developments, Zimbabwe, Botswana and South Africa should adopt a responsive regulatory regime enabling them to reap the financial inclusion benefits emanating from widespread use of cryptocurrencies.[121]

Lamentably, central banks in South Africa, Botswana and Zimbabwe have issued either official statements or position papers on cryptocurrencies re-asserting that they are the sole authority legally permitted to issue legal tender and that cryptocurrencies are not legal tender in their respective jurisdictions.[122] Typical examples are the 2014 Position Paper on Virtual Currency and the 2019 Consultation Paper on Policy Proposals for Crypto Assets issued by South Africa, which state that crypto asserts are not recognised as legal tender in South Africa.[123] The position of the South African Reserve Bank is informed by sections 1 and 17 of the South African Reserve Bank (SARB) Act[124] as well as section 15 (3)(c) of the

---

[116] Bernadette et al. (2019).

[117] Baur et al. (2018), p. 181.

[118] CoinStaker (2018).

[119] United States Congress (2018).

[120] Renteria and Esposito (2021).

[121] The Crypto Assets Regulatory (CAR) Working Group (2021).

[122] South African Reserve Bank (2014).

[123] South African Reserve Bank (2014); and Crypto Asset Regulation Group (2019).

[124] Act 90 of 1989. Section 17 (a) of the SARB Act defines legal tender as 'a tender by the bank itself, of a note of the Bank or of an outstanding note of another bank for which the bank has assumed liability in terms of section 15 (3)(c) of the Currency and Banking Act or in terms of any agreement entered into with another bank before or after commencement of this Act; and (b) a tender by the bank itself, of an undefaced and unmutilated coin which is lawfully in circulation in RSA and of current mass.'

Currency and Banking Act[125] which exclusively limit legal tender to banknotes, bank-based digital currencies and coins issued only by the SARB. Similarly, sections 22 and 23 of the Bank of Botswana Act[126] and sections 40, 41 and 44 of the Reserve Bank of Zimbabwe Act[127] limit legal tender to conventional currencies declared as such by central banks. It is submitted that the refusal by the central banks of South Africa, Botswana and Zimbabwe to recognise cryptocurrencies as legal tender may amount to a *de facto* ban on cryptocurrencies or an attempt to discourage their usage.[128] In either of the scenarios, such a stance creates problems of regulatory arbitrage and competition.[129] For instance, when the People's Bank of China on 25 September 2021 outlawed all crypto-related mining and transaction activities, the exodus of the cryptocurrency industry from China to more conducive jurisdictions intensified as did the emergence of underground cryptocurrency black-markets.[130] Many cryptocurrency dealers have found habitat in the US state of Texas where conducive cryptocurrencies policies and laws are being introduced and implemented.[131] These developments demonstrate that efforts to either impose a blanket ban or to undermine cryptocurrencies may not be the most plausible regulatory approach.[132]

While there are people and organisations in South Africa, Botswana and Zimbabwe using cryptocurrencies, such transactions fall outside of the domestic financial markets' regulatory framework and there is no right of convertibility of cryptocurrencies transactions in the financial markets.[133] The implication is that cryptocurrencies are currently unregulated. Those using cryptocurrencies in South Africa, Botswana and Zimbabwe therefore bear the accompanying financial risks, without protection from the law.[134] However, by establishing the Intergovernmental Fintech Working Group (IFWG) in 2016, South Africa seems to have taken preliminary steps towards developing an amicable policy approach towards cryptocurrencies and other fintech matters.[135]

Notwithstanding the above, one of the greatest challenges facing regulators in South Africa, Zimbabwe and Botswana is how to effectively regulate a decentralized

---

[125] Act 31 of 1920.

[126] Act 191996.

[127] Act 3 of 2016 (Part XCV).

[128] Marian (2015), pp. 53–61.

[129] PWC (2015).

[130] China has not enacted any legislation regulating cryptocurrencies. However, Chinese regulators have not recognised cryptocurrencies as legal tender or an instrument of payments, and the country's banking sector is not accepting any existing cryptocurrencies or providing related services. Nonetheless, the Chinese central bank has been minting plans to introduce a government backed centralised cryptocurrency. BBC News (2021a).

[131] Washington Post (2021). See also BBC News (2021b).

[132] Department of Financial Services (2015). See also South African Government (2021).

[133] World Economic Forum (2021c).

[134] IFWG (n.d.).

[135] IFWG (n.d.).

cryptocurrencies' ecosystem which is largely antithetical to the current centralised orthodox financial regulation prevalent in these countries.[136] In searching for an appropriate cryptocurrencies regulatory model, the wisdom embedded in the current centralised conventional financial system regulatory model should be considered.[137] That model is premised on regulating against market failure, with a thematic focus on the idea that "regulation should begin where the market failures can potentially occur".[138] The orthodox approach to financial sector governance is deployed towards minimising risks in financial markets emanating from the market participants and other sources.[139] Such risks can originate from conduct such as market manipulation, fraud, consumer exploitation, cryptocurrencies' volatility, tampering with the ledgers' system, anti-competitive acts and oligopolies, tax evasion issues, governance problems, and other forms of risk connected to the issue of central bank backed digital currencies and microeconomic instability.[140] Similarly, these risks also plague cryptocurrency transactions and markets. Due to the virtual nature of cryptocurrency transactions, risks such as privacy and identity theft concerns can be added.[141]

Although the orthodox approach to financial sector governance has been instrumental in dealing with the aforementioned systemic risk in the financial sector, it remains largely inapplicable to the regulation of cryptocurrencies in South Africa, Botswana and Zimbabwe.[142] With its centralisation premise, the orthodox approach to financial regulation would be ill-suited and counterproductive.[143] This approach would only address cryptocurrencies' market failure or effect behavioural change through regulating developers, miners, prototype layers and codes.[144] These cryptocurrencies' market participants in South Africa, Botswana and Zimbabwe would be compelled, by the threat of sanctions, to adhere to the dictates of the rule of law and financial market laws.[145] However, the orthodox approach becomes difficult to apply in circumstances where the participants have no real time presence or representation or a place of domicile.[146] This problem can largely be avoided

---

[136] Financial Action Task Force (2019).

[137] Coetzee and de Bee (2016), p. 93.

[138] Francis (1993), p. 1.

[139] Baldwin et al. (2012), p. 14.

[140] Demertzis and Wolf (2018).

[141] Peters et al. (2015), p. 15.

[142] Mazikana (2018).

[143] Athanassiou (2018), p. 38.

[144] Yeoh (2017), p. 200.

[145] This is based on the command control theory which underpins most legal rules. Proponents such as John Austin argued that human beings only obey the law because of the threat of sanctions. See Austin (1832), p. 123.

[146] White (2005).

through the development of a regime consisting of indirect decentralised cryptocurrencies regulation.[147]

A decentralised indirect cryptocurrencies regulation in South Africa, Zimbabwe and Botswana would be anchored on identifying the financial institutions who offer precise points of connection between the cryptocurrencies world and the real time world.[148] Such an approach would then be premised upon new and some old elements drawn from the current regulatory mechanisms, including the twin peaks model in South Africa and the financial prudential supervision and management systems existing in Botswana and Zimbabwe.[149] Instead of targeting the cryptocurrency technologies, prototype layers and codes, this amalgamated financial regulation mechanism would largely govern cryptocurrency applications, users and use-points.[150] Other traditional gatekeepers such as cryptocurrency banks, lenders, exchanges and wallet providers, custodians and merchant acceptance facilities would be regulated as well.[151] Such a decentralised hybrid regulatory approach would rely on the central banks in South Africa, Botswana and Zimbabwe designing rules for the intermediaries enforced through the known traditional institutions such as banks, payment services providers, exchanges, miners and other new participants.[152] This approach circumvents direct regulation of coders whose identity maybe unknown.[153]

The envisaged decentralised indirect cryptocurrencies regulatory framework would necessitate the introduction of the following changes to the existing financial system related policies and laws in South Africa, Botswana and Zimbabwe.[154] First, the South African Reserve Bank (SARB), Bank of Botswana and Reserve Bank of Zimbabwe, being central banks, should be authorised to have a supervisory and regulatory responsibility to monitor cross-border financial outflows in respect of various crypto assets.[155] This would require the amendment of section 10(4) of the Exchange Control Regulations to include cryptocurrencies in the definition of 'capital' for the purposes of exchange control regulation in South Africa.[156] Changes to inter alia, section 2(d) of the Zimbabwe Exchange Control Act[157] should be made to authorise dealers to facilitate and report transactions involving transfer of foreign currency for the purpose of purchasing cryptocurrencies abroad.[158]

---

[147] Nabilou (2019), p. 281.

[148] For a further discussion of the concept of decentred regulation, see Finck (2019), p. 172.

[149] FSCA (2018).

[150] Dewey (2018), p. 59.

[151] Finck (2018), p. 689.

[152] Nabilou and Prüm (2019), p. 1.

[153] International Organisation of Securities Commissions (2020).

[154] Carstens (2021).

[155] The Crypto Assets Regulatory (CAR) (2021).

[156] The Crypto Assets Regulatory (CAR) Working Group (2021).

[157] 109 of 1996 Chapter 22:05.

[158] The Crypto Assets Regulatory (CAR) Working Group (2021).

Further, a plethora of legislative amendments should be made declaring cryptocurrencies as a financial product via the Financial Advisory and Intermediary Services Act[159] (South Africa), Botswana's Banking Act[160] and Non-Bank Financial Institutions Regulatory Authority Act[161] and Zimbabwe's Securities Act.[162] This would require cryptocurrency service providers to become licenced intermediaries and provide for the rendering of advice by such entities.[163] Such a development allows for regulatory oversight and will assist in addressing the risk of exploitation of consumers by unscrupulous entities.[164] Additional changes to the legislation governing traditional payment systems including South Africa's National Payment Systems Act,[165] Botswana's National Clearance and Settlement Systems Act[166] and Zimbabwe's National Payment Act[167] favouring cryptocurrencies' acceptance and widespread uptake would create more opportunities for these three countries to reap the financial inclusion benefits and potential of cryptocurrencies.[168]

6 Theoretical, Practical and Policy Implications of Developing a Decentralised Cryptocurrencies' Regulatory Regime

It is noteworthy that a decentralised regime of cryptocurrencies' regulation remains the most efficient and effective regulatory strategy for mitigating the risks associated with the use of cryptocurrencies in South Africa, Zimbabwe and Botswana.[169] Clearly, the current orthodox model for regulating instruments of payment and investments, with its highly centralised command and control characteristics, is inadequate for cryptocurrencies' regulation.[170] South Africa, Botswana and Zimbabwe should deploy a decentralised regime of cryptocurrencies' regulation thereby strengthening the institutional competence of their regulators.[171] Such a regulatory model will contribute towards minimising the risks associated with cryptocurrencies

---

[159] Act 37 of 2002.

[160] Act 19 of 1996.

[161] Act of 2006.

[162] Act 17 of 2004 Chapter 24:25.

[163] Murray (2019).

[164] Broader changes can be considered such as the strengthening of consumer protection legislation in South Africa, Botswana and Zimbabwe. Benoit (2018).

[165] Act 78 of1998.

[166] Act 2003 Chapter 46:06.

[167] Chapter 24:23 of 2001.

[168] Jabotinsky (2020).

[169] Nabilou (2019), p. 289.

[170] Shirakawa (2019).

[171] Marian (2015), p. 68; Peters et al. (2015), p. 5.

use and the declaration of cryptocurrencies as legal tender.[172] Further, such a development will allow people in South Africa, Botswana and Zimbabwe to use cryptocurrencies as instruments of payment, investment and for accessing financial services and products.[173]

7 Conclusion

This chapter has demonstrated that the adoption and use of cryptocurrencies has the potential to facilitate financial inclusion in South Africa, Botswana and Zimbabwe.[174] The idiosyncratic characteristics of cryptocurrencies enables them to be deployed as *sui generis* instruments of payment, assets and investments, enabling them to challenge conventional financial tools for transacting, storing and transferring economic value.[175] It has been shown that cryptocurrencies, being denationalised peer-to-peer-based instruments, could result in unbanked persons located in emerging market economies being attracted to their use and adoption. Cryptocurrencies can promote financial inclusion by enlarging the space for monetary innovation in South Africa, Zimbabwe and Botswana, thereby lowering the cost of transactions, making the countries less dependent on the traditional use of cash, and promoting the transnational mobility of money.[176]

It has also been argued that South Africa, Botswana and Zimbabwe should develop a decentralised indirect cryptocurrencies' regulatory model in order for them to reap the financial inclusion benefits emanating from the adoption of cryptocurrencies' technology.[177] Such a model of decentralised regulation would be the most optimal regulatory approach to governing decentralised cryptocurrencies' transactions.[178] The absence of visible target institutions and the anonymity accompanying most cryptocurrency transactions makes the orthodox regulatory approach prevalent in the financial sector unsuitable for cryptocurrencies' regulation.[179] A decentralised regulatory model would target known institutions such as banks, payment services providers, exchanges, miners, cryptocurrencies e-wallet providers and other emerging intermediaries.[180] In this context, the underlying regulatory rationale would be two-fold, namely, the reduction of systemic risk

---

[172] OECD (2019a, b).

[173] deVries (2016), p. 6.

[174] Lee (2018), p. 254.

[175] Lee (2018), p. 255.

[176] Global Legal Research Center (2018).

[177] Grinberg (2011), p. 160.

[178] Armour et al. (2016), p. 101.

[179] Athanassiou (2018), p. 38.

[180] Black (2001), p. 106.

as well as maintaining the integrity and safety of cryptocurrency transactions.[181] This could result in a significant deepening and strengthening of the ongoing initiatives aimed at ensuring that financial inclusion becomes a reality in South Africa, Botswana and Zimbabwe.[182]

Bibliography

Abdulbaseet Q (2021) Personal Data, the eNaira, and Matters of Digital Transaction Confidentiality. https://enaira.com/news/insights/personal-data-the-e-naira-and-matters-of-digital-transaction-confidentiality. Accessed 10 Dec 2021

Abrahams L (2017) Regulatory imperatives for the future of SADC's digital complexity ecosystem. Afr J Inf Commun 20:3

Ajifowoke M (2021) Central Bank Digital Currencies Differ from Crypto. Here's How they Work. https://techcabal.com/2021/07/13/central-bank-digital-currencies-differ-from-crypto-heres-how-they-work/. Accessed 10 Dec 2021

Alonso NLS (2021) Cryptocurrency mining from an economic and environmental perspective. Anal Most Least Sustain Countr Ener 14:1

Ammous S (2017) Can Cryptocurrencies Fulfil the Functions of Money? https://capitalism.columbia.edu/files/ccs/workingpage/2017/ammous_cryptocurrencies_and_the_functions_of_money.pdf. Accessed 27 Nov 2021

Ana I (2018) Digital identity: the current state of affairs. https://www.bbvaresearch.com/wp-content/uploads/2018/02/Digital-Identity_the-current-state-of affairs.pdf. Accessed 12 Jan 2022

Ankalkoti P, Santhosh SG (2017) A relative study on bitcoin mining. Imp J Interdiscip Res 3:1362

Armour J et al (2016) Principles of financial regulation. Oxford University Press, Oxford

Athanassiou PL (2018) Digital innovation in financial services: legal challenges and regulatory policy issues. Juta, Cape Town

Austin J (1832) The province of jurisprudence determined. John Murray

Aziz A (2019) Cryptocurrency: evolution and legal dimension. Int J Bus Econ Law 18:31

Baldwin R et al (2012) Understanding regulation: theory, strategy and practice. Oxford University Press, Oxford

Bank of Botswana Act 19 1996

Bankable Frontier Associates (2018) Landscaping a digital financial identity for SADC. https://bfaglobal.com/wp-content/uploads/2018/02/FMT-Digital-ID-landscape-report-1.pdf. Accessed 11 Nov 2021

Baur DG et al (2018) Bitcoin: medium of exchange or speculative assets? J Int Financ Mark Inst Money 54:177

BBC News (2021a) China Declares All Crypto-Currency Transactions Illegal. https://www.bbc.com/news/technology-58678907. Accessed 11 Nov 2021

BBC News (2021b) Why China's bitcoin miners are moving to Texas. https://www.bbc.com/news/world-us-canada-58414555. Accessed 18 Nov 2021

Bech M, Garratt R (2017) Central Bank Cryptocurrencies. https://www.bis.org/publ/qtrpdf/r_qt1709f.htm. Accessed 10 Dec 2021

Benoit C (2018) The Future of Financial Market Infrastructures: Spearheading Progress Without Renouncing Safety. https://www.ecb.europa.eu/press/key/date/2018/html/ecbsp180626.en.html. Accessed 11 Nov 2021

---

[181] Payne (2015), p. 3.

[182] Nair and Cachanosky (2017), p. 4.

Benson EA (2021) 3 Days After Launch, It's Been a Rough Patch for the eNaira; Here's What You Need to Know. https://africa.businessinsider.com/local/markets/3-days-after-launch-its-been-a-rough-patch-for-the-enaira/3d1ckgj. Accessed 11 Nov 2021

Bernadette J et al (2019) Cryptocurrency Regulations: Institutions and Financial Openness. https://www.adb.org/sites/default/files/publication/513726/adbi-wp978.pdf. Accessed 12 Jan 2022

Bierer T (2016) Hashing it out: problems and solutions concerning cryptocurrency used as article 9 collateral. J Law Technol Internet 7:79

Bill and Melinda Gates Foundation (2012) Financial services for the poor: a policy overview. https://docs.gatesfoundation.org/Documents/fsp-strategy-overview.pdf. Accessed 11 Nov 2021

Black J (2001) Decentring regulation: the role of regulation and self-regulation in a "Post Regulatory". Curr Leg Probl 54:103

Blemus S (2017) Law and blockchain: a legal perspective on current regulatory trends worldwide. Corp Financ Capital Mark Law Rev 4:1

Blockchain Africa (2019) Blockchain Technology: Moving Africa Forward. https://blockchainafrica.co/blockchain-africa-conference-cape-town-2/. Accessed 11 Nov 2021

Boehm F, Pesch P (2014) Bitcoin: A First Legal Analysis - with Reference to German and US-American Law. https://www.zar.kit.edu/DATA/veroeffentlichungen/237_BTC_final_camready_437e610.pdflaw. Accessed 11 Nov 2021

Bourreau M, Valletti T (2015) Enabling Digital Financial Inclusion through Improvements in Competition and Interoperability: What Works and What Doesn't? http://www.cgdev.org. Accessed 10 Dec 2021

Cai CW (2018) Disruption of financial intermediation by FinTech: a review on crowdfunding and blockchain. Account Finance 58:965

Carletti AFE et al (2014) The African financial development and financial inclusion gaps. J Afr Econ 23:614

Carstens A (2021) Digital Currencies and the Future of the Monetary System. https://www.bis.org/speeches/sp210127.pdf. Accessed 11 Nov 2021

Cermeño JS (2016) Blockchain in Financial Services: Regulatory Landscape and Future Challenges for its Commercial Application. https://www.bbvaresearch.com/wp-content/uploads/2016/12/WP_16-20.pdf. Accessed 11 Jan 2021

Chason ED (2018) How bitcoin functions as property law. Seton Hall Law Rev 49:129

Chen W (2021) Financial inclusion in China: an overview. Front Bus 15:1

Chidochashe ML (2009) The economic decline of Zimbabwe. Gettysburg Econ Rev 9:110

Chitimira H, Ncube M (2020) Legislative and other selected challenges affecting financial inclusion for the poor and low-income earners in South Africa. J Afr Law 64:337

Christopher CM (2016) The bridging model: exploring the roles of trust and enforcement in banking, bitcoin, and the Blockchain. Nevada Law J 17:140

Chuen DLK, Deng R (eds) (2017) Handbook of blockchain, digital finance, and inclusion. Elsevier

CNB (2021) El Salvador looks to become the world's first country to adopt bitcoin as legal tender. https://www.cnbc.com/2021/06/05/el-salvador-becomes-the-first-country-to-adopt-bitcoin-as-legal-tender-.html. Accessed 11 Nov 2021

Coetzee J, De Bee J (2016) Financial regulation in the South African banking industry Cape Town. Juta

CoinStaker (2018) Cryptocurrency Legal Status by Individual Nations. https://www.coinstaker.com/cryptocurrency-legal-status/. Accessed 10 Nov 2021

Congressional Research (2015) Bitcoin: Questions, Answers and Analysis of Legal Issues. https://sgp.fas.org/crs/misc/R43339.pdf. Accessed 9 Nov 2021

Congressional Research Service (2020) Cryptocurrency: the economics of money and selected policy issues. https://sgp.fas.org/crs/misc/R45427.pdf. Accessed 9 Nov 2021

Crypto Asset Regulation Group (2019) Consultation Paper on Policy Proposals for Crypto Assets. http://www.treasury.gov.za/comm_media/press/2019/CAR%20WG%20Consultation%20paper%20on%20crypto%20assets_final.pdf. Accessed 13 Nov 2021

Currency and Banking Act 31 of 1920

Cvetkova I (2018) Cryptocurrencies legal regulation. BRICS Law J 5:150

Das MD (2016) social inclusion in macro-level diagnostics: reflecting on the World Bank Group's early systematic country diagnostics. https://openknowledge.worldbank.org/handle/10986/24630. Accessed 10 Dec 2021

Das MD, Espinoza SA (2020) Inclusion matters in Africa. World Bank Group

Demertzis M, Wolf GB (2018) The economic potential and risks of crypto assets: is a regulatory framework needed? https://www.bruegel.org/wp-content/uploads/2018/09/PC-14_2018.pdf. Accessed 10 Dec 2021

Department of Financial Services (2015) Regulations of the Superintendent of Financial Services, Part 200. Virtual Currencies. http://www.dfs.ny.gov/legal/regulations/adoptions/dfsp200t.pdf. Accessed 11 Nov 2021

DeVries PD (2016) An analysis of cryptocurrency, bitcoin, and the future. Int J Bus Manage Commer 1:1

Dewey J (ed) (2018) Blockchain and cryptocurrency regulation. Rory Smith

Diphoko W (2021) Nigeria Becomes the First Country in Africa to Launch A Digital Currency. eNaira. https://www.iol.co.za/technology/nigeria-becomes-the-first-country-in-africa-to-launch-a-digital-currency-enaira-664948c2-3fc6-4c36-b43a-92cddcb4322b. Accessed 18 Nov 2021

Dullien S et al (2010) The financial and economic crisis of 2008–2009 and developing countries. UNCTAD

Dzomira S (2014) Analysis of Bank failures during financial tumult in Africa-Zimbabwe: a historical review. J Gov Regul 3:75

Erdina E et al (2020) A bitcoin payment network with reduced transaction fees and confirmation times. Comput Netw 172:1016

European Parliament (2018) Cryptocurrencies and Blockchain. https://www.europarl.europa.eu/cmsdata/150761/TAX3%20Study%20on%20cryptocurrencies%20and%20blockchain.pdf. Accessed 11 Nov 2021

Fatás A (ed) (2019) The economics of fintech and digital currencies. CEPR Press

Financial Action Task Force (2019) Guidance_For_A_Risk-Based Approach to Virtual Currencies. https://www.fatf-gafi.org/media/fatf/documents/reports/Guidance-RBA-Virtual-Currencies.pdf. Accessed 11 Nov 2021

Finck M (2018) Blockchains: regulating the unknown. German Law J 19:666

Finck M (2019) Blockchain governance in Europe. Cambridge University Press, Cambridge

Francis J (1993) The politics of regulation. Cambridge University Press

Freund A (ed) (2017) Handbook of blockchain, digital finance, and inclusion. Elsevier

FSCA (2018) Regulatory strategy of the financial sector conduct authority. https://www.fsca.co.za/Documents/FSCA_Strategy_2018.pdf. Accessed 11 Nov 2021

G20 Leaders Statement (2010) Principles and Report on Innovative Financial Inclusion from the Access through Innovation Sub-Group of the G20 Financial Inclusion Experts Group. https://www.gpfi.org/publications/g20-principles-innovative-financial-inclusion-executive-brief. Accessed 19 Nov 2021

Girasa R (2018) Regulation of cryptocurrencies and blockchain technologies - national and international perspectives. Palgrave

Global Commission on Internet Governance (2017) Beyond access: addressing digital inequality in Africa https://media.africaportal.org/documents/GCIG_no.48_0.pdf. Accessed 8 Nov 2021

Global Legal Research Center (2018) Regulation of Cryptocurrency Around the World. https://www.loc.gov/law/help/cryptocurrency/cryptocurrency-world-survey.pdf. Accessed 10 Nov 2021

Goldenfein J, Hunter D (2017) Blockchains, orphan works, and the public domain. Columbia J Law Arts 41:1

GPFI (2010) G20 Principles for Innovative Financial Inclusion. https://www.gpfi.org/publications/g20-principles-innovative-financial-inclusion-executive-brief. Accessed 11 Nov 2021

Granot E (2018) On the Origin of the Value of Cryptocurrencies. https://www.intechopen.com/chapters/62430. Accessed 11 Nov 2021

Griffin J, Shams A (2020) Is bitcoin really untethered? J Financ 74:1

Grinberg R (2011) Bitcoin: an innovative alternative digital currency. Hast Sci Technol Law J 4:159

Grinberg R (2012) Bitcoin: an innovative alternative digital currency. Hast Sci Technol Law J 4:159

Guégan D, Sotiropoulou A (2017) Bitcoin and the challenges for financial regulation. Oxf Capital Mark Law J 12:466

Härdle WK (2019) Understanding Cryptocurrencies, RTG 1792 Discussion Paper 2019 1 4 https://ies.keio.ac.jp/upload/20191125econo_Wolfbang_wp.pdf. Accessed 18 Nov 2021

Harwick C (2016) Cryptocurrency and the problem of intermediation. Indep Rev 20:569

Henderson R, Prinsloo L (2021) South African Brothers Vanish, and So Does $3.6 Billion in Bitcoin. https://www.bloomberg.com/news/articles/2021-06-23/s-african-brothers-vanish-and-so-does-3-6-billion-in-bitcoin. Accessed 10 Dec 2021

Hernandez J (2021) El Salvador Just Became the First Country to Accept Bitcoin as Legal Tender. https://www.kalw.org/npr-news/2021-09-07/el-salvador-just-became-the-first-country-to-accept-bitcoin-as-legal-tender. Accessed 10 Jan 2022

Hofman A (2014) The Dawn of the National Currency – An Exploration of Country-Based Cryptocurrencies. https://bitcoinmagazine.com/articles/dawnnational-currency-exploration-country-based-cryptocurrencies-1394146138. Accessed 11 Nov 2021

IFWG (n.d.) South Africa Fintech Vision. https://www.ifwg.co.za/wp-content/uploads/South_Africa_FinTech_Vision.pdf. Accessed 12 Jan 2022

International Monetary Fund (2018) FinTech in Sub-Saharan African Countries A Game Changer? https://www.elibrary.imf.org/abstract/IMF087/25592978148438566l/25592978148438566l/25592978148438566. Accessed 10 Jan 2022

International Organisation of Securities Commissions (2020) Issues, Risks and Regulatory Considerations Relating to Crypto-Asset Trading Platforms. https://www.iosco.org/library/pubdocs/pdf/IOSCOPD649.pdf. Accessed 12 Jan 2022

Isakul A, Tantua B (2021) Financial Inclusion in developing countries: Applying Financial Technology. https://www.Financial%20Inclusion%20in%20Developing%20Countries%3A%20Applying%20Financial%20Technology%20as%20a%20Panacea,January%202021South%20Asian. Accessed 15 Nov 2021

Islam MR et al (2018) Cryptocurrency vs Fiat Currency: Architecture, Algorithm, Cash flow and Ledger Technology on Emerging Economy. https://www.publication/329565339_Cryptocurrency_vs_Fiat_Currency_Architecture_Algorithm_Cashflow_Ledger_Technology_on_Emerging_Economy. Accessed 10 Dec 2021

Jabotinsky HY (2020) The Regulation of Cryptocurrencies - Between a Currency and a Financial Product. https://core.ac.uk/download/pdf/363913093.pdf. Accessed 12 Jan 2022

Johnson KN (2021) Decentralised finance: regulating cryptocurrency exchanges. William Mary Law Rev 62:1911

Kasahara, S and Kawahara, J (2016) Effect of Bitcoin Fee on Transaction-Confirmation Process https://arxiv.org/pdf/1604.00103.pdf. Accessed 7 Jan 2022

Kasradze T (2020) Challenges facing financial inclusion due to the COVID-19 pandemic. Eur J Market Econ 3:67

Kozak S (2019) Bitcoin as An Electronic Payment Tool, Zeszyty Naukowe Uniwersytetu Przyrodniczo-Humanistycznego w Siedlcach Seria Administracja i. Zarządzanie 47:33

Kshetri N (2017) Will blockchain emerge as a tool to break the poverty chain in the global south? Third World Q 8:1710

Lee J (2018) Distributed ledger technologies (blockchain) in capital markets: risk and governance. J Bus Technol Law 14:252

Lee L (2016) New kids on the blockchain: how Bitcoin's technology could reinvent the stock market. Hast Bus Law J 12:81

Liang J (2018) Evolutionary dynamics of cryptocurrency transaction networks: an empirical study. PLoS One 13:1

Lim J (2015) A facilitative model for cryptocurrency regulation in Singapore. In: Chuen K, Lee D (eds) Handbook of digital currency: bitcoin, innovation, financial instruments, and big data. Elsevier

Ly MK (2014) Coining Bitcoin's legal bits: examining the regulatory framework for bitcoin and virtual currencies. Harv J Law Technol 27:588

Marian O (2015) A conceptual framework for the regulation of cryptocurrencies. Univ Chicago Law Rev 82:54

Matshane O (2021) Fintech Working Group Position on Cryptocurrency, IFWG CAR Working Group position paper on crypto assets, 11 June 2021

Mazikana AT (2018) The impact of cryptocurrencies in Zimbabwe. Anal Bitcoins. https://doi.org/10.2139/ssrn.3376307. Accessed 11 Nov 2021

Mike T (ed) (2016) History of money: from barter to bitcoin. Lean Stone Publishing

Murray W (2019) The Applicability of the Financial Advisory and Intermediary Services Act to Cryptocurrency Assets. https://financialregulationjournal.co.za/2019/08/08/theapplicability-of-the-financial-advisory-and-intermediary-services-act-to-cryptocurrency-assets/. Accessed 18 Nov 2021

Nabilou A, Prüm A (2019) Ignorance, debt and cryptocurrencies: the old and the new in the law and economics of concurrent currencies. J Financ Regul 1:1

Nabilou H (2019) How to regulate bitcoin? Decentralised regulation for a decentralised cryptocurrency. Int J Law Technol 27:266

Nahorniak I et al (2016) Cryptocurrency in the context of development of digital single market in European Union. J Int Eur Law 3:109

Nair, M and N Cachanosky N (2017) 'Bitcoin and entrepreneurship: breaking the network effect. Rev Austrian Econ 30:1

Ncube N (2020) Why it's time for africat adopt a regional digital financial identity. https://nextbillion.net/africa-regional-digital-financial-identity/. Accessed 10 Dec 2021

Noack (2018) Cryptocurrency mining in Iceland is using so much energy, the electricity may run out. https://www.washingtonpost.com/news/worldviews/wp/2018/02/13/cryptocurrencymininginiceland-is-using-so-much-energy-the-electricity-may-run-out/. Accessed 10 Dec 2021

Non-Bank Financial Institutions Regulatory Authority Act of 2006

Obiezu T (2021) Nigerians skeptical about new digital currency days after launch. https://www.voanews.com/a/nigerians-skeptical-about-new-digital-currency-days-after-launch/6289378.html. Accessed 10 Jan 2022

OECD (2019a) Advancing the Digital Financial Inclusion of Youth' Report Prepared for the G20 Global Partnership for Financial Inclusion by the OECD. https://www.oecd.org/finance/advancing-the-digital-financial-inclusion-of-youth.pdf. Accessed 7 Dec 2021

OECD (2019b) Initial Coin Offerings (ICOs) for SME Financing. https://www.oecd.org/finance/ICOs-for-SME-Financing.pdf. Accessed 7 Dec 2021

OECD (2021) Shared Values: Building a Green and Inclusive Future. https://www.oecd.org/newsroom/media-advisory-oecd-2021-ministerial-council-meeting-31-may-1-june.htm. Accessed 7 Dec 2021

Okeahalam CC (1998) The political economy of Bank failure and supervision in the Republic of South Africa. Afr J Polit Sci 3:29

Omar MA, Inaba K (2020) Does financial inclusion reduce poverty and income inequality in developing countries? A panel data analysis. J Econ Struct 37:1

Omarova ST (2019) New tech vs. new Deal: fintech as a systemic phenomenon. Yale J Regul 36:735

Ozturk L, Sulungur E (2021) The Regulation Problem of Cryptocurrencies. In: Cobanoglu C, Corte VD (eds) Advances in Global Services and Retail Management. https://digitalcommons.usf.edu/cgi/viewcontent.cgi?article=1127&context=m3publishing. Accessed 7 Jan 2022

Payne J (2015) The role of gatekeepers. In: Moloney N et al (eds) The Oxford handbook of financial regulation. Oxford University Press, Oxford

Peters G, Panayi E, Chapelle A (2015) Trends in cryptocurrency and blockchain technologies: a monetary theory and regulation perspective. J Financ Persp 3:1

PWC (2015) Money is No Object: Understanding the Evolving Crypto-Currency Market. http://www.pwc.com/fsi. Accessed 11 Dec 2021

Quach K (2021) Three things that Have Vanished: $3.6bn In Bitcoin, A Crypto Investment Biz, and the Two Brothers Who Ran It. https://www.theregister.com/2021/06/23/africrypt_bitcoin_disappearance/. Accessed 11 Jan 2021

Raymaekers W (2015) Cryptocurrency bitcoin: distribution, challenges and opportunities. J Payments Strategy Syst 9(1):30–46

Renteria N, Esposito A (2021) El Salvador's World-First Adoption of Bitcoin Endures Bumpy First Day. https://www.reuters.com/business/finance/el-salvador-leads-world-into-cryptocurrency-bitcoin-legal-tender-2021-09-07. Accessed 10 Dec 2021

Reserve Bank of Zimbabwe Act 3 of 2016 (Part XCV)

Robberson SJ, McCoy MR (2018) A bit like cash: understanding cash-for-bitcoin transactions through individual vendors' risk. J Digital Forensic Secur Law 13:1

Roestoff M (2016) Payment systems. In: Sharrock R (ed) The law of banking and payment in South Africa, Cape Town. Juta

Roy A (2021) In El Salvador, more people have Bitcoin Wallets than traditional bank accounts. https://www.forbes.com/sites/aviksaroy/?sh=19008f3962fb. Accessed 11 Nov 2021

Rueckert C (2019) Cryptocurrencies and fundamental rights. J Cybersecur 5:1

Salami I (2021) Nigeria's Digital Currency: what the Enaira is for and why it's not perfect. https://theconversation.com/nigerias-digital-currency-what-the-enaira-is-for-and-why-its-not-perfect-1 71323. Accessed 12 Jan 2022

Sari K, Pujiyono S (2019) The use of cryptocurrency as a payment instrument, advances in economics. Bus Manage Res 130:366

Sarma M, Pais J (2011) Financial inclusion and development. J Int Dev 23:613

Scott B (2016) How Can Cryptocurrency and Blockchain Technology Play a Role in Building Social and Solidarity Finance? United Nations Institute for Social Development 4

Shannon, RP (2014) Disruptive Innovation Requires Delicate Regulation. http://www.law360.com/articles/595081/disruptive-innovation-demandsdelicate-regulation. Accessed 27 Nov 2021

Shirakawa JBR (2019) Cryptocurrency Regulations: Institutions and Financial Openness Asian Development Bank Institute. https://www.adb.org/sites/default/files/publication/513726/adbi-wp978.pdf. Accessed 11 Jan 2021

Silver L, Johnson C (2018) Internet Connectivity Seen as Having A Positive Impact on Life in Sub-Saharan Africa. https://www.pewresearch.org/global/2018/10/09/internet-connectivity-seen-as-having-positive-impact-on-life-in-sub-saharan-africa/. Accessed 10 Dec 2021

Soederberg S (2013) Universalising financial inclusion and the securitisation of development. Third World Q 34:593

South Africa's National Payment Systems Act 78 of 1998

South African Parliament (2021) A guide to Understanding Major Cryptocurrency Issues and Regulatory Frameworks. https://www.parliament.gov.za/storage/app/media/PBO/Analysis_and_Reports/2021/june/03-06- 2021/May_2021_PBO_Select_Finance_Committee_Cryptocurrency_25_May.pdf. Accessed 10 Jan 2021

South African Reserve Bank (2014) Position Paper on Virtual Currencies. http://www.treasury.gov.za/comm_media/press/2014/2014091801%20%20User%2Alert%20Virtual%20currencies.pdf. 13 January 2021

South African Reserve Bank (SARB) Act 90 of 1989

The AFI Financial Inclusion Strategy Peer Learning Group (2017) Defining Financial Inclusion https://www.afi-global.org/working-groups/fis/. Accessed 18 Nov 2021

The Crypto Assets Regulatory (CAR) (2021) Working Group "Position Paper on Crypto assets". http://www.treasury.gov.za/comm_media/press/2021/IFWG_CAR%20WG_Position%20paper%20on%20crypto%20assets_Final.pdf. Accessed 18 Nov 2021

United States Congress (2018) Regulation of Cryptocurrency in Selected Jurisdictions. https://www.hsdl.org/?view&did=812853. Accessed 18 Nov 2021

Varadarajan T (2017) The Blockchain is the Internet of Money. https://www.wsj.com/articles/the-blockchain-isthe-internet-of-money-1506119424. Accessed 10 Jan 2022

Vincent O, Evans O (2019) Can cryptocurrency, Mobile phones, and internet herald sustainable financial sector development in emerging markets? J Transnatl Manage 24:1

Washington Post (2021) Why Bitcoin Entrepreneurs are Flocking to Rural Texas. https://www.washingtonpost.com/technology/2021/07/08/bitcoin-mining-texas-electricity/. Accessed 18 Nov 2021

Wazvaremhaka T, Osode P (2018) The implications of *Truworths Limited v Minister of Trade and Industry* 2018 (3) SA 558 (WCC) for access to credit by historically disadvantaged and low-income consumers, law. Democr Dev 23:1

WB (2019) Financial Inclusion Global Initiative. https://www.worldbank.org/en/topic/financialinclusion/brief/fig. Accessed 18 Nov 2021

WB (2020) Financial Inclusion is A Key Enabler to Reducing Poverty and Boosting Prosperity. https://www.worldbank.org/en/topic/financialinclusion/overview. Accessed 18 Nov 2021

White RW (2005) The Need for a Longer Policy Horizon: A Less Orthodox Approach. http://citeseerx.ist.psu.edu/viewdoc/download?doi=10.1.1.545.4190&rep=rep1&type=pdf. Accessed 27 Nov 2021

World Bank (2015) Zimbabwe Diagnostic Review of Consumer Protection and Financial Literacy. https://documents1.worldbank.org/curated/en/700761483944795457/pdf/111758-WP-P1514 50Public-V1-Abstract-Sent ZimbabweCPFLDiagReviewVolumeIFINAL.pdf. Accessed 18 Nov 2021

World Bank Group (2018) South Africa Retail Banking Diagnostic Treating Customers Fairly in Relation to Transactional Accounts and Fixed Deposits. http://www.treasury.gov.za/publications/other/SA%20Retail%20Banking%20Diagnostic%20Report.pdf. Accessed 18 Nov 2021

World Economic Forum (2021a) Cryptocurrencies Can Enable Financial Inclusion. Will You Participate?

World Economic Forum (2021b) Navigating Cryptocurrency Regulation: An Industry Perspective on the Insights and Tools Needed to Shape Balanced Crypto Regulation. https://www3.weforum.org/docs/WEF_Navigating_Cryptocurrency_Regulation_2021.pdf. Accessed 18 Nov 2021

World Economic Forum (2021c) Why We Need New Rules and Tools for Cryptocurrencies. https://www.weforum.org/agenda/2021/07/new-rules-tools-cryptocurrencies/. Accessed 18 Nov 2021

Yeoh P (2017) Regulatory issues in blockchain technology. J Financ Regul Compl 25:200

Zheng Z et al (2018) Blockchain challenges and opportunities: a survey. Int J Web Grid Serv 14(4):352–375

Zimbabwe Exchange Control Act 109 of 1996 Chapter 22:05

Zimbabwe's National Payment Act Chapter 24:23 of 2001

Zimbabwe's Securities Act 17 of 2004 Chapter 24:25

Shelton T. Mota Makore is a Post-doctoral fellow and law lecturer in the Nelson Mandela Faculty of Law, at the University of Fort Hare, in South Africa. He has lectured law for a period of more than 6 years. In this capacity, he has lectured various law modules such as, legal research and writing, insolvency law, social security law, family law, instruments of payment, law of delict, law of evidence, law of succession, commercial law 2b and introduction to law. Further, he has also served as an academic intern for approximately 5 years at the Centre for Transdisciplinary Studies (CTS) within the same institution. Academically, he is a holder of a doctoral degree earned from the University of Fort Hare, since 2019. His doctoral thesis entitled "Constructing an alternative World Trade Organisation agricultural trade liberalisation model for the protection of the human right to food." argues that liberal rules in agriculture, particularly those contained in Agreement on

Agriculture (AoA), to a larger extent, impede the realisation of the human right to food in developing countries. The study proposed recommendations for re-theorising and re-orienting liberal rules governing trade in agriculture to promote the availability, accessibility and affordability of food in developing countries such as South Africa. Further, his dissertation entitled "Expanding access to essential medicines through the right to health: A case study of South Africa" was loudly endorsed by examiners as an apt research which offers contemporary thoughts on how to increase access to patented essential medicines under intellectual property rules in South Africa thereby ensuring that people living with HIV/AIDS and other pandemics have access to essential medicines. He is endowed with a passion to promote social justice through interdisciplinary and transdisciplinary research methodologies. This probably has to do with the humility of my background. As opposed to the majority of law graduates who have a strong bias towards interdisciplinary studies in commercial law or criminal law only, his passion and special interest lies in utilising transdisciplinary research methodologies which transcends borders of learning and, in the promotion of social justice which is capable of directly assisting developing countries to accelerate their holistic transformation through a number of mechanism that deter the abuse of public power, create domestic and trans juridical liability, accountability norms and the protection of vulnerable interests through economic, socio- legal instruments.

Patrick C. Osode has been Professor of Mercantile Law at the Nelson R Mandela School of Law, University of Fort Hare, South Africa, since 2004. He holds the degrees of LLB (University of Jos, Nigeria), LLM (University of Lagos, Nigeria) and SJD (University of Toronto, Canada). His teaching and research interests are in Corporate Law, Securities Regulation, International Trade Law, Public Procurement Law, and Government Liability. He is: Co-author of a book (with Chuks Okpaluba) entitled: *Government Liability – South Africa and the Commonwealth* (2010); co-editor of a volume (with Graham Glover) entitled: *Law and Transformative Justice in Post-Apartheid South Africa* (2010); and author/co-author of numerous law journal articles and book chapters. Professor Osode was admitted as a member of the International Academy of Commercial and Consumer Law (IACCL) in 1996. He was Dean of the Law School at the University of Fort Hare from 2002 to 2011; served as Honorary Secretary for the Society of Law Teachers of Southern Africa between 1999 and 2003; and is currently Managing Editor of *Speculum Juris*, a DHET-accredited electronic open-source law journal.

Nombulelo Lubisi holds a Baccalareus Legum (LLB), Advanced Certificate in Labour Law from UNISA, (LLM) in Labour Law, and (LLD) from the University of Fort Hare. She is the former Dean of Law at University of Fort hare. She has taught a number of modules at undergraduate level lecturing various modules such as, Law of Evidence, Criminal Procedure, Legal Research Methodology, Labour Law, Administrative Law, Advanced Constitutional Law, Advanced Administrative Law, Social Security Law, Bill of Rights, Constitutional Law and Labour Law to students registered for the Diploma in Local Government and Administration. In 2000, she was appointed as judges' researcher at the constitutional Court of South Africa. In 2002, she worked as a researcher for National Association of Democratic Lawyers (NADEL), and later on at the National Institute for Crime Prevention and the Reintegration of Offenders (NICRO)and. In 2003 she worked for the Department of Justice at George Magistrate Court from where she was appointed at the University of Fort Hare as a Lecturer. Dr. Lubisi has been involved in many activities coordinating treaties, acquisition of books for the faculty and Co-ordinator for both internal and external Moot Court and Mock Trials competition, and played a crucial role in preparing students, with considerable success. On certain occasions she has been invited to talk on a number of issues. For example, invitation by the Moral Regeneration Movement and South African Police service in Alice. She also co-facilitated community workshops organised by the UNESCO Oliver Tambo Chair of Human Rights. During 2008 she developed a training booklet for community training on issues of human rights. This booklet has four parts, these include, domestic violence, maintenance, gender issues and social grants. In 2005 she was appointed as a Head of Department: Adjectival Law, in 2007 as a coordinator Quality Assurance and 2011 coordinator of Law Foundation Programme and Faculty

Community Engagement Champion. In 2007 I served as a Research Scholar in Law and participated in the Clerkship Exchange Program first established between the Rutgers Law School and the Constitutional Court of South Africa, United States District Court (the Federal court) in Camden, New Jersey. Subsequently, I was also granted a scholarship by the Netherlands National UNESCO Commission as a visiting researcher at the Centre for Human Rights of Maastricht University, Netherlands. During 2008 I was appointed by the Minister of Justice to serve on an advisory committee of the South African Law Reform Commission's Project 25 on Statutory Revision, which we were tasked to scrutinise labour statutes. In 2015 she was appointed to serve on a committee of inquiry at the Bisho Legislature. In 2013–2015 Dr. Lubisi was appointed as a Deputy Dean: Teaching & Learning and Community Engagement, and from July 2016 acted as the Dean of Law. During this period, she had to prepare for the National LLB Review site visits that were scheduled to commence in September 2016. Dr. Lubisi has supervised and co-supervised postgraduate students and acted as an external examiner for LLB courses and Masters, and PHDs theses for various institutions. She has been a reviewer journal articles for publications, hosting postdoctoral fellows, and author of various articles in accredited journals. She presents papers at national conferences and also the additional member of the Editorial board South African Judicial Institute. Nombulelo Lubisi-Bizani was a member of council for the Eastern Cape Community Colleges of the Department of Higher Education. Currently she serves on the Council member of the South African Judicial Education Institute. She is also a member of Speculum Juris Journal.

The Role of Corporate Directorship in Financial Inclusion Within Selected SADC Countries

Tshepo H. Mongalo

Abstract Most of the Southern African Development Community (SADC) countries' corporate statutes are similar to the United States of America's (USA) state corporate laws and relevant USA federal legislation in prohibiting legal entities (including partnerships and close corporations) from being appointed as corporate directors. There are, however, a number of other SADC countries—mainly civil law countries—which allow corporate directors. This chapter contends that arguments against the use of corporate directors, as advanced in major developed countries of USA and UK, are overstated. The clearly defined role of the board in SADC countries' companies means that available resources in corporate entities that can potentially be deployed in corporate boards are prevented from being so used due to the blanket ban on corporate directors. This unjustifiably prevents legitimate participants in the governance of corporate entities from appropriately benefiting in the proper running of those entities. The blanket ban against corporate directors further reduces the chances of preventing the malaise of corporate governance failures in selected SADC countries. The chapter aims to contribute to the establishment of an industry of board service suppliers as supported by some leading commentators in USA.

1 Introduction

The chapter addresses a thorny issue of whether legal entities should be allowed by statutes of selected SADC countries to serve as directors of companies. Thus, in this chapter the term corporate director refers to a company director that is appointed to serve as a director in its capacity as a legal entity, not as an individual. Although the term is capable of being used to refer to any director of a company, whether as an

T. H. Mongalo (✉)
School of Law, University of the Witwatersrand, Johannesburg, South Africa
e-mail: Tshepo.Mongalo@wits.ac.za

individual or as a legal entity, in this context, it is limited to legal entities serving as directors of companies. Fiduciary services refer to services that are offered to clients to enhance the latter's role as a steward of other people's resources or assets in the execution of their fiduciary responsibilities. Board service suppliers is a collective term for all legal entities that may provide board services to corporate clients, primarily as members of the boards of directors. In this chapter the role of corporate director is essentially that of a non-executive director and not an executive director.

Corporate directors in the jurisdictions of the Southern African Development Community (SADC) have the potential to facilitate financial inclusion of individuals within entities involved in the provision of management consulting and/or fiduciary services. The latter services are core to the functions expected of corporate boards and their availability within a number of services companies within SADC countries means they essentially remain underutilized as corporate boards are prohibited. The potential for these companies, particularly from disadvantaged communities, to provide these services as corporate boards remain untapped. This potential to provide necessary board services notwithstanding, the influence of leading capitalist economies,[1] particularly the USA,[2] on the relevant SADC community countries,[3]

---

[1] For example, section 201B(1) of Australia's Corporations Act, 2001, provides that: "[o]nly an individual who is at least 18 may be appointed as a director of a company." Furthermore, section 105(1)(c) of the Canadian Business Corporations Act, 1985, also disqualifies any "person who is not an individual" from serving on a corporate board of directors. As for New Zealand, section 151(1) of its Companies Act, 1993, states that only a "natural person" who is not otherwise disqualified "may serve as a director".

[2] The Model Business Corporation Act 1999–2021 ('MBCA'), which has been adopted by more than half of the states of United States of America, limits corporate directorship to natural persons. It does so in a somewhat convoluted manner by providing, in section 8.03, that a board "must consist of one or more individuals" and, in section 1.40, by defining an individual as "a natural person." Furthermore, section 141(b) of the Delaware General Corporation Law ('DGCL'), described as the unofficial corporate law of the U.S.A, categorically states that each member of the board of directors "shall be a natural person." Clearly, in most, if not all, of the United States, non-natural legal persons—such as companies and other forms of legal entities—cannot serve as members of a board of directors.

[3] Out of the sixteen SADC countries, ten have statutes with a blanket ban against corporate directors. They include the following: Botswana, in terms of whose statute corporate directors are prohibited, in terms of section 146(2) of the Companies Act, 2007, which disqualifies persons under 18 years of age' from being directors. Eswatini, in which body corporates are among those disqualified from occupying the position of a director in terms of section 198(1)(a) of the Kingdom of Eswatini Companies Act, 2009. Lesotho, as per section 57(3)(a) of the Kingdom of Lesotho's Companies Act, 2011 (Act No. 18 of 2011), which prohibits body corporates from occupying the position of director. Malawi, in accordance with section 164(2), makes it clear that a person is only allowed to be appointed, or to hold office, as a director of a company if he or she is a natural person, except in the case of a state-owned company. Mauritius, as per section 133(1) of its Companies Act, 2001, the appointment of directors is limited to 'natural persons.' Namibia, in terms of section 225-(1) Companies Act, 2004 (Act No. 28 of 2004), permits only individual directors for Namibian companies by disqualifying body corporates from serving as directors of companies. South Africa's section 69(1) of its Companies Act, 2008 (Act No. 71 of 2008), renders 'a juristic person' ineligible to be a director of a company. Tanzania, pursuant to section 194(1) of its Companies Act, 2002, prohibits the appointment to directorship if the person is below the age of 21 or above the age of 70.

has led to the enactment of corporate statutes, which prohibit corporate directorships in these SADC jurisdictions. This chapter shows that there is an unjustifiable widespread ban on corporate directors within some SADC countries, particularly in South Africa, Botswana, Namibia and Zimbabwe. The chapter argues that this ban is largely as a result of the influence of industrialized Common-Law countries such as USA, Australia and New Zealand. Relying mainly on the research of Bainbridge & Henderson in 2014[4] and of Bainbridge in 2018,[5] the chapter demonstrates that this widespread ban has the effect of excluding, unjustifiably, appropriately positioned individuals in entities qualified to provide board services to corporate entities. This legal ban unfairly deprives these entities of the opportunity to gain financially and in skills development for their constituent members.

Given the potential benefits of corporate directors—which arguably outstrip the disadvantages—the chapter argues that the reconsideration of the ban and its removal by the concerned SADC legislatures will go a long way to facilitate financial inclusion. This is because a large number of legal entities can potential qualify for the provision of board services as the functions expected of directors are well established by legislation, codes of corporate governance and practice.

Furthermore, the provision of board supplier services by these corporate directors will also have the indirect benefit of improving entrepreneurial skills of the individuals and employees connected with these corporate directors. This will, in turn, potentially contribute to the growth of the economy as more and more well-run institutions can be formed by these individuals and former employees of corporate directors who decide to pursue careers in entrepreneurship.

The chapter is divided into five sections: Sect. 1 sets out an introduction. Section 2 sets out an overview of functions of directors and the suitability of corporate directors to undertake those functions. Section 2 demonstrates the existence of a widespread ban on corporate directors across SADC countries by referring to relevant statutory provisions of business statutes that prevent or allow corporate directors in the relevant jurisdictions. This section also reveals that most of these statutes are inherited from jurisdictions from which they are based. Section 3 deals with the widespread ban against, and limited Permission of, corporate directors across the whole SADC region. Section 4 deals with the possible role of corporate directorships in facilitating financial inclusion of vulnerable groups or previously disadvantaged persons within selected SADC countries. Section 5 concludes the discussion by pointing out the documented perceived disadvantages of corporate directorship and the analysis of such perceived disadvantages, based on available research.

Zambia restricts the appointment of directors to natural persons in line with section 92 (1) of its Companies Act, 2017 (Act No. 10 of 2017). Finally, Zimbabwe includes, in terms of section 173(1) (a) of the its Companies and other Business Entities Act [Chapter 24:31], 2020, 'body corporates' among persons who are disqualified from being appointed directors of a companies.

[4]Bainbridge and Henderson (2014), pp. 1051–1119.

[5]Bainbridge (2018), p. 65.

2 Overview of Functions of Directors and Suitability of Corporate Directors to Perform Those Functions

Although none of the four selected SADC countries'[6] corporate legislation specifically list the powers or functions of the board in detailed specificity, those functions are well documented and well accepted in corporate governance circles[7] Also, these functions can be deduced from the broad powers of the board specified in each of the statutes of the selected SADC jurisdictions.[8]

The Companies Act, 2007,[9] of Botswana comes closer to enumerating all functions of the board than those of Namibia, South Africa and Zimbabwe. Moreover, corporate statutes of Namibia and Zimbabwe do not directly provide for directors' functions and the only way that these two jurisdictions attempt to provide for the functions of directors is in their Schedules to their statutes.[10] South Africa cryptically provides for the functions of directors in section 66(1) of the Companies Act, 2008,[11] but it is section 127 of the Botswana's Companies Act, 2007, which provides more clarity on the accepted functions of directors.

---

[6] That is, Botswana, Namibia, South Africa, and Zimbabwe.

[7] For example, in Bainbridge (2017), pp. 65–68.

[8] In this regard, see Section 127 of the Botswana Companies Act, 2007; Art 59 of Table A and Art 60 of Table B of the Namibian Companies Act, 2004; section 66(1) of the Companies Act, 2008; and Art 81 of Table A of the First Schedule of the Zimbabwean Companies Act, 2020 [Chapter 24: 03].

[9] Botswana Companies Act, 2007 (Chapter 42:01).

[10] For Namibia, Article 59 of Table A and Article 60 of Table B of Schedule 1 of the Companies Act, 2004, provides thus: "[t]he business of the company shall be managed by the directors who may pay all expenses incurred in promoting and incorporating the company, and may exercise all such powers of the company as are not by the Act, or by these articles, required to be exercised by the company in general meeting, subject to these articles, to the provisions of the Act, and to such regulations, not inconsistent with the aforesaid articles or provisions, as may be prescribed by the company in general meeting, but no regulation prescribed by the company in general meeting shall invalidate any prior act of the directors which would have been valid if such regulation had not been prescribed." With regard to Zimbabwe, Article 81 of Table A of the First Schedule of the Companies Act, 2020 [Chapter 24:03], provides that: "The business of the company shall be managed by the directors, who may pay all expenses incurred in promoting and registering the company, and may exercise all such powers of the company as are not, by the Act or by these regulations, required to be exercised by the company in general meeting, subject, nevertheless, to any of these regulations, to the provisions of the Act and to such regulations, being not inconsistent with the aforesaid regulations or provisions, as may be prescribed by the company in general meeting; but no regulation made by the company in general meeting shall invalidate any prior act of the directors which would have been valid if that regulation had not been made".

[11] Section 66(1) of the Companies Act, 2008, provides that:

> [t]he business and affairs of a company must be managed by or under the direction of its board, which has the authority to exercise all of the powers and perform any of the functions of the company, except to the extent that this Act or the company's Memorandum of Incorporation provides otherwise.

Essentially, the role of directors in the Common-Law world consist of three interrelated functions. Firstly, management is at the forefront of directors' functions.[12] Although it is common cause that the day-to-day operations in a company are delegated to the company's management, the board retains the residual role of management as the directing mind of the organisation. In fact, there are certain management functions which are reserved for the board as a whole, rather than management. These management functions, in the South African context in particular, include approval of financial transactions such as distributions,[13] mergers and amalgamations,[14] and voluntary business rescue commencements.[15]

Even in relation to the UK, Bainbridge acknowledges that the board does have certain managerial functions.[16] The position in the USA, particularly in Delaware, is no different as Bainbridge and Henderson concede that the delegation of day-to-day operations to company management does not mean that directors have no management role because they remain obligated to make fundamental decisions, "like hiring and firing the managers, setting compensation incentives, raising capital, and entering into mergers and acquisitions."[17]

Secondly, another function of the board is that of providing advice and guidance to top managers. This is particularly important as the director's knowledge of the industry and key players within the relevant industry invariably renders his or her experience extremely invaluable to the company. Consequently, the advice and guidance given can help the company to pursue business opportunities that contribute to its profitability and success. This role is not specifically set out in the South African corporate statute, but it can be deduced from the catch-all authority invested in the board of directors to exercise all of the powers and perform any of the functions of the company. Botswana's Companies Act specifically authorises the board with all the powers necessary for managing and for directing the management of the business and affairs of the company,[18] which undoubtedly include the power to provide advice and guidance to management. The wider the experience and networks of the director, the richer the advice and guidance that can be provided

---

[12]This is expressly provided for in both the Botswana and South African statutes. In particular, section 127(1) of the Botswana Companies Act, 2007, and section 66(1) of the South African Companies Act, 2008.

[13]Section 46(1)(a)(ii) of the Companies Act, 2008.

[14]Section 113(4)(a) of the Companies Act, 2008, requires the board of each amalgamating or merging company to consider whether, upon implementation of the agreement, each proposed amalgamated or merged company will satisfy the solvency and liquidity test before the merger or amalgamation can be referred to the shareholders for approval.

[15]Section 129(1) of the Companies Act, 2008.

[16]Bainbridge (2017), p. 71.

[17]Bainbridge and Henderson (2014), p. 1053.

[18]See section 127(2) of Botswana's Companies Act, 2007.

to a company.[19] As will be discussed later on in this chapter, such an extensive breadth of experience and network is better found among individuals who form part of a body corporate that can serve as a director, if possible, than in an individual person serving as a director. The latter position is not only a norm in SADC countries that follow common-law legal system, it is actually mandatory, notwithstanding the practical viability of the former position.

Thirdly, directors' role is to monitor or supervise management. Of all the functions of the directors, the provision of oversight over management is the common one. Notwithstanding the popularity of this role in corporate governance circles,[20] of the four SADC countries in focus in this chapter, only Botswana makes reference to supervision of management by the board.[21] In Botswana, the legislation makes it clear that in addition to the role of managing the company, the board has powers necessary for supervising the management of the business and affairs of the company.[22] This role is not made explicit from the statutory arrangements of the other SADC countries of Namibia, South Africa and Zimbabwe, but the applicable law in all these jurisdictions affirm the application of the oversight or supervisory role of the board.[23] Interestingly, supervision of management is, essentially, the practical manifestation of the function of directors to manage the company. This function is ordinarily delegated to management with attendant responsibility by the board to monitor its execution.

These functions of boards of directors necessitate a question of whether they (board the functions) can, as Common-Law SADC legislators would have us believe,[24] only be fulfilled by individual directors and not corporate directors. The reality is that these roles of directors cannot only be ably fulfilled by natural persons, as most SADC countries' statutes prescribe.[25] A better view, supported by Bainbridge & Henderson,[26] is that there are legitimate reasons for companies to use corporate directors in the execution of these functions. This is particularly so as the economies of scale brought by the use of corporate directors generally make the execution of the functions quicker and thorough.

In this regard, Bainbridge & Henderson mention that firms which specialize in board service are better positioned to make better decisions than individual

---

[19] As far as this role of directors is concerned, Bainbridge refers to research by Stiles and Taylor (2001), p. 52, who view this function as invaluable in ensuring the 'opening of doors' for firms through the use of directors' contacts.

[20] Particularly in corporate statutes, case laws and corporate governance codes.

[21] Section 127(2) of the Botswana's Companies Act, 2007.

[22] Ibid.

[23] See *Fisheries Development Corporation of South Africa Ltd v Jorgensen* 1980 4 SA 156 (W) (*Fisheries Development Corporation*), at 166.

[24] The restrictions on the nature of persons who can serve as board members are set out hereunder in respect of all 16 SADC countries.

[25] Ten of the sixteen SADC countries only allow natural persons to serve as directors of companies.

[26] Bainbridge and Henderson (2014). See also Bainbridge (2017).

directors.[27] They argue that such corporate directors "would have better information, access to specialists with fewer conflicted interests, more person-hours available for exercising judgment, better incentives, to name but a few of the advantages.[28] Bainbridge further maintains that since a lot of decisions that boards of directors have to make in the exercise of their managerial functions involve a mere exercise of critical evaluative judgment,[29] groups are superior to individuals at making such judgments.[30] He correctly observes that this is due to these decisions being essentially about assessing proposals put forward by management, instead of exercising original thinking.[31]

Admittedly, as most of the companies that can potentially serve as corporate directors have multiple employees and directors themselves, a corporate director will invariably bring to the boardroom table combined knowledge and expertise of multiple individuals.[32] In the same vein, the advantage of having numerous individuals connected to the potential corporate director means that the number of work hours devoted by each director in the boardroom can increase exponentially, as opposed to when a single individual acts as a director.

As already mentioned, the role that the corporate director can play in providing advice and guidance to top managers, eclipses that of an individual director and there are obvious advantages that may be derived from that arrangement. For instance, the process of raising much-needed funds for the business can be made easier when it is approached collectively through the efforts of multiple individuals who are the constituent members of the corporate director. The good names associated with experts within the corporate director can help the company raise its reputation in the community by association with those individuals. Stiles and Taylor observe that the corporate director can also be of assistance in helping the company to deal with threats in the external environment.[33]

On leveraging business networks, the advantage of a corporate director is that it is able to facilitate access to mission critical resources by specifically "providing introductions, formal and informal communication channels, and helping coordinate ongoing relationships."[34] Bainbridge observes that "[a] corporate director with multiple employees and directors, each of whom has their own network of clients and associates, should be far better at building a network of resources on which the firm can draw than are their individual counterparts."[35]

---

[27] Bainbridge and Henderson (2014), p. 1097.

[28] Bainbridge and Henderson (2014), p. 1097.

[29] In this regard, see Bainbridge (2002), p. 30.

[30] Bainbridge (2017), p. 77.

[31] Bainbridge (2017), p. 77.

[32] Bainbridge (2017), p. 77.

[33] Stiles and Taylor (2001), p. 52.

[34] Bainbridge (2017), p. 78.

[35] Bainbridge (2017), p. 78.

It is doubtful that the utility of individual directors would surpass that of corporate directors when it comes to the role of monitoring management.[36] In fact, literature indicates that in this regard the advantages of corporate directors may eclipse those of individual directors.[37] More importantly, reputational incentives for corporate directors, and individuals associated with them, play a crucial role in encouraging directors to effectively monitor management better than individual directors would.[38] This is because corporate directors have more to lose in the event of management's behaviour caused by, for example, cheating and shirking. Misconduct by management has serious consequences and can potentially lead to allegations of disloyalty or insufficient care by directors. As a result, this is something which directors cannot afford to dent their reputations.[39] This is particularly glaring from the perspective of ensuring effective corporate governance for those who are occupying the position of directors and it is of less relevance whether resulting lawsuits for breaches of duty by management ends up in an adverse judgment or mere settlement. To augment this argument, Bainbridge asserts that individual directors "are fairly limited since they capture so little of any gains and suffer so little of any losses from the decisions they make,"[40] as compared to corporate directors. Indeed, in monitoring management, reputation incentives may be instrumental in driving corporate directors to be more active, than individual directors. There are still other reasons why corporate directors can potentially be more likely to outstrip individual directors in monitoring management. For example, corporate directors may be very useful for foreign investors to serve as local nominee directors in order to facilitate prompt handling of business matters such as signing documents. This is, for example, the case in Hong Kong where local corporate directors are regularly called upon to serve in this manner.[41] Another advantage of a corporate director is its ability to designate someone to attend to the matters of the corporate client company, as opposed to the inability of individual director in a case where such a director travels frequently. For practical business reasons, it is advantageous to have a holding company serve as a director for its subsidiary,[42] if corporate directors are allowed.[43]

---

[36] Bainbridge and Henderson (2014), pp. 1098–1099.

[37] Bainbridge and Henderson (2014), pp. 1081–1096.

[38] Bainbridge and Henderson (2014), pp. 1088–1093.

[39] Bainbridge and Henderson (2014).

[40] Bainbridge (2017), p. 78.

[41] Bainbridge (2017), pp. 78–79.

[42] Whether alone or jointly with other corporate and/or individual directors.

[43] Bainbridge (2017), p. 79.

3 Widespread Ban Against, and Limited Permission of, Corporate Directors Across the Whole SADC Region

3.1 Introduction

In relation to the treatment of corporate directors, the difference between various SADC corporate statutes is that the approach taken by these countries directly mirror the applicable legal system in each of these jurisdictions. SADC Countries that follow the civil-law legal system are generally receptive to the idea of corporate directors and those that follow the common-law system are generally dismissive of the idea.

i. Angola

Angola, like its former colonial master, Portugal, has a legal system based on civil-law, rather than common-law. Largely due to the country's different corporate law traditions, Angola envisages the appointment of corporate directors when it provides, in its Commercial Companies Law,[44] for broad qualifying criteria of corporate directors. Due to its Civil-Law legal system, Angola does not share common-law traditions with many other SADC countries, which subscribe to Common-Law legal system.

The statutory permission for corporate directors is evidenced, inter alia, by a provision in Art. 410 (2), which provides that "[e]xcepting a stipulation in the articles of incorporation stating otherwise, a director can be any person enjoying full legal capacity, whether they are a shareholder of the company or not". The article further provides clarity on this matter by stating, in art. 410(3) that, "[i]f a corporate entity is nominated as a director, it must name an individual person to hold the respective office." While this kind of qualification is familiar in common-law jurisdictions like South Africa, in respect of external auditors, it is fascinating that Angola makes it clear that directorship is not limited to individuals.

It must be pointed out, however, that if the individual person to hold the respective office of a corporate director is limited to just one person, then the 'corporate director' as envisaged in the Angolan statute would not prove to be better than 'individual director' since both are natural persons. That is why it is argued in this chapter that the proposed corporate directors should not be limited to designating single individuals as persons to hold office of a director. Such designated representative should merely be the accountable people on behalf of the legal entity, which is essentially the corporate director. According to the chapter, therefore, the legal entity serving as a corporate director should merely send the name of the most qualified person as its representative, but may still designate other qualified individuals to act on its behalf as a director.

---

[44]Commercial Companies Law 1 of 2004.

ii. Botswana

As a country based on the Common-Law legal system as far as it relates to corporate Law, Botswana, like most SADC countries, allows only natural persons to be appointed as directors of companies in terms of its Companies Act, 2007.[45] The restriction of directorships to natural persons is further bolstered by section 146(2) which disqualifies "a person who is under 18 years of age" from being a director.[46] Since a legal entity acquires legal capacity on incorporation and does not have to wait 18 years to perform juristic acts, it is clear that the only persons who can serve as directors in Botswana are individuals.[47] An argument can be made that the prescription of age limit is not necessarily a bar against corporate directors as, even in some civil-law countries, corporate directors must essentially be represented by a natural person as well. It is argued, however, that even if the legal entity is represented by a natural person, it is the corporate entity, and not the individual, who is legally designated as a director. As such, the question of age does not even have to arise.

iii. The Comoros

As a Civil-Law jurisdiction, the Comoros follows in the trajectory as other Civil-Law jurisdictions within the SADC. In addition to being a member state of the SADC, the Union of the Comoros is one of the 17-member states of the Organization for Business Law Harmonization in Africa (Organisation pour l'Harmonisation en Afrique du Droit des Affaires (OHADA).

The Uniform Act on Commercial Companies and Economic Interest Groups Law[48] governs the incorporation and general operation of the companies in member states of OHADA including the Union of the Comoros.[49] Just like the Angolan Companies Law 1 of 2004, the Uniform Act on Commercial Companies envisages the appointment of corporate directors in public companies registered within OHADA member states.[50]

---

[45] Section 146(1) of the Botswana Companies Act, 2007, titled 'Qualifications of directors' provides that "[a] natural person who is not disqualified by subsection (2) of this section may be appointed as a director of a company."

[46] Section 146(2) of the Botswana Companies Act, 2007.

[47] See section 146(2) of Botswana's Companies Act, 2007.

[48] The Commercial Companies and Economic Interest Groups Law came into effect in 2014.

[49] The Act is known as the Uniform Act Relating to Commercial Companies and Economic Interest Groups, 1997.

[50] Art. 421 of the Uniform Act on Commercial Companies and Economic Interest Groups, 1997, is quite interesting and extensive and provides that: "A corporate person may be appointed director. It shall, on its appointment, nominate, by hand delivered letter with acknowledgement of receipt or by registered letter with acknowledgement of receipt addressed to the company, a permanent representative for its term of office. Although the permanent representative so nominated is not personally a director of the company, he shall be subject to the same conditions and obligations and shall incur the same civil and criminal liabilities as if he were director in his own name, without prejudice to the joint and several liability of the corporate person he represents. A permanent representative may or may not be a shareholder of the company."

iv. Democratic Republic of Congo

The Democratic Republic of Congo, as one of the two-member states of OHADA within the SADC,[51] has a law that is the same as that which is applicable in the Union of the Comoros, discussed above.

However, just like the Comoros, the DRC appears to take the concept of transparency and accountability of corporate director representative to a whole new level. In this regard, the Angolan statutory provision of requiring corporate directors to name an individual person to hold the respective office on its behalf would have been understandable from the perspective of ensuring transparency and, possibly, accountability.

All OHADA member states' statutory positions, however, go further than that as the Uniform Act on Commercial Companies and Economic Interest Groups, 1997, and require the corporate director to nominate a permanent representative for its term of office. This permanent representative is not personally a director of the company, but is subject to the same conditions and obligations (including civil and criminal liabilities) as if he were director in his own name.[52] It is argued that this may act as a disincentive for companies in OHADA member states to appoint corporate directors as the identification of the permanent representative, as required by the law, may prove to be a challenge. Also, this chapter's recommendation for selected SADC countries to consider permitting corporate directors does not envisage the model of OHADA member states as explained above.

v. Kingdom of Eswatini

The law governing the incorporation and general operation of companies in the Kingdom of Eswatini is the Companies Act, 2009, which came into operation on 01 April 2010. Just like the Companies Act of Botswana, body corporates are, unsurprisingly, among those disqualified from occupying the position of a director in the Kingdom of Eswatini.[53] What is interesting about the countries which prohibit body corporate to serve as directors is that all of them, including Eswatini, allow the role of a company secretary to be undertaken by a legal entity.[54]

vi. Kingdom of Lesotho (Lesotho)

In Lesotho, just like the rest of the Common-Law countries in the SADC, body corporates are included in the list of persons who are disqualified from being appointed or holding office as a director of a company.[55]

---

[51] Formerly known as the Republic of Zaire.

[52] Art. 421 of the Uniform Act on Commercial Companies and Economic Interest Groups, 1997.

[53] This is provided for in s 198(1)(a) of the Kingdom of Eswatini Companies Act, 2009.

[54] For example, in Eswatini, section 2(1) of the Companies Act, 2009, defines a secretary to include "any official of a company by whatever name...designated, including a body corporate, who or which is performing the duties normally performed by a secretary of a company".

[55] In particular, section 57(3)(a) of the Kingdom of Lesotho Companies Act, 2011 (Act No. 18 of 2011) provides that "[t]he following persons are disqualified from being appointed or holding office as a director of a company - (a) a body corporate..."

This provision is further bolstered by the limitation of persons who can serve as directors to natural persons.[56] Regardless of the regulatory approach that frowns upon the appointment of a body corporate as a director, like Eswatini, Lesotho also permits the appointment of a corporate entity as a company secretary.[57]

vii. Republic of Madagascar

Like other civil-law countries within the SADC, Madagascar also allows the appointment of legal entities as directors.[58] Presumably with the purpose of enhancing transparency and, possibly, accountability, Madagascar, requires that the full name, address, profession and nationality of the natural persons who are permanent representatives of the corporate entities that are members of the board of directors be identified.[59] This requirement is not particularly unique to civil-law countries, except that in common-law countries it is applicable to individual members of the board.

viii. Republic of Malawi

The Malawian Companies Act, 2013[60] regulates qualifications of directors in the same way as the other countries with laws based on the Common-Law statutes. In particular, the Act specifically mandates companies to only appoint natural persons as directors.[61] The Act further clarifies this position by making it clear that a person shall only be allowed to be appointed, or to hold office, as a director of a company if he or she is a natural person, except in the case of a state-owned company.[62]

The rationale for only allowing state owned companies to have corporate directors is not clear. However, it would have been quite a welcome development if the Malawian Companies Act extended this permission to other companies. While the exemption for corporate directors may be justifiable in the case of state-owned companies on the basis of collective governance through other state-controlled or state-owned entities, the same justification could be extended to companies operating in the private sector. This is particularly true where, as it is often the case with multinational companies, corporate entities operate within intricate group structures.

---

[56] Section 57(1) of the Kingdom of Lesotho's Companies Act, 2011, provides that "[a] natural person who is not disqualified by subsection (3) may be appointed as a director of a company."

[57] Section 2(1) of Lesotho's Companies Act, 2011, provides that "secretary" includes an official of a company performing the duties normally performed by a secretary of a company."

[58] Art. 417(3) of Madagascar's Law No. 2003-036 on Commercial Companies.

[59] Art. 417(2) of Madagascar's Law No. 2003-036 on Commercial Companies.

[60] 15 of 2013.

[61] Section 164(1) of the Malawian Companies Act, 2013, provides that "[a] company shall appoint a natural person as director".

[62] Section 164(2) of the Malawian Companies Act, 2013, provides that "[n]o person shall be appointed, or hold office, as a director of a company if he is a person who. . .is not a natural person save in the case of State-Owned Companies. . .".

ix. Republic of Mauritius

Like company statutes of other Common-Law jurisdictions, the Mauritian Companies Act, 2001[63] limits to natural persons, those who can serve the company as directors.[64] Mauritius is consistently ranked in the top 20 countries, globally, for ease of doing business.[65] That stellar performance notwithstanding, the country continues to prohibit corporate directorships. This is, obviously, a legacy issue rather than business consideration, as the country is part of the Commonwealth and operates under the Common-Law legal regime. Even though according to the *Africa Wealth Report* (2019), Mauritius boasts the second fastest-growing wealth market globally (after China),[66] growing 124% between 2008 and 2018, the continued limitation of board membership to individuals is a step in the wrong direction by the country.

x. Republic of Mozambique

In clear contrast to the many SADC countries with legislation based on Common-Law corporate statutes, Mozambique's legislation allows for both individuals and corporate bodies with full legal capacity to serve as directors of companies.[67] The statute, however, makes reference to corporate bodies with full legal capacity,[68] which is odd as there is no age of maturity for corporate bodies. Because of juristic personality, these entities acquire full legal capacity upon incorporation. It may be that full legal capacity in this regard refer to proper and formal authorisation by the corporate body's decision-making authority for the corporate body to perform juristic acts.[69] These juristic acts include consenting to act or serve as a director of another corporate entity.

---

[63] 15 of 2001.

[64] Section 133(1) of the Mauritian Companies Act, 2001, provides that "[a] company shall appoint a natural person as director".

[65] In the latest World Bank's Ease of Doing Business (2021) rankings, Mauritius' overall position was 13, one position above Australia (another Common-Law country) and 25 positions above the other highest ranked African country, Rwanda, at Position 38.

[66] Africa Wealth Report (2019).

[67] Article 149(1) of the Mozambique Commercial Code (Decree 2/2005 of 27 December 2015) provides that: "[d]irectors may be individuals and corporate bodies with full legal capacity."

[68] Ibid.

[69] According to Sharrock (R. Sharrock, *Business Transactions Law* 9ed (2016), at 1, a juristic act is an act which is intended to have, and has, legal consequences. The author goes further to assert that "[w]hen a juristic act is performed, a legal relationship [including appointment as a director] is created, altered or terminated. It is worth noting that a juristic act may be unilateral or bilateral/ multilateral. The example of the former type of juristic act is making a will or cancelling a contract for breach. The appointment of a director is an example of the latter type of a juristic act as it essentially involves the conclusion of a contractual relationship between the corporate director and the concerned company.

xi. Republic of Namibia

In keeping with the Common-Law corporate statutes, the Namibian Companies Act, 2004,[70] permits only individual directors for Namibian companies by disqualifying body corporates from serving as directors of companies.[71] The current Namibian Companies Act, 2004, is a mirror image of the repealed South African Companies Act, 1973,[72] which also provided for the prohibition of corporate directors.[73] The position under the home-brewed statute is likely to be clarified under the new Companies Act of Namibia as the country is in the process of reviewing its corporate laws.[74] It is advisable for policy makers to consider accommodating corporate directors under the new corporate legislation in Namibia.

xii. Republic of Seychelles

As a result of the seesawing of the Islands of Seychelles between Civil-Law and Common-Law legal systems,[75] the regulation of director qualification status would have gone either way. Unsurprisingly, the Seychelles is one of the few SADC members that allow corporate directorships by making it clear that a board of directors may consist of one or more persons who may be individuals or companies.[76]

xiii. Republic of South Africa

Even after the enactment of the new Companies Act, which took effect from 01 May 2011 following an extensive corporate law reform process, the Companies Act, 2008 (71 of 2008) of South Africa prohibits juristic persons from occupying the position of director.[77] The section prohibiting corporate directors under the Companies Act,

---

[70] 28 of 2004. Although this statute was enacted in 2004, it is a verbatim re-enactment of the previous Companies Act, 1973 (61 of 1973), of the Republic of South Africa.

[71] Section 225(1) of the Namibian Companies Act, 2004 (28 of 2004) provides that "[a]ny of the following persons are disqualified from being appointed or acting as a director of a company...(a) a body corporate."

[72] 61 of 1973.

[73] It provided for such disqualification in terms of section 218(1)(a) of the Act.

[74] To the author's knowledge, the process for revamping corporate laws in Namibia is being undertaken in accordance with 'Terms of Reference (ToR) for a Consultancy to review, simplify and modernize the Close Corporations Act, 1988 (Act 26 of 1988) and Companies Act, 2004 (Act No. 28 of 2004)' as issued on 18 October 2019 under the auspices of the Ministry of Industrialisation, Trade and SME Development (MITSMED) and the Deutsche Gesellschaft für Internationale Zusammenarbeit (GIZ).

[75] Mainly due to its difficult history of having been a colony of France (a Civil-Law country) and of Great Britain (a common-Law country).

[76] According to section 41 of the Seychelles Companies Act (Consolidated to 01 December 2014), "[s]ubject to any limitations in its Memorandum or Articles, the business and affairs of a company incorporated under this Act shall be managed by a board of directors that consists of one or more persons who may be individuals or companies."

[77] Section 69(1) of the South African Companies Act 71 of 2008 provides that: "[a] person is ineligible to be a director of a company if the person... (a) is a juristic person."

2008, appears to be an exact restatement of the previous section under the repealed Companies Act, 1973.[78] This position reflects that of other Common-Law based SADC countries. Although the 1973 Companies Act did not substantially depart from the U.K. Companies Act, 1948, in application at the time,[79] the provision on disqualification of directors was, and continues to be, markedly different from the equivalent provision of the applicable Companies Act.[80]

Although the current Companies Act, 2008, of South Africa was hailed as exemplary for other countries wanting to improve their basic company legislation for the twenty-first century,[81] its continued prohibition against the appointment of corporate directors is nothing short of a deleterious progress. It is in this vein that this chapter acknowledges the progress that South Africa achieved through her relatively recent corporate law reform process, but is not blind to the shortcomings of that celebrated process. It is, thus, not unexpected that the recommendations for the introduction of corporate directors in the SADC do not exempt the Republic of South Africa.

xiv. United Republic of Tanzania

Section 194(1) of the Tanzanian Companies Act, 2002, prohibits the appointment to directors if the person is below the age of twenty-one or above the age of 70. The way in which this provision is phrased (by specifying the age of appointees to the office of director) makes it apparent that only natural persons can become directors of companies in the United Republic of Tanzania.[82] This is because a juristic person, like a company, does not need to be of a particular age to perform juristic acts.

xv. Republic of Zambia

Zambia's corporate legislation fails to distinguish itself from other Common-Law countries when it comes to the qualification for directorship in companies. In terms

---

[78] Above, note 72. Section 218(1)(a) of the Companies Act, 1973, specifically provided that "[a]ny of the following persons shall be disqualified from being appointed or acting as a director of a company: (a) [a] body corporate. . ."

[79] That is, [t]he Companies Act 1948 (11 & 12 Geo.6 c.38) (as amended).

[80] Under s 155 of the UK Companies Act, 2006, only one director of a company is required to be a natural person. However, in 2015, the UK Parliament approved legislation containing a ban— subject to some yet to be defined exemptions—of corporate directors. This is in accordance with s 87 of the Small Business, Enterprise and Employment Act, 2015, which proposes to insert section 156A and 156B in the Companies Act, to, respectively, 'require each company director to be a natural person' and 'provide for exceptions from requirement that each director be a natural person.' This amendment has, however, not been implemented and, as such, section 155 is still in force on or before 05 November 2021. Once implemented, the law will make it a requirement for all company directors to be natural persons. (On the undesirability of pursuing the course of action as per the proposed amendment, see Bainbridge 2018.)

[81] Hanks (2010), p. 147.

[82] See section 194(1) of the Companies Act, 2002 (12 of 2002) of the United Republic of Tanzania.

of section 92 (1) of the Zambian Companies Act, 2017 (Act No. 10 of 2017), "[a] company shall appoint a natural person as director".[83]

xvi. Zimbabwe

Like the neighbouring South Africa, Zimbabwe also disqualifies body corporates from occupying or being appointed as directors of Zimbabwean companies.[84] This is not surprising, as the country follows the trend of SADC countries with Common-Law legal systems.

The Zimbabwean Companies and other Business Entities Act, 2020, is the latest of all companies' statutes of the SADC countries. That notwithstanding, the Zimbabwean legislation still ascribes to the uniform ban of corporate directors, which is synonymous with corporate statutes of most of the SADC countries. Even though Zimbabwe, like South Africa, has consistently aligned its corporate statutes with those of England over almost two centuries,[85] the country has specifically refrained from following the example of the UK in respect of corporate directors. This is specifically clear from the current 202 statutes, which 'turned a blind eye' to the 2006 UK Companies' Act's authorisation of corporate directors.[86]

4   The Possible Role of Corporate Directorships in Facilitating Financial Inclusion of Vulnerable Groups or Previously Disadvantaged Persons Within Selected SADC Countries

As mentioned earlier on, the focus of this chapter is on the SADC countries of Botswana, Namibia, South Africa and Zimbabwe. In these countries, programmes for indigenisation of economic development are compelling, given the application of discriminatory laws under colonial and apartheid regimes, which were synonymous with this southern part of Africa.

---

[83] Section 92(1) of the Zambian Companies Act, 2017 (10 of 2017).

[84] Section 173(1)(a) of the Zimbabwean Companies and other Business Entities Act [Chapter 24: 31], 2020, includes "body corporates among persons who are disqualified from being appointed directors of a company."

[85] Firstly, the Ordinance for facilitating security of shares in joint-stock companies of 1846 was an almost verbatim iteration of the similar Joint-Stock Companies, 1844 of the U.K. Subsequent to that, the Act to limit the liability of members of certain joint-stock companies of 1861 came on the heels of the UK's Joint-Stock Companies Act of 1856, which incorporated the Limited Liability Act of 1855. All other subsequent Zimbabwean corporate statutes—including the Companies Ordinance, 1895; the Companies Ordinance, 1907; the Companies Ordinance, 1895 and Amendment Ordinance, 1921—followed closely the equivalent UK corporate statutes enacted few years prior to each of these colonial statutes.

[86] Under section 155 of the UK Companies Act, 2006, which came into operation in 2009—full 11 years before the enactment of the Zimbabwe's Companies and Other Business Entities Act, 2020.

Financial inclusion in the context of corporate directorships comes into play when one considers compensation incentives of corporate directors. It is common cause that director compensation, particularly in listed companies, consists primarily of a mix of cash and equity grants in the company. In order to align the interests of directors and those of the residual claimants (shareholders), a company would ordinarily use the incentive of equity grants. In the case of individual directors, these equity grants are invariably small, in comparison to the total capitalisation of the company concerned. In fact, critics maintain that as the amounts are routinely so small, they do little to meaningfully align shareholder and board incentives.[87]

If this approach to compensation incentivisation is followed even in the case of corporate directors, the result may be far reaching than in the case of individual board members.[88] To lend credence to this potential reality, Bainbridge & Henderson[89] state that if a corporate director designates a number of individuals to be responsible for performing the functions of directors, the company might simply replicate the current pay structure of the underlying client company. This can be achieved by remunerating directors by means of a fixed salary (equal to the company's current annual retainer) and, in addition, reward those individual employees of the corporate director by means of equity in the client company. The financing of such equity stake can then be structured in such a way that empowers qualifying individuals who are constituent members of the corporate director. For example, if anyone of the individuals qualifies as a designated person in terms of the applicable equity legislation aimed at advancing the interests of a group within the client company,[90] the latter may provide financial assistance in accordance for the acquisition of the equity stake. In the instance of South Africa, this can be done in line with the provisions of section 45 of the Companies Act, 2008.[91] An equivalent provision in selected SADC countries may be employed to achieve this.

The importance of financial inclusion cannot be overstated. In fact, within the selected SADC countries of Botswana, Namibia, South Africa and Zimbabwe, there are many corporate entities which exists that can offer board supplier services as corporate directors in companies.[92] If one were to assess the feasibility of

---

[87] In this regard, see Bebchuk and Fried (2010), pp. 11–12.

[88] Bainbridge and Henderson (2014), p. 1082.

[89] Bainbridge and Henderson (2014), p. 1082.

[90] Such as those who are defined as being "black people" in the Broad Based Black Economic Empowerment Act, 2013 (Act No. 53 of 2003) as amended, in the context of South Africa, to promote broad-based black economic empowerment initiative, including ownership of stakes in enterprises. For a more detailed analysis of measures aimed at indigenisation and transformation of the economies of South Africa and Zimbabwe, see, inter alia, Marazanye (2016).

[91] Act No. 71 of 2008. The extensive discussion of section 45 and its advantages and disadvantages is outside the scope of this chapter, but deserves further analysis and should form part of future research on the empowerment of designated individuals in equity stake acquisitions and their inclusion in mainstream economy.

[92] The empirical study to investigate the number of entities that exist within the four jurisdictions that can offer board supplier services is far beyond the scope of this chapter, and in any event, the

establishing corporate directors within selected SADC countries' corporate statutes, the multiplier effect of the use of compensation incentives will be relatively more tangible when the current board compensation structure applicable in respect of individual board members can be extended to designated persons within corporate bodies supplying board services within companies.

5 Conclusion

The dominant arrangement regarding qualification for supplying board services within SADC countries is characterised by a blanket prohibition against the appointment of corporate boards. The potential benefits, including the benefit of financial inclusion of previously disadvantaged individuals in board supplier services, are immense. As indicated earlier, the three primary roles of corporate boards are; (a) to manage the business and affairs of a company, (b) to provide advice and guidance to top managers, and (c) to monitor or supervise management with a view to ensuring the operationalisation of the corporate strategy. All these functions are arguably capable of being undertaken by a wide range of corporate entities doing business in the services industry.[93] It can be surmised that that such corporate entities exist in abundance in the selected SADC countries. However, none of those corporate entities would be able to supply those board services as each of the corporate statute within selected SADC countries only allow natural persons to serve as board members.

If legal entities are allowed to serve as corporate directors, the potential number of beneficiaries can increase exponentially as legal entities that serve as corporate directors are able to designate more than one individual to provide board services on behalf of the corporate client. The multiplier effect of remuneration to multiple individuals connected to the corporate entities, as opposed to when an individual director is appointed, is quite obvious. Moreover, as the board functions explained herein are capable of being undertaken by a large number of professional services legal entities in selected SADC countries, the benefit to a number of people who would ordinarily not have been considered for the board role can be quite tangible.

---

best that anyone can offer without the in-depth survey is an estimation. However, for the purposes of proving my recommendation feasible, it is absolutely necessary to accept that since board services are known to primarily consist of the managerial, advisory and supervisory services, quite a number of body corporates operating within the services industry can potentially qualify for appointment as corporate directors. These entities will be justifiably benefited should the blanket ban against their appointment as directors be lifted in the selected SADC countries. Of importance here, in relation to the facilitation of financial inclusion of previously disadvantaged persons and, possibly, vulnerable individuals is that the current board compensation structure can easily be achieved in the professional services firm setting explained herein.

[93] Bainbridge and Henderson (2014), p. 1075, accept that "nearly every other professional service has the option of being provided by any type of business association."

The apprehension for using corporate entities on the basis of being unable to ensure transparency and accountability is overrated. In this regard, the experience of Civil-Law jurisdictions within the SADC is instructive. This is particularly because the Civil-Law SADC countries' insistence on identifying certain individuals as permanent or designated suppliers of board services effectively endeavour to address the problem of (possible lack of) transparency. As regards the possible inability to ensure accountability as corporate boards enjoy the benefits of separate legal personality—which will presumably insulate individuals associated with corporate directors from liability—that, too, is overrated as the combination of piercing the corporate veil and direct liability are capable of effectively resolving the challenge.

The main objections raised with regard to allowing corporate directors relate to the challenge of ensuring transparency and accountability.[94] The argument made is that since a corporate director is a legal person with separate legal personality, , the potential impossibility to look behind the legal entity in observance of the separate legal personality principle will possibly limit transparency with regard to who actually serves as a board member.

In attempting to provide a solution to this perceived problem, Bainbridge states that appropriate mandatory disclosure should deal with potential lack of transparency.[95] In this regard, he argues that potential lack of transparency could be addressed through disclosure and substantive regulation without sacrificing the benefits provided by corporate directors.[96]

The concern of separate legal personality of the corporate director standing in the way of holding constituent individuals can also be resolved as there exists the possibility of piercing the corporate veil. In the South African context, that can be done in line with the guidelines provided in section 20(9) of the Companies Act, 2008. In other SADC countries, a similar provision in statute or at common law, read in line with applicable case law, can be adhered to.[97]

Bibliography

Australia's Corporations Act, 2001
Bainbridge SM (2002) Why a board? Group decision-making in corporate governance. Vand Law Rev 55(1):30

---

[94] Referencing the United Kingdom Department for Business, Innovation, and Skills Report (2014) Transparency & Trust: Enhancing the Transparency of UK Company Ownership and Increasing Trust in UK Business—Government Response, p. 44, Bainbridge (2017), p. 75–76, observes that "[t]he stated rationale for restricting the use of corporate directors was that they "bring about a lack of transparency and accountability with respect to the individuals influencing the company".

[95] Bainbridge (2017).

[96] Ibid, at 82.

[97] See, in particular, *Ex Parte: Gore NO and Others* 2 All SA 437 (WCC).

Bainbridge SM (2017) Corporate directors in the United Kingdom. William Mary Law Rev Online 59:75–76. Article 3. Available at https://scholarship.law.wm.edu/pageswmlronline/vol59/iss1/3

Bainbridge SM (2018) Corporate directors in the United Kingdom. William Mary Law Rev Online 59:65

Bainbridge SM, Henderson TM (2014) Boards-R-Us: reconceptualizing corporate boards. Stanford Law Rev 66:1051–1119

Bebchuk LA, Fried JM (2010) Tackling the managerial power problem: the key to improving executive compensation. Pathways:9–12

Broad Based Black Economic Empowerment Act 53 of 2003

Commercial Companies and Economic Interest Groups Law, 1997

Delaware General Corporation Law

Ex Parte: Gore NO and Others (2013) 2 All SA 437 (WCC)

Fisheries Development Corporation of South Africa Ltd v Jorgensen 1980 4 SA 156 (W)

Hanks JJ Jr (2010) The new legal capital regime in South Africa. In: Mongalo TH (ed) Modern company law for a competitive South African economy. Juta, Claremont

Kingdom of Eswatini Companies Act, 2009

Kingdom of Lesotho's Companies Act, 2011 (Act No. 18 of 2011)

Madagascar's Law No. 2003-036 on Commercial Companies

Malawian Companies Act, 2013

Marazanye K (2016) An analysis of indigenisation and economic empowerment in Zimbabwe' an unpublished thesis submitted for the degree Masters in Public Administration in the Faculty of Economic and Management Science, Stellenbosch University

Mauritius Companies Act, 2001

Model Business Corporation Act

Mozambique's Commercial Code (Decree 2/2005 of 27 December 2015)

Namibian Companies Act 28 of 2004

New Zealand Companies Act, 1993

Seychelles Companies Act (Consolidated to 01 December 2014)

South African Companies Act 61 of 1973

South African Companies Act 71 of 2008

Stiles P, Taylor B (2001) Boards at work: how directors view their roles and responsibilities. Oxford University Press, Oxford

Tanzania's Companies Act 12 of 2002

United Kingdom Company Ownership and Increasing Trust in UK Business—Government Response' (2014)

Zambia's Companies Act 10 of 2017

Zimbabwe's Companies and other Business Entities Act [Chapter 24:31] 2020

Tshepo H. Mongalo Professor Tshepo Mongalo B.Proc (*summa cum laude*), LLB (University of KwaZulu-Natal); LLM (University of Cambridge); Cert. in Legal Writing (Cape Town); Cert. in Law, Social Thought & Global Governance (Brown); Cert. in Global Law, Economic Policy & Social Justice (Harvard); PhD (Cape Town). Professor Mongalo is an Associate Professor of Law at the University of the Witwatersrand, Johannesburg. He is also an adjunct lecturer for Postgraduate Diploma in Business Administration (PDBA) and Master of Business Administration (MBA) at Wits Business School in Johannesburg. He is the former Associate Professor and Head of the Department of Law at Monash South Africa, a private higher education institution based in Roodepoort, Johannesburg. Prof Mongalo is the Deputy Chairperson of the Specialist Committee on Company Law in South Africa and a non-executive director of Eskom Holdings (SOC) Ltd and a member of its Audit & Risk Committee (ARC) and a member and Chair of its People & Governance (P&G) committee. Prof Mongalo is the former Project Manager and Lead Expert of the Corporate Law Reform in South Africa. As Project Manager (2003–2008), Prof Mongalo was instrumental in the development of the Companies Act, 2008. His research interests are in Corporate Law &

Corporate Governance, Securities Regulation, Regulatory Framework Design and Social Enterprise Law. Prof Mongalo is currently involved in a couple of book projects on Functional Company Law for South Africa (with Prof. Michael Katz of ENS Africa), Corporate Law & Corporate Governance (with Dr. Tshepiso Scott of the University of Pretoria), and Social Enterprise Law (with Prof. Steven Dean of Brooklyn Law School). Prof. Mongalo was a contributor to the internationally acclaimed publication by Cambridge University Press entitled 'Cambridge Handbook on Corporate Law, Corporate Governance and Sustainability.

Financial Inclusion and Persons Living with Disabilities in Zambia: Reality Versus Rhetoric

Herbert Kawadza and Sharon Handongwe

Abstract While Zambia has made strides in setting up legal and structural mechanisms aimed at enriching the lives of persons living with disabilities, these on their own are inadequate. More particularly, although these benevolent intentions are commendable, however, in an environment where these efforts are not supported by mechanisms that promote the financial independence of the disabled these will not avail much. This chapter considers the civil justice issue of the financial exclusion of persons with living with disabilities in Zambia. It contends that their inability to access financial services bars them from participating in wealth creation and therefore impedes the transformation of their livelihoods. In as far as it exposes such barriers, this chapter is vital in providing a platform upon which further research into social-economic justice in Zambia can be undertaken.

1 Introduction

For a while now, Zambia has boasted a myriad pieces of legislation and policies which seek to undergird social-economic protection and the economic equality of its citizens.[1] The obligation to usher economic equality is premised on the well-founded belief that inequality is related to, among many other social ills, poverty and a distortion of patterns of economic growth.[2] However, much as countries, "including Zambia, are keen to ensure service provision has equity, equality and quality, there is

---

[1] See e.g. Chirwa and Odhiambo (2017), p. 1; United Nations Population Fund (2015); Hikaumba (2012), p. 1.

[2] United Nations General Assembly, 2013.

H. Kawadza (✉)
School of Law, University of the Witwatersrand, Johannesburg, South Africa
e-mail: Herbert.kawadza@wits.ac.za

S. Handongwe
Cheshire Homes Society of Zambia National Office, Lusaka, Zambia

a tendency to leave out other players especially the vulnerable and marginalized groups. . . people with disabilities are most affected."[3] In fact, "reducing inequality is Zambia's principal development challenge"[4] as it is characterized as one of the most unequal societies.[5] Statistically, percentages relating to the exclusion of persons living with disabilities have been consistently high.[6]

More precisely, an area where inequality is manifested in Zambia is in relation to the inability of certain quarters of the Zambian community to access financial services and products. As central bank, the Bank of Zambia notes, approximately 41 percent (more than 3.5 million) of the Zambian adult population do not have access to financial services or products.[7] Similarly, a large percentage (approximately 60 percent) of those who do have such access undertake financial activities through unregulated financial providers.[8] The risks that come with that are enormous. For instance, the lack of standardized and legal financial institutions that can offer financial services for persons with disabilities renders them vulnerable to the risk unscrupulous financial activities and services such as ponzi schemes usurious lending.[9]

Growing pressure to transform that scenario has resulted in noticeable policy announcements. In its new policy document—a document which is referred to as amounting to a "renewed commitment to financial inclusion"[10]—the Bank of Zambia underscores the need "to achieve universal access and usage of a broad range of quality and affordable financial services that meet the needs of both individuals and enterprises."[11] Much as that high sounding document is noteworthy, in so far as it is not disability-inclusive and is bare on the determinants or underlying causes of financial exclusion, the interventions it suggests will only benefit certain social groups to the exclusion of others. More specifically, because the document does not address the specific factors that create barriers to disabled persons from enjoying the benefits of financial inclusion, it is fair to assert that the strategies and interventions will not avail much of the intended objectives and will in fact, run the risk of entrenching the existing exclusion.

This chapter adopts a qualitative method and argues that there is a knowledge gap relating to the drivers of financial exclusion in Zambia. The aim, therefore, is to add

---

[3] United Nations (n.d.-a).

[4] United Nations (n.d.-b).

[5] Kragelund (2017), p. 51.

[6] Bhorat (2016).

[7] BOZ (2017–2022).

[8] BOZ (2017–2022).

[9] Special Needs Alliance (2019).

[10] BOZ (2017–2022).

[11] BOZ (2017–2022). The aspiration is that "all Zambians will reap the full benefits of financial inclusion: that is, individuals will be able to use appropriate savings, credit, payment, insurance, and investment services to manage risks, plan for the future, and achieve their goals, and firms will be able to access affordable financing to facilitate innovation and firm growth and create employment." At xi.

to the sparse literature on this issue by examining the inequality-generating factors through an examination of financial exclusion for persons living with disabilities. It argues that financial constraints arising from the lack of attention to economic exclusion has driven the disabled to the periphery of Zambia's economic geography and the policy makers' attention. Failure to reflect on the processes by which those with disabilities are excluded undermines efforts aimed at engendering social capitalism. More specifically, the lack of commitment and vigour towards addressing their exclusion is a major flaw in efforts of minimising the chronic poverty that assails that demography of the Zambian population. Furthermore, this chapter postulates that despite the commonly cited social justice issues, there are measurable economic losses that a country exposes itself to which arise from the exclusion of persons with disabilities from formal employment.[12] It also avers that a failure to integrate persons living with disabilities would be a travesty not only to that demography's financial needs but also to their potential to contribute towards the country's economic development agenda.

This Chapter proceeds as follows. Immediately after the introduction, the second section highlights the link between financial exclusion, disability and poverty and the third section three outlines the state of financial marginalisation in Zambia and reviews existing theoretical studies that describe the poverty of the people living with disability. The fourth section hypotheses some of the personal and extra personal factors that directly or indirectly impede the participation persons living with disabilities in the financial sector. Section five makes recommendations for regional policymakers to enhance the participation of disabled persons in the financial sector and the sixth section concludes.

2 Contextualising Disability, Financial Exclusion and Poverty

The transformative effect of inclusive financial environments as accelerators of individual economic development especially in less developed countries is a well-established fact[13] and will only be mentioned in passing. Over the years scholars have emphasised that "financial inclusion contributes to faster and more equitable macroeconomic growth, reduces poverty, and promotes income equality in developing countries by providing access to formal financial services."[14] Other scholars contend that the systemic restriction of financial services in developing countries is a significant obstacle to the agenda of accomplishing sustainable growth in Africa.[15] In sum, there is an interaction between higher financial inclusion and reduced

---

[12] International Labour Organisation (2010).

[13] Giné et al. (2012); Chmelíkova and Redlichova (2020), p. 457; Lusardi and Mitchell (2011).

[14] Omar and Inaba (2020), p. 21; World Bank Group (2016).

[15] Kostov et al. (2012), p. 397.

poverty rates and higher equality.[16] By extension, a significant number of studies have established a relationship between disability, financial exclusion and poverty.[17] The contention is that while the condition of disability on its own has an effect of catalysing deprivation, the levels of deprivation are exacerbated in environments that are statistically characterised by limited or non-existent access to financial services and products.[18] It is also common cause that an inability to participate in mainstream economic activities fortifies a disabled person's material disadvantages and entrenches their susceptibility to poverty.[19] Put differently, the material deprivation of persons living with disabilities can be attributed to their distorted or non-existent access to the core economic resources such as financial services and financial products.[20]

For instance, a corollary of the barriers or restrictions which disability imposes on the people is their incapacity to access wealth-accruing systems such as employment, home ownership and life insurance. However, where such insurance is offered, the disabled are usually saddled with high premiums, hence effectively restricting access to such services.[21] As will be shown in detail below, there is generally an entrenched stigma and "negative attitudes towards disabled people's employment potential,"[22] and where it is provided, such employment is often low-skill, demanding but less rewarding and comes with rigid conditions and with minimal chances of promotion.[23] In the absence of an effective welfare system, the burden of caring for the disabled can indirectly exacerbate the poverty or the margins of poverty of the immediate family since the family is forced to channel any available resources towards the upkeep of the person with a disability.[24] That may take the form of dipping into savings to supplement such care or dropping from employment to take care of a disabled relative. In Zambia, women bear the greater load of caring for those with disabilities because, culturally, taking care of a sick person is placed on women.[25]

What emerges from the above discussion is a rich corpus of scholarship demonstrating that financial inclusion is a key driver of economic inclusion, hence the efforts to do away with impediments to access to low-cost and safe financial services.

---

[16]Park and Mercado (2018).

[17]See for instance Hanass-Hancock et al. (2017), p. 280; Pinilla-Roncancio (2015), p. 113; Honohan (2004).

[18]Omar and Inaba (2020), p. 1; Hewitt (2018).

[19]Townsend (1979).

[20]Townsend (1979).

[21]Townsend (1979).

[22]Honey (1993); Dench (1996).

[23]Lonsdale (1990); Walker (1982).

[24]Muller-Kluits and Slabbert (2018), p. 493; Barros et al. (2019), p. 380.

[25]Ghazawy et al. (2020), p. 20; Bakas (2004), p. 95.

3 A Primer on Zambia

In the Zambian context, the financial exclusion narrative places emphasis more on low income and poor people than those living with disabilities.[26] For instance, Zambia's 2021 national budget, by comparison to the previous year's budget, drastically cut services that are targeted towards persons with disabilities.[27] This is satirical considering that those with disabilities are supposed to equally benefit, if not more, than their non-impaired peers. This flies in the face of myriad pieces of legislation seeking to uplift the welfare of the disabled and in fact, is an apt demonstration of theory not translating into practice.

In 2010 Zambia ratified the United Nations Convention on the Rights of Persons with Disability (UNCRPD). Its ratification was followed by the enactment of the Persons with Disabilities Act[28] Another notable enactment is the Citizen Economic Empowerment Commission Act, 2008 which empowers people with disabilities to be economically independent through start-up businesses which are expected to provide employment for others. Similarly, Article 112(f) of the Zambia's Constitution (1991 as amended) requires the state to provide to social benefits and amenities that meet their needs and are just and equitable. Further, section 9 of the Persons with Disabilities Act provides for the protection of the rights of persons with disabilities who encounter law enforcement agents and the judiciary.

The creation of the Zambia Agency for Persons with Disabilities (ZAPD) was a culmination of the enactment of the Persons with Disabilities Act to promote the rights of persons with disabilities. Ancillary bodies include the Zambia Federation of Disability Organizations (ZAFOD) which is the umbrella organisation representing several organisations that represent the needs of those living with disabilities in Zambia. Likewise, the National Social Protection Policy (NSSP)[29] aims to cushion the vulnerable from economic challenges by providing income security for that demography's basic needs as well as to offer protection from economic risks and shocks. Similarly, through the Social Cash Transfer (SCT)[30] mechanism the government seeks to safeguard the poor and vulnerable households that have one or more incapacitated members by way of an unconditional cash transfer.

Zambia is also member of the Alliance for Financial Inclusion. However, what disheartening revelation in *Attorney General v Roy Clarke*[31] where the Supreme Court of Zambia's acknowledged disability-related international treaties signed by Zambia are not binding but merely persuasive. This, therefore, means that there is no

---

[26]World Bank (2017); Cramm and Finkenflügel (2008), p. 15.

[27]2021 Budget Address by Honourable Dr Bwalya KE Ng'andu, MP, Minister of Finance, Delivered to the National Assembly on Friday, 25th September.

[28]6 of 2012.

[29]Handa (2018), p. 42; Government of the Republic of Zambia (2017).

[30]Arruda and Dubois (2018); Costa (2016); Beazley and Carraro (n.d.).

[31](2008) AHRLR 259 (ZASC 2008).

guarantee that the international obligation to comply with the conventions which promote or reinforce the economic and human rights of the disabled will be met.

Also lamentable is that despite the rich vein of purportedly inclusion-engendering polices, legislation and institutions, much remains to be done. Furthermore, while these programs are laudable, their efficacy and impact towards the intended group still leave a lot to be desired. The main weakness is that government's ownership of the programs is nominal primarily because these programs are donor dependent, and their efficacy depends on the availability of donor resources.[32]

4 A Taxonomy of Obstacles to Financial Inclusion

As one Joseph posits, "the main focus of society should be to solve problems directly, addressing root origins. . . a true philanthropic desire to promote the welfare of others [should] seek to alter the preconditions"[33] that seek to create inequalities. In the Zambian context efforts towards aligning economic rights with a view to accomplishing financial inclusion are hampered by multidimensional factors which include self-exclusion, discrimination, exclusion by design, harsh credit conditions, lack of social capital, negative staff attitudes, no or insufficient training, and absence of an integrated approach. Besides these, barriers can be attributed to subjective factors which hamper the disabled individual from navigating and enjoying the market for financial services. Below are a few of such factors.

4.1 Discrimination

There is sufficient theoretical evidence for hypothesizing that 'it is society which disables physically impaired people'[34] through attitudes, perceptions and values. Therefore, a person is only considered to be incapacitated because of a limitation imposed by the environment or the system. Unlike other jurisdictions, Zambia does not specifically spell out the economic rights of the disabled. It is no wonder therefore that the financial barriers the disabled face are less about the economic capacity of the country but more about how the financial sector regards those living with disabilities. In other words, 'as a group, people with perceived impairments encounter economic and social deprivation. . .these disadvantages are the consequence of a particular ideology or ideologies which justify and perpetuate them'.[35] Therefore, because of discrimination, impairments and limitations exist.

---

[32] Kampamba et al. (2019).

[33] Joseph (2017), p. 107.

[34] UPIAS (1976), p. 14.

[35] Barnes and Mercer (2010), p. 80.

A germane example of discrimination and the lack of an all-encompassing rights-based approach to disability is the recent case of *Frankson Musukwa & 2 Others v The Road Transport and Safety Agency*[36] in which deaf petitioners sought to challenge the Road Transport and Safety Agency's refusal to grant them driving licences and permits. Despite passing all physical tests, the licences were denied due to the operation of a section in the Road Traffic Act which empowers the agency to deny a person a licence or permit if they fail to pass a physical test that includes hearing. The petitioners' contention was that denying them licences and permits because their disability was a breach of their constitutional rights to movement, equality, and freedom from discrimination unconstitutional as it interfered with their right to movement. The Court dismissed their petition and ruled that although discriminatory, public safety made it necessary to shield the public from the risk that comes from allowing deaf people to drive as they would not be able to hear emergency sounds such as sirens and hooting. It is worth noting that by contrast, neighbouring countries such as Zimbabwe, South Africa, Namibia, Congo, Tanzania, and Botswana permit the hearing-impaired people to drive.[37]

That case underlines the paternalistic social relationship which 'enables the dominant elements of a society to express profound and sincere sympathy for the members of a minority group while, at the same time, keeping them in a position of social and economic subordination. It has allowed the nondisabled to act as the protectors, guides, leaders, role models, and intermediates for disabled individuals who, like children, are often assumed to be help-less, dependent, asexual, economically unproductive, physically limited, emotionally immature, and acceptable only when they are unobtrusive'.[38] This attitude is echoed in the financial sector's reluctance to integrate the non-abled into the financial system.

4.2 Fragmented Policy Implementation

In as much as commendable policies exist, programs aimed at alleviating financial exclusion are not adequately implemented. The very same disabled people's organisations (DPO) or the focal institutions under the umbrella of the Zambia Federation of Disability Organizations (ZAFOD) which are supposed to be the champions of their constituents' rights are hampered by a "lack awareness of disability rights and the actual provisions of the CRPD. Furthermore, the framework within which they are supposed to operate has not been established."[39] This aggravates and perpetuates the *status quo*. This failure is partly attributable to poor coordination among Non-Governmental Organizations (NGOs), Disabled People Organizations (DPOs)

---

[36] (2019/HP/1832) [2021] ZMHC 5 (4 June 2021).
[37] See also World Federation of the Deaf (n.d.).
[38] Hahn (1986), p. 130. See also Daley (2018), p. 55.
[39] Banda and Kalaluka (2014).

and people with disabilities. The lack of a harmonized approach to protecting the rights of the disabled means that there is no collective voice to achieve the particularly the 2030 Agenda for Sustainable Development under the auspices of Goals 1 and 10 of the United Nations Sustainable Development Goals,[40] which champion the inclusion of the disabled *inter alia,* within the formal financial sector.

There is need to equip the DPOs with technical and financial skills which they can impart to their constituents. Furthermore, the poor collaboration and engagement between these bodies in terms of policy implementation is a major hindrance to uplifting the financial status of those with disabilities. The dearth of evidence-based research aimed at broadening implantation strategies and lessons which government agencies can utilise in policy formulation whose effect might be to aggravate the existing problem.

4.3 Self-Stigmatization

The 'internalised oppression' of those living with disabilities can result in self-exclusion. It is argued that "impairment, by definition, is functionally limiting...This means many disabled people, because they cannot conform to a 'nondisabled' ideal and stigma, experience low self-esteem or internalized oppression."[41] This culminates in lack of confidence and insecurity both which often lead to risk-avoiding behaviorism and is depicted in situations where the disabled believe, for example, that applying for a financial products is a fruitless exercise because of the ever-present perception that owing to their state, they will be denied financial products. In essence therefore, self-exclusion is a constraint on their capacity to believe that financial products and services are attainable to them. This in turn results in the disabled resorting to grants rather than self-generating income development for sustenance and being less motivated than others.[42]

Self-stigmatisation is reinforced by negative perceptions which society harbours towards the disabled.[43] The feeling of shame and ignorance about the cause of disability tends to generate feelings of shame among families. For example, surveys conducted in Zambia and other African countries show that 38% of respondent caregivers of children with disabilities tend to hide their child with a disability from public view, or barring them such children from participating in social activities or even school as a means of protecting them from the stigma of disability.[44] The crux of the matter, therefore, self-stigmatisation contributes to the low uptake of financial products among those living with disabilities in Zambia.

[40] International Disability Alliance (2021).
[41] Barnes and Mercer (2010).
[42] Simanowitz (2001).
[43] Parsons et al. (n.d.).
[44] United Nations (n.d.-a). See also Watermeyer and Görgens (2014), p. 253.

4.4   Moral Hazard of Aid

Related to self-exclusion is the moral hazard of dependency that comes with the lack of initiative on the part of the disabled. As mentioned above, much of the resources for disability-related projects and sustenance in Zambia depend on donor funding[45] which is disbursed either directly to the disabled by the donor agencies or thorough the intermediation of quasi government departments falling under the Ministry of Community Development and Social Welfare. The proliferation of aid as a mechanism of supplementing government-assisted welfare mechanism has been noted to be associated with several risks, chief of which is that handouts limit individual initiative, negate empowerment and liberation.[46] It has also been contented that although supportive, public welfare initiatives aimed at assisting the disabled come with a residual risk of tainting the victims as helpless and oblivious about what is best for them.[47] In essence, therefore, such paternalism discourages economic self-sufficiency, and is a disincentive to independence and culminates in a 'benefit trap' which in turn inhibits efforts to embark on wealth enhancing strategies such as participating in the financial sector.[48] Without a consistent income and short of any hope for one, the disabled have no incentive to engage with the financial sector.

4.5   Unemployment

It is trite that the greater proportion of the poverty of the disabled can be attributed to the uneven or limited access to the main wealth accumulating and economic resources system which is characterised by the labour market and wage system.[49] Through their inability to be part of this system, the disabled are left without an income and are therefore tangentially excluded from attaining an economic status which enables them to make use of the financial system and its products. In an environment where they are denied full participation in social life and are not participants in mainstream industrial capitalism where reward is a by-product of economic activities, expecting the disabled to be integrated into the financial system and to be financially independent will remain an elusive quest. Several statistical researches have concluded that in Zambia unemployment percentages are significantly higher among persons with disabilities.[50] Such an environment is attributed to several interlinked factors including low skill levels due to inadequate education, employers' discriminatory attitudes and the absence of policies to support the

---

[45] United Nations (n.d.-b).

[46] Moonga and Green (2016), p. 350; Holmes (2007).

[47] Brown (2011), p. 313; Moonga and Green (2016), p. 350.

[48] Guo et al. (2019); Soffer (2010), p. 376; Stapleton (2006), p. 701.

[49] Townsend (1979).

[50] UNICEF (2018).

employment of persons living with disabilities. Although the Persons with Disabilities Act proscribes any form of discrimination aimed at persons living with disability, this part of the Zambian population continues to encounter barriers in the employment space.[51] Lack of employment means no income and, in that environment, opening a bank account becomes impossible, if not deemed to be a luxury. As such, financial products become unaffordable and inaccessible to the disabled. Similarly, without an income this demographic is unlikely to benefit from Fintech and, in fact, digital exclusion arising from waning use of physical banks emanating from the proliferation of mobile money will only serve to widen the current barriers.

4.6   Lack of Security

"Not only do disabled people have lower social status. They also have lower incomes and fewer assets. Moreover, they tend to be poorer even when their social status is the same as the non-disabled."[52] Without an income, persons with disabilities cannot acquire assets. Without assets which are the 'qualifier' for credit they are driven further from the credit institutions and financial products. Thus, limited access to capital is an added constraint which hinders persons with disabilities not only enjoying financial services and products but also from contributing effectively towards the economic development of the country. In the absence of a policy to ensure access to resources, persons living with disabilities have limited chances of being integrated in the mainstream financial sector.[53]

4.7   Illiteracy

There is a correlation between lack of education and the risk of poverty and an inability to participate in economic activities among people with disabilities.[54] Lack of sufficient education impedes full participation in industrial capitalism and ultimately widens the gap of financial exclusion through the division of society into those who can work and those who cannot.[55] In that environment those endowed with educational qualifications or skills are preferred over those without such attributes and because of the sociological factors that deny them access to education, the incapacitated end up without marketable skills.[56]

---

[51] Zambia Agency for Persons with Disabilities (2019).

[52] Townsend (1979), p. 711.

[53] Zambia Agency for Persons with Disabilities (2019).

[54] Liao and Zhao (2013), p. 230.

[55] Barnes and Mercer (2010).

[56] Muzata (2020), p. 71.

In Zambia, much as the Persons with Disabilities Act 2012 provides for free primary, higher, and vocational education, as well as ensuring that physical impediments to accessing educational structures are eliminated, these measures however, have not been fully implemented. The number of persons with disabilities not being able to attain an educational qualification remain high and the ideal of removing barriers to inclusive education is still far from achievable. The ratio of persons with disabilities who had never attended school was higher (34.4%) as compared to those without disabilities (20.9%).[57] Generally speaking, therefore, their academic performance and retention levels are poor.[58] A high percentage of persons with intellectual and psychosocial disabilities are excluded from education on the basis that they are deemed to be incapable of being trained or on the pretext of the unavailability of specialized teachers, infrastructural inadequacies to meet the needs of the student and insufficient financial resources to cater for their training.[59] In short, the learning environments are not adapted to include those with disabilities.

An aggravating factor is the non-justiciability factor relating to the constitutional provisions pertaining to access to education.[60] This therefore means that access to education cannot be enforced before courts of law. In addition, provisions requiring the inclusion of the disabled in education system are rarely implemented owing to the absence of prescribed guidelines or guidelines. Without an education people with disabilities are not only poorer but more in need of social protection.

5 The Way Forward

The exclusion from mainstream financial services which of persons living with disabilities are subjected to is a social justice issue and needs an emancipatory approach. A constructive approach towards tackling such barriers should start with an acknowledgment of the sociological certainty that impairment does not amount to a biological or mental difference, but rather, that it is a social construction or condition.[61] Neither should disability be equated to inability. In other words, "it is the society which disables physically impaired people."[62] With that in mind, it would arguably be possible to shape the socio-political economy of financial product deprivation which is steeped in the functionally limiting perception that the impaired are 'unfortunate, useless different...and sick."[63] Also in need of purging is the mindset that because they do not add value to the economic good of society, persons

---

[57] Zambia Agency for Persons with Disabilities (2019), p. 1.

[58] UNICEF (2018); Miles (2011), p. 1087.

[59] Banda and Kalaluka (2014).

[60] Zambia Civic Education Association (2012); Chanda (2003), p. 1.

[61] Barnes and Mercer (2010).

[62] Union of the Physically Impaired Against Segregation (1976), p. 14.

[63] Hunt (1996), p. 146.

with disabilities are not deserving of the benefits of financial inclusion.[64] What is needed is a radical overhaul of the manner in which various economic players hamper the endeavour of the disabled and making them dependent and unable to participate in economic activities.

This theoretical discussion calls for important policy implications. A cautionary recommendation is that in its endeavour to bring about a new paradigm focusing on financial inclusion to the disabled, Zambia needs to be critical of the manner it approaches efforts to bring about economic equality. More specifically, its sociology of disability should be informed by local conditions. This should entail avoiding copying western-style ideologies and initiatives that mirror policies and institutions imposed by its former colonial powers. To start with, Zambia is not well resourced to replicate these, rather "the policies and institutions that support disabled people must emerge from local knowledge and expertise, indigenous resources and cultures."[65]

For instance, Zambia's financial institutions should innovate to incorporate need-based formal financial services which meet the requirements of the disabled segments of the Zambian population. Because most of the disabled people live in rural areas, the Zambian government, needs to craft an approach which could lead to the development of an infrastructure which supports the penetration of financial services and products which the disabled could be exposed to. The low hanging fruit would be the existing mobile networks and phones upon which the provision of financial literacy to raise an awareness and eventually an enjoyment of financial products could piggyback.

The efficacy of such mechanisms would be boosted in an environment of wider financial information availability. The elimination of information asymmetry would be a convenient tool towards minimising involuntary financial exclusion among persons living with disabilities. For persons with disabilities, special and deliberate strategies and actions need to be made to help them open bank accounts and to ensure that online and physical banking feature such as ATMs are accessible.

Equally, policies should initiate necessary actions regarding specific socio-economic constraints, and financial system inefficiencies to promote a more inclusive financial system. Perhaps an additional innovative approach would entail incentivizing the formation of social banking platforms whose aim is not profit maximisation but the attainment of social values such as the promotion of access to credit and financial products for the unbankables.[66] Lessons drawn from other jurisdictions which have managed to minimise the financial exclusion of people living with disabilities through specific banks whose mandate is to usher economic justice through investment would be instructive. The Charity Bank[67] in the UK, for example, exists specifically to make available affordable loans and financial advice

---

[64] Hunt (1996) p. 152.

[65] Barnes and Mercer (2010), p. 225.

[66] Weber and Remer (2011).

[67] See <https://charitybank.org/>. Accessed 20 July 2021.

to disadvantaged community groups. Similarly, the Ekobanken[68] of Sweden promotes a social economy based on the understanding that money is a facilitative forum for the attainment of public good. Such banks are spurred by corporate values steeped in social sensitivity and especially the development of better quality of life for their account holders. Thus, social banks "with their activity and financing priorities, play a pivotal role in allocating financing resources to those urgent needs, helping to move towards a new scenario of integrated general economic equilibrium"[69] could be ushered.

The existence of banks with such priorities and values in Zambia would engender a trickle-down of economic values to the currently marginalised population. Fintech offering fair, safe and low-cost mechanisms of receiving, storing and spending finance for and by the disabled and the development of institutions whose mandate is to minimize financial exclusion, banks which offer products and services that are inclusive of the underserved disability groups need to be explored. It remains to be seen whether anthropological reductionism which is manifested in the self-interest and profit-maximisation agenda of existing institutions, would to be accommodative of the non-profit objectives aimed at supporting financial inclusion of people living with disabilities in Zambia. Suffice to say that the Zambian government will have to provide a litany of incentives and facilitative infrastructure to the financial sector to induce the emergency of 'philanthrocapitalism'[70] and to spur the institutions to experiment with some aspects of social financing. Inducements should be in place to ensure that such institutions are not perceived as the usual run-of-the-mill philanthropic organisations and that they offer superior products and infrastructure have a direct impact on the financial needs of people living with disabilities. Similarly, the Zambian government should champion that ecosystem through an assortment of fiscal policies, regulations, and state-owned financial institutions whose products are tolerant of the cause of those living with disabilities.

It is worth highlighting that some commendable headway seems to be in evidence. For instance, in 2020 Zambia signed a grant worth SEK 40 million (4,628,120,00 US Dollars) with Sida which is aimed at to promoting financial inclusion and capabilities for women, youth and people with disabilities and to promote their access to basic financial services.[71]

---

[68] See <https://www.gabv.org/members/ekobanken>. Accessed 23 July 2021.

[69] Weber and Remer (2011), p. 51.

[70] Bishop and Green (2015), p. 113; McGoey (2012), p. 185; Rogers (2011), p. 376.

[71] See <https://www.fsdzambia.org/news-item/fsd-zambia-signs-a-sek-40000000-grant-with-sida-to-promote-financial-inclusion-and-capabilities-for-women-youth-and-people-with-disabilities/>. Accessed 20 July 2021.

6 Conclusion

One of the key factors to the lasting exclusion of persons with disabilities is the perception or "the enduring belief that it is unfortunate personal circumstances which are holding disabled people back."[72] It is that mindset that needs to change so that policy makers can appreciate what is at the core of the financial marginalisation of persons living with disabilities. Much as there have been efforts to bolster the participation of the incapacitated in the formal financial sector, there is little attention to the factors that cause exclusion.

Through a theoretical discussion this chapter focused on financial exclusion and the resultant poverty among person living with disabilities in Zambia. By focusing on the interplay of such elements, this chapter suggests that current policies are ineffectual in guaranteeing universal access financial services and products. If at all change is to be realised, a policy shift is vital. Change through actual solutions should transcend humanitarian rhetoric and, in its place, should be practical solutions that are steeped in an understanding of how the current architecture foments financial exclusion. Unless an equalization of access to financial products and services within Zambia's financial sector is achieved this demography will continue to be denied social and economic participation and in the absence of a practical and visible change the disabled will remain 'helpless or forced to submit to the institutionalised system of abuse'.[73]

Bibliography

Arruda P, Dubois L (2018) A brief history of Zambia's Social Cash Transfer Programme <https://ipcig.org/pub/eng/PRB62_A_brief_history_of_Zambia_s_social_cash_transfer_programme.pdf>. Accessed 20 July 2021

Bakas T, Austin JK, Jessup SL, Williams LS, Oberst MT (2004) Time and difficulty of tasks provided by family caregivers of stroke survivors. J Neurosci Nursing 36:95

Banda N, Kalaluka L (2014) Zambia. <http://rodra.co.za/images/country_reports/reports/adry_2014_2_zambia.pdf>. Accessed 20 July 2021

Barnes C, Mercer G (2010) Exploring disability: a sociological introduction, 2nd edn. Polity Press, Cambridge

Barros ALO, de Gutierrez GM, Santos M (2019) Quality of life and burden of caregivers of children and adolescents with disabilities. Spec Care Dentist 39:380

Beazley R, Carraro L (n.d.) Zambian social cash transfer programme: assessment of the targeting mechanisms and proposed harmonised approach. <https://www.opml.co.uk/files/Publications/8049-zambia-social-protection/zambian-social-cash-transfer-programme-briefing-note.pdf?noredirect=1>. Accessed 20 July 2021

Bhorat H, Oosthuizen HM, Yu D, Kachingwe N (2016) Understanding growth-income inequality interactions in Zambia. Development Policy Research Unit, University of Cape Town

---

[72] Barnes and Mercer (2010), p. 123.
[73] Raw (2019).

Bishop M, Green G (2015) Philanthrocapitalism comes of age. In: Nicholls A, Paton R, Emerson J (eds) Social finance, p 11

BOZ (2021) National Financial Inclusion Strategy 2017–2022. <https://www.boz.zm/National-Financial-Inclusion-Strategy-2017-2022.pdf>. Accessed 20 July 2021

Brown K (2011) Vulnerability: handle with care. Ethics Soc Welf 5(3):313

Budget Address by Honourable Dr. Bwalya KE Ng'andu, MP, Minister of Finance, Delivered to the National Assembly on Friday, 25th September, 2020. <https://www.mof.gov.zm/?wpfb_dl=2 78>. Accessed 20 July 2021

Chanda A (2003) Gaps in the law and policy in the implementation on the rights of the child in Zambia. Zambia Law J 32:1

Chirwa T, Odhiambo N (2017) Macroeconomic policy reform and economic growth in Zambia. EuroEconomica 35(2):1

Chmelíkova G, Redlichova R (2020) Is there a link between financial exclusion and over-indebtedness? Evidence from Czech peripheral municipalities. J Rural Stud 78:457

Costa M, Gyoeri M, Veras Soares F (2016) Scaling up cash transfer programmes: good practices and lessons learned from Kenya, Tanzania and Zambia' Community of Practice on Cash Transfers in Africa. Policy Brief, No. 1

Cramm JM, Finkenflügel H (2008) Exclusion of disabled people from microcredit in Africa and Asia: a literature study. Asia Pac Disabil Rehabil J 19(2):15

Daley A, Phipps S, Branscombe NR (2018) The social complexities of disability: discrimination, belonging and life satisfaction among Canadian youth. Populat Health 5:55

Dench S, Meagerand N, Morris S (1996) The recruitment and retention of people with disabilities, institute for employment studies, Report 301, ISBN: 978-1-85184-227-8

French S (1994) On equal terms: working with disabled people. Butterworth Heinemann, Oxford

Ghazawy ER, Mohammed SE, Mahfouz ME, Abdelrehim MG (2020) Determinants of caregiver burden of persons with disabilities in a rural district in Egypt. BMC Public Health 1156:20

Giné X, Menand L, Townsend RM, Vickery J (2012) Financial Inclusion—A Pathway to Financial Stability? Understanding the Linkages. <http://www.gpfi.org/knowledge-bank /publications>. Accessed 20 July 2021

Government of the Republic of Zambia Integrated Framework of Basic Social Protection Programmes (2017). https://www.ilo.org/wcmsp5/groups/public/%2D%2D-africa/%2D%2D-ro-abidjan/%2D%2D-ilo-lusaka/documents/publication/wcms_671566.pdf.   Accessed 20 July 2021.

Guo C, Luo Y, Tang X, Ding R, Song X, Zheng X (2019) Poverty and youth disability in china: results from a large, nationwide, population-based survey. PLoS One 14(4):e0215851

Hahn H (1986) Public support for rehabilitation programmes: the analysis of U.S. disability policy. Disabil Handicap Soc 1(2):121

Handa SL, Seidenfeld ND, Tembo G, Davis B (2018) Can unconditional cash transfers raise long-term living standards? Evidence from Zambia. J Dev Econ 133:42

Hewitt J (2018) Disability, development and financial exclusion: a study of the socio-economic barriers to accessing microfinance encountered by people with physical disabilities in Kampala, Uganda, PhD thesis. University of Nottingham

Hikaumba L (2012) Socioeconomic Policies for Inclusive Growth, Sustainable Economic Development and Decent Work. <https://www.imf.org/external/np/seminars/eng/2012/zambia/pdf/hik.pdf>. Accessed 20 July 2021

Holmes R (2007) Social Protection and Low-Capacity Households in Zambia

Honey S, Meager N, Williams N (1993) Employers' attitudes towards people with disabilities. Institute of Manpower Studies, Brighton

Hunt P (1996) Stigma: the experience of disability. Geoffrey Chapman

International Disability Alliance (2021) The 2030 Agenda for Sustainable Development. <https://www.internationaldisabilityalliance.org/content/2030-agenda-sustainable-development-0>. Accessed 10 July 2021

International Labour Organisation (2010) The Price of Excluding People with Disabilities from the Workplace.   https://www.ilo.org/skills/pubs/WCMS_149529/lang%2D%2Den/index.htm. Accessed 10 July 2021

Joseph P (2017) The new human rights movement: reinventing the economy to end oppression. BenBella Books

Kampamba R, Pellerano L, Banda C, Musama O (2019) Financing the Zambia social cash transfer scale-up: a tax benefit microsimulation analysis based on microzamod. https://doi.org/10.35188/UNU-WIDER/2019/653-1. Accessed 10 July 2021

Kostov P, Tarun A, Annim S (2012) Determinants of access to finance: an investigation into the mzansi intervention. Eur J Dev Res 24:397

Kragelund P (2017) The making of local content policies in Zambia's copper sector: institutional impediments to resource-led development, resources policy. Elsevier, p 51

Liao J, Zhao J (2013) Rate of returns to education of persons with disabilities in rural China. In: Proceedings of the International Conference on Applied Social Science Research, August 2013

Lonsdale S (1990) Women and disability. Macmillan

Lusardi A, Mitchell OS (2011) Financial literacy and planning: implications for retirement wellbeing. In: Lusardi A, Mitchell OS (eds) Financial literacy: implications for retirement security and the financial marketplace. Oxford University Press, Oxford

McGoey L (2012) Philanthrocapitalism and its critics. Poetics 40:185

Miles S (2011) Exploring understandings of inclusion in schools in Zambia and Tanzania using reflective writing and photography. Int J Incl Edu 15:1087

Moonga F, Green S (2016) Risks and vulnerabilities of children in Zambia: mooting responsive social protection interventions. Social work (Stellenbosch. Online) 52(3):350

Muller-Kluits N, Slabbert I (2018) Caregiver burden as depicted by family caregivers of persons with physical disabilities. Soc Work 54:493

Muzata K (2020) Interrogating parental participation in the education and general development of their deaf children in Zambia, African Disability Rights Yearbook, p 71

Omar AMD, Inaba K (2020) Does financial inclusion reduce poverty and income inequality in developing countries? A panel data analysis. J Econ Struct 9(37):1

Park C, Mercado RV (2018) Financial inclusion: new measurement and cross-country impact assessment ADB Economics Working Paper Series 539/2018. Manila, Philippines https://www.adb.org/sites/default/fles/publicatio n/408621/ewp-539-fnancial-inclusion.pdf. Accessed 12 July 2021

Parsons JA, Bond VA, Nixon SA (n.d.) Are We Not Human?' Stories of Stigma, Disability and HIV from Lusaka, Zambia and Their Implications for Access to Health Services. https://journals.plos.org/plosone/article?id=10.1371/journal.pone.0127392. Accessed 12 July 2021

Raw A (2019) Abusive Laws and the fight for reform, SALC. https://www.southernafricalitigationcentre.org/2019/06/28/salc-in-the-news-abusive-laws-and-the-fight-for-reform/. Accessed 12 July 2021

Rogers R (2011) Why Philantho-policymaking matters. Society 48:376

Simanowitz A (2001) Microfinance for the poorest: A review of issues and ideas for contribution of Impact, CGAP Microfinance Gateway 2001: www.microfiancegateway.or/files/3395Anton.dom. Accessed 12 July 2021

Soffer M, McDonald KE, Blanck P (2010) Poverty among adults with disabilities: barriers to promoting asset accumulation in individual development accounts. Am J Commun Psychol 46(3–4):376

Special Needs Alliance (2019) Financial Abuse of Individuals with Disabilities. https://www.specialneedsalliance.org/the-voice/financial-abuse-of-individuals-with-disabilities/. Accessed 14 July 2021

Stapleton DC, Day LO, Livermore B, Imparato AJ (2006) Dismantling the poverty trap: disability policy for the twenty-first century. Milbank Q 84(4):701

Townsend P (1979) Poverty in the United Kingdom. Penguin Books

UNICEF (2018) Qualitative Study from Zambia on Barriers to and Facilitators of Life-Long Learning (Summary of Results)

Union of the Physically Impaired Against Segregation (UPIAS) (1976)

United Nations (2016) Toolkit on disability for Africa: Culture, Beliefs, and Disability

United Nations (n.d.-a) Zambia – Foreign Aid and Democratic Consolidation. https://www.wider.unu.edu/sites/default/files/RB2013-Zambia%20%E2%80%93%20Foreign%20Aid%20and%20Democratic%20Consolidation.pdf. Accessed 14 July 2021

United Nations (n.d.-b) Zambia Country Analysis Summary' http://zm.one.un.org/sites/default/files/un_country_analysis_report.pdf. Accessed 14 July 2021

United Nations Population Fund (2015) Accelerating economic growth & policy reforms to optimise Zambia's demographic dividend. https://zambia.unfpa.org/sites/default/files/pub-pdf/Policy%20Brief_Accelerating%20economic%20policy%20reforms%20%28final%29_0.pdf. Accessed 14 July 2021

Walker W (1982) Unqualified and underemployed handicapped young people and the labour. Palgrave Macmillan

Watermeyer B, Görgens T (2014) Disability and internalized oppression. In: David EJR (ed) Internalized oppression: The psychology of marginalized groups. Springer, p 253

Weber O, Remer S (2011) Social banks and the future of sustainable finance. Routledge International Studies in Money and Banking. Routledge

World Bank (2017) Zambia Makes Steady Progress in Financial Inclusion but Many Women Still Excluded. <https://www.worldbank.org/en/news/feature/2017/11/08/zambia-makes-steady-progress-in-financial-inclusion-but-many-women-still-excluded>. Accessed 15 July 2021

World Bank Group (2016) Poverty and shared prosperity 2016: Taking on inequality. <https://openknowledge.worldbank.org/bitstream/handle/10986/25078/9781464809583>. Accessed 15 July 2021

Zambia Agency for Persons with Disabilities (2019) Strategic Plan 2017 - 2021 Promoting Inclusive and Sustainable Development. <https://www.un.org/development/desa/disabilities/wp-content/uploads/sites/15/2019/10/Zambia_DISABILITY-STRATEGIC-PLAN-2017-2021.pdf>. Accessed 15 July 2021

Zambia Civic Education Association (2012) Advancement of Children's Rights and the Education Budget in Zambia. <https://resourcecentre.savethechildren.net/node/8048/pdf/advancement_of_childrens_rights_and_the_eeducation_budget_in_zambia.pdf>. Accessed 15 July 2021

Hebert Kawadza is an Associate Professor in Banking and Finance Law in the School of Law of the University of the Witwatersrand, Johannesburg in South Africa. I hold a PhD from the University of Manchester, Masters from the University of London and an LLB (Hons) from the University of Zimbabwe. Areas of expertise include capital markets regulation, regulation of finance in emerging economies, corporate law, banking and finance law, prevention of various types of financial crimes. Have published extensively in several local and international journals. A former legal practitioner with extensive experience in various financial products and general advocacy in spheres such as the linkages between human rights, corporations and poverty. Consultant for several global financial institutions on local and international financial law.

Sharon Handongwe is vastly experienced development worker with speciality in disability inclusion. She is Zambia's Community Based Rehabilitation (CBR) representative for CBR Africa. Further, Zambia's Enhanced CBR Response coordinator and is currently attached to Cheshire Homes Society of Zambia National office as a manager.

The Prospects and Challenges for Mobile Money Regulation and the Promotion of Financial Inclusion in Zimbabwe

Howard Chitimira and Menelisi Ncube

Abstract Zimbabwe experienced a financial crisis from around 2005 to date which was characterised by hyperinflation, currency instability and a collapse of the formal financial sector. This situation has impoverished many and led to the categorisation of many people in Zimbabwe as poor, informally employed and low-income earning. Additionally, as result of this financial crisis, mobile money services like Ecocash, Telecash, Mycash and Onemoney were established. These mobile money services have substantially promoted the financial inclusion of most people in Zimbabwe to date. Mobile money services have come in handy for most informal workers who account for approximately 85% of the workers in Zimbabwe who do not have formal bank accounts. About 90% of the adult Zimbabwean population uses Ecocash for mobile money transfers and for urban to rural money remittances for family support, payment for goods and services in retail settings. Apart from Ecocash, which has various savings, investments and loan provision services, it is evident that other mobile money services in Zimbabwe like Telecash, Mycash and Onemoney do not promote savings as conventional banking institutions would. Additionally, there has been rampant misuse of mobile money services in Zimbabwe including practices of money laundering. This status quo appears to result from the lack of a legislative framework for mobile money services in Zimbabwe. To date, the Reserve Bank of Zimbabwe (RBZ) and Postal and Telecommunications Regulatory Authority of Zimbabwe (POTRAZ) are responsible for the supervision of mobile money operations in Zimbabwe and their regulation through the Statutory Instrument Banking (Money Transmission, Mobile Banking and Mobile Money Interoperability) Regulations. To this end, this research will investigate the challenges surrounding mobile money services in Zimbabwe in a bid to promote financial inclusion in Zimbabwe.

H. Chitimira (✉) · M. Ncube
Faculty of Law, North-West University, Potchefstroom, South Africa
e-mail: Howard.Chitimira@nwu.ac.za

© The Author(s), under exclusive license to Springer Nature Switzerland AG 2023
H. Chitimira, T. V. Warikandwa (eds.), *Financial Inclusion and Digital Transformation Regulatory Practices in Selected SADC Countries*, Ius Gentium: Comparative Perspectives on Law and Justice 106,
https://doi.org/10.1007/978-3-031-23863-5_6

1 Introductory Remarks

Mobile money may be defined as digital payment platform which enables financial transactions and services to be carried out using a mobile device such as a mobile phone, tablet, laptop and any other related technological gadget.[1] Mobile transactions included herein are airtime purchases, bill payments and remittances.[2] Mobile money technology has high chances for the betterment of savings mechanisms of rural people, especially where appropriate banking systems are inaccessible and unaffordable for the majority in developing countries.[3] The wide reception of mobile money technologies has generally promoted financial inclusion of most people in most global communities globally.[4]

Generally, mobile money technology has high chances of promoting saving mechanisms of rural people, especially where appropriate banking systems are inaccessible and unaffordable for the majority in developing countries.[5] In this regard, Zimbabwe is not an exception.[6] Financial consumers in Zimbabwe have, over the years, experienced challenges including hyperinflation, cash shortages, high withdrawal fees, low withdrawal limits and the mistrust of the formal banking sector.[7] As a result of this, most people have been left unemployed, impoverished and engaged in informal trading for sustenance in Zimbabwe.[8] To this end, mobile money services have come in handy to the populace of Zimbabwe in enabling the swift and convenient transfer of money for mostly urban to rural money remittances in line with family support and the payment for goods and services in retail settings.[9] In 2019, from 1 billion payment transactions that were made in Zimbabwe, 85.33% were carried out through mobile money platforms.[10] In the same year, the number of active mobile phone subscribers increased exponentially. This goes to say that about 13.2 million out of a total population of approximately 15 million (equivalent to 88% of the population) had mobile cellular subscriptions whilst the internet penetration rate was 59.8% in Zimbabwe.[11] This suggests that mobile money services have been widely adopted by most financial consumers and are most likely to promote financial inclusion for the poor, informally employed and low-income earners in Zimbabwe. Poor people and low-income earners are referred to those individuals who sustain

---

[1] Asongu (2021), p. 2; Donovan (2012), pp. 61–62.

[2] Tengeh and Talom (2020), pp. 5; Shrier (2016), pp. 2–23.

[3] Nan et al. (2020), pp. 1–2; Batista and Vicente (2020), pp. 1–2.

[4] Ahmad et al. (2020), pp. 755–756; Madise (2019), pp. 99; Qureshi (2020), p. 211.

[5] Akinyemi and Mushunje (2020), p. 4; Mhlanga and Denhere (2020), p. 40.

[6] Mazambani et al. (2018), p. 132; Murendo et al. (2021), p. 87; Kabala et al. (2021), p. 60.

[7] Simatele and Mbedzi (2021), p. 6; Dumbu (2018), p. 30.

[8] Dzawanda et al. (2021), p. 2; Hove (2017), pp. 46–47.

[9] Simatele and Mbedzi (2021), p. 6; Ngwenya et al. (2018), p. 14.

[10] Maune et al. (2020), pp. 195, 198.

[11] Simatele (2021), p. 5; Ngondo (2019), p. 7.

their livelihoods under what is considered as the Total Consumption Poverty Line.[12] However, several factors negatively affect the optimum operation of mobile money in Zimbabwe. These include poor internet network coverage in some rural areas, illiteracy of some adults, electricity outrages and low-income levels.[13]

Notably, mobile money is a contemporary technological development which has revolutionised and made banking practices more convenient to financial consumers while promoting financial inclusion of the poor, informally employed and low-income earners in Zimbabwe.[14] This follows the fact that conventional banking mostly involved transacting and/or the transferring money physically from the banks whilst mobile money enables a person to transfer money instantly and anywhere globally through the use of a mobile phone or computer that is connected to the Internet.[15] Financial inclusion is generally defined by numerous scholars as the development and provision of affordable and suitable financial products and services to all persons in a country by the relevant government, banks and other related role-players.[16] Inversely, financial exclusion refers to the lack of access by some individuals in any given country to common, suitable and affordable financial services including savings accounts, loans, cashless transactions, credit, and other related traditional banking services.[17] Financial inclusion plays a pivotal role in curbing the growth of informal sources of finance which often tend to be exploitative to the poor, informally employed and the low-income earners as has been the case in Zimbabwe.[18] Therefore, there is a need to robustly promote financial inclusion by the Reserve Bank of Zimbabwe (RBZ) and other relevant bodies in Zimbabwe.

2 Historical Aspects of Mobile Money in Zimbabwe

The Zimbabwe telecommunications industry commenced operations in 1996 with the establishment of NetOne, a private limited telecommunications company largely owned by the government of Zimbabwe (GoZ).[19] Later on in 1996, Telecel was established as another telecommunications services provider which was largely also owned by the GoZ in Zimbabwe.[20] In 1998, Econet Wireless Zimbabwe was established as a privately owned telecommunications company in Zimbabwe.[21]

---

[12]ZimStats (2021), p. 1.

[13]Coulibaly (2021), p. 18; Chitimira and Torerai (2021), p. 6.

[14]Bara (2013), pp. 345–346.

[15]Chaimaa et al. (2021), p. 1060.

[16]Chitimira and Ncube (2021b), pp. 67–68; Senyo and Osabutey (2020), p. 2.

[17]Ozili (2021), pp. 4–7; Ababio et al. (2019), p. 44.

[18]Dube and Chummun (2019), p. 421; Nyagadza (2019), p. 2; Zikhali (2020), pp. 11–12.

[19]Marumbwa (2014), p. 73.

[20]Marumbwa (2014), p. 73.

[21]Marumbwa (2014), p. 73.

Even to date, Netone, Telecel and Econet Wireless Zimbabwe are the providers of telecommunication services in Zimbabwe. However, the inception of mobile money services in Zimbabwe can be traced back to 2011.[22] This follows the establishment of NetOne's OneWallet/OneMoney, Telecel's Skwama, and Econet's EcoCash as mobile money services in Zimbabwe.[23] OneWallet provides a mobile money platform for sending and receiving money, payment for various utility bills and airtime purchase in Zimbabwe.[24] Telecash is a mobile money service which allows Telecel mobile phone users to deposit money (physical cash) through an agent, bank, or Telecel shop into a Telecash account.[25] Consequently, such deposited money becomes e-money which can be transferred electronically to other mobile phone users without the need to visit any bank.[26] EcoCash is a mobile money service platform which allows users to perform financial transactions including sending money, buying prepaid airtime or data and paying for goods and services.[27]

According to a financial consumer survey conducted by the RBZ in 2014, 22% of Zimbabweans were financially excluded adult Zimbabweans.[28] Out of these, 30% had access to and utilised formal banking services whilst only 20% were using formal savings channels in Zimbabwe. By 2016 however, mobile money users in Zimbabwe increased exponentially owing to the crisis of hyperinflation and the subsequent cash shortages.[29] In 2018, mobile phone usage had reached about 93% equally increasing the levels of mobile money services in Zimbabwe.[30] Notably, it appears that most people living in rural areas of Zimbabwe who make up a bulk of the unbanked persons in Zimbabwe have largely adopted mobile money services for carrying important transactions like buying essential goods and services.[31] This position has also been promoted by the poor expansion of banking institutions and related automatic teller machines (ATM) into rural areas in Zimbabwe.[32] In light of the above, it remains a great concern to the RBZ and other relevant bodies to tackle challenges which affect the optimum adoption of mobile money services in Zimbabwe. It is submitted that robust measures by the RBZ and other relevant bodies aimed at addressing the financial exclusion of most people who in any case, reside in

---

[22] Gupta and Thakur (2020), p. 5.

[23] Kufandirimbwa et al. (2013), pp. 96; 259.

[24] Moyo et al. (2017), p. 750.

[25] Moyo et al. (2017), p. 750.

[26] Moyo et al. (2017), p. 750.

[27] Robb (2017), p. 219; EcoCash *EcoCash* https://www.ecocash.co.zw/about accessed 14 July 2021-page number unknown.

[28] Reserve Bank of Zimbabwe (2016), p. 65; Nyanhete (2017), p. 257.

[29] Mavaza (2019), p. 6; Bara and LeRoux (2018), p. 230.

[30] Gukurume and Mahiya (2020), pp. 1203–1204.

[31] Gukurume and Mahiya (2020), pp. 1203–1204.

[32] Gukurume and Mahiya (2020), p. 1205; Muzurura and Chigora (2019), p. 331.

the rural parts of Zimbabwe,[33] has the potential to achieve optimum levels of financial inclusion especially in line with the Zimbabwe Vision 2030 in Zimbabwe.

3 The Regulatory Framework for Mobile Money in Zimbabwe

To date, there is no express legislation that regulates mobile money services in Zimbabwe.[34] This position stems from the fact that mobile money services involve the financial sector and the telecommunications sector which are distinctly regulated in Zimbabwe.[35] As an example, monetary aspects of mobile money services involve prudential regulation which is often concerned with promoting systemic and market related controls in order to preserve a functional banking sector as a whole.[36] Prudential regulation is mostly concerned with banking institutions' adherence to adequate minimum capital measures, sufficient credit control risks to avoid their insolvency which would otherwise affect the entire banking sector.[37] On the other hand, the use of mobile networks in mobile money services involves the regulation of the telecommunications sector which is mostly concerned with laws that govern the exchange of information over significant distances by electronic means, often referring to all types of voice, data and video transmission.[38] Such information transmitting devices include cell phones, microwave communications, fiber optics, satellites, radio and television broadcasting, the Internet and telegraphs.[39] The laws regulating the conduct of banking institutions in Zimbabwe including the Reserve Bank of Zimbabwe Act[40] and the Banking Act[41] do not explicitly provide for the regulation of mobile money services in Zimbabwe.

Companies which carry on telecommunication business in Zimbabwe like NetOne, Telecel and Econet Wireless Zimbabwe are supervised by the Postal and Telecommunications Authority of Zimbabwe (POTRAZ).[42] Although the RBZ is the apex regulator of the financial sector of Zimbabwe to date,[43] there is no express

---

[33] Maune et al. (2020), pp.198–200.

[34] Chitimira and Torerai (2021), p. 5; Mbengo and Phiri (2015), p. 198.

[35] See related discussion by Chibango (2014), p. 65; Chitimira and Torerai (2021), p. 11.

[36] See related discussion by Ahmad et al. (2020), p. 772; Chitimira and Torerai (2021), p. 11.

[37] See evidence from the global financial crisis as according to Hlaing and Kakinaka (2018) pp. 225–226; Cargill (2017), p. 188; Almaw (2020), p. 1364.

[38] Paelo and Robb (2020), pp. 3–4.

[39] Singh (2020), p. 228.

[40] Reserve Bank of Zimbabwe Act 5 [Chapter 22:15] of 1999 (RBZ Act), see s6 on the functions of the RBZ Act.

[41] Banking Act 9 [Chapter 24:20] of 1999 (Banking Act), see long title of the Banking Act.

[42] Chigwende and Govender (2020), pp. 80–81.

[43] Section 6 of the RBZ Act.

provision in the RBZ Act which mandates the RBZ to regulate mobile money network operators who conduct the mobile money business. However, the RBZ is, by virtue of its powers in the issuance of licensing to anybody or person offering banking services in Zimbabwe, responsible for issuing operating licences to mobile money service providers in Zimbabwe.[44] The National Payments System Division within the RBZ is responsible for the regulation of mobile money services under the auspices of the National Payment System Act in Zimbabwe.[45] Additionally, the NPSA also does not expressly mention the regulation of mobile money services as inference is drawn from the fact that mobile money services also fall into the category of payments and settlements system regulated by the NPSA. The RBZ seems to follow a bank-based model on the regulation of mobile money products and innovations, even for those which are offered by non-bank institutions like NetOne, Telecel and Econet.[46] In context, a bank-based model in this regard refers the regulation of banking institutions in the traditional manner not including telecommunication organisations providing banking products and services to financial consumers. In this way, the RBZ only regulates the risk management and compliance aspects of mobile money when regulating mobile money services in Zimbabwe.[47] This means that the RBZ does not possess any regulatory powers of mobile money service providers in Zimbabwe.

However, guidelines established by the RBZ in 2020, assert some level of regulation of mobile money services and seem to promote financial inclusion of all including the poor, informally employed and low income-earners in Zimbabwe.[48] As an example, the Banking Regulations of 2020[49] requires that all money transmission providers and mobile banking providers money transmission rendering money transmission services and mobile banking to be registered under the Postal and Telecommunication Act.[50] Additionally, the Banking Regulations of 2020[51] obligates all mobile money providers to be connected to a national payment switch in order to afford easy surveillance to the RBZ in the transactions carried out by mobile money service providers in Zimbabwe. Moreover, the Banking Regulations of 2020[52] imposes an embargo on levying, amending or reviewing any mobile

---

[44] Section 6 of the RBZ Act.

[45] National Payment System Act 21 [Chapter 24:23] of 2001 (NPSA), ss 3–10; Simatele and Mbedzi (2021), p. 6.

[46] Bara (2013), p. 347.

[47] Bara (2013), p. 347.

[48] See sections 3-5 of the Banking (Money Transmission, Mobile Banking and Mobile Money Interoperability) Regulations, 2020 (Banking Regulations of 2020); Chitimira and Torerai (2021), p. 15.

[49] Section 3 of the Banking Regulations of 2020; see related discussion by Chitimira and Torerai (2021), p. 15.

[50] Postal and Telecommunications Act 4 [Chapter 12:05] of 2000 (Postal and Telecommunications Act), see section 4(d).

[51] Section 4 of the Banking Regulations of 2020.

[52] Section 5 of the Banking Regulations of 2020.

money transaction charges by a mobile money service provider without the prior consent of the RBZ in Zimbabwe. This is perhaps a safeguard against the undue levying, amending or reviewing any mobile money transaction charges by mobile money service providers to the prejudice of mobile money users.

Notably, Banking Regulations of 2020,[53] introduced interoperability which currently allows for transactions to be carried out across different mobile different mobile money service providers unlike the position in the past wherein transactions could only be done between users of the same mobile money service provider. It could be said that such interoperability between mobile money service providers has improved convenience in mobile money usage and promoted some sense of financial inclusivity among financial users in Zimbabwe. The researchers submit that there is a need to enact comprehensive legislation to incorporate both aspects of mobile money which are; banking and telecommunication. Mobile money usage is a growing practice globally which serves to alleviate the financial exclusion of many especially people living in poor communities. Thus, there is need for Zimbabwe to enact legislation that will regulate mobile money services comprehensively. Perhaps the establishment of a division within the RBZ to specifically and strictly supervise the functioning of mobile money services in Zimbabwe in order to achieve optimum financial inclusion for all especially the poor, informally employed and low-income earners in Zimbabwe is necessary.

4   The Regulatory Framework for Financial Inclusion in Zimbabwe

The promotion of financial inclusion for the poor, informally employed and low-income earners is not expressly provided in any laws in Zimbabwe. However in 2016, the Ministry of Finance and Economic Development launched the National Financial Inclusion Strategy (NFIS) from 2016 to 2020.[54] Primarily, the NFIS sought to expand financial consumer education and increase the overall access of formal financial services from 69% in 2014 to at least 90% by 2020 in Zimbabwe.[55] The NFIS sought to achieve 90% formal financial access by increasing the proportion of banked adults from 30% in 2014 to at least 60% by 2020.[56] To this end, the GoZ established the Zimbabwe Women's Micro-Finance Bank which sought to reduce the inequalities of female adults in line with promoting financial inclusion in Zimbabwe.[57] Therefore varied financial products including joint liability group loans,   group   savings,   micro-farming   loans/micro-enterprising   loans   and

---

[53] Section 2 of the Banking Regulations of 2020.

[54] Ngoma (2019), pp. 78–79.

[55] Chitiyo (2016), p. 18.

[56] Reserve Bank of Zimbabwe (2017), p. 32.

[57] Siwela (2021), pp. 66–69; Chivasa and Simbanegavi (2016), p. 54.

non-financial services including business management training, financial education were offered to qualifying women by the Zimbabwe Women's Micro-Finance Bank.[58] Notably, the Zimbabwe Women's Micro-Finance Bank facilitated financial inclusion by decentralising the banking system so that it becomes accessible to the majority of informally employed women who reside in the rural areas and carry out numerous economic activities to earn a living.[59]

Consequently, women's access to bank credit improved by 39% while direct loans to women from banks increased 12% from 2017 to 2018 in Zimbabwe.[60] The above shows that the GoZ made commendable efforts in improving the financial inclusion of women in Zimbabwe from 2017 to 2018. Likewise, mobile phone usage had reached about 93% of the total population of Zimbabwe by 2018,[61] while financial inclusion in the form of new bank accounts for adults increased exponentially from 1.5 million in 2016 to 8.5 million in 2020.[62] The above statistics evidently show a commendable increase in the financial inclusion of people in Zimbabwe during the stated period. However, the receipt and adoption of other facets of financial inclusion (especially in savings for longer periods and credit acquisition by financial consumers in Zimbabwe during the same period) remained low. This status quo stemmed from the lack of collateral, documentation and other prerequisites required under the Know-Your-Client (KYC) regulations by most financial consumers to acquire loans from banks in Zimbabwe.

5 Factors Influencing the Contemporary Challenges of Financial Exclusion in Zimbabwe

Numerous impediments currently hinder the optimum reception and adoption of mobile money services for the promotion of financial inclusion of many informally employed, poor and low-income earning people in Zimbabwe. Firstly, a comprehensive definition of financial inclusion involves making sure that all initiatives that make formal financial services such as savings, credit, payment and risk management products (like interest rate swap) that are available, accessible and affordable to everyone in any given country.[63] In this regard, for as long as the poor, informally employed and low-income earners in Zimbabwe fail to make use of some mobile money services like accessing credit through mobile money and long term saving, they remain financially excluded.[64] While mobile money has received wide

---

[58] Reserve Bank of Zimbabwe (2021), pp. 42–43; Tarinda (2019), p. 8.

[59] Tarinda (2019), p. 8.

[60] Tarinda (2019), p. 15.

[61] Tarinda (2019), p. 15.

[62] Hawthorne et al. (2020), p. 12.

[63] Ozili (2021), pp. 251–260, 252–254.

[64] Reserve Bank of Zimbabwe (2016), p. 16; Ngoma (2019), pp. 78–79.

coverage amongst adults in Zimbabwe, subscribers tend to underutilise some services offered by the mobile money service providers as the majority only uses it simply for sending or receiving money.[65] It is submitted that the use of mobile money for saving and loan acquisition is not very popular. The images below illustrate the use of mobile money services in Zimbabwe.

Figure 1 is a screenshot from Ecocash mobile money services. Figure 1 depicts the landing page for EcoCash. From it, it is evident that currently, Ecocash does not offer any loan related service to financial consumers affiliated to the mobile money service. On the other hand, Fig. 1 also shows that Ecocash provides a savings service (Kashagi Savings Club) which is also shown in Fig. 2. However, this savings service does not offer interest on savings to financial consumers use it. Moreso, the savings option does not deter the premature withdrawal of savings as conventional banking methods would through charging hefty penalties for such practices. As a result, a

Fig. 1 Landing Page on EcoCash. Source: Authors' compilation based on the EcoCash Mobile Money Application

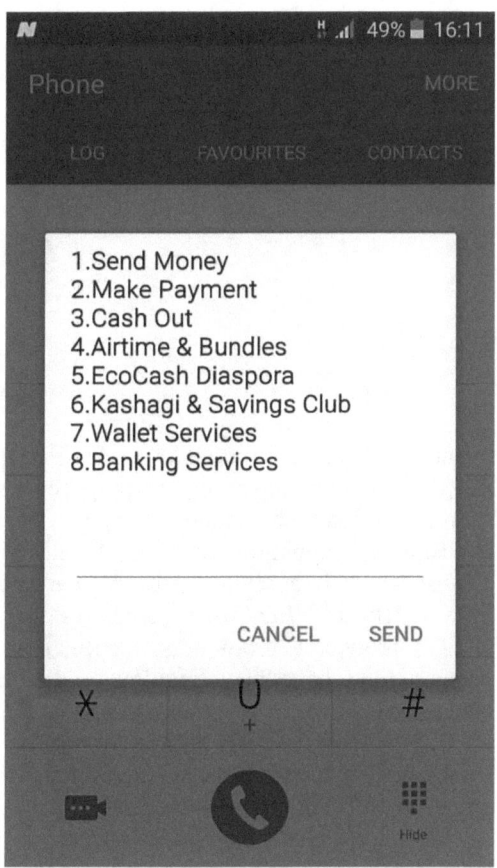

---

[65] Ngoma (2019), pp. 78–79.

Fig. 2 Landing Page on
EcoCash Kashagi and
EcoCash Savings Club.
Source: Authors'
compilation based on the
EcoCash Mobile Money
Application

financial consumer can transfer money into the savings account and withdraw it at
any time thereby subverting the purpose of saving. In this regard, the researchers
submit that Ecocash mobile money service does not optimally promote financial
inclusion in Zimbabwe. In 2013, Econet Wireless introduced the EcoCashSave
service which is a savings account that operates under Econet Wireless's bank;
Steward Bank.[66] EcoCashSave allows the mobile service user to save money
without producing proof of residence, payslip or any other form of paperwork
which would have been required under the KYC formalities in Zimbabwean
banks.[67] However, it is worth noting that EcoCashSave is not directly linked with
EcoCash. Figure 3 shows the varied mobile money services offered by OneMoney.
From Fig. 3, it is apparent that OneMoney mobile service is a payment and receipt of
money mobile money service. This means that OneMoney does not provide any
savings and/or credit facilities for users in Zimbabwe. As a result, the researchers

---

[66] Mago and Chitokwindo (2014), p. 223.

[67] Shambira (2020), p. 121; Chitimira and Torerai (2021), p. 7.

Fig. 3 Landing Page on
OneMoney Service. Source:
Authors' compilation based
on the OneMoney Service

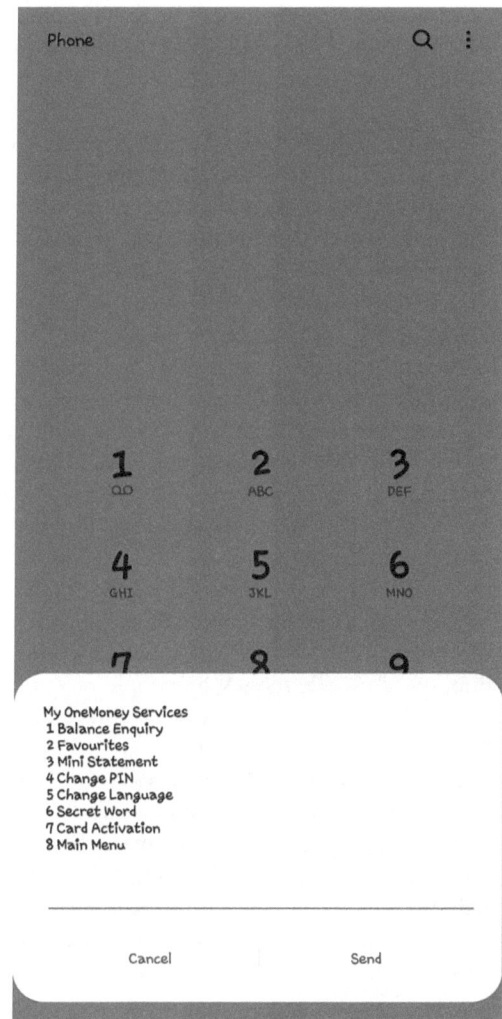

submit that mobile money in Zimbabwe does not optimally provide for the financial inclusion of the poor, informally employed and low-income persons.

Secondly, there seems to be no legislation that expressly regulates mobile money in Zimbabwe to date.[68] Chitimira and Torerai opine that a myriad of incoherent laws are used to regulate and supervise innovative financial services and products in Zimbabwe.[69] There is thus a need for the enactment and robust enforcement of legislation specifically and expressly regulating mobile money services in Zimbabwe. This follows the case in point wherein RBZ suspended some Ecocash agents. In

---

[68] Shambira (2020), p. 121; Chitimira and Torerai (2021), p. 7.

[69] Chitimira and Torerai (2021), p. 11.

casu, it was alleged that some Ecocash agents were creating fictitious mobile money platforms which converted such mobile money into cash in order to facilitate the purchasing of foreign currency on the black market and to launder the money out of Zimbabwe.[70]

Thirdly, mobile money payments are not widely accepted by some service providers in Zimbabwe as currently, the ZUPCO bus company (which is currently the sole authorised local public transporter) does not allow mobile money payments from passengers. As a result of this, financial consumers have to withdraw cash for from mobile money agents in order to pay for such services in Zimbabwe. What exacerbates this position is the fact that due to scarcity of hard currency in Zimbabwe to date, mobile money agents illicitly charge commission rates of up to about 40% of the money withdrawn.

Furthermore, since mobile money services utilise electricity for network boosters, electricity outrages which are often rampant in Zimbabwe hinder the efficient use of mobile money services in Zimbabwe thereby perpetuating financial exclusion of some people in Zimbabwe.[71] It is submitted that electricity challenges must be resolved by the GoZ in order to allow the consistent operation of mobile money services in order to help bolster financial inclusion for those people staying in rural areas.

Moreover, limits in payments allowable and set by mobile money service providers ostensibly to curb money laundering further hinder the efficient use and adoption of mobile money by people in Zimbabwe. Such limits result in challenges to financial consumers as at times, necessary basic needs cannot be purchased at once. The researchers submit that this position is merely caused by the poor regulation of mobile money services in Zimbabwe than a measure to curb money laundering. At the time of conducting tis research, EcoCash had a one-time transactional limit of $5000 Zimbabwean Dollars (ZWL) for sending money but they were lifted to $20,000 ZWL for bill payments and merchant payments.[72] This position prejudices financial consumers who would otherwise wish to transact more than this amount as such consumers will have to incur more charges in excess transactions.

6   Concluding Remarks

This chapter has discussed the reception of mobile money for the promotion of financial inclusion in Zimbabwe. To date, it is evident that optimum levels of financial inclusion have not yet been achieved in Zimbabwe. As a result, this research recommends firstly, the enactment of enabling legislation for mobile

---

[70] Zikhali (2020), p. 13; Chitimira and Ncube (2021a), p. 10.

[71] Muparadzi and Rodze (2021), p. 1177.

[72] Dzoma (2021).

money services in order to improve the regulation of mobile money services in Zimbabwe. Additionally, this research recommends the strict enforcement of such enacted mobile money services' legislation in order to curb the illicit practices of some unscrupulous mobile money agents who overcharge financial consumers due to cash shortages often leading to the commodification of cash in Zimbabwe. Moreover, the regulators of mobile money services need to constantly and reasonably review limits for one-time transactions of consumers. This will aid in matching the cost of the basic needs of consumers with such limits in order to curb the burden of charges per transaction otherwise incurred by consumers for numerous transactions aimed at acquiring sufficient basic needs. It is hoped that these recommendations will enhance financial inclusion for all people in Zimbabwe especially the poor, informally employed and low-income earners.

Bibliography

Ababio JO et al (2019) Financial inclusion and human development in frontier countries. Int J Finance Econ 42–59

Ahmad AA, Green C, Jiang F (2020) Mobile money, financial inclusion and development: a review with reference to african experience. J Econ Surv 753–792

Akinyemi BE, Mushunje A (2020) Determinants of mobile money technology adoption in rural areas of Africa. Cogent Soc Sci 6:1–21

Asongu SA, Agyemang-Mintah P, Nting RT (2021) Law, mobile money drivers and mobile money innovations in developing countries. Technol Forecast Soc Change 1–9

Banking (Money Transmission, Mobile Banking and Mobile Money Interoperability) Regulations, 2020

Banking Act 9 [Chapter 24:20] of 1999

Bara A (2013) Mobile Money for Financial Inclusion: Policy and Regulatory Perspective in Zimbabwe. Afr J Sci Technol Innov Dev 5:345–354

Bara A, LeRoux P (2018) Technology, financial innovations and bank behavior in a low-income country. J Econ Behav Stud 10:221–234

Batista C, Vicente PC (2020) Adopting mobile money: evidence from an experiment in rural Africa. Institute of Labor Economics Discussion Paper, pp 1–11

Cargill TF (2017) The Financial System, Financial Regulation and Central Bank Policy 1st edn. Cambridge University Press

Chaimaa B, Najib E, Rachid H (2021) E-banking overview: concepts, challenges and solutions. Wireless Personal Commun 117:1059–1078

Chibango C (2014) Mobile money revolution: an opportunity for financial inclusion in Africa. Int J Human Soc Stud 2:59–67

Chigwende S, Govender K (2020) Corporate brand image and switching behavior: case of mobile telecommunications customers in Zimbabwe. Innov Market 16:80–90

Chitimira H, Ncube M (2021a) Towards ingenious technology and the robust enforcement of financial markets laws to curb money laundering in Zimbabwe. PER/PELJ 24:1–47

Chitimira H, Ncube M (2021b) Overview legislative flaws hampering the promotion of financial inclusion for the poor and low-income earners in South Africa. Interdiscip J Bus Econ Law 10: 67–87

Chitimira H, Torerai E (2021) The Nexus between mobile money regulation, innovative technology and the promotion of financial inclusion in Zimbabwe. PER/PELJ 24:1–33

Chitiyo K, Vines A, Vandome C (2016) The domestic and external implications of Zimbabwe's economic reform and re-engagement Agenda. Chatham House Working Paper 1–48

Coulibaly SS (2021) A study of the factors affecting mobile money penetration rates in the West African economic and Monetary Union (WAEMU) compared with East Africa. Financ Innov 7: 1–26

Donovan K (2012) Mobile money for financial inclusion. The World Bank Information and Communications for Development 61–73

Dube T, Chummun BZ (2019) Effects of mobile money usage on rural consumers' Livelihoods in Zimbabwe. Afr Rev Econ Finance 11:420–454

Dumbu E (2018) Banking the unbanked: perceptions of the international cross border women entrepreneurs in Beitbridge, Zimbabwe. London J Res Manage Bus 18:23–32

Dzawanda B et al (2021) Impact of virtual cash economy on livelihood outcomes of informal cross border traders in Gweru, Zimbabwe. J Borderlands Stud 1–19

Dzoma G (2021) Ecocash Calculator, Fees and Limits-November 2021. https://www.google.com/search?client=firefox-b-d&q=Ecocash+transactional+limit. Accessed 20 Nov 2021

EcoCash *EcoCash* (year unknown) https://www.ecocash.co.zw/about accessed 14 July 2021 page number unknown

Gukurume S, Mahiya IT (2020) Mobile money and the (Un) making of social relations in Chivi, Zimbabwe. J South Afr Stud 1203–1217

Gupta S, Thakur KS (2020) Performance evaluation of financial inclusion in India: with special reference to Pradhan Mantri Jan Dhan Yojana (PMJDY). In: Innovation and emerging trends in business management and information technology. Jiwaji University May 2020 India, 1–23

Hawthorne R et al (2020) Zimbabwe: Financial Inclusion Refresh. FinMark Trust 1–102

Hove M (2017) Endangered human security in cash strapped Zimbabwe, 2007–2008. Afr Stud Q 17:45–65

Kabala E et al (2021) An ethnological analysis of the influence of mobile money on financial inclusion: the case of Urban Zambia. Zambia Soc Sci J 7:53–76

Kakinaka M (2018) Financial crisis and financial policy reform: crisis origins and policy dimensions. Eur J Polit Econ 55:224–243

Kufandirimbwa O et al (2013) Mobile money in Zimbabwe: integrating mobile infrastructure and processes to organisation infrastructure and processes. Online J Soc Sci Res 2:92–110

Madise S (2019) The regulation of mobile money: law and practice in Sub-Saharan Africa, 1st edn. The Palgrave Macmillan Studies in Banking and Financial Institutions

Marumbwa J (2014) Exploring the moderating effects of socio-demographic variables on consumer acceptance and use of mobile money transfer services (MMTs) in Southern Zimbabwe. Am J Ind Bus Manage 4:71–79

Maune A, Matanda E, Mundonde J (2020) Does financial inclusion cause economic growth in Zimbabwe? An empirical investigation. Acta Universitatis Danubius Œconomica 16:195–215

Mavaza T (2019) E-banking adoption by Zimbabwe banks: an exploratory study. PM World J 8:1–10

Mazambani L, Rushwaya TJ Mutambara E (2018) Financial inclusion: disrupted liquidity and redundancy of mobile money agents in Zimbabwe. Investment Manage Financ Innov, pp 131–142

Mbengo P, Phiri MA (2015) Mobile banking adoption: a rural Zimbabwean marketing perspective. Corp Ownership Control 13:195–204

Mhlanga D, Denhere V (2020) Determinants of financial inclusion in Southern Africa. Studia Universitatis Babes-Bolyai Oeconomica 65:39–52

Moyo M et al (2017) Irrigation development in Zimbabwe: understanding productivity barriers and opportunities at Mkoba and Silalatshani irrigation schemes. Int J Water Resour Dev 33:740–754

Muparadzi T, Rodze L (2021) Business continuity management in a time of crisis: emerging trends for commercial banks in Zimbabwe during and post the covid-19 global crisis. Open J Bus Manage 9:1169–1197

Murendo C et al (2021) Financial inclusion, nutrition and socio-economic status among rural households in Guruve and Mount Darwin Districts, Zimbabwe. J Int Dev 33:86–108

Muzurura J, Chigora F (2019) Consumers' behavioural intention to adopt mobile banking in rural Sub-Saharan Africa using an extension of technology acceptance model: lessons from Zimbabwe. Int J Bus Econ Manage 6:316–334

Nan WV, Zhu XC, Markus ML (2020) What we know and don't know about the socioeconomic impacts of mobile money in Sub-Saharan Africa: a systematic literature review. Electr J Inform Syst Dev Countr 1–22

National Payment System Act 21 [Chapter 24:23] of 2001

Ngoma G (2019) Financial inclusion and its determinants in Zimbabwe. Int J Innov Res Multidiscip Field 5:78–87

Ngondo PS (2019) An exploratory study: digital and social media use by Zimbabwean public relations practitioners. Public Relat J 12:1–26

Nyagadza B (2019) Conceptual model for financial inclusion development through agency banking in competitive markets. Africanus: J Dev Stud 49:1–22

Nyanhete A (2017) The role of international mobile remittances in promoting financial inclusion and development. Eur J Sustain Dev 6:256–266

Nyoni T, Bonga WG (2017) Cashless transacting economy: a necessary evil for development! A Zimbabwean Scenario!. Dyn Res J 2:1–10

Ozili PK (2021) Financial inclusion-exclusion paradox: how banked adults become unbanked again. Financ Internet Q 1–13

Paelo A, Robb G (2020) Comparative approaches to key issues in the economic regulation of telecommunications markets in South Africa, Tanzania, Zambia, and Zimbabwe. United Nations University World Institute for Development Economics Research, pp 1–28

Postal and Telecommunications Act 4 [Chapter 12:05] of 2000

Reserve Bank of Zimbabwe (2016) Reserve Bank of Zimbabwe 2014 Annual Report. Reserve Bank of Zimbabwe, pp 1–71

Reserve Bank of Zimbabwe (2021) Zimbabwe National Financial Inclusion Journey 2016–2020. Reserve Bank of Zimbabwe Report 1–148

Reserve Bank of Zimbabwe Act 5 [Chapter 22:15] of 1999

Robb G, Tausha I, Vilakazi T (2017) Competition and regulation in Zimbabwe's emerging mobile payments markets. In: Klaaren J, Roberts S, Valodia I (eds) Competition law and economic regulation in Southern Africa, 1st edn. Wits University Press, pp 215–233

Senyo PK, Osabutey ELC (2020) Unearthing antecedents to financial inclusion through FinTech innovations. Technovation, pp 1–16

Shambira L (2020) Exploring the adoption of artificial intelligence in the Zimbabwe banking sector. Eur J Soc Sci Stud 5:110–124

Shrier D (2016) Mobile money & payments: technology trends. In: Shrier D, Canale G, Pentland A (eds) Mobile money & payments technology trends. Massachusetts Institute of Technology, pp 2–27

Simatele M (2021) E-Payment instruments and welfare: the case of Zimbabwe. J Transdiscip Res South Afr 17:1–11

Simatele M, Mbedzi E (2021) Consumer payment choices, costs, and risks: evidence from Zimbabwe. Cogent Econ Finance, 1–23

Singh AK (2020) Digital Era in the Kingdom of Saudi Arabia: novel strategies of the telecom service providers companies. Webology 17:227–245

Siwela G (2021) Opportunities and challenges for digital financial inclusion of females in the informal sector through mobile phone technology: evidence from Zimbabwe. Int J Econ Commer Manage 9:60, 66–69

Tarinda S (2019) Gender, women's economic empowerment and financial inclusion in Zimbabwe. Alliance Financ Inclusion, 1–22

Tengeh RK, Talom FSG (2020) Mobile money as a sustainable alternative for SMEs in less developed financial markets. J Open Innov Technol Mark Compl, 1–21

Zikhali W (2020) Changing money, changing fortunes: experiences of money changers in Nkayi Zimbabwe. Canadian J Afr Stud 1–19

ZimStats (26 July 2021) Poverty Datum Lines – July 2021. *ZimStats*

Howard Chitimira (co-editor of the book) - Howard Chitimira is a full Professor of Law and Research Professor at the Faculty of Law, North-West University. He is also an advocate of the High Court of South Africa and a National Research Foundation (NRF) rated legal scholar. Prof Chitimira holds the degrees Bachelor of Laws (LLB) (Cum Laude) from the University of Fort Hare (UFH); Master of Laws (LLM) from UFH and Doctor of Laws (LLD) from the Nelson Mandela Metropolitan University (NMMU). For his doctorate, he specialised in securities and financial markets law. To date, he has published three books and over 50 journal articles in this field. Prof Chitimira is a reviewer and editorial board member of several law journals in South Africa and elsewhere, as well as an external examiner for LLB, LLM and LLD degrees at several universities. He serves on editorial boards of journals and a member of several academic and related associations. For instance, Prof Chitimira is an assistant editor of the Potchefstroom Electronic Law Journal and an editorial board member of the Journal of Corporate & Commercial Law & Practice. He has acted a guest editor for the Interdisciplinary Journal of Economics and Business Law and the Namibia Law Journal. He was appointed by the Academy of Science of South Africa (ASSAF) on behalf of the Department of Higher Education and Training (DHET) to serve on an ad hoc ASSAF Consensus Panel to peer review new applications and re-applications of journals for DHET accreditation on 11 October 2019. To date, he has delivered numerous keynote speeches on Securities and Financial Markets Law in South Africa and elsewhere. Prof Chitimira was invited to comment on the Financial Action Task Force's Recommendation 1 on Risk-Based Measures to Proliferation Financing in August 2020. He successfully launched the annual Corporate and Financial Markets Law Conference in 2019.

Menelisi Ncube completed his primary and high school in Bulawayo Zimbabwe. Thereafter in 2014, he enrolled for an LLB Degree at the North-West University in South Africa. He completed it in 2017 and pursued his Master of Laws (LLM) in Mercantile Law at North-West University in 2018, which he completed in the same year. Currently, he is a 3rd year LLD candidate in Mercantile Law at the North West University and involved in a number of mercantile law related book and article writing related projects. Menelisi is a multi-facetted, self-motivated, dedicated and enthusiastic young man. As part of his University life, he has been involved in; *inter alia*, numerous community outreach projects under the banner of Golden Key International Honour Society where he served as a President in the North West University Mafikeng Chapter in 2019. Additionally, he volunteered as a student legal advisor at the North West University Community Law Centre in 2016. Menelisi's academic and professional interests are with company law, insolvency law, banking law, intellectual property law, civil litigation, and some related aspects of competition law. Against this background, Menelisi has presented in various academic and/or colloquiums, which have improved his writing and presentation skills in law related subjects. Furthermore, Menelisi was a temporary lecturer at the North West University in the field of law of contracts and introduction to company/entrepreneurial law. Above all, Menelisi is an aspiring renowned academic who has, to date, co-authored numerous articles that have been published in both internationally and nationally accredited journals.

Land Reform and Financial Inclusion Challenges in South Africa

Clemence Rusenga and Emmanuel Ndhlovu

Abstract This chapter addresses the experiences of land reform beneficiaries in South Africa, in relation to financial in/exclusion. It highlights that the government largely subject land reform beneficiaries to agricultural production within a costly agribusiness model without adequate access to financial and material resources. The chapter notes that black farmers continue to face obstacles when trying to access financial services, including within government agencies responsible for supporting agricultural development. Both public and private agencies are biased towards large-scale commercial producers in their distribution of financial resources and support. Consequently, land beneficiaries' production is negatively affected by lack of resources, affecting access to better-rewarding markets and their income. Using a case study from the Limpopo province of South Africa, the chapter provides empirical evidence demonstrating how financial exclusion negatively impacts the livelihoods of land beneficiaries. The argument is that a combination of financial exclusion and effects of the imposed costly agribusiness model promoting large-scale production have undermined the production and livelihoods of land beneficiaries.

1 Introduction

The land and agrarian reforms in South Africa have been acknowledged as critical for rural development, livelihoods and economic transformation.[1] In its land reform policy, the post-apartheid government committed itself to, *inter alia*, redistribute

---

[1] Department of Land Affairs (DLA) (1997), p. 24.

C. Rusenga (✉)
School for Policy Studies, University of Bristol, Bristol, UK

E. Ndhlovu
Vaal University of Technology, Vanderbijlpark, South Africa

© The Author(s), under exclusive license to Springer Nature Switzerland AG 2023   141
H. Chitimira, T. V. Warikandwa (eds.), *Financial Inclusion and Digital Transformation Regulatory Practices in Selected SADC Countries*, Ius Gentium: Comparative Perspectives on Law and Justice 106,
https://doi.org/10.1007/978-3-031-23863-5_7

land to formerly disadvantaged black Africans as part of its poverty reduction strategy. While literature on the potential impacts of land reform on the broader economy abounds,[2] there is limited focus on financial inclusion in the context of land reform. This key element in political economy of agrarian transformation is overshadowed by debates on dynamics behind slow progress in transfer of land to black beneficiaries. Blind spots also exist in terms of how financial inclusion can be broadened to capture the context of circumstances, such as the needs for land reform recipients. Since the institution of land reform, the government has struggled to facilitate access to financial resources for the land reform beneficiaries. On one hand this is partly due to the exorbitant costs involved in facilitating land transfer using the market-based willing seller, willing buyer principles which consume government budgets leaving little for post-settlement support. On the other, private sector financiers such as banks continue to focus on established white dominated commercial agriculture at the neglect of the new black entrants into the agricultural sector.

While financial inclusion is important for economic development, according to Hall '[D]espite the introduction of some agricultural support and funds for land reform beneficiaries... the agriculture departments have remained biased in favour of commercial farming and unsupportive of smallholder farming and the production systems of the poor.'[3] The departments continue to mirror the colonial and apartheid policies which built white-dominated agrarian capitalism on the basis of exploitation of cheap black labour, biased state support and political intervention.[4]

Despite the potential impact of financial inclusion on agrarian transformation,[5] land beneficiaries continue to be marginalised as a result of neoliberal approaches being implemented by the government.[6] Paradoxically, the government expects land beneficiaries to be successful commercial farmers without the requisite support that was central to the development of white commercial farmers historically.[7] It is for this reason that Rusenga[8] argued that the government is setting land beneficiaries up for failure.

The chapter starts by situating financial inclusion in the context of agrarian reform in the era of neoliberal capitalism. The next section provides a brief outline of land and agrarian reform in South Africa, highlighting the challenges of financial inclusion and their effects on rural livelihoods and economic development. The case study of the Elangeni project is then presented, noting the beneficiaries' experiences and the impact of limited post-settlement support on their production. The conclusion then sums up the key findings, arguing that a combination of financial exclusion

---

[2]Gumede (2014), p. 9; Masilela and Weiner (1996), p. 244; Maphoto (2012), p. 3; Hall (2009a), p. 23.
[3]Hall (2009b), p. 6.
[4]Rusenga (2017), p. 44.
[5]Mhlanga and Denhere (2021), p. 7; Cartier and Louis (2017), p. 11.
[6]Mpandeli and Maponya (2014), p. 4.
[7]DLA, General Conditions for All Land Reform Grants. (2008) Version 1. (Government Printers).
[8]Rusenga (2020), p. 382.

and enforcement of the capital-intensive agribusiness model negatively affect the livelihoods of the land beneficiaries in South Africa.

2 Agriculture, Land Reform and Financial Exclusion in South Africa: Continuities and Discontinuities

The challenges that South Africa experiences regarding black farmers' access to financial services are similar to their counterparts on the African continent, given the shared history of colonialism and racial discrimination. The concept 'financial inclusion' was first introduced by some geographers in the 1990s who sought solutions to the lack of physical access to banking services due to closure of bank branches.[9] The financial inclusion criteria, introduced by the European Commission and the World Bank respectively, included aspects such as access to savings, credit, insurance, remittance and banking.[10] Financial inclusion is broadly understood as the delivery of financial services such as access to banking,[11] including to the poor,[12] at an affordable cost. Given its critical importance, Amoah, Korle, and Asiama[13] consider financial exclusion as a major socio-economic challenge in contemporary economics. Where access is facilitated, benefits include poverty alleviation, job creation, and equity especially for the poor sections of the population.[14] In addition, financial inclusion has benefits for society at large, such as reduced levels of corruption, good governance, accountability and political sustainability.[15]

The inadequate financing of agriculture is a central component of the African agrarian question which concerns itself with how to improve agriculture and its contribution to livelihoods and economies.[16] In the former settler societies of southern Africa (Namibia, South Africa and Zimbabwe) where extensive alienation of land belonging to black Africans took place, Mafeje[17] argues that land reform is central to addressing poverty and economic development in those parts of Africa. However, the land question has spread throughout the whole African continent[18] driven by global financial capital's hunger for new farmland—resulting in land shortages for African residents. For Amin,[19] the contemporary agrarian question is

---

[9]Mhlanga and Dunga (2021), p. 6.

[10]Claessens (2006), p. 9; World Bank Group (2017), p. 9.

[11]Demirguc-kunt et al. (2018) p. 112.

[12]Louis and Chartier (n 6), p. 4.

[13]Amoah (2020), p. 7.

[14]Mhlanga and Denhere (2021), p. 2.

[15]Eldomiaty (2020), p. 2; Omar and Inaba (2020), p. 4.

[16]Mafeje (2003), p. 77; Mafeje (2003), p. 88.

[17]Mafeje (2020), p. 1.

[18]Moyo (2003), p. 1.

[19]Amin (2012), p. 11.

about the increasing gap in productivity between modern capitalist agriculture and the peasant farming systems—itself a product of how neoliberal capitalist development produces inequalities including in access to financial services.

The poor are excluded from sources of agricultural finance which are critical for production, given state policies that favour agriculture dominated by local elites and agribusiness.[20] However, Mafeje[21] argued that the development strategy based on large-scale farming has failed in sub-Saharan Africa. Further, in Southern Africa large-scale farming as a model for agrarian transformation has caused suffering and chronic rates of unemployment among the land-starved blacks.[22] Even where land reforms were instituted with goals of broad-based poverty reduction, like in Zimbabwe, state bureaucrats manipulate access to state resources at the expense of the poor. For instance, new evidence on the distribution of the Reserve Bank of Zimbabwe Farm Mechanisation resources showed that access was politicised and biased in favour of ruling Zimbabwe African National Union—Patriotic Front (ZANU–PF) elites.[23]

From its inception in the Cape Colony in the second half of the seventeenth century, commercial agriculture was founded on racial and material inequalities.[24] Its emergence was built on state support (for white farmers), exploitation of cheap black labour (facilitated by the state and laws) and political intervention. The success of black farmers was actively discouraged and mechanisms were put in place to undermine their production and access to land, markets and resources. As observed by Colin Bundy,[25] when a class of black commercial farmers emerged in the late 1800s in the Cape, taking advantage of industrial and urban development as suppliers of food, its success was reversed through state intervention including the institution of the Native Land Act of 1913. Additionally, sharecropping and tenancy arrangements that followed the extensive expropriation of Africans' land also served to promote white farmers at the expense of blacks.[26] However, it was during the mechanisation process of the 1940s to the 1980s where the financial exclusion of black farmers became well-defined.[27] After 1948, when the National Party took over the government, white commercial farmers were provided with extensive financial, material and marketing support that facilitated mechanisation of agriculture.[28] This process was accompanied by various state programmes to facilitate white farmers' access to cheap black labour.[29] No similar support mechanisms were implemented

---

[20] Rusenga (2021), p. 197.

[21] Mafeje (2003), p. 23.

[22] Mafeje (2003), p. 27.

[23] Gono (2020) and Magaisa (2020).

[24] Rusenga (2017), p. 77.

[25] Bundy (1979), p. 17.

[26] Duncan (1997), p. 145.

[27] Rusenga (2017), p. 177.

[28] Bernstein (1996), p. 9.

[29] Rusenga (2017), p. 44.

for black tenants who were increasingly driven to the crowded homelands.[30] Exclusion from financial and material support were not the only consequences suffered by black people in the twentieth century. They also bore the negative effects of agricultural mechanisation such as job shedding and loss of land.[31]

The above is the context in which land and agrarian reform in South Africa should be understood. The South African land reform programme emerges from Section 25 (5) of the Constitution which obligates the state to '. . .take reasonable legislative and other measures, within its available resources, to foster conditions which enable citizens to gain access to land on an equitable basis.'[32] Land reform was recognised as key to rural development, employment creation, increasing rural incomes, and dealing with overcrowding.[33] This was consequently expected to translate into improved livelihoods and the emergence of a broad-based rural economy.[34] Land reform was thus adopted with a rural development focus. However, even though land reform was implemented, the challenge remains on how to fundamentally change South Africa's distorted agrarian structure, including the racially-prejudiced financial access as well as the institutions that influence access to components of the agricultural arrangement other than land, such as inputs, technology, expert knowledge, finance, water rights and markets of diverse kinds.

Between 1995 and 1999 the government provided R16,000 per household under the Settlement and Land Acquisition Grant (SLAG) programme to enable poor households to purchase land on the market.[35] SLAG was replaced by the Land Redistribution for Agricultural Development (LRAD) programme in 2001, which required land applicants to contribute to the land cost. The contribution was between R5000 and R400,000 and 'depending on the level of this contribution, would be eligible for a matching grant of between R20,000 and R100,000, on a sliding scale.'[36] Considerations were also made to allow the poor to contribute through labour provision instead of cash. The LRAD was later replaced by the Proactive Land Acquisition Strategy (PLAS) with the focus now drifting towards the creation of a class of black commercial farmers with resources to finance their own activities. With most acquired lands not subdivided, coupled with financial constraints and a large-scale agribusiness model being extended to land reform beneficiaries, most encountered a myriad of challenges including limited access to financial resources.[37]

---

[30] Ncapayi (2013), p. 144.

[31] Marcus (1989), p. 44.

[32] *Constitution of the Republic of South Africa*, 1996.

[33] DLA (1997), p. 19; Department of Rural Development and Land Reform (DRDLR) (2013a), p. 22.

[34] DLA (1997), p. 23.

[35] Boudreax (2009), p. 4.

[36] Hall (2004), p. 3.

[37] Rusenga (2017), p. 382.

Credit availability, among other things, is a challenge for many black farmers in South Africa.[38] Consequently, this affects small-scale producers' access to water and production equipment.[39] According to Chisasa and Makina,[40] the performance of emerging farmers in South Africa lags behind their global counterparts due to credit accessibility challenges.

On the other hand, large-scale farmers, mostly white, have better credit access and support provided by various credit institutions including commercial banks.[41] However, emerging farmers, particularly blacks, are deemed high risk.[42] Another factor affecting black farmers is the lack of clear land rights,[43] especially in the former homelands. As a result, they cannot use their land as collateral for financing. Lack of access to credit and infrastructure constitutes barriers that, in turn, affect access to formal markets due to production, quality and standard issues.[44] Below we present and discuss data from the Elangeni project in Limpopo province of South Africa to illustrate the financial challenges black farmers experience and their implications for agrarian transformation.

3 Description of the Case Study

The Elangeni project is located in Tzaneen and was established in December 2007 constituted by nine members of a single family. However, its history goes back to the turn of the twenty-first century when one of its members, Sophie M, retired from her primary school teaching job to start a fruit and vegetable market shop in Mooketsi, near Tzaneen town. It was in the process of conducting this business that in 2004 'an idea struck her that she needed to acquire a piece of land in the form of a farm' to sell her own products.[45] Initially, Sophie M wanted to do a joint venture with her local female pastor. After approaching the local office of the then DLA, the women were told to abandon the idea of a joint venture and apply separately with their family members (Interview with Sophie M on 18 July 2012). It seems the DLA discouraged joint ventures given the problems associated with group projects.[46] Consequently, in 2004 Sophie M mobilised her husband (retired teacher), six children (some in professional jobs) and her elderly mother to form a family trust and apply for a

---

[38] Kirsten and Van Zyl (1998), p. 551. Cousins (2015), p. 77; Aliber and Cousins (2013), p. 148; Boudreax (2009), p. 2.

[39] Von Loeper et al. (2016), p. 1.

[40] Chisasa and Makina (2012), p. 109.

[41] Gaanakgomo (2015), p. 77.

[42] Chisasa and Makina (2012), p. 20.

[43] Gaanakgomo (2015), p. 115.

[44] Rusenga (2017), p. 128.

[45] Elangeni Farm Profile Brochure (2013), p. 2.

[46] Anseeuw and Mathebula (2008), p. 14.

farm through the DLA. The inclusion of the children is important given the limited post-settlement support from the state. A trust is one of the legal entities used to hold land on behalf of beneficiaries in South Africa.[47]

After applying to the DLA in October 2004[48] the beneficiaries received a call from the Department of Rural Development and Land Reform's (DRDLR, formerly DLA) Polokwane office in December 2007, instructing them to go and view a farm in the Deerpark area of Tzaneen. The farm was immediately leased to them in accordance with the PLAS terms before its final allocation to them in December 2009 (Title Deed Number: T82954/2009) in terms of the LRAD programme.[49] The farm was purchased in 2007 by the South African government from the Aanbreek Beleggings Pty Ltd. for R2,150,000.[50]

The Elangeni Project is portion 40 of Grey Stones 469 LT which is 165 hectares in size.[51] The farm had approximately 10,000 mango trees on 17 hectares and about 3000 avocado trees on 10 hectares.[52] The inherited land uses inclined the beneficiaries towards capital-intensive, large-scale farming. To succeed, more resources were needed to support production. After struggling for many years to sustain production in a context of limited state support, the beneficiaries sold their farm in 2018.

This case study draws from qualitative data collected from land reform beneficiaries, representatives of agribusiness markets and government officials actively involved in agrarian reform programmes. Primary data on subtropical production and markets, generated by the South African Subtropical Growers' Association (Subtrop) based in Tzaneen, Limpopo province, South Africa, is also used. The chapter also make use of secondary data from government reports and academic publications. The data was collected between 2012 and 2021.

4 Challenges of Capital-Intensive Production

Having inherited high-value subtropical fruits upon occupation of the farm, the beneficiaries required a lot of resources to sustain production. The government expected them to maintain the land uses on the farm, but did not prohibit them from adding more. Towards that objective, government officials carried out inspections on the farm in the formative years when the farm was leased to the beneficiaries. Such inspections also served the purpose of determining if the beneficiaries were the right candidates to be allocated the farm permanently. Victor M argued that '[O]nce someone is there you would want to up production on the farm. But where a

---

[47]DRDLR (2010), p. 4.

[48]DRDLR (2013a), p. 4.

[49]DRDLR (2013a), p. 4.

[50]Equivalent to US$135 366,26 at the Rate of US$1: R15,8800 on 2/12/2021 (www.xe.com).

[51]DRDLR (2011), p. 4.

[52]Elangeni Farm Profile Brochure (2013).

farm has actually been on a commercial basis before transfer we would like to maintain that standard, the commercial basis' (Interviewed on 22 May 2013).[53] Another officer from the Limpopo Department of Agriculture (LDA) Tzaneen Office concurred with Victor M arguing that the beneficiaries should maintain the agribusiness model (large-scale, capital-intensive) at the farm. He argued that '[T]hey are running commercial farms. That is why we try to appoint the people who are skilled. The most important thing is to establish the international market because depending on the quality of the farm produce, say you are producing bananas and mangoes, you must produce quality' (Interviewed on 2 July 2012).

Clearly, the various government agencies preferred continuation of the agribusiness model in the projects—with some even targeting supplying international markets. However, the government preferences were not backed with availability of financial and material resources required for achievement of such objectives. Instead, the government used its control of the title deed during the lease period to exert pressure on beneficiaries to strive towards unrealisable targets. The only support availed was non-material.

To ensure continuity, the Department of Agriculture, Forestry, and Fisheries (DAFF) sent Sophie M to attend a Market Development Programme at the South African Agri Academy (SAAA) in Cape Town (South Africa) immediately after the farm was allocated to Elangeni Trust, and received her certificate in February 2008.[54] The course targeted 'emerging black farmers focused on export and market readiness.'[55] Modules included global good agricultural practices (GLOBALGAP), the hazard analysis and critical control points (HACCP), the British Retail Consortium (BRC), Market Access Regulations, MRL's/Quality Standards/Phytosanitary Requirements, tracking and tracing which are prerequisites for the supermarkets and export trade chain.[56] These standards had to be integrated into the production process when targeting lucrative markets controlled by agribusiness.

The course empowered the beneficiaries with invaluable knowledge. However, this is evidence that production for commercial markets is knowledge-intensive. Further, given the limited external support most beneficiaries receive[57] and the lack of skills for most of them, access to financial resources becomes a critical requirement for successful production. All these developments were taking place without financial support from the state. At Elangeni the first monetary support from the government, a grant of R500,000, was only made available to the beneficiaries in 2011 despite there having been at the project since 2007. Thus, producing fruits using the capital-intensive agribusiness model was tantamount to setting beneficiaries for failure.[58]

---

[53] Land Reform Officer at the DRDLR, Limpopo Office.

[54] SAAA Certification Programme (2008).

[55] SAAA Course Outline (2014).

[56] Rusenga (2017), p. 81.

[57] Aliber et al. (2013), p. 25; Rusenga (2017).

[58] Rusenga (2017), p. 96.

To complicate their production experience, the beneficiaries suggested that banks, and in particular, the Land Bank, had a problem with the title deed registered in the Trust. Sophie M said:

> [I]f we go to the Land Bank right now to apply for a loan, they will deal with us as individuals. As Elangeni, they will want my husband's assets, my assets . . . all of us as individuals. They do not treat you as Elangeni, as a group . . . This is what they do. You will not get help there (Interviewed on 5 June 2013).

It is possible that the bank's scepticism may have been fuelled by the reported loan repayment defaults by some beneficiaries of land reform.[59] While it is a norm that lending institutions demand collateral for loans provided, the beneficiaries' shock at such demands shows a lack of experience with banking and taking out loans—which are important elements of capitalist agriculture. Nevertheless, the limited access to financial resources negatively affects beneficiaries' production and livelihoods. While land beneficiaries in South Africa are exposed to harsh production conditions some, within the government, accuse them of unproductivity (Interview with Mr. Mooketsi on 3 July 2020).[60]

To put the discussion into context, while beneficiaries at Elangeni started production in December 2007, the first financial support from the government was availed in 2011, 4 years after they first occupied the farm. However, even where financial access was facilitated poor packaging of the support and questionable decision-making on the part of the state affected the impact of the support on land beneficiaries' production. In 2011 the DRDLR released the balance of the grant, totalling R500,000, to the beneficiaries. The balance of the grant is the money that remains after the cost of the farm has been subtracted from the total allocated grant. Little flexibility on how the money should be spend saw the DRDLR using the grant to buy a few implements including a tractor that cost R400,000 and a bakkie (that cost R70,000).[61] In 2012 the beneficiaries successfully applied for a grant worth R350,000 from the Department of Trade and Industry (DTI) under the Cooperative Incentive Scheme (CIS). However, this grant also imposed conditions of use that restricted the resources towards the purchase of farm equipment.

The state spent R3,000,000 in total at Elangeni alone, which is substantial expenditure on one farm. However, 72% of that sum went towards the purchase of the farm alone. This confirms the view of some scholars[62] who posit that the government is charged higher prices for the purchase of land for agrarian purposes. The remaining R850,000 was spent on, or reserved for, the purchase of farm implements only with operational costs for labour, inputs, electricity, fuel and maintenance coming either from agricultural savings or off-farm income invested on the farm. This shows that the support could have had a better impact had the

---

[59] Aliber et al. (2013), p. 24.

[60] Pseudonym. Agricultural Extension officer at the Department of Agriculture office in Tzaneen, Limpopo province.

[61] Rusenga (2017), p. 109.

[62] Andrews (2007), p. 202; See also Rusenga (2017), p. 90.

resources been used differently. For instance, a second-hand tractor could have been purchased to save resources to ensure support for agricultural production. Thus, production costs, other than farm equipment, were financed mostly through off-farm income (parents' pension and salaries of the children). If the beneficiaries struggled for operational capital despite the state having invested R3 million on the farm, surely the agribusiness model is not financially-feasible. With many beneficiaries not as fortunate as those at Elangeni in terms of mobilising production resources,[63] this means that they will likely be less successful in a context where the state promotes large-scale production.[64]

Against this backdrop, the state has introduced joint ventures (commonly known as strategic partnerships in South Africa) where agribusinesses are seconded by the government as business partners for the land reform beneficiaries.[65] Strategic partnerships have been introduced as a solution that can unlock potential access to credit services for land reform beneficiaries.[66] However, they have been criticised for marginalising land beneficiaries as production, marketing decisions and benefits are dominated by the agribusiness partners.[67]

4.1 Impact of Financial Exclusion on Fruit Production

Elangeni produced the Tommy Atkins and Saber mango cultivars and the Fuerte avocado cultivar.[68] With limited access to financial resources, the beneficiaries struggled to sustain the various essential activities in subtropical fruit production. Such activities include weeding, irrigation, spraying, pruning and harvesting. For instance, inadequate weeding of orchards affects the output as 'the grasses . . . absorb everything under the tree', taking the food away from it (Marius P, interviewed on 27 August 2013).

From 2011, when the tractor was purchased, the beneficiaries used the tractor pulled slasher to weed the grasses between and under the fruit trees. For instance, the Subtropical Growers' Association (Subtrop) estimated tractor costs for a hectare of avocadoes in 2020 to be R1 224,81.[69] This cost is not limited to weeding only, but includes transport obligations. With 27 hectares under mango and avocado production, in 2020 beneficiaries would have needed around R33,000 for tractor costs only. Without adequate income to cover the high costs, the beneficiaries struggled to weed the whole farm. Such inadequacies in the production of fruits did affect the

---

[63] Anseeuw and Mathebula (2008), p. 14.

[64] Hall and Kepe (2017), p. 122.

[65] Rusenga (2021), p. 197.

[66] Hall and Kepe (2017), p. 122.

[67] Hall and Kepe (2017), p. 122; Fraser (2007), p. 299.

[68] Elangeni SWOT Analysis Document (2013), p. 2.

[69] Subtrop (2020).

beneficiaries' ability to satisfy standards such as Global GAP which emphasises clean production environments (Interview with Mr. Moses on 16 August 2013).[70] The risks associated with overgrown orchards include the quick spread of veld fires. One such fire broke out at the farm in August 2012 and burnt mango orchards (blocks 1, 4, 5, 6 and 7), the water pump, irrigation pipes, and the electricity meter box thereby also affecting vegetable production which the beneficiaries practiced alongside fruit production.[71] The inferno lasted 6 days. Because of that veld fire, the affected trees took longer to recover as the beneficiaries did not have adequate financial resources to tend to the orchards.

The orchards were also not irrigated. Water facilitates the absorption of nutrients to ensure that more leaves and fruits are produced. It aids optimal fruit development and tree recovery from harvest shock.[72] Therefore, irrigation is very important in fruit production. However, the beneficiaries' off-farm income was too little to support the irrigation of the subtropical fruits. With the limited external support having been restricted towards the purchase of equipment, irrigation remained a big problem.

Another essential activity that was affected by the lack of resources was pruning. Pruning is the cutting off of branches from a plant so that it grows better in the future. The process enables sunlight penetration and leaf and flower development.[73] Marius P stated that without leaves the tree cannot produce fruits even if flower development takes place. He said:

> You do not farm mangoes but you farm leaves. The more leaves that are there, the more fruits you will have ... I think for each mango on the tree, that mango needs something like 60 to 70 leaves (Interviewed on 27 August 2013).

Pittaway[74] has shown that most flowers occur on one-year-old bearing branches with older ones bearing less. Pruning 13,000 trees at Elangeni required huge capital investment which the beneficiaries did not have. The Subtrop projected, for avocadoes alone, that R580 was needed for pruning and plant growth regulation.[75] That figure is certainly more for mango orchards as they hold more trees (476) per hectare than a hectare of avocadoes (203).[76] Samuel M confirmed that pruning 27 hectares required more capital. He argued that hiring the pruning machines was expensive. As a result, they resorted to use of hacksaws to prune the trees, a process that is time consuming (Samuel M, interviewed on 15 August 2013). The beneficiaries' off-farm income and farm savings were woefully inadequate to serve the purpose. The problems extend to other activities, such as harvesting. The above shows that

---

[70] Not his real name.

[71] Elangeni Farm Book (2013).

[72] Elangeni Fruit Spray Programme (2013).

[73] Pittaway (2002), p. 17.

[74] Pittaway (2002), p. 17.

[75] Subtrop (2020).

[76] Subtrop (2020).

financial access is important if land beneficiaries are to improve their production, especially as most come from poor backgrounds with no history of capitalist agricultural production.[77]

At Elangeni, the spraying of fruit trees was not prioritised, with the beneficiaries arguing that the fruits were grown organically. Where spraying of fruits takes place, Subtrop estimated that R2500 was required for pest control per hectare in 2006.[78] That figure would differ for mango and avocado orchards because the former has more trees per hectare. Although grown organically, the beneficiaries did spray copper to control worms in mangoes and black spots on avocados. However, the use of copper only was determined more by the limited availability of financial resources than the fact that the fruits were grown organically.

The basic spraying programme has three stages in the season, focusing on disease and pest control. During the flower bud development stage (May to July) a sanitisation spray should be done to control fungal and bacterial diseases.[79] In the flowering and fruit set stage (August to October), diseases such as powdery mildew and pests such as gall fly should be controlled. From fruit growth up to harvest (October to February) diseases such as anthracnose and pests, such as termites and fruit flies, should be controlled through sprays.[80] Not all diseases can be ignored as some can destroy the whole crop if not controlled. Marius P said:

> What is very important is the addressing of the flowering stage and to get it right. Diseases such as Powdery Mildew ... you have to spray and you know you have your crop viable because we [agribusiness markets] can only work with fruit that is of a good quality (Interviewed on 27 August 2013).

Spraying also protects flowers from diseases and ensures that fruits are formed. Nkhetheni B of Granor Passi argued that:

> There is a disease called powdery mildew. If you do not control that disease now while the mangoes are still at flowering stage, that disease destroys all the flowers. And if the flowers are destroyed you will not get the fruit because the fruits come from the flowers (Interviewed on 16 August 2013).

While spraying is essential, inadequate resource availability ensured the beneficiaries could not strictly follow the required spraying programme. The limited availability of financial resources undermined production at Elangeni project. As reported elsewhere by Aliber et al.[81] and Hall and Kepe,[82] production in land reform projects has been undermined by the government's failure to properly facilitate land beneficiaries' access to post-settlement support, including access to credit for production. Thus, the combination of limited access to financial resources, among other things,

---

[77] Rusenga (2017); Hall and Kepe (2017), p. 122; Aliber et al. (2013), p. 1; Rusenga (2021), p. 197.

[78] Subtrop (2013).

[79] Elangeni Fruit Spray Programme (2013).

[80] Elangeni Fruit Spray Programme (2013).

[81] Aliber et al. (2013).

[82] Hall and Kepe (2017), p. 122.

and the enforcement of the capital-intensive agribusiness model negatively affected the beneficiaries' production.

4.2 Financial Exclusion Affects Access to Lucrative Produce Markets

Because of the challenges the beneficiaries faced in production, their access to better-paying markets were affected. With regards to mangoes, the beneficiaries supplied achar processors who ranked lowest in terms of prices per ton.[83] There were nine to ten achar processors in Tzaneen. Achar processors were preferred because they did not apply strict standards, such as the spraying requirement. Where minimal requirements were applied, they were flexibly enforced. Sophie M remarked that '[T]he mangoes for achar do not need to be sprayed with chemicals because you send them whilst they are still green. They will cut them into achar' (Interviewed on 5 June 2013). Nkhetheni B concurred with Sophie M stating that many African farmers in Tzaneen preferred the achar processors for the same reasons as the beneficiaries at Elangeni. He said:

> That is why the majority of farmers when it comes to mango they will go to the achar market because they know in achar they will not wait for their fruits to ripen. They will just pick those small green mangoes and send them to the market (Interviewed on 16 August 2013).

Because the achar processors flexibly enforced their standards, they were easily accessible for the beneficiaries. However, their accessibility was off-set by the low prices they offered per ton of mangoes. While the average price of achar mango was around R1000 in 2013 (David N, interviewed on 18 August 2013), the national average price per ton of mango sold in the domestic market in the same season was R7000.[84] The average domestic mango price per ton rose to R10,000 during the 2015/16 mango season. The prices were even much higher for those targeting the export markets (close to R20,000 in 2013 and R22,500 in 2016).[85] Thus, land reform beneficiaries' access to lucrative markets is affected by failure to meet the standards and grades in such markets.[86]

The ripened mangoes were supplied to Letaba Citrus Processors (LCP) and Granor Passi. The former is in Nkowankowa and the latter, in Letsitele. LCP extracts, concentrates, processes and blends citrus and other subtropical fruits.[87] Granor Passi processes all citrus varieties, mangoes, and guavas into concentrate

---

[83] Subtrop (2020).

[84] DAFF (2017), p. 8.

[85] DAFF (2017), p. 9.

[86] Rusenga (2017), p. 128.

[87] Hilton-Barber (2011).

juices.[88] The mango processing season started in mid-December and ended at the beginning of February. Juice processors applied several standards that farmers were required to observe before accessing the market. The two companies were guided by Global GAP and food safety requirements as some of their produce were exported. They required their suppliers to observe standards that enabled their juice to access any market. Nkhetheni B explained some of the standards Granor Passi required its suppliers to observe. He said:

> If a farmer is complying with Global GAP standards they can automatically supply to Granor Passi. . . . On the side of Granor Passi, we say the market is available. What you need to do is to comply with our standards (Interviewed on 16 August 2013).

Even at LCP Marius P confirmed that there are standards the company adheres to in order for it to access its domestic and international markets. Such standards include the need to use registered pesticides, crop varieties and the physical quality of the fruit (Interviewed on 27 August 2013). While Granor Passi emphasised Global GAP certification and the use of pack houses, LCP did not adhere much to those requirements. However, such standards made the juice processing market less accessible for those farmers struggling with production viability.[89]

The standards discussed above are part of the reason why the land beneficiaries primarily supply the mangoes to the achar processors. The production constraints they experienced when using the agribusiness model undermined their ability to produce fruits that were compliant with the market standards. And because of the enormous challenges beneficiaries experienced in their production, including limited access to financial services, their production and livelihoods were affected.

As for avocado production, the problems were more similar. The lack of finance capital for investment in the orchards affected the land beneficiaries' ability to produce viable quantities of avocados, on one hand, and the quality required to access better-rewarding markets such as the Fresh Produce Markets and the retailer supermarkets. Consequently, the land beneficiaries at Elangeni relied on informal sector operators as the main market for the avocados. The advantages of the informal market are that there are limited marketing costs and standards compared to other formal sector markets. The main disadvantage, however, was that the informal traders' prices were too low thereby affecting farmers' profitability. Sophie M lamented the low prices arguing that it was tantamount to giving the produce for free (Interviewed on 5 June 2013). Data produced by DAFF[90] show that the National Fresh Produce Markets (NFPMs) paid on average R7000 per ton during the 2013/14 season, rising to over R12,000 per ton during the 2017/18 season. However, the failure of the land reform beneficiaries to access such lucrative markets, partly due to limited access to finance for production, affected their revenue and livelihoods.

---

[88] Granor Passi Corporate Profile (2013), p. 4.

[89] Rusenga (2017), p. 128.

[90] DAFF (2019).

5   The Implications of Financial Exclusion on Land Beneficiaries' Livelihoods: Towards a Conclusion

The chapter has discussed the importance of access to finance in the context of the land reform programme in South Africa. It noted that financial inclusion is important for the land reform beneficiaries to improve their production and meet the market standards and grades requirement in lucrative markets.[91] However, as argued by Ruth Hall[92] many land reform beneficiaries are marginalised from financial opportunities as both government agencies and private sector players continue to favour established commercial farmers, mostly white farmers.

The government has vacillated between extreme positions in its interpretation of the challenges affecting land reform since the onset of agrarian reform in the 1990s. On one hand, some within the national departments overseeing land and agrarian reform accused the land reform beneficiaries of unproductivity (Mr. Mooketsi, interviewed on 3 July 2020). In line with that thinking the government introduced what came to be known as the 'use it or lose it principle' which sought to repossess those farms deemed to be not productive.[93] Such approach was critiqued by academics and activists for its failure to appreciate the complex experiences of land reform beneficiaries including the inadequate access to financial resources needed for viable production.[94]

On the other hand, the government's adoption of the recapitalisation and development policy[95] is acknowledgement of the challenges land reform beneficiaries face regarding access to financial resources. It is in that context that strategic partnerships and mentorships were introduced as solutions to facilitate access to capital, skills and markets.[96] The idea is that the business partners (mostly agribusiness) mobilised by the government on behalf of land beneficiaries will play a critical role in achieving the goals of improving production, access to capital and markets. However, as observed by Fraser[97] and Hall and Kepe[98] the most strategic partnerships have failed to improve the production experiences of most land beneficiaries. Instead, strategic partnerships served to facilitate white commercial farmers and agribusiness' access to public resources through the back door – mostly at the expense of the real land beneficiaries.[99]

---

[91] Rusenga (2017), p. 128.

[92] Hall (2004), p. 6.

[93] DLA (1997).

[94] Rusenga (2017); Aliber and Cousins (2013).

[95] DRDLR (2013b).

[96] DRDLR (2013c); C Rusenga (2021), p. 197.

[97] A Fraser (2007), p. 299.

[98] Hall and Kepe (2017), p. 122.

[99] Friedman (2019).

The case study discussed in this chapter highlights the experiences of land beneficiaries at one farm in Limpopo province of South Africa. It draws attention to the combined effect of limited access to finance and the enforcement of large-scale production on land beneficiaries' ability to produce as well as access to lucrative produce markets. It noted that as a result the production of land reform beneficiaries is negatively affected leading to the undermining of their livelihoods. It is against this backdrop that Aliber and Cousins[100] have argued that there is a general consensus that land reform in South Africa is failing to improve lives. With production affected by limited access to financial resources, among other things, the land beneficiaries struggle to sustain their livelihoods, especially where production is undertaken through the large-scale model.[101] Data from the Elangeni project suggest that production using the agribusiness model promoting large-scale production amplify the negative effects of financial exclusion. On the contrary, studies by Chitonge and Ntsebeza,[102] Ncapayi[103] and Aliber et al.[104] show that when land is utilised outside the agribusiness model (large-scale production), its contribution to livelihoods increases.

Bibliography

(2020) The Big Saturday Read Blog
Aliber M, Maluleke T, Manenzhe T, Paradza G, Cousins B (2013) Land Reform and Livelihoods: Trajectories of Change in Northern Limpopo Province, South Africa. Human Sciences Research Council
Aliber N, Cousins B (2013) Livelihoods after land reform in South Africa. J Agrar Chang 13(1): 140–165
Amin S (2012) Contemporary imperialism and the agrarian question. Agrarian South J Polit Econ 1(1):11–26
Amoah A, Korle K, Asiama KK (2020) Mobile money as a financial inclusion instrument: what are the determinants? Int J Soc Econ 47(10):1–16
Andrews M (2007) Struggling for a Life in Dignity. In: Ntsebeza L, Hall R (eds) The land question in South Africa: the challenge of transformation and redistribution. HSRC
Anseeuw W, Mathebula N (2008) Evaluating Land Reform's Contribution to South Africa's Pro-Poor Growth Pattern. Research paper No. 2008/1
Bank (2018)
Bernstein H (1996) How white agriculture (re)positioned itself for a New South Africa. Crit Sociol 22(9):120–145
Boudreax K (2009) Land Reform as Social Justice: The Case of South Africa. Working Paper no. 09-37 October 2009, The Mercatus Center at George Mason University
Bundy C (1979) The Rise and Fall of the South African Peasantry. David Phillip

---

[100] Aliber and Cousins (2013), p. 148.

[101] Rusenga (2017).

[102] Chitonge and Ntsebeza (2012), p. 87.

[103] Ncapayi (2013).

[104] Aliber et al. (2013).

Cartier F, Louis L (2017) Financial inclusion in South Africa: an integrated framework for financial inclusion of vulnerable communities in South Africa's regulatory system reform. J Comp Urban Law Policy 1(13):170–196

Chisasa J, Makina D (2012) Trends in credit to smallholder farmers in South Africa. University of Pretoria

Chitonge H, Ntsebeza L (2012) Land reform and rural livelihoods in South Africa: does access to land matter? Rev Agrarian Stud 2(1):87–111

Claessens S (2006) Access to financial services: a review of the issues and public policy objectives. World Bank Res Obs 2(21):207–240

Constitution of the Republic of South Africa, 1996

Cotula L, Vermeulen S, Leonard R, Keeley J (2009) Land grab or development opportunity? Agricultural investment and international land deals in Africa. FAO

Cousins B (2015) Through a Glass Darkly: towards Agrarian reform in South Africa. In: Cousins B, Walker C (eds) Land divided, land restored: land reform in South Africa for the 21st century. Jacana

DAFF (2017) A profile of the South African Avocado Market value chain. Government Printer

Demirguc-kunt A, Klapper L, Singer D, Ansar S, Hess J (2018) The Global Findex Database 2017: Measuring Financial Inclusion and the Fintech Revolution. The World Bank

Department of Agriculture, Forestry and Fisheries (DAFF) (2017) A Profile of the South African Mango Market Value Chain. Government Printer

Department of Land Affairs (DLA) (1997) White paper on South African Land Policy. Government Printers

Department of Rural Development and Land Reform (DRDLR) (2010) The State of Communal Property Associations and Other Legal Entities for Land Reform Projects. Briefing to the Portfolio Committee on Rural Development and Land Reform (Government Printers 2013)

DLA (2008) General Conditions for All Land Reform Grants. Version 1. Government Printers

DRDLR (2013a) Deeds Register (Farm History) for Portion 40 of Grey Stones 469 LT. Government Printers

DRDLR (2013b) Mopani Land Reform Database, 1994 – December 2011. Government Printers

DRDLR (2013c) Policy for the Recapitalisation and Development Programme of the Department of Rural Development and Land Reform. Government Printers

Duncan D (1997) Farm Labor and the South African State, 1924–1948. In: Jeeves AH, Crush J (eds) White farms, black labour: the state and Agrarian Change in Southern Africa, 1910–1950. Heinemann

Eldomiaty T, Hammam R, El-bakry R (2020) Institutional determinants of financial inclusion: evidence from world economies. Int J Dev Iss 19(2):1–12

Gaanakgomo T (2015) Challenges and opportunities facing emerging farmers in North West Province, South African Case Study: DR. Kenneth Kaunda District Municipality-Ventersdorp Local Municipality. North West University-Mafikeng, South Africa

Gono G (2020) Gideon Gono: The Truth About RBZ Debt and Farm Mechanisation

Gumede V (2014) Land reform in post-apartheid South Africa: should South Africa follow Zimbabwe's footsteps? Int J Afr Renaissance Stud 9(1):50–68

Hall R (2004) A political economy of land reform in South Africa. Rev Afr Polit Econ 31(100): 213–227

Hall R (2009a) A Fresh Start for Rural Development and Agrarian Reform? Policy Brief 29

Hall R (2009b) Land reform for what? Land use, production and livelihoods. In: Hall R (ed) Another country? Policy options for land and Agrarian reform in South Africa. PLAAS

Hall R (2011) Land grabbing in southern Africa: the many faces of the investor rush. Rev Afr Polit Econ 38(128):193–214

Hall R, Kepe T (2017) Elite capture and state neglect: new evidence on South Africa's land reform. Rev Afr Polit Econ 44(151):122–130

Hilton-Barber D (2011) Footprints: on the trail of those who shaped Tzaneen's history. Theron Books

https://www.bigsr.co.uk/single-post/2020/07/18/BSR-EXCLUSIVE-Beneficiaries-of the-RBZ-
Farm-Mechanisation-Scheme Accessed 12 November 2021
Kirsten JF, Van Zyl J (1998) Defining small-scale farmers in the South African context. Agrekon
37(4):551–562
Mafeje A (1988) The Agrarian Question and Food Production in Southern Africa. In: Prah KK
(ed) Food security issues in Southern Africa: selected proceedings of the conference on food
security issues in Southern Africa. Institute of Southern African Studies, National University of
Lesotho
Mafeje A (2003) The Agrarian question, access to land, and peasant responses in Sub-Saharan
Africa. UNRISD
Mafeje A (2020) The land and the Agrarian Question in Southern Africa. Rethinking Africa series
Occas Occasional Paper No. 2
Magaisa A (2020) BSR EXCLUSIVE: Beneficiaries of the RBZ Farm Mechanisation Scheme
Maphoto TA (2012) Land Claims in South Africa: Progress Report by Minister, from Parliamentary
Monitoring Group. 3 www.pmg.org.za. Accessed 11 Oct 2021
Marcus T (1989) Modernising super-exploitation: restructuring South African Agriculture. Zed
Books
Masilela C, Weiner D (1996) Resettlement planning in Zimbabwe and South Africa's rural land
reform discourse. TWPR, West Virginia
Mhlanga D, Denhere V (2021) Determinants of financial inclusion in Southern Africa. Studia
Universitatis Babes-Bolyai Oeconomica 65(3):39–52
Mhlanga D, Dunga SH (2021) Financial inclusion in agriculture: lessons from Zimbabwe. Acad
Account Financ Stud J 25(2):48–58
Mkodzongi C, Rusenga C (2022) The Idea of a "Rainbow Nation" and the Persistence of Agrarian
Injustices in Post-apartheid South Africa. In: Ndlovu-Gatsheni SJ, Ngcaweni B (eds) The
contested idea of South Africa. Routledge
Moyo S (2003) The land question in Africa: Research perspectives and questions. Draft paper
presented at Codesria Conferences on Land reform, the Agrarian Question and Nationalism in
Gaborone, Botswana (18–19 October 2003) and Dakar, Senegal (8–11 December 2003)
Mpandeli NS, Maponya PI (2014) Constraints and challenges facing the small-scale farmers in
Limpopo Province. J Agric Sci 6(4):135–143
Ncapayi F (2013) Land and changing social relations in South Africa's former reserves: the case of
Luphaphasi in Sakhisizwe Local Municipality, Eastern Cape. Unpublished PhD Thesis, Uni-
versity of Cape Town
Omar MA, Inaba K (2020) Does financial inclusion reduce poverty and income inequality in
developing countries? A panel data analysis. J Econ Struct 9(1):2–25
Pittaway T (2002) An investigation of the effect of time of pruning on the growth and fruiting of
lemons [Citrus limon (L) Burmann f.] cv. Eureka. Unpublished Master's Thesis, Port Elizabeth
Tecknikon
Rusenga C (2017) The socio-economic consequences of the agribusiness model on the land reform
beneficiaries in Greater Tzaneen Municipality, South Africa: the case of Elangeni Project.
Unpublished PhD Thesis, University of Cape Town
Rusenga C (2019) The agribusiness model in south African land reform? Land use implications for
the land reform beneficiaries. Agrarian South: J Polit Econ 8(3):440–461
Rusenga C (2020) Setting them up to fail: enforcement of the agribusiness model on land reform
projects in South Africa. Rev Afr Polit Econ 47(165):382–398
Rusenga C (2021) The Reincarnation of Apartheid: strategic partnerships and land reform in
South Africa. In: Nhemachena A, Chitimira HT, Warikandwa TV (eds) Global Jurisprudential
Apartheid in the twenty-first century: universalism and particularism in international law.
Lexington Books

The Herald, Harare. https://www.zimlive.com/2020/07/19/gideon-gono-the-truth-about-rbz-debt-and-farm-mechanisation/downloaded. Accessed 12 November 2021

Vink N, Van Rooyen J (2009) The economic performance of Agriculture in South Africa since 1994: implications for food security. Development Planning Division Working Paper Series No. 17

Von Loeper W, Musango J, Brent A, Drimie S (2016) Analysing challenges facing smallholder farmers and conservation agriculture in South Africa: a system dynamics approach. SAJEMS Asset Res 19(5):747–763

World Bank Group (2017) Achieving effective financial inclusion in South Africa: a payments perspective. Government of South Africa

Clemence Rusenga holds a PhD in Sociology from the University of Cape Town, South Africa. He researches on land and agrarian development in Africa, and the nexus between cannabis and development in Africa. He is currently a Research Associate on the Cannabis Africana project based at the University of Bristol. The project looks at cannabis and development on the African continent, focusing on four case study countries - South Africa, Zimbabwe, Kenya and Nigeria.

Emmanuel Ndhlovu is a peasant scholar-activist who writes on land reform issues, political economy, peasant livelihoods, migration, food sovereignty, and on the decolonisation of development. He holds a PhD in Development Studies from the University of South Africa. Emmanuel is currently with the Vaal University of Technology as a postdoc researcher.

Exploring Digital Financial Inclusion Strategies for Urban and Rural Communities in Botswana, Namibia, South Africa and Zimbabwe

Tendai D. Svotwa, Charles Makanyeza, and Eukeria Wealth

Abstract This chapter explores digital financial inclusion strategies for rural and urban communities in Botswana, Namibia, South Africa, and Zimbabwe. Financial inclusion has taken centre stage in academic discourses due to its criticality in enhancing socio-economic development. Digital financial services refer to services that are made available through mobile phones and the internet. The World Bank indicates that in developing countries, more households own mobile phones as compared to those who access water and electricity which highlights high mobile penetration rates in developing countries. Digital financial services are key in enhancing financial inclusion, by including the previously marginalised people into the formal financial system. Statistics reveal that more than 60 percent of the global population now has access to digital financial services hence regulators and policymakers must focus on this burgeoning issue. Huge disparities are evident in the levels of digital financial inclusion between the rural and urban communities for the countries under study, largely because of the marginalisation of rural communities and their depressed spending patterns. Proposed digital financial strategies should, therefore, address this anomaly and include the rural communities into the manifold of digital services to ameliorate the vagaries of poverty rampant in rural communities.

T. D. Svotwa
Department of Graduate Studies, Botho University, Gaborone, Botswana
e-mail: douglas.svotwa@bothouniveristy.ac.bw

C. Makanyeza (✉)
Namibia Business School, University of Namibia, Windhoek, Namibia
e-mail: cmakanyeza@unam.na

E. Wealth
School of Accounting, Faculty of Commerce, Management and Law, University of Namibia, Windhoek, Namibia
e-mail: ewealth@unam.na

1   Introduction

This chapter explicates how digital technologies are aiding the development of digital financial services. A plethora of studies has focused on financial inclusion in the past two decades due to the multiplicity of benefits it offers to the socio-economic development of a country. Countries across the globe are now focusing on the promotion and uptake of financial inclusion in their respective domains as a bulwark for addressing a myriad of challenges confronting them from an economic, political, and social dimension. Financial inclusion refers to a situation where businesses and individuals have access to useful financial products and services which are affordable in meeting their multi-faceted needs in terms of transactions, payments, savings, credit, and insurance that are offered in a responsible and sustainable manner.[1] Furthermore, The World Bank posited that from the 2018 global population of 3.8 billion people, 1.7 billion were financially excluded,[2] implying that they do not have bank accounts to access formal financial services, and have no access to mobile money providers. It is also noteworthy that most of the financially excluded people are from developing countries, mostly African countries. Financial inclusion has been witnessed to be a major catalyst for attaining the United Nations Sustainable Development Goals, that includes the eradication of poverty and enhancement of gender equality. Furthermore, financial inclusion has also been confirmed to play a significant role in ameliorating the levels of social inclusion in a diversity of societies across the globe. In view of all these benefits, policy makers have been seen committing substantial financial resources in their countries to increase the levels of financial inclusion.[3]

Related to financial inclusion is digital financial inclusion (DFI). Studies confirm that DFI is an extension of financial inclusion which employs technology and enables people to have access to financial services such as savings, lending, insurance and advance economic growth and progress in underserved segments of the market,[4,5] especially those who live below the poverty line. DFI is further defined by other scholars as referring to those financial services that can be accessed through the usage of electronic devices in a cashless manner without exerting much effort, through which both the service providers and receivers can benefit.[6] In the current age of the Fourth Industrial Revolution(4IR) that we are in, DFI is the way to go in alignment with the new technological realities that are prevailing in the current volatile, uncertain, complex and ambiguous (VUCA) environment. DFI has created a myriad of positive changes to the unbanked and underbanked global population in

---

[1] World Bank (2018).

[2] Demirgüç-Kunt et al. (2020), p. 4.

[3] Ozili (2020), pp. 1–23.

[4] Shen et al. (2021), p. 219.

[5] Chu (2018), p. 131.

[6] Klapper (2017).

accessing financial services through digital technologies, for instance mobile phones.

The use of mobile technologies and mobile phones globally has experienced phenomenal growth from 750 million users in 2000 to 6 billion users by 2011. A distinction should be made between mobile money and mobile banking. Mobile money is normally run by mobile network operators (MNOs) and includes transactions that are performed using mobile phones by accessing the funds for the customer stored by the MNO. As for mobile banking, it refers to the usage of mobile phones to access a bank account and services offered by the bank, and this is mostly run by the banks and other financial service providers. In addition, DFI has been progressing well which has resulted in some people especially the poor and rural communities being financially included in countries such as India, China, and Sub-Saharan Africa (SSA).[7] Billions of people now able to communicate using mobile phones and transact in some instances by employing the internet. Across the globe, people are now making use of mobile phones to purchase agricultural products, send money in and outside the country through mobile platforms, as well as executing other purchases, for instance, groceries. However, it should be noted that while DFI offers a multiplicity of benefits, there are some challenges which come with it such as constrained infrastructural capacities which inhibit transacting due to intermittent networks and high levels of financial illiteracy in some countries.

The advent of the Covid-19 pandemic in December 2019 ushered in a new era in which digital platforms are mostly sought after in view of the threats posed by the virus most especially when people are in proximity. Governments across the globe instituted policies and measures that were meant to curtail and contain the spread of the virus which include lockdowns, imposition of curfews, and restrictions in business trading hours. The impact of the pandemic on the economy has been severe. This chapter, therefore, argues that DFI plays a critical role as a pillar of resilience to absorb the external shocks brought about by Covid-19, while ultimately reaching the generality of the population, most especially the underserved population who need access to these financial services as confirmed in literature.[8] This view is also buttressed by the World Bank which postulates that the importance of DFI in providing secure, low-cost and contactless financial tools to individuals and businesses has become more pronounced in the Covid-19 era. In addition, the current pandemic has magnified the urgency in the provision of DFI targeted at the most vulnerable rural populations.[9] DFI strategies will be explored in the four countries under review which are Botswana, Namibia, South Africa, and Zimbabwe. The next sections of the chapter provide an overview of digitisation from a global perspective and delve into digitisation efforts in the countries under discussion. Policy recommendations will be proffered at the end of the chapter.

---

[7] Chu (2018), p. 132.

[8] Ayadi and Shaban (2020), p. 1. See also Financial Inclusion Global Initiative (FIGI) (2019).

[9] World Bank (2019).

2   Global Overview of Digitisation

The information and communication revolution that has evolved considerably over time has resulted in a marked increase in DFI. The rapid deployment of mobile technology has accelerated global mobile inclusion in both developed and developing countries,[10] and this has had far reaching consequences on DFI. As postulated by the World Bank President Jim Yong Kim in 2016, more than 40% of the global population had access to the internet, with previous statistics indicating the tripling of the number of people who had access to the internet in 2005 standing at 1 billion, skyrocketing to 3.2 billion in 2015. He also noted that among those who are classified as the poorest 20% of households, nearly seven out of every ten people own a mobile phone, while these poorest households are likely to have access to mobile phones than to toilets or clean water,[11] which reflects high mobile penetration rates. By 2017, one billion financially excluded adults already owned a mobile phone,[12] offering opportunities for expanding financial and DFI.

Digital technologies that encompass the internet, mobile phones and all other tools that are used to store and analyse data have phenomenally grown in the last decade, with results showing a marked increase in the introduction of new products and services to the financial services system. The usage of the internet has resulted in an increase in conducting trade, coupled with the low cost of doing business globally, resulting in improved business efficiencies, as well as enhanced customer service.

Globally, DFI has been on an upward trajectory for a considerable period, although more than 300 million people globally are excluded from digital financial services. Africa and Asia and The Pacific have outpaced other continents in terms of the growth of DFI, for the period 2014–2017.[13] For Africa, there has been greater reception to mobile phones and mobile technologies, resulting from the high mobile penetration rates. The major gainers for the 2014–2017 period were Ghana, Kenya, Benin, and Senegal while China, Bangladesh and Malaysia led in the Asia and Pacific group. Latin America, Dominican Republic and Chile dominated in Latin America and the Caribbean.[14]

Despite the marked differences in terms of DFI discussed above obtaining in different continents, there are positive impacts on the globe envisaged by 2025. DFI is expected to boost the global Gross Domestic Product (GDP) by 6% which translates to $3.7 trillion; the creation of 95 million jobs, the attraction of $4.2 trillion in new deposits, coupled with the DFI of 1.6 billion people.[15] Based on these statistics, one could argue that DFI is a catalyst of financial inclusion, social development, and

---

[10]Chu (2018), pp. 131–144.

[11]World Bank (2016).

[12]Demirgüç-Kunt et al. (2018), p. xii.

[13]Khera et al. (2021), p. 12.

[14]Khera et al. (2021), p. 12.

[15]Manyika et al. (2016), p. 3.

a source of economic growth.[16] Based on the preceding information, and previous research studies, DFI presents the following benefits to a country:[17]

- DFI assists banks lower costs by reducing queuing lines in banking halls, reduce manual paperwork and documentation and resultantly have fewer bank branches. This comes about because of people using their mobile phones in conducting business transactions, hence there will not be any need for visiting banks, thus limiting customers from social interactions in this Covid-19 era.
- With DFI, many depositors can easily switch banks within minutes; and this forces banks to provide superior services to their customers or risk losing depositors to competitors. Resultantly, customers will benefit from the enhanced customer service provided by banks, coupled with the fact that there will be choices for selecting efficient banks who deliver the best service resulting in customer delight.
- Regarding financial and monetary system regulators, DFI also helps to curb inflationary pressures on the economy by reducing the amount of physical cash in circulation especially in poor and developing countries. This will be made possible through the usage of mobile and internet transactions, and other related mobile technologies.
- DFI can improve the welfare of both businesses and individuals that possess reliable digital platforms to have access to funds in their bank accounts and transact without visiting the physical structures of the banks. Customers may derive the maximum payoff of using digital platforms when the costs of acquiring the digital transactional platforms are very low, coupled with instances where a digital transactional platform requires the use of personal computers, mobile phones, personal computers, and related digital devices.
- Related to the above, mobile technologies capacitate the unbanked by enabling them to have access to digital financial services. Therefore, mobile phones can be used in addressing and solving the local problems and needs of the unbanked and underbanked members of the population. Mobile technologies can assist the unbanked with basic access to a bank account, or somewhere to store their money and perform financial transactions.
- Digital financial transactions offer great security and convenience to a wide array of stakeholders such as individuals, business entities and governments across the globe. For individuals, there will not be any need for carrying huge sums of money which can be risky. For businesses and governments, digital transaction costs are less than handling cash which is costly in terms of handling and insurance.
- DFI has resulted in customers having confidence and trust with tech-based financial solutions, offered through the usage of mobile phones and personal computers. Resultantly, there has been an upsurge in the demand for customized

---

[16]Manyika et al. (2016), p. 3.
[17]Ozili (2018), p. 330; Saal (2017), p. 2; Klapper (2017), p. 2; Chu (2018), p. 142 and Demirgü-ç-Kunt et al. (2018), p. 1.

products and services. In this regard, FinTech companies are offering these products and services at a low cost and implementing convenient ways to transfer money, borrow, and invest, thus enhancing financial activities in the formal financial services sector.

- Digital payment systems allow entrepreneurs to make payments for goods and services using electronic means and methods such as mobile phones, the internet, and retail point of sales, as compared to using cash or cheques which may not be readily available. As a result, this measure assists the government in curbing the spread of the Covid-19 virus through limiting movements and contact of people.
- Digital financial services can also help people manage financial risk, especially the vulnerable poor rural communities by making it easier for them to collect money from distant friends and relatives when they fall on hard times, mostly during economic hardships.

Whilst DFI offers innumerable benefits, it is critical to have a balanced view and have a cursory analysis of the downside of DFI. Several research scholars have put forth some of these challenges as evidenced below:[18]

- Infrastructural challenges pose a great strain on digital payments. This issue may not be prevalent in developed economies but in most developing and poor African countries, there are indeed infrastructural challenges associated with the delivery of digital services. Electricity is a major challenge that constrains the powering of mobile phones and cell towers, limitations in mobile network coverage, coupled with poor transport networks that hinder the expansion of digital financial services, most especially in remote rural areas.
- Furthermore, to open a bank account, mobile money account or utilising digital financial systems require that one provides the banks or mobile phone operators with the relevant identification documents such as national identity cards or birth certificates. However, prior research carried out by the World Bank in 2014 revealed that more than 2 billion people globally did not possess any form of identity. By 2019, women were disproportionately affected: 45 percent of women in low-income countries, mostly Africa lacked a formal ID compared with only 30 percent of men.[19] Considering this, enhancing DFI becomes a mammoth task to national governments across the globe.
- The low levels of financial literacy, digital literacy and numeracy among the global populations also militate against the usage of digital financial systems which ultimately hinder the progression of DFI in an economy. Previous research established that 33% of adults in 140 countries had difficulty in interpreting simple financial statements which results in poor financial decision making. The Organisation for Economic Cooperation and Development (OECD) also found out that low levels of financial inclusion normally result from low levels of financial literacy.

---

[18] Klapper (2017), p. 6. See also Chetty et al. (2019), pp. 2–3; and Banna (2020), p. 133.
[19] Bill and Melinda Gates Foundation (2019), p. 9.

- The rapid increase of DFS by both bank and non-bank financial institutions may disrupt the regulatory and supervisory activities by regulatory authorities in different countries, confidential data may also be leaked in cyberattacks, money laundering and financing in terrorism may increase. Resultantly, this may compromise the financial system of a country and expose it to several vulnerabilities.
- In East and Southern African countries, the mobile-wallet transaction costs for low-value transfers are astronomically high for the low-income segment. Based on the unstable incomes prevalent in the informal sectors of these countries and the high costs of mobile devices and intermittent internet access, the costs of mobile transactions are unaffordable for the poor segment of society, resulting in limited usage of the products.
- Another challenge has been the regulatory environment especially in the Southern and East African regions. Normally regulations are instituted to protect and standardise the financial-services ecosystem in a country. On the other hand, restrictive regulations will negatively impede on innovations. The regulatory frameworks in these sub-regions remain hazy and opaque, resulting in innovators being unaware of how to develop new technologies that are in sync with the regulatory requirements and needs of a country.
- Products are not designed appropriately for the needs of the low-income segment. Instead, the products are normally designed for the middle- and top-income group hence the low-income consumers have not been able to save, access credit or have access to insurance in the formal financial system.

Having considered the benefits and challenges associated with DFI, the next section presents the status of DFI in Africa, with a particular focus on Botswana, Namibia, South Africa, and Zimbabwe.

3   The State of DFI in Africa

African governments are employing different strategies to enhance the usage of digital technologies to build inclusive economies. Research shows that more than 400 million adults in Africa and 60 percent of them being women lack access to digital financial services, especially the rural poor.[20] The G20 Global Partnership for financial inclusion encouraged governments in 2017 to promote a digital approach for financial inclusion, and this has resulted in a marked improvement in the levels of financial inclusion globally. Recent data by the Findex database show that 69% of adults globally own a bank account or another type of account at a financial institution or have reported personally using a mobile money service in the past 12 months. In Africa, mobile money accounts have been successful in reaching individuals who are otherwise excluded from the formal financial system on the

---

[20]Bill and Melinda Gates Foundation (2019), p. 8.

continent. For instance, in Kenya, when the M-Pesa service was launched in 2007, 73% of adults reported using mobile money.[21] M-Pesa was the first mobile money service scheme introduced by Safaricom, an MNO in Kenya that has been a success story in Africa.

The 2017 Global Findex highlights that SSA has demonstrated the power of financial technology in expanding access to and the use of accounts, with 21% of adults now having a mobile money account.[22] These mobile money accounts are important in transacting, which could be in the form of making deposits, withdrawing from a bank account, or making online payments using mobile phones. Within the Southern African Development Community (SADC), statistics indicate that 45.8 million people are financially excluded in the region.[23] Furthermore, in the SADC region, the sophistication of a country's Information Technology (ICT) sector positively impacts financial inclusion.[24] Countries with high levels of financial inclusion, such as Botswana, South Africa, Mauritius, Namibia, and Lesotho tend to have high rates of mobile penetration, which suggests a more developed ICT sector, and the size of the existing user base. Furthermore, as countries broaden their financial service offerings such as mobile money, the demand is met for these products and services through the offering of digital platforms which widen and deepen the levels of financial inclusion by creating a wider customer base.[25] The discussion below focuses on the state and level of DFI in the four selected countries under discussion in this chapter.

3.1   South Africa

South Africa is an upper middle-income country and has one of the most complex and advanced financial system in Africa and leads in the SSA region. In fact, the country has the highest level of access to financial facilities in emerging economies. Paradoxically, customers experience concomitant challenges in accessing the financial facilities, resulting in the low rates of usage for these financial services and huge dependence on cash. Based on the high rates of access to a banking account or mobile-wallet facility, the rates of poverty in the country have remained high, and the expected benefits of financial services for the low-income strata have not materialized,[26] twenty-seven years after democracy. The financial services sector is well regulated and stable, that withstood the global 2008 turmoil. The sector has provided access to numerous financial products and services through the usage of a

---

[21] Ayadi and Shaban (2020), p. 4.

[22] Shipalana (2019), p. 15.

[23] Finmark Trust (2019), p. 3.

[24] SADC (2016), p. 29.

[25] SADC (2016), p. 31.

[26] Chetty (2019), p. 2.

wide physical and digital network. There have been great strides made in financial inclusion, especially the previously marginalised and excluded people. These positive developments have been largely attributed to the advent of digital channels which have contributed to widening access to the sector and improving efficiency in the financial service sector.

Despite being one of the financially advanced economies, it remains one of the most unequal countries in the world due to the high levels of poverty, with almost half of the population living below the poverty datum line. Literature further supports the fact that improved digital services are not available everywhere, for instance, rural areas. The low-income segment of the population cannot afford these services, which results in them financially and digitally excluded.[27] Statistics reveal that about 30 million South Africans, mainly the previously marginalised black population are still living in poverty and some of them face hurdles in accessing financial services and financial products due to lack of the required documentation to open a bank account, low incomes, lack of trust in the banks, exorbitant bank fees, coupled with financial illiteracy.[28]

A significant number of South Africans make use of digital payments monthly (approximately 37 percent), and despite an increase in the number of smartphone users, about 40 percent tend to use their smartphones in conducting various transactions on their smartphones.[29] South Africa has high mobile penetration rates, with about 150 subscriptions per 100 people, which indicates multiple ownership of mobile phones per individual. In South Africa, all the big banks offer mobile banking, as an additional access channel to existing bank accounts, and such mobile banking models, like WIZZIT and MTN Mobile Money are predominant in the financial services sector.

Based on the operations of these models, a customer's bank account is fully integrated with the mobile phone, thus allowing the customer to use the mobile phone as an additional access channel as well as a conduit for effecting payments.[30] Despite South Africa's digitisation efforts, high mobile penetration, and lower transaction costs for using digital distribution channels, most customers still prefer to transact on a face-to-face basis through branches. This fact may be attributed to a lack of digital literacy, and the fear of fraud involving Automated Teller Machines (ATMs) and mobile/internet banking.[31]

---

[27] Shipalana (2019), *South African Institute of International Affairs* 13.

[28] Chitimira and Ncube (2020), p. 339. See also Allen et al. (2016), pp. 18–27.

[29] Abrahams (2017), p. 648.

[30] Bara (2013), p. 351.

[31] Financial Sector Conduct Authority (2019).

3.2 Botswana

Research conducted in 2015 showed that more than two-thirds of Batswana adults were formally served in the financial services sector, with a further 8% usage in informal services only, and 20% were totally excluded. The usage was mainly driven by savings products, followed by remittances, insurance and credit.[32] The Botswana Financial Inclusion Roadmap Strategy 2015–2021 laid the foundation for the enhancement of financial inclusion, which is implemented by the Ministry of Finance and Economic Development. The report indicated that some groups which are more financially excluded than others include women, rural poor, and other remote or hard-to reach populations, as well as informal micro and small businesses are also affected.[33] Informal employees have a great challenge in accessing the formal banking products and services hence they are digitally excluded. Previous research studies in Botswana regarding financial inclusion show that most people who are financially included are males who reside in urban areas. Results showed that financial inclusion is higher among adults who reside in cities/towns, with 86 percent being financially included compared to urban villages (78 percent) and rural areas (64 percent), while males (79 percent) were mostly financially included as compared to 73 percent of females.[34] These results confirm that the poor, rural communities are financially and digitally excluded to a greater extent as compared to the urban population.

Commercial banks have been found to be fuelling the high levels of financial exclusion of the rural population due to the limited number of bank branches and ATMs operating in the rural areas. In addition, banking regulations have been outlined yet another reason that contributes to financial exclusion in Botswana. The Know Your Customer (KYC) drive by banks require establishing the source of your income which precludes people in informal employment to have access to bank accounts and credit facilities and consequently resort to loan sharks who fleece customers by charging exorbitant rates.[35]

The Botswana population census survey of 2017 showed that 33.4% of the adult population lived in the rural areas which are serviced by 50 Post offices, one commercial bank branch and 60 mobile money operators.[36] These glaring statistics confirm the extent and magnitude of an underserved market, the rural poor community which is highly excluded in terms of financial access and digital financial access. However, to a lesser extent, the use of digital technologies such as internet banking, mobile banking and mobile money appear to have reduced the need for physical

---

[32] Making Access Possible (2015), p. xv.

[33] Botswana Stock Exchange Limited News (2019), p. 10.

[34] Molefhi (2019), p. 9.

[35] Botswana Stock Exchange Limited News (2019), p. 10.

[36] Finmark Trust (2019), p. 35.

structures such as banking halls since there was a slight reduction in the proportion of bank branches per 100,000 adults.

Since mobile money has been confirmed to play a significant role in enhancing the level of financial inclusion, it is worth mentioning that between 2017 and 2018, there has been a reduction in the number of mobile money agents, from 91 to 77. This confirms that in the context of Botswana, digital financial services are mainly driven by commercial banks as opposed to mobile money.[37] On a positive note, the financial services system is highly integrated due to the interoperability between mobile money access points and commercial banks. Therefore, to increase the level of access to digital financial services, possibly the mobile money agents could intensify their presence in the rural areas to serve the financially, and digitally excluded people.

3.3 Namibia

Namibia since gaining independence in 1990 has come up with policies that are meant to increase the levels of financial inclusion to the previously disadvantaged majority. This resulted in the country crafting its Financial Sector Strategy for 2011–2021 to address the inherent weaknesses in the Namibian financial system. This was meant to bring changes in the country's financial sector to positively contribute to the socio-economic development of Namibia through poverty reduction and increased access to financial services as contained in developmental plans, such as National Development Five (NDP5) and Vision 2030.

However, despite the Government of Namibia's efforts to increase the levels of financial inclusion, access to DFI has remained limited, especially for previously disadvantaged low-income group, and small and medium enterprises (SMEs). The high cost of services coupled with the limited outreach of commercial banks, especially in the rural areas of the country implies that the rural poor remain unserved.[38] This implies that some segments of the populace remain digitally excluded and would not be able to participate in the formal economy by enjoying the benefits available in the financial services sector.

Regarding financial inclusion, Namibia is among a few SADC countries that exhibit women being more financially included as compared to men, which is not the norm on the Africa continent. Prior studies conducted in Namibia regarding DFI indicate that it is observed that on average, 75% of Namibians have a formal account with a financial institution, 62% have savings at a financial institution and only 16% could access formal credit from a financial institution around May 2017, when data

---

[37] Finmark Trust (2019), p. 35.
[38] Haiyambo (2016), p. 75.

collection for the study started in October 2017.[39] The above statistics imply that a greater proportion of the population relies on credit from the informal sector which in most instances charges punitive rates for cash lending.

Furthermore, literature confirms that in countries such as Botswana and Namibia, two thirds of adults have a bank account, there are already more mobile phone subscriptions than inhabitants and yet the volume of mobile money transactions is extremely low.[40] In this regard, mobile infrastructure is not the major constraint, therefore digital financial inclusion has a high unrealised potential in many countries, including these two countries.

3.4   Zimbabwe

Zimbabwe crafted the National Financial Inclusion Strategy in March 2016 (2016–2020) that was geared at ensuring the existence of an inclusive financial sector, catering for the needs of everyone in the population in accessing and using financial services which would ultimately translate into positive socio-economic development. The major stakeholders in the implementation of strategy are government ministries and agencies, financial institutions, regulatory bodies, development partners, business associations and MNOs.[41] The promulgation of the National Financial Inclusion Strategy highlights the commitment of the Government of Zimbabwe in making sure that every individual within the population has total access and usage of formal financial services, thus reducing the levels of financial exclusion.

Mobile money services have been evidenced as major contributors to financial inclusion since they can be used for the payment of goods and services, wages, and government related payments. Zimbabwe is among the top ten countries in Africa utilising mobile money (number three), with Kenya topping the list, thus enhancing financial and DFI. It is also apparent that in all the ten African countries highlighted, males constitute a larger percentage of those who owned a mobile account.[42] All banks in Zimbabwe are capitalising on the high mobile phone penetration rate of over 90% by partnering MNOs to offer a range of efficient, fast, safe digital financial services to different segments of the market, thereby widening the choices of consumers. In addition, prior studies reveal an exponential increase in the total number of mobile money agents from 40,950 in 2014 to 49,663 in 2018. Mobile money has been seen as an alternative to the traditional banking models and has been viewed as a catalyst in broadening and expanding DFI.[43]

---

[39] Mukong et al. (2020), p. 155.

[40] Stijns et al. (2017), p. 7.

[41] Reserve Bank of Zimbabwe (2016), p. 3.

[42] Machasio (2020), p. 1.

[43] Finmark Trust (2019), 30.

Statistics provided by the Reserve Bank of Zimbabwe in 2016 for the last Finscope Survey carried out in 2014 highlight that the level of financial inclusion is skewed in favour of the urban population (89%) as opposed to the rural population (62%). Paradoxically, more than two thirds of the country's population (67%) are in rural areas. The view above is also supported by other researchers who echoed that usually the most financially excluded in Zimbabwe are the low income individuals and or households in marginal areas such as the rural areas, those engaged in agriculture, microenterprises as well as the informal sector.[44] Furthermore, most of Zimbabwe's adult population rely on informal savings as opposed to formal savings as only 20% of the adult population made use of formal savings channels in 2014, whilst 23% utilised informal channels.[45] These statistics reveal that people who make use of informal channels for savings are both financially and digitally excluded from the financial services system, hence are denied the benefits which accrue from these formal systems which include having access to short term loans and financing.

Commercial banks work very closely with MNOs hence this interoperability has resulted in an increase in the value of bank to wallet transfers especially during the period 2014–2018. Since all banks are linked to the mobile network operators, this ultimately gives bank customers flexibility and choice to access their funds and bank accounts using the mobile platforms anytime, which also enhances the levels of DFI.

4   Opportunities for DFI in Africa

DFI has grown in the last decade and continues to grow in the foreseeable future. DFI poses many opportunities within the context of Africa, and particularly to the four countries under study. The following are some of the envisaged benefits of DFI based on extant literature:[46]

(a) Africa is the second largest continent with an expected population of 2.5 billion people by 2050, whose median age is 18 years. Given such a youthful population which is techno savvy, opportunities abound on this continent especially in terms of product offerings through DFI, which are more likely to be embraced by the youth.

(b) Low levels of formal financial services: Innovations such as mobile money can take hold more completely in emerging markets where there is a strong need and no incumbent service to displace. Building on the mobile money ecosystem, innovative mobile service providers are offering customised services to serve the underserved population and outcompete traditional brick and mortar structures.

(c) Low- income levels: Setting up and operating bank branches is expensive in both emerging and developed markets, and the use of digital channels in offering

---

[44] Masiyandima et al. (2017), p. 8.

[45] Reserve Bank of Zimbabwe (2016), p. 10.

[46] Saal et al. (2017), p. 7; UN Population Division (2019); and Machasio (2020), p. 4.

digital financial services helps reach more customers at lower cost across different market segments.

(d) Weak infrastructure: In instances where the financial infrastructure is lacking, the networks and infrastructure of the operational banks still have significant value. Banks must leverage their position of already having payments, identity and trust assets in place as new infrastructure comes online. Banks can collaborate with Fintechs (technology companies which assist in the delivery of digital financial services) based on their resource capabilities, customer bases, and brands to expand rapidly fill gaps in banks' channels, product sets, and processing capabilities.

(e) Global Findex data found that about 1.1 billion adults are unbanked globally. Two thirds of those without an account possess a mobile phone, which presents a great opportunity for unbanked households to directly embrace mobile payments and the benefits associated with financial services.

The preceding information attests to the fact that DFI remains a force to reckon with, in any country given the innumerable benefits that if offers in aiding to the enhancement of financial inclusion efforts by various governments.

5   Policy Recommendations for DFI

Given the socio-economic contributions of DFI, governments need to make concerted efforts in digitizing the financial services sector and a host of other sectors in service delivery which ultimately benefits most of the population. Based on the discussions in the previous sections, the following policy recommendations are proffered to increase the levels of DFI in the countries under study:

(i) Given the ravages of the current Covid-19 pandemic, more concerted efforts should be put on accelerating the levels of digital technologies hence eliminate the need for direct contact. Mobile money services such as MTN Mobile Money (MoMo) in South Africa, Ecocash in Zimbabwe, Orange Money in Botswana, and Mobipay in Namibia could enhance DFI swiftly as compared to the traditional banking operations. Botswana hugely presents a great opportunity especially in terms of increasing the number of mobile agencies particularly in the rural areas which are underserved, with very few MNOs and commercial branch networks.

(ii) Governments should enhance the formalization of services by promoting the use of mobile saving platforms such as digital wallets and other digitalization services that could also support inclusion.[47] Governments which offer pension payments through account transfers could incorporate digital pension payments to pensioners monthly. A case in point in Zimbabwe is the National Social

---

[47] Saal et al. (2017), p. 7; UN Population Division (2019); and Machasio (2020), p. 4.

Security Agency (NSSA), which is an organisation dealing with social security issues that pays pensioners through crediting savings accounts when payments fall due. Some people must travel to cities and towns to access their monthly pension, yet digital technologies can be employed to speed up the process by directly transferring the money into a mobile account which is easily accessible.

(iii) Related to e-wallets, many SMEs in developing countries are using cash and cheques to pay salaries.[48] In this instance, there is a need to promote the use of digital wallets to support the unbanked members of the population who are financially excluded and rely on cash transactions.

(iv) One of the impediments to DFI is the lack of financial literacy among some segments of the population. In this regard, there is a need by Government agencies to intensify the level of digital awareness to enhance financial literacy. People should be encouraged to adopt the use of mobile and digital financial services. The merits of using such platforms should be communicated to the vulnerable groups, the less educated and poor, who are financially excluded using various media platforms and fora. Financial literacy programmes can also be introduced in schools, even starting at the primary level to acquaint the future generations with the financial tools which they should be prepared to use in future. Communities should also be involved in the process, hence the need to identify community-based trainers.

(v) Infrastructural challenges have been identified as exerting a great strain on the efficient and effective utilisation of digitisation as earlier stated. Considering this, governments should make firm commitments on infrastructural spending, especially the marginalised rural communities to enhance digital and internet connectivity, to make sure that the internet is readily available to everyone in the country. Related to this aspect, there is also a need to step up electrification programmes in the rural communities so that the MNOs can offer digital services without resorting to the use of generators which may become expensive to offer the services.

(vi) Working with regulators: A recent study in East and Southern Africa found out that respondents were of the view that there is a need to cultivate a healthy relationship between the regulators (who are mostly government agencies) and fintech companies which play a great role in DFI.[49] In that regard, the regulators would clarify to the fintech operators how they are supposed to comply with the policy requirements of digital financial services; and that regulators should be kept informed of the technological trends and their possible impact on the operations of the financial services sector. Furthermore, digital financial inclusion efforts of a country should not be conducted in isolation but should be anchored in a country's broader digital framework/strategy, from efforts aimed at expanding the electricity grid to policies to enhance broadband coverage.[50]

---

[48] Ayadi and Shaban (2020), p. 16.

[49] Chetty et al. (2019), p.10.

[50] Bill and Melinda Gates Foundation (2019), p. 14.

6 Conclusion

This chapter explored the strategies employed in the provision of digital financial services in the rural and urban communities of Botswana, Namibia, South Africa and Zimbabwe. DFI has been proven to play a significant role in the socio-economic growth of a country and acts as a catalyst to financial inclusion. Evidence from the four selected countries in SADC indicates that the rural marginalised population still bears the brunt of digital financial exclusion as exemplified by the low rates of financial service operators and mobile agencies operating in rural areas as compared to their urban counterparts. This calls for deliberate policy prescriptions that are geared towards the amelioration of digital financial services in the rural areas since most of the population reside in rural areas except for Botswana which has a high number of urban dwellers in cities and towns, there is a need to boost infrastructural development in rural areas to increase network availability and increased use of the internet. Truly, mobile money plays a greater role in increasing the level of DFI, hence it should be promoted further in the selected four countries. MNOs can leverage on interoperability which exists between themselves and banking institutions.

Poverty levels in the four selected countries are astonishing and have reached alarming levels despite these countries possessing huge mineral deposits, and the rural poor are the ones who suffer most. The Government of Botswana, Namibia, South Africa and Zimbabwe need to come up with friendly regulatory policies that are pro-poor which encourage businesses to invest heavily in remote, rural areas and offer them lucrative incentives meant to uplift the standards of living of the poor. These rural communities have suffered for a long time and have been marginalised especially regarding DFI, hence this is the right time to act so that everyone enjoys the benefits that are offered by the financial services sector. Residents of towns and cities are the major beneficiaries of these financial products and services. To attain this goal which is related to the United Nations Sustainable Development Goals, especially number one (eradication of poverty), concerted efforts should be made by the respective Governments in educating the rural communities on the benefits of financial literacy, financial inclusion, products, and services offered by financial institutions, and DFI. This is the era for DFI, given the ravages brought about by the Covid-19 pandemic. Products and services can be accessed remotely through the utilisation of digital financial technologies, regardless of one's location.

Bibliography

Abrahams R (2017) Financial inclusion in South Africa: a review of the literature. South Afr Account Assoc 632–661
Allen F, Klapper L, Demirgüç-Kunt A, Peria MSM (2016) The foundations of financial inclusion: understanding ownership and use of formal accounts. J Financ Intermed 27(1):18–27

Ayadi R, Shaban M (2020) Digital financial inclusion: a pillar of resilience amidst Covid-19. Euro-Mediterranean Econ Assoc 1–16

Banna H, Hassan MK, Alam MR (2020) Digital financial inclusion, Islamic banking stability and sustainable economic growth. Islamic Persp Sustain Financ Syst 131–152.

Bara A (2013) Mobile money for financial inclusion: policy and regulatory perspective in Zimbabwe. Afr J Sci Technol Innovat Dev 5(5):345–354

Bill and Melinda Gates Foundation (2019) A G7 partnership for Women's digital financial inclusion in Africa. Bill and Melinda Gates Foundation, pp 1–24

Botswana Stock Exchange Limited News (2019) Advancing Financial Inclusion. Botswana Stock Exchange Limited News, pp 1–58

Chetty K, Josie J, Siswana B, Mashotola E, Kariuki K, Johnson C, Luo M (2019) Review of fintech strategies for financial inclusion in Sub-Saharan Africa. International Financial Architecture for Stability and Development/Crypto–Assets and Fintech 1–14

Chitimira H, Ncube M (2020) Legislative and other selected challenges affecting financial inclusion for the poor and low-income earners in South Africa. J Afr Law 64(3):337–355

Chu AB (2018) Mobile technology and financial inclusion. In: Handbook of Blockchain, digital finance, and inclusion. Academic Press, pp 131–144

Demirgüç-Kunt A, Klapper L, Singer D, Ansar S, Hess J (2018) The Global Findex Database 2017: Measuring Financial Inclusion and the Fintech Revolution. World Bank 1–151

Demirgüç-Kunt A, Klapper L, Singer D, Ansar S, Hess J (2020) The Global Findex Database 2017: measuring financial inclusion and opportunities to expand access to and use of financial services. World Bank Econ Rev S2–S8

Financial Inclusion Global Initiative (2019) Financial Inclusion. Available at <https://www.worldbank.org/en/topic/financialinclusion/brief/figi> Accessed 8 July 2021

Financial Sector Conduct Authority (2019) Financial Inclusion Strategy. Available at <www.fsca.co.za> Accessed 10 April 2021

Finmark Trust (2019) Measuring Progress 2019: Financial Inclusion in SADC. Available at <https://finmark.org.za/system/documents/files/000/000/183/original/ME_Report_2019.pdf?1601964365> Accessed 18 July 2021

Haiyambo E (2016) An Impact Assessment of the Regulation of Microfinance Institutions in Namibia. Doctoral Thesis, Stellenbosch University

Khera P, Ng S, Ogawa S, Sahay R (2021) Measuring digital financial inclusion in emerging market and developing economies: a new index. IMF Working Paper No. 21 1–33

Klapper L (2017) How Digital Payments Can Benefit Entrepreneurs. IZA World of Labour available at <https://wol.iza.org/articles/how-digital-payments-can-benefit-entrepreneurs/long> Accessed 14 July 2021

Machasio IN (2020) COVID-19 and Digital Financial Inclusion in Africa. World Bank, pp 1–7

Making Access Possible (2015) Botswana - Demand, Supply, Policy and Regulation. Diagnostic Final Report 1–247

Manyika J, Lund S, Singer M, White O, Berry C (2016) Digital finance for all: powering inclusive growth in emerging economies. McKinsey Global Institute, pp 1–24

Molefhi K (2019) Financial inclusion and its impact on employment creation in Botswana. Botswana Institute for Development Policy Analysis pp 1–28

Mukong A, Shiwayu N, Kaulihowa T (2020) A decomposition of the gender gap in financial inclusion: evidence from Namibia. Afr J Bus Econ Res 15(4):149–164

Ozili PK (2020) Financial inclusion research around the world: a review. Forum Soc Econ 1–23

Reserve Bank of Zimbabwe (2016) National Financial Inclusion Strategy 2016–2020. Reserve Bank of Zimbabwe 1–62

Saal M, Starnes S & Rehermann T (2017) Digital Financial Services. IFC Available at <https://openknowledge.worldbank.org/bitstream/handle/10986/30368/118736-BRI-EMCompass-Note-42-DFS-Challenges-and-Opportunities-PUBLIC.pdf?sequence=1>   Accessed 16 July 2021

Shen Y, Hu W, Hueng CJ (2021) Digital financial inclusion and economic growth: a cross-country Study. Proc Comput Sci 218–223

Stijns JP, Borysko S, Marchitto B (2017) Banking in Sub-Saharan Africa: interim report on digital financial inclusion. Regional Studies and Roundtables European Investment Bank, pp 1–25

UN Population Division (2019) World Population Prospects 2019. Available at <https://esa.un.org/unpd/wpp/Publications/Files/WPP2017_KeyFindings.pdf>. Accessed 16 July 2020

World Bank (2016) World Development Report 2016: Digital Dividends. World Bank. Available at <http://www.worldbank.org/en/publication/wdr2016> Accessed 10 July 2021

World Bank (2018) Financial Inclusion is a Key Enabler to Reducing Poverty and Boosting Prosperity. Available at <https://www.worldbank.org/en/topic/financialinclusion/overview>. Accessed 8 July 2021

World Bank (2019) Financial Inclusion Global Initiative. Available at <https://www.worldbank.org/en/topic/financialinclusion/brief/figi>. Accessed 8 July 2021

Tendai Douglas Svotwa holds a Bachelor of Business Studies *(Honours)*, a Master of Business Administration (MBA) degree from the University of Zimbabwe and a PhD in Business Management from North-West University, Mafikeng, South Africa. Dr Svotwa is also a seasoned banker with more than 12 years' experience working in the Corporate sector, mainly in the Treasury Department. He is also an accomplished researcher, having published extensively in peer reviewed journals and has presented at local and international Conferences such as Botswana, Namibia, South Africa, Tanzania, Morocco, and France. Dr Svotwa is also a renowned academic, who has taught at tertiary institutions since 2009, starting off his teaching career at the University of Zimbabwe. He is a Senior Lecturer at Botho University, Graduate Studies and Research Department, Gaborone, Botswana where he teaches and supervises postgraduate students. His research interests are in the fields of strategy, leadership, general management, entrepreneurship, family businesses and marketing management. He is a member of The European Academy of Management (EURAM), Africa Academy of Management (AFAM), South African Association of Public Administration and Management (SAAPAM), and a Life-time member of the Golden Key International Honour Society. In 2017, he was one of the two African scholars selected to represent Africa in Rabat, Morocco, at the PhD Doctoral Colloquium: EURAM Early Career Colloquium (EECC), facilitated by EURAM. Currently he is part of a 10-member team engaged as a Co-Country Investigator (CCI) in Botswana for the Global Leadership and Business Effectiveness (GLOBE) survey focusing on organisational culture, trust, and leadership in more than 110 countries across the globe.

Charles Makanyeza is a senior academic, researcher and consultant who commands respect among his peers. At the time of writing, Charles has more than eleven years of teaching experience at university level, more than five years of experience in university administration, and more than ten years of industry experience. He holds the following qualifications: PhD Marketing, Executive MBA, MSc Marketing, Postgraduate Diploma in Project Management, BCom Marketing, Diploma in Agriculture, Certificate in International Computer Driving Licence (ICDL), and Training and Resources in Research Ethics Evaluation (TRREE) Certificates in Introduction to Research Ethics; Research Ethics Evaluation; Informed Consent; Good Clinical Practice; HIV Vaccine Trials; Adolescent Involvement in HIV Prevention Trials; Public Health Research Ethics; and South Africa. Charles is currently an Associate Professor of Marketing and Strategy at the Namibia Business School, University of Namibia. His specialisation and research areas of interest include marketing, strategy, entrepreneurship and quantitative research. Before joining the University of Namibia, he served as Director of the Graduate Business School, Acting Dean, Deputy Dean, Programme Coordinator, Associate Professor, Senior Lecturer and Lecturer at Chinhoyi University of Technology. Charles has also served as a Senior Lecturer and Lecturer and various institutions both full-time and part-time. His recent key projects include (i) Causes of lack of professionalism and poor organisational performance at Apple Valley Primary School and appropriate solutions (ii) Conducted, in partnership with CeDRE International Africa, an evaluation of the project on strengthening smallholder farmer incomes and rural social infrastructure in Chimanimani district of Zimbabwe in 2016. The project was commissioned by the TSURO Trust in cooperation with BFDW – EED. The major components of the project were on transparent community planning, monitoring and governance processes, community managed social and health care, local healthy food products and market development.

Eukeria Wealth is an established, competent and proficient lecturer with more than 11 years teaching experience at university level. Eukeria holds the following qualifications; PhD Accounting Sciences, Master of Commerce in Accounting, Bachelor of Commerce in Accounting, Post Graduate Diploma in Tertiary Education (PDTE), Post Graduate Diploma in Applied Taxation (ICTAZ), Certified Public Accountant (ICPAZ), Certified Tax Accountant (ICTAZ), Registered and Practicing Accountant (RPAccZ) with PAAB. Eukeria is currently a senior lecturer in the School of Accounting, University of Namibia. She has specialised in Accounting and taxation, and her research interests include transfer pricing, taxation, financial inclusion and diversification. Before joining the university of Namibia, she was the Head of department for the department of Accounting at Midlands State University. Her flagship projects include (i) Accounting education for fourth industrial revolution accountants in Africa, commissioned by African Accounting and Finance Association (AAFA) in collaboration with Pan-African Federation of Accountants (PAFA) (2020), (ii) Experiences in the Zimbabwe Hotel Industry during Hyperinflation sponsored by the Macro-economic and Financial Management Institute of Eastern and Southern Africa (MEFMI) (2016), (ii) Illicit Trade, Economic Growth and the Role of Customs as commissioned by the World Customs Organisation (2014).

A 'Social Justice' Movement in the Banking Industry? Banking, Competition and Financial Inclusion in South Africa with Insights from Zimbabwe

Tinashe Kondo

Abstract While social justice conversations seem to have been fading in philosophical arenas over the last decade, there remain legitimate reasons to keep them alive. In law, social justice debates have, by and large, been confined to human rights corridors. However, as will be argued in this chapter, social justice is about the organisation of society and the realisation of equality in material conditions. These aspirations cannot be realised if members of society are limited by 'markets' and 'banking institutions. Therefore, there is a place for social justice within the banking sector, and more broadly, in other economic fields (including their regulation too). This chapter drives financial inclusion as a concept to advance this agenda. Financial inclusion seeks to expand the availability and equality of access for banking products. Safe to say, financial inclusion is about (social) justice in relation to banking products. Once established, this paper then explores the impact of competition in the banking industry in South Africa on financial inclusion. The paper finds, using a review of the literature and existing secondary data from empirical studies, that there is a definite correlation between an increase in competition in the industry and improved access and product ranges for consumers, as competitors attempt to garner new clients and markets. Oddly enough, competition law and financial inclusion are deemed to be strange bedfellows, sharing a common interest in transformation. The chapter recommends that further deliberate efforts, through law and policy, be taken to enforce competition within the banking sector and advocate for better financial inclusion.

T. Kondo (✉)
Department of Mercantile and Labour Law, University of the Western Cape, Cape Town, South Africa
e-mail: tkondo@uwc.ac.za

1   Introduction

> In a real sense, all life is interrelated. The agony of the poor impoverishes the rich; the
> betterment of the poor enriches the rich. We are inevitably our brother's keepers because we
> are our brother's brother. Whatever affects one directly affects all indirectly.[1]

The above were the words of Martin Luther King in his last book published in 1967,
"Where Do We Go from Here: Chaos or Community?". In this particular book, he
explained that, at the heart of the civil rights movement, was the broad recognition of
the humanity of black people and the accomplishment of true equality for this
group.[2] In a 2017 commentary on the book, Bennet argued that the painful truth
was that most of the concerns King had in 1967 remained true to this very day.[3]
Bennet's comments are not far from the truth. It is a truism that the rich continue to
prey on the poor, especially in capitalist societies. As a result, many advocates, such
as this author, continue to fight for social justice.

Theories of distributive justice are however plenty, but divergent from each
other.[4] As a result, what is considered to be social justice is a point of contention.
In contributing to this debate on conceptualising social justice, prominent English
Professor of Political Theory, David Leslie Miller,[5] advanced that:

> social justice has been the animating ideal of democratic governments throughout the
> twentieth century. Even those who oppose it recognize its potency. Yet the meaning of
> social justice remains obscure, and existing theories put forward by political philosophers to
> explain it have failed to capture the way people in general think about issues of social
> justice.[6]

This notwithstanding, Miller proposed a general conception of social justice that
could be useful. He proffered that a crude understanding of social justice could be
understood as being the sharing of losses and successes of humanity by all its
members.[7] Accordingly, he argued that there are multiple sources of justice, basing
his argument on a multifaceted approach, integrating philosophical and empirical
approaches.[8] However, despite the topical nature of his findings, Miller failed to
develop a theory of justice.[9] Consequently, his contributions have been subject to
criticism.

One vociferous critic is Alice Baderin. In a publication titled '*Who Cares What
People Think? Revisiting David Miller's Approach to Theorising About Justice*', the

---

[1] Saxon (2019).

[2] Burnett (2017).

[3] Burnett (2017).

[4] Miller (2017).

[5] Professor Miller is a Professor of Political Theory at the University of Oxford and a fellow of the
Nuffield College in Oxford.

[6] Miller (2002), p. 1.

[7] Miller (2002), p. 1.

[8] Oppenheimer (2002), p. 296.

[9] Oppenheimer (2002), p. 296.

author argued that while Miller's approach of integrating theories of social justice with a broad data set on popular attitudes was initially appealing, it was fundamentally flawed because of the fact that it based its findings on problematic empirical assumptions about the nature of public attitudes.[10]

Another prominent author, worth mentioning, who shares different views to Miller, is American moral and political philosopher, John Rawls.[11] Rawls was a critical figure in social justice, whose work led to the renaissance of the political philosophy on justice.[12] Rawls, like many other contemporary philosophers, couched social justice as being part of distributive justice.[13] One of his notable works was '*A Theory of Justice* and *Political Liberalism*'.[14] Within this work developed what has come to be known as Rawls theory of justice—with many students subscribing to this school (students of Rawlsian Philosophy).

The work sketches two crucial principles of social justice that strive for a well-ordered society. The first principle pertains to political institutions. It avers that every person has an equal claim to a full adequate package of basic rights (equality principle).[15] This entails that everyone has access to basic liberties that are non-derogable. The conception of the first principle is more useful for human rights analysis. However, the second principle has more persuasive value for the purposes of this chapter. It concerns social and economic institutions. It provides that:[16]

> social and economic inequalities are to satisfy two conditions: first, they are to be attached to offices and positions open to all under conditions of fair equality of opportunity; and second, they are to be to the greatest benefit of the least-advantaged members of society (the Difference Principle).

This difference principle prescribes that social inequalities should be regulated in order to better the conditions of the most disadvantaged. The argument is therefore that there should be a relative equality of material conditions.[17] When one ponders on this, two questions are likely to come to mind. These are: Is life fair? Is life just?[18] These questions are often the subject of many contemporary social justice debates. They challenge us to critically reflect on society and its institutions. Harold Pinter reflected on this matter and was of the view that:

---

[10] Baderin (2018), p. 4.

[11] John Rawls taught at Harvard for almost 40 years and trained some of the leading scholars in moral and political philosophy.

[12] Oppenheimer (2002), p. 295.

[13] Miller also discusses distributive justice. He argues that, for distributive justice to be successful, there must be a shared communal identity. This involves tax-payers identifying themselves as being beneficiaries of distributive justice. See De Schutter and Tinnevelt (2008), p. 370.

[14] Rawls (1971).

[15] Upadhyay (1993), p. 388.

[16] Upadhyay (1993), p. 388.

[17] Lockhart (1994), p. 29.

[18] Van Soest (2001), p. 181.

> There exists today widespread propaganda which asserts that socialism is dead. But if to be a
> socialist is to be a person convinced that the words "the common good" and "social justice"
> actually mean something; if to be a socialist is to be outraged at the contempt in which
> millions and millions of people are held by those in power, by "market forces," by
> international financial institutions; if to be a socialist is to be a person determined to do
> everything in his or her power to alleviate these unforgivably degraded lives, then socialism
> can never be dead because these asportations never die.[19]

Pinter raises very contentious but valuable points. To begin, he centres his argument on socialism and attempts to deconstruct the connections between social justice and socialism, as advocated by what he terms 'propaganda'. Importantly, he notes vital aspects of social justice such as the abuse of people by market forces and international financial institutions and the need to uplift those living in degraded conditions.

Financial institutions in South Africa, have in the past, been accused of doing little to improve the conditions of the poor and underprivileged in society. In 2013, the World Bank noted that, despite South Africa's well-developed banking infrastructure, particularly in relation to mobile technologies, the progress made in reducing poverty and inequality has been disappointing.[20] Then World Bank Director for South Africa, Asad Alam, was of the view that, in order to harness the full power of South Africa's developed banking infrastructure.[21]

The transformative power of financial inclusion in South Africa should not be underestimated. Improved access to finance by poor households and micro enterprises can unlock income earning opportunities and self-reliance for many.

Against this backdrop, this paper traverses the role of financial inclusion, as a social justice concept, in improving conditions for poor and previously disadvantaged persons. The major question under review is whether competition in the banking industry can help improve financial inclusion, thereby, ultimately, improving conditions for those at the bottom of society?

The early parts of the chapter, may, as a result of the natural progression of the chapter seem disjointed, dissecting competition issues separately from banking issues and financial inclusion. Conceptually, these units are fundamentally distinct and need to be approached from this dichotomy. Nevertheless, in later stages, the chapter reveals an appreciation for points of intersection in these concepts, emphasising on the core values and spirit.

It will be demonstrated that, in the context of competition law, specifically in relation to the Harvard School of thought, a central idea is that of promoting social objectives such as inclusion, redistribution, and equality, tenets of which are at the core of financial inclusion. As a result, it is unsurprising that an increase in competition in the banking industry promotes better financial inclusion.

---

[19] Quoted in Gallagher (2015), p. 53.
[20] The World Bank (2013).
[21] The World Bank (2013).

2 Financial Inclusion

2.1 Conceptualising Financial Inclusion

A growing social justice movement within the financial sector is that of financial inclusion.[22] However, to better understand financial inclusion, it is first important to set out financial exclusion.[23] This is because financial inclusion postures itself as a solution to financial exclusion, and therefore, focuses on the solution and not the problem.[24] This type of logic may potentially force anyone analysing the challenge of financial inclusion to derail.[25]

Financial exclusion describes a situation where access to financial products such as bank accounts, insurance and credit is limited.[26] Such exclusion occurs in varying degrees, ranging from partial exclusion, to total exclusion for certain sections of a population. Carbo *et al* exquisitely summarise this, broadly defining financial exclusion as: "[T]he inability of and/or reluctance of particular social groups to access mainstream financial services."[27]

The text by Carbo *et al* describes financial exclusion as an important and problematic challenge of our time.[28] This is particularly true because the effects of financial exclusion can be devastating, especially in the case of systematic exclusion from financial services. This type of exclusion, particularly in the case of the working poor, reduces them and their communities to a life where they are relegated to the fringes of the economy and society. Despite a concerted effort to tackle this challenge, financial exclusion remains a persistent problem. According to the 2017 Global Findex Database, at least 1.7 billion adults across the world remained unbanked, without access to any bank accounts or mobile money services.[29]

Having dispensed with this preliminary debate, it then becomes important to navigate the subject matter of this debate, namely 'financial inclusion'. Financial inclusion, as a concept, was articulated over 30 year ago by Nobel Laureate,

---

[22] See generally, Zauro et al. (2020), pp. 558–562. See also Zulkhibri (2016), p. 306.

[23] Ikdal (2017).

[24] Doolittle (2018).

[25] Doolittle (2018).

[26] Garg and Agarwal (2014), p. 52.

[27] Carbo et al. (2005), p. 1. Abrahams, in relation to financial exclusion, suggests that: 'To enhance one's understanding of the concept of financial inclusion, a definition of financial exclusion is warranted. Warsame (2009, p. 17) explains that financial exclusion can be defined in either a narrow sense or a broad sense. In the narrow sense, it is the exclusion of individuals from particular sources of credit and financial services, such as insurance, bill payment services and accessible and appropriate deposit accounts (Warsame 2009, p. 17). In the wider sense, financial exclusion refers to the factors which effectively shut out the less fortunate of society from any access to the mainstream money services (Warsame 2009, p. 17)'. See Abrahams (2017), p. 635.

[28] Carbo et al. (2005), p. 1.

[29] The Global Findex Report (2017), p. 35.

Mohammed Younus.[30] Younus thought that the long-standing challenge of poverty could not be addressed without resolving difficulties with regard to access to finance, particularly for the poor, marginalised and historically underprivileged.[31] It could be said that, in the narrow sense, financial inclusion describes the relationship of the general public with financial institutions in as far as it relates to vital services such as bank accounts, credit and insurance.[32]

More broadly, however, it could also be argued that financial inclusion is all about equity, fairness, transparency and the reduction of costs associated with banking services.[33] This approach is reinforced, to a larger degree, by the definition of financial inclusion stipulated by the National Treasury in South Africa. The definition states that financial inclusion involves the provisioning of banking services, at an affordable rate, to those that have been historically disadvantaged.[34] There is growing evidence that financial inclusion has significant benefits for members of a community that are poor, and previously disadvantaged, with special regards to women in these categories.[35]

A widely employed definition of financial inclusion,[36] derived from the World Bank's 2017 Global Findex,[37] avers that financial inclusion:

> [M]eans that individuals and businesses have access to useful and affordable financial products and services that meet their needs – transactions, payments, savings, credit and insurance – delivered in a responsible and sustainable way.[38]

Consequently, financial inclusion is vital to improving the quality of living and standards of living for the poor and marginalised in our community. Given the potential of financial inclusion in addressing poverty, financial inclusion is also a potential tool for propelling inclusive development and promoting sustainable development goals (SDGs).[39] Of interest, for this purpose, are SDGs 1 and 10, which speak to eradication of poverty and reduction of inequality.

---

[30] Shipalana (2019), p. 4.

[31] Shipalana (2019), p. 4.

[32] Bagli and Dutta (2012), p. 3.

[33] Paramasivan and Ganeshkumar (2013), p. 45.

[34] National Treasury (2020), p. 1.

[35] Ozili (2020), p. 1.

[36] Doolittle (2018).

[37] World Bank Group (2018), p. 1.

[38] World Bank (2018).

[39] SAIIA (2019). In 2015, the United Nations adopted the SDGs as a means of promoting peace and prosperity on the globe. The SDGs focus is on ending poverty and other pressing challenges that are holding back humanity. The specific SDGs are: (1) no poverty, (2) zero hunger, (3) good health and well-being, (4) quality education, (5) gender equality, (6) clean water and sanitation, (7) affordable and clean energy, (8) decent work and economic growth, (9) industry, innovation and infrastructure, (10) reduced inequalities, (11) sustainable cities and communities, (12) responsible consumption and production, (13) climate action, (14) life below water, (15) life on land, (16) peace, justice and strong institutions, and (17) partnership for the goals. The SDGs are therefore aspirational goals, providing a blueprint for nation states to move towards a better future. The SDGs, at a local level,

The suggestions above are not without basis. Recent research conducted by various scholars seems to adopt the view that there are many developmental benefits emanating from financial inclusion, especially from the use of digital services such as mobile money, payment cards and other related technologies.[40] This allows the poor, marginalised and excluded to, inter alia, engage in investments in health, education, business and finance, thus allowing them to unshackle the laborious collars of poverty.[41] Used appropriately, financial inclusion can be applied as an innovative technique to improve the banking habits of the previously disadvantaged, thus enhancing their participation and opportunities for success in the formal economy.[42] While studies demonstrating the developmental side of financial inclusion are now available, one cannot overlook a significant number of other studies that argue that financial inclusion does not always yield positive results.[43]

2.2 Financial Inclusion in South Africa

A fair assessment of the state of financial inclusion in South Africa will reveal that, despite its challenges, South Africa has done well to improve financial inclusion. Data gathered or collected over the last two decades reflects positively on the country. Available data reveals that, from 2004 to 2016, financial inclusion increased from 61% to 89%, in the 12-year period.[44] The National Treasury in the 2030 National Development Plan further noted that

> at least 91% of South African adults have been formally included in its financial system, with only about 2.9 million still excluded. Of those included, 81% have a bank account, 78% use other non-bank channels, and approximately 61% still use informal channels. If South Africa's nearly 5.3 million social grant beneficiaries are excluded from banking institutions, then only 68% of adults are considered banked.[45]

It is clear from these statistics that South Africa has done well to improve financial inclusion in the country. South Africa's success in improving financial inclusion has, however, not been accidental. In 2004, the government decided to respond to the slow development of the low-income market segment by committing to the Financial Sector Charter (FSC).[46] The FSC is a voluntary agreement facilitated

---

therefore, have to be read together with other strategies related to health and education in order to fully realise change. They are the work of various member states and the United Nations over decades. See United Nations Department of Economic and Social Affairs, 'The 17 Goals' <https://sdgs.un.org/goals> accessed on 9 February 2021.

[40] World Bank Group (2018), p. 1.

[41] World Bank Group (2018), p. 1.

[42] Paramasivan and Ganeshkumar (2013), p. 45.

[43] World Bank Group (2018), p. 1.

[44] Abrahams (2017), p. 656.

[45] National Treasury (2021), p. 1.

[46] Global Partnership for Financial Inclusion (2014), p. 5.

through the National Economic Development and Labour Council (NEDLAC)[47] and is based on the Broad-Based Black Economic Empowerment [BBBEE] Act 53 of 2003.[48] The aim of the FSC is to:

> ...actively [promote] a transformed, vibrant, and globally competitive financial sector that reflects the demographics of South Africa, and contributes to the establishment of an equitable society by effectively providing accessible financial services to black people and by directing investment into targeted sectors of the economy.[49]

The 2004 draft of the FSC succeeded in improving access to financial services in the Republic. However, this document was not successful in stimulating broader transformation in all spheres of the industry. Then, acting Chief Director of the Department of Trade and Industry (DTI) portfolio on Black Economic Empowerment, Liso Steto, told the Parliament's Standing Committee on Finance that while access to financial services had improved, levels of ownership and control by black persons in the industry had declined. As a result, the Amended Financial Sector Code, 2017, was published.[50] The amended Financial Sector Code harmonised the DTIs Amended Codes of Good Practice (CoGP) and the Financial Sector Code published in 2012.[51] The Amended Financial Sector Code features enhanced recognition of certain categories of black people such as those with disabilities, black youth, black women, black people living in rural areas and black people who are unemployed in terms of the Financial Institution Scorecard.[52]

South Africa's progress in financial inclusion has been spurred on by a well-developed (although as noted above, untransformed) institutional set-up. The Banking Sector in South Africa has 42 banking institutions, excluding foreign bank representatives registered with the Prudential Authority.[53] Currently, there are at least 30 foreign banks that have established offices within the country and have registered representatives. The market is, however, dominated by the big five largest banks: Standard Bank, First Rand, Absa, Nedbank and Investec. This can be illustrated in terms of their market share.[54]

In the South African context, where youth unemployment is currently at 55.75% (as of 2020),[55] financial inclusion can be a useful tool to address the plight of youth unemployment.[56] But more broadly, South Africa has a poverty challenge. A 2018

---

[47]NEDLAC is a platform that facilitates dialogue between government, labour, business and non-governmental organisations. The aim is to cooperate, through problem solving, on critical issues facing the country, related to the economy, labour and business.

[48]The Banking Association of South Africa (n.d.).

[49]The Banking Association of South Africa (n.d.).

[50]See Amended Financial Sector Code (2017).

[51]Amended Financial Sector Code (2017), p. 3.

[52]Amended Financial Sector Code (2017), p. 16.

[53]Businesswire (2019).

[54]Businesstech (2021a).

[55]Statista (2021).

[56]Mathe (2019).

Word Bank Report titled "Overcoming Poverty and Inequality in South Africa: An Assessment of Drivers, Constraints and Opportunities", exposed that South Africa, by 2015 had a gini-coefficient of 0.63.[57] This means that South Africa can be characterised as one of the most unequal societies on the globe.[58] South Africa's unemployment rate speaks to this tragedy. This figure has been steadily on the rise over the last decade, with unemployment figures pegged at 25.1% in 2015, 27.7% in the third quarter of 2017, and finally, 30.1% by 2020.

However, Khulekani Mathe, Head of Financial Inclusion at the Banking Association South Africa, noted that while financial inclusion was one of the ways to mitigate unemployment and grinding poverty, a huge challenge in the South African situation was that of limited financial literacy.[59] This he noted, emanated from challenges with regard to accessibility and usability which would have improved through financial inclusion strategies, as financial inclusion would be meaningless to consumers who are unable to evaluate or understand products in the market.[60]

The challenge raised above by Mathe is not the only limiting factor to financial inclusion in South Africa. Ikdal, a Senior Partner and Managing Director at BCG South Africa, identified 6 challenges to financial inclusion in South Africa.[61] First, Ikdal notes that there is a generally a perception existing among consumers of banking services in South Africa that there are high fee structures. According to this scholar, this is supported by statistics that South Africa's banking fee structure is three to four times higher than other countries such as Germany, Australia and India.[62] Second, Ikdal notes that there is the general mistrust of the motives of banks in South Africa. Low-income earners, in particular, feel that banks expose them to a fear of exploitation. This is as a result of unscrupulous marketing and selling of financial products which are not appropriate for certain clients.

Third, while cashless transactions increase convenience, the fear of fraud, which has been stoked by fraud at automated teller machines (ATMs) and via internet/cellphone banking has customers experiencing a phobia of banking innovation. For example, the South African Banking Risk Information Center (SABRIC) released statistics for 2019 which confirmed that digital banking fraud in South Africa had increased by 8% with a gross loss of R284.4 million.[63] Incidents of digital banking fraud also increased 20% from 23,206 to 27,928.[64] This is indicative of the fact that there are high risks to customers' money in digital transactions.

---

[57] World Bank (2018), p. xii.

[58] BusinessTech (2020).

[59] Mathe (2019).

[60] Mathe (2019).

[61] Ikdal (2017).

[62] BusinessTech (2018).

[63] SABRIC, *Annual Crime Stats 2019* (2020), p. 16.

[64] SABRIC, *Annual Crime Stats 2019* (2020), p. 16.

Fourth, many South Africans have already built relationships of trust with their advisors.[65] Ikdal refers to the case of stokvels, which, as estimated by the National Stokvel Association of South Africa, are being used by 40% of the households in the country. Rightfully, stokvels are vehicles for saving and offer a flexible platform for low-income earners.[66] Stokvels are defined by Matuku and Kaseke as "self-help initiatives designed to respond to the problems of poverty and income insecurity in communities".[67] Thus, stokvels are a form of social security, albeit an informal source of social security.[68] Research results show that, by 2019, there were at least 820,000 stokvels, with at least 11 million members, boasting of a collective saving effort of R44 billion.[69] As a result, while stokvels play this positive discretionary savings role, inadvertently, they also undermine the financial inclusion project.

Fifth, banks are crippled by a long-standing challenge of bureaucracy.[70] Customers are required to fill in many forms in order to access financial products such as loans. Businesstech notes that:[71] The financial services industry has created substantial barriers for individuals to access products such as loans. Banks require payslips and bank statements, and approval can take a long time. This is restrictive to people in the low-income segment that often need money on the same day and do not have access to these documents.

Furthermore, the response times of these financial institutions are quite slow, with many (potential) customers requiring immediate solutions to their challenges. This makes banks an unattractive solution to financial difficulties. While modernisation and digitisation have streamlined many of the processes, regulatory dictates still make it difficult for processes to be speedy and free of paperwork. Banks, inter alia, must still ensure that they are compliant with the Financial Intelligence Centre Act 38 of 2001 (FICA) and are not implicitly participating in money laundering as prohibited by the Prevention of Organised Crime Act 121 of 1998 (POCA).

Finally, a significant amount of business in South Africa is conducted informally.[72] While the size of the informal economy in the country is smaller than that of other similarly situated countries, it remains a major consideration during policy development.[73] The latest Quarterly Labour Force Survey (QLFS) showing figures for the fourth quarter of 2020, published on the 23rd of February 2021, states that informal sector employment in the quarter had grown by 65,000, with over 4 million people employed in the informal sector.[74] These persons are unable to produce any

---

[65] BusinessTech (2018).

[66] Businesstech (2018).

[67] Matuku and Kaseke (2014), p. 503.

[68] Matuku and Kaseke (2014), p. 503.

[69] Dlamini (2019).

[70] Ikdal (2017).

[71] Businesstech (2017).

[72] Ikdal 2017.

[73] Rogan (2018).

[74] Stats SA (2021), p. 18.

formal documentation when engaging with financial institutions, which makes it difficult for them to access banking products such as bank accounts and loans, products of which typically require completion of a lot of formal documents.

2.3 Financial Inclusion in Zimbabwe

Financial inclusion in Zimbabwe has been formalised through the National Financial Inclusion Strategy (NFIS) 2016–2020 which was launched by the Minister of Finance and Economic Development in 2016. While the NFIS completed its cycle in 2020, it is informative to understand what the aims and objectives of the strategy were. To begin, the overarching aim of the NFIS was to create a platform for the identification of barriers to financial inclusion in Zimbabwe and the implementation of strategies to address these.[75] The barriers noted were classified into three categories, namely; demand-side, supply-side and regulatory barriers.[76] On the demand side, challenges to financial inclusion include; low income levels, irregular income streams, high barriers to opening new accounts, inadequate information on financial services and products, lack of confidence in the financial system,[77] financial illiteracy and inflexible implementation of anti-money laundering (AML) procedures.[78]

On the supply side, challenges included were; the absence of robust credit information systems, poor infrastructure in rural areas and a lack of skills to understand the dynamics of projects of poor people. In terms of regulatory barriers, the absence of a nationally coordinated policy and strategy on financial inclusion was noted, a weak consumer protection regulatory framework was also highlighted, and capacity and resource constraints identified.[79] To address these challenges, the NFIS identifies 4 strategies: financial innovation, financial capability, financial consumer protection and microfinance.[80] In implementing these strategies, the NFIS called for the incorporation of a financial inclusion measurement framework whose task was to provide a prognosis on the state financial inclusion.[81]

While by design, the NFIS appeared as sound and promising, but there were challenges with the framework. Halfway through its implementation, the three major

---

[75] Reserve Bank of Zimbabwe: National Finance Inclusion Strategy 2016–2020 (2016), p. 2.

[76] Reserve Bank of Zimbabwe: National Finance Inclusion Strategy 2016–2020 (2016), p. 11.

[77] The lack of confidence in the banking system in Zimbabwe is a huge issue. In the 2000s, the country was plunged into hyperinflation because of a number of factors, including inflation and price distortions caused by price controls. The printing of money to, amongst other things, purchase money on the black-market worsened things. This led to a situation in which currency after currency was printed and introduced into the market. At the end of it all, most people lost their life's' savings and pensions. Since then, trust in the banking system in Zimbabwe has been eroded. See Kavila and Le Roux (2017), pp.131–159.

[78] Reserve Bank of Zimbabwe (2016), p. 11.

[79] Reserve Bank of Zimbabwe (2016), p. 11.

[80] Reserve Bank of Zimbabwe (2016), p. 2.

[81] Reserve Bank of Zimbabwe (2016), p. 2.

financial regulatory authorities, that is, the RBZ, the Insurance & Pensions Commission and Securities and Exchange Commission of Zimbabwe, in collaboration with the FinMark Trust, organised a two-day forum to unpack, reflect and learn from the first two years of the NFIS.[82] This event, titled "Strengthening Financial Inclusion in Zimbabwe, from Policy to Practice: Lessons and Way Forward" was held from the 19th to the 20th of February 2019 in Harare.

A number of issues were identified at this forum. Some of the issues identified included: (a) a lack of understanding of the NFIS from the major players, (b) a failure by capital markets to develop indicators to monitor progress in implementing the NFIS, (c) a failure to develop regulatory technology, (d) inadequate checks and balances for consumer protection by regulators, (e) a lack of incentives for the private sector to participate in financial inclusion processes, (f) a failure to collaborate by key stakeholders in ensuring financial inclusion for previously disadvantaged groups such as women and the youth, (g) high levels of bureaucracy running contrary to the spirit of financial inclusion, (h) a need to restore confidence in the banking sector so as to improve financial inclusion, and (i) the failure by microfinance institutions (MFIs) to access financial inclusion funds.[83] This was demonstrative of the fact that, while theoretically the NFIS looked impressive, its implementation was riddled with problems.

The above notwithstanding, by and large, as noted above, financial inclusion in Zimbabwe has improved considerably. This has partly been as a result of some of the positive strides made by the NFIS, but to another degree, this has been through innovation in the market,[84] particularly in the development of mobile banking services.[85] The Reserve Bank of Zimbabwe (RBZ) estimated that, by April 2020, at least 15.3 million people would be using mobile money services in Zimbabwe, with at least 5.3 million accounts being active.[86] This has been supported by the growing number of financial institutions in Zimbabwe. As at 30 June 2020, there were also 19 banking institutions and 222 other institutions under the supervision of the Reserve Bank.[87] This is indicative of the robust nature of the banking sector in Zimbabwe. It is not surprising that, with this architecture, penetration of banking services has improved.

Studies concluded before the implementation of the NFIS demonstrate that financial inclusion was already increasing. A 2014 qualitative research project conducted in Masvingo Province by Mago and Chitokwindo on the impact of mobile banking on financial inclusion revealed that poor people in Zimbabwe had been traditionally situated in the informal sector in Zimbabwe where they barely benefited

---

[82] Finmark Trust (2019).

[83] Report on the Financial Inclusion Forum (2019), p. 13, 15.

[84] For example, between 2011 and 2014, financial inclusion increased from 60 per cent to 77 per cent. See Finmark Trust (2020).

[85] Gambe and Sandada (2018), p. 63.

[86] Finmark Trust (2020).

[87] Reserve Bank of Zimbabwe (2020), p. 3.

from banking services.[88] However, the study found that the penetration of mobile banking services has created an opportunity for these categories of people to access banking services, even from remote areas, at a cheaper cost, and in a more accessible and convenient manner.[89] As a result, financial activity, and consequently, economic growth, improved within rural areas.[90] This was galvanised by an impressive mobile penetration rate in the country. According to the Postal and Telecommunication Regulatory Authority of Zimbabwe (POTRAZ), by 2015, mobile cellphone usage was pegged at 103%.[91]

Interestingly, there are some studies which argue that progress in financial inclusion in Zimbabwe has been too slow. One such study was conducted by Mbengo and Phiri in 2015. The study found that, despite the fact that the Zimbabwean banking sector was slowly turning to mobile banking as a service driver,[92] the degree of financial inclusion remained low in comparison to neighbouring countries. A few questions can be raised regarding the accuracy and fairness of the study. A first challenge to this study is that the study was qualitative in nature, reviewing 50 articles on mobile banking—thus basing its findings on secondary data.[93] By contrast, the earlier study by Mago and Chitokwindo was based on a quantitative research methodology, collecting data from 270 participants in Masvingo Province.[94] It is important to note that while a study of this nature could be conducted using a qualitative approach, a quantitative study is often deemed more instructive.

A second challenge that may be raised is that the main data relied upon was a 2012 FinScope Consumer Survey which reflected financial inclusion in Zimbabwe at a rate of 24%, as opposed to neighbouring countries such as Botswana, Swaziland, Namibia and South Africa, providing figures of 41%, 44%, 62% and 63%, respectively.[95] While the FinScope Consumer Survey is widely cited and its contents are considered accurate, an argument can be made that the specific survey relied upon 2012 data and was therefore outdated. A more relevant study which could have been utilised, the 2014 FinScope Consumer Survey, revealed that financial inclusion in Zimbabwe in 2014 had increased to 77%, with mobile money being the key contributor to this growth.[96]

More recent data, from the 2017 FinScope Consumer Survey now suggests that only 10% of the population was excluded from financial products and services.[97] While only 30% of the population was banked, 69% had access to financial products

---

[88] Mago and Chitokwindo (2014), p. 221.

[89] Mago and Chitokwindo (2014), p. 221.

[90] Ibid Mago and Chitokwindo (2014), p. 229.

[91] Mbengo and Phiri (2015), p. 198.

[92] Mbengo and Phiri (2015), p. 198.

[93] Mbengo and Phiri (2015), p. 196.

[94] Mago and Chitokwindo (2014), p. 224.

[95] Mbengo and Phiri (2015), p. 198.

[96] Finmark Trust (2020).

[97] Mavaza et al. (2020), p. 3.

and services, demonstrative of the contribution of cellphone banking to financial inclusion.[98] Against this background, it can be argued that financial inclusion in Zimbabwe has improved. While the government could have taken better steps in implementing the NFIS, actions such as the mid-implementation review of the NFIS were welcome.

3 Competition in the Banking Industry in South Africa

3.1 History of Competition in the Banking Industry

Competition between banks is important because of the central role banks play within a society. Typically, the operation of banks improves economic efficiency by diverting funds deposited by clients into investment vehicles for the benefit of the clients and the bank. The services delivered by banks provide economies with an opportunity to grow both at macro and micro levels.[99] Competition between these banks is important because it improves efficiency and makes banks more productive, ultimately producing benefits for the economy more broadly.[100] Therefore, it is important to ensure that banks participate in a competitive environment. A failure to maintain adequate competition within this industry has the potential to create a crisis relationship between banks and society. This is because, if people cannot trust the banks to provide them with credible, fair and competitive rates for their services, there will be a crisis of legitimacy.

As a result, it is vital to assess the measurement and evolution of the competitiveness of the banking industry.[101] In many of these studies,[102] it was revealed that, in many markets, there is a clear lack of competition. For example, a qualitative study conducted within the Jordanian banking sector between 2000 and 2014 revealed that, during the entire period under review, Jordanian banks operated under monopolistic conditions.[103] This followed a review of thirteen banks within the industry. To make this finding, the researchers employed the often applied Panzar-Rosse approach which is founded on a micro-economic approach that analyses the relation between the revenue of banks and their cost-structures.[104] Ideally, the market, if functioning well, an increase in costs would lead to a change in the total revenue, indicative of firm earning normal profits.[105]

---

[98] Mavaza et al. (2020), p. 3.

[99] Khalaf et al. (2015), p. 294.

[100] Bank of England (n.d.).

[101] Khalaf et al. (2015), p. 294.

[102] Northcott (2004), pp. 1–34, Moyo (2018), p. 14 and Akins (2016), p. 28.

[103] Khalaf et al. (2015), p. 286.

[104] Khalaf et al. (2015), p. 286.

[105] Khalaf et al. (2015), p. 286.

3.2   The Challenge of South Africa's Oligopolistic Banking Industry

While it is clear elsewhere that there is a dearth of competition within the banking industry, the question arises whether this is also the case in the South African context? A relevant study in this regard by Verhoef noted that: 'The banking sector in South Africa has been dominated by British-owned banks since the second half of the 19th century, both in nature and in size'.[106]

Verhoef raises two major points to substantiate his assertions. A number of these will be listed here. Firstly, in 1865, 1876, 1881 and 1890 there were four consecutive bank disasters in the then Cape Colony.[107] These disasters diminished competition in the market from independent banks, leaving two British Banks, Bank of Africa and Standard Bank operating, and with an assailable position in the market.[108] By the end of the final crisis, only seven banks remained in the Cape Colony's banking industry.[109]

Second, the British banks also acquired domination by acquiring competing banks. Standard Bank acquired the African Banking Corporation after the formation of the Union of South Africa in 1910, while The National Bank of South Africa acquired the Natal Bank, and the National Bank of the Orange Free State.[110] In 1926, Barclays Bank acquired the National Bank, cementing the position of British Banks within the national market. Later on, other banks were established, challenging the position of these banks in the market. These banks were however set to dominate the market for the rest of the century (ending in 2000).[111]

As evidenced above, before the turn of the new millennium, the banking sector was traditionally dominated by an oligopoly of British banks such as Standard Bank and Barclays Bank.[112] Recent studies have also produced similar results. For example, a study conducted by Mishi et al, set out to investigate industry concentration and risk taking in the South African banking sector.[113] The study found that South Africa has a highly sophisticated and concentrated banking sector".[114] This was calculated using the Herfindahl-Hirschman Index (HHI),[115] surveying a total

---

[106] Verhoef (2009), p. 157.

[107] Verhoef (2009), p. 157.

[108] Verhoef (2009), p. 157.

[109] Verhoef (2009), p. 157.

[110] Verhoef (2009), p. 157.

[111] Verhoef (2009), p. 157.

[112] Mishi et al. (2016), p. 115.

[113] Mishi et al. (2016), p. 112.

[114] Verhoef (2009), p. 157.

[115] The HHI index, otherwise known as the Herfindahl–Hirschman index, is a statistical and commonly accepted measure of market concentration. This index can be applied in a variety of contexts including the banking sector. In this regard, it is one indicator in a toolkit on the analysis of the competitiveness of banks. It is a vital indicator because of the importance in determining market

number of twenty-one banks.[116] It was found that the sector was dominated by the 'big four' banks (Standard Bank, Absa, FNB and Nedbank) which represented at least 84% of the industry balance sheet.[117] Interestingly Standard Bank and Absa[118] are part of the 'legacy oligopolistic infrastructure' in the market.[119]

The question then becomes: what is problematic about the existence of an "oligopoly" within the banking industry? To understand and interrogate this question, it is vital to firstly define what an oligopoly is and then to demonstrate how it fits into this particular scenario. Theoretically, an oligopolistic market structure is one in which a small group of companies dominate. This means that, even if there are a number of other competitors, there will be major players that control the bulk of the market. Within economic theory, where a market is dominated by a few firms, that market is deemed to be highly concentrated. For example, in the United Kingdom, in 2017, the 'Big Six' energy suppliers dominated the market, accounting for at least 78% of the electricity supply.[120] This was notwithstanding the fact that, at the time, there were at least 54 active suppliers. On the basis of this illustration, one can conclude that South Africa's banking market falls within the same category. The market only has 'four big players' and 34 registered banks (2017 data).[121] This creates an opportunity for some of these 'larger' players to abuse their dominance.

Further, oligopolistic conditions may affect competition within the market as there are few strong competitors. These conditions are also not suited for innovation as there is no incentive to provide new product offerings. Inevitably, there will be a reduction in efficiency and losses to consumer welfare in the market. Interestingly, in such oligopolistic conditions, firms may also seek to follow trend and price setters who seek to set prices not connected to their marginal costs. This is in order to maximise profit in a market where there is a general propensity among the key players to want to collaborate. These partnerships eventually lead to higher prices in the market which are also unfavourable for consumers. It is unlikely that a key firm in an oligopolistic market will refuse an offer to collaborate, because such a refusal may trigger a price war which will lead to losses for everybody within the market. Rather, these companies would invest money into research and advertising, in an effort to demonstrate to consumers why their product is superior.[122]

---

concentration in assessing the competitiveness of a particular market. In other contexts, it has also been used to show cooperation and collaboration within a market. To calculate this index, the market share of each competing firm in the market is squared, and thereafter, the sum of these figures is computed. The higher the result of calculation, the less the competition in the market. See Matsumoto et al. (2012), p. 181.

[116] Matsumoto et al. (2012), p. 181.

[117] Matsumoto et al. (2012), p. 181.

[118] Barclays Group was renamed Absa Group Limited.

[119] The firms discussed above which controlled the banking market, pre-2000.

[120] Economics Online (2020).

[121] Statista (2018).

[122] Corporate Finance Institute (n.d.).

3.3 The Potential of Digital Disruptions to Change the Competition Structure

In recent times, technological disruptions have impacted competition in the global banking industry,[123] with the potential to increase efficiency and consumer welfare. In South Africa, digital banks entered the market, becoming instant game-changers.[124] Three new banks were registered in 2017, namely; Discovery, Bank Zero and Tyme Digital.[125] The introduction of these banks immediately ignited a price war as the newcomers drastically slashed banking fees, placing legacy banks under pressure.[126] *Prima facie*, this is indicative of the patent benefits of new competitors in the market to competition in the banking industry.

However, this is an over-simplification of the actual proceedings. The benefits of competition in the banking industry have to be evaluated in the context of the industry specific challenges. Despite a history of steady growth, South Africa's largest banks have been receiving flat earnings in the past few years. This is as a result of significant competition from new players who have variable cost structures and business models.

These flexible new players are eroding the established profitable business areas of the large banks. Tymebank, for example, South Africa's first fully-digital transactional bank, claims to be registering an average of 110,000 clients per year and hopes to reach 4 million clients by 2022.[127] The bank, since commencing with operations in February 2019, had already attracted 2.8 million clients by February 2021. This rapid expansion has been driven by innovative packages designed for consumers. Tymebank is offering consumers a zero-fee account, a product completely unique to the market.[128]

Traditional banks have therefore been forced to respond to these new innovations with new market offerings. Standard Bank has created a new account offering (MyMo bank account), while FNB, Capitec and Nedbank have reduced their banking fees.[129] This may however not be enough to mitigate the pressure these banks are under. In addition, fin-tech start-ups are also offering significant competition in areas previously serviced by banks. This brings to the fore the issue of the delicate balance between competition and stability of the banking industry.

---

[123] OECD (2020), p. 7.
[124] Chisoro-Dube (2018).
[125] Moyo (2019).
[126] Moyo (2019).
[127] Kenen-Okafor (2021).
[128] McKane (2021).
[129] Businesstech (2021b).

4 The Nexus Between Competition in Banking and Financial Inclusion

Given the above, it is not surprising that, in recent times, the issue of financial inclusion has received a great deal of attention. This paper would be incomplete without considering the implications of competition in the banking industry to financial inclusion. On face value, there are definitely potential points of intersections between the two concepts. To begin, foundationally and philosophically, there is a familiar idea in both concepts in the form of transformation.

From the prism of competition law, one can consider the Harvard and Chicago schools of antitrust analysis which form the foundation of competition law. Competition regulators in every country have to decide which school is appropriate for their purpose. The Chicago school of thought focuses on consumer welfare/efficiency within a market. Proponents of this school believe that markets are self-correcting without the intervention by governments or competition authorities.[130] The Harvard school of thought, on the other hand, proposes that market concentration results in the likelihood of anti-competitive behaviour.[131] A key aspect of the Harvard school of thought is the focus on the plurality of welfare goals. The thinking in this regard is that market imperatives such as efficiency have to be considered together with social objectives.

South Africa has adopted Harvard school of thought to its regulation of competition within markets. This is evident in its position outlined in the Competition Act. Section 2 of the Competition Act sets out the purpose of the Act. The first two *provisos* in the section speak to efficiency in the market. Section 2(a) of the Competition Act provides that the aim of the Act is to promote efficiency, adaptability and the development of the economy, while section 2(b) of the Competition Act provides that the aim of the Act is to provide consumers with competitive prices and options. In the 2018 Amendment to the Competition Act, the legislators also inserted section 2(g) into the Act which recognises the detection and resolution of market conditions where competition is likely to be impeded, restricted, or distorted in relation to the acquisition or supply of goods or services. This *proviso* recognises the need to eliminate any shortcomings within the market which would otherwise render the market inefficient by allowing anti-competitive behaviour.

However, later *provisos* in the section relating to social objectives are enunciated. Section 2(c) of the Act, for example, provides that the objective of the Act is to promote employment and advance the social and economic welfare of South Africans. A more interesting objective is found in section 2(d) of the Act which affords that the Act strives to widen opportunities for locals in the world market, while recognising the need for foreign competition. This in principle, is similar to section 2(f) of the Act which provides that the Competition Act aims to

---

[130] Piraino (2007), p. 350.
[131] Piraino (2007), p. 349.

promote a greater spread of ownership, particularly focusing on increasing the ownership stakes of historically disadvantaged persons.[132]

As discussed in detail in the introductory section, social justice is about bettering the lives of persons in a country, particularly the poor and disadvantaged. Social justice is, according to articulations from some scholars, also about freeing the masses from market forces which may be undermining their position.[133] The transformational component of social justice does not require a belaboured debate as it is implied and evident in its name. It is clear from this discussion that at the centre of both competition regulation and financial inclusion in South Africa, is the transformation agenda. Both concepts seek to improve the position of previously disadvantaged persons within the markets.

Bearing this conversation in mind and deliberations in the foregoing section, it can be said with conviction that competition within the banking sector is an important ingredient in the realisation of financial inclusion in South Africa. This is because competition amongst banks compels them to innovate. Innovation entails the creation of new banking products that improve the quality of the service experienced by the customer. Many of the services reach out to customers who were previously excluded from service cover such as those in rural or remote areas.

The introduction of new banks such as Capitec, Discovery, Bank Zero and Tyme bank has entrenched these ideas. Customers are able to access banking services without the need for physically visiting banks. Existing products such as mobile banking, e-wallet services and loan facilities have also been improved as a result. Traditional banks such as Standard Bank, which have enjoyed oligopolistic privileges over many years, have had to improve their service delivery and product lines.

For instance, Standard Bank customers are able to apply for loans telephonically or online, with same day delivery of the loan in many instances. Mortgages can now also be pre-approved online, a service also offered by many other banks. A new account called MyMo can now be opened for a monthly fee of R4.95, with no minimum monthly income required to hold the account. Accordingly, competition in the industry has led to an overhaul of the product basket and an overall decrease in the cost of products.

The introduction of these new banks has undoubtedly transformed the market and fostered a better environment for financial inclusion. Before, this, as explained above, the monopolistic nature of the banking sector in South Africa had not provided much incentive for innovation. While there was general innovation of some products, this was mostly in response to global trends and changing market conditions, particularly as a result of the growth of the internet. The Global Partnership for Financial Inclusion (GPFI) summarised the connections well, explaining that:

> The financial services sector in South Africa is well developed and characterised in most sectors by well-established private companies, with significant infrastructure and

---

[132] See also section 2(e) of the Competition Act.

[133] Gallagher (2015), p. 53.

sophisticated operational capabilities, a wide range of products covering multiple market segments and typically well-capitalized. The banking sector was a prime example of this, with the four major retail banks at the time dominating the local retail market with a market share of approximately 90%. The banks were cautious at that stage though, as the consequences of a credit bubble implosion has just led to a run on some smaller banks and the demise of one of the most prominent smaller banks. Although there were some notable movements to engage lower-income segments, the banks by-and-large focussed on middle- and upper-income individuals and established business and corporate clients. The concentrated nature of the industry also did not engender a sufficiently competitive environment promoting innovation, which meant that new business models and innovative access means were not high on the agenda.[134]

An important observation from the excerpt above is that competition in the banking industry has had an effect on the product offerings in the banking industry, and ultimately financial inclusion. This has been the agenda of the democratic government in South Africa.

Whilst the establishment of democracy in 1994 and the resultant constitutional changes and developmental initiatives gave hope to millions of people, economic exclusion was still the reality for a large proportion of South Africans. The Government recognized at the time that access to financial services is one of the key stepping stones on the path to sustainable economic development. As a clear governmental policy objective was (and remains) redressing the skewed development of the past, increasing pressure was being brought to bear on financial service providers to actively extend access and improve usage of appropriate financial services by all South Africans.[135]

Accordingly, the South African government will need to continue to open up the banking sector, to undo the skewed development of the past, and in so doing enhance financial inclusion.

5 Conclusion

As discussed in this paper, financial inclusion is one of several crucial tools in reducing poverty in a modern society. This notwithstanding, nearly two billion people remain unbanked across the globe.[136] This means that they lack access to vital services such as bank accounts, insurance and credit. Thus, at a global level, there are high rates of financial exclusion. However, as demonstrated in this paper, despite the many challenges South Africa faces with regards to achieving financial inclusion, the country has made great strides in including previously excluded persons in the banking sector. A major contributor to this success has been the increasing role of technology in the banking sector. This development is not unique

---

[134] Global Partnership for Financial Inclusion (2014), p. 4.

[135] GPFI (2014).

[136] Shipalana (2019), p. 5.

to South Africa. As indicated in the paper, even in Zimbabwe, a vast number of unbanked persons in remote areas have been included via banking services over cellular networks such as Econet.

However, an important, but less often talked about factor, has been that of competition in the banking industry. This has been the subject matter of this paper. This chapter has advanced the position that while competition and financial inclusion seem to be wholly irreconcilable concepts, actually, at the core, these concepts do share a common DNA. The commonality is the fact that both concepts (at least competition law when viewed from the Harvard school of thought) seek to foster transformation, focusing in particular on previously disadvantaged persons. This leads one to consider whether the one concept has an impact on the other?

The finding of this chapter is that competition within the banking industry, undeniably, improves financial inclusion in the sector. As more players are allowed to enter into the market, they need to provide new product offerings, including offering new products geared for low-income and previously unbanked groups. Through this process, these groups are included within the mainstream financial sector. Therefore, it is important that the laws (rules) relating to the entry of new firms in the banking sector be carefully considered so as to remove barriers which may prevent new players from entering the market. However, caution must be used, as flooding the market with competitors could collapse this delicate but critical sector.

Bibliography

Abrahams R (2017) Financial Inclusion in South Africa. Biennial International Conference Proceedings of the Southern African Accounting Association, pp 170–196

Akins B, Li L, Ng J, Rusticus TO (2016) Bank competition and financial stability: evidence from the financial crisis. J Financ Quant Anal 51:1–28

Baderin A et al (2018) Who cares what people think? Revisiting David Miller's approach to theorising about justice. Contemp Polit Theory 17:69–104

Bagli S, Dutta P (2012) A study of financial inclusion in India. Radix Int J Econ Bus Manage 1:1–18

Bank of England. (n.d.) Why is Competition Important in Banking' available at <https://www.bankofengland.co.uk/knowledgebank/why-is-competition-important-for-banks>. Accessed 25 Jan 2021

Broad-Based Black Economic Empowerment [BBBEE] Act 53 of 2003

Burnett B (2017) Martin Luther King Jr asked Chaos or Community. <https://www.commondreams.org/views/2017/10/06/martin-luther-king-jr-asked-chaos-or-community>. Accessed 16 Dec 2021

Businesstech (2017) High Prices, Fraud and Four Other Reasons Why South Africans Don't Trust SA Banks. <https://businesstech.co.za/news/banking/173527/high-prices-fraud-and-four-other-reasons-why-south-africans-dont-trust-sa-banks/>. Accessed 25 Mar 2021

BusinessTech (2018) South Africa's Banking Fees vs the World. <https://businesstech.co.za/news/banking/236517/south-africas-banking-fees-vs-the-world/>. Accessed 28 Mar 2021

BusinessTech (2020) South Africa's Unemployment Rate Climbs to 30.1%. <https://businesstech.co.za/news/government/409897/south-africas-unemployment-rate-climbs-to-30-1/#:~:text=Stats%20SA%20has%20published%20its,first%20quarter%20of%20the%20year>. Accessed 3 Feb 2021

Businesstech (2021a) 2021 South African Banking Fees Compared: Capitec vs Absa vs Standard Bank vs Nedbank vs FNB. <https://businesstech.co.za/news/banking/456642/2021-south-african-banking-fees-compared-capitec-vs-absa-vs-standard-bank-vs-nedbank-vs-fnb/>. Accessed 25 Mar 2021

Businesstech (2021b) How South Africa's 5 biggest banks continue to dominate. <https://businesstech.co.za/news/banking/506740/how-south-africas-5-biggest-banks-continue-to-dominate/>. Accessed 12 Dec 2021

Businesswire (2019) South Africa Banking Industry Report 2019. <https://www.businesswire.com/news/home/20191014005441/en/South-Africa-Banking-Industry-Report-2019%2D%2D-ResearchAndMarkets.com>. Accessed 13 Feb 202

Carbo S et al (2005) Financial exclusion. Springer, New York

Chisoro-Dube S (2018) Digital Banks: Game-Changers in South Africa's Banking Industry. <https://www.competition.org.za/ccred-blog-competition-review/2018/5/30/digital-banks-game-changers-in-south-africas-banking-industry>. Accessed 25 Mar 2021

Competition Act 89 of 1998

Corporate Finance Institute. (n.d.) Oligopolistic Market. Available at <https://corporatefinanceinstitute.com/resources/knowledge/economics/oligopolistic-market-oligopoly/>. Accessed 25 Jan 2021

De Schutter H, Tinnevelt R (2008) David Millers theory of global justice. A brief overview. Crit Rev Int Soc Polit Philos 11:69–104

Dlamini S (2019) SA Stockvels Collectively Save R 44bn Annually. <https://www.iol.co.za/business-report/economy/sa-stokvels-collectively-save-r44bn-annually-25814087>. Accessed on 25 March 2021

Doolittle L (2018). Defining Financial Exclusion: Why We Need to Focus on the Problem and Not Just the Solution. <https://medium.com/s3idf/defining-financial-exclusion-w,hy-we-need-to-focus-on-the-problem-not-just-the-solution-37117b8f6507>. Accessed 2 Jan 2021

Economics Online (2020) Oligopoly. <https://www.economicsonline.co.uk/Business_economics/Oligopoly.html>. Accessed 25 Jan 2021

Financial Intelligence Centre Act 38 of 2001

Financial Sector Code, 2017 (as amended)

Finmark Trust (2019) Zimbabwe Financial Inclusion Forum 2019 Report. <http://finmark.org.za.dedi517.jnb2.host-h.net/zimbabwe-financial-inclusion-forum-2019-report/>. Accessed 3 Feb 2021

Finmark Trust (2020) Interest on Mobile Money in Zimbabwe: 'Paying the Customer their Dues. <https://finmark.org.za/knowledge-hub/blog/interest-on-mobile-money-in-zimbabwe-paying-the-customer-their-dues?entity=blog>. Accessed 2 Feb 2021

Gallagher K (2015) Responsible art and unequal societies: towards a theory of drama and the social justice Agenda. In: Freebody K, Finneran M (eds) Drama and social justice: theory, research and practice in international texts. Routledge, Oxfordshire

Gambe B, Sandada M (2018) The effectiveness of selected financial inclusion strategies. Acta Universitatis Danubius Œconomica 3:59–64

Garg S, Agarwal P (2014) Financial inclusion in India – a review of initiatives and achievements. IOSR J Bus Manage 16:52–61

Global Partnership for Financial Inclusion (2014) Global Partnership for Financial Inclusion (GPFI) country case studies: VOLUME 1 - The Use of Financial Inclusion Data in South Africa, the Philippines and Peru. <https://www.afi-global.org/wp-content/uploads/publications/gpfi_country_case_studies_volumn_1_-_the_use_of_financial_inclusion_data.pdf>. Accessed 16 Dec 2021

Ikdal A (2017) Improving Financial Inclusion in South Africa. <https://www.bcg.com/publications/2017/globalization-improving-financial-inclusion-south-africa>. Accessed 16 Feb 2021

Kavila W, Le Roux P (2017) The role of monetary policy in Zimbabwe's hyperinflation episode. Afr Rev Econ Financ 9:131–166

Kenen-Okafor T (2021) South African Digital Bank TymeBank Lands $109 from UK and Philippines Investors. <https://techcrunch.com/2021/02/23/south-african-digital-bank-tymebank-lands-109m-from-uk-and-phillippines-investors/>. Accessed 25 Mar 2021

Khalaf BA et al (2015) The evolution of bank competition: have conditions been changed in the Jordanian banking sector. Int J Acad Res Bus Soc Sci 5:2222–6990

Lockhart C (1994) Social constructed conceptions of distributive justice: the case of affirmative action. Rev Polit:29–49

Mago S, Chitokwindo S (2014) The impact of mobile banking on financial inclusion in Zimbabwe: a case for Masvingo Province. Mediterranean J Soc Sci 5:221–221

Mathe K (2019) Can financial inclusion be the key to end poverty. <https://www.iol.co.za/personal-finance/can-financial-inclusion-be-the-key-to-end-poverty-26590443>. Accessed 6 Feb 2021

Matsumoto A et al (2012) Notes on applying the Herfindahl-Hirschman index. Appl Econ Lett 19:181–184

Matuku S, Kaseke E (2014) The role of Stokvels in improving people's lives: the case of Orange farm in Johannesburg. Social Work/Maatskaplike Werk 50:504–515

Mavaza T et al (2020) An insight into financial inclusion of the informal sector in Masvingo Zimbabwe. PM World J IX:1–8

Mbengo P, Phiri MA (2015) Mobile banking adoption: a rural Zimbabwe marketing pespective. Corp Ownership Contr 13:195–204

McKane J (2021) No-Monthly-Fee Bank Accounts in South Africa Compared. <https://mybroadband.co.za/news/banking/384488-no-monthly-fee-bank-accounts-in-south-africa-compared.html>. Accessed 25 Mar 2021

Miller D (2002) Principles of social justice. Harvard University Press, Massachusetts

Miller D (2017) Justice. <https://plato.stanford.edu/entries/justice/>. Accessed 15 Feb 2021

Mishi S et al (2016) Industry concentration and risk taking: evidence from the South African banking sector. Afr Rev Econ Financ 8:113–136

Moyo A (2019) Digital Newcomers Spark Price War Among SA Banks. <https://www.itweb.co.za/content/KA3WwqdlL1aqrydZ>. Accessed 25 Mar 2021

Moyo B (2018) An analysis of competition, efficiency and soundness in the South African banking sector. South Afr J Econ Manage Sci 21:1–14

National Treasury (2021) 2030 National Development Plan Draft: An all Inclusive Sector for All. <http://www.treasury.gov.za/comm_media/press/2020/Financial%20Inclusion%20Policy%20-%20An%20Inclusive%20Financial%20Sector%20For%20All.pdf>. Accessed 7 Feb 2020

Northcott CA (2004) Competition in banking: a review of the literature. 2004 Bank of Canada Working Paper 1–34

OECD (2020) Digital disruption in banking and its impact on competition. OECD Publishing, Paris

Oppenheimer J (2002) Considering social justice: a review of david miller's principles of social justice. Soc Just Res 12:295–311

Ozili PK (2020) Financial inclusion research around the world: a review. Forum Soc Econ, pp 1–23

Paramasivan C, Ganeshkumar V (2013) Overview of financial inclusion in India. Int J Manage Dev Stud 2:45–49

Piraino TA (2007) Reconciling the Harvard and Chicago Schools: a new antitrust approach for the 21st century. Indiana Law J 82:345–410

Prevention of Organised Crime Act 121 of 1998

Rawls J (1971) A theory of justice. Harvard University Press, Massachusetts

Report on the Financial Inclusion Forum (2019)

Reserve Bank of Zimbabwe (2020) Banking Sector Report for Quarter Ended 30 June 2020

Reserve Bank of Zimbabwe: National Finance Inclusion Strategy 2016-2020 (2016)

Rogan M (2018) Informal economies are diverse: South Africa needs policies to recognise this. <https://theconversation.com/informal-economies-are-diverse-south-african-policies-need-to-recognise-this-104586#:~:text=The%20informal%20economy%20in%20South,of%20total%20non%2Dagricultural%20employment>. Accessed 25 Mar 2021

SA (23 February 2021) Quarterly Labour Force Survey: Q 4 – 2020

SABRIC (2020) Annual Crime Stats 2019

SAIIA (2019) Digitising Financial Services: A Tool for Financial Inclusion in South Africa. <https://saiia.org.za/research/digitising-financial-services-a-tool-for-financial-inclusion-in-south-africa/>. Accessed 9 Feb 2021

Saxon J (2019) Reflections on Truth and Compassion Mark Martin Luther King Jr. Day Celebration. <https://www.princeton.edu/news/2019/01/22/reflections-truth-and-compassion-mark-martin-luther-king-jr-day-celebration>. Accessed 10 Feb 2021

Shipalana P (2019) Digitising Financial Services: A Tool for Financial Inclusion in South Africa. 2019 SAIIA Occasional Paper 301

Statista (2018) Number of Banks Registered in South Africa from 2006 – 2017. <https://www.statista.com/statistics/915598/number-registered-banks-south-africa/#:~:text=In%202017%2C%20there%20were%2034,the%20country%20of%20South%20Africa>. Accessed 25 Jan 2021

Statista (2021) South Africa: Youth Unemployment Rate from 1999 to 2020. Available at https://www.statista.com/statistics/813010/youth-unemployment-rate-in-south-africa/.   Accessed 3 Feb 2021

The Banking Association of South Africa (n.d.). Financial Sector Charter Code. <https://www.banking.org.za/consumer-information/consumer-information-legislation/financial-sector-charter-code/>. Accessed 10 Feb 2021

The Global Findex Report (2017)

The World Bank (2013) South Africa Update: Financial Inclusion Critical for South Africa's Poor. Available <https://www.worldbank.org/en/country/southafrica/publication/south-africa-economic-update-financial-inclusion-critical-for-south-africa-s-poor>. Accessed 15 Feb 2021

United Nations Department of Economic and Social Affairs. The 17 Goals. <https://sdgs.un.org/goals>. Accessed 9 Feb 2021

Upadhyay AK (1993) Rawlsian concept of two principles of justice. Indian J Polit Sci 54:388–395

Van Soest D (2001) Review of principles of social justice david miller reviewed by Dorothy Van Soest. J Sociol Soc Welfare 28:181–183

Verhoef G (2009) Concentration and competition: the changing landscape of the banking sector in South Africa 1970 – 2007. South Afr J Econ Hist 24:157–197

World Bank (2018) Overcoming poverty and inequality in South Africa: an assessment of drivers, constraints and opportunities. World Bank Publications, Washington DC

World Bank. Financial Inclusion: Financial Inclusion is a Key Enabler to Reducing Poverty and Boosting Prosperity. <https://www.worldbank.org/en/topic/financialinclusion/overview>. Accessed 2 Feb 2021

World Bank Group (2018) The global findex database 2017: measuring financial inclusion and the fintech revolution. World Bank Publications, Washington DC

Zauro NA, Saad RAJ, Sawindi N (2020) Enhancing socio-economic justice and financial inclusion in Nigeria: the role of Zakat, Sadaqah and Hassan. J Islamic Account Bus Res 11:558–562

Zulkhibri M (2016) Financial inclusion, financial inclusion policy and islamic finance. Macroecon Financ Emerg Mark Econ 9:303–320

Tinashe Kondo is a lecturer in the Department of Mercantile and Labour Law at the University of the Western Cape where he teaches Insolvency Law, Competition Law and Cyber-Law. He also supervises a number of masters and doctoral students in a variety of field in Mercantile Law. He holds a Bachelor of Commerce in Law with an economics specialisation, a Bachelor of Laws degree, a Master of Laws specialising in Mercantile Law, and a Doctor of Laws degree specialising in Investment Law (UWC). His doctoral thesis was titled "Investment Law in a Globalised Environment: A Proposal for a New Foreign Direct Investment Regime in Zimbabwe". The thesis focused on rethinking the law of foreign direct investment in Zimbabwe. After his studies, he completed a two-year postdoctoral fellowship on constitutional theory with the Centre for Humanities Research at the University of the Western Cape. The focus of this fellowship was to investigate how humanities considerations could be infused within legal research. Since his studies, Dr Kondo is now a tenured academic at the aforesaid institution and focuses his research on Banking Law, Investment Law, Competition Law and Social Justice. His most recent project was a book published by UWC Press, a joint project between African Sun Media and the University of the Western Cape, titled "Law and Investment in Africa: The Governance of Foreign Direct Investment in Zimbabwe". The book builds on his doctoral study and traverses' recent developments such as the Zimbabwe Investment and Development Agency African Continental Free Trade Area. Many of his current projects include collaborative work with various academics and practitioners on infusing social justice debates within contemporary literature and fields. The aim and hope of this research theme is to change the organisation of society, in particular, economic structures, and aim at the realisation of equality in material conditions.

Financial Inclusion, Intra-African Trade and the AfCFTA: A Law and Economics Perspective

Tapiwa Victor Warikandwa

Abstract It is challenging to calculate the value of Sub-Saharan Africa's contribution to global trade because of the continent's low financial inclusion, which mostly finances trade through the informal financial system. Although access to more affordable and effective formal financial services can help boost intra-African trade, small traders in Africa cannot afford to use official financial channels for cross-border transactions. Almost no official trade is conducted between African nations. The average exports and imports between nations on the same continent between 2015 and 2017 was only 2% in Africa, compared to 47%, 61%, 67%, and 7% in America, Asia, Europe, and Oceania, respectively. This is because although intra-African trade makes up more than 60% of regional trade, it is typically unregulated and thus informal. The African Continental Free Trade Agreement (AfCFTA) provides an opportunity to regularise such trade. The AfCFTA was ratified by 36 of the 54 African nations. On January 1, 2021, it was formally started with the intention of unifying the African market by removing 90% of tariffs and enabling free trade in commodities, services, and capital. In order to lower the cost of international transfers and contribute to the success of the AfCFTA, this chapter will argue that using mobile money to expand financial inclusion for individuals working in the informal sector is decisive.

T. V. Warikandwa (✉)
School of Law, University of Namibia, Windhoek, Namibia
e-mail: twarikandwa@unam.na

© The Author(s), under exclusive license to Springer Nature Switzerland AG 2023
H. Chitimira, T. V. Warikandwa (eds.), *Financial Inclusion and Digital Transformation Regulatory Practices in Selected SADC Countries*, Ius Gentium: Comparative Perspectives on Law and Justice 106,
https://doi.org/10.1007/978-3-031-23863-5_10

1 Introduction

Issues around financial services in the AfCFTA and Intra-African Digital Trade are crucial for the development of Africa.[1] However, due to low levels of financial inclusion in Africa, trade is largely financed through the informal financial system, making it difficult to measure the value of Sub-Saharan Africa's share of global trade.[2] The formal financial channels for cross-border transactions are too expensive for small traders in Africa, access to cheaper and more efficient formal financial services can help to boost intra-African trade.[3] There is very little formalised trade going on between African countries. This is because intra-African trade is largely informal, yet it accounts for over 60% of regional trade.[4] This trade is usually conducted by small businesses and individual traders in goods which may be legal on one side of the border and illicit on the other side due to not having been subjected to statutory border formalities such as customs clearance.[5] Informal trade can be beneficial to those living near borders as it provides livelihoods, contributes to job creation and ensures food security through the trade of agricultural products, but it comes at the cost of reduced tax revenue and undermines policy-making efforts.[6]

The World Bank forecasts $292 billion in income gains from greater trade facilitation, such as cheaper cross-border transfers, for the AfCFTA to succeed, but the high cost of moving cash across African is a hurdle to success.[7] Sending money to Sub-Saharan Africa (SSA) is more expensive than sending money to any other region on the planet. According to World Bank data, sending money to Sub-SSA costs 8.9% of the total cost, which is more than the global average of 6.8%.[8] Sending money from South Africa to China cost 25.1% on average in 2019, while sending money from Cameroon to Nigeria cost 15.5%.[9] Due to a lack of statutory border formalities like customs clearance, small businesses and individual traders commonly engage in this trade in goods that are lawful on one side of the border but illegal on the other. Through the interchange of agricultural products, informal trade can help communities living close to borders by generating income, assisting in the creation of jobs, and maintaining food security. However, this is done at the expense of tax revenue and undermines efforts to make policy.

In the framework of the AfCFTA, it is necessary to examine the relationship between economic growth and financial inclusion or between economic growth and trade openness. In this chapter, a one-way causal relationship between commerce,

---

[1] Banga (2021).

[2] Triki and Faye (2013), Part 1.

[3] Agbelusi (2022).

[4] African Union (2022a).

[5] Brenton and Soprano (2018).

[6] Brenton (n.d.).

[7] The World Bank (2020a).

[8] Economist Intelligence Unit (2020).

[9] Heitzig (2020).

economic expansion, mobile money, and financial inclusion in Africa is presented. The link between commerce and growth is particularly supported by expanding financial inclusion in the financial sector. It is advised that policymakers in Africa concentrate on pro-growth measures in order to improve financial inclusion, which fuels the continent's primarily informal trade (under the auspices of the AfCFTA).

2   Contextual Background

The main goal of the AfCFTA is to establish a unified continental African market for goods and services with unrestricted trade in investments and services.[10] When fully implemented, the AfCFTA will cover a market of more than 1.2 billion people and have a combined gross domestic product (GDP) of more than US$3.4 trillion, making it the largest free trade area in the world by the number of participating nations since the World Trade Organization (WTO) was founded.[11] On March 21, 2018, 44 African Union (AU) members signed the AfCFTA Agreement in Kigali, Rwanda, establishing the AfCFTA. As of July 2019, 30 of the 55 AU member nations had ratified the AfCFTA Agreement, which had been signed by 54 of the 55 AU members. The AfCFTA Agreement was supposed to start trading on July 1, 2020, but this date has been delayed because of the Covid-19 pandemic's global effects on commerce and economic activity. A new time has not yet been determined.

The advantages of an effective AfCFTA implementation vastly outweigh the drawbacks. The delay in the start of commerce will provide member nations the chance to further up their preparations for the AfCFTA's implementation. There will be winners and losers despite the AfCFTA's overall advantages. This chapter examines the effects of financial inclusion on the prospects of the success or failure of the AfCFTA. Countries in Africa had Regional Existing Communities (RECs) prior to the AfCFTA.[12] The RECs, proposed by the Abuja Treaty of 1991 establishing the wider African Economic Community and the Lagos Plan of Action for the Development of Africa in 1980, had the goals of facilitating economic integration among and between members of the individual regions with a view to eventual continental integration.[13]

The Arab Maghreb Union (AMU), the Common Market for Eastern and Southern Africa (COMESA), the East African Community (EAC), the Economic Community of Central African States (ECCAS), the Economic Community of West African

---

[10] Article 3 of the Agreement Establishing the African Continental Free Trade Area, adopted 21 March 2018.

[11] The World Bank (2020a).

[12] See Articles 3(c), 5(b) and (i) of the Agreement Establishing the African Continental Free Trade Area.

[13] African Union (2022b).

States (ECOWAS), the Intergovernmental Authority on Development (IGAD), and the South African Development Community (SADC) are the eight RECs that are acknowledged as the foundation of the African Union (AU).[14] The AU adopted the Decision to Establish a Continental Free Trade Area in January 2012 at its eighteenth ordinary session in Addis Ababa, Ethiopia, after realizing the importance of promoting intra-African trade for long-term economic growth, employment, and effective integration of Africa into the global economy.[15] By an indicative deadline of 2017, the Continental Free Trade Area (CFTA) was supposed to be operational. However, the AfCFTA's operative phase did not begin until July 2019 after 27 ratifying countries had submitted the document at the Chair of the African Union Commission (depositary).

The AfCFTA aims to liberalise markets for goods and services, create a single market for goods and services that is facilitated by the movement of people in order to further the economic integration of the African continent, contribute to the movement of capital and natural persons and facilitate investment, and lay the groundwork for the eventual creation of a Continental Customs Union.[16] Over the past ten years, Africa's trade growth has been among the weakest among the world's major regions, primarily due to falling commodity prices, competition, a lack of foreign exchange liquidity, issues with regulations, and a lack of access to trade finance.[17] Even though banks still frequently fund trade, participation rates have declined. Despite the ongoing huge trade financing imbalance, commerce remains a key driver of Africa's social and economic development. Development finance institutions like the African Development Bank and the African Export-Import Bank have been looking for ways to boost intra-African trade.[18] Due to a lack of legal documentation, small and medium-sized businesses (SMEs) in Africa are unable to prove their validity to banks, service providers, and other firms.[19] As a result, millions of people struggle to forge alliances and obtain trade financing, particularly in emerging economies.

It is vital to assess if the implementation of the AfCFTA will strengthen digital business identity across the continent in order to close the trade finance gap in Africa. This approach will help establish whether improving digital business identity can increase financial inclusion for SMEs and informal businesses on the continent in order to ensure the growth of the African financial sector. AfCFTA must address the high cost of cross-border payments. The AfCFTA intends to integrate the African market by eliminating 90% of tariffs and enabling free flow of capital, products, and services, but it cannot be successful without a robust and inclusive financial sector.[20]

---

[14] African Union (2022c).

[15] See the Assembly of the Union Eighteenth Ordinary Session (2012).

[16] See Articles 3 and 4 of the Agreement Establishing the African Continental Free Trade Area.

[17] Meyer and Stratton (2022).

[18] Meyer and Stratton (2022).

[19] Ackah and Vuvor (2011).

[20] Abrego et al. (2020), p. 17.

This is because the World Bank estimates that increased trade facilitation, such as more affordable cross-border payments, could generate income gains of $292 billion, but that success is constrained by the high cost of sending money across Africa.[21] Sub-Saharan Africa (SSA) is the most expensive place in the world to transmit money than any other region. Sending money to SSA carries costs at a rate of 8.9% percent, higher than the 6.8% global average, according to World Bank data.[22] In 2019, the average transaction fee for transfers from South Africa to China was 25.1%, and the average fee for transactions from Cameroon to Nigeria was 15.5%.[23] Mobile money must be used to integrate those working in the unorganized sector of society into the financial system in order to reduce the cost of cross-border payments.

2.1 Financial Inclusion and Mobile Money in Africa

Only 20% of people in SSA have bank accounts, compared to 92% in industrialized nations and 38% in less developed ones, according to the World Bank.[24] People turn to informal channels due to the high expense of traditional financial services. The Centre for Financial Regulation and Innovation (CENFRI) believes that an additional 50% of remittance value is sent informally, making Nigeria's diaspora remittance ($25.3 billion as of 2019) the biggest in Africa.[25] Such large economic activity occurring outside of the established system raises the dangers of money laundering and financing terrorism, as well as denying the unbanked the advantages of access to financial services including higher consumption and investment in the productive economy.

Mobile money is on the increase in Africa and can help more individuals access formal financial services thanks to the accessibility of affordable mobile devices and the high mobile phone penetration rate. In 2019, 50 million people in sub-Saharan Africa opened a mobile-money account using a phone, a rise of 12% from the previous year that brought the region's total number of users to 469 million.[26]

---

[21] The World Bank (2020b) Digital Financial Services and Cross-Border Payments, Remarks delivered at the G20 Finance Ministers and Central Bank Governors Meeting, Riyadh, Saudi Arabia, 23 February 2020, by Anshula Kant, Managing Director and World Bank Group Chief Financial Officer.

[22] Esser and Cooper (2020), pp. 1–41.

[23] Agbelusi (2022).

[24] Calderon et al. (2018), pp. 1–45.

[25] Nevin and Omosomi (2019).

[26] Velluet (2020).

Mobile money wallets from providers like Paga[27] and Safaricom[28] have become a quick and affordable replacement for traditional banking institutions, which lack the manpower and equipment necessary to effectively service rural areas. For instance, Nigeria only has 16.93 ATMs and 4.3 commercial bank branches per 100,000 adults, preventing a sizable portion of the rural population from access to formal financial services.[29]

2.2 Improving Cross-Border Payments

It is challenging for African banks to fulfill their duty for monetary stability due to the high number of cross-border transfers made outside of the formal financial system. Driving financial inclusion will reduce financial exclusion and encourage trade inside Africa.[30] Thus, an emphasis on identity management via the Bank Verification Number, payment system, agent banking, and mobile banking may be necessary. Sadly, the goal of considerably lowering financial exclusion in Africa has frequently fallen short. This has been ascribed to the usage of bank-led mobile money solutions in the majority of African nations. Most adult mobile phone users will therefore continue to be financially excluded. In order to address this, the banks may need to develop systems similar to Nigeria's Payment Services Banks, which permit mobile network companies to offer consumers basic financial services.[31] All mobile phone owners should be able to be registered using the current Subscriber Identity Module registration database, which will address the identity management issue.[32]

The AfCFTA will only be successful if its payments system is robust and inclusive. Therefore, by advancing financial inclusion on the continent and democratizing cross-border payments, financial regulators in Africa may significantly contribute to the success of AfCFTA. It may thus be imperative to question if

---

[27] In order to make it easier for one billion people to access and use money, Tayo Oviosu founded Paga in early 2009, in Nigeria. Paga has done away with the use of cash in transactions and opening up access to financial services. It is an ecosystem for banking and payment services throughout Africa. Its main goals are to make it easier for buyers and sellers to pay, receive payment, and use financial services. Paga accomplishes this objective directly as well as through our Platform-as-a-Service, which enables other third parties to use the substantial infrastructure we have established for countless opportunities.

[28] Kenyan mobile network operator Safaricom PLC has its corporate headquarters at Safaricom House in Nairobi. It is one of the most successful businesses in East and Central Africa and the biggest telecommunications operator in Kenya.

[29] The World Bank (2020a).

[30] For instance, the National Financial Inclusion Strategy (NFIS) in Nigeria, which was amended in 2018, began a campaign to promote financial inclusion in Nigeria in 2012. As a result, in 2018 Nigeria's rate of financial exclusion decreased from 46.3% to 36.8%.

[31] Creemers et al. (2020).

[32] Oladipo et al. (2018).

African banks are prepared to compete in the market for trade financing. To date, mostly Pan-African organisations, particularly Moroccan ones, are gradually beginning to take market share for trade financing in Africa.[33] As these organisations assist businesses, invest in financial inclusion, and adopt digital advances, they are gradually gaining in stature. The organisations are steadily becoming more influential as they invest in financial inclusion, support entrepreneurs and take up digital innovations. However, it is important to note that African banks frequently lack the capital required to assume the risk associated with some of the larger agreements and must therefore turn to the major international banks, which charge a premium for their services.[34]

2.3   Trade Financing in Africa

Due to the AfCFTA's implementation and the projected increase in intra-African commerce, African banks will likely be more comfortable with expanding trade lending than their foreign competitors.[35] Once the AfCFTA gets into full swing and intra-African commerce really takes off, African banks will be more at ease developing trade credit than their international competitors. Banks must emphasize promoting and/or helping entrepreneurs who are venturing into new markets because Africa is a significant source of development.[36]

2.4   A Digital Shift to Trade in Africa

Paper for administrative purposes is a big part of trade finance hence alternative approaches are therefore required to encourage trading on digital platforms. Another component of the solution is digital innovation.[37] One of Africa's potential future growth sectors could be blockchain-based trade digital platforms. The processing of a trade negotiation from the beginning of the trade contract to settlement is made possible by trade digital platforms.[38] Currently being explored in several of our African subsidiaries is Komgo, a different digital platform that specializes in trade financing and is utilized by more than 160 businesses and 40 banks in Europe.[39] African participants have shown their proficiency with digital documents and mobile

---

[33] Faujas (2021).

[34] Nyantakyi and Sy (2015), pp. 1–16.

[35] The World Bank (2022).

[36] Hawkins and Mihajek (n.d.).

[37] Feyen et al. (2021a), pp. 1–53.

[38] Benjelloun (2021).

[39] Faujas (2021).

banking in particular. They will rely on technology that can analyze contracts, bill of lading documents, invoices, and more in order to facilitate compliance monitoring.

2.5 Using Digital Currency in Africa

Banks do not seem to be interested in making it easier to make payments or settle contracts. They are mainly focused on raising the ISO 20022 standard for the SWIFT interbank payment system by 2025.[40] The market for trade financing in Africa has enormous potential with new participants having a solid reputation because they are new to the commodities market. As Asia's influence grows, continental banks are being compelled to increase their presence in East Africa and English-speaking Africa.[41] Positive trends appear to be helping African banks. First, there is the derisking phenomena, which discourages certain major banks from funding agreements deemed too complex, such as contracts relating to the Democratic Republic of Congo.[42] Smaller banks are benefiting from this.

African banks are replacing large institutions that are leaving the continent, like BNP Paribas.[43] They are setting up offices in London and Paris to cut costs. They recognized that because their balance sheets differed from those of Deutsche Bank, they had to grow in order to compensate for their low capital ratio.[44] They realized that in order to gain market share, they needed to improve their technological and human resources, master the regulatory environment, and customize their strategies to the demands of their various portfolios.

There are various groups that make up Africa's trade finance champions. European banks like Société Générale and CACEIS (Crédit Agricole), as well as their affiliates in the European trade corridor, make up one group.[45] Large US banks like Citi and JP Morgan that dominate the US corridor make up another group. Mitsubishi, Standard Chartered, HSBC, and ICBC control the Asian corridor.[46] The group of sizable African banks-often Moroccan-like Bank of Africa (BOA, formerly BMCE), Ecobank, *Banque Centrale Populaire*, Attijariwafa,[47] and Absa, are steadily gaining influence on the global stage. Despite the possibility of US and European penalties, they are less hesitant to do business with Chinese exporters and importers. Above all, once the AfCFTA is implemented and intra-African commerce picks up, they will be more at ease establishing trade financing than their foreign

---

[40] Bank of Namibia (2021).

[41] Faujas (2021).

[42] European Investment Bank (2020).

[43] M'Bida and Mieu (2022).

[44] M'Bida and Mieu (2022).

[45] Faujas (2021).

[46] Faujas (2021).

[47] Berrada et al. (2021).

rivals. Parties will develop regulatory cooperation arrangements in priority sectors as part of the AfCFTA service negotiations.

2.6 Supporting AfCFTA Objectives Through Regulatory Cooperation

The interaction between the regulation and regulators in other nations to achieve the goals of regulatory policy is referred to as cooperation, which is a broad phrase. Information sharing and harmonisation are both examples of cooperation. Dialogue, information sharing, partnerships, recognition, networks negotiated agreements, collaborative rule-making, integration, and harmonisation through supranational bodies are all included in the Organization for Economic Co-operation and Development's taxonomy of regulatory cooperation.[48]

The regulatory treatment of the services can be more significant in the context of trade-in-services than the explicit market access and national treatment promises included in services schedules (which themselves often also relate to the regulatory treatment of certain businesses).[49] The regulatory standards, particularly for providers of financial services, are frequently stringent and can differ greatly from one nation to the next.[50] The majority of nations do not regulate or impose restrictions on the use of financial services abroad.[51]

Cross-border supply is frequently severely constrained; normally, governments forbid the sale of financial services from overseas to citizens within their borders, but this is typically reflected in service schedules.[52] Country A, for instance, categorizes all financial services as unconstrained. Natural persons' presence is frequently restricted horizontally; people can only conduct business in Country A if other conditions are met (typically in line with immigration law). The licensing and registration procedures, however, may present an additional obstacle to a person's ability to conduct business once they have been given permission to do so because typically financial services providers must be licensed or registered.

---

[48]Lazo and Sauve (2017), pp. 575–607. See also Lezotre (2014), and Organisation for Economic Co-operation and Development (2020).

[49]The framework agreement (the Articles of the Agreement), its Annexes, the schedules of members' individual commitments, and the lists of Article II (Most Favoured Nation) exclusions provided by WTO members make up the General Agreement on Trade in Services (GATS). The Agreement's schedules and exemption lists are essential components.

[50]Claessens and Rojas-Suarez (2016).

[51]Pasini (2011), pp. 4–24. See also Key (1999), pp. 61–75.

[52]Blumberg et al. (2016).

The most liberalised method of providing financial services is commercial presence.[53] While this method occasionally has schedules with restrictions on equity levels or local incorporation, the majority of the roadblocks are rules that apply to financial service providers operating in the nation, such as capital requirements, reporting requirements, conduct rules, and others.[54] These are not discriminatory, but they nevertheless put a lot of barriers in the way of international financial service providers entering new markets, which lessens competition in any particular market.

Foreign service providers complicate the job of regulators and supervisors because they must comprehend and analyse enterprises in other jurisdictions but might not have access to all the information they require or regulatory authority over all aspects of the business. However, foreign competitors may be crucial to achieving regulatory and policy objectives for the financial sector, such as promoting competition, bringing down costs, opening up new categories of financial services, and enhancing access to these services.[55] These regulatory frameworks are likely to make trade in financial services between African countries easier than the liberalization commitments themselves, which are unlikely to go beyond the current levels of liberalization, given the low-level ambition for liberalization of the services sectors (GATS-plus).[56] Two different reporting formats or conflicting conduct rules are just two issues that make trade in financial services difficult from the perspective of service providers and risky from the perspective of regulatory authorities.[57] Coordination between regulators and the integration of regulatory systems, both of which are significant aspects of cooperation, can address these issues.

A more favourable environment for the trade of financial services on the continent will be created by working to enhance the experience for the suppliers of financial services as well as to reassure regulators, which will assist countries achieve their financial sector goals.[58] Transparency in regulation is also a key component of enhancing access for foreign providers, and transparency should be required as part of the AfCFTA's regulatory framework as a unilateral rather than cooperative action.[59] If there is no procedure for applying for a license, a financial service provider cannot hope to comply with requirements it cannot identify. Additionally, it is critical that governments engage widely and are open-book about regulatory changes. Free trade agreements are increasingly referencing these "good regulatory practices," and the AfCFTA's financial services regulatory framework should do the

---

[53] The General Agreement on Trade in Services (GATS) 1869 UNTS 183; 33 ILM 1167 (1994) agreement's Annex on Financial Services contains detailed information about the actions that authorities may take with regard to financial services. A non-exhaustive list of the banking, insurance, and other financial services that are subject to GATS laws and commitments is also included in the Annex (Article 5).

[54] OECD (2015), pp. 1–29.

[55] Feyen et al. (2021b), pp. 1–64.

[56] Matoo (2018), pp. 1–31.

[57] Hope (2020).

[58] Hope (2020).

[59] Hope (2020).

same.[60] Making these requirements legally binding by committing to specific actions will guarantee that the initiatives actually expand access.

3 Coordination and Integration of Regulations

Regulatory results, such as efficient supervision and enforcement, are achieved through coordination, which is more concentrated on the operational and supervisory components of regulation.[61] The core of regulatory coordination is information sharing, although coordination can also involve joint action and mutual assistance in supervision and enforcement (for instance, when Namibian authorities need to learn more about a certain financial service provider with a base in Botswana) (for example a joint taskforce to address a cross-border regulatory problem). The process by which specific components or aspects of one regulatory system are acknowledged by, or incorporated into, another regulatory system to create a single, integral system that operates on a cross-border basis, is known as integration and is more concerned with the structural aspects of regulation.[62]

The most comprehensive type of regulatory integration, referred to as harmonization, often entails not just a single set of regulations but also a single supervisory authority. Common rules could be the application of the same laws, but not necessarily the same oversight and policing. This might be the case, for instance, if two nations adopt a model law or a global norm. Harmonization and the application of similar norms can both take place on a global scale or in specific subsectors, but the latter is more frequent. Harmonization across the board, like that of the European Union, is intermittent.[63]

The AfCFTA's new regulatory frameworks should be ambitious in terms of both coordination and integration, but they should also be considered as only one of several levels of collaboration between the continent's financial systems. These include "hard" legal instruments of collaboration, such as treaties (including free trade agreements), agreements for mutual recognition, memoranda of understanding between regulators, and unofficial agreements for sharing knowledge. Although agreements like free trade agreements are legally binding contracts between nations, their promises to regulate are not always enforceable.[64] This is due to the fact that treaties frequently employ hortatory language like "will endeavour" and "will encourage," which indicates that the legal instruments are "hard" but the obligations themselves are "soft."[65]

---

[60] Baiker et al. (2021), pp. 2–48.

[61] Llewellyn (2006), pp. 1–45.

[62] Hope (2020).

[63] Dahlberg et al. (2020).

[64] Benson and Judd (2021) e.

[65] Drexl et al. (2014), pp. 41–57.

Other levels of cooperation include adhering to international standards like the International Financial Reporting Standards,[66] the Basel Core Principles,[67] and the Objectives and Principles for Securities Regulation of the International Organization for Securities Commissions,[68] as well as regional standards like those created by regional cooperation mechanisms like the Organization for the Harmonization of Business Law in Africa.[69] Regulatory frameworks must therefore be created "where necessary, for each of the sectors, taking into account the best practices and acquis from the RECs".[70]

Since the RECs[71] have attained varied degrees of integration and coordination, it is crucial to highlight that the Southern Africa Customs Union, a monetary union, shares monetary policy but may not always do so with financial regulatory policy.[72] On the other hand, countries such as Benin, Burkina Faso, Cote d'Ivoire, Guinea-Bissau, Mali, Niger, Senegal, and Togo are members of Economic Community of West African States (ECOWAS) and operate under a unified regulatory framework known as the West African Economic and Monetary Union. However, the ECOWAS region as a whole is less tightly connected, with regulatory limitations on cross-border market involvement and separate regulatory agencies in each of the other ECOWAS nations.[73] Even though it is not (yet) a monetary union, the East African Community (EAC) has achieved relatively deep financial regulatory integration compared to ECOWAS.[74] For instance, the EAC countries are working toward common banking regulation rules based on adherence to international standards, including the Basel Banking Core Principles, but regional supervision or licensing is not yet in place.[75]

The mechanisms that will be put into place as a result of the AfCFTA do not take the place of current processes; rather, they provide another layer of coordination and integration to the continent's financial sector. Additionally, they will serve as a crucial foundation for greater integration planned under the Abuja Treaty.[76] In the end, a fully integrated African Community will have financial sector-wide

---

[66]The International Accounting Standards Board and the IFRS Foundation together publish the accounting standards known as "International Financial Reporting Standards," or "IFRS."

[67]The minimal international standards for competent prudential regulation and supervision of banks are outlined in the Core Principles for Effective Banking Supervision (CPs). They were first released in 1997 and have since been revised in 2006 and 2012.

[68]International Organisation of Securities Commissions (2017).

[69]Organisation pour l'Harmonisation en Afrique du Droit des Affaires (OHADA) is a system of business laws and implementing institutions adopted by sixteen West and Central African nations.

[70]Erasmus (2022).

[71]See Article 1(t) of the AfCFTA Agreement.

[72]Seoela (2022), pp. 35–53.

[73]Torres and Seters (2016), pp. 1–95.

[74]Krapohl and Van Huut (2020), pp. 565–582.

[75]Beck and Rojas-Suarez (2019), pp. 1–89.

[76]Abuja Treaty Establishing the African Economic Community, adopted 3 June 1991 and entered into force on 12 May 1994.

harmonised regulations and unified supervisory authorities, allowing for frictionless business travel across African borders. However, this dream is a long way off. AfCFTA regulatory framework drafters can learn from the pockets of harmonisation that some of Africa's monetary unions already offer, but at the continental level, more focused harmonisation and other types of regulatory cooperation and integration should be prioritized. This will be more manageable than complete harmonisation, and it will also allow drafters, regulators, and policymakers to focus their efforts on the policy objectives that will have the biggest an impact on the financial sector (and more broadly). The following common rules should be developed with priority:

(a) Consumer protection is a crucial policy consequence and a key component of reassuring regulators that consumers will be safe while doing business with foreign suppliers. This can be done by having a set of regulations that are universal and cross-border.
(b) The standards for financial reporting should be uniform, even though this extends beyond the banking industry. This will facilitate information sharing between regulators and be crucial for providers conducting cross-border business because they will only need to maintain one set of books.
(c) It is important to harmonize new areas of financial regulation, especially those governing digital financial services like mobile money, crowdfunding, and blockchain-based services. Financial inclusion is significantly impacted by digital financial services. Due to their propensity for global mobility, digital services are also significant. They are frequently also start-ups and lack the tools that established financial institutions have to handle a variety of legislation. Given that these are new areas for regulation, this should also be more feasible than harmonizing already-existing regulations.

The following must be emphasized in relation to areas of mutual recognition:

(a) The ability to offer securities throughout the continent using a single offer document should be prioritized.
(b) Broker-dealers and financial advisers must be qualified and licensed in every member state, by the relevant regulatory authorities. The recognition throughout the continent would be made easier as a result.
(c) There are many financial markets on the continent which lack depth. Mutual recognition would allow stock exchanges (financial markets) to open to trading throughout the continent.

Emphasis should also be placed on regulatory cooperation as follows:

(a) It is necessary to establish supervisory colleges for pan-African banking organizations. Cross-border banking can provide dangers, particularly in the host country because, in some situations, pan-African banks have systemic importance, even though bank supervision is expected to remain national (or regional, in other cases) for the foreseeable future. Cooperation in governing these institutions is therefore crucial.

(b) On the continent, underinsurance is a big problem, particularly for homes and small enterprises. Markets and insurance regulations are still in their infancy. Collaboration can be used to build stronger regulatory systems.

Considering the disparate levels of both regulatory capability and regulatory frameworks, regulatory frameworks will be easier to achieve by concentrating on priority areas for shared sets of norms, mutual recognition, and regulatory cooperation. The financial sector policy objectives will likewise be most impacted by this.

4   AfCFTA Implementation and Covid-19

Africa has a rare opportunity to establish the largest trade area in the world based on the number of members, together with the associated economic benefits, through the implementation of the AfCFTA. The AfCFTA offers opportunities for a larger market for goods and services produced on the continent, increased labour mobility across the continent, increased participation of women in formal business, and quicker and deeper development due to the ease of interconnection between and among Small and Medium-Term Enterprises (SMEs) on the African continent. The AfCFTA's initial implementation date of July 1, 2020, was chosen. The AfCFTA trading date was delayed without a new date being set because of Covid-19's impact on international commerce and economic activity, particularly in regard to African trade.[77] African nations were debating the best ways to address the difficulties that the AfCFTA's implementation would face prior to its suspension.

Barriers to the AfCFTA's successful implementation include both tariff and non-tariff ones. One of the many issues working against the successful implementation of the AfCFTA is inefficient bureaucracy, poor infrastructure, persistent non-tariff barriers and other protectionist measures, heavy reliance on traditional export crops and commodities, lack of cross-border rule and regulation harmonisation, lengthy delays at road border crossings for cargo trucks, and poorly functioning rail systems.[78] As a result, concerns have been expressed over whether Africa is ready for the AfCFTA. The AfCFTA's trading date being delayed because of Covid-19 does not mean everything is lost. The delay allows African leaders more time to continue their negotiations and ultimately come to agreements on the specifics of removing non-tariff and physical trade barriers, two significant obstacles to the successful implementation of the AfCFTA. Moreover, the delay offers African nations the chance to implement trade and investment policies while accelerating investment through the development of local capacity for crucial commodities and

---

[77] Asiedu (2021).
[78] Trade Mark East Africa (2020).

services. Increased international trade is good to the economy of all the participating nations, as evidenced by the advantages of a successful AfCFTA implementation.[79]

5 Financial Inclusion as a Tool for Winning Under the AfCFTA

The majority of the adult population in Africa is still unbanked, creating a significant untapped opportunity for financial inclusion services.[80] The free movement of goods and services always necessitates the ease of the movement of capital, making the financial services sector a crucial one in the continental market of Africa. People who would typically have been excluded from financial products are now more readily available in Africa. For example, the percentage of people who have access to financial services is already 83% in Kenya,[81] up from 27% in 2006, while the ambitious target for Nigeria is 80% financial inclusion by 2020.[82] More people will have easier access to funds that they can utilize for their enterprises when there is greater financial inclusion. Only the development and widespread use of technology, particularly mobile and internet-based devices, will enable financial inclusion. When trade under the AfCFTA begins, a nation that has neglected or refused to create essential technological infrastructure risks losing.

5.1 Lessons from COMESA: Supporting Digital Financial Inclusion by Working with the Trade and Development Bank

On January 20, 2021, in Kigali, Rwanda, the Common Market for Eastern and Southern Africa (COMESA) Business Council (CBC) and the Trade and Development Bank (TDB) organized a high-level public-private dialogue with the theme "Towards the COMESA Digital Integrated Common Payment Policy for Micro Small and Medium-sized Enterprises (MSMEs)".[83] The TDB and the CBC joined forces to advance digital financial inclusion in the area, with an emphasis on Small and Medium Enterprises (SMEs). More specifically, the collaboration intends to validate the COMESA digital integrated common payment policy and framework for SMEs.

---

[79] Kende-Robb (2021).
[80] World Bank (2018).
[81] Reuters Staff (2019).
[82] Udo (2019).
[83] COMESA Business Council (2021a), pp. 1–18.

Nine pilot-study countries, central bank governors, finance ministers, ICT regulators, manufacturers, mobile network operators, commercial banks, and MSMEs participated in the public-private discussion to discuss and validate the COMESA Digital Integrated Common Payment Policy and Framework for SMEs.[84] Partnerships, regulatory discussion, and consumer protection were all considered to be crucial success elements for SMEs' digital financial inclusion during the discussion. The foundation of the infrastructure that will help African SMEs develop into successful firms over the future years will be the establishment of the policy on Digital Integrated Common Payment. With potential advantages in development of regional trade (sourcing and supply), which is currently below 20%, digital payment system platform dividend for COMESA and Africa at large can be substantial.[85] However, it will take the combined efforts of our governments, the private sector, and development partners to make this enormous promise a reality.

In order to support the design, development, and deployment of an integrated, low-cost, and fraud-resistant digital financial services infrastructure that serves Micro, Small, and Medium-sized Enterprises, particularly women and youth who are at the base of the financial pyramid, CBC has been implementing the Digital Financial Inclusion Program. The TDB emphasized that numerous parties, including policymakers, regulators, the commercial sector, employers, educational institutions, communities, and individuals, are involved in financial inclusion. Increasing MSMEs' engagement in digital financial inclusion can have positive effects on the economy, the efficacy of macroeconomic policy, and job creation.

During the public-private conversation, the draft model policy regulation guidelines/rulebook for a digital integrated regional common payment plan for SMEs was presented and validated. Prior to the second conference to validate the edited report of the common policy framework, national committee meetings will take place.

5.2   Pan-African Payment and Settlement System

The Pan-African Payment and Settlement System will be advantageous for Africa. A deal that, if completely implemented, would link about 1.3 billion people in 55 nations with a $3.4 trillion global GDP.[86] The World Bank estimated in 2020 that the implementation of the AfCFTA could increase African exports by $560 billion while raising the continent's revenue by $450 billion by 2035.[87] Stronger trade facilitation measures to cut red tape, streamline customs processes, and make it simpler for African enterprises to join into global supply networks would account for

---

[84] COMESA Business Council (2021b).

[85] COMESA (2021).

[86] Ogbalu III (2022).

[87] The World Bank (2020c).

$292 billion of the $450 billion.[88] One such measure is the creation of a centralized payment and settlement infrastructure to support trade in this new agreement. This infrastructure will be known as the Pan-African Payment and Settlement System and will be led by the Africa Export-Import Bank in collaboration with the AfCFTA Secretariat (PAPSS).[89] Payment facilitators in Africa, including banks and new Fintech start-ups, will be able to connect with PAPSS and use it to make safe and quick payments on behalf of their clients.[90]

A well-functioning payment infrastructure is often referred to as an economy's circulatory system, even if money is often considered its lifeblood. Therefore, PAPSS implementation is crucial to enabling the seamless operation of a continent-wide market and provides advantages to key players in the African private sector. Instant payments and receipts will help companies throughout Africa, boosting trust and trade volumes while freeing up time traditionally lost to payment confirmation delays.[91] For example, a design firm in Accra would be able to pay promptly and in its own local currency if it wanted to buy kikoy cloth from a tiny fabric maker in Kenya. The Kenyan fabric producer would avoid the already frequent delays in customs and tax procedures and receive money promptly into its bank account in local currency, freeing up time to quickly fulfill the Accra order.[92]

The successful implementation of PAPSS means lower liquidity needs for settlements as well as for African commercial banks engaged in payment clearing and settlement.[93] As a result, there will be less restrictions on the monies they hold for settlements, releasing more funds for other initiatives and value-added services. More significantly, these institutions would no longer be forced to seek for scarce hard currency in order to facilitate trade between two African markets. The successful implementation of PAPSS could aid policymakers in tracking informal small-scale cross-border trade, which is a crucial component of African economies but is infrequently fully captured and reported in official trade statistics.[94] This is in addition to streamlining value exchange procedures. Therefore, when making judgments, foreign investors and policymakers frequently overlook these typical interactions, which results in financial exclusion and underestimate of the export potential of African nations.

FinTechs with the highest growth rates and most innovative technologies may be found all over Africa, but particularly in Egypt, Nigeria, Kenya, South Africa, and other countries.[95] Thousands of individuals and small enterprises that are typically

---

[88] The World Bank (2020c).
[89] Ogbalu III (2022).
[90] African Union (2022c).
[91] Ogbalu III (2022).
[92] Ogbalu III (2022).
[93] Ogbalu III (2022).
[94] Usman and Csanadi (2022).
[95] Musewe and Hiebert (2022).

inaccessible by traditional banking structures now have last-mile access thanks to these FinTechs.[96] Imagine the profound economic impact of PAPSS when clients of commercial banks and FinTechs in Africa are linked to a single, immediate payment rail.

If the Covid-19 pandemic has taught us anything as a continent, it is that investing in regional commerce is essential for assisting African countries in absorbing future economic shocks as well as for promoting long-term sustainable economic growth and development. The AfCFTA must be fully implemented by African governments, but PAPSS is in a position to encourage and hasten this process. This gives confidence that Africa's future is bright, even in a post-Covid-19 world; a future that is lined with innovation, financial inclusion, prosperity, and economic policy reform.

6 Conclusion

This chapter has made the case that using mobile money to increase financial inclusion for all Africans (particularly those who are marginalised or are in informal sectors) is crucial for lowering the cost of international transfers and aiding in the success of the AfCFTA. It is inadequate for a nation to merely ratify the AfCFTA agreement. In the world of commerce, there are winners and losers. For a nation to profit when commerce under the AfCFTA begins, it must have made investments in two crucial infrastructure areas, namely power and financial inclusion. Imagine a continent without borders, where trade between countries is unrestricted and goods and services can be exchanged for the best price possible without being hampered by complex and frequently expensive customs procedures and tariffs. This expanding, free-flowing mosaic of information, goods, and capital will definitely alter the economies of African countries, leading African governments to revaluate their policies, lower trade costs, give their marginalised people more power, and seize new opportunities. The financial services sector is essential to the continent of Africa since the free flow of goods and services always requires the free flow of cash. As a result, in order for the AfCFTA to be successful, financial inclusion mechanisms in Africa must now provide access to financial services to those who would ordinarily be excluded from them.

---

[96] Musewe and Hiebert (2022).

Bibliography

Abrego, L, de Zamaroczy, M, Gursoy, T, Issoufou, S, Nicholls, GP, Perz-Saiz, H and Rosas, J (2020) The African Continental Free Trade Area: Potential Economic Impact and Challenges, IMF Staff Discussion Note, SDN/20/04, p 17

Abuja Treaty Establishing the African Economic Community, adopted 3 June 1991 and entered into force on 12 May 1994

Ackah J, Vuvor S (2011) The Challenges faced by Small and Medium Enterprises (SMEs) in Obtaining Credit in Ghana. https://www.diva-portal.org/smash/get/diva2:829684/FULLTEXT01.pdf;The. Accessed 4 July 2022

African Union (2022a) Boosting Intra-African Trade https://au.int/en/ti/biat/about. Accessed 6 June 2022

African Union (2022b) Regional Economic Communities (RECs). https://au.int/en/organs/recs. Accessed 1 July 2022

African Union (2022c) The Pan-African Payments and Settlement System. https://au-afcfta.org/operational-instruments/papss/. Accessed 11 July 2022

Agbelusi M (2022) Financial Services and AfCFTA. https://digitalbankerafrica.com/financial-services-afcfta/. Accessed 6 June 2022

Agreement Establishing the African Continental Free Trade Area, Adopted 21 March 2018, entered into force on 30 May 2019

Article 3 of the Agreement Establishing the African Continental Free Trade Area, adopted 21 March 2018

Asiedu E (2021) Continental Free Trade Area (AfCFTA): Exploring Potential Impacts and Developmental Implications. https://www.intechopen.com/chapters/76462. Accessed 13 July 2022

Assembly of the Union Eighteenth Ordinary Session, 29-30 January 2012 Addis Ababa, Ethiopia. https://au.int/sites/default/files/decisions/9649-assembly_au_dec_391_-_415_xviii_e.pdf. Accessed 5 July 2022

Baiker L, Bertola E, Jelitto M (2021) Services Domestic Regulation – Locking in Good Regulatory Practices: Analysing the Prevalenece of Services Domestic Regulation Disciplines and their Potential Linkage with Economic Performance. World Trade Organisation Economic Research and Statistics Division, pp 2–48. https://www.wto.org/english/res_e/reser_e/ersd202114_e.pdf. Accessed 11 July 2022

Banga K, MacLeod J, Mendez-Parra M (2021) Digital Trade Provisions in the AfCFTA: What can we learn from South-South Trade Agreements? https://repository.uneca.org/bitstream/handle/10855/43949/b11990405.pdf?sequence=1&isAllowed=y. Accessed 11 July 2022

Bank of Namibia (2021) Guidance Note on the Migration to ISO 20022 Messaging Standards for both Domestic and Cross-Border Payments in the National Payment System. https://www.bon.com.na/CMSTemplates/Bon/Files/bon.com.na/53/53d72437-02d1-4ca9-a339-c329a12df99e.pdf. Accessed 10 July 2022.

Beck T, Rojas-Suarez L (2019) Making Basel III Work for emerging markets and developing economies: a GCD task force report. Center for Global Development, pp 1–89

Benjelloun R (2021) Opinion: How Blockchain can Boost Trade in Africa. https://www.devex.com/news/opinion-how-blockchain-can-boost-trade-in-africa-101615. Accessed 10 July 2022

Benson E, Judd L (2021) Trade Laws of Nature: Biodiversity Provisions and the AfCFTA. Center for Strategic and International Studies. https://www.csis.org/analysis/trade-laws-nature-biodiversity-provisions-and-afcfta. Accessed 12 July 2022

Berrada E, Assoko JT, Toulemonde M (2021) BCP, BMCE, Attijariwafa: Will Morocco's top 3 banks see a recovery in 2021? TheAfricaReport, 8 April 2021

Blumberg RL, Malaba J, Meyers L (2016) Traders in Southern Africa: Contributions, Constrains, and Opportunities in Malawi and Botswana. https://banyanglobal.com/wp-content/uploads/2017/05/ICBT-Gender-Assessment-Report_Final_4-30-2016_DEC.pdf. Accessed 7 July 2022

Brenton P, Soprano C (2018) Small-scale cross-border trade in Africa: why it matters and how it should be supported. https://www.tralac.org/news/article/13116-small-scale-cross-border-trade-in-africa-why-it-matters-and-how-it-should-be-supported.html. Accessed 5 June 2022

Brenton P, Gamberoni E, Sear C (n.d.) Women and Trade in Africa: Realising the Potential. https://
    openknowledge.worldbank.org/bitstream/handle/10986/16629/825200WP0Women00Box3
    79865B00PUBLIC0.pdf. Accessed 3 July 2022
Calderon C, Cantu C, Chuhan-Pole P (2018) Infrastructure Development in Sub-Saharan Africa: A
    Scorecard. World Bank (Office of the Chief Economist, Africa Region) Policy Research
    Working Paper 8425, pp 1–45
Claessens S, Rojas-Suarez L (2016) Financial Regulations for Improving Financial Inclusion: A
    CGD Task Force Report. https://www.cgdev.org/sites/default/files/CGD-financial-regulation-
    task-force-report-2016.pdf. Accessed 6 July 2022
COMESA (2021) COMESA Secretariat signs Sub-Delegation Agreement with Malawi to upgrade
    Mchinji Boder Post. https://www.comesa.int/wp-content/uploads/2021/01/e-COMESA-News
    letter-650.pdf. Accessed 11 July 2022
COMESA Business Council (2021a) CBC Regional Advocacy Agenda 2021, Policy Brief A
    COMESA Business Council Annual Publication, CBC Sector Report Series 003 – 12/2021,
    pp 1–18
COMESA Business Council (2021b) Digital Financial Inclusion for MSMES. https://
    comesabusinesscouncil.org/wp-content/uploads/2021/05/DFI_Insider5.pdf.   Accessed
    12 July 2022
Creemers T, Murugavel T, Boutet F, Omary O, Oikawa (2020) Five Strategies for Mobile-Payment
    Banking in Africa. https://www.bcg.com/publications/2020/five-strategies-for-mobile-pay
    ment-banking-in-africa. Accessed 7 July 2022
Dahlberg E, Naess-Schmidt S, Virtanen L, Marcuss S, Di Salvo M, Pelkmans J, Dalla Pzza V,
    Kubovicova K (2020) Legal obstacles in Member States to Single Market rules, Publication for
    the committee on Internal Market and Consumer Protection, Policy Department for Economic,
    Scientific and Quality of Life Policies. European Parliament, Luxembourg
Drexl J, Ruse-Khan HG, Nadde-Phlix S (eds) (2014) EU bilateral trade agreements and intellectual
    property: for better or worse? Springer, pp 41–57
Economist Intelligence Unit (2020) Africa weekly brief: Pandemic leads to slump in Remittances.
    http://country.eiu.com/article.aspx?articleid=1630038146&Country=Tanzania&topic=Econ
    omy_1. Accessed 1 July 2022
Erasmus G (2022) Does the AfCFTA Protocol on Trade in Services allow for Flexibilities? Tralac
    7 March 2022
Esser A, Cooper B (2020) Exploring the barriers to remittances in sub-Saharan Africa, removing the
    barriers to remittances in sub-Saharan Africa. Recommendations 7:1–41
European Investment Bank (2020) Banking in Africa: Financing Transformation amid uncertainty.
    https://www.eib.org/attachments/efs/economic_report_banking_africa_2020_en.pdf. Accessed
    8 July 2022
Faujas A (2021) Are African Banks ready to take on the Trade-Finance Market? TheAfricaReport
    17 May 2021
Feyen E, Frost J, Gambacorta L, Natarajan H, Saal M (2021a) Fintech and the Digital Transfor-
    mation of Financial Services: Implications for Market Structure and Public Policy, Bank for
    International Settlements- Papers 117, pp 1–53
Feyen E, Frost J, Gambacorta L, Natarajan H, Saal M (2021b) Fintech and the digital Transforma-
    tion of Financial Services: Implications for Market Structure and Public, Bank for International
    Settlements Papers No 117, pp 1–64
Hawkins J, Mihajek D (n.d.) The Banking Industry in the Emerging Market Economies: Compe-
    tition< Consolidation and Systematic Stability – An Overview. https://www.bis.org/publ/
    bppdf/bispap04a.pdf. Accessed 10 July 2022
Heitzig C (2020) Figure of the week: Remittance flows to sub-Saharan Africa expected to slow after
    years of growth. Africa In Focus, 25 June 2020
Hope A (2020) Cooperation on Financial Services Regulation under the AfCFTA, TRALAC
    27 March 2020

International Organisation of Securities Commissions (2017) Objectives and Principles of Securities Regulation. https://www.iosco.org/library/pubdocs/pdf/IOSCOPD561.pdf. Accessed 12 July 2022

Kende-Robb C (2021) 6 Reasons why Africa's new free trade area is a global game changer. https://www.weforum.org/agenda/2021/02/afcfta-africa-free-trade-global-game-changer/. Accessed 14 July 2022

Krapohl S, Van Huut S (2020) A missed opportunity for regionalism: the disparate behaviour of African countries in the EPA-negotiations with the EU. J Eur Integr 42(4):565–582

Lazo RP, Sauve P (2017) The treatment of regulatory convergence in preferential trade agreements. World Trade Rev 17(4):575–607

Lezotre P (2014) State of Play and Review of Major Cooperation Initiatives, International Cooperation, Convergence and Hamonisation of Pharmaceutical Regulations. https://www.ncbi.nlm.nih.gov/pmc/articles/PMC7182102/pdf/main.pdf. Accessed 11 July 2022

Llewellyn DT (2006) Institutional structure of financial regulation and supervision: the basic issues. Paper presented at a World Bank seminar Aligning Supervisory Structures with Country Needs Washington DC, 6th and 7th june, 2006, pp 1–45

M'Bida A, Mieu B (2022) Sub-Saharan Africa is no longer a priority for BNP Paribas, TheAfricaReport 1 April 2022

Matoo A (2018) Services globalisation in an age of insecurity: rethinking trade cooperation. World Bank Policy Research Working Paper 8579, pp 1–31

Meyer L, Stratton L (2022) Africa: Trade Finance and the Efforts to Boost Intra-African Trade. Baker and McKenzie, 14 March 2022

Musewe T, Hiebert K (2022) The future of fintech is unfolding in Africa. Centre for International Governance Innovation 25 July 2022.

Nevin AS, Omosomi O (2019) Strength from abroad: The Economic Power of Nigeria's Diaspora. https://www.pwc.com/ng/en/pdf/the-economic-power-of-nigerias-diaspora.pdf. Accessed 10 July 2022

Nyantakyi EB, Sy M (2015) The banking system in Africa: main facts and challenges. Afr Econ Brief 6(5):1–16

OECD (2015) Opportunities and Constraints of Market-Based Financing for SMES. OECD Report to G20 Finance Ministers and Central Bank Governors, pp 1–29

Ogbalu III M (2022) Boosting the AfCFTA: the role of the Pan-African Payment and Settlement System. Africa in Focus 11 February 2022

Oladipo FO, Abdu H, Obansa A (2018) Integrated Subscriber Identification Module Registration. https://www.researchgate.net/publication/336073326_Integrated_Subscriber_Identification_Module_Registration. Accessed 7 July 2022.

Organisation for Economic Co-operation and Development (2020) OECD Best Practice Principles on International Regulatory Cooperation. https://www.oecd.org/gov/regulatory-policy/public-consultation-best-practice-principles-on-international-regulatory-cooperation.pdf. Accessed 11 July 2022

Organisation pour l'Harmonisation en Afrique du Droit des Affaires (OHADA) is a system of business laws and implementing institutions adopted by sixteen West and Central African nations

Pasini FL (2011) The International Regulatory Regime on Capital Flows, Asian Development Bank Institute Working Paper Series No 338 December 2011, pp 4–24. See also Key SJ (1999) Trade Liberalisation and Prudential Regulation: The International Framework for Financial Services. Int Aff 75(1): 61–75

Reuters Staff (2019) M-Pesa helps drive up Kenyans' access to Financial Services – study Reuters 3 April 2019

Seoela BN (2022) Efficacy of monetary policy in a currency union? Evidence from Southern Africa's Common Monetary Area. Quant Financ Econ 6(1):35–53

The General Agreement on Trade in Services (GATS) 1869 UNTS 183; 33 ILM 1167 (1994)

The World Bank (2020a) Commercial bank Branches (per 100,000 adults) – Nigeria. https://data.
    worldbank.org/indicator/FB.CBK.BRCH.P5?locations=NG. Accessed 6 July 2022
The World Bank (2020b) Digital Financial Services and Cross-Border Payments, Remarks deliv-
    ered at the G20 Finance Ministers and Central Bank Governors Meeting, Riyadh, Saudi Arabia,
    23 February 2020, by Anshula Kant, Managing Director and World Bank Group Chief Financial
    Officer
The World Bank (2020c) The African Continental Free Trade Area. https://www.worldbank.org/en/
    topic/trade/publication/the-african-continental-free-trade-area. Accessed 3 July 2022
The World Bank (2022) Free Trade Deal Boosts Africa's Economic Development. https://www.
    worldbank.org/en/topic/trade/publication/free-trade-deal-boosts-africa-economic-development.
    Accessed 12 July 2022.
Torres C, Seters J (2016) Overview of Trade and Barriers to Trade in West Africa: Insights in
    Political Economy Dynamics, with Particular Focus on Agricultural and Food Trade. European
    Centre for Development Policy Management Discussion Paper No 195, pp 1–95
Trade Mark East Africa (2020) Is Africa ready for the AfCFTA? https://www.trademarkea.com/
    news/52419-2/. Accessed 13 July 2022
Triki T, Faye I (eds) (2013) Financial Inclusion in Africa, African Development Bank, Ghana,
    Part 1
Udo B (2019) Nigeria targets 80% adult financial inclusion by 2020 Premium Times
    14 January 2019
Usman Z, Csanadi A (2022) Latest Milestone for the African Continental Free Trade Area: The
    Pan-African Payment and Settlement System, Carnegie Endowment for International Peace
    7 February 2022
Velluet Q (2020) Africa: Over 500 million mobile-money users expected in 2020. TheAfricaReport
    8 April 2020. https://www.theafricareport.com/25846/africa-over-500-million-mobile-money-
    users-expected-in-2020/. Accessed 5 July 2022
World Bank (2018) Digital Access: The Future of Financial Inclusion in Africa. https://documents1.
    worldbank.org/curated/en/719111532533639732/pdf/128850-WP-AFR-Digital-Access-The-
    Future-of-Financial-Inclusion-in-Africa-PUBLIC.pdf. Accessed 12 July 2022

Tapiwa Victor Warikandwa (co-editor of the book) - Tapiwa Victor Warikandwa holds a Doctor
of Laws in International Trade Law. He is a Senior Lecturer and former Head of Department in the
Faculty of Law at the University of Namibia. He specialises in International Trade Law, Labour
Law, Indigenisation Laws, Mining Law and Constitutional Law amongst other disciplines. Prior to
coming to Namibia, Dr. Warikandwa worked as a legal officer and later legal advisor in the Ministry
of Public Service Labour and Social Welfare in Zimbabwe. Key amongst his duties was legal
drafting. Dr Warikandwa worked with the law reviser of the Ministry of Justice in Zimbabwe in
reviewing laws administered by the Ministry of Public Service Labour and Social Welfare. Dr
Warikandwa also completed an ordinary and advanced training in Labour Law Making at the
International Labour Organization's International Training Centre in Turin Italy. On numerous
occasions, Dr. Warikandwa was actively involved in the activities of the Cabinet Committee on
Legislation on behalf of the Ministry of Public Service Labour and Social Welfare. Dr. Warikandwa
has since written books on labour law and women's rights in South Africa and Namibia amongst
others, as well as publishing articles in accredited peer reviewed journals such as Law, Develop-
ment and Democracy, Speculum Juris, Journal for Black Studies, Potchefstroom Electronic Law
Journal, Comparative International Law Journal for Southern Africa and the African Journal of
International and Comparative Law, Juridical Tribune, amongst others. He was also a Post-doctoral
Fellow and has also worked as a senior lecturer at the University of Fort Hare in South Africa. Dr
Warikandwa studied for his Bachelor of Laws, Master's degree and Doctoral degree at the
University of Fort Hare in South Africa. He currently is the Chief Editor of the Namibian Law
Journal.

Retirement Funding and Financial Inclusion in South Africa: A Contrary Policy Approach

Clement Marumoagae

Abstract This chapter illustrates that the South African government has narrowly approached the financial inclusion debate by failing to include retirement funding in its understanding of this concept. It argues that failure to identify retirement funding as one of the priority financial inclusion products, prevented the government from creating a platform that will enable those currently excluded from retirement funding to access important financial products offered by retirement funds. The chapter further argues that there is a need to establish a national retirement fund that would focus on those who are currently excluded from retirement funding. Moreover, this chapter argues that the membership of this retirement fund should be voluntary for those who currently have retirement funding but compulsory for those who earn a living but not currently saving for their retirement through retirement funds. This will prevent financial dependence on the state when people reach retirement age. This initiative must be accompanied by efforts to eradicate retirement financial illiteracy through provision of dedicated retirement funding education to all retirement fund members and future members.

1 Introduction

Participation in retirement funding is a major contributor towards financial independence during old age.[1] People who contribute towards retirement funding accumulate retirement benefits over a long period of time. This enables them to adequately

---

[1] Snyman et al. (2017), p. 206. See also Kim (2014), p. 1, where it is stated that '[m]any developed countries have introduced several types of pension scheme for wage earners to diminish expected economic difficulties after their retirement'.

C. Marumoagae (✉)
School of Law, University of the Witwatersrand, Johannesburg, South Africa

Faculty of Law, University of Lesotho, Maseru, Lesotho
e-mail: Clement.Marumoagae@wits.ac.za

© The Author(s), under exclusive license to Springer Nature Switzerland AG 2023
H. Chitimira, T. V. Warikandwa (eds.), *Financial Inclusion and Digital Transformation Regulatory Practices in Selected SADC Countries*, Ius Gentium: Comparative Perspectives on Law and Justice 106,
https://doi.org/10.1007/978-3-031-23863-5_11

provide for themselves when they reach retirement. The adequacy of retirement income is determined by the number of years spent saving for retirement relative to the life expectancy during retirement.[2] Retirement benefits play a crucial role of minimising reliance on the state upon reaching retirement age. Despite these seemingly obvious advantages, the South African government is yet to seriously consider the future budgetary impact of those who reach retirement without having contributed to retirement funds.[3] South Africa has not yet established a focused policy dedicated at broadening access to retirement funding which can be implemented to assist the working class to accumulate adequate financial resources required to meet their retirement financial needs.[4] This is despite many individuals being concerned about adequate income during retirement, which is an important factor they consider when choosing an age to retire.[5]

Compared to countries with established retirement funding systems, there is relatively wide retirement funding coverage in South Africa for those in formal employment.[6] However, substantial number of people in both formal and informal employment lack access to an affordable retirement funding vehicle.[7] Notwithstanding this, the South African government is yet to put measures in place to expose more people to retirement funding. It is also disappointing that, in its draft policy document titled 'An Inclusive Financial Sector for All',[8] the South African government through the National Treasury does not identify retirement funding as one of the tools that can effectively ensure desired financial inclusion as expressed in the National Development Plan 2030 document. In the latter document, it is stated that to promote economic inclusion and social stability, government adopted an integrated vision of social policy which includes pension and provident funds as its key elements.[9] National Development Plan 2030 document identifies financial inclusion as one of the tools that can address structural challenges such as poverty,[10] which is a constant challenge for people who reach retirement age without having contributed

---

[2] See Antolin (2009), p. 5.

[3] See Stewart and Yermo (2009), who argue that participation in retirement funding can alleviate government costs by reducing government expenditure on those who reach retirement age. See also National Treasury (21 September 2012), where the government identified retirement funding as a tool that can be used to 'reducing potential reliance on the state'.

[4] Bomikazi et al. (2020), p. 2.

[5] Snyman et al. (2017), p. 204.

[6] Malherbe (2013), p. 107.

[7] National Treasury (December 2004), p. 5.

[8] National Treasury (2004). See also Mahalika et al. (2021), p. 1.

[9] National Planning Commission (n.d.). See also Mhlanga et al. (2021), p. 1, who argue that '[t]he National Development Plan Vision 2030 of South Africa, acknowledges financial inclusion as one of the important tools that will contribute towards the realisation of its goals of eliminating poverty, inequality and unemployment through decent work and sustainable livelihoods'.

[10] National Planning Commission (n.d.).

towards retirement funding.[11] An Inclusive Financial Sector for All draft policy document fails to locate the financial inclusion debate around retirement funding, thereby perpetuating financial exclusion of majority of the working class by denying them viable savings vehicles in the form of retirement funds.

The purpose of this chapter is not only to highlight the omission of retirement funding in the government's understanding of financial inclusion but also to demonstrate why retirement funds are ideal vehicles to secure financial inclusion in South Africa. This will be done by first evaluating the concept of poverty during old age and how the South African government has attempted to address this pandemic. Second, a contextual understanding of what financial inclusion entails will be provided. Herein, it will be demonstrated that the South African government has conceptualised financial inclusion in a narrow way, which will delay the process of including those currently excluded into the retirement funding system. Third, it will be shown why retirement funding should be at the centre of financial inclusion policy directive in South Africa. An argument will be made that there is a need to broaden access to retirement funding in South Africa to prevent the working class from being unable to financially care for themselves when they reach retirement age and thereby fall back on the state.[12] The fourth section addresses the need for retirement fund products to be made easy to understand and affordable to encourage more people to contribute towards retirement funding. Available alternative options that can be explored to prevent financial exclusion from retirement funding will be discussed. An argument will also be made that for retirement funds to be viable tools for financial inclusion, government should focus of retirement fund financial education to decisively eradicate retirement funding financial illiteracy. Given the dearth of academic literature on the topic discussed in this article and its social relevance, where necessary, I will refer to media reports were experts in academia and practice have responded to the proposals made by the Department of Social Development.

---

[11] See Foster (2011), p. 344, where it is argued that '[t]he quality of life an individual can expect in retirement is considerably affected by material circumstances and experience of income poverty'.

[12] See Pask and Marx (2018), p. 1, where it is argued that only about 10% of South Africans can financially sustain themselves when they retire. See also Dhlembeu (MCom Mini-Dissertation, UP 2018) 1, where it is stated that '[t]he low retirement savings rate among South African citizens has serious repercussions on the economy and communities in general. If South Africans do not effectively plan for retirement, the government faces the burden of having to financially support its citizens through social grants and other schemes. This will result in less funds being available for social and physical infrastructure development needs; thus, stifling the growth of the economy. Furthermore, the elderly in society end up depending on the younger generation for financial support, which affects the ability of the benefactors to plan and save for their own retirement'.

2   Initiatives Aimed at Fighting Poverty on Retirement

One of the major threats to human existence is lack of the financial resources for a minimum standard of living.[13] Lack of financial means often leads to poverty, inequality, vulnerability, indigency and ultimate exclusion from economic activities.[14] The South African government adopted various post-apartheid policies intended to eradicate poverty, all of which failed dismally.[15] In 2018, the study conducted by the World Bank in collaboration with the South African Department of Planning, Monitoring and Evaluation as well as Statistics South Africa, established that more than half of the South African population is poor and lives beyond the poverty line.[16] Poverty can be tackled through job creation, which has been negatively affected by corruption and poor economic growth in South Africa.[17] However, South African government, through either the Department of social development or National Treasury, has from time to time adopted and issued several policy documents that were released for public comment. These policy documents, some of which will be discussed below, sought to address widespread poverty in the country by creating an environment where more people would participate in the country's financial systems to boost economic growth.[18]

---

[13] Aduda and Kalunda (2012), p. 96.

[14] National Treasury (27 February 2007), p. 12.

[15] See Kgatle (2007), p. 4, where it is stated that '[t]here has been an attempt by the post-1994 South African government to address the challenge of poverty. There have been different economic approaches to this challenge. The economic approaches include the RDP, the GEAR, ASGISA, NGP and the NDP'. See also Pauw and Mncube (August 2007), p. 4, where it is stated that 'Past discriminatory policies have left a large proportion of the population outside the economic mainstream and relatively poor compared to an elite minority. Since the transition to democracy in 1994 various policies of redistribution, mainly through labour and capital markets, were put in place, including affirmative action and broad-based Black Economic Empowerment (BEE). However, even with these policies in place, it appears that overall inequality has increased further, albeit not necessarily along racial lines'.

[16] World Bank (2018), p. xii.

[17] See Mohammad et al. (2020), p. 623, argue that '[c]orruption could be a hurdle to economic development and thereby intensify poverty through a number of channels. It weakens national institutions and increases economic inefficiencies, reduces economic growth hampers the productivity of the public sector reduces private sector investment, reduces FDI in developing countries, causes a decline in personal incomes, intensifies income inequality and poverty, lowers expenditure on health and education, and more generally hampers economic development. Corruption is economically damaging as resources are transferred to unproductive activities' (references omitted). See also Bhorat and van der Westhuizen (November 2012), p. 12, where it is stated that '[t]here is very little debate, if any, amongst economists around the notion that a high level of economic growth is essential for poverty reduction. Indeed, increased growth rates, effectively measured by rising per capita incomes, would appear to make this link clear and simple: If you increase economic growth, poverty levels will fall in the society'.

[18] See National Treasury (2019). See also Kruger (2011), p. 207, where it is explained that the democratic government adopted the Black Economic Empowerment policy designed to overcome

In August 2021, the Department of Social Development released a green paper on Comprehensive Social Security and Retirement Reform (Green Paper).[19] This Green Paper, among others, highlighted the fact that millions of employees in South Africa are excluded from lifestyle preserving retirement coverage.[20] The Green Paper misleadingly stated that the exclusion from retirement coverage is due to the structural complexity and high costs of private retirement funds.[21] The reality is that participation in occupational retirement funds, most of which are operating in the private sector is not dependent on employees' knowledge of the structural design of such retirement funds or the costs and charges associated with the administration thereof.[22] Participation in both public and private retirement funding depends on the type of employer and whether the employer in its employment package offers retirement funding.[23] Some employers are participating in retirement funds and offer retirement benefits to their employees.

For selected employers, usually participation in retirement funding is compulsory and employees do not have an opportunity to assess and compare which retirement fund can best deliver the pension promise to them, particularly for employers that participates in only one retirement fund.[24] There are however, some employers who operate in sectors such as chemicals, municipality and retail that may be participating in more than one retirement fund.[25] It is possible for such employers to invite all the retirement funds in which they participate to provide information regarding their

---

the economic legacy of the apartheid government with a view to broaden participation in the economy.

[19] Department of Social Development 'Green Paper on Comprehensive Social Security and Retirement Reform' Consolidated Government Paper: Public Consultation Version (03 August 2021) Government Gazette No 45006 (18 August 2021) (hereafter 'Green Paper').

[20] Department of Social Development (2021).

[21] Department of Social Development (2021).

[22] See Lonescu and Robles (2014), pp. 1–44, who state that '[a]dministrative and other charges are not always explained clearly to pension fund members'.

[23] The South African Labour Guide (n.d.), where it is correctly stated that '[u]sually it is compulsory to become a member of a fund. This means that a worker does not choose whether to belong to the fund or not, the worker must belong to the fund if the employer has a fund'.

[24] Marumoagae (2020), p. 214, where it is argued that '[t]here are, however, industries where it is compulsory for all employees employed in such industry to participate in the recognised industry retirement funds. For example, it is compulsory for every employee and employer in the private security sector to contribute to the Private Security Sector Provident Fund'. See also Budlender and Sadeck (2007), p. 27. These authors observe that the Government Employees Pension Fund '. . . . was established in 1996, and membership is compulsory for all employees of national and provincial governments who are not required by legislation to become a member of another pension fund, or excluded from the pension fund'.

[25] See *Municipal Employees Pension Fund v Natal Joint Municipal Pension Fund (Superannuation) & others* [2016] 4 All SA 761 (SCA) para 2.

pension products so that employees can choose which among them they wish to become members thereof.[26]

Most formally and all informally employed persons do not have retirement fund coverage because the government has not yet prioritised retirement funding in South Africa and not because of the reasons outlined in the Green Paper.[27] According to the Green Paper, the complexity of private retirement funds and their associated high costs '... contributes to significant reductions in income at retirement, which results in old age poverty and reliance on the social grant system as the only source of income in old age'.[28] In this Green Paper, the government interestingly did not deal with the costs and complexities associated with retirement funds in which it participates, such as the GEPF. Unfortunately, the Green Paper does not address the government's failure to improve the economy to absorb more employees in the public sector who can contribute towards public sector retirement funds such as the Government Employees Pension Fund (hereafter GEPF). It is public knowledge that by international standards, there is a shortage of key public servants such as nurses, doctors, police officials and teachers who could be savings towards their retirement through the GEPF in South Africa.[29]

Nonetheless, the Green Paper claims that there is consensus that the challenges identified in this discussion paper '... must be addressed by introducing a mandatory retirement, death and disability insurance for all workers ... provided through a publicly offered National Social Security Fund (NSSF); operated on the principles of risk pooling and social solidarity'.[30]

The proposal is to design the conceptualised NSSF as a broad social insurance vehicle that will 'insure' mainly formally employed persons against retirement, unemployment, health challenges arising from employment and accidents on the

---

[26] See *Sasol Limited v Chemical Industries National Provident Fund* (20612/2014) [2015] ZASCA 113 (7 September 2015) para 2 where it is stated that '[i]n response to pressure from employees to transfer, Sasol decided to offer them an opportunity to do so during a 'window period'. Consequently, on 31 August 2012, Sasol wrote to the CINPF. It recorded that many employees wished to transfer and that a window period would open from 1 October 2012 to 30 November 2012 during which employees would be permitted to transfer. An objection period would run from 1 to 31 December 2012. In order to inform employees of the benefits offered by the different funds, they would be given an opportunity to attend information sessions during the window period at which presentations would be made by all the relevant funds. On 13 September 2012, Sasol instructed all of its plants to display a notice informing employees of the window period and the forthcoming information sessions'.

[27] See IOPS, p. 3 <http://www.iopsweb.org/rbstoolkit/SOUTH-AFRICA.pdf>. Accessed on 30 October 2021, where an observation is made that notwithstanding having a well-developed occupational retirement funding system, there is a limited coverage of the working population. Further that '[p]roblems with coverage and 'leakage' have led to the government proposing reforms for the South African pension system, including the possible introduction of mandatory individual accounts'.

[28] Green Paper, p. 8.

[29] See Rasool and Botha (2011), p. 1. See also, Writer (2020), Wagner (n.d.), and Maphalala and Mpofu (n.d.).

[30] Green Paper, p. 8. See also Angeloni (n.d.).

roads.[31] The Green Paper proposed that all employees who earn R 22 320.00 or more per annum should be compelled to contribute between 8 to 12% of their monthly earnings to the NSSF.[32] Given the fact that the proposal is to cover different contingent events, it is not clear what percentage of the collected contribution will be allocated to which contingent event. This raises a challenge of whether the NSSF will collect enough contributions for every member to be adequately covered. The proposal that if the desired 40 per cent replacement income is not achieved when a member retires, such a member may receive old age grant,[33] suggests that government may have realised that this fund may not collect enough retirement funding contributions that may render members self-sufficient during retirement. It is further proposed that the high earning members of this fund will be encouraged to 'make supplementary contributions [to approved funds] during their careers if they are to achieve an adequate retirement pension'.[34]

The fact that the Green Paper proposed that employees should be forced to be members of NSSF and merely encouraged to supplement their contributions through private retirement funds,[35] has been justifiably criticised. For instance, it has been argued that by seeking to protect the proposed fund from private retirement funding competition, this amounts to the removal of agency and the power of self-determination by employees whose employers, bargaining councils and unions may be associated with private retirement funds, to which they may wish to belong.[36] The consequence of this proposal is that this arrangement will have devastating impact on the South African retirement fund industry. Forcing members of retirement funds to join this fund will make it difficult for these members to continue contributing to their established funds, thereby negatively affecting the business of such retirement funds. Members have established relationships with their current funds which also have established reputation and there is no need to disrupt the current retirement funding system in favour of an untested proposed public fund. This proposal aims to eliminate competition and force members to place their trust on a new entity that has not proven itself and will only develop expertise as it goes along.[37] It is submitted that to require employees to transfer their savings from their current retirement funds to this proposed new fund is totally ill-advised.

It is submitted that a better approach would be for the proposed NSSF to target employees who are not currently contributing to retirement funds and not those who are currently contributing towards retirement funding. In other words, current members of retirement funds should not be obliged to be members of NSSF, but should merely be encouraged to top-up or supplement their savings with this

---

[31] Ibid. See also van den Heever (2021).

[32] Ibid 12.

[33] Ibid 48.

[34] Ibid.

[35] Ibid 58. See Majola (2021).

[36] Ibid.

[37] Anon (2021).

proposed fund, to the extent to which they can afford. These members may however, be compelled to contribute a reasonable percentage for the purposes other contingencies such as unemployment and health related issues at work.

The Green Paper also proposed the establishment of the NSSF default fund that will cater for self-employed and informal sector employees as well as employees whose employers are unable to provide an occupational fund, which will be established within the main proposed NSSF.[38] It is not clear however, what formula or criteria would be used for the collection of contributions that self-employed and informally employed persons would be expected to make to the default fund given their irregular income. While the proposed mandatory NSSF is proposed to be a defined benefit fund with the state as the sponsor, the NSSA default fund is intended to be a separate fund administered by the mandatory fund on a defined contribution basis, where members will bear the risk of investment.[39]

Providing access to retirement funding to self and informally employed persons is long overdue.[40] It is important to note that government generally use Green Papers to provide the public with its general thinking with a view to start a discussion on a particular policy direction, which in this case is the establishment of the NSSF.[41] In other words,, a Green Paper is a draft policy document for consultation that is not expected to contain all the relevant details pertaining to the proposed policy.[42] However, it is not unreasonable to expect this specific Green Paper to be sufficiently detailed because it follows an investigation and report produced by the Inter-Departmental Task Team on Social Security and Retirement Reform on the same subject released in 2016, which also recommended the establishment of the NSSF.[43] In this report, the Inter-Departmental Task Team highlighted the need to extend retirement funding to informally employed persons but did not provide details on how that should be achieved.[44] It is not clear whether the Department of Social Development when preparing the Green Paper consulted members of Inter-Departmental Task Team to understand some of the challenges that led to their proposals not being implemented, particularly that relating to the establishment of the NSSF and extending retirement funding to informal and self-employed

---

[38] Green Paper, p. 57.

[39] Ibid 55.

[40] See National Treasury (December 2004) 6, were the government acknowledged that despite wide occupational pension coverage, '... many people lack effective access to an affordable retirement funding vehicle' in South Africa and necessary reforms should be effected to extend coverage.

[41] Parliament <https://www.parliament.gov.za/how-law-made>. Accessed on 30 October 2021.

[42] UCT <http://www.governmentpublications.lib.uct.ac.za/gov-pubs-types>. Assessed on 30 October 2021.

[43] Comprehensive Social Security in South Africa: Discussion Document' Version 11.9 (March 2012).

[44] Ibid 29. Inter-Departmental Task Team merely stated that '[t]he Government will consider establishing a low-cost pension fund to run alongside the NSSF and the approved funds. An administratively simple, low-cost arrangement would benefit self-employed or informal-sector workers, for example'.

employees. It is also not clear whether the Department of Social Development conducted research before compiling the Green Paper not only on the feasibility of the establishment of the NSSF in South Africa but also on how retirement funding should be extended to informal and self-employed employees. It is thus, disappointing that Green Paper does not provide details as to how these employees will covered by the proposed NSSF, particularly when they do not have regular income. From the Green Paper, it is not clear what percentage of the self and informally employed persons' income will be used to insure any of the identified contingencies.

It is further not clear how the NSSF default fund will deal with inability to pay contributions for any period before retirement. If this fund does not consider the irregular nature of the income received by self and informally employed members with a view to creating member specific portfolios that would enable them to contribute in a long term based on their personal circumstances, it will fail these members. It is submitted that, at least for retirement savings, there is a need for a separate fund that will collect contributions from these type of employees on a flexible basis in accordance with their earnings. These employees should know what percentage of their earnings should be contributed to the fund for the purposes of retirement in any given year. Failure to design a retirement fund that is specifically focused on the nuances of self-employed and informally employed employees will lead to these employees' continued financial exclusion from retirement funding. Fortunately, after wide and warranted criticism, the South African government decided to withdraw this flawed Green Paper.[45]

3 Narrow View of Financial Inclusion in South Africa

According to the World Bank, '[f]inancial inclusion means that individuals and businesses have access to useful and affordable financial products and services that meet their needs – transactions, payments, savings, credit and insurance – delivered in a responsible and sustainable way'.[46] From this definition, it can be argued that access to affordable financial products is important. In South Africa, there are various financial products such as bank accounts, insurance policies, investment products, credit facilities, securities, derivatives, commodities, and currencies offered by several services providers.[47] The importance of these products on consumers varies depending on factors such knowledge and awareness of their exis-

---

[45] Department of Social Development (1 September 2021).

[46] World Bank 'Financial Inclusion' <https://www.worldbank.org/en/topic/financialinclusion/overview>. Accessed on 30 June 2021.

[47] See Lunn et al. (2018), p. iii; Demirguc-Kunt et al. (2017), p. 4 and Chui (2012), p. 3.

tence, their complexities, location of consumers, affordability, and consumers' needs.[48] Section 1 of the Financial Advisory and Intermediary Services Act,[49] broadly defines the phrase 'financial product' to mean securities and instruments, participatory interest in one or more collective investment schemes, insurance contract or policy, a benefit provided by a friendly society, a foreign currency, a health service benefit, and a benefit provided by a pension fund organization. This statutory definition, if considered in line with the definition provided by the World Bank, clearly denotes that retirement funds should be included in the broader understanding of financial inclusion. Retirement funds collect and invest members' contributions and thus, provide financial products to their members.[50]

The Organisation for Economic Co-operation and Development (OECD) views financial inclusion as a 'process of promoting affordable, timely and adequate access to a wide range of regulated financial products and services ...'.[51] Access to financial products appear to be a common factor in most definitions of financial inclusion. There is a global realisation that financial products are important tools of bettering people's lives and further that they are not currently accessible to everyone in any country.[52] Some researchers have called for the broadened use of financial products 'by all segments of society through the implementation of tailored existing and innovative approaches ... with a view to promote financial well-being as well as economic and social inclusion'.[53]

It is important for the government to create an economic environment that will enable financial service providers to be innovative and put measures in place that will ensure that the poor and financially marginalised have adequate access to crucial financial services. Some of the major financial service providers also offer retirement funds related products and constantly seek methods of improving their services.[54]

---

[48] Elizabeth et al. (2018), p. 1.

[49] 37 of 2002.

[50] Section 13A of the Pension Funds Act 24 of the 1956 (PFA).

[51] Atkinson and Messy (2013), p. 11.

[52] See Shankar (2013), p. 61 and Tounwendé et al. (2018), p. 142, where it is argued that '... while financial accessibility can contribute to increased private investment, economic growth in developing countries, the individual must still have access to financial services and products and be able to use them efficiently. Thus, there is a need to consider the factors or indicators of financial accessibility that contribute to increased private investment in developing countries'.

[53] Atkinson and Messy (2013), p. 11. See also OECD 'Advancing the digital financial inclusion of youth' Report prepared for the G20 Global Partnership for Financial Inclusion by the OECD (2020) 17, where policy makers are urged to ensure '... availability and accessibility of financial products for all youth, and especially most vulnerable youth, regardless of ethnicity, religion, gender, ability, education, location or other criteria will be needed, for truly inclusive societies'. See also Antunes (2021), p. 11, where it is observed that '[a]ccess to financial services is critical to the achievement of the 2030 Agenda for Sustainable Development. Despite progress in recent years, significant gap remains between developed and developing economies. ... The poor, less educated, youth and women tend to be more excluded'. See also Nguyen (2021), p. 81.

[54] See for instance Old Mutual 'Retirement Ready' <https://www.oldmutual.co.za/personal/solutions/retirement-plans/>. Accessed on 27 October 2021.

These financial institutions can play an important role of ensure that domestic savings and domestic capital can be mobilised through investments with a view to channel resources into productive activities that will protect those who are contributing towards retirement funding when they retire.[55] It is submitted that the government must also work with these institutions to develop a workable framework that can be used to include those who are currently excluded from retirement funding. Retirement funding can play an important role in ensuring self-sufficiency upon retirement. However, financial inclusion in South Africa has narrowly been conceptualised to exclude retirement funding.

The National Treasury on its proposed policy on financial inclusion narrowly locates its understanding of the concept on the historical circumstances of the country where majority of the people of the country were prevented from accessing some of the financial products.[56] National Treasury views financial inclusion as part of the provision of affordable financial services to the broader population, particularly those who were historically not serviced by the formal financial sector.[57] The National Treasury regards financial inclusion as a tool that can positively address historical imbalances by bringing the historically economically marginalised to participate in the mainstream economy.[58] To achieve this, core-financial services should be provided to the rural parts of the country.[59] The National Treasury identified five main financial products that it believes will promote financial inclusion in South Africa: needs-oriented and affordable transactional accounts; responsible access to credit; insurance products; savings products and remittances.[60] This illustrates that, in South Africa, financial inclusion is mainly understood through the lens of the banking sector because most of the financial products identified as critical to financial inclusion are provided by the banks.[61]

Research in South Africa points out that '[t]he financial product usage hierarchy is grounded in the field of saving and savings behaviour'.[62] This explains why in the

---

[55] Imboden (2005), p. 66. See also Phalatse (2021), p. 10, where it is argued that mobilisation of substantial private savings driven by pension funds and insurance companies can lead to profit from investments in strategic infrastructure.

[56] National Treasury, p. 1.

[57] Ibid. The National Treasury further observes that '[i]n the South African context, the segments of society that underutilise financial services are inadequately provided for. Even if the services exist, they are often not easily accessible to the excluded and under-served. Furthermore, financial services are a significant enabler for a society's social and economic development. Effectively, including people in the financial sector not only requires the availability of financial products and services, it also needs them to be convenient, affordable, fair and trusted. In addition, most South Africans must be able to use them'.

[58] Ibid.

[59] See Chitimira and Ncube (2020), p. 345, where the challenge of uneven concentration of banking services in South Africa is highlighted.

[60] National Treasury, p. 21.

[61] See generally Lawack (2013), p. 317.

[62] Stedall and Venter (2016), p. 312.

South African context, emphasises on financial inclusion has been on consumers'
access to bank related products.[63] It must be pointed out that to achieve greater
financial inclusion, it is important to view the financial sector broadly to include
access to retirement funding. Dasgupta[64] argues that '[f]inancial services do not
mean the provision of credit alone, but the provision of all other services, especially
savings, insurance and remittance facilities'. Most importantly for this chapter, on its
report, the committee on financial inclusion in India noted that '[t]he ideal definition
[of financial inclusion] should look at people who want to access financial services
but are denied the same'.[65] Thus, to increase participation in the financial sector,
there is a need to include other financial services such as retirement funds in the
broader understanding of financial inclusion.

While it is important for the greater population has access to banking related
products such as banking accounts and ability to access much needed credit, there is
also a need for the government to consider other financial products, such as retirement funding, as an integral part of financial inclusion. The National Treasury noted
that the route to financial inclusion is different for most people and is influenced by
their individual circumstances but emphasised that the starting point is the acquisition of a basic transactional account.[66] The reality is that one can have access to the
banking system and remain financially excluded when they do not have any means
of income. It appears as if the National Treasury assumes that once people have
acquired transactional accounts, they will either be able to acquire credit to carry out
their projects or at the very least start saving.

In its attempt to make out a case for savings, the National Treasury in its draft
financial policy document uses stokvels[67] as a method of saving that has been used
in South Africa. Stokvels can be used as high budget financial institutions that assist
their members to save and invest.[68] 'Stokvels can provide a platform for periodic
collective savings for members, whereby the total amount collected during a year is
either reserved on behalf of the members or disbursed as a lump sum on an equal
share'.[69] National Treasury is of the view that the arrangement of stokvels should be

---

[63] In fact, there are those who have restricted the concept of financial inclusion to pure banking. See
Dev (2006), p. 4310, who defines financial inclusion '... as delivery of banking services at an
affordable cost to the vast sections of disadvantaged and low-income group'.

[64] Dasgupta (2009), p. 41.

[65] Rangarajan (2008), p. 12.

[66] National Treasury, p. 11.

[67] See Verhoef (2001), p. 263, who states that '[a] stokvel is a type of credit union in which a group
of people, by voluntary mutual agreement, regularly contribute money to a common pool and
circulate the pool among the group'. See also Lukhele (1990), for a comprehensive discussion on
stokvels. For the evolution of Stokvels and the modern risks related thereto in South Africa see,
Mokoena et al. (2021), p. 1.

[68] Matuku and Kaseke (2014), p. 506.

[69] Bophela and Khumalo (2019), p. 27.

changed to allow them to yield better returns for their members because most of the money derived from these stokvels is held in low-interest bank accounts.[70]

In principle, it is not wrong for the National Treasury to refer to a stokvel which is a short-term savings tool for those who participate in it and has a measure of flexibility. It is surprising however, that the National Treasury in its discussion for the need to save over a long period does not identify retirement funds as the potential long-term savings tool that can ensure effective financial inclusion. This is despite the fact that over the years, the South African government has released several reports and discussion papers indicating that majority of South Africans do not participate in retirement funding.[71] Further, that lack of participation in retirement funding has denied those who reach retirement age the ability to be self-sufficient post their retirement, thereby forcing them to rely on the state. It is not clear why the National Treasury omitted retirement funding as one of the main tools that can be used to facilitate financial inclusion in South Africa. I submit that to truly realise financial inclusion, South Africa's understanding of this concept should be broadened. To prevent poverty and marginalisation in old-age, it will be ideal for financial inclusion in South Africa to be understood not only to include banking services and access to credit but also financial products that relate to contingency planning and wealth creation such as different types of investment products, insurance and most importantly, retirement funding. Access to retirement benefits and periodic annuity payments received from retirement funds during retirement can smooth consumption and provide reliable income and ultimately reduce old-age poverty.[72] Hence, it is important that South Africans are not only made aware of the concept of retirement funding and its potential benefits, but the government should create an environment where they can meaningfully participate by saving towards their retirement irrespective of whether they are self, formally or informally employed. Failure to do so amounts to financial exclusion from retirement funding.

---

[70] National Treasury, p. 60.

[71] See among others: National Treasury 'The South African Retirement Funds Landscape' Retirement Fund Reform: A discussion Paper (December 2004); Committee of Investigation into a Retirement Provision System for South Africa (1988); The Commission of Inquiry into Certain Aspects of the Tax Structure of South Africa, Katz Commission, 1994); The Committee on Strategy and Policy Review of Retirement Provision in South Africa (Smith Committee, 1995); and Transforming the Present – Protecting the Future: Report of the Committee of Inquiry into a Comprehensive System of Social Security for South Africa Taylor (Commission, 2002) and well as Inter-Departmental Task Team on Social Security and Retirement Reform 'Comprehensive Social Security in South Africa: Discussion Document' Version 11.9 (March 2012).

[72] Bloom and McKinnon (2013), p. 5.

4   Financial Inclusion Through Retirement Funding

4.1   Overview

In African countries such as Zimbabwe[73] and Zambia,[74] as is the case in South Africa, many people do not have access to financial services and the ever-expanding assets in the financial sector are concentrated in the hands of few people.[75] There is a need for the financial sector to be inclusive and be redesigned to offer those currently excluded therefrom to have sustainable access thereto. The establishment of an inclusive retirement funding system that will enable any person who is able to earn a living to contribute thereto and save towards their retirement in accordance with their means can broadening access to the financial sector in South Africa. Retirement funds play an important role in the country's financial sector through the development of capital markets, advancement of economic growth, increasing savings and increasing the availability of long-term capital.[76] Participation in retirement funding is essential for self-sufficiency during retirement.[77] Most of those who are not participating and contributing early to retirement funds during their working lives may not be able to save enough to financially care for themselves during retirement.

It is submitted that the South Africa government through legislative reform, should create an environment which will enable self, formally and informally employed persons to access retirement funding themselves. This can be achieved by making it easier for these employees to join retirement annuity funds and umbrella funds, which should be legislatively empowered to create specific contributions plans for those who wish to join them. Alternatively, government should consider establishing a dedicated retirement fund that is tailor made to cater for the specific circumstances of self and informally employed persons. Contributions can be determined and informed by the pattern of income that these employees receive and market conditions within their respective sectors. Their income should determine how much they should contribute to the fund. It is submitted that it should be compulsory for all these employees to have a bank account and regularly submit the statement of their income to this fund. The board of this fund must continuously remind members that saving through this fund is for their benefit and emphasise the importance of regular contributions where this is possible.

Government should also encourage small business owners to also join umbrella funds with a view of extending retirement funding to their employees to enable them to save towards self-sufficiency in retirement. This requires not only political will but also government's commitment through the adopted policies and legislative framework that can be used to enable the development of an inclusive retirement fund

---

[73]Chivasa and Simbanegavi (2016), p. 57.

[74]Silimina (2021).

[75]Imboden (2005), p. 65.

[76]Thomas and Spataro (2016), pp. 1–33.

[77]See Ketkaew et al. (2019), p. 2.

industry to promote financial inclusion. Policy and law makers should officially recognise retirement funding as one of the effective tools for financial inclusion. They should also develop and implement initiatives that can ensure that more informally, self-employed, and formally employed persons save towards their retirement through retirement funds. Retirement funds can play an important role in the attainment of economic stability, sustainable and inclusive economic growth, advancement of income equality, creation of employment generation, poverty eradication in South Africa.[78] Access to retirement annuity funds, umbrella funds or a dedicated retirement fund that considers the personal circumstances of self and informally employed persons will lead to the financial inclusion of these employees through retirement funding. It is submitted that failure to use retirement funding as a tool for financial inclusion amounts to government missing a golden opportunity to broaden participation in the financial sector in South Africa.

4.2 Benefits Provided by Retirement Funds

Retirement funds are financial schemes that enable members to contribute part of their income which are duly invested over a long period of time during their working days.[79] Retirement funds are financial schemes that are managed and administered by boards of management. The boards of management are legislatively mandated to take decisions that would ensure that retirement funds are sustainable and can meet all the claims of their members. In terms of section 7C(2)(f) of the PFA board members owe fiduciary duties to their funds and members of such funds as well as beneficiaries of such members in respect of accrued retirement benefits. Board members also have a fiduciary duty to ensure that these funds are managed and governed in accordance with the law and the respective rules of their funds.[80] Board members are also obliged to manage retirement funds in a sustainable manner by constantly collecting contributions and prudently investing such contributions for the benefit of their members. Investment performance, particularly for defined contribution funds which are sponsored by members themselves, is an important factor that influence retirement funds' financial sustainability.[81] The boards, when carrying out their duties, must adhere to good corporate governance principles to ensure that retirement funds meet their obligations in respect of their members and other stakeholders.[82]

---

[78] Tran et al. (2021), p. 95.

[79] Section 13A of the PFA.

[80] Section 7C(2)(f) of the PFA.

[81] Delsen and Lehr (2019), p. 240.

[82] See The Institute of Directors in Southern Africa (IoDSA) and the King Committee Fourth King Report on Corporate Governance in South Africa (King IV) 96. See also Marumoagae (2021b), p. 18.

In South Africa, there are stand-alone, sector-based, umbrella funds and retirement annuity funds that formally employed persons can join with a view to contributing towards retirement savings.[83] A standalone retirement fund is the type of fund established by a single employer designed to allow only the employees of such employer to contribute to that fund with a view to save towards their retirement during the period of their employment.[84] An umbrella fund is a financial scheme usually established by large financial institution that enables several employers to participate and register their employees as members so that they can contribute towards saving for their retirement.[85] Umbrella funds are structured and designed in such a way that if used effectively, having regard to their flexibility, can play an important role in broadening access to retirement funding.[86] Unlike a standalone fund which accept as members only the employees of the employer who is participating in the fund, umbrella funds accept employees from different employers.[87] In other words, umbrella funds are catering for different employers and their employees. It is submitted that the fact that umbrella funds are not tied to any particular employer, demonstrates that they can also be used to cater for people with irregular income such as self and informally employed persons. For instance, within umbrella funds, sub-funds catering for domestic workers and farm workers can easily be established to enable those rendering these services to save towards their retirement.

A retirement annuity fund is a non-occupational based retirement fund that allows anyone, irrespective of their employment status, to invest for their retirement.[88] It

---

[83] Generally, retirement funds are structured as either defined benefit funds or defined contribution funds. In *ICS Pension Fund v Sithole* 2009 ZAGPHC 6 (13 January 2009) para 3, the court held that '. . . a defined benefit fund is a pension fund whose pension benefits are determined in accordance with a formula contained in the rules of the fund and which are underwritten by the participating employer. If the investments made by such a fund perform well, the members do not benefit proportionately. However, if the investments perform poorly, members have the advantage that their pension benefits remain guaranteed by the employer. The employer carries the risk of the investments and the members' pension benefits are secure'. The court further held that 'In a defined contribution fund, the benefits are not underwritten by the employer but the members have the advantage that if the fund performs well, it would reflect in their pension benefits. If the fund performs poorly, the members' pension benefits are reduced accordingly. In short, the members carry the risk of the investments, both good and bad, and their benefits are not guaranteed by the employer' (para 4).

[84] See ASISA 'Introduction to umbrella fund' <https://www.asisa.org.za/media/s5gnn0im/atleha-edu_umbrella-funds-cfe-publication.pdf>. Accessed on 02 July 2021, where it is stated that '[t]his type of fund needs to be managed by a board of trustees consisting of both employer and member-elected representatives'.

[85] Ibid.

[86] See Cloete (2021), p. 24, who argues that '[s]ome umbrella funds consciously design flexibility into the benefits available to members. Once the employer has made certain initial choices at group level, which they believe are suitable for their employees, flexibility at member level allows employees to shape their retirement and insurance benefits according to their specific needs'.

[87] Old Mutual (n.d.).

[88] Kieran Godden (2010), p. 24.

has been argued that this retirement scheme is ideal for those who: are self-employed; don't have access to a work-place pension or provident fund through their employer; want to supplement their retirement savings to earn significant amounts of non-pensionable income.[89] Retirement annuity funds are also regulated by the PFA. The boards of these funds have the responsibility to collect contributions from members with a view to invest them so that members can receive adequate benefits upon retirement.[90] Retirement funds play an important role in ensuring that members engage in low-risk long term investment, and in the process ensure that members do not run a risk of not having enough financial resources to care for themselves during their retirement.[91] Retirement funds hold large bond and equity holdings which have increased the magnitude of assets managed by these funds for the benefits of their members.[92] Thus, retirement funds should be used as viable financial inclusion tools. Retirement funds also play an important role in the development of the stock or local securities market and provide an important source of capital in financial markets that can be used to drive national priorities such as reduction of poverty.[93]

On 9 July 2012, the National Treasury noted that at the time '. . . only an estimated 6 per cent of South Africans are able to maintain their lifestyle and replace their income fully at retirement'.[94] According to the research conducted by 10X Investments, many people have not formally financially planned their retirement and do not know whether they will be self-sufficient in retirement.[95] Statistic South Africa in its quarterly labour force survey of the second term of 2021, clearly demonstrated that unemployment rate increased in South Africa with low participation in retirement funding.[96] Those who are out of work will not be able to save enough for immediate consumption let alone their retirement. There are however, self, informally and formally employed persons who are currently not saving towards their retirement through retirement fund who, when provided with an opportunity to do so, can participate in retirement funding. The South African government has not yet dedicated time to assess how those who are currently excluded from retirement funding can effectively be incorporated into the retirement funding system based on their respective earnings. It is for this reason that the South African government in its draft financial inclusion policy must also focus on retirement funds to ensure that deliberations regarding how those who are currently

---

[89] 10x Investments 'What is a retirement annuity?' <https://www.10x.co.za/faq/retirement-annuity/what-is-a-retirement-annuity>. Accessed on 1 July 2021.

[90] Section 13A of the PFA.

[91] Regulation 28 of the Pension Funds Regulations.

[92] See generally Wepener (MCom Dissertation UCT, 2014), for a detailed discussion on asset investment allocation. See also generally Bikker et al. (2010), p. 54.

[93] Moleko and Ikhide (2017), pp. 135 and 148.

[94] National Treasury 'Statement on the Impact of the Proposed Retirement Reforms' (n.d.).

[95] 10X Investments (2020).

[96] Stats SA (2021), p. 72.

excluded from retirement funding can be accorded retirement benefits in the form of retirement, withdrawal, disability, funeral, and housing benefits, can occur within South Africa. Failure to urgently attend to the retirement needs of those currently excluded from retirement funding amounts to financial exclusion that prevents them from accessing formal financial system in the form of retirement funds.[97]

Broadening access to retirement funding through easy access to retirement annuity funds, umbrella funds or a specialised retirement for self and informally employed persons will enable many people in South Africa to save using retirement fund. This will also provide a good case study for government and the financial sector to understand how best to expand the South Africa retirement funding system in a manner that makes it easier for those excluded to participate. For instance, as Hardy and Shuey correctly argue '[a]ccess to employer-sponsored pensions can provide an additional source of retirement income, but pension coverage does not guarantee more income in retirement'.[98] It is however, important to qualify this submission. The potential threat to retirement benefits during retirement is the retirement funds' members ability to contribute to their funds consistently over the entire period of their employment. This is not always the case because people change jobs, resign, or can be dismissed or retrenched. Some people are even married in community of property and when they divorce their spouses are entitled to share in their retirement benefits which can substantially reduce their benefits.[99] To address this issue, the legislature has provided tax benefits to encourage those who resigned, are dismissed, or retrenched to transfer their withdrawal benefits from their current retirement funds to preservation funds, while they are still looking for alternative employment.[100] 'No tax is levied on pension or provident fund transfers into a preservation fund, and investment returns in the fund are tax-free'.[101]

Regarding retirement benefits, the legislature has introduced amendments that force those who retire to purchase an annuity that they will use to receive periodic payments during their retirement days. The Taxation Laws Amendment Act of 2020 (TLAA) was promulgated to amend section 1 of the Income Tax Act.[102] This amendment introduced compulsory annuitisation of retirement benefits received by provident fund members when they retire.[103] In the same way as pension fund members, provident fund members are no longer allowed to take their full retirement benefits as lumpsum upon retirement.[104] This applies only to contributions that were

---

[97] Wentzel et al. (2016), p. 203.

[98] Hardy and Shuey (2000), p. 271.

[99] *Ndaba v Ndaba* 2017 (1) SA 342 (SCA) para 25–27. See also Marumoagae (2017), p. 1.

[100] Section 1 of the Income Tax Act 58 of 1962.

[101] Judy Gilmour (2021). See also section 1 of the Income Tax Act 58 of 1962.

[102] 58 of 1962.

[103] Section 75(1)(*c*)(iii)(*dd*) of the TLAA.

[104] Ibid. See also Marumoagae (2021a), p. 1.

made after 1 March 2021. This is an attempt by government to ensure that retirement fund members have sufficient money during their retirement days. These initiatives cover those who are already participating in retirement funds. It is submitted that the concept of financial inclusion demands that initiatives should be made to also cover those who are not participating in standalones, umbrella, and retirement annuity funds. Apart from retirement and withdrawal benefits, those who are excluded from the retirement funding miss out from other benefits that are provided by retirement funds thus, rendering them effectively excluded from the financial sector.

There are also various products that are provided by retirement funds that can promote financial inclusion in South Africa. Some retirement funds provide disability benefits for their members. The rules of retirement funds that provide disability benefits differ.[105] Some retirement funds provide their boards the authority to decide whether members claiming to be disabled are indeed disabled.[106] The rules of other retirement funds leave mandate insurance companies that underwrite such benefits to make decision regarding whether members who are claiming disability benefits are disabled.[107] Some retirement funds provide their members with funeral benefits that can assist such members to withstand the financial difficulties with which they are faced on the death of their loved ones.[108] Most importantly, funeral benefits provided by retirement funds provide members' beneficiaries financial comfort when members die. Section 19(5) of the PFA makes it possible for members of retirement funds regulated by this Act to access credit for housing purposes.[109]

---

[105] See generally *Nkomombini v Municipal Workers' Retirement Fund and another* [2021] 2 BPLR 540 (PFA) and *Makhanya and others v Municipal Employees Pension Fund and others* [2016] JOL 36561 (PFA).

[106] See generally *Nkomombini v Municipal Workers' Retirement Fund and another* [2021] 2 BPLR 540 (PFA); *Sebalo v Municipal Workers Retirement Fund* [2021] 2 BPLR 575 (PFA); and *Nonyane v Municipal Employees Pension Fund and another* [2021] 2 BPLR 545 (PFA). See also Mhango (2007), p. 1472.

[107] See generally *Nkomombini v Municipal Workers' Retirement Fund and another* [2021] 2 BPLR 540 (PFA); *Sebalo v Municipal Workers Retirement Fund* [2021] 2 BPLR 575 (PFA); and *Nonyane v Municipal Employees Pension Fund and another* [2021] 2 BPLR 545 (PFA). See also Mhango (2007), p. 1472.

[108] See *Makhanya and others v Municipal Employees Pension Fund and others* [2016] JOL 36561 (PFA); *Mthembu and others v Municipal Employees Pension Fund and others* [2016] JOL 36565 (PFA).

[109] Section 19(5)(*b*)(iv) of the PFA. See also *Khumalo v Coca Cola Canners Provident Fund and Others* [2003] 10 BPLR 5220 (PFA) and *Erasmus v Rentmeester Assurance Ltd and Others (2)* [2000] 8 BPLR 878 (PFA).

5   Retirement Funding Financial Literacy

There is a need for improved financial literacy to promote financial inclusion in South Africa.[110] This may assist most financially excluded people in South Africa to actively participate in the formal economy.[111] Should my proposal that the government should focus on retirement funding as a viable tool for financial inclusion be acceptable, the government should undertake initiatives aimed at providing information regarding the operations of retirement funds in South Africa. Knowledge relating to those who manage retirement funds and how they are appointed or elected should be made readily available. It is also important to highlight the duties and functions of those who manage retirement funds and how they go about making their decisions. Information regarding the nature of investments made and investment destinations should also be made readily available. The general procedure to remove board members from office must be articulated clearly.

Most importantly, general information relating to how contributions members of these funds are expected to make are calculated must be easy to understand. Retirement fund members rights and obligations in retirement funds must also be made absolutely clear to members and potential members. It is also crucial that benefits which retirement fund members are likely to receive are adequately defined. Information regarding contributions, membership, rights and duties, investments, and other relevant aspects of the administration of retirement funds is usually contained in the rules of retirement funds.[112] It is advisable for the government to develop a legislative framework that would require retirement funds to make their rules public to create awareness of their operations. It is submitted that provision of knowledge of retirement funds as financial schemes and how they can assist those who use them to save for retirement to be self-sufficient when they retire is an important component of making more people interested in investing with retirement funds. In other words, it is not only about access to retirement funds but also how they operate. It is important to provide retirement fund related financial knowledge to the broader community to make them understand how their monies can be invested and managed through retirement funds. Those who may find it difficult to understand the information provided, they should at the very least have the basic information which they can use to obtain expert advice on.[113] Notwithstanding, the

---

[110] See Rootman and Antoni (2015), p. 478.

[111] Roberts et al. (2018), p. 87.

[112] Regulation 30(2) of the PFA Regulations prescribes what should be contained in the retirement fund rules, the discussion of which is beyond the scope of this paper.

[113] See Prast and van Soest (2016), p. 116, who convincingly argue that '[k]nowledge about pensions, the complexity of the provided information and the choice problem are important – even pension-literate people will only make conscious pension decisions if the choices presented to them are not overly complex. In addition, it is crucial to get people involved. For example, young people who lack the motivation to think about retirement because it is too far off will not make conscious pension decisions'.

complexities inherent in retirement funds administration, available research demonstrates that retirement fund knowledge in many countries is limited.[114]

Members must be financially included by being provided on-going education that can enlighten them on the fees and charges associated with their funds,[115] tax implications at different stages which they may choose to exit their funds,[116] and the role of important service providers such as asset managers in the investment of their contributions.[117] Financial education can also provide relevant information regarding the characteristics of various retirement funds which members can use to better understand the rights, duties and choices they have in those retirement funds.[118] Dedicated retirement funding financial education should become a powerful tool that can effectively eradicate retirement financial illiteracy, thereby ensuring adequate retirement planning. To ensure greater financial inclusion, adopted educational initiatives must improve retirement fund members' understanding of different products offered by retirement funds and empower them to be conscious of the inherent risks and opportunities generally associated with retirement funds.[119] It is thus, submitted that the South African government should reconsider their narrow approach and consider a more flexible and broader approach to financial inclusion and include through including retirement funding in its financial inclusion policy. By so doing, adequate arrangements can be made to redesign the South African retirement funding system to cater for every person who earns an income, and not only selected formally employed persons whose employers have provided them with retirement benefits.

6 Conclusion

This chapter argued that South Africa must broaden its understanding of financial inclusion to include retirement funding which can play a pivotal role in ensuring greater financial inclusion in the country. Further that failure to focus on retirement funding prevents the government from creating a platform that will enable those currently excluded from retirement funding from accessing benefits that can be offered by retirement funds. This chapter also demonstrated that the South African government has not yet shown commitment to broadening retirement fund coverage

---

[114] Ibid.

[115] See generally National Treasury 'Charges in South African Retirement Funds' Technical Discussion Paper A for public comment (11 July 2011).

[116] SARS (n.d.).

[117] Marumoagae (2021b), p. 22.

[118] OECD 'Financial Education and Saving for Retirement' (n.d.), p. 12.

[119] See Dovie (2018), p. 33, where it is argued that '[a]dequate planning for retirement requires extensive information, and an understanding of the elaborate rules governing social security and private pensions'.

and participation and, in the process, lessen reliance on the state during old-age. Instead, the South African government, through its various departments, continues to release discussion papers and reports, proposals of which are hardly implemented. It further illustrated that the current policy position regarding the establishment of the National Social Security Fund, while noble, it will not adequately cater for retirement funding.

A better proposal in relation to retirement funding, would have been to establish a national retirement fund that would focus on those who are currently excluded from retirement funding. Unlike the proposal that every employee, irrespective of whether he or she is currently contributing to a retirement fund, must join and contribute to the National Social Security Fund, the national retirement fund should make its membership voluntary for those who have retirement funding and wish to supplement their savings in this fund. It was further argued in this chapter that for greater financial inclusion, efforts must be made to eradicate retirement financial illiteracy through the provision of dedicated retirement fund education to all retirement fund members.

Bibliography

Aduda J, Kalunda E (2012) Financial inclusion and financial sector stability with reference to Kenya: a review of literature. J Appl Finance Bank 2(6):95–120

Alain ST, Mbatina NN, Zelezny-Green R (2018) Financial accessibility and private investment in developing countries. Int J Innov Sci Res Technol 9(3):141–150

Antolin P (2009) Private pensions and the financial crisis: how to ensure adequate retirement income from DC pension plans. OECD J 2:1–21

Antunes B (2021) Financial inclusion for development: better access to financial services for women, the poor, and migrant work. United Nations Conference on Trade and Development

Atkinson A, Messy F (2013) Promoting financial inclusion through financial education: OECD/INFE evidence, policies and practice. OECD Working Papers on Finance, Insurance and Private Pensions No. 34

Atkinson A, Messy F (2020) Promoting financial inclusion through financial education: attitudes and intentions. J Econ Financ Sci 13:1–55

Bhorat H, van der Westhuizen C (2012) Poverty, inequality and the nature of economic growth in South Africa. DPRU Working Paper 12/151 (November 2012)

Bikker JA, Broeders DWGA, de Dreuc J (2010) Stock market performance and pension fund investment policy: rebalancing, free float, or market timing? Int J Cent Bank 6(2):54–78

Bloom DE, McKinnon R (2013) The design and implementation of public pension systems in developing countries: issues and options. IZA Policy Paper No. 59 (May 2013)

Bophela MJK, Khumalo N (2019) The role of stokvels in South Africa: a case of economic transformation of a municipality. Probl Perspect Manag 17(4):26–37

Chitimira H, Ncube M (2020) Legislative and other selected challenges affecting financial inclusion for the poor and low-income earners in South Africa. J Afr Law 64(3):337–355

Chivasa S, Simbanegavi P (2016) Financial inclusion in Zimbabwe post hyper inflationary period: barriers and effects on societal livelihoods, a qualitative approach: a case of Matebeleland North. J Sustain Dev Africa 18(1):53–72

Chui M (2012) Derivatives markets, products and participants: an overview. In: IFC Bulletin No 35. Data requirements for monitoring derivative transactions (2012: People's Bank of China and the Irving Fisher Committee)

Cloete R (2021) Standalone versus umbrella funds: what to tell your clients. Money Market 5:24

Delsen L, Lehr A (2019) Value matters or values matter? An analysis of heterogeneity in preferences for sustainable investments. J Sustain Finance Invest 9(3):240–261

Demirguc-Kunt A, Klapper L, Singer D (2017) Financial inclusion and inclusive growth: a review of recent empirical evidence. Policy Research Working Paper 8040: Finance and Private Sector Development Team (April 2017)

Dev SM (2006) Financial inclusion: issues and challenges. Econ Polit Wkly 41:4310–4313

Dovie DA (2018) Financial literacy in an African society: an essential tool for retirement planning. Contemp J Afr Stud 5(2):26–59

Foster L (2011) Older people, pensions and poverty: an issue for social workers? Int Soc Work 54(3):344–360

Godden K (2010) Pension funds, provident funds and retirement annuities. TAXTalk 22:24–25

Hardy MA, Shuey K (2000) Pension decisions in a changing economy: gender, structure, and choice. J Gerontol 55B(5):271–277

Imboden K (2005) Building inclusive financial sectors: the road to growth and poverty reduction. J Int Aff Editorial Board 58(2):65–86

Ketkaew C, van Wouwe M, Vichitthamaros P, Teerawanviwat D (2019) The effect of expected income on wealth accumulation and retirement contribution of Thai wageworkers. SAGE Open 9(4):1–20

Kgatle MS (2007) A practical theological approach to the challenge of poverty in post-1994 South Africa: apostolic faith mission as a case study. Theol Stud 73(3):1–9

Kim JY (2014) Empirical analysis of retirement pension and IFRS adoption effects on accounting information: glance at IT industry. Sci World J:1–6

Kruger LP (2011) The impact of Black Economic Empowerment (BEE) on South African businesses: focusing on ten dimensions of business performance. South Afr Bus Rev 15(3):207–233

Lawack VA (2013) Mobile money, financial inclusion and financial integrity: the South African case. Wash J Law Technol Arts 8(3):317–346

Lonescu L, Robles EA (2014) Update of Iops work on fees and charges. IOPS Working Papers on Effective Pensions Supervision, No. 20, pp 1–44

Lukhele AK (1990) Stokvels in South Africa: informal saving schemes by Blacks for the Black Community. Johannesburg

Lunn P, Mcgowan F, Howard N (2018) Do some financial product features negatively affect consumer decisions? A review of evidence. Research Series Number 78

Mahalika R, Matsebula V, Yu D (2021) Investigating the relationship between financial inclusion and poverty in South Africa. Dev South Afr 38(5):1–23

Malherbe K (2013) Retirement reform in South Africa: the influence of international social security standards and human rights instruments. Int J Comp Labour Law Ind Relat 29:105–128

Marumoagae C (2017) The law regarding pension interest in South Africa has been settled! Or has it? With reference to Ndaba v Ndaba (600/2015) [2016] ZASCA 162. PER 20:1–22

Marumoagae C (2020) Retirement funds rivalry, voluntary withdrawal of membership. S Afr Merc Law J 32:205–233

Marumoagae C (2021a) Pensions: January to March 2021. Juta Q Rev:1–4

Marumoagae C (2021b) The need to adopt preventative measures to combat the misappropriation of retirement fund assets. PER/PELJ 24:1–35

Matuku S, Kaseke E (2014) The role of stokvels in improving people's lives: the case in Orange Farm, Johannesburg, South Africa. Soc Work 50(4):504–515

Mhango M (2007) When should a pension fund require a member to undergo medical treatment as a condition for receiving permanent disability benefits? A critical review of the pension fund adjudicator's determinations. Ind Law J 28:1472–1483

Mhlanga D, Dunga SH, Moloi T (2021) Understanding the drivers of financial inclusion in South Africa. Econ Financ Sci 14(1):1–8

Mokoena K, Dickason-Koekemoer Z, Ferreira-Schen S (2021) Analysing the risk tolerance levels of stokvel investors. Cogent Soc Sci 7(1):1–13

Moleko N, Ikhide S (2017) Pension funds evolution, reforms and trends in South Africa. Int J Econ Finance Stud 9(2):134–151

Nanziri EL, Leibbrandt M (2018) Measuring and profiling financial literacy in South Africa. S Afr J Econ Manag Sci 21(1):1–17

Nguyen TTH (2021) Measuring financial inclusion: a composite FI index for the developing countries. J Econ Dev 23(1):77–99

OECD (2020) Advancing the digital financial inclusion of youth. Report prepared for the G20 Global Partnership for Financial Inclusion by the OECD

Pask AE, Marx J (2018) Mitigating the South African retirement-income shortfall crisis. Econ Financ Sci 11(1):1–10

Phalatse S (2021) The role of private finance in infrastructure development in South Africa – a critical assessment. (18 January 2021) Institute for Economic Justice Working Paper Series, No. 6

Prast H, van Soest A (2016) Financial literacy and preparation for retirement. Intereconomics 51(3): 113–118

Rasool F, Botha CJ (2011) The nature, extent and effect of skills shortages on skills migration in South Africa. SA J Hum Resource Manag 9(1):1–12

Roberts B, Struwig J, Gordon S, Radebe T (2018) Financial literacy in South Africa: results from the 2017/18 South African Social Attitudes Survey round. Report prepared by the Human Sciences Research Council on behalf of the Financial Sector Control Authority

Rootman C, Antoni X (2015) Investigating financial literacy to improve financial behaviour among black consumers. J Econ Financ Sci 8(2):474–494

Salahuddin M, Vink N, Ralph N, Gow J (2020) Globalisation, poverty and corruption: retarding progress in South Africa. Dev South Afr 37(4):617–643

Shankar S (2013) Financial inclusion in india: do microfinance institutions address access barriers? ACRN J Entrep Perspect 2(1):60–74

Stedall C, Venter JMP (2016) Financial products used by South African households at different life stages. J Econ Financ Sci 9(1):310–325

Stewart F, Yermo J (2009) Pensions in Africa. OECD Working Papers on Insurance and Private Pensions, No. 30, pp 1–32

Thomas A, Spataro L (2016) The effects of pension funds on markets performance: a review. J Econ Surv 30(1):1–33

Tran T, Le T, Thi H (2021) The impact of financial inclusion on poverty reduction. Asian J Law Econ 12(1):95–119

Verhoef G (2001) Informal financial service institutions for survival: African women and stokvels in urban South Africa, 1930—1988. Enterp Soc 2(2):259–296

Wentzel JP, Diatha KS, Yadavalli VSS (2016) An investigation into factors impacting financial exclusion at the bottom of the pyramid in South Africa. Dev South Afr 32(2):203–214

Zeka B, Rootman C, Krüger J (2020) Retirement funding adequacy: the influence of provisions, attitudes and intentions. J Econ Financ Sci 13(1):1–9

World Bank (2018) Overcoming poverty and inequality in South Africa: An Assessment of Drivers, Constraints and Opportunities

National Treasury An inclusive financial sector for all: draft for consultation (2020)

The Institute of Directors in Southern Africa (IoDSA) and the King Committee Fourth King Report on Corporate Governance in South Africa (King IV)

National Treasury 'Retirement Fund Reform: A Discussion Paper' (December 2004)

National Treasury 'The Measurement of Poverty in South Africa Project: Key issues' (27 February 2007)

National Treasury 'The South African Retirement Funds Landscape' Retirement Fund Reform: A Discussion Paper (December 2004)

Committee of Investigation into a Retirement Provision System for South Africa (1988)

The Commission of Inquiry into Certain Aspects of the Tax Structure of South Africa, Katz Commission, 1994)

The Committee on Strategy and Policy Review of Retirement Provision in South Africa (Smith Committee, 1995)

National Treasury 'Charges in South African Retirement Funds' (11 July 2011) *Technical Discussion Paper A for Public Comment*

National Treasury 'Preservation, Portability and Governance for Retirement Funds' (21 September 2012) Technical Discussion Paper C for Public Comment

Transforming the Present – Protecting the Future: Report of the Committee of Inquiry into a Comprehensive System of Social Security for South Africa Taylor (Commission, 2002)

Inter-Departmental Task Team on Social Security and Retirement Reform 'Comprehensive Social Security in South Africa: Discussion Document' Version 11.9 (March 2012)

Rangarajan Report 'Report of the Committee on Financial Inclusion' (January 2008)

Department of Social Development 'Green paper on Comprehensive Social Security and Retirement Reform' Consolidated Government Paper: Public Consultation Version (03 August 2021) Government Gazette No 45006 (18 August 2021)

Department of Social Development 'Department of Social Development Withdraws the Green Paper on Comprehensive Social Security and Retirement Reforms' (1 September 2021) Media Statement

Stats SA 'Statistical release P0211' Quarterly Labour Force Survey Quarter 2 (2021)

Dhlembeu NT (2018) The relationship between retirement planning and financial literacy in South Africa. MCom Mini-Dissertation, UP

Wepener CW (2014) Optimal asset allocation for retirement funds: a South African perspective. MCom Dissertation UCT

Sasol Limited v Chemical Industries National Provident Fund (20612/2014) [2015] ZASCA 113 (7 September 2015)

Ndaba v Ndaba 2017 (1) SA 342 (SCA)

Nkomombini v Municipal Workers' Retirement Fund and another [2021] 2 BPLR 540 (PFA)

Sebalo v Municipal Workers Retirement Fund [2021] 2 BPLR 575 (PFA)

Nonyane v Municipal Employees Pension Fund and another [2021] 2 BPLR 545 (PFA)

Makhanya and others v Municipal Employees Pension Fund and others [2016] JOL 36561 (PFA)

Mthembu and others v Municipal Employees Pension Fund and others [2016] JOL 36565 (PFA).

Khumalo v Coca Cola Canners Provident Fund and Others [2003] 10 BPLR 5220 (PFA)

Erasmus v Rentmeester Assurance Ltd and Others (2) [2000] 8 BPLR 878 (PFA)

Municipal Employees Pension Fund v Natal Joint Municipal Pension Fund (Superannuation) & others [2016] 4 All SA 761 (SCA)

ICS Pension Fund v Sithole 2009 ZAGPHC 6 (13 January 2009)

Financial Advisory and Intermediary Services Act 37 of 2002

Pension Funds Act 24 of 1956

Taxation Laws Amendment Act of 2020

Tax Act 58 of 1962

ASISA 'Introduction to Umbrella Fund' <https://www.asisa.org.za/media/s5gnn0im/atleha-edu_umbrella-funds-cfe-publication.pdf> accessed on 02 July 2021

Brits W 'Health Care Nearing Crisis Due to Shortage Of Nursing Staff' <https://solidariteit.co.za/en/health-care-nearing-crisis-due-to-shortage-of-nursing-staff/> accessed on 28 June 2021

Silimina D 'Financial Inclusion: Taking it to the Bank' (2021) <https://www.dandc.eu/en/article/zambia-has-set-itself-goal-universal-access-financial-services> accessed on 27 October 2021.

Gilmour J 'Preservation Funds: Secure A Good Retirement, Defer Tax' <https://www.sygnia.co.za/press/preservation-funds-secure-a-good-retirement-defer-tax> accessed on 5 July 2021

Maphalala M, Mpofu N 'South Africa Battling with Shortage of Teachers in Public Schools' <https://www.iol.co.za/the-star/opinion-analysis/opinion-south-africa-battling-with-shortage-of-teachers-in-public-schools-37696438> accessed on 28 June 2021

National Treasury 'Inclusive Financial Sector for All' Draft for consultation <http://www.treasury.gov.za/comm_media/press/2020/Financial%20Inclusion%20Policy%20-%20An%20Inclusive%20Financial%20Sector%20For%20All.pdf> Accessed on 26 June 2021

National Treasury 'Statement on the Impact of the Proposed Retirement Reforms' <http://www.treasury.gov.za/comm_media/press/2014/2014070901%20-%20Statement%20on%20the%20Impact%20of%20the%20Proposed%20Retirement%20Reforms.pdf> accessed 5 July 2021

National Planning Commission 'National Development Plan 2030: Our Future- Make it work' 118 <https://www.gov.za/sites/default/files/gcis_document/201409/ndp-2030-our-future-make-it-workr.pdf> accessed on 26 June 2021

Old Mutual 'Retirement Ready' <https://www.oldmutual.co.za/personal/solutions/retirement-plans/> accessed on 27 October 2021

OECD 'Financial Education and Saving for Retirement' <https://www.oecd.org/finance/private-pensions/39197801.pdf> accessed on 10 July 2021

Parliament 'How Law is Made' <https://www.parliament.gov.za/how-law-made> assessed on 30 October 2021

SARS 'Tax and Retirement' <https://www.sars.gov.za/individuals/tax-during-all-life-stages-and-events/tax-and-retirement/> accessed on 10 July 2021

Wagner G 'Police Staff Shortages Negatively Affecting Crime Levels' <https://www.westerncape.gov.za/news/police-staff-shortages-negatively-affecting-crime-levels>   accessed   on 28 June 2021

World Bank 'Financial Inclusion' <https://www.worldbank.org/en/topic/financialinclusion/overview> accessed on 30 June 2021

Writer S 'South Africa is Facing A Doctor Shortage – Here's Why' BusinessTech (20 October 2020) <https://businesstech.co.za/news/government/346538/south-africa-is-a-facing-a-doctor-shortage-heres-why/> accessed on 28 June 2021

10x Investments 'What is a Retirement Annuity?' <https://www.10x.co.za/faq/retirement-annuity/what-is-a-retirement-annuity> accessed on 1 July 2021

10X Investments '10X South African Retirement Reality Report 2020' <https://f.hubspotusercontent00.net/hubfs/3390004/Retirement%20Reality%20Report/10X%20Retirement%20Reality%20Report%20-%202020.pdf> accessed on 05 July 2021

Clement Marumoagae is an Associate Professor at the University of the Witwatersrand. He holds the following qualifications: LLB LLM Diploma in Corporate Law (Wits); LLM (NWU); PhD (UCT) and AIPSA Diploma in Insolvency Law (UP). Clement is also a practising attorney at Marumoagae Attorneys Inc, specializing in pension law and family law. Clement's main area of research is mercantile law and pension law. He also researches in family law, insolvency law and procedural law. Clement is a councilor of the Legal Practice Council and the inaugural chair of its education committee. He is also passionate about the development of candidate legal practitioners and conducts research that is aimed at eradicating artificial barriers meant to restrict entry to the legal profession. Furthermore, he is also a member of the advisory committee of the South African Law Reform Commission, project 144 which is mandated to investigate the possibility of introducing a single marriage statute in South Africa.

Mobile Fin-Tech Ecosystem Shaping Financial Inclusion in Zimbabwean Banking and Financial Services Markets

Brighton Nyagadza, Dumisani R. Muzira, and Tinashe Chuchu

Abstract The purpose of this chapter is to explore mobile financial technology ecosystem shaping financial inclusion in Zimbabwean banking and financial services markets. The chapter is based on a narrative approach of secondary data sources, mainly peer reviewed reputable journal articles. The purpose being to draw conclusions and identifying the research gaps that exist within the banking and financial services markets in Zimbabwe. The chapter is based on a structural analysis methodology to frame the categories of the major analysis in combination with scientific rigour to a broad and complex problem. Research results proved that the mobile financial technology ecosystem shaping financial inclusion in Zimbabwean banking and financial services markets is a necessity for sustainable economic growth and development. Implications to contemporary banking and financial services industry business leaders include bringing-in present day digital financial technologies, incubating survival plans of actions or strategies so as to fully operationalise mobile financial technology seamlessly. In addition to this, establishing technological innovation appetite is meant to address, respond and navigate within the associated financial digital disruptive complexities for the sustenance of banking and financial services markets in Zimbabwe. The study results underscore the necessity of understanding mobile financial technology ecosystem so as to design relevant strategies in a bid to carve financial inclusion in Zimbabwean banking and financial services markets. With its novelty, the chapter conceptually examines how mobile financial technology ecosystem can shape financial inclusion

B. Nyagadza (✉)
Department of Marketing, Marondera University of Agricultural Sciences and Technology, Marondera, Zimbabwe

D. R. Muzira
Department of Agribusiness & Management, Marondera University of Agricultural Sciences and Technology, Marondera, Zimbabwe

T. Chuchu
Marketing Division, University of Witwatersrand, Johannesburg, South Africa

© The Author(s), under exclusive license to Springer Nature Switzerland AG 2023
H. Chitimira, T. V. Warikandwa (eds.), *Financial Inclusion and Digital Transformation Regulatory Practices in Selected SADC Countries*, Ius Gentium: Comparative Perspectives on Law and Justice 106,
https://doi.org/10.1007/978-3-031-23863-5_12

in Zimbabwean banking and financial services markets. It contributes to literature and theoretical novel introspections into the depth and breadth of how mobile financial technology can contribute to the development of financial inclusion in the Zimbabwean banking and financial markets.

1 Introduction

The key terms such as financial inclusion, m-banking, mobile money and financial technology are defined for readers to have an appreciation of these terms as they are used in this chapter. Financial inclusion is defined as delivery of financial and banking services at an affordable cost to most of the disadvantaged and low-income groups.[1] It involves activity that facilitating the accessibility, obtainability of services and use of the formal financial system for all individuals that participate in of an economy. It is the ability of communities to access essential financial and banking services.[2] M-banking is the interaction of the customers and the bank through a mobile device like a cell phone, smartphone, or a tablet.[3] Financial technology refers to the innovative ways used by banks to improve financial services through the use of technology.[4] In this case the technology that supports the mobile banking systems.

Financial inclusion is a major issue in most developing countries such as Malawi, Kenya, Zambia and Zimbabwe. In some countries such as United States, they have introduced inclusive legislation, the United Kingdom has since launched a task force that monitors financial inclusion and in France, a law was introduced to protect the individual's right to open a bank account.[5] The determinants of financial inclusion in Zimbabwe include age, education, financial literacy, income, and internet connectivity as positively related to inclusion while those negatively related to inclusion are the documentation required to open bank accounts and the distance to the nearest access point.[6] It can be suggested that a certain age, level of education, access to resources would limit one's ability in being included financially in a countries economy. The ability to open bank accounts is limited to certain members of the economy and the distance to the nearest access points adds to this financial exclusion. The most excluded members of an economy are the rural population. These rural communities have limited access to banking services as they reside far from services that officer such services. The mostly excluded population being the rural population because of the long distances to access points and the youth because they are viewed by banks as risky clients, low income groups that live on hand to mouth,

---

[1] Dev (2006), pp. 4310–4313.

[2] Cruz-García (2021), pp. 1496–1526.

[3] Laukkanen (2017), pp. 1042–1043.

[4] Leong and Sung (2018), pp. 74–78.

[5] Changchit et al. (2017), pp. 239–261.

[6] Sanderson et al. (2018), pp. 1–8.

micro small and medium scale enterprises (MSMEs), small holder farmers, and people with disabilities.[7] This chapter will look at mobile financial technological ecosystem practices shaping financial inclusion in Zimbabwean banking and financial services markets. This also includes the technological change and policy and regulatory frameworks.

The quality of life is fast changing the whole world wide due to advancement in technology and dynamics in economic systems.[8] These changes are being triggered by forces of Fourth Industrial Revolution (4IR)[9] and this plays a bigger role in production improvement, cost reduction and customer services enhancement. The Fourth Industrial Revolution (4IR) is concerned with the integration and accumulation of effects of multiple advances in technologies which include artificial intelligence (intelligence demonstrated by machines).[10] World of work and the art of doing business has since changed and expanding corporate boundaries.[11] These 4IR disruptive technologies are going to unlock the potential for sustainable financial services innovation in emerging economies such as Zimbabwe through facilitating the inter-linkages in the enhanced service production process.[12] However, the effect of the novel pandemics such as the Coronavirus disease (COVID-19) is forcing individuals to opt to go for the sustainable emerging technologies adoption as a gateway to convenience in a bid to access services such as m-banking (m-banking). COVID-19, stands for Corona Virus 2019 which is a human respiratory infectious disease. M-banking is fast being accepted in Africa with Nigeria, Tanzania, and South Africa leading other countries as result of their larger population base.[13] Banking and financial institutions have since invested in the development of m-banking applications over the years.[14] This is in response to the demand for m-banking as a result of changes caused by the volatile, uncertain, complex and ambiguous business environment. The challenges of m-banking may include, but not limited to sufficiency issues related to maturity befitting disruption and whether there can be affordability to the costs faced for interoperability reasons.[15]

In Zimbabwe, banks have adopted m-banking facility with Econet Wireless' Ecocash on top of the rank, followed by OneMoney of NetOne Wireless, CABS's TextaCash, FBC Mobile Moola, CBZ Bank's Touch M-banking application and others. While the worldwide mobile penetration stood at 78.2%[16] with an unfortunate bancarisation lower rate of 9%, despite the current 103% mobile penetration in

---

[7]Reserve Bank of Zimbabwe (RBZ) (2016), p. 40.

[8]Changchit (2017), p. 239.

[9]Nyagadza et al. (2021), p. 89.

[10]Nyagadza et al. (2021), p. 89.

[11]Zhao (2013), pp. 123–152.

[12]Mcafee and Brynjolfsson (2017), p. 64.

[13]UNCTAD (2017), p. 56.

[14]Rauch (2016), pp. 1–16.

[15]Micheler et al. (2019), pp. 503–528.

[16]Nyagadza (2021).

Zimbabwe,[17] m-banking adoption remains deplorable. This could have been as a result of poor financial inclusion development strategies by banking and financial services institutions in Zimbabwe. Devising strategies and tactics to enhance the banks viability in making an increase in demand for m-banking[18] under COVID-19 pandemic situation is very necessary. Further to this, the degree to which m-banking is being adopted in developing countries such as Zimbabwe, is not as equivalent as expected and currently taking place in developed countries.[19]

Evidence from literature review depicts that researchers such as[20] (from developing countries), (from developed countries)[21] have carried out researches in almost similar areas associated with m-banking adoption intention which is very different from the current study. They could not proffer research inquiries that link sustainability, m-banking and its adoption with a perspective from a developing country like Zimbabwe.

2   Mobile Money and Financial Inclusion

Most banks in Zimbabwe are concentrated in the urban areas with just a few, the likes of POSB, Agribank and CBZ having their presence in the rural areas. This could be because most industries and businesses that push volumes in banking transactions are concentrated in the urban centres. The few banks that are in the rural areas have the government as part of its shareholders so it could be that the government is influencing them to have banks there probably as a way of promoting financial inclusion to the rural population. The other reason could be that, Agribank and CBZ offer loans to farmers and most farming activities are done away from the central business district hence these banks' presence in the rural areas to be close to these farmers as part of their customers. Despite having access to few banking services in the rural areas, working age population is more in rural than urban areas in Zimbabwe. Working age rural population constitutes 64% and 36% in the urban areas,[22] meaning that those who are economically active are concentrated in Zimbabwe's rural areas. This then makes m-banking a solution for financial inclusion because it can be easily accessed even from remote rural places, easy to use, secure and convenient too.[23] In their study in Zimbabwe, Mutsonziwa and Maposa found out that 45% of adult population use mobile money services because it is

---

[17] Changchit and Chuchuen (2016), pp. 1–9.

[18] Changchit et al. (2017), p. 240.

[19] Makanyeza (2017), p. 997.

[20] Laukkanen (2008), pp. 440–455.

[21] Laforet and Li (2005), pp. 362–380.

[22] Zimbabwe National Statistics Agency (2019), p. 15.

[23] Mago and Chitokwindo (2014), pp. 221–230.

cheap and it is the only accessible service in the areas of Zimbabwe they live.[24] This makes m-money services a feasible option to enhance financial inclusion. The main mobile money platforms used in Zimbabwe being Ecocash a product of Econet Wireless, Onemoney a product of NetOne, and Telecash a product of Telecel. The antecedents, drivers and inhibitors of mobile money and financial inclusion are discussed in the succeeding sections.

3 Antecedents of Mobile Money (M-Money)

Antecedents of mobile money sets the environment in which the introduction of mobile money has its drivers and inhibitors. These antecedents set the favourable or unfavourable context that existed before the introduction of mobile money in Zimbabwe. The need for easy access to financial services for making payments, sending, and receiving money, access to micro loans created room for the development of m-banking to financial inclusion. Most of the Zimbabwean population are not formally employed, have no bank accounts, and faced difficulties in accessing loans such that mobile platforms such as Kashagi became convenient as they provide easy access to micro loans without waiting periods and the bureaucracy of loan approvals.[25] The innovation and technological advancement in Zimbabwe also provided fertile ground for mobile money and m-banking Innovations. High literacy level of Zimbabweans which stood at 97.4% in 2019[26] could also have set a good environment that could support the use of mobile phones to perform most services that would ordinarily require a bank teller's assistance. Most Zimbabweans can therefore easily follow m-banking instructions. More so, some mobile phone platforms have an option of choosing the language of preference to be used in transacting making it even more user friendly.

4 Drivers of Mobile Money

The drivers of mobile money can be grouped as factors that arise from the benefits offered by mobile money and those that emanate from the challenges in the traditional banking system.[27] Some of the benefits of mobile money are that there are no monthly fees and membership does not expire as is the case with the banking system that has monthly fixed charges over and above other transaction costs.[28] Some of the

---

[24] Mutsonziwa and Maposa (2016), pp. 45–56.

[25] Mago and Chitokwindo (2014), p. 221.

[26] Zimbabwe National Statistics Agency (2019), p. 23.

[27] Masocha and Dzomonda (2018), pp. 1–11.

[28] Masocha and Dzomonda (2018), pp. 1–11.

drivers of mobile money usage are the mobile money agents, collaboration between banks and mobile services providers, the need to cut costs, and the need to increase customer base. Mobile money agents provide more access points to mobile services such as ecocash cash in and cash out, World Remit, Mukuru, Subscriber Identification Module card (SIM card) sales, line registration, and airtime sales. Collaboration between banks and mobile services providers in offering services such as bank to wallet, wallet to bank transfers, interbank and intrabank transfers, balance enquiry and even account statement requests have since increased in Zimbabwe, in a bid to increase financial inclusivity and equality. The need to cut costs by leveraging the infrastructure that banks and telecommunications use as well as a wider customer base by leveraging on telecom and bank customers can drive mobile money usage.[29] The convenience of using mobile money to pay city council bills, Zimbabwe National Road Administration (ZINARA) payments of toll gates, Zimbabwe Electricity Supply Authority (ZESA), Zimbabwe Revenue Authority (ZIMRA) payments, Registrar General's office payments for marriage licences, marriage banns, and other payments that have to do with birth certificate replacement, Identification card replacements led to its increased usage. In addition, most supermarkets such as OK, Spar, Pick 'n' Pay are also linked to mobile money platforms. One can pay grocery bills from these supermarkets by just confirming a point sale bill using their mobile money pin. This has destroyed the distance barrier as one is able to pay for a bill from wherever they are provided there is network connection. The most used function on m-banking is that of sending and receiving money[30] showing that mobile money is standing in the gap that has been left by traditional banking system.

5 Inhibitors of Mobile Money

The inhibitors of mobile money include merchants that refuse mobile money to pay goods and services, and those that price highly when using mobile money.[31] This has resulted in commodities having three price tags, the United States dollar price, Zimbabwean dollar cash price, ecocash price and swipe price (payment using a bank card). Ecocash and swipe prices are usually pegged very high. This then has discouraged people from using mobile money as they try to cut on costs. The high transaction fees associated with the use of mobile money has also negatively affected the use of mobile money. Connectivity challenges brought about by the high cost of data, high cost of smart phones that are compatible in supporting the m-banking applications. However, the mobile money service providers try to alleviate the high costs of data by offering discounted data packages such as private Wi-Fi bundles, data bouquets, weekend hourly bundles, e-learning bouquets, and voice-voice

---

[29]Mutsonziwa and Maposa (2016), pp. 45–56.
[30]Mago and Chitokwindo (2014), p. 221.
[31]Mutsonziwa and Maposa (2016), pp. 45–56.

bundles of joy. Power-cuts also hinder the use of mobile money since mobile network connectivity relies on power supply. These power outages at times lead to incomplete transactions and at times multiple charges for a single transaction that are difficult to follow through for them to be reversed. Since the gadgets used for m-banking needs power supply, when there is no electricity for some time the batteries can go flat, and potential business is lost when customers fail to transact because the point-of-sale machines will have switched off for lake of power. In this regard, power-cuts then become a hindrance to mobile money usage. Other studies have lack of awareness of mobile money benefits, anxiety towards new technology, lack of technology skills and complexity of new technology as inhibitors of mobile money usage.[32]

6   Technological Change and Financial Inclusion

Information, communication, and technology (ICT) is essential for financial inclusion to succeed.[33] Resisting the changes that technology brings results in missed opportunities.[34] Technological change is discussed using access to ICT services and equipment. These services can be accessed using a computer, internet, and mobile phones.[35] The places where technology is used include the home, work, church, and school. Remote working from home, online teaching and learning, online church services using zoom, google meet and other online platforms are a result of technology usage. Smart phones are the mobile phones that are compatible with most mobile money platforms. Access to Internet whether fixed/wired broadband or mobile broadband is needed to support financial inclusion. The individuals using technology also need to have the relevant computer and internet skills to use and understand the digitalised financial services.

7   Policy and Regulatory Frameworks for Financial Inclusion

Policies and regulations are essential to maintain sanity in the financial sector. Other studies[36] suggest that policymakers should focus on improving technological infrastructure and amenities that help to clear grey areas and information asymmetry in

---

[32] Sharma et al. (2018), pp. 52–63.

[33] Wellalage et al. (2021), pp. 1–13.

[34] Nyagadza (2019), pp. 235–252.

[35] RBZ (2016), p. 40.

[36] Agyekum (2021), pp. 1–15.

the supply of credit to SMEs in developing economies.[37] The regulators should protect customer deposits, promote and maintain confidence and minimise financial crises risk by curbing cyber security issues.[38] However, in Zimbabwe there is need for balance such that the regulations do not end up being a barrier to telecommunication. Policies such as the Zimbabwe's national financial inclusion strategy commissioned in 2016,[39] the anti-money laundering policy, Credit Guarantee Scheme for SMEs are some of the policies that have been put in place in Zimbabwe to support financial inclusion. The introduction of Zimbabwe Women's Microfinance Bank and Empower Bank for the youth was done as a way of empowering the youth and women and as a way of promoting financial inclusion of women and youth. In an Act of Parliament, the war veterans were given 20% of the mining claims,[40] artisanal miners to be officially registered such that they do not need middlemen to sell their minerals,[41] Members of Parliament given money to start income generating projects such as bakeries, fisheries, horticulture, and poultry farming to promote financial inclusion in different parts of the country. The Central bank (Reserve Bank of Zimbabwe) is recommended to supervise non-bank led m-banking models and manage their cash holding limits and cost structures.[42]

8 Financial Inclusion Mobile Fin-Tech Adoption Intention Model

In line with technology acceptance, this chapter adopts the Unified Theory of Adoption and Use of Technology model 2 (UTAUT2). The UTAUT2 model extended[43] provides a better explanation and fit to the current research study of financial inclusion as it depicts behavioural intentions and technology use than the prior model(s) like Technology Acceptance Model (TAM). Justification for the use of UTAUT2 in this financial inclusion chapter is based on its application in technology adoption such as mobile applications software social network sites,[44] online games internet banking, near field communication (NFC), mobile payments robotics and travel and tourism.[45] In the current chapter, the UTAUT model is applied in investigating m-banking service adoption intention determinants under COVID-19 conditions (Fig. 1).

---

[37] Agyekum (2021), pp. 1–15.

[38] Lumsden (2018), pp. 1–45.

[39] Nyagadza (2020), pp. 1–19.

[40] National Assembly (2021), p. 62.

[41] The Herald (2021).

[42] Mago and Chitokwindo (2014), p. 221.

[43] Venkatesh et al. (2012), pp. 157–178.

[44] Kim (2009), pp. 283–311.

[45] Chao (2019), pp. 1–14.

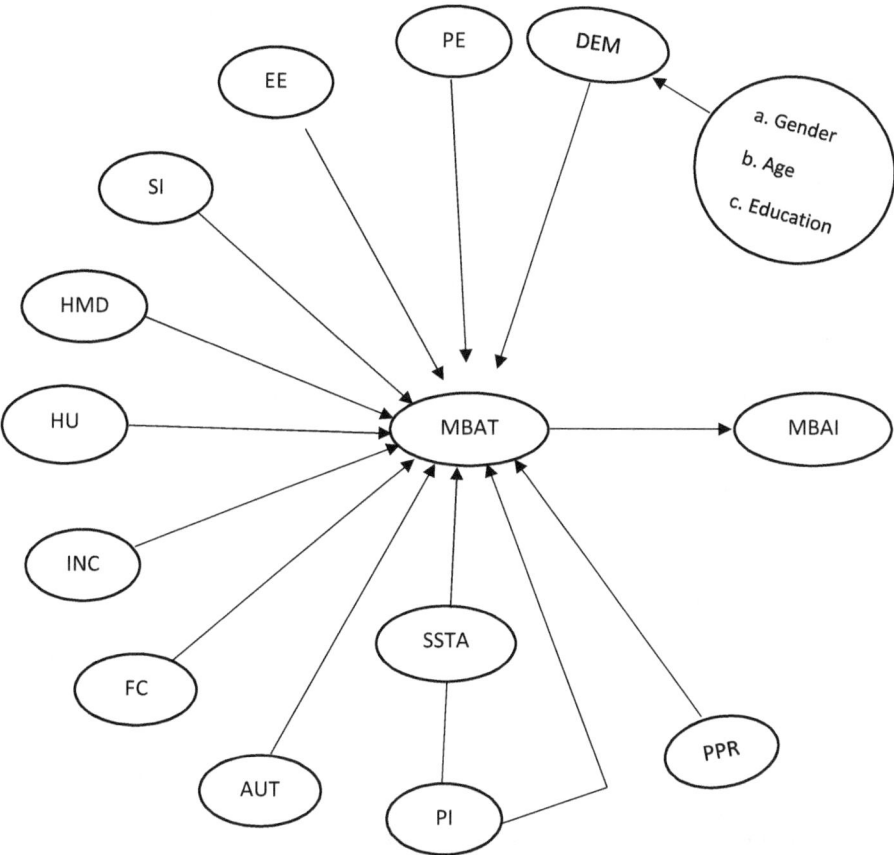

Fig. 1 Mobile fin-tech adoption intention conceptual model. Source: Authors' conception (2021). **Key**: Predictor Variables—Pe: performance expectancy; EE: effort expectancy; SI: **social influence; HM**: hedonic motivations; HU: habitual use; INC: inconvenience; **FC**: facilitating conditions; AUT: automation; PPR: perceived privacy risk; PI: **perceived innovativeness; SSTA**: attitude towards Self-Service Technologies (SSTs). **Mediator Variable**— **Mbat**: M-Banking Adoption' Trust. **Moderator**: Dem—Demographic Factors—Age, Gender; Education; Income. **Response Variable—MBAI**: M-banking Adoption' Intention

8.1 Performance Expectancy

Performance expectancy discusses an individual's perception of how their performance can be improved by a system. The extent to which the usage of technology benefitting customers in the performance of certain activities define performance expectation and its link to financial inclusion. Evidence from research depicts that the greatest predictor of technology acceptance (for example m-banking customer service) is performance expectancy.[46] This concept is built upon, five constructs: Perceived usefulness, relative advantage, job-fit, extrinsic motivation and outcome expectations.[47]

8.2 Effort Expectancy

Effort expectancy can be defined as the extent of ease associated with the use of the technology system.[48] Basic antecedents of effort expectancy include ease of use and complexity.[49] In this chapter, effort expectancy refers to the belief and trust that the banking customers hold in the ease of use of m-banking in e-banking customer service.[50] Effort expectancy is deemed to be a direct determinant of trust in m-banking by customers.[51] Effort expectancy is founded on the notion that there are connections between the effort put forth at work, the performance achieved from that effort, and the benefits gained from the effort.[52]

8.3 Social Influence

Social influence refers to the change in an individual's thoughts, feelings, attitudes or actions that ultimately influence that individual's interaction with others. M-banking have great social influence or social presence.[53] Social influence can be viewed as other people's degree of salience in an interaction and the consequent salience of interpersonal relationships. The social influence represents a sense of sociability, which in m-banking customer service and e-commerce affect the level of trust[54] and usage intention in future.[55] This tends to impact how financial inclusion tends to develop at any given circumstance. Customers trust in m-banking is affected by their social influence or presence during the process of transactions. Social influence of m-banking has a positive impact on consumers' use intention and determine their trust levels.[56]

---

[46] Khalilzadeh (2017), pp. 460–474.
[47] Chao (2019), pp. 1–14.
[48] Chao (2019), pp. 1–14.
[49] Cheng and Jiang (2020), pp. 592–614.
[50] Herrero and San Martín (2017), pp. 209–217.
[51] Onaolapo and Oyewole (2018), pp. 95–115.
[52] Cheng and Jiang (2017), p. 592.
[53] Sheehan (2018).
[54] Han (2021), pp. 46–65.
[55] Ho et al. (2020), pp. 133–151.
[56] Mimoun et al. (2017), pp. 545–559.

8.4   Hedonic Motivations

Hedonic motivations are considered to have a direct effect on one's intention to search and an indirect association with an individual's purchase intention as well as the level and/or extent of financial inclusion diffusion. Gratification associated with transacting over m-banking is another important aspect that influences hedonistic desire and trust by customers when they use them for e-banking transactions.[57] Some customers can find m-banking as fun, enjoyment and as a diplomatic way of killing time.[58] When m-banking become more hedonically interactive, there is higher chance of being influential in determining customers' trust levels, and subsequently the intention to use them will be fostered with increase in financial inclusivity.[59]

8.5   Habitual Usage

M-banking systems application can be habitually used on a daily basis by customers when making e-banking financial transactions.[60] Customers' habit is directly related to their past and present behaviour,[61] which in turn affects their levels of trust in the m-banking usage intention.[62] M-banking facilitates several transactions at different intervals simultaneously[63] with natural language, which enhancing interactivity and inclusivity with customers.[64] Due to their operation of 24 h a day and 7 days a week, m-banking systems applications give bank customers the room to be transact whenever they want.[65]

8.6   Perceived Innovativeness

M-banking perceived innovativeness is directly related to utilitarian gratification, whereby individuals' technology utility needs are known to be information seeking and/or self-presentation.[66] In this chapter, m-banking perceived innovativeness is the

---

[57] Cheng and Jiang (2020), p. 614.

[58] Chao (2019), pp. 1–14.

[59] Alraja et al. (2016), pp. 930–934.

[60] Morosan and Defranco (2016), pp. 17–29.

[61] Herrero and San Martín (2017), pp. 209–217.

[62] Xu (2014), p. 55.

[63] Weißensteiner (2018), p. 65.

[64] Michiels (2017), pp. 70–78.

[65] Chave and Gerosa (2021), pp. 729–758.

[66] Papacharissi and Mendelson (2011), p. 230.

willingness of customers to try out new technologies.[67] Customers tend to differ in the way they use information technology for financial inclusion, as some adopt it and some may delay ADOPTION OR REJECT IT, DUE TO THE LEVEL OF TRUST THAT THEY PLACE.[68]

8.7 Attitude Towards Self-Service Technologies (SSTs)

If customers get the rightful experience they perceive m-banking positively,[69] and normally their trust is increased if the innovativeness tallies with their expectations.[70] Self-Service Technologies (SSTs) like m-banking systems applications are more acceptable to the millennials than any other age group and their attitude is shaped by the associated trust. Some customers perceive that interaction with the Interactive Voice Response (IVR) is frustrating. Hence, experience and trust levels might be affected as a result of this issue,[71] leading to poor development of financial inclusion.

8.8 Inconveniences

Due to the fact that m-banking may be better skilled in the human conversations imitations, hackers can capture the information, which may end up being a security risk concern to the concerned banking customers,[72] which further affects the development of financial inclusion as customers' trust is reduced. Further to this, chatbots do not have own personality or identity, even feelings and emotions like people,[73] who may need more words, longer words and words associated with positive emotions.[74] Errors may increase and banks' brand image will be damaged.[75] Such kind of inconveniences lead to phishing of confidential information, since m-banking use open internet protocols.[76]

---

[67] Alalwan et al. (2018), pp. 125–138.
[68] Lovakov and Agadullina (2021), pp. 485–504.
[69] Parker et al. (2016), p. 65.
[70] Dehghani (2018), pp. 145–158.
[71] Yen and Chiang (2020), pp. 1177–1194.
[72] Wang (2020).
[73] Dehghani (2018), p. 158.
[74] Papacharissi and Mendelson (2011), p. 230.
[75] Michiels (2017), pp. 70–78.
[76] Yen and Chiang (2020), pp. 1177–1194.

8.9 Facilitating Conditions

Research has proved that people are more likely to be inclined to engage with technology that give them experience which facilitate features through aesthetic cues.[77] This is the similar case for m-banking in engaging customers for e-banking service. Other research studies[78] have indicated that facilitating conditions for financial inclusion in m-banking system design increases customers' trust and affects their intentions to use them in the future. Language style and names as cues in m-banking systems software increases influence on customers' attitudes, satisfaction[79] and emotional connection to the bank's brand[80] which offers m-banking service.

8.10 Automation

Jobs with higher automation have proved to be of higher job insecurity and associated with poor health.[81] Technology, further to this has been seen as highly linked to displacement of people from work, therefore reducing the room for financial inclusion. Naturally, customers may have a negative attitude over the use of m-banking as it is perceived to be predictively going to replace humans.[82]

8.11 Perceived Privacy Risk

Perceived risk can be viewed as the m-banking users' uncertainty about the negative outcomes related to revealing of customers' personal information.[83] Under normal circumstances customers are concerned about privacy issues when they do transactions of e-banking either via an official website or social media platforms, as revealed by a variety of scholars.[84] Privacy and security trust in m-banking is a major issue of concern, especially when dealing with personal information such as email addresses, cell numbers, names, or physical addresses.[85]

---

[77] Han (2021), p. 65.

[78] Nyagadza et al. (2020), pp. 1–22.

[79] Wang (2020).

[80] Nyagadza et al. (2020).

[81] Brandtzaeg and Følstad (2017), p. 40.

[82] Arenas et al. (2015), pp. 1–23.

[83] Cheng and Jiang (2020), p. 614.

[84] Pang and Choy (2020), pp. 133–151.

[85] Alalwan et al. (2018), pp. 125–138.

8.12 Trust and M-Banking Fin-Tech Adoption Intention

Intention can be defined as the person's subjective probability that they will perform an actual behaviour.[86] Trust levels in financial inclusion have been operationalized in prior research[87] as the customers' integrity, benevolence and ability in relation perception of m-banking. The intention to use m-banking is highly related to the trust that customers place on them in transacting and receiving e-banking services. Further to this, trust and intention to use the m-banking is connected to the level of loyalty to a given corporate brand of the bank and associated satisfaction levels together with financial inclusion.[88]

8.13 Customers' Age, Gender and M-Banking Fin-Tech Adoption Intention

In developing countries, the variation in age-gender socialisation roles accorded to men and females has been used to explain variation in performance of environmental and technological sustainable behaviours.[89] The Gender Socialisation theory posits that women are more apt to engage in pro-social behaviours than men towards technology.[90] However, it is not known whether this translate to the customers' trust and intention to use m-banking. Thus, a question is raised: will the young (men or women), digital native banking customers use m-banking as anticipated.[91]

9 Discussion, Implications and Conclusion

Theoretical, practical and future research implications as well as limitations of the study findings are discussed in this section.

---

[86]Bae (2018), pp. 137–153.

[87]Morosan and Defranco (2016), pp. 17–29.

[88]Lovakov and Agadullina (2021), pp. 485–504.

[89]Flavian et al. (2019), pp. 547–560.

[90]Chung et al. (2018), pp. 627–643.

[91]Chung et al. (2018), pp. 627–643.

9.1   Theoretical Implications

The model developed in this chapter has managed to comprehensively integrate predictors from the existing literature, in connection with exploratory, empirical, conceptual and anecdotal literature conducted in the m-banking research stratification for financial inclusion. The major theoretical contribution of our research is that the current study is unique and different from previous ones due to the fact that it is anchored on how Zimbabweans may intend to use m-banking amidst COVID-19 pandemic situations sustainably. Further to this, prior studies focused on post adoption intentions, but ours is aimed at adoption determinants in adoption stage. The current model for this research study can be used as a baseline future m-commerce (mobile commerce) research studies. M-banking is highly influenced by ICTs such as computers, mobile phones, and internet technology as well as SSTs. Due to the fact that customers do many transactions through m-banking, proper customer service is a necessity.

For banks to foster financial inclusion, there is need to make sure that they decelerate system downtimes and ensuring that the system operates seamlessly as expected, even during high times of high usage volumes by customers. If there is no good security and privacy, rejection probability will be so high. Swift response to m-banking transaction problems by concerned banks offering the service is key in maintaining closer customer relationships management. Mobile fin-tech banking adoption study is a complicated phenomenon in financial inclusion, which may require more than one model to test its validity and reliability, than the UTAUT theoretical model explicated in the current study. A results comparison with the extant literature is anchored on the hypothetical context incubated to address the main research objectives.

9.2   Practical Implications

The chapter's practical implications are for banking industry and management. The research has determined useful contributions to banking practice and implications for pushing the agenda of sustainable m-banking fin-tech adoption in Zimbabwe, as well as its usage in uncertain pandemics prevalence such as the COVID-19 situations. This is so because majority of developed countries are already enjoying the benefits of m-banking. The determinants identified in the current research can be used by banking policy formulators to influence m-banking adoption so as to manipulate and control customer retention.

Managers of banks and relevant financial services corporates need to encourage and or emphasise benefits associated with m-banking and m-money, and decelerate its customers' perception on potential risk. This implies that banks need to design effectively m-banking fin-tech systems to support positive credibility in a bid to enhance customers' attitudes towards m-banking adoption intentions. If the customers feel more competent in using the m-banking system, they would enjoy the benefits effectively. Collaborative customer education campaigns and marketing communications promotional efforts by banks offering m-banking services are necessary in risk reduction perception. This may shape confidence and trust in the system and banks' brand images in a move towards financial inclusion.

9.3   Study Limitations and Future Research Implications

The study has limitations which may affect the generalisability of the results, since they can only be applied to the population and country or area studied under the COVID-19 pandemic situation. Future research studies can include evaluating other relevant theoretical frameworks in customers' sustainable m-banking services adoption intention theory determinants amidst COVID-19 pandemic.

10   Conclusion

Complementary research studies can be done in other parts of the world to be able to come up with cross-cultural comparisons, as well as methodological validation. Another limitation was nature of the study (conceptual cross sectional) which does not allow conclusions to be made about the development of customers' sustainable m-banking services adoption intention for financial inclusivity. In future, longitudinal research study inquiries can be made in order to check different variations of economic situations in other relevant studies.

Despite the limitations of the chapter, the results have contributed to the better understanding of customers' sustainable m-banking services adoption intention. The results hopefully may influence further future research study inquiries. The chapter offers valuable insights on how to achieve sustainable m-banking fin-tech customer base for financial inclusion. In line with this, it will enhance successful m-banking and establish a non-volatile velocity circulation of m-money which directly affects national economic development positively, and accelerates GDP growth.

Bibliography

Agyekum FK, Reddy K, Wallace D, Wellalage NH (2021) Does technological inclusion promote financial inclusion among SMES? Evidence from South-East Asian (SEA) countries. Glob Finance J:1–15

Alalwan AA, Dwivedi YK, Rana NP, Algharabat R (2018) Examining factors influencing Jordanian customers' intentions and adoption of internet banking: extending UTAUT2 with risk. J Retail Consum Serv 40:125–138

Alraja MN, Hammami S, Chikhi B, Fekir S (2016) The influence of effort and performance expectancy on employees to adopt E-Government: evidence from Oman. Int Rev Manag Market 6(4):930–934

Arenas GJ, Peral PB, Ramón JM (2015) Elderly and internet banking: an application of UTAUT2. J Internet Bank Commerce 20(1):1–23

Bae M (2018) Understanding the effect of the discrepancy between sought and obtained gratifications on social networking site users' satisfaction and continuance intention. Comput Hum Behav 79:137–153

Brandtzaeg PB, Følstad A (2017) Why people use chatbots. In: Proceedings of the 4th international conference on internet science. Thessaloniki, Greece

Changchit C, Chuchuen C (2016) Cloud computing: an examination of factors impacting users' adoption. J Comput Inf Syst:1–9

Changchit C, Lonkani R, Sampet J (2017) M-banking: exploring determinants of its adoption. J Organ Comput Electron Commerce 27(3):239–261

Chao CM (2019) Factors determining the behavioural intention to use mobile learning: an application and extension of the UTAUT model. Front Psychol 10:1–14

Chave AP, Gerosa MA (2021) How should my chatbot interact? A survey on social characteristics in human–chatbot interaction design. Int J Hum–Comput Interact 37(8):729–758

Cheng Y, Jiang H (2020) How do AI-driven chatbots impact user experience? Examining gratifications, perceived privacy risk, satisfaction, loyalty, and continued use. J Broadcast Electron Media 64(4):592–614

Chung N, Lee H, Kim JY, Koo C (2018) The role of augmented reality for experience-influenced environments: the case of cultural heritage tourism in Korea. J Travel Res 57(5):627–643

Cruz-García P, Palacios D, Macedo MDC, Tortosa-Ausina E (2021) Financial inclusion and exclusion across Mexican municipalities. Reg Sci Policy Pract 13(5):1496–1526

Dehghani M (2018) Exploring the motivational factors on continuous usage intention of smartwatches among actual users. Behav Inf Technol 37(2):145–158

Dev SM (2006) Financial inclusion: issues and challenges. Econ Polit Wkly:4310–4313

Flavian C, Ibañez-Sanchez S, Orús C (2019) The impact of virtual, augmented and mixed reality technologies on the customer experience. J Bus Res 100:547–560

Han MC (2021) The impact of anthropomorphism on consumers' purchase decision in chatbot commerce. J Internet Commerce 20(1):46–65

Herrero A, San Martín H (2017) Explaining the adoption of social networks sites for sharing user-generated content: a revision of the UTAUT2. Comput Hum Behav:209–217

Ho J, Pang C, Choy C (2020) Content marketing capability building: a conceptual framework. J Res Interact Market 14(1):133–151

Khalilzadeh J, Ozturk AB, Bilgihan A (2017) Security-related factors in extended UTAUT model for NFC based mobile payment in the restaurant industry. Comput Hum Behav:460–474

Kim G, Shin B, Lee HG (2009) Understanding dynamics between initial trust and usage intentions of M-banking. Inf Syst J 19(3):283–311

Laforet S, Li X (2005) Consumers' attitudes towards online and M-banking in China. Int J Bank Market 23(5):362–380

Laukkanen T (2017) Mobile banking. Int J Bank Market 35(7):1042–1043

Laukkanen P, Sinkkonen S, Laukkanen T (2008) Consumer resistance to internet banking: postponers, opponents and rejectors. Int J Bank Market 26(6):440–455

Leong K, Sung A (2018) Fintech (Financial Technology): what is it and how to use technologies to create business value in fintech way. Int J Innov Manag Technol 9(2):74–78

Lovakov A, Agadullina AE (2021) Empirically derived guidelines for effect size interpretation in social psychology. Eur J Soc Psychol:485–504

Lumsden E (2018) The future is mobil: financial inclusion and technological innovation in the emerging world. Stanford J Law Bus Finance 23(1):1–45

Mago S, Chitokwindo S (2014) The impact of M-banking on financial inclusion in Zimbabwe: a case for Masvingo Province. Mediterr J Soc Sci 5(9):221–230

Makanyeza C (2017) Determinants of consumers' intention to adopt M-banking services in Zimbabwe. Int J Bank Market 35(6):997–1017

Masocha R, Dzomonda O (2018) Adoption of mobile money services and the performance of small and medium enterprises in Zimbabwe. Acad Account Financ Stud J 22(3):1–11

McAfee A, Brynjolfsson E (2017) Machine, platform, crowd: harnessing our digital future. W.W. Norton & Co, New York

Micheler S, Goh YM, Lohse N (2019) Innovation landscape and challenges of smart technologies and systems – a European perspective. Prod Manuf Res 7(1):503–528

Michiels E (2017) Modelling chatbots with a cognitive system allows for a differentiating user experience. POEM Doctoral Consortium, pp 70–78

Mimoun MSB, Poncin I, Garnier M (2017) Animated conversational agents and E-consumer productivity: the roles of agents and individual characteristics. Inf Manag 54(5):545–559

Morosan C, Defranco A (2016) It's about time: revisiting UTAUT2 to examine consumers' intentions to use NFC mobile payments in hotels. Int J Hosp Manag 53:17–29

Mutsonziwa K, Maposa OK (2016) Mobile money-a catalyst for financial inclusion in developing economies: a case study of Zimbabwe using finscope survey data. Int J Financ Manag 6(3): 45–56

National Assembly (2021) Hansard Parliament of Zimbabwe (17 June 2021)

Nyagadza B (2019) Responding to change and customer value improvement: pragmatic advice to banks. Market Rev 19(3–4):235–252

Nyagadza B (2020) Search engine marketing and social media marketing predictive trends. J Digit Media Policy:1–19

Nyagadza B (2021) Futurology reorientation nexus: fourth industrial revolution. In: Kazeroony H, Tsang D (eds). Routledge, p 34

Nyagadza B, Kadembo EM, Makasi A (2020) Exploring internal stakeholders' emotional attachment & corporate brand perceptions through corporate storytelling for branding. Cogent Bus Manag 7(1):1–23

Nyagadza B, Kabonga I, Hlungwani PM, Chigora F, Rukasha T (2021) The fourth industrial revolution and the imperatives of African States' sovereignty over natural resources. In: Nhemachena A, Kangira J, Chiripanhura M (eds) From #RhodesMustFall Movements to #HumansMustFall Movements: African liberation movements in the age of the transhumanist geographies of death. Langaa Research & Publishing Common Initiative Group, p 89

Onaolapo S, Oyewole O (2018) Performance expectancy, effort expectancy, and facilitating conditions as factors influencing smart phones use for mobile learning by postgraduate students of the University of Ibadan, Nigeria. Interdiscip J E-Skills Lifelong Learn:95–115

Papacharissi Z, Mendelson A (2011) Toward a new(er) sociability: uses, gratifications and social capital on facebook. In: Papathanassopoulos S (ed) Media perspectives for the 21st century. Routledge, p 230

Parker GG, Van Alstyne MW, Choudary SP (2016) Platform revolution: how networked are transforming the economy – and how to make them work for you. W.W. Norton and Co., New York, p 65

Rauch M, Wenzel M, Wagner HT (2016) The digital disruption of strategic paths: an experimental study. In: International conference on information systems. Dublin

Sanderson A, Mutandwa L, Le Roux P (2018) A review of determinants of financial inclusion. Int J Econ Financ Issues 8(3):1–8

Sharma SK, Mangla SK, Luthra S, Al-Salti Z (2018) Mobile wallet inhibitors: developing a comprehensive theory using an integrated model. J Retail Consum Serv 45:52–63

Sheehan BT (2018) Customer service chatbots: anthropomorphism, adoption and word of mouth. Doctoral Dissertation, Queensland University of Technology

The Herald (2021) RBZ to Formalise 1.5 million Artisanal Miners (11 November 2021)

UNCTAD (2017) Trade and development report: Ch. 3. Robots, Industrialization and Inclusive Growth

Venkatesh V, Thong JY, Xu X (2012) Consumer acceptance and use of information technology: extending the unified theory of acceptance and use of technology. MIS Q 36(1):157–178

Wang CL (2020) Contemporary perspectives on fandom research: an introduction. In: Wang CL (ed) Handbook of research on the impact of fandom in society and consumerism. IGI Global

Weißensteiner AAA (2018) Chatbots as an approach for a faster enquiry handling process in the service industry. Master's Dissertation, Modul University, Vienna, Austria

Wellalage NH, Hunjra AI, Manita R, Locke SM (2021) Information communication technology and financial inclusion of innovative entrepreneurs. Technol Forecast Soc Change 163:1–13

Xu X (2014) Understanding users' continued use of online games: an application of UTAUT2 in social network games. In: Lorenz P (ed) The sixth international conferences on advances in multimedia. MMEDIA: IARIA, p 55

Yen C, Chiang MM (2020) Trust me, if you can: a study on the factors that influence consumers' purchase intention triggered by chatbots based on brain image evidence and self-reported assessments. Behav Inf Technol:1177–1194

Zhao X, Xue L, Whinston AB (2013) Managing interdependent information security risks: cyberinsurance, managed security services, and risk pooling arrangements. J Manag Inf Syst 30(1):123–152

Zimbabwe National Statistics Agency (2019) Labour force and child labour survey

Brighton Nyagadza is a full-time lecturer and A/Chairperson department of Marketing (Digital Marketing) at Marondera University of Agricultural Sciences & Technology (MUAST), Zimbabwe, Full Member of the Marketers Association of Zimbabwe (MAZ), an Associate of The Chartered Institute of Marketing (CIM), United Kingdom and Power Member of the Digital Marketing Institute (DMI), Dublin, Ireland. He has published several book chapters in Routledge Books of Taylor & Francis Publishers, New York (USA), Lexington Books of the Rowan & Littlefield Publishers, Maryland (USA), Langaa Publishers (Cameroon) and in reputable global journals such as *Journal of Environmental Media* (Intellect, Bristol, UK), *Journal of Asian & African Studies* (SAGE, London, UK), *Journal of Digital Media & Policy* (Intellect Publishers, Bristol, UK), *Youth & Society* (SAGE, London, UK), *Cogent Business & Management, Cogent Psychology, Cogent Social Sciences* (Taylor & Francis, England & Wales, UK), *Communicare* (University of Johannesburg, South Africa), *The Marketing Review* (Westburn Publishers, Scotland), *Retail and Marketing Review* (UNISA), *Africanus* (UNISA Press), *Amity Journal of Entrepreneurship* (Amity University Press) and others. Currently, he is editing a book on *Social Media Marketing Strategy Post COVID-19 Pandemic: Ethics, Challenges & New Directions*, to be published by Vernon Press Publishers, Wilmington, Delaware (USA).

Dumisani R. Muzira is currently a lecturer in the Faculty of Agribusiness and Entrepreneurship at Marondera University of Agricultural Sciences and Technology (MUAST); Adjunct Lecturer for Solusi University and an online course instructor for Canada Summer Overseas (China) and Unicaf University. She worked as Group Accountant for S & I Valve Company, Group Accountant for Electric Motor Centre, Accountant for Anglo-Dutch Motors, Accountant for Tedco Management Services, and Training officer for Public Service Commission. She is a reviewer of journals and a university programme content reviewer for Zimbabwe Council for Higher Education (ZIMCHE) for Accounting and Finance degrees. Her research interests are in Integrated reporting, Forensic auditing, Change management, and Curriculum studies. She attained her PhD in Business-Emphasis Accounting (Adventist International Institute of Advanced Studies, Philippines); Master of Commerce in Applied Accounting (Great Zimbabwe University, Zimbabwe); Master of Science in Finance and Investment (National University of Science & Technology, Zimbabwe), Bachelor of Business Administration -Major in Accounting (Solusi University, Zimbabwe), and Post Graduate Diploma in Education-Accounting (Zimbabwe Ezekiel Guti University, Zimbabwe). She is married to Dr Robert Muzira, a pastor and an educationist. They are blessed with three children.

Tinashe Chuchu holds a Doctorate in Marketing from the University of the Witwatersrand. Currently, he works as a Senior Lecturer in the Marketing Division of the School of Business Sciences at the University of the Witwatersrand, South Africa. Previously, he worked as a Senior Lecturer in the Department of Marketing Management, University of Pretoria, South Africa. He is a consumer behaviour and tourism scholar who has published numerous studies in these fields in top journals and has presented at international conferences. Dr. Chuchu has published and reviewed for major publishing outlets, which include Wiley, Taylor & Francis, Elsevier, Emerald Publishing, SAGE and presented at the premier conference for marketing academics (the American Marketing Association Conference) which was held in Chicago, USA in 2019. He is a member of The Academy of Business and Retail Management Conferences based in the United Kingdom. He was a recipient of the South African government's National Research Foundation Doctoral Scholarship in 2015. In 2019, Dr. Chuchu was awarded the Best Junior Researcher in Management Sciences at the University of Pretoria, South Africa. He sits on the editorial board of the Retail and Marketing Review as well as the African Journal of Business and Economic Research.

Financial Inclusion Challenges and Prospects During the COVID-19 Pandemic: Insights from Botswana, Namibia, South Africa and Zimbabwe

Charles Makanyeza, Eukeria Wealth, and Tendai D. Svotwa

Abstract Financial inclusion is a process that enables the ease of access, availability and usage of formal financial services for all members of an economy. It is a United Nations Sustainable Develop Goal (SDG) earmarked to alleviate poverty and income inequality. As such, financial inclusion has attracted the attention of many researchers and policymakers. However, the outbreak of the COVID-19 pandemic has brought the whole world to a standstill. It has impacted many facets of the economy. The pandemic has reshaped the financial services sector. Financial inclusion is one facet of the economy that has been affected positively and negatively by the pandemic. This chapter explores the literature on financial inclusion and its challenges and opportunities induced by COVID-19. The chapter further explains the challenges and prospects of financial inclusion due to the COVID-19 pandemic. It concludes by illuminating future research directions.

1 Introduction

COVID-19 is a disease caused by the coronavirus. The disease originated in China in December 2019. Since then, the disease has spread all over the world. The disease has become a global pandemic. Many people have fallen ill, and many have died in

C. Makanyeza (✉)
Namibia Business School, University of Namibia, Windhoek, Namibia
e-mail: cmakanyeza@unam.na

E. Wealth
School of Accounting, Faculty of Commerce, Management and Law, University of Namibia, Windhoek, Namibia
e-mail: ewealth@unam.na

T. D. Svotwa
Department of Graduate Studies, Botho University, Gaborone, Botswana
e-mail: douglas.svotwa@bothouniveristy.ac.bw

both developing and developed countries. The disease spreads very fast and can infect many people within a short space of time. Since its outbreak, countries have instituted measures to contain the disease such as lockdowns, social distancing, sanitising and wearing of face masks. Of late, nations have discovered vaccines and have started vaccinating their citizens. Developing countries lag behind developed nations in terms of the number of people vaccinated. COVID-19 containment measures such as social distancing and lockdowns have disrupted supply chains and slowed the growth of financial markets and economies. Many people have lost their jobs. Many businesses have either closed down or retrenched many of their employees. The most affected are low-income earners and informal businesses that typically lack financial reserves to cushion themselves during the pandemic. This has the potential to increase poverty, widen income inequality and reverse the progress made over the years on financial inclusion.[1]

Financial inclusion is described as a process that enables ease of access, availability and usage of formal financial services by all members of society, including the poor, low-income earners, vulnerable members of the population, informal businesses, and small, micro and medium enterprises.[2] Financial inclusion is a tool that can be used to achieve sustainable economic development, alleviate poverty and reduce income inequality. Thus, financial inclusion fosters inclusive economic development.[3] Although financial inclusion is still low in Botswana, Namibia, South Africa and Zimbabwe, there has been significant progress towards improving it over the past few years.[4] This upward financial inclusion trajectory has been spurred by the increased use of digital financial solutions such as mobile money services.

This chapter reviews the literature on financial inclusion. The chapter explores challenges and prospects on financial inclusion as a result of the COVID-19 pandemic. Insights are drawn from Botswana, Namibia, South Africa and Zimbabwe. The chapter recommends future research directions and the way forward on achieving financial inclusion in a COVID-19 pandemic environment.

2   Understanding Financial Inclusion

It is concerned with the delivery of and access to financial services at reasonable costs to all members of society, including the poor and disadvantaged.[5] It fosters ease of access, availability and usage of the formal financial system for the members

---

[1] Arunachalam and Crentsil (2020), p. 33. See also Mogaji (2020), pp. 57–63; and Ozili (2020).

[2] Sarma and Pais (2011), p. 613. See also Matongela (2014), p. 71.

[3] Kasradze (2020), p. 74.

[4] Ayadi and Shaban (2020).

[5] Matongela (2014), p. 71.

of society.[6] The scope of financial inclusion is broad and encompasses business enterprises. Thus, financial inclusion can broadly be defined as the ease of access, availability and usage of formal financial services by individuals and enterprises in an economy.[7] A situation where members of a society do not have access to a formal financial system is called financial exclusion. Financial exclusion can be voluntary or involuntary. Voluntary financial exclusion takes place when members of society willingly decide not to use services in a formal financial system. This decision could be triggered by many factors such as cultural, religious, personal or lack of need. On the other hand, involuntary financial exclusion takes place when members of a population do not have access to formal financial services due to barriers such as high cost of transactions, insufficient income, high-risk profile, market failure and imperfection, and discrimination. An inclusive financial system should increase the availability of, access to and usage of formal financial services while minimising involuntary financial exclusion.[8] Policy interventions should be directed towards involuntary financial exclusion, which can be addressed by appropriate financial reforms and policies.[9]

Financial inclusion fosters sustainable economic development; hence it has been dubbed a key enabler for the attainment of seven of the 17 United Nations Sustainable Development Goals.[10] Financial inclusion has been considered a strategic tool to reduce poverty and ameliorate income inequality.[11] It leads to inclusive economic growth. Similarly, where there is financial exclusion, economic growth only benefits a few members of the economy.[12] Without an efficient financial system, it is difficult for the economy to allocate resources to productive sectors efficiently. As a result, it becomes difficult to achieve economic growth.

Although financial inclusion is still low in Botswana, Namibia, South Africa and Zimbabwe, significant strides have been made towards improving it over the past few years.[13] Over the period 2004 to 2018, the financial inclusion index has increased from 0.165 to 0.219 in Botswana, from 0.085 to 0.306 in Namibia, from 0.148 to 0.313 in South Africa, and from 0.0726 to 0.1086 in Zimbabwe.[14] Technology has played a pivotal role in this upward trajectory in these countries. The growth of ICT and increased use of mobile broadband technologies have resulted in increased financial inclusion in Botswana, Namibia, South Africa and Zimbabwe. The four countries have witnessed increased usage of mobile phones among the citizens, including low-income earners. This technology has enabled the low-income

---

[6]Demirgüç-Kunt and Klapper (2013), p. 280.

[7]Khan et al. (2021). See also Menyelim et al. (2021), p. 1.

[8]Turegano and Herrero (2018), p. 4.

[9]Park and Mercado (2018), p. 2.

[10]Gutiérrez-Romero and Ahamed (2020), p. 37.

[11]Ayadi and Shaban (2020).

[12]Kasradze (2020), p. 74.

[13]Ayadi and Shaban (2020).

[14]Gutiérrez-Romero and Ahamed (2020), p. 37.

earners and the other vulnerable members of society to send and receive money without even opening bank accounts that are relatively more expensive than mobile money services. Mobile money services lower transaction costs and increase money transfers.[15]

3   COVID-19 Induced Challenges of Financial Inclusion

COVID-19 has resulted in negative growth of economies and financial markets, and increased unemployment as organizations lay off people.[16] Thus, COVID-19 is not just a pandemic, it is a global economic crisis because of the measures taken to contain it. It disrupts supply chains.[17] COVID-19 has negative socio-economic impacts. It slows down economies. It disrupts the production and movement of goods and services locally and internationally. The movement of people and social gatherings are banned. This includes postponement of sporting events which can also stimulate economic growth for economies. As such, the COVID-19 pandemic has the potential to reverse the financial inclusion progress made in many developing countries before it worsens poverty and income inequality. Financial inclusion is a tool that can be used to alleviate poverty. Hence, the disruption caused by the pandemic has the potential to cause increased poverty and income inequality. COVID-19 induced restrictions such as lockdowns, albeit at varying levels, have increased poverty levels by as much as 56% in developing countries. This worsens the poverty situation and financial vulnerability in these countries. The COVID-19 pandemic has severely affected many African countries more than in any other region in the world. Lockdowns and social distancing restrictions have reduced social interaction and economic activities, thereby increasing financial exclusion.[18]

COVID-19 has both economic and health impacts, especially in the developing world. With increasing COVID-19 cases in many African countries, including Botswana, Namibia, South Africa and Zimbabwe, many people fell sick. This put pressure on the already relatively underdeveloped health care systems. As a result, the health care systems in these countries could not cope, resulting in many people dying. With many people falling sick, they could not continue to go to work, thereby worsening poverty and financial vulnerability.[19]

The impact of COVID-19 was ubiquitous. The whole global economy was disturbed and negatively impacted. Many businesses in Botswana, Namibia, South Africa and Zimbabwe were affected. Many businesses retrenched their

---

[15] Hasheela (2013), p. 12. See also Mukong et al. (2020), p. 151.

[16] Manyati and Mutsau (2021).

[17] Arunachalam and Crentsil (2020), p. 33.

[18] Manyati and Mutsau (2021). See also Ozili (2020).

[19] Ozili (2020).

employees, further worsening poverty, income inequality and financial exclusion in these countries.[20]

Countries increased national budgets for the health sector to cope with the increased number of COVID-19 related illnesses. This placed a burden on the already constrained financial resources in developing countries. This implies decreased support towards financial inclusion initiatives, thereby worsening financial inclusion.[21]

COVID-19 has placed a burden on both individuals and businesses. This has left developing countries much more vulnerable. The greatest impact is likely to be left by the less resilient such as informal businesses and vulnerable members of the society.[22] The informal sector is high in developing countries such as Botswana, Namibia, South Africa and Zimbabwe. Zimbabwe has the second biggest informal sector in the world, with more than 60% of the total economy.[23] The most affected part of the economy is the informal sector. Many people in developing countries such as Botswana, Namibia, South Africa and Zimbabwe are employed in the informal sector. The informal sector typically survives on daily incomes and lacks such benefits as pension, and usually lacks support in terms of access to credit lines to sustain businesses during the pandemic. As such, COVID-19 induced lockdowns imply that the majority of the people employed in the informal sector cannot go to work and will not have an income. For example, informal cross-border trading, the mainstay of livelihoods of many Zimbabweans, has been put on hold due to the COVID-19 related restrictions. In Namibia, such vendors as *kapana* traders have found it difficult to conduct business. The market has dwindled due to social distancing measures. These traders don't have financial reserves to cushion themselves during these trying times. This has resulted in the loss of livelihoods, resulting in increased financial exclusion and income inequality.[24]

Apart from posing a global health crisis, COVID-19 has become a global economic crisis, damaging the livelihoods of people all over the world.[25] Most affected are poor people and other vulnerable members of society. These people typically do not have stable and alternative sources of income. They survive mainly from hand to mouth. Therefore, COVID-19 containment measures such as social distancing and ban on public gatherings immediately switch off the main source of income. This implies loss of income despite the need to meet financial obligations such as buying food and health care products, paying school fees, paying utilities, etc. With little to no income reserves, poor people become more financially

---

[20] Ozili (2020).

[21] Ozili (2020).

[22] Arner et al. (2020).

[23] Manyati and Mutsau (2021).

[24] Arunachalam and Crentsil (2020), p. 33. See also Dzingirai (2021) Chapter 3; Gutiérrez-Romero and Ahamed (2020), p. 37; Manyati and Mutsau (2021); Ozili (2020).

[25] Ayadi and Shaban (2020), p. 16.

vulnerable. This increases poverty and widens income inequality. It also worsens pre-existing financial exclusion.[26]

4 COVID-19 Induced Prospects of Financial Inclusion

Despite the detrimental effects of COVID-19 on financial inclusion, it has also brought prospects. Technology is redefining the landscape of the financial sector. At the height of COVID-19 containment measures such as social distancing, technology has given birth to new opportunities in the form of digital financial services. Digital financial technology can be leveraged to achieve financial inclusion, thereby providing a sigh of relief in ensuring financial inclusion during the COVID-19 pandemic.[27] This process is known as digital financial inclusion.[28] Digital financial inclusion involves "capitalising on cost-saving digital technologies and the widespread use of mobile phones to reach the financially excluded and enhance access to formal affordable financial services in a sustainable manner".[29] Thus, digital financial inclusion plays a pivotal role as a resilience tool to financial instability caused by the pandemic.

The challenges posed by COVID-19 containment measures such as social distancing and lockdowns resulted in the closure of banking halls and other financial services providers. Nation governments in many countries, including Botswana, Namibia, South Africa and Zimbabwe, advocated for increased use of cashless and contactless transactions to minimise the spread of the disease. This has increased the use of mobile financial services. It has also been observed that Sub Saharan Africa has recorded the greatest number of mobile financial services usage between 2010 and 2019. This has coincided with the increased demand for cashless transactions due to social distancing.[30]

Cash has always been responsible for spreading diseases. Although the Zimbabwean situation seems to be different because cash has become a sought-after commodity because of its scarcity, the general public tends to be reluctant to accept cash[31] in Botswana, Namibia and South Africa. Thus, cashless and contactless payment systems can be the solution during the pandemic. This technology is easily accessible to the poor and rural folks that seem to have limited financial access to

---

[26] Knotek II et al. (2020). See also (2020), p. 7; Mogaji (2020), pp. 57–63; Nguer and Powell (2020), p. 83.

[27] Jhunjhunwala (2020), pp. 157–161.

[28] Arner et al. (2020), p. 23. See also Sahay et al. (2020).

[29] Ayadi and Shaban (2020), p. 16.

[30] Machasio (2020), p. 7.

[31] Arunachalam and Crentsil (2020), p. 33.

formal financial services, thereby increasing financial access to these disadvantaged members of society.[32]

Digital financial services such as mobile money services are cheaper, fast and more efficient than conventional financial services such as banking. As such, digital financial services are easily accessible to small enterprises, informal businesses and low-income and other disadvantaged members of the society such as the unbanked. Financial technology enables contactless and cashless transactions which auger well with COVID-19 containment measures. This facilitates transacting during the COVID-19 pandemic. Digital financial services can also be used to facilitate efficient distribution of government's financial support to affected members of the society such as small businesses and low-income earners.[33,34] Similarly, digital financial solutions accelerate access to financial services by the informal sector and disadvantaged and vulnerable members of the society such as the poor and rural inhabitants. Thus, financial inclusion can be used as a tool to withstand the shocks caused by COVID-19.[35]

Digital financial technology has the potential to increase economic growth, alleviate poverty and lessen income inequality.[36] In this regard, research has shown that digital financial inclusion fosters increased economic growth. Thus, digital financial inclusion can be used to dampen the detrimental effects of COVID-19 on the economy and the well-being of people. Increased financial access by small businesses and vulnerable members of society through financial technology can lead to inclusive economic growth.[37]

Despite significant strides made by digital financial services in promoting financial inclusion in Botswana, Namibia, South Africa and Zimbabwe, there is a risk of asymmetry in information and access to digital infrastructure. Lack of information and such infrastructure as mobile phones, computers and the internet could also lead to another form of exclusion which can be worsened as the adoption of digital financial services increases during the COVID-19 pandemic. The cost of data can be a major stumbling block in these countries. Efforts are being made to alleviate the cost of data on mobile financial transactions. For example, mobile financial applications are being zero-rated so that members of society will no longer require data to use mobile financial applications. Financial institutions that have zero-rated their mobile applications include FNB in Namibia, Ozow in South Africa and Stanbic Bank in Zimbabwe. Increased financial services can also result in financial instability if the financial services providers are not properly regulated. In Zimbabwe, mobile money services such as EcoCash have been accused by the government of fuelling increases in prices and parallel foreign exchange rates. This led to further tightening

---

[32] Arner et al. (2020), p. 23.

[33] Machasio (2020).

[34] Sahay et al. (2020).

[35] Ayadi and Shaban (2020), p. 16.

[36] Machasio (2020), p. 7.

[37] Sahay et al. (2020).

of regulations against mobile money operators. Increased growth in digital financial services also poses risks. Increased adoption of digital solutions raises consumer safety and cybersecurity issues. These risks have the potential to worsen financial exclusion and income inequality.[38]

5 Conclusion

COVID-19 has brought financial inclusion challenges and opportunities in Botswana, Namibia, South Africa and Zimbabwe. The disease has become a global crisis because of the measures taken to contain it. These include social distancing and lockdowns. These containment measures have resulted in negative economic growth. Financial markets have also been severely affected and are experiencing stunted growth. Supply chains have been disrupted. There has been increased closure of businesses. Individuals have lost their jobs, their main source of livelihood. With many people falling sick, it means they cannot go to work and this is a loss of income. The most affected are informal businesses and micro, small and medium enterprises. The informal sector constitutes a significant chunk of the economy in Botswana, Namibia, South Africa and Zimbabwe. Similarly, poor and vulnerable members of society are severely affected because they lack resilience in the form of other sources of income. As such, the COVID-19 pandemic has reversed the financial inclusion progress made in these developing countries over the past few years. This situation has worsened poverty and income inequality, thereby accelerating financial exclusion. The spread of COVID-19 has affected the Chinese economy. Many businesses in Botswana, Namibia, South Africa and Zimbabwe depend on imports from China. A slowing Chinese economy coupled with failure to import goods from China due to lockdowns resulted in many businesses retrenching their employees. This situation further worsened poverty, income inequality and financial exclusion in these countries. With increased budgets for the health sector to cope with the increased number of COVID-19 related illnesses, countries were left with fewer resources directed towards supporting financial inclusion initiatives. This also worsened financial inclusion.[39]

Notwithstanding its detrimental effects on financial inclusion, COVID-19 has also brought opportunities in terms of accelerating digital financial inclusion. Digital financial technology has emerged as the main solution to facilitate transactions midst of COVID-19 containment measures such as social distancing and lockdowns. Therefore, digital financial inclusion has played a major role as a resilience tool to financial instability caused by the pandemic. Botswana, Namibia, South Africa and Zimbabwe have encouraged cashless and contactless transacting to minimise the spread of COVID-19. This has increased the use of mobile financial services. Digital

---

[38] Sahay et al. (2020).
[39] Ozili (2020).

financial services such as mobile money services are cheaper, fast and more efficient than conventional financial services such as banking. They are easily accessible to small enterprises, informal businesses and low-income and other disadvantaged members of the society such as the unbanked. Thus, digital financial inclusion can be used as a tool to withstand the shocks caused by the COVID-19 pandemic. It results in inclusive economic growth.

However, digital financial services have inherent risks that need to be managed to ensure that this innovation is a success in promoting financial inclusion. Lack of information to other members of the society, usually the poor and informal sector businesses, can be a barrier to financial inclusion. Digital financial infrastructure can also be elusive to poor and disadvantaged people. Such infrastructure as mobile phones, computers and the internet might be inaccessible and too expensive to these members of the society. The cost of data might not be affordable. This calls for innovation. One such innovation is the zero-rating of mobile financial applications so that members of society will no longer require data to use mobile money financial applications. Increased digital financial solutions can also result in financial instability if the financial service providers are not properly regulated. As such, there is a need for increased and appropriate digital financial regulations to ensure financial stability. Digital financial services also raise consumer safety and cybersecurity issues. These risks have the potential to worsen financial exclusion and income inequality. There is a need to enact consumer safety and cybersecurity laws designed to protect consumers and digital financial services providers.

6   Recommendations

This chapter illustrated the impact of COVID-19 on financial inclusion by focusing on challenges and opportunities. However, there is a lack of empirical research that has been conducted to ascertain the extent to which COVID-19 has affected financial inclusion in Botswana, Namibia, South Africa and Zimbabwe. Still, there is an unanswered question. For example, do the prospects of COVID-19 on financial inclusion outweigh the challenges? Therefore, it is recommended that empirical studies be conducted in these countries to ascertain the extent to which COVID-19 has impacted financial inclusion.

The chapter suggests possible ways of improving financial inclusion in a COVID-19 pandemic environment. There is a need for increased collaboration between financial technology companies, financial institutions and governments. These entities should have concerted efforts directed towards increased financial inclusion.[40]

Digital financial technology has emerged as an effective solution. Therefore, there is a need to promote cashless and contactless transactions through mobile money and other electronic financial solutions. Countries should invest in affordable

---

[40] Sahay et al. (2020).

digital financial infrastructure, targeting vulnerable groups and people in marginalised areas such as rural areas. This can be achieved by increasing internet connectivity and provision of cheaper data, and zero-rating of mobile financial applications. The acceptance and use of digital currencies also present an opportunity. Digital currencies that can be used to facilitate transactions are known as cryptocurrencies. An example is Bitcoin which can be used to purchase goods and services.[41]

There is a need to increase digital financial awareness to boost digital financial inclusion. This can be achieved by providing digital financial education through various channels such as mass media and social media. Financial education could be targeted to vulnerable groups such as low-income earners, informal traders and micro, small and medium enterprises.[42]

The promotion of digital financial solutions should be accompanied by increased financial regulation to ensure financial stability. If not properly regulated, digital financial services can cause financial instability which might worsen the plight of the poor and vulnerable members of society. This has the potential to worsen financial exclusion.[43]

There is a need to encourage cash withdrawals at the point of sale in-store to cater for situations where cash is required.[44] Poor and vulnerable people should be allowed to withdraw money when they need it. As such, financial institutions such as banks should remain accessible to vulnerable groups, especially in marginalised areas such as rural and remote areas where digital financial solutions might be limited.[45]

Main affected businesses include micro, small and medium enterprises and informal businesses. As such, there is a need to provide short-term to medium-term financial assistance to low-income individuals and businesses.[46] There is a need for the provision of ease of access to prompt and efficient credit facilities at affordable interest rates to affected business end individuals. This can be strengthened by the provision of government credit guarantee schemes. This will protect vulnerable individuals and affected businesses from informal sector lenders such as loan sharks that usually charge exorbitant interest rates. The continued survival of these businesses preserves employment. These initiatives can be augmented with physical policies that enhance inclusive growth such as fiscal packages to rescue businesses and favourable tax regimes that promote business recovery and growth.[47]

It is also recommended that governments provide financial relief packages to households that have lost their incomes. Directed financial assistance is needed to at

---

[41] Arner et al. (2020).

[42] Gutiérrez-Romero and Ahamed (2020), p. 37.

[43] Ayadi and Shaban (2020), p. 16.

[44] Kasradze (2020), p. 74.

[45] Ozili (2020).

[46] Gutiérrez-Romero and Ahamed (2020), p. 37.

[47] Arner et al. (2020), p. 23.

least maintain the welfare of vulnerable members of society. This is useful in stimulating demand for goods and services which in turn spurs economic growth.[48]

Financial institutions also require assistance. This can be achieved by easing existing capital and liquidity requirements. This will enable financial service providers to offset potential losses and still have enough resources to continue to offer credits to affected individuals and businesses.

Bibliography

Ahamed M, Gutiérrez-Romero R (2021) COVID-19 response needs to broaden financial inclusion to curb the rise in poverty. World Dev 138:1–37

Arner DW, Barberis JN, Walker J, Buckley RP, Dahdal AM, Zetzsche DA (2020) Digital finance and the COVID-19 crisis. University of Hong Kong Faculty of Law Research Paper 2020/017. https://ssrn.com/abstract=3558889

Arunachalam RS, Crentsil GLK (2020) Financial inclusion in the era of Covid-19. The Financial Inclusion Advocacy Centre, pp 1–33

Ayadi R, Shaban M (2020) Digital financial inclusion: a pillar of resilience amidst Covid-19 in the Mediterranean and Africa. EMEA Policy Paper 1. www.euromed-economists.org

Demirgüç-Kunt A, Klapper L (2013) Measuring financial inclusion: explaining variation in use of financial services across and within countries. Brookings Papers on Economic Activity, pp 279–340

Dzingirai M, Chagwesha M, Mudzurandende F (2021) Challenges and opportunities from COVID-19 vis-à-vis informal cross-border women entrepreneurs scenario in Zimbabwe. In: Handbook of research on sustaining SMEs and entrepreneurial innovation in the post-COVID-19 era. IGI Global, pp 40–59

Hasheela ET (2013) Access to finance and financial inclusion in Namibia. Master of Business Administration, University of Stellenbosch

Jhunjhunwala A (2020) Role of telecom network to manage COVID-19 in India: Aarogya Setu. Trans Indian Natl Acad Eng:157–161

Kasradze T (2020) Challenges facing financial inclusion due to the COVID-19 pandemic. Eur J Market Econ 3(2):50–63

Khan I, Khan I, Sayal AU, Khan MZ (2021) Does financial inclusion induce poverty, income inequality and financial stability: empirical evidence from the 54 African countries? J Econ Stud [Volume and page numbers ahead-of-print]. https://doi.org/10.1108/JES-07-2020-0317

Knotek ES II, Schoenle R, Dietrich A, Kuester K, Müller G, Myrseth KOR, Weber M (2020) Consumers and COVID-19: a real-time survey. Economic Commentary 2020-08. https://doi.org/10.26509/frbc-ec-202008

Machasio IN (2020) COVID-19 and digital financial inclusion in Africa: how to leverage digital technologies during the pandemic. World Bank 1(4):1–7

Manyati TK, Mutsau M (2021) Leveraging green skills in response to the COVID-19 crisis: a case study of small and medium enterprises in Harare, Zimbabwe. J Entrepreneurship Emerg Econ [Volume ahead-of-print]. https://doi.org/10.1108/JEEE-07-2020-0236

Matongela AM (2014) Understanding the state of financial inclusion in Namibia. Res J Finance Account 5(23):171–175

---

[48] Arner et al. (2020), p. See also Nuguer and Powell (2020), p. 83.

Menyelim CM, Babajide AA, Omankhanlen AE, Ehikioya BI (2021) Financial inclusion, income inequality and sustainable economic growth in Sub-Saharan African countries. Sustainability 13(4):1–15

Mogaji E (2020) Financial vulnerability during a pandemic: insights for Coronavirus Disease (COVID-19). Research Agenda Working Papers, pp 57–63

Mukong A, Shiwayu N, Kaulihowa T (2020) A decomposition of the gender gap in financial inclusion: evidence from Namibia. Afr J Bus Econ Res 15(4):149–169

Nuguer V, Powell A (2020) Inclusion in times of Covid-19. Inter-American Development Bank, pp 1–83

Ozili P (2020) COVID-19 in Africa: socio-economic impact, policy response and opportunities. Int J Sociol Soc Policy [Volume ahead-of-print]. https://doi.org/10.1108/IJSSP-05-2020-0171

Park CY, Mercado R Jr (2018) Financial inclusion, poverty, and income inequality. Singap Econ Rev 63(01):185–206

Sahay MR, von Allmen MUE, Lahreche MA, Khera P, Ogawa MS, Bazarbash M, Beaton MK (2020) The promise of Fintech: financial inclusion in the post COVID-19 era. International Monetary Fund. https://books.google.com.na/books?id=UqwYEAAAQBAJ&source=gbs_navlinks_s

Sarma M, Pais J (2011) Financial inclusion and development. J Int Dev 23(5):613–628

Turegano DM, Herrero AG (2018) Financial inclusion rather than size is the key to tackling income inequality. Singap Econ Rev:167–184

Charles Makanyeza is a senior academic, researcher and consultant who commands respect among his peers. At the time of writing, Charles has more than eleven years of teaching experience at university level, more than five years of experience in university administration, and more than ten years of industry experience. He holds the following qualifications: PhD Marketing, Executive MBA, MSc Marketing, Postgraduate Diploma in Project Management, BCom Marketing, Diploma in Agriculture, Certificate in International Computer Driving Licence (ICDL), and Training and Resources in Research Ethics Evaluation (TRREE) Certificates in Introduction to Research Ethics; Research Ethics Evaluation; Informed Consent; Good Clinical Practice; HIV Vaccine Trials; Adolescent Involvement in HIV Prevention Trials; Public Health Research Ethics; and South Africa. Charles is currently an Associate Professor of Marketing and Strategy at the Namibia Business School, University of Namibia. His specialisation and research areas of interest include marketing, strategy, entrepreneurship and quantitative research. Before joining the University of Namibia, he served as Director of the Graduate Business School, Acting Dean, Deputy Dean, Programme Coordinator, Associate Professor, Senior Lecturer and Lecturer at Chinhoyi University of Technology. Charles has also served as a Senior Lecturer and Lecturer and various institutions both full-time and part-time. His recent key projects include (i) Causes of lack of professionalism and poor organisational performance at Apple Valley Primary School and appropriate solutions (ii) Conducted, in partnership with CeDRE International Africa, an evaluation of the project on strengthening smallholder farmer incomes and rural social infrastructure in Chimanimani district of Zimbabwe in 2016. The project was commissioned by the TSURO Trust in cooperation with BFDW – EED. The major components of the project were on transparent community planning, monitoring and governance processes, community managed social and health care, local healthy food products and market development.

Eukeria Wealth is an established, competent and proficient lecturer with more than 11 years teaching experience at university level. Eukeria holds the following qualifications; PhD Accounting Sciences, Master of Commerce in Accounting, Bachelor of Commerce in Accounting, Post Graduate Diploma in Tertiary Education (PDTE), Post Graduate Diploma in Applied Taxation (ICTAZ), Certified Public Accountant (ICPAZ), Certified Tax Accountant (ICTAZ), Registered and Practicing Accountant (RPAccZ) with PAAB. Eukeria is currently a senior lecturer in the School of Accounting, University of Namibia. She has specialised in Accounting and taxation, and her research interests include transfer pricing, taxation, financial inclusion and diversification. Before joining the university of Namibia, she was the Head of department for the department of Accounting at Midlands State University. Her flagship projects include (i) Accounting education for fourth industrial revolution accountants in Africa, commissioned by African Accounting and Finance Association (AAFA) in collaboration with Pan-African Federation of Accountants (PAFA) (2020), (ii) Experiences in the Zimbabwe Hotel Industry during Hyperinflation sponsored by the Macro-economic and Financial Management Institute of Eastern and Southern Africa (MEFMI) (2016), (iii) Illicit Trade, Economic Growth and the Role of Customs as commissioned by the World Customs Organisation (2014).

Tendai D. Svotwa holds a Bachelor of Business Studies *(Honours)*, a Master of Business Administration (MBA) degree from the University of Zimbabwe and a PhD in Business Management from North-West University, Mafikeng, South Africa. Dr Svotwa is also a seasoned banker with more than 12 years' experience working in the Corporate sector, mainly in the Treasury Department. He is also an accomplished researcher, having published extensively in peer reviewed journals and has presented at local and international Conferences such as Botswana, Namibia, South Africa, Tanzania, Morocco, and France. Dr Svotwa is also a renowned academic, who has taught at tertiary institutions since 2009, starting off his teaching career at the University of Zimbabwe. He is a Senior Lecturer at Botho University, Graduate Studies and Research Department, Gaborone, Botswana where he teaches and supervises postgraduate students. His research interests are in the fields of strategy, leadership, general management, entrepreneurship, family businesses and marketing management. He is a member of The European Academy of Management (EURAM), Africa Academy of Management (AFAM), South African Association of Public Administration and Management (SAAPAM), and a Life-time member of the Golden Key International Honour Society. In 2017, he was one of the two African scholars selected to represent Africa in Rabat, Morocco, at the PhD Doctoral Colloquium: EURAM Early Career Colloquium (EECC), facilitated by EURAM. Currently he is part of a 10-member team engaged as a Co-Country Investigator (CCI) in Botswana for the Global Leadership and Business Effectiveness (GLOBE) survey focusing on organisational culture, trust, and leadership in more than 110 countries across the globe.

Financial Inclusion and the Small-Scale Fisheries Sector in Namibia: A Contemporary Legal Perspective

Tapiwa Victor Warikandwa, Elize Shakalela, and Eugene L. Libebe

Abstract The small-scale fisheries (SSF) sector in Namibia has largely been financially excluded and mostly characterised by a limited access to financial services, and scarcity of financial resources for investment fishing projects. This is attributed to the fact that most of fisherman constituting Namibia's SSF sector are from marginalised coastal communities owing to a limited or restricted access to marine resources and amongst the most marginalized communities such as the Topnaar community. Their low social status is a result of poverty as well as exploitation by middlemen and merchants. Middlemen have control over credit and fish marketing, which drains away the surplus generated and often make them indebted. A combination of variability in catch, technology upgrades, over capitalization, rising costs, aggressive fishing, overcrowding, amongst other issues, have made economics of fishing and fishing related occupations uncertain. The overall output remains almost the same but the investment and operational costs have gone up considerably. This has resulted in fishermen getting increasingly dependent on loans to finance their expenditures and also using loans as coping mechanism. There is a widely held belief that Namibia has no marine artisanal fishery. Fisheries legislation provides for commercial fishing, dominated by a large-scale industrial fleet, and recreational fishing (from which the sale of catches is prohibited). At the fringes of both these fisheries, however, there are a small number of individuals who operate in a way that would be described as artisanal elsewhere in the world. This chapter argues for the use of financial inclusion mechanisms as a means to empower the SSF sector in Namibia.

T. V. Warikandwa (✉)
School of Law, University of Namibia, Windhoek, Namibia
e-mail: twarikandwa@unam.na

E. Shakalela · E. L. Libebe
School of Law, Faculty of Commerce, Management and Law, University of Namibia, Windhoek, Namibia
e-mail: eshakalela@unam.na; elibebe@unam.na

1 Introduction

Small-scale fishers (SSF)[1] in Namibia have for long remained unable to obtain funding or take advantage of formalization's advantages and prospects due to economic and cultural hurdles. The livelihood of the community and the sustainability of the ecosystem are directly impacted by the decisions made by fishermen, who are the guardians of the ocean.[2] Due to their position, SSF should be well-positioned to access various funding sources and money for projects, which can encourage sustainability and resilience and meet a number of United Nations Sustainable Development Goals (SDGs).[3] Namibia's SSF frequently face challenges from getting the funding that would make the most difference due to limitations caused by policy and legal framework. SSF associations like the Hanganeni Artisanal Fishing Association (HAFA) and marginalized, possibly economically excluded coastal communities like the Topnaar are frequent features of Namibia's SSF sector.

Few, if any, Financial service providers (FSPs) have historically been able to interact with Namibia's SSF. This is largely attributed to high levels of perceived risk and low levels of fisher formalization in the nation. In the past, not much was done to help the underprivileged and marginalised communities of coastal towns such as Walvis Bay, Swakopmund and Lüderitz. Due to their capacities, only a select few registered large corporations and FSPs participated in the rights applications to benefit from the fishing resources. The Ministry of Fisheries and Marine Resources assisted in the establishment of the Hanganeni Artisanal Fishing Association (HAFA), one of the few member-based associations, in 2003.[4] HAFA mainly operates in Henties Bay and has a traditional fishing community of an estimated 500 persons.[5] The HAFA administration employs 14 people, of whom 11 work in management and three are supported by fringe perks including housing, cellphones, health plans, and pensions, for a combined yearly salary of almost N$1.6 million.[6] The HAFA membership is largely concentrated in Swakopmund, Walvis Bay, and Lüderitz. Task forces were created to organize anglers in such communities. Every year, the association adds between 80 and 140 new members. The Fisheries and Marine Resources Act, 2000,[7] policies, and regulations are all followed by HAFA because it is governed by and operates under the custodianship of the Ministry of Fisheries and Marine Resources.

FSPs are still hesitant to invest much in the SSF. The majority of SSF operate without a formal corporate structure or fiscal registration, in addition to frequently

---

[1]Food and Agriculture Organisation of the United Nations (2022).
[2]Brugère et al. (2008).
[3]Rice (2017).
[4]Batty and Tjipute (2005).
[5]Daniels (2020).
[6]Daniels (2020).
[7]Fisheries and Marine Resources Act, 2000 (Act 27 of 2000).

lacking the required sanitary and fishing licenses.[8] Without formalization or business savvy, SSF might not be able to effectively apply for and manage the cash and investment. Even governmental subsidies meant to encourage innovation in the SSF and aquaculture sectors have heavily favored commercial fisheries and aquaculture projects, mainly because few impoverished SSF communities are able to meet investment requirements and obtain the matching funds needed to qualify.[9]

Namibia has reasonably sound banking and financial systems, including a thriving and sizable microfinance sector, as well as forward-thinking Fintech and digital wallet environments that are supported by a strong regulatory framework.[10] Nevertheless, due to a lack of digital and banking cultures in rural regions, SSF financial inclusion through these means is likely to remain uncommon. Rural and commercial banks, as well as credit and savings institutions, are the financial institutions that lend to fishermen the most frequently among those that do serve borrowers from the fisheries industry, while loans to fisheries still make up less than one percent of their portfolios.[11] These institutions reduce the risks by requiring larger down payments, higher lending rates, and stringent formalities such as collateral requirements.

More than ever, the difficulties in providing funding to SSF were made obvious. The Namibian government created emergency stimulus funding and unique low-interest credits expressly for corporates in response to the COVID-19 crisis,[12] but even these had difficulty efficiently reaching and supporting their intended populations. The government's current lack of express provision of the necessary financial assistance to the SSF, when they most need it, brings to light the same obstacles that fishermen typically encounter when attempting to obtain any kind of official finance.[13] These obstacles make the task of a potential funder more difficult since they limit fishermen's capacity to execute projects successfully and their preparedness for investment. Due to obstacles and constraints on both sides of the problem, there is still a formal financial inclusion gap for SSF in Namibia.

In this chapter, we look at the financial landscape today and the challenges of helping SSF. Fishing households and their enterprises have few choices for financing and managing cash flow for personal necessities or business investments because to a lack of access to banking institutions. Informal lenders, who may also be the main consumers of fish or the boat owners, fill the access gap. Financial inclusion, usually referred to as access to formal financial services,[14] can strengthen the financial resilience of rural and coastal SSF households in Namibia.

---

[8]FAO (2020a, b, c).

[9]FAO (2020a, b, c).

[10]Bank of Namibia (2021).

[11]Bank of Namibia (2001).

[12]Marenga and Amupanda (2021), pp. 206–225.

[13]Perhaps this position will change with the adoption in June 2022 of a National Plan of Action for the SSF in Namibia. See Oirere (2022).

[14]Nekwaya-Okafor (2022).

The chapter discusses the current obstacles to financial inclusion for small-scale fishing households, including their lack of formal identity, low financial literacy and capability, lack of collateral assets, and distance from banking institutions. Additionally, it discusses ways to overcome these obstacles, such as promoting financial literacy, de-risking financial institutions, gathering financial data, offering a variety of financial services besides credit, and comprehending the needs of the client, all of which will help fishing households maintain control over their income and savings. Improved economic resilience can be achieved by reducing the various vulnerabilities of underprivileged fishing households and rural communities.

2 Contextual Background

SSF are central to achieving SDG 14 on sustainable oceans, specifically target 14.b[15] on access for small-scale artisanal fishers to marine resources and markets. Additionally, sustainable small-scale fisheries are essential for achieving a range of other SDGs, most directly SDG 1 (no poverty), SDG 2 (no hunger), SDG 3 (good health and well-being), SDG 5 (gender equality), SDG 8 (decent work and economic growth) and SDG 10 (reduced inequalities), and generally support the achievement of the entire 2030 Agenda.[16] SSF therefore make an important contribution to nutrition, food security, rural livelihoods, and poverty alleviation.[17] It is no wonder that SSF is central to the call for recognizing the human rights of SSF's marginalised coastal communities through the Blue Justice agenda. The Blue Justice agenda focuses on the following aspects: (a) Calling for the governments' attention to fairness and equity for the SSF especially the most marginalized and vulnerable groups; (b) Investigating pressure on the SSF from the Blue Growth/Blue Economy Agenda; and (c) Assessing how the rights and wellbeing of SSF and their communities are compromised.

The United Nations (UN) acknowledged the significance of SSF by designating 2022 as the International Year of Artisanal Fisheries and Aquaculture (IYAFA 2022). Access to financial services is essential for fostering SSF in Africa in a long-term fashion. Financial service providers (FSPs) in Namibia should increase the availability of their services to SSF in order to achieve the aforementioned SDGs. Sixty-four percent of the FSPs who participated in a recent survey in Africa said they

---

[15] SDG 14.b makes provision for, "... access of small-scale artisanal fishers to marine resources and markets".

[16] See the United Nations General Assembly Resolution adopted on September 2015. The 2030 Agenda for Sustainable Development specifically affirms that the SDGs 'seek to realize the human rights of all' (A/RES/70/1: http://undocs.org/A/RES/70/1) https://www.un.org/en/development/desa/population/migration/generalassembly/docs/globalcompact/A_RES_70_1_E.pdf. Accessed 11 January 2022.

[17] FAO (2020a, b, c). See also Niner et al. (2022), pp. 25–35.

provide their services to SMEs engaged in SSF and aquaculture.[18] However, less than ten percent of the FSPs' portfolios are made up of the credit programs accessible to fisheries and aquaculture enterprises.[19] Thirty-five percent of FSPs have specific loan programs for the aquaculture or fisheries industries (or both). Thirty-one to Fifty-two percent of FSPs rated the financial performance of their lending services to the fisheries and aquaculture sectors as "good" or "very good" between 2016 and 2019.[20]

The Blue Justice agenda is concerned with the following aspects: (a) urging the government to pay attention to fairness and equity for SSF, especially the most vulnerable and marginalized groups; (b) looking into the pressure the Blue Growth/ Blue Economy Agenda is putting on the SSF; and (c) determining how the rights and wellbeing of SSF and their communities are jeopardized. The Blue Justice agenda's five guiding principles are inclusive government, social justice, human rights, equal opportunity, and environmental sustainability. There are seven actions that must be taken in order to combat injustice: (1) Supporting the SSF guidelines' implementation; (2) Highlighting SSF as an important factor in sustainable ocean development, particularly post-Covid-19; (3) Including SSF in discussions of all Sustainable Development Goals; (4) Supporting coordinated application of laws and regulations that support SSF; (5) Promoting cross-sectoral collaboration and strengthening SSF networks; (6) Encouraging governance reform to recognize SSF rights and assist in realizing their potentials; (7) Raising general knowledge of SSF's values and significance.

2.1 Significance of the SSF Industry to Namibia

Namibia's economic and social progress is indirectly driven by the SSF industry. For thousands of people living in impoverished and distant coastal and inland locations, the SSF industry provides employment and a means of subsistence. SSF frequently sells its caught fish for a reasonable price on the local and international markets. The industry plays a crucial role in preserving food security and well health by providing an unreplaceable source of highly nutritious food.[21] Over 280,000 Namibians, or over 11% of the nation's total population, have indirect support from the SSF subsector in Namibia. Income, employment, socioeconomic advantages, food security, and nutrition security are all examples of livelihood assistance.[22] A total of 46,500 fisherfolks in SSF are anticipated to get direct support in the form of jobs and

---

[18]FAO (2022a, b). See also FAO in Namibia (2022) Mapping women in small-scale fisheries https://www.fao.org/namibia/news/detail-events/ru/c/1492150/. Accessed 10 July 2022.
[19]FAO (2022a, b).
[20]FAO (2022a, b).
[21]FAO (2014), pp. 1–119. See also Ankintola and Fakoya (2017), pp. 1–17.
[22]Moyo (2022).

direct livelihoods, of which 45,000 work in the inland fisheries sector and 1500 in the coastal small-scale fisheries sector.[23] Over 15,000 direct employment are supported by it, making it Namibia's third-largest employer after mining and agriculture.[24] N$9 billion is added to Namibia's Gross Domestic Product (GDP) each year by the nation's fishing industry.[25] More than 20% of the nation's overall export revenue comes from the fishing industry, which also generates a large number of direct and indirect jobs.[26] Fish products are the second-largest export product category after commodities, making up 13% of overall exports on average.[27]

According to the Food and Agriculture Organization (FAO), SSF are crucial to people's everyday life because they support livelihoods in the production sector (through direct fishing), the post-harvest sector (through fish processing), and through local, national, and international marketing.[28] Dried and salted Namibian fish is exported to markets as far as the Democratic Republic of Congo and Zambia, and fish production in the Zambezi region alone is estimated at 5000 metric tonnes annually and valued at N$150 million.[29] Due to the importance of SSF to Namibia, the Government of Namibia committed to developing its National Plan of Action for Small-Scale Fisheries (NPOA-SSF) in September 2020 through the implementation of the Voluntary Guidelines for Securing Sustainable SSF in the Context of food Security and Poverty Eradication (SSF Guidelines).[30] The nearly two years long NPOA-SSF development process was collaborative and participative, and it has raised awareness of the significance of SSF in the lives of Namibian people that depend on rivers and fishing. Through the Directorate of Inland Fisheries and Aquaculture, the Ministry of Fisheries and Marine Resources has launched a sub-program titled "Implementing the Small-Scale Fisheries Guidelines for gender equitable and climate resilient food systems and livelihoods." The SSF Guidelines promote gender equitable development strategies for small-scale fisheries.

A small-scale fishing right may only be granted to one cooperative per small-scale fishing community, and that cooperative must include all of the confirmed small-scale fishermen in that community as members.[31] Small-scale fishing villages must develop secondary cooperatives with other small-scale fishing communities in order to better benefit small-scale fishermen and strengthen their negotiating position.[32] A small mullet beach-seine fishery and a decreasing number of ski-boats utilizing handline gear are two examples of commercial fishing operations that exhibit the

---

[23] FAO (2022a, b).
[24] FAO (2022a, b).
[25] Moyo (2022).
[26] Moyo (2022).
[27] Moyo (2022).
[28] FAO (2022a, b).
[29] Shigwedha (2022), p. 11.
[30] The Namibian (2021), p. 7.
[31] FAO (2012).
[32] Stacey et al. (2021), pp. 1–12.

traits of an artisanal fishery.[33] Anglers, divers, and gatherers who depend on their catches for food and cash are also included among fishermen working from the beach (with or without recreational fishing licenses).[34] The sale of their catches had previously been "informal," but in 2003, a group of beach fishermen received a fishing permit for experimental purposes.[35] Today, these fishermen are now able to function as an association for artisanal fishing with government funding. Nevertheless, the socio-economic makeup of unlicensed fishermen and their motivation in obtaining official, legal access to marine resources are still both poorly understood. In terms of catches, employment, and economic worth, this artisanal fishery pales in comparison to the industrial and recreational fisheries. It is based in part on the resources from fisheries that help the recreational fishery.

2.2   Small-Scale Fishers' Barriers to Access Financing

The fishing sector is very important to many related industries, including engineering, transportation, logistics, and medicine, to name a few. The fishing sector is anticipated to grow by up to 3.6 percent in 2022 after experiencing a record-breaking loss of −9.4 percent in 2020.[36] Indeed, the recovery of the fishing industry following the disruption caused by the Covid-19 outbreak is good news for the struggling economy.[37] Over 30% of Namibian imports to the European Union are made up of fish and fishery products.[38] The inland fishing sector in Namibia is highly active locally. Large freshwater bodies in the country's northern areas enable inland fisheries. More than 40,000 Namibians, according to the FAO, depend on small-scale fisheries for their livelihoods.[39] These livelihoods include those that are supported in the production sector (through direct fishing), the post-harvest sector (through fish processing), and through marketing that takes place locally, nationally, and regionally.

For a variety of factors, SSF are unable to obtain formal financing sources. The least formalized of these is the most significant, although it is also influenced by other elements including organizational governance and cultural norms. Ensuring regulatory compliance may not be regarded as required or even typical given that the majority of artisanal fishers in Namibia operate informally. Formalization is one of the prerequisites that funders would not budge on, despite the fact that the bulk of the

---

[33] Tubino et al. (2007), pp. 187–197.

[34] Batty and Tjipute (2005).

[35] Batty and Tjipute (2005).

[36] Moyo (2022).

[37] Moyo (2022).

[38] Moyo (2022).

[39] FAO (2022a, b).

small-scale fleet has not been able to adopt it.[40] This requirement has strong foundations because formalization offers two essential components necessary for formal finance mechanisms to function: transparency in the capital recipient's fiscal and financial situation, and recognition and capitalization of assets to be used as collateral to leverage credit. Therefore, it will be essential to address and promote formalization at every level, from the individual fisher to the boat owner, commercializer, and association, for efforts that aim to organize money for investment and project development in small scale fisheries.

The effects of the barriers vary depending on the structure and growth of the fishery.[41] However, when it comes to funding for working capital, the majority of SSF funding in Namibia presently originates from unofficial sources. In order to offset the cost of risk, these informal lenders, who are frequently buyers, other supply chain intermediaries, or input suppliers, offer capital at rates higher than formal lenders, but they typically have flexible repayment terms, do not impose formality requirements, and do not require collateral. As a result, fishermen incur debt, become dependent on their line of work, struggle to maintain control over business and investment decisions, and are unable to access formal financial resources.

The ability to establish formal market relationships, particularly in high-value fisheries, which would show the potential financial flow to attract finance, is another key impediment.[42] Again, informality is the norm in fishing ports, where sales are frequently tied to buyers and intermediaries who act as informal lenders and are conducted on a daily basis through verbal agreements and cash transactions. Fishers in these unofficial settings are vulnerable to market volatility, which makes it harder for them to forecast their cash flow. The ability of fishermen to become investment-ready is further hampered by this unpredictability as well as the absence of official purchase orders and established market relationships.[43]

The capacity of artisanal fishermen to access formal money is also severely impacted by a number of other social and environmental challenges.[44] Fishing club members frequently join for purely social reasons and are unaware of the additional economic advantages of cooperative and aggregation structures. Producers frequently lack financial education and business savvy, and they frequently lack access to information about the supply chain and the market that would enable them to form strategic alliances, launch new business ventures, and develop detailed business plans that would improve their chances of obtaining financing. Fishers' financial flow, ability to save money, and ability to repay loans on time are all significantly impacted by the intense volatility in the amounts captured as a result of climate change and worsening environmental circumstances, as well as swings in the

---

[40]FAO (2020a, b, c).

[41]Bertheussen et al. (2021), pp. 1–9.

[42]United Nations Conference on Trade and Development (UNCTAD) (2022), pp. 1–64.

[43]Rocca (2021).

[44]UNCTAD (2022).

prices fishers are able to secure. Furthermore, there are restrictions on the funders' side of the gap that prevent them from efficiently allocating capital to the artisanal fisheries industry. Funders who operate in silos miss out on collaborative solutions that can involve important local system such like anchor companies, public programs or supplier providers, or blended finance models. These kinds of partnerships could assist donors in reducing risk and offering additional forms of assistance, like financial literacy programs or capacity building, to complement and guarantee the sustainability of their investments.

Lack of information and a general awareness of the needs and realities of fishermen are further consequences of informality. This causes a mismatch between the amounts and types of money supplied to and sought by the sector, and it may also cause grant programs for technical support and capacity building to be overlooked, which are essential for the advancement and sustainability of projects. Small-scale fishers in Namibia frequently face obstacles that prevent them from accessing financing and from taking use of formalization's advantages and prospects, including both cultural and economic ones.[45] Namibian experts in rural finance and fisheries must consult in order to increase small-scale fishers' access to financial services. Small-scale fishermen play a significant role in Namibian society by supporting the country's food security, nutrition, employment, coastal livelihoods, and export revenues.[46] These small-scale fishermen lack access to official financial services including microfinance, savings, credit, and insurance, while a sizable majority of them do. There are various reasons why they cannot, including the minimal collateral they can offer, their restricted ability to invest, the geographical dispersion of coastal fishing settlements, and the high rates of illiteracy among fishers.[47]

On the other hand, financial institutions frequently lack the industry expertise necessary to evaluate the risks involved and may view the subsector as having poor prospects for both commercial and financial gain. Additionally, the situation in communities of fishermen and their unique demands are frequently ignored by government financial policies and legislation. Namibians must be able to learn the necessary skills through training if they are to take advantage of the opportunities presented by the expansion of the fishing sector. Additionally, supporting policies and programs are required for the distribution of fishing rights and quotas in order to increase the role that Namibian firms play in the sector. By enhancing the fishing industry's capabilities for research and training, this objective will be accomplished.

The Policy Statement on the Granting of Rights of Exploitation to Utilise Marine Resources and on the Allocation of Fishing Quotas of 8 July 1993 provided details on the new system of long-term fishing rights and vessel quotas. Amongst the critical issues raised in this policy is the Namibianisation of the fisheries sector. To achieve the Namibianisation of the fisheries sector that does not exclude the SSF. To ensure

---

[45] Chiripanhura and Teweldemedhin (2016), pp. 1–84.

[46] Shigwedha (2022), p. 7.

[47] Brugère et al. (2008), pp. 1–39.

effective financing plans for small-scale fisherman in Namibia, it is necessary to consider the potential for formulating recommendations for micro-finance, loans, and insurance for small-scale fisheries. To increase the availability of financial services to small-scale fisheries, it is advisable to develop a capacity-building program and follow practical principles for greater access to financial services.[48]

Lessons learned from the joint FAO and Asia-Pacific Rural and Agricultural Credit Association (APRACA) expert workshop, which took place from May 7–9, 2019, in Bangkok, could provide guidance on SSF funding in Namibia.[49] It was brought up during this workshop that certain APRACA members provide credit to SSF. The need for capacity building for numerous rural banks in the area to serve the financial needs of small-scale fishers and their communities was also brought up. Namibia could gain from the workshop's exchange of experiences and lessons learned from other nations and international experts regarding the guidelines created in collaboration with FAO to assist APRACA members in effectively providing credit to small-scale fishermen.

Dr. Raymon van Anrooy, a senior fisheries officer for the FAO, stated at the workshop that the guidelines for insurance and credit will make it easier to implement the 2014 voluntary guidelines for securing sustainable small-scale fisheries in the context of achieving food security and the reduction of poverty.[50] They will also help to achieve SDG 14: Conserve and sustainably use the oceans, seas, and marine resources for sustainable development. The SSF in Namibia (and elsewhere in Africa and the rest of the world) will be able to invest in more principled fishing operations and technology, lessen overfishing, contribute to fisheries management, and put into action climate change adaption measures by having access to financial services. The experts at the APRACA/FAO workshop discussed financial inclusion and financial services programs for small-scale fishers, finalized guidelines to help them get better access to financial services, and created a capacity-building program to increase the availability of financial and insurance services to small-scale fisheries.[51]

There are a lot of possible areas for development, and the following are some generally accepted observations:

(a) In most developing countries, SSF have restricted access to microfinance, lending, and insurance services compared to the availability of financial services for farmers and other rural sectors;
(b) SSF finance has many similarities to rural and agricultural finance, but also differs in some ways (such as having unique daily working capital requirements, seasonality, labour risks, moral hazard, limited collateral, perishable goods, and some declining markets), all of which must be considered when promoting increased access;

---

[48] FAO (2021a, b).
[49] FAO (2020a, b, c).
[50] FAO (2019).
[51] FAO (2019), pp. 3–32.

(c) Some programs successfully address the financial requirements of small-scale fishermen, and they could serve as models for the area; and

(d) Most developing nations still have low levels of financial literacy among SSF, which limits their access to financial products and their understanding of the financial status of their fishing business, cash flows generated, and business hazards associated.[52]

The primary expenses for the SSF would be: (1) capital expenses for the acquisition of boats, launches, nets, and engines, among other things; (2) running expenses for ice, gasoline, and supplies; and (3) additional expenses for medical, emergency, and other outlays for the family, including schooling.[53]

SSF employees may have no other option for obtaining formal institutional credit than money lenders. As a result, the SSF continues to rely on money lenders, financiers, chit funds, borrowing from friends and family, and other sources to cover expenses such as housing, children's education, setbacks, and crises. They frequently have to rely on unregulated financial markets, such as traders, merchants, and money lenders, even for production-related needs. SSF have historically been among the poorest and most marginalized groups, frequently being taken advantage of by middlemen and traders.[54] The power that middlemen have over finance and fish marketing sucks away the surplus produced and frequently leaves them in debt. The lives of coastal small-scale fishermen and aquaculturists can be improved via microfinance.

The only option available to fishermen in the lack of appropriate institutional credit is the informal credit system, which comes at a significant cost in the form of hefty interest expenses and the need that they sell their best catch for a fixed price that may be less than half the market price.[55] Furthermore, there is no insurance or social security to fall back on for operations requiring severe risks to life, property, and uncertainty regarding the availability of catch and market-related vagaries. Nearly none of the numerous credit plus services are available. In light of this, microfinance services should be seen as essential to Namibia's SSF.

A relatively small percentage of financial policies in Namibia and Africa specifically mention microfinance, despite its potential relevance as a tool for financial inclusion and for reducing poverty.[56] Evidence from evaluation studies of previous initiatives suggests that formal credit programs through rural banks and cooperatives, frequently supported by donor agencies, frequently fail, both in terms of the viability of lending institutions in outreach and the capacity of intended beneficiaries to access more affordable sources of credit. Because they are more accessible to the users, more flexible, have user-friendly processes and procedures, and are more

---

[52] FAO (2019).

[53] FAO (2019).

[54] Macusi (2022).

[55] Shrestha (n.d.).

[56] The World Bank (2016).

tailored to the client's microcredit needs, informal savings schemes and credit markets are widely developed in many countries.

These developments may positively contribute to granting access to capital or assets. As a result, the microfinance industry is being more recognized as a vital development instrument for financial inclusion and poverty alleviation, however official fisheries policies have yet to completely take this into account. In this context, microfinance is understood to include the provision of a wide array of financial services, including deposits, loans, payment services, money transfers, and insurance, and is most frequently characterized by micro/nano loans to cover unexpected urgent family costs.[57] Few commercial banks or microfinance organizations exist that are ready and able to offer small loans to small-scale fishermen at interest rates significantly lower than those offered by middlemen.[58] Due to complicated documentation requirements and lending standards based on collateral, fishermen also view the perception of banks' inflexibility as a major hindrance to timely access to financing.

Women make up the majority of microfinance customers globally, mostly due to their stellar track records of loan repayment and micro-savings. They are essential members of fishing communities, carrying out social and economic obligations both within and outside of their own homes. Women are disproportionately active in income-generating activities outside of the fishing industry that are directly related to the production, processing, and sale of fish.[59] Because they frequently need modest loans, SSF are suitable microfinance customers. Due to their infrequent access to institutional finance, there is a need for savings and credit services among fishermen that is rarely satisfied. The households require microfinance in order to enhance their revenue through fishing and other sources of income. Additionally, it is necessary to smooth out consumption patterns and meet social demands relating to a person's quality of life, particularly in lean and off-seasons when little to no food or revenue is produced. Microfinance also aids in risk management and lessens social and economic vulnerability.

3 Policy Issues

Namibia has a number of fisheries policies; however, they say little about issues related to financial inclusion. It is important to recognize that Namibia's financial inclusion agenda prioritizes three areas: (1) access to financial services and products, (2) financial literacy, and (3) consumer protection.[60] The primary goals of the financial services and products dimension are to increase consumption and access

---

[57]Beck (2015), pp. 1–59.
[58]Karmakar et al. (2009).
[59]Kusakabe and Thongprasert (2022).
[60]Nekwaya-Okafor (2022).

to financial products and services. However, the rural and informal sectors are still underserved or excluded from the Namibian economy (these are the categories within which SSF is situated).[61]

Consumer protection in the context of financial inclusion refers to safeguarding consumers through effective regulation, oversight, and enforcement of market behaviour by financial service providers.[62] It is one of the most important facilitators for improving financial inclusion goals and policies in a nation. Consumer empowerment, which comprises empowering consumers to make more educated financial decisions through the provision of information, education, and efficient channels for redress, goes hand in hand with consumer protection. When it comes to creating an environment where consumers can prosper, there are two main components that make up consumer empowerment: first, the resources and tools available to them for making informed decisions, such as reliable information and the knowledge to use these tools effectively; and second, the institutions, such as consumer protection laws and regulatory bodies, that back up consumers and help shape the market. Namibia should put safeguards in place for customers and create a proper and effective regulatory framework for consumer protection in the financial industry, according to the 2011–2021 Namibia Financial Sector Strategy.[63] Namibia does not yet have a consumer protection law.

The Guidelines for Filing Complaints, published in 2013 by the Bank of Namibia and the Bankers Association of Namibia, provide instructions for customers on how to file complaints about commercial banks.[64] In a similar vein, the banking sector created the code of banking practice, which establishes guidelines for ethical behaviour for banks to adhere to while interacting with clients. But there is still much work to be done before the financial sector has the proper structure in place for consumer protection, especially now that the tide of digital change is sweeping the industry.

The mix of awareness, information, skills, attitude, and behaviours required to make wise financial decisions in order to eventually achieve individual financial well-being is referred to as financial literacy. According to the 2017 Namibia Financial Capability Survey, 52.9 percent of Namibians are financially literate.[65] This indicates that either less than half of the Namibian population is well informed to make wise financial decisions or that consumers' attitudes toward financial decision-making and management are generally negative. This is a matter for concern, especially in light of the second financial literacy gap that has been created by the financial technology industry's rapid advancements, known as digital financial literacy, which has the potential to widen literacy gaps among different demographic sectors. This emphasizes the necessity of ongoing financial literacy activities to help consumers effectively utilize cutting-edge financial goods and services.

---

[61] Nekwaya-Okafor (2022).

[62] The World Bank (2021).

[63] Ministry of Finance (2011).

[64] Bank of Namibia (n.d.).

[65] Bank of Namibia (2017).

An admirable start in the right direction was the launch of Namibia's financial literacy project, a national platform designed to improve financial education for individuals and small enterprises by raising awareness of financial services and products.[66] One of the few nations in the area with such a body in place is Namibia. The platform must, however, step up its efforts to deliver the essential consumer education and put in place efficient structures to guide the national financial education agenda.

Namibia has made progress in its efforts to increase financial inclusion overall, compared to its peers, with an overall financial inclusion rate of 78 percent. This is especially true in terms of formal account ownerships and a few initiatives targeted at providing access to finance for micro, small, and medium-sized businesses. The underserved rural population still faces significant transportation expenses to use Automated Teller Machines, bank offices, and other formal financial services, therefore much work needs to be done to improve access and usage. To reach these groups, regulators, politicians, innovators, and financial service providers must use agent networks and digital financial services. Some of the policies that are important to the SSF are described in this chapter's section. The Strategic Plan for the Ministry of Fisheries and Marine Resources will be discussed first.

3.1 Ministry of Fisheries and Marine Resources Strategic Plan

The Ministry of Fisheries and Marine Resources (MRMR) Strategic Plan,[67] referred to as the "Fisheries Policy," is the primary fisheries policy of Namibia. It refers to "small-scale fishermen" but does not define the term. According to this strategy, the Ministry of Fisheries and Marine Resources must carry out its fundamental duties by executing strategic initiatives and key performance indicators that are evaluated yearly and converted into management plans. SSF are one of the primary stakeholders in the strategic plan. In accordance with Vision 2030, the Harambee Prosperity Plan, and the National Development Plan, the primary objective of the strategic plan is to establish a sustainable and economically inclusive fisheries that aids Namibia in achieving its national goal of ending poverty.

The Republic of Namibia's Constitution,[68] a number of policy and regulatory documents, and a cabinet directive that established the MFMR in 1991 all serve as the foundation for the strategic plan's mandate.[69] As a result, among other things, the

---

[66]Namibia Financial Institutions Supervisory Authority (2018).

[67]Ministry of Fisheries and Marine Resources Strategic Plan (2017–2018–2021/22).

[68]The Constitution of the Republic of Namibia, 21 March 1990, https://www.refworld.org/docid/4 7175fd361.html. Accessed 7 July 2022.

[69]The primary policy and regulatory instruments for MFMR which are: (1) The Marine Resources Act 2000 (Act No. 27 of 2000); (2) The Marine Resources Regulations (Government Notice

strategic plan works in tandem with the policies and laws mentioned above. The Namibianisation of the fishing industry was one program the government implemented in addition to the strategic plan to help people become key players in their local economy. A recent analysis found that Namibians control 90–95 percent of the local fishing business, illustrating the sector's growing Namibianisation.[70] Since it is impressive how rapidly a previously foreign-dominated fishing industry was converted for a developing country like Namibia, the Namibianisation program has also garnered recognition from other nations. The Namibianisation Policy was a tool employed by the MFMR to resurrect Namibia's fishing industry. Initially, the Namibianisation strategy had the following goals: (1) to promote local ownership of fishing vessels and businesses; (2) to create new jobs; (3) to replace foreign labor with Namibian labor; and (4) to develop a domestic processing sector.

In order to right historical wrongs and give Namibians long-term relief regarding their marine resources, the Namibianisation strategy was created. Initially, it seemed that there were two ways to do this: (1) using command and control by seizing and distributing fishing rights to previously underprivileged Namibians, or (2) putting in place a just and equitable incentive-based system that promoted economically motivated relocations.

3.2   National Plan of Action for the SSF

SSFs are crucial to the development of local economies in the BCLME region. Marine and inland fisheries make to the region's fisheries sector (rivers, dams, amongst others). The small-scale fishing industry is believed to be the primary source of income, employment, food security, and nutrition for over 100,000 small-scale or artisanal fisherman. Namibia's NPOA-SSF, with the theme of building resilient small-scale fisheries systems together toward sustainable natural resource utilisation, co-governance, and viable communities, was introduced by the Ministry of Fisheries and Marine Resources from June 8–10, 2022, at the MFMR Auditorium in Swakopmund.[71]

The three-day launch of the NPOA-SSF gave participants the opportunity to: (i) validate the significance and importance of small-scale fisheries in Namibia and the BCLME region; (ii) better understand the current status of the sector—both

---

No. 241, Regulations relating to the exploitation of Marine Resources, 2001); (3) Namibia's Marine Resources Policy: Towards Responsible Development and Management of the Marine Resources Sector (August 2004); (4) The White Paper on the Responsible Management of the Inland Fisheries of Namibia (1995); (5) Inland Fisheries Resources Act (No. 1 of 2003); (6) Aquaculture Policy; (7) Aquaculture Act 2002 (Act No.18 of 2002); and (8) Aquaculture Regulation on Licensing.

[70]Chiripanhura and Teweldemedhin (2016).

[71]World Ocean's Day and the International Year of Artisanal Fisheries and Aquaculture (IYAFA 2022) were also celebrated by MFMR in cooperation with the Food and Agriculture Organization (FAO) and the Benguela Current Convention (BCC).

inland and marine; (iii) raise awareness of the sector's significance and viability; and (iv) promote capacity building and support for sustainable resource utilization and improved governance for artisanal and small-scale fisheries. Namibia became one of the first African countries to implement the SSF Guidelines through the MFMR by creating a national plan of action for SSF. SSF from 14 regions of Namibia validated the NPOA-SSF before it was officially introduced.

3.3 White Paper on Responsible Development of the Fisheries Sector

The primary goal of the government of Namibia's White Paper on Responsible Development of the Fisheries Sector[72] is to guarantee that the nation's fisheries resources and related industries are used sustainably over the long term in order to support the nation's economy and meet development goals. This White Paper highlights the Namibian government's commitment to rebuilding exhausted fisheries stocks by regulatory measures such adjusting fisheries exploitation levels, effort limits by reducing fleet sizes, limiting harvesting hours, and restricting access to specific locations. Maximising Namibians' advantages from the fisheries sector and expanding meaningful engagement in the fishing business and control over marine resources are other major goals of the White Paper. Thus, the White Paper called for a Namibianisation policy that aimed to correct historical inequities and unequal management of fisheries assets, especially the involvement of foreign fleets.[73]

Namibianisation, which has a strong economic incentive, aims to enhance Namibian ownership and control of the fisheries industry through encouraging industry reform. By offering priority quotas to applicants who demonstrate a significant level of Namibian ownership and investment, Namibianisation specifically targets previously disadvantaged groups. Important factors that influence the quota right allocation given to the corporation include the percentage of Namibian ownership of a vessel, the make-up of the crew, and the quantity of catch landed and processed in Namibian ports.[74]

Although the Namibianisation Policy in the White Paper is focused on enhancing access to marine resources for Namibia's historically underserved individuals and groups, it also acknowledges the significance of foreign investment, which is mostly promoted through joint ventures. By offering significant tax savings for Namibian-owned vessels and further reductions if the fish is processed on land, an incentive structure has been established. These mechanisms help this system further encourage (local) control and ownership as follows: (1) Giving 90 percent Namibian-owned businesses longer-term rights (10 years) than joint ventures (7 years); (2) providing

---

[72] MFMR (1991).
[73] Erastus (2002).
[74] Erastus (2002).

further levies reductions for fish processed locally, which would increase local employment opportunities; and (3) encouraging new entrants or companies (not previously engaged in fisheries) to enter the industry.[75]

New entrants may include people with entrepreneurial abilities, who may also be involved in diverse sectors of the economy and who may have little knowledge of the fishing business in order to balance and broaden the advantages from Namibia's fishing sector. Everyone who has experienced disadvantage is welcome to participate, but the objective is to support potential black business owners who might be able to compete in the commercial fishing sector. The new entrants may include business professionals as well as community and traditional leaders. Great prospects to increase engagement in the Namibian fishing industry have been made possible by the Namibianisation Policy.

The White Paper makes no specific provisions for artisanal and subsistence fishers, which is particularly pertinent to this chapter. As stated in the White Paper's first paragraph, the available resources, lack of natural harbours, lack of artisanal fishing industry, and lack of significant domestic fish market restrict development choices.[76] The paragraph goes to state that because Namibian Fisheries will be almost entirely export-oriented, it will need to be competitive and responsive to economic and technological changes. The structures of the future fleet as well as the land-based processing activities will naturally depend on various technical and economic factors.[77] Such factors are largely out of the reach of SSF.

4 The Legal Context

Financial inclusion is crucial for achieving SDG targets, especially among the SSF, as this chapter has already alluded to. The great majority of SDG targets are based on clauses in international human rights agreements that subject States that have ratified them to duties under the law. Additionally, the overarching principle of "leaving no one behind" represents the basic tenets of equality and non-discrimination in human rights. Generally speaking, there is a mutually reinforcing relationship between human rights and the SDGs. More specifically, a number of human rights must be realized in order for SDG goal 14.b to be implemented effectively and adequately. It also has the ability to help these rights become a reality.

The financial services sector is essential to the global economy, has significant influence over the fisheries sector and its related commercial endeavours, and is crucial to ensuring widespread corporate observance of human rights. The United Nations Guiding Principles on Business and Human Rights (UNGPs) has placed focus and emphasis on development finance, including, but not limited to,

---

[75]Erastus (2002).

[76]MFMR (1991), paragraph 1, pp. 25–26.

[77]MFMR (1991), p. 25.

multilateral, bilateral, and national development finance institutions; microfinance institutions; community development financial institutions; and revolving loan funds. These different financing mechanisms are crucial to financial inclusion for the SSF. However, for financing of the SSF to take place, there must be formal recognition of the SSF from a policy and regulatory perspectives.

As things stand, Namibia has just developed and launched a National Plan of Action on the SSF. This is a deliberate effort by the Namibian government to formally recognise the SSF. By addressing foreign dominance of the fisheries, increasing Namibian ownership in fishing companies, promoting opportunities for historically disadvantaged people to enter the fishing sector, creating jobs for the Namibian people, and generating government revenue and export earnings, the Namibianisation policy has significantly contributed to the transformation of the fishing industry. However, a policy does not have the same effect as law. However, there are certain complaints of the process of implementing policy, particularly the absence of financial and technical support for the less wealthy and technologically advanced segments of individuals belonging to the formerly disadvantaged group. Lack of clear legal channels for underprivileged communities, individuals, and small-scale fishermen who lack the financial means and essential tools to acquire access to marine resources as a source of livelihood is a major challenge in terms of upholding regional duties. The fisheries ministry, the Marine Resources Act 27 of 2000 and the Inland Fisheries Resources Act 1 of 2003 recognise artisanal and recreational fishing but do not include SSF. This section will look at the different legal instruments and analyse how they recognise SSF and financial inclusion, if at all they do.

4.1   The Constitution of Namibia

A democratic Constitution founded on the rule of law and human rights governs the Republic of Namibia. The Constitution creates a framework that upholds international law, fulfills its treaty responsibilities, and promotes the peaceful resolution of international issues.[78] Chapter 11, "Principles of state policy," which mandates the government to adopt policies aimed at maintaining ecosystems, crucial ecological processes, and Namibia's biological diversity as well as ensuring the sustainable use of natural resources for the benefit of all Namibians, is pertinent to the management of national resources.[79] In accordance with Article 100 of the Constitution, the state is the exclusive owner of all national resources, whether they are found on land, in the water, or both, unless they are otherwise lawfully possessed. Article 100's overall significance is that the state must hold title to the country's natural resources in the name of all Namibians, including the SSF. Although the SSF have not yet been

---

[78] See Erasmus (1089–1990), p. 81. See also Szasz (1989–1990), pp. 65–80.
[79] Article 95 (l) of the Constitution.

expressly recognized in the present legal system, the government of Namibia's intention to grant them the ability to use natural resources is indicated by the National Plan of Action on the SSF's recent approval.

4.2 The Marine Resources Act 27 of 2000

The Marine Resources Act (MRA) calls for the sustainable use, conservation, protection, and promotion of maritime resources as well as the preservation of the marine ecosystem.[80] Regulations Relating to the Exploitation of Marine Resources have been published by the Minister of Fisheries and Marine Resources (the Minister) in accordance with section 61(1) of the MRA.[81] The Fisheries Act 29 of 1992 was completely repealed by the MRA.[82] Simplifying and streamlining the many laws pertaining to marine resources was one of the goals of the MRA.

4.3 Artisanal and Subsistence Fisheries

Artisanal fisheries are not defined by the MRA; hence the Act lacks any provisions that would formally allow this group of fishers access to marine resources. The MRA and the Regulations make a distinction between the harvesting of marine resources for commercial and recreational uses. The MRA gives a broad definition of "commercial purposes," which encompasses harvesting "with the intention of selling, trading, or pledging" as well as "exceeding the limits set for the collection of marine resources for private use."[83] Harvesting for dietary purposes is included in the concept of "recreational purpose".[84] Given the expansive definition of "harvesting marine resources for commercial reasons," persons who fish for subsistence are not allowed to sell or trade any surplus catches and are only allowed to harvest marine resources for "own use," which implies personal or consumptive uses. In particular, section 8.5 of the Regulations enables a person without a fishing license to harvest and keep for personal use a number of designated marine resources.[85]

The Marine Resources Regulations' Annexure K lists the amount or mass that may be taken without a fishing license.[86] Therefore, even while measures for the administration of this sector are not provided, subsistence fisheries and subsistence

---

[80] MFMR (2000) Preamble to Marine Resources Act.

[81] Regulations Relating to the Exploitation of Marine Resources No. 241 of 2001.

[82] Section 64(1) read with the Amendments schedule.

[83] Part 1 of the MRA No.27 of 2000.

[84] Part 1 of the Regulations relating to the exploitation of marine resources No.241 of 2001.

[85] Section 8(5).

[86] MFMR, 2001, Annexure K of Marine Resource Regulations 241.

fishers are not explicitly defined in the MRA, the Regulations imply that resource collection for subsistence use is recognized as a valid activity. However, it is clear that the government does not view the subsistence sector as a separate group of fishers needing specific management attention because subsistence use is covered by the legislation governing recreational fishing.

4.4 Recreational Fishing

The Namibian coast is becoming a well-liked tourist destination in large part due to the growing popularity of recreational fishing in Namibia. According to the Regulations, taking advantage of maritime resources for recreation involves doing so "for sport, leisure, or subsistence." Recreational fishermen must have a permit and are subject to a number of regulations, including those relating to the methods of harvest, daily bag limits, and forbidden species of bait. Anyone who violates or disobeys any of the regulations' provisions is guilty of an offense and must pay a fine.[87] Recreational fishermen do not need permits for a number of marine resource types.

As previously indicated, these Regulations give subsistence fishermen a chance to get access to marine resources for exclusive consumption. Potential subsistence users may encounter barriers due to the administrative processes needed to obtain these resources, the costs associated with using them, and the penalties associated with breaking the law. Furthermore, it is unknown if those who consider themselves to be subsistence fishermen are aware of these possibilities to obtain access to marine resources through the regulations governing fishing for recreational purposes.

4.5 Commercial Fisheries

The fishing industry in Namibia has grown over the years to become one of the country's most significant economic sectors and the only one to do so since independence. The MRA focuses on the management and control of persons who participate in resource harvesting for profit. Below are several provisions pertinent to commercial exploitation that are highlighted because they are pertinent to some artisanal-level small-scale fishing operations. It is worthwhile to look more closely at the meaning of "commercial purposes".[88] The phrase "commercial purposes" has a

---

[87]Regulations 7 and 8.

[88]"Commercial purposes" with respect to harvesting marine resources means: (1) "with the intention of selling, bartering, pledging or otherwise disposing of, or delivering or offering to do any of the things mentioned in this paragraph in respect of resources"; (2) "using purse seine, trawl or long line, or such other fishing or harvesting methods as may be prescribed"; and/or (3) "exceeding the limits prescribed for the harvesting of marine resources for own use."

very broad definition. As a result, when someone goes over the restrictions set forth for the personal use of marine resources, that individual will have engaged in commercial fishing activities. Therefore, a fisher would be considered to be fishing for a commercial purpose and as such would need the required licence or quota if they occasionally sell or barter their excess catch or go beyond the limitations set for the gathering of marine resources for their own use.

Fishers and operations that can be categorized as artisanal fishing should also be aware of some parts in Part VI, Commercial Harvesting of Marine Resources. The requirements and/or prerequisites for exploiting marine resources are outlined in Section 32. No one is allowed to exploit marine resources for commercial use without a right, an exploratory right, or a fisheries agreement, according to Sub-sections 1 to 6. Additionally, any vessel used to extract marine resources for profit needs a license, and some marine resources are subject to limitations.[89]

Because there are no express provisions in the statute providing for artisanal fishers, it is difficult for fishermen who may be considered artisanal fishers in other jurisdictions to participate in the fishing business. Additionally, these fishermen would be considered commercial fishermen under Namibian law and would be required to abide by the aforementioned legal criteria. It is significant to note that Namibia's coastal waters lack traditional artisanal fisheries, according to the government.[90]

In light of the information presented by Holtzhausen, this is questionable development[91] which implied that small boats engaged in inshore activities in the Walvis Bay region in the 1970s and 1980s utilizing handlines and set-nets. Hampton also refers to a small group of people who frequently fish with a rod and line with the intention of selling their catches.[92] The hard and hostile coastal environment and powerful Benguela current are cited as the primary causes of Namibia's lack of traditional artisanal fishing. Other concerns include the lack of local seafood markets

---

[89]The parameters that the Minister may consider while evaluating an application for a right are outlined in Section 33. The section provides as follows: (1) "whether or not the applicant is a Namibian citizen;" (2) "where the applicant is a company, the extent to which the beneficial control of the company vests in Namibian citizens;" (3) "the beneficial ownership of any vessel which will be used by the applicant;" (4) "the ability of the applicant to exercise the right in a satisfactory manner;" (5) "the advancement of persons in Namibia who have been socially, economically or educationally disadvantaged by discriminatory laws or practices which were enacted or practiced before the independence of Namibia;" (6) "regional development within Namibia;" (7) "co-operation with other countries, especially those in the Southern African Development Community;" (8) "the conservation and economic development of marine resources;" (9) "whether the applicant has successfully performed under an exploratory right in respect of the resource applied for;" (10) "socio-economic concerns;" (11) "the contribution of marine resources to food security"; and (12) "any other matter that may be prescribed."

[90]MFMR, 1991, White Paper on Responsible Development of the Fisheries Sector paragraph 1, p. 26.

[91]Holtzhausen (1999).

[92]Hampton (2003).

and rural coastal villages. These factors have caused the fishing sector to become completely industrialized and export-focused.

A study on a related BCLME Project on information pertinent to the artisanal fisheries sector in the BCLME region suggests that there are two to three fisheries in Namibia that could be classified as artisanal fisheries, despite the lack of legal recognition of a separate artisanal or small-scale commercial fisheries sectors. The Hanganeni Association Line Fishery in Henties Bay and the Beach Seine Fishery in Walvis Bay are the two fisheries that exhibit the traits of artisanal fisheries. An additional artisanal fishery that operates off of Walvis Bay and Swakopmund is the ski-boat line fishery.[93] Ski-boat fishing and line fishing are both legal for both recreational and commercial use. Fishing is done with actual equipment, mostly focusing on varieties of fish found along the coast.

In addition to the general ban on collecting marine resources for commercial purposes (unless under a right, an exploration right, or a fisheries agreement), the Act and Regulations' broad definitions[94] or quota, if the resource has been put subject to a quota), further restricts poor coastal residents' access to marine resources. However, the Minister may consider a variety of things when deciding whether to grant a right, such as the applicant's nationality, the advancement of people who had previously faced adversity, socioeconomic issues, and the value of maritime resources in ensuring food security.[95]

Furthermore, it is possible to request an exception from any or all of the MRA's provisions by using section 62 of the Act. According to Section 62(1)(b), "a particular category of people authorised or required to conduct any act under any legislation which would or might result in a contravention of this Act" may be exempted in writing by the Minister. Artisanal, subsistence, and small-scale commercial fishermen can petition to be exempted from any onerous MRA regulations that prevent them from engaging in such activities within the bounds of the law. Together with the Namibianisation policy, these provisions, do provide historically underprivileged people the opportunity to work in the commercial fishing industry.

Various problems and constraints exist which hamper the effective enforcement of fisheries legislation in Namibia. These include:

- high operational costs required for the effective deployment of operational resources (surveillance aircraft, patrol vessels and vehicles for the coastal inspection);
- vast geographical areas to be covered;
- inadequate training of fisheries inspectors; and
- omissions and legal loopholes in the MRA and Regulations.

---

[93] Batty and Tjipute (2001).

[94] MFMR, 2000, MRA, Article 32 (1).

[95] MFMR, 2000, MRA Article 33 (4) a-j.

5 Public Consultation

Through the Namibianisation process, previously disadvantaged individuals and coastal communities have been empowered to participate more actively in the fishing industry. However, the extent to which the poor from the coastal communities have actually gained access to benefits from the Namibianisation process, and have specifically gained direct access to marine resources, is unclear. The government promotes the Namibianisation of the fishing sector by encouraging the Namibianisation of the fishing fleet and processing and employment-creation on shore, but coastal subsistence and artisanal fishing communities are not recognised as a distinct fishing sector in Namibian.

Through the introduction and development of an Aquaculture Policy, Aquaculture Act and Aquaculture Strategic Plan, Ministry of Fisheries and Marine Resources Strategic Plan, and most recently the National Plan of Action on the SSF, the MFMR has started a number of initiatives for greater participation in the marine fisheries resources. The introduction and creation of policies that are responsive to the SSF has taken precedence for the Namibian government. This is clear from the creation of the National Plan of Action on the SSF, the establishment of an Aquaculture division within MFMR, the selection of an Aquaculture expert advisor to the Ministry, and recent statements by the Minister regarding Aquaculture policy and awareness campaigns published in regional newspapers. These regulations give the MFMR the chance to actively help coastal SSF and artisanal fishermen buy processing equipment and facilities and open up access to local markets. Subsistence, artisanal, and SSF are not sufficiently recognized under Namibia's present marine fisheries legislation as having unique rights and obligations. Regarding this, the legislation does not demonstrate or offer quantifiable conformance to the terms of numerous international law accords.

6 Inland Fisheries Resources Act 1 of 2003

The inland water resources of Namibia play an important role in providing food and a source of livelihood to thousands of rural dwellers and/or families. The inland fisheries are described as largely subsistence although there is increasing use of modern gear, and the implementation of fishing effort is shifting this fishery into a small-scale commercial operation. Aspects of the inland fisheries policy and legislation are described and discussed because of their relevance to artisanal fisheries.[96] The Namibian inland water resources cover approximately 50,000 km^2. Inland fish production was estimated at 2800 met in 1994 and the potential production is estimated at 15,000 mt.

---

[96]MFMR (1995) Responsible Management of the Inland Fisheries of Namibia.

Inland fisheries are mainly subsistence in nature, and are labour intensive.[97] General surveys indicate that mainly women, children and older men use traditional fishing gear with low efficiency. It would appear that the inland fishery sector in Namibia seems to be in a state of rapid transition from subsistence to becoming increasingly commercialised. The increase in commercialisation of these inland fisheries has the social consequences of a widening gap between the majority small-scale subsistence fishers and minority commercial fishers, increasingly excluding women and children from this sector.[98]

The Inland Fisheries Act was promulgated in 2003 and is in early stages of implementation. The Pre-amble to the Act states as follows: "to provide for the conservation and protection of aquatic ecosystems and the sustainable development of inland fisheries resources; to provide for the control and regulation of inland fishing and to provide for related matters."[99] This Act came into effect on 23 April 2003 and is thus in its infant stage of implementation. The Act does define "subsistence fisheries" as "those fishing activities whose fishers regularly catch fish using traditional fishing gear for personal and household consumption and engage from time to time in the local sale or barter of excess catch."[100] The Act furthermore provides that the provisions relating to fishing licences and the registration of nets do not apply to subsistence fisheries by means of traditional gear.[101] Thus, subsistence fishers are provided for in terms of the Act and are allowed to sell or barter their excess catch. However, the Regulations make no mention of subsistence fishers and have failed to further regulate this category of fishers. There is no specific mention of artisanal fishers in the Act or the Regulations.

In general terms, the Namibian fisheries policies and laws are in conformity with the Namibian Constitution, UN Fish Stocks Agreement and, to some extent, through the Namibianisation policy, the FAO Code of Conduct for Responsible Fisheries. However, the Namibian fisheries policies and laws which govern marine resources do not recognise artisanal fishers as a legitimate category of fishers, and in this regard do not comply with certain principles and provisions in the FAO Code of Conduct for Responsible Fishers and the SADC Protocol on fisheries. The official position of the Ministry of Fisheries and Marine Resources in Namibia is that there is no artisanal fisheries sector in the country because environmental conditions are not conducive to such a sector. Consequently, the fishing industry is highly industrialised and export oriented. However, the Marine Resources Act and associated Regulations do make provision for harvesting resources for subsistence use in

---

[97]MFMR (1995) Responsible Management of the Inland Fisheries of Namibia, paragraph 2.1, p. 11.

[98]MFMR (1995) Responsible Management of the Inland Fisheries of Namibia, paragraph 2.1, p. 11.

[99]MFMR (1991) White Paper on Towards Responsible Development of the Fisheries Sector.

[100]Part 1 (Definitions) of the Inland Fisheries Resources Act.

[101]Section 31 (2) of the Inland Fisheries Resources Act.

terms of the Regulations governing recreational fishing, although no sale or barter of excess catch is permitted.

7   Human Rights Issues Informing Access to Finance

This section will discuss some of the most prominent human rights underpinning SDG target 14.b and resultantly financial inclusion. The right to work and to free choice of employment is a fundamental human right enshrined in the Universal Declaration of Human Rights (UDHR)[102] and the International Covenant on Economic, Social and Cultural Rights (ICESCR),[103] among others. The right to work is the foundation for the realisation of other human rights and includes the opportunity to earn a livelihood by work freely chosen or accepted.[104] In realising this right, States (including Namibia) are obliged to ensure the availability of technical and vocational guidance and develop an enabling environment for productive employment opportunities in a non-discriminatory manner.[105] Likewise, ILO Convention No. 111 on discrimination in employment and occupation aims to eliminate discrimination and lack of equal opportunities in accessing work and employment. Hence, this Convention is relevant not only in addressing discrimination within the small-scale fisheries sector, but also in addressing discrimination against the sector, as the Convention prohibits discrimination against traditional occupations such as fisheries. Once employed, one has access to financial services and credit.

7.1   Adequate Standard of Living

The right to an adequate standard of living is a fundamental human right enshrined the UDHR, the ICESCR, and numerous other instruments. The right to an adequate standard of living encompasses a series of more specific rights necessary for upholding health and well-being, such as the rights to food; housing; medical care; social services; and security in the event of unemployment, sickness, disability, widowhood, old age or other lack of livelihood.[106]

---

[102] UN General Assembly, Universal Declaration of Human Rights, 10 December 1948, 217 A (III).

[103] UN General Assembly, *International Covenant on Economic, Social and Cultural Rights*, 16 December 1966, United Nations, Treaty Series, volume 993, p. 3.

[104] See section 3 of the Namibia Labour Act 11 of 2007; See also Article 9(3)(a)(e) of the Namibia Constitution on the Prohibition of Forced Labour.

[105] United Nations Committee on Economic, Social, and Cultural Rights (2006), General Comment 18, E/C.12/GC/18.

[106] Universal Declaration of Human Rights, article 25.

Many small-scale fishermen live in poverty with insufficient income to ensure an adequate standard of living, due to adverse impacts of commercialisation, overfishing, climate change and unfair distribution of access to marine resources between large-scale and small-scale fishers. Ensuring ethical and fair business practices in trade are also critical. Loss of fishing resources and incomes for coastal communities is particularly problematic in many developing countries and has considerable negative impacts on the use of fish as a source of food security for the most vulnerable and marginalised.[107] Moreover, many small-scale fishers and fish workers do not have access to social security, which could help mitigate the effects of, for example, climate change, shocks and disasters, overfishing, fishing bans and conservation measures, and discriminatory regulations and policies.

In Namibia, Article 95 of the Constitution of Namibia makes provision for the Promotion of the Welfare of the People.[108] The fisheries ministry, with technical support from the FAO, has committed to implementing voluntary guidelines for securing sustainable small-scale fisheries in the context of food security, poverty alleviation and access to financial services. The end result of the immediate above outlined approach is that a NPOA-SFF for Namibia has been developed.

7.2   Equality and Non-discrimination

Financial inclusion also ensures the SSF's access to rights to equality and non-discrimination. These are fundamental human rights principles enshrined in

---

[107] Chan et al. (2019), pp. 17–25.

[108] This Article is provided for under Chapter 11 of the Constitution which deals with Principles of State Policy. The State shall actively promote and maintain the welfare of the people by adopting, inter alia, policies aimed at the following: (1) enactment of legislation to ensure equality of opportunity for women, to enable them to participate fully in all spheres of Namibian society; in particular, the Government shall ensure the implementation of the principle of non-discrimination in remuneration of men and women; further, the Government shall seek, through appropriate legislation, to provide maternity and related benefits for women; (2) enactment of legislation to ensure that the health and strength of the workers, men and women, and the tender age of children are not abused and that citizens are not forced by economic necessity to enter vocations unsuited to their age and strength; (3) . . .; (4) . . .; (5) . . .; (6) . . .; (7) . . .; (8) a legal system seeking to promote justice on the basis of equal opportunity by providing free legal aid in defined cases with due regard to the resources of the State; (9) ensurance that workers are paid a living wage adequate for the maintenance of a decent standard of living and the enjoyment of social and cultural opportunities; (10) consistent planning to raise and maintain an acceptable level of nutrition and standard of living of the Namibian people and to improve public health; (11) encouragement of the mass of the population through education and other activities and through their organisations {organizations} to influence Government policy by debating its decisions; (12) maintenance of ecosystems, essential ecological processes and biological diversity of Namibia and utilization of living natural resources on a sustainable basis for the benefit of all Namibians, both present and future; in particular, the Government shall provide measures against the dumping or recycling of foreign nuclear and toxic waste on Namibian territory.

all international instruments. In many parts of the world, the commercialisation of fisheries has led to or exacerbated discrimination and marginalisation of small-scale artisanal fishers and fish workers. This happens through many mechanisms, inter alia, financial exclusion, disproportionate subsidies for industrial fishing, privatisation of access to marine fisheries, corruption in the management of fisheries, exploitation in value chains, overfishing and different forms of illegal fishing. Moreover, while fisheries provide employment to millions of people and generate a highly valuable trade, unfair benefit-sharing and exploitative labour practices mean many workers in small-scale fisheries face high levels of poverty.

Moreover, patterns of discrimination against particular groups of rights-holders—based on characteristics or 'grounds of discrimination' such as ethnicity, gender, migratory or social and economic status—are often reflected or exacerbated within the sector. Men, for example, are most at risk of human trafficking, while women often are less represented in organisations, do 'invisible' pre- and post- harvest work, have less access to skills training, are paid low wages and are subject to sexual harassment. Article 10 of the Constitution of Namibia provides as follows: (1) All persons shall be equal before the law. (2) No persons may be discriminated against on the grounds of sex, race, colour, ethnic origin, religion, creed or social or economic status.

7.3   Recognition of Labour Rights

Recognition of labour rights can also lead to financial inclusion. Both international human rights instruments and the core labour conventions of the International Labour Organization (ILO) protect freedom of association and collective bargaining, as well as prohibit discrimination, child labour and forced labour. Commonly identified labour issues in small-scale fisheries relate to: Occupational safety and health as certain types of fishing are considered among the most hazardous occupations in the world); limited access to health care; gender-based discrimination; no or weak work agreements, leading to insufficient rest and remuneration; and barriers to accessing social security. Moreover, child labour is widespread in the fisheries sectors,[109] including the worst forms of child labour when fishing is hazardous and labour-intensive,[110] critical thinking and application around employment creation needs to be explored to change the status quo.

Artisanal fisheries can help create employment and economic activities in both coastal and in riverine communities especially where job options remain limited. These opportunities can only be explored once provisions for "Artisanal fisheries" are made in the MRA. There are eminent amendments of the MRA. Such strategic amendments for incorporating the SSF in the MRA could have a potential impact on

---

[109] FAO (2021a, b).

[110] International Labour Organisation (2013).

the local economy. The recognition of the rights of indigenous peoples could also be a vehicle to realising financial inclusion of the SSF in Namibia.[111] The Constitution of Namibia prohibits discrimination on grounds of ethnic or tribal affiliation. However, the constitution does not specifically recognize the rights of Indigenous Peoples or minorities, and there is no national legislation that deals directly with Indigenous Peoples.[112]

7.4 Cultural Rights

The ICESCR reaffirms that everybody has the right to take part in cultural life and that minorities have a right to enjoy their own culture, to profess and practise their own religion and to use their own language. Communities of small-scale fishers and fish workers often represent specific but diverse ways of life and hold rich knowledge systems of global significance for sustainable development. Hence, respect for the cultures of fishing communities, their forms of organisation, and traditional knowledge and practices is a precondition for the sustainable development of the sector.

8 Recommendations

The following recommendations are advanced to ensure financial inclusion for the SSF in Namibia:

(a) There is need to amend the current fisheries legislation to recognise SSF. In this way SSF can become formalized and be able to access financial services. The recently adopted National Plan of Action is not adequate to achieve the fundamental objective of ensuring that SSF access financial services in Namibia.
(b) There is need to secure SSF in the Context of Poverty Eradication and Food Security (SSF Guidelines), as endorsed by the 31st Session of the FAO Committee on Fisheries in 2014, and particularly its article 6.4 which provides that there is need to "support the development of and access to other services that are appropriate for SSF communities with regard to, for example, savings, credit and insurance schemes, with special emphasis on ensuring the access of women to such services".

---

[111] Rights to indigenous people are enshrined in the UN Declaration on the Rights of Indigenous Peoples and ILO Convention No. 169. Indigenous peoples have rights to lands, territories and resources (including marine resources) that they have traditionally owned or otherwise occupied and used.
[112] Chiripanhura and Teweldemedhin (2016).

(c) Rural and agriculture finance institutions, fisheries and finance authorities, Non-Governmental Organisations and other stakeholders in Namibia need to endorse, as relevant, and actively promote access of SSF to insurance services in Namibia, and access to micro-finance and credit programmes in support of SSF in Namibia.

(d) The government of Namibia together with FAO must develop the Programme on Capacity building for small-scale fisheries in micro-finance, credit and insurance services and seeks support from micro-finance, credit and insurance institutions and other industry actors, for its implementation in Namibia.

(e) The MFMR must collect and make available production information, socio-economic data of fishers (including a fishers registration/record) and loss and damage assessment reports following natural disasters, specifically on SSF, to facilitate financial services market and risks assessments.

(f) The MRMR, in close consultation with relevant ministries, make third party liability insurance (where available) mandatory for obtaining and renewal of respectively fishing vessel registrations, fishing licenses and authorizations to fish.

9 Conclusion

While the Namibianisation Policy has resulted in several direct and indirect benefits to Namibian citizens, there is still lack of support, both financial and technical, for previously disadvantaged individuals, in particular new black entrants, entering the fishing sector for the first time. It is apparent that neither subsistence nor artisanal fishers or these fishery sectors are clearly defined in the legislation governing marine resources management in Namibia. Besides the support provided to the Hanganeni Fishermen's Association, other subsistence and artisanal fishers have not received adequate consideration, protection and support. However, despite the current inadequacies in the legislation to address the needs and interests of existing and potential coastal artisanal and subsistence fishers, the current legislation does provide the Minister with sufficient discretion and powers to accommodate subsistence fishing and artisanal sectors as a separate category of resource users.

There are also inadequate mechanisms available to previously disadvantaged fishers, in particular the poor and marginalised people living in coastal communities, for gaining access to marine resources as a means of livelihood. This is exacerbated by the fact there is currently no formal legal mechanism for coastal communities or small-scale fishers to gain access to marine resources so as to contribute to their livelihoods and generate a modest income. Although subsistence fishers can harvest resources if they obtain recreational fishing permits, the application processes and permit fees may be too onerous for this group of fishers, effectively excluding them from benefiting from marine resources.

There is a clear need for legislative review regarding the MRA and its regulations so as to recognise SSF as a separate category of fishers with defined rights and responsibilities. Financial assistance should be provided to subsistence coastal fishing communities by means of the development of viable projects which provide training to develop SSF business ventures. Once the SSF is recognised in the existing fisheries legislation, microfinance programmes which have a social impact on the SSF could be introduced. Micro finance programmes promote investment in human capital and contribute to increased awareness of reproductive health among poor families. Adult literacy rate is significantly higher among the eligible participants. Such microfinance programmes are also likely to have a positive impact on women empowerment. Women in the SSF will be able to acquire assets of their own and exercise power in household decision making. They will also realise a significant increase in their access to credit. Microcredit programmes make women come to the center meeting and that helps build their confidence. Microcredit allows a woman to handle money. Domestic violence might also be significantly reduced due to women's personal influence in income generation and through group action. Microcredit programmes can also increase women's participation in the activities of local government. Some women microcredit clients can elected as Chairpersons and members of various SSF committees.

Ensuring access to financial services for the SSF may also positively impact on the local economy. Financial inclusion programmes related to the SSF may have spillover effects in local economies, thereby increasing local village welfare. Microfinance not only affects the welfare of participants and non-participants, but also facilitates aggregate welfare at village level. Access to financial services for the SSF may also lead to commercial viability and Self-reliance. The issue of regulation and supervision of the SSF's access to financial services is also crucial. Regulation would protect the interest of SSF members when they access credit. If they operate under a proper regulatory authority, the monitoring system will develop to comply with certain regulatory requirements. Government programs and commercial banks' participation in microfinance to the SSF are now required in Namibia, as they play useful promotional and development roles in this sector. The important observation is that the microfinance operations are now more self-reliant than before; it has funded half of its operation from local sources that comprise members' savings and service charges on loan.

Bibliography

Ankintola SL, Fakoya KA (2017) Small-scale fisheries in the context of traditional post-harvest practice and the quest for food and nutritional security in Nigeria. Agric Food Secur 6:1–17. https://doi.org/10.1186/s40066-017-0110-z
Aquaculture Act 18 of 2002
Bank of Namibia (2001) Optimal Financial Structure for Namibia. https://www.bon.com.na/CMSTemplates/Bon/Files/bon.com.na/bb/bb4b1702-a266-4ebc-9b3f-48b0ac170bbb.pdf. Accessed 12 Jan 2022

Bank of Namibia (2017) Namibia Financial Capability Survey. http://www.fli-namibia.org/cms/wp-content/uploads/2018/11/namibia-financial-capability-survey-2017.pdf.   Accessed 10 July 2022

Bank of Namibia (2021) Financial Technology (FINTECH) Innovations Regulatory Framework. https://www.bon.com.na/CMSTemplates/Bon/Files/bon.com.na/e8/e833f19c-86ca-4eea-a801-638b912ae6f8.pdf. Accessed 12 Jan 2022

Bank of Namibia (n.d.) Guidelines for Filing Customer Complaints. https://www.bon.com.na/Bank/Banking-Supervision/Guidelines-for-Lodging-Customer-Complaints.aspx.   Accessed 10 July 2022

Batty M, Tjipute M (2001) Information on Resources for Namibia, Draft BCLME Report

Batty M, Tjipute M (2005) Overview and Analysis of Social, Economic and Fisheries Information to Promote Artisanal Fisheries Management in the BCLME Region – Namibia: Final report and Recommendations. http://archive.iwlearn.net/bclme.org/projects/docs/Final%20report%20AFSE-03-01%20Namibia%20overview.pdf. Accessed 11 Jan 2022

Beck T (2015) Microfinance-A Critical Literature Survey. Independent Evaluation Group Working Paper 2015/4, pp 1–59

Bertheussen BA, Dreyer BM, Hermansen O, Isaksen JR (2021) Institutional and financial entry barriers in fishery. Mar Policy 123:1–9

Brugère C, Holvoet K, Allison E (2008) Livelihood diversification in coastal and inland fishing communities: misconceptions, evidence and implications for fisheries management. Working paper, Sustainable Fisheries Livelihoods Programme (SFLP). Rome, FAO/DFID, pp 1–39

Chan C, Tran N, Pethiyagoda S, Crissman CC, Sulser TB, Phillips MJ (2019) Prospects and challenges of fish for food security in Africa. Global Food Secur 20:17–25

Chiripanhura B, Teweldemedhin M (2016) An analysis of the fishing industry in Namibia: the structure, performance, challenges, and prospects for growth and diversification. African Growth and Development Policy Working Paper 0021, pp 1–84

Daniels O (2020) HAFA Drives Job Creation. https://www.erongo.com.na/news/hafa-drives-job-creation-2020-02-25. Accessed 12 Jan 2022

Erasmus G (1089–1990) The Namibian Constitution and the application of international law. S Afr Yearb Int Law 15:81

Erastus AN (2002) The development of the Namibianisation Policy in the Hake Subsector, 1994-1999. The Namibian Economic Policy Research Unit (NEPRU) Research Report No. 82, June 2002

FAO (2012) Cooperatives in small-scale fisheries. https://www.fao.org/family-farming/detail/en/c/273930/. Accessed 12 Jan 2022

FAO (2014) Policy Support and Governance Gateway, Sustainable Fisheries and Aquaculture for Food Security and Nutrition A Report by the High-Level Panel of Experts on Food Security and Nutrition June 2014. HLPE Report 7, pp 1–119

FAO (2019) Guidelines for Increasing Access of Small-scale Fisheries to Insurance Services in Asia: a handbook for Finance and Fisheries Stakeholders. https://www.apraca.org/wp-content/uploads/2019/07/ssf-insurance_Apraca_FAO.pdf. Accessed 9 July 2022

FAO (2020a) Implementing the SSF Guidelines in Asia and the Pacific. https://www.fao.org/voluntary-guidelines-small-scale-fisheries/news-and-events/detail-zh/zh/c/1272959/. Accessed 9 July 2022

FAO (2020b) Legislating for Sustainable Small-Scale Fisheries – a guide and considerations for implementing aspects of the Voluntary Guidelines for Securing Sustainable Small-Scale Fisheries in the Context of Food Security and Poverty Eradication in national legislation. Rome. https://doi.org/10.4060/cb0885en. Accessed 12 Jan 2022

FAO (2020c) The State of World Fisheries and Aquaculture 2020. Sustainability in action. Rome. https://doi.org/10.4060/ca9229en. Accessed 11 Jan 2022

FAO (2021a) Global network for Capacity Building to increase access of small-scale fisheries to financial Services (CAFI SSF Network). https://www.fao.org/voluntary-guidelines-small-scale-fisheries/news-and-events/detail/en/c/1396376/. Accessed 10 Jan 2022

FAO (2021b) Tackling child labour in fisheries and aquaculture, Background paper. Rome. https://doi.org/10.4060/cb7159en. Accessed 14 July 2022

FAO (2022a) Financial Services Provision to Small-scale Fisheries. https://www.fao.org/publications/card/en/c/CB9021EN/. Accessed 10 July 2022. See also FAO in Namibia (2022) Mapping women in small-scale fisheries. https://www.fao.org/namibia/news/detail-events/ru/c/1492150/. Accessed 10 July 2022

FAO (2022b) Namibia's National Plan of Action for small-scale fisheries (NPOA-SSF). https://www.fao.org/voluntary-guidelines-small-scale-fisheries/news-and-events/detail/en/c/1492006/. Accessed 12 July 2022

Fisheries and Marine Resources Act 27 of 2000

Food and Agriculture Organisation of the United Nations (2022) Voluntary Guidelines for Securing Small-Scale Fisheries in the Context of Food Security and Poverty Eradication. https://www.fao.org/voluntary-guidelines-small-scale-fisheries/en/. Accessed 10 Jan 2022

Hampton I (2003) Harvesting the Sea, Chapter 5. In: Molloy, Kainan R (eds) Namibia's Marine Environment. Directorate Environmental Affairs, Windhoek

Holtzhausen H (1999) Population dynamics and life history of West Coast Steenbras. PhD Dissertation, University of Port Elizabeth

Inland Fisheries Resources Act 1 of 2003

International Labour Organisation (2013) Caught at Sea: Forced Labour and Trafficking Guidelines. https://www.ilo.org/wcmsp5/groups/public/%2D%2D-ed_norm/%2D%2D-declaration/documents/publication/wcms_214472.pdf. Accessed 10 July 2022

Karmakar KG, Mehta GS, Ghosh SK, Selvaraj P (2009) Review of the development of microfinance services for coastal small scale fisheries and aquaculture for South Asia countries (including India, Bangladesh & Sri Lanka) with special attention to women, Paper presented in the Asia Pacific Fisheries Commission (APFIC) Regional Consultative Workshop "Best Practices to Supporting and Improving Livelihoods Small Scale Fisheries and Aquaculture Households", 13–15 October 2009, Manila, Philippines

Kusakabe K, Thongprasert S (2022) Women and men in Small-scale Fisheries and Aquaculture in Asia: barriers, constraints and opportunities towards equality and secure livelihoods. https://www.fao.org/3/cb9527en/cb9527en.pdf. Accessed 9 July 2022

Macusi ED, Siblos SKV, Betancourt ME, Macusi ES, Calderon MN, Bersaldo MJI, Digal LN (2022) Impacts of COVID-19 on the catch of small-scale fishers and their families due to restriction policies in Davao Gulf, Philippines. Front Mar Sci 8:770543. https://doi.org/10.3389/fmars.2021.770543

Marenga R, Amupanda J (2021) The coronavirus and social justice in Namibia. S Afr J Polit Stud 48(2):206–225

MFMR (1991) White Paper on Towards Responsible Development of the Fisheries Sector. http://the-eis.com/elibrary/sites/default/files/downloads/literature/White_Paper_on_the_Responsible_Management_of_the_Inland_Fisheries_of_Namibia.pdf. Accessed 15 July 2022

Ministry of Finance (2011) Namibia Financial Sector Strategy: 2011-2021. https://www.bon.com.na/CMSTemplates/Bon/Files/bon.com.na/e7/e7e69c6d-b02b-4109-8d3d-5b41a79f9d89.pdf. Accessed 10 July 2022

Ministry of Fisheries and Marine Resources Strategic Plan (2017–2018–2021/22). https://mfmr.gov.na/documents/411764/436229/Strategic+Plan+2017+-+2021.pdf/76a029eb-8aa3-061b-545b-2d48459b8350. Accessed 10 July 2022

Moyo T (2022) Fishing Industry Resurgence 2022, The Namibian 28 April 2022

Namibia Financial Institutions Supervisory Authority (2018) The Financial Literacy Initiative: A New National Platform to Enhance Financial Education. https://www.namfisa.com.na/educates/the-financial-literacy-initiative-a-new-national-platform-to-enhance-financial-education/. Accessed 15 July 2022

Namibia Labour Act 11 of 2007

Namibia's Marine Resources Policy: Towards Responsible Development and Management of the Marine Resources Sector (August 2004)

National Plan of Action for the SSF, June 2022

Nekwaya-Okafor S (2022) The Importance of Financial Inclusion, The Namibian 8 June 2022

Niner HJ, Barut NC, Baum T, Diz D, del Pozo DL, Laing S, Lancaster A, McQuaid KA, Mendo T, Morgera E, Maharaj PN, Okafor-Yarwood I, Ortega-Cisneros K, Warikandwa TV, Rees S (2022) Issues of context, capacity and scale: essential conditions and missing links for a sustainable blue economy. Environ Sci Policy 130:25–35

Oirere S (2022) Namibia launches plan to support small-scale fisheries, SeafoodSource 20 June 2022

Regulations Relating to the Exploitation of Marine Resources No 241 of 2001

Rice J (2017) Achieving and Maintaining Sustainable Fisheries. https://www.un.org/en/chronicle/article/achieving-and-maintaining-sustainable-fisheries. Accessed 11 Jan 2022

Rocca C (2021) Promoting Financial Inclusion of Small-scale Fisheries in Peru, Future of Fish, 8 January 2021

Shigwedha A (2022) Nam to promote Artisanal Fisheries and Aquaculture, The Namibian Business, 2 January p 11

Shrestha BP (n.d.) Institutional Credit for Fisheries Development in Nepal: A Case Study. https://www.fao.org/3/t0274e/T0274E08.htm. Accessed 5 July 2022

Stacey N, Gibson E, Loneragan NR, Warren C, Wiryawan B, Adhuri DS, Steenbergen DJ, Fitriana R (2021) Developing sustainable small-scale fisheries livelihoods in Indonesia: trends, enabling and constraining factors, and future opportunities. Mar Policy 132:1–12

Szasz PC (1989–1990) Succession to treaties under the Namibian. Constitution 15:65–80

The Constitution of the Republic of Namibia, 21 March 1990. https://www.refworld.org/docid/47175fd361.html. Accessed 7 July 2022

The Marine Resources Act 27 of 2000

The Marine Resources Regulations (Government Notice No 241, Regulations relating to the exploitation of Marine Resources, 2001)

The Namibian (2021) National Plan of Action for small scale fisheries being mooted, The Namibian (Agriculture News) 25 June 2021, p 7

The White Paper on the Responsible Management of the Inland Fisheries of Namibia (1995)

The World Bank (2016) Financial Inclusion in Namibia: Summary Note. https://view.officeapps.live.com/op/view.aspx?src=https%3A%2F%2Fdocuments1.worldbank.org%2Fcurated%2Ffr%2F376661479214149670%2F1478722578918-000022351-Namibia-Output-P147539-2016-10-28-04-51.docx&wdOrigin=BROWSELINK. Accessed 12 July 2022

The World Bank (2021) Key facts Statement Testing: Options, Methodologies, and Tools – Financial Inclusion Support Framework: Technical Brief. https://responsiblefinance.worldbank.org/en/responsible-finance/financial-consumer-protection. Accessed 20 Mar 2022

Tubino R, Monteiro-Neto C, de Souza Moraes LE, Paes E (2007) Braz J Oceanogr 55(3):187–197

UN General Assembly, Universal Declaration of Human Rights, 10 December 1948, 217 A (III)

UN General Assembly, International Covenant on Economic, Social and Cultural Rights, 16 December 1966, United Nations, Treaty Series, volume 993, p 3

United Nations Committee on Economic, Social, and Cultural Rights (2006), General Comment 18, E/C.12/GC/18

United Nations Conference on Trade and Development (UNCTAD) (2022) Harnessing Fishery Resources for Socio-Economic Development: Lessons for Angola and Haiti, UNCTAD/ALDC/INF/2021/5, pp 1–64

United Nations General Assembly Resolution adopted on September 2015. The 2030 Agenda for Sustainable Development specifically affirms that the SDGs 'seek to realize the human rights of all' (A/RES/70/1: http://undocs.org/A/RES/70/1). https://www.un.org/en/development/desa/population/migration/generalassembly/docs/globalcompact/A_RES_70_1_E.pdf. Accessed 11 Jan 2022

Tapiwa Victor Warikandwa (co-editor of the book)—Tapiwa Victor Warikandwa holds a Doctor of Laws in International Trade Law. He is a Senior Lecturer and former head of department in the Faculty of Law at the University of Namibia. He specialises in International Trade Law, Labour Law, Indigenisation Laws, Mining Law and Constitutional Law amongst other disciplines. Prior to coming to Namibia, Dr. Warikandwa worked as a legal officer and later legal advisor in the Ministry of Public Service Labour and Social Welfare in Zimbabwe. Key amongst his duties was legal drafting. Dr Warikandwa worked with the law reviser of the Ministry of Justice in Zimbabwe in reviewing laws administered by the Ministry of Public Service Labour and Social Welfare. Dr Warikandwa also completed an ordinary and advanced training in Labour Law Making at the International Labour Organization's International Training Centre in Turin Italy. On numerous occasions, Dr. Warikandwa was actively involved in the activities of the Cabinet Committee on Legislation on behalf of the Ministry of Public Service Labour and Social Welfare. Dr. Warikandwa has since written books on labour law and women's rights in South Africa and Namibia amongst others, as well as publishing articles in accredited peer reviewed journals such as Law, Development and Democracy, Speculum Juris, Journal for Black Studies, Potchefstroom Electronic Law Journal, Comparative International Law Journal for Southern Africa and the African Journal of International and Comparative Law, Juridical Tribune, amongst others. He was also a Post-doctoral Fellow and has also worked as a senior lecturer at the University of Fort Hare in South Africa. Dr Warikandwa studied for his Bachelor of Laws, Master's degree and Doctoral degree at the University of Fort Hare in South Africa. He currently is the Chief Editor of the Namibian Law Journal.

Elize Shakalela is a Law Lecturer and environmental justice advocate for the University of Namibia. Elize Shakalela has experience teaching environmental law and promoting sound environmental practices through advocacy. She is currently working on research focused on implementing effective environmental justice activities and raising awareness of the importance of international and national laws on environmental protection. Elize will be placed at Western Environmental Law Center in Eugene, to advance environmental justice in affected communities.

Eugene L. Libebe is a former magistrate and lectures in the Faculty of Law, Department of Public Law and Jurisprudence, at the University of Namibia. He holds a B. Juris degree, Bachelor or Laws Honours (LLB) and Master of Law in International Law. His areas of interest include public international law, economic law, climate change law and policy, African jurisprudence and decolonization, law of evidence, family law, sociology, political philosophy, leadership, communal conservancies and natural resources law.

Barriers to Integrating Financial Inclusion for Coastal Small-Scale Fishermen into Namibian Fisheries Policies and Regulatory Frameworks

Alex T. Kanyimba and Martha N. Jonas

Abstract The Ministry of Fisheries and Marine Resources has been applauded intercontinentally for laying the groundwork to develop the Namibian fisheries sector since the dawn of the country's independence in 1990. However, there are no financial inclusion policies for small scale artisanal fishermen. This paper aims to report on barriers to integrating financial inclusion for coastal small-scale fishermen into the Namibian fisheries policies and regulatory frameworks. This chapter reviews the understanding of financial inclusion, the elements of financial inclusion such bank inclusion and financial credit schemes breaks for the economically marginalized small-scale fishermen and access to fish markets for the small-scale fishermen. It provides a review of various international policies and regulatory frameworks that should guide financial inclusion of the small-scale fishermen. Among, the international policies, it is shown that the FAO guidelines for Securing Sustainable Small-Scale Fisheries in the Context of Food Security, the Sustainable Development Goals 14, target 14b and 17 have the potential to promote and strengthen financial inclusion for the small-scale fishermen. The national level policies and regulatory frameworks do not make specific reference to the small-scale fishermen. However, the development of the National Plan of Action for the small-scale fishermen in Namibia will be a potential for including small-scale fishermen into the Namibian policies and regulatory frameworks, although the aspect of financial inclusion is still unclear. The barriers to financial inclusion are that financial institutions are hesitant to run into business with the small-scale fishermen because the majority of them do not have collateral and bank accounts, they do not have access to the market for their harvest, they lack education, training and capacity, and have limited production capacity. There is also the skewed perception that the recognition of the small-scale fishermen will result in the over exploitation of marine resources if their capacity to catch more fish is enhanced. The small-scale fishermen are urged to set-up support

A. T. Kanyimba (✉) · M. N. Jonas
Department of Higher Education and Lifelong Learning, University of Namibia, Windhoek, Namibia
e-mail: akanyimba@unam.na; mnjonas@unam.na

© The Author(s), under exclusive license to Springer Nature Switzerland AG 2023
H. Chitimira, T. V. Warikandwa (eds.), *Financial Inclusion and Digital Transformation Regulatory Practices in Selected SADC Countries*, Ius Gentium: Comparative Perspectives on Law and Justice 106,
https://doi.org/10.1007/978-3-031-23863-5_15

organisations to promote representative participation in the development of policies and vouch for financial inclusion. The Government of Namibia is urged to set-up schemes to provide financial credit guarantees for the small-scale fishermen. Moreover, capacity strengthening among small-scale fishermen are recommended to provide expertise in post-harvest handling, preservation, processing, and marketing of marine products as well as providing an integral relationship with markets.

1 Introduction

The Namibian literature displays two main institutional frameworks that guide the management of fishing activities in the country. These are the marine-based sub-sector, and aquaculture sector respectively.[1] The marine based sector is capital intensive and include commercial Fishing activities and Recreational Fishing Activities.[2] Aquaculture includes fresh water fisheries and Mari-culture and the products thereof are geared towards the local market and food security. The aforementioned assertions seem to suggest that Namibia does not have a well-developed concept of the Small-Scale Fishermen (SSF) into the marine sub-sector. However, there seems to be consensus in Namibia that the term SSF is captured through the concept of Recreational Fishermen or Anglers. This scenario creates a semantic and conceptual inaccuracy because Recreational Fishing is primarily seen as fishing for enjoyment as opposed to Small Scale fishing whose main purpose is the production of subsistence food and other products.[3] Moreover, the literature shows that not all Non-commercial fishing around the world can be described as purely 'recreational'.[4] Some coastal fishermen in Namibia may wish to engage into coastal fishing to derive economic benefits at a relatively limited range. The authors hereby embrace the concept of SSF in this chapter because it is viewed as structurally different from large-scale commercial fishermen and semantically different from recreational fishermen.

The SSF are seldom explicitly mentioned in policies and regulatory frameworks around the world while they find themselves intertwined in weak socio-economic circumstances and poverty situations.[5] The publication by Bronnmann et al., explains that the SSF do not have the potential to sell their catch to the international markets and have very limited recognition by established financial institutions.[6] This scenario occurs locally and internationally despite that the fact that the SFF were accorded special recognition by the FAO code of conduct for responsible Fisheries

---

[1] Batty et al. (2005).
[2] Batty et al. (2005).
[3] Pawson and Padda (2008), pp. 339–350.
[4] Ibid.
[5] Sowman (2020).
[6] Bronnmann et al. (2020).

as important contributors to employment, income and food security.[7] The code of conduct States and all those engaged in fisheries management should, through an appropriate policy, legal and institutional framework, adopt measures for the long-term conservation and sustainable use of fisheries resources, conservation and management measures.[8] The FAO, Voluntary Guidelines for Securing Sustainable Small-Scale Fisheries in the Context of Food Security and Poverty Eradication explain that the Small-scale fisheries provide nutritious food for local, national and international markets and generate income to support local and national economies.[9]

The review of fisheries data in Namibia, does not reveal a policy or regulatory framework that extends financial inclusion benefits such as bank inclusion, credits and access to markets to the SSF. At the global level, the SSF were categorized by the International Labor Organization (ILO) as production units operated by single individuals or households that are not constituted as separate legal entities independent of their owners and in which capital accumulation and productivity are low.[10] These authors also explain that the SFF are engaged in informal labour activities that require access to financial services. This assertion is further supported by Sowman and Cardoso[11] who argue that there is a need for financial inclusion of the subsistence fishermen around the world. The view of the authors is that building financial inclusion for the SSF is Namibia will help to address the matter of inequality and economic marginalization and assert their contribution to the provision of nutritious food for local and national markets and generate income to support local and national economies. This would enhance a holistic approach encompassing dimensions of financial inclusion.[12] The holistic approach to financial inclusion moves beyond extending financial products to large scale fishermen but to also to small scale fishermen.

Presently, there is no universal definition of the SFF concept in Namibia. Owing to the lack of definition, the following criteria captured in the Batty et al. report is hereby used to understand the SSF concept. These criteria explain that the SFF in Namibia are small scale, privately owned, low technology, limited fishing range and catches used partly for subsistence.[13]

The above criteria show that the SSF Namibia is understood in terms of size, fishing gear and subsistence use only. Smith and Basurto argue that issue of the definition often presents a stumbling block for efforts to achieve mutual dialogue and consensus agreements on fisheries governance at national, regional, and global levels.[14] The authors Jentoft et al., explain that the SSF are by no means 'small',

---

[7] Soltanpour et al. (2017), pp. 425–428.

[8] FAO (2009).

[9] FAO (2018).

[10] Pomeroy et al. (2020), p. 118.

[11] Sowman and Cardoso (2010).

[12] Sowman (2020), p. 1.

[13] Batty et al. (2005).

[14] Smith and Basurto (2019).

on the contrary, they are much larger than previously thought and appear to have an outsized impact on human health and nutrition, poverty alleviation, job creation, and the structure of seafood markets.[15] This is not say that the SFF must operate at the level of large scale commercial fishermen but their aforementioned roles should be acknowledged, to facilitate the expansion and financial inclusion opportunities created nationally.

The SSF in Namibia need not be perceived as 'small' locally because globally, the financial contribution is critical from an employment and livelihoods perspective and simultaneously important for livelihoods.[16] Therefore, the Namibian coastal SSF need to have both the economic and physical benefit of sustainable catch of fish in order to help orientate them from predominantly subsistence fish harvesting to a developmental focus. The need for shift from subsistence fish harvesting to a development focus is captured in the Kanyimba, Tshininingayame and Jonas 2020 Report.[17] The report emphasizes that the Namibian coastal SSF require an enabling environment in terms of policies and legislation as key implementation mechanisms of ocean policy which in turn contributes to enhancing socio-economic development that is targeted to the benefit of all Namibians, and not only commercial fishermen. The authors of this chapter believe that this should be one of reasons for including sustainable principles of financial inclusion practices of the SSF into the Namibian Fisheries Policies and Regulatory Frameworks. This view is in line with the Sustainable Development Goal 14b (SDG 14B) that calls for the "provision of access for small-scale fishers to marine resources and markets".[18] The authors makes reference to the SDGs for the reason that most of the states, including Namibia, have adopted the SDGs, where the achievement of Sustainable Development (SD) is seen to a process to advance the economic, social, and ecological aspects of peoples livelihoods.[19]

This Chapter reports data collected through document analysis and an integration of qualitative data collected from participants in three coastal towns, namely Swakopmund, Walvisbay and Hentiesbay during November 2020–January 2020. The qualitative findings are captured and reported in Sect. 4 of this chapter. The population comprised of informal coastal community groups, the semi-formal community groups and multi-stakeholder groups. The informal coastal community group are participants who lived at the coast or migrated to the coast. The semi-formal community groups are participants that have been registered with local authorities. These include, women, youth, small-scale fishing associations, as well as mussel and shell collectors. The multi-stakeholder group comprised of the three local authorities (Walvisbay, Swakopmund and Hentiesbay), the representatives of the Hanganeni

---

[15] Jentoft et al. (2017).

[16] Finkbeiner (2015), pp. 139–152.

[17] Kanyimba et al. (2020).

[18] Sustainable Development Solutions Network https://indicators.report/targets/14-b/ accessed on 13 July 2021.

[19] UN General Assembly (2015).

Small scale fishing association, the TopNaar traditional authority and the Benguela Current Large Marine Ecosystem (BCLME).

Purposive sampling was used to select the stakeholders described above. Interviews were audio recorded and later transcribed. Informed Consent was sought from each and every participant in the study. Assurance and reassurance of their confidentiality and anonymity throughout data collection phase was explained in detail and time was taken to ensure participants understood and comprehend what was expected of them in the study. Participants were aware that their involvement was strictly voluntary, and they had the freedom to stop participating whenever they felt uncomfortable.

The purpose of this chapter is to undertake an evaluation of the barriers to integrating financial inclusion among coastal SSF into the Namibian fisheries policies and regulatory frameworks. Within this context, the term 'barriers' refers to obstacles that prevents access to financial capital while 'regulatory framework' is seen as conventions, laws, regulations, codes of conduct and control agreements[20] that should shape the development of the SSF. The rest of the sections of this chapter follow this sequence. First, section presents the understanding of financial inclusion, indicators of financial inclusion and reasons why the SFF experience financial exclusion in policies and regulatory frameworks. This is followed by an overview of the policy and regulatory frameworks that should govern the financial inclusion for the SSF. This section addresses policies and regulatory frameworks at international level and national level. Moreover, the chapter presents barriers to integrating indicators and dimensions of financial Inclusion into the Namibian policies and regulatory frameworks. The final section is about the way forward, which are some of the means to address barriers to financial inclusion for the coastal SSF in Namibia.

2 Understanding Financial Inclusion, Key Indicators and Dimensions of Financial Inclusion, Reasons Why the SFF Experience Financial Exclusion

The term 'financial inclusion' is an alien concept in context of the SSF in Namibia. For the sake of the objectives of this chapter, the term financial inclusion is seen as the practice of ensuring that access to appropriate financial services from established financial institutions are available to the SSF. The purpose of financial inclusion is to assist and realise the full potential of the SSF, and to develop their capacity and strengthen their fishing technology, skills-set so that they are able to engage in income-generating fishing activities, as well as manage risks associated with subsistence livelihoods of those associated with small scale fishing. The term financial inclusion has three dimensions: These are: access to financial services; usage of

---

[20]Rabeau (2021).

financial services, and quality of financial products and related service delivery.[21] Moreover, Box 1 shows some definitions of financial inclusion that may be relevant to the SSF in the Namibian context:

Box 1 Definitions of Financial Inclusion[22]
1. [To] be open and accepting the diversity of stakeholders and to expand opportunities and public access to finance industries.
2. Banking inclusiveness is a process of ensuring access to appropriate financial products and services needed by all sectors of the society and by vulnerable groups, such as the less advantaged socio-economic and low-income groups,
3. A state in which all working-age adults have effective access to credit, savings, payments, and l insurance from formal service providers.
4. Financial inclusion involves providing financial access to an adequate range of safe, convenient and affordable financial services to disadvantaged and other vulnerable groups that include low-income, rural and undocumented persons, who have been poorly or excluded from the formal financial sector
5. A process to ensure the access for the poor who are marginalized to various services of the financial system

The key indicators of financial inclusion that the authors adopt from Box 1 are financial diversity, bank inclusion and adequate credit services. Access to local fish market for the SSF is also another key indicator for financial inclusion. This indicator is not alluded to in Box 1 but contained in the Kanyimba, Tshiningayamwe and Jonas 2020 report as a financial inclusion measure.[23] For the sake of the purposes of this chapter, a fish market conceived as a place for the retail of fish and fish products harvested by the Coastal SSF. These indicators are chosen because it is believed that their holistic integration can create sustainable financial opportunities for the SSF, to enable them secure financial loans to purchase items relating to adequate fishing gear, to acquire fishing permits and acquire other related fishing expenses. In particular, diversity is the practice of including or involving different stakeholders into the financial sector, credit is the practice of securing sustainable loans. The notion of bank inclusion relates to the process of broadening the banking services prospects to include the marginalised members of the community and in this case, the SFF. Langenheim, reported that millions of Small-Scale Fishermen are facing economic exclusion because most national and international fishery and trade rules

---

[21] Shipalana (2019).

[22] Yuliana (2016), p. 24.

[23] Kanyimba et al. (2020).

are made with the industrial sector in mind.[24] This assertion is also augmented by the by Sowman and Cardoso publication.[25] Several reasons are cited in the literature that are primary causes for this financial exclusion. Box 2 presents several reasons why the SFF experience financial exclusion:

Box 2 Several Reasons for Why the SFF Experience Financial Exclusion[26]

1. [They] lack physical and livelihood assets, including land, that can be used as collateral;
2. Lack of education and financial literacy;
3. Inadequate savings organizational mechanisms;
4. They tend to be more individualistic orientated, are not functionally organized;
5. they do not have a credit history;
6. Low cultural willingness and/or inability to save;
7. Political and economic marginalization; and
8. Lack of bank accounts

Although the concepts of 'financial inclusion' SSF concept is relatively new in Namibia, the need to incorporate this term into the Namibian policies and regulatory frameworks is gathering momentum. The view of the authors is that positioning this term 'financial inclusion' into the Namibian policies and regulatory framework will be severely hampered by the lack of access to the financial markets among[27] the SFF because their catch is meant for domestic consumption.[28] The Report by Kanyimba, Tshininingayame and Jonas[29] indicated that one of the major challenges that the Namibian SSF have is that of paying for expensive fishing permits while their harvest is only for daily domestic consumption. This scenario implores the following question: How would the SSF afford to sustain acquisition of expensive permits and maintain a sustainable livelihood, if their catch is only for daily domestic consumption?

The above scenario requires that financial inclusion relating to bank inclusion and extending adequate credit and local fish markets, be positioned into the Namibian policies and regulatory frameworks to help the SFF earn credit for acquiring fishing permits and meet family financial needs and meet other expenses related to their fishing activities. The authors embrace the view that developing of financial

---

[24]Langenheim (2017).

[25]Sowman (2020).

[26]Pomeroy et al. (2020), p. 118.

[27]Kanyimba et al. (2020).

[28]Batty et al. (2005).

[29]Kanyimba et al. (2020).

inclusion in the Namibian policies and regulatory frameworks is important because it is a key enabler to reducing poverty, boosting financial capacity and promote inclusive development as well as address the SDG14, target 14b.[30] The World Bank and the United Nations recognize that financial inclusion can support overall economic growth by creating more stable financial systems and sustainable economies, mobilising financial domestic resources through national savings, and helping to boost government revenue.[31]

3 Policies and Regulatory Frameworks That Should Govern Financial Inclusion of SSF in Namibia

The discussion of the policy landscape and policy framework that should govern financial inclusion of the SSF in Namibia will cover the international and national policies. The authors will also attempt to reflect on ways in which these policies and legislative frameworks are governing and guiding the financial inclusion and help to reduce the barriers among the SFF in Namibia. The purpose of this exercise is to ascertain whether policies and regulatory frameworks have an aspect or a clause that can support financial inclusion for the SFF. This will then help in determining and highlighting existence of financial barriers or lack thereof of in those policies and regulatory frameworks.

3.1 International Policies and Regulatory Frameworks That May Govern Financial Inclusion of the Small-Scale Fishermen in Namibia

Namibia is part of the international community and therefore guided by international conventions. This section will discuss some international conventions that are of strategic influence to the Namibian policy landscape and regulatory frameworks, including the SFF. The discussion in this section will specifically include the following: The 1982 United Nations Convention on the Law of the Sea (UNCLoS), the Voluntary *Guidelines* for Securing Sustainable *Small-Scale Fisheries* in the Context of Food Security and Poverty Eradication and the UN 2030 Agenda for Sustainable Development (UNASD). The Convention, the FAO Guidelines and some aspects of the SDGs were selected for the review to offer guidance and to portray the international profile of the SSF paradigm that could justify need for financially including the SFF in Namibian policies and regulatory frameworks.

---

[30]Yin et al. (2020), p. 2524.
[31]Pomeroy et al. (2020), p. 118.

3.1.1   The United Nations Convention on the Law of the Sea

United Nations Convention on the Law of the Sea became binding in Namibia on the 16th of November 1994.[32] The convention sets out a legal framework within which all activities pertaining to the oceans need to be undertaken and established guidelines for businesses and environmental defenders on matters of sustainable managing of littoral and marine resources. In particular, section 61 (Conservation of the living resources) and section 62 (Utilization of the living resources). Article 61 states the following.[33]

> [The] coastal State shall determine the allowable catch of the living resources in its exclusive economic zone. The coastal State, taking into account the best scientific evidence available to it, shall ensure through proper conservation and management measures that the maintenance of the living resources in the exclusive economic zone is not endangered by over-exploitation. . .Such measures shall also be designed to maintain or restore populations of harvested species at levels which can produce the maximum sustainable yield, as qualified by relevant environmental and economic factors, including the economic needs of coastal fishing communities and the special requirements of developing States [. . .]

Article 62 explains the following[34]

> [The] coastal State shall promote the objective of optimum utilization of the living resources in the exclusive economic zone without prejudice to article. . .In giving access to other States to its exclusive economic zone under this article, the coastal State shall take into account all relevant factors, including, inter alia, the significance of the living resources of the area to the economy of the coastal State concerned and its other national interests, the provisions of articles 69 and 70, the requirements of developing States in the sub region or region in harvesting part of the surplus and the need to minimize economic dislocation in States whose nationals have habitually fished in the zone or which have made substantial efforts in research and identification of stocks [. . .]

There are two ways in which the above excerpts from the convention also alludes to the idea of financial inclusion. Firstly, it is through the idea of minimizing economic dislocation which may mean that people who have been trimmed of their cultures and economic activities through unfavorable policies and regulatory frameworks are provided socio-economic opportunities for financial recovery. Secondly, it is through the notion of national economic interest. The concept of national economic interest has long been manifested as a category used by political leaders to unite citizens towards achieving socio-economic development.[35] The view of the authors is that the national economic interest concept promotes inclusion because it urges coastal regions to promote economic activities.

---

[32] Warikandwa 'Notes Presented at the FAO and OOH Workshop on Legal Training on the Use of Diagnostic Tool for Small Scale Fishermen' (n.d.) Unpublished Notes, FAO & OOH.

[33] United Nations Convention on the Law of the Sea (n.d.).

[34] Ibid.

[35] FAO (2018).

3.1.2 Voluntary Guidelines for Securing Sustainable Small-Scale Fisheries in the Context of Food Security and Poverty Eradication

The Voluntary Guidelines for Securing Sustainable Small-Scale Fisheries in the Context of Food Security and Poverty Eradication were developed by FAO.[36] The following are objectives of the Voluntary Guidelines for Securing Sustainable Small-Scale Fisheries in the Context of Food Security and Poverty Eradication as shown in Box 3.

Box 3 The Objectives of the Voluntary Guidelines for Securing Sustainable Small-Scale Fisheries in the Context of Food Security and Poverty Eradication[37]

1. to enhance the contribution of small-scale fisheries to global food security and nutrition and to support the progressive realization of the right to adequate food,
2. to contribute to the equitable development of small-scale fishing communities and poverty eradication and to improve the socio-economic situation of fishers and fish workers within the context of sustainable fisheries management,
3. to achieve the sustainable utilization, prudent and responsible management and conservation of fisheries resources consistent with the Code of Conduct for Responsible Fisheries (the Code) and related instruments,
4. to promote the contribution of small-scale fisheries to an economically, socially and environmentally sustainable future for the planet and its people,
5. to provide guidance that could be considered by States and stakeholders for the development and implementation of ecosystem friendly and participatory policies, strategies and legal frameworks for the enhancement of responsible and sustainable small-scale fisheries, and
6. to enhance public awareness and promote the advancement of knowledge on the culture, role, contribution and potential of small-scale fisheries, considering ancestral and traditional knowledge, and their related constraints and opportunities

---

The nature and scope of the above objectives of the Voluntary Guidelines for Securing Sustainable Small-Scale Fisheries raises an international profile of SFF. Accordingly, the SSF Guidelines support the visibility, re-cognition, and enhancement of this globally important small-scale fisheries sector and promote socially inclusive small-scale fisheries by calling for an equitable distribution of fishing

---

[36]Isomov (2020), p. 2.
[37]FAO (2018).

rights and raise the importance of protecting all forms of legitimate marine tenure rights, from formal to informal, particularly for women that have been discussed and promoted globally.[38] Moreover, the FAO guidelines promote an important notion of public awareness and advancement of knowledge on the culture and potential of small-scale fisheries. The SSF Guidelines offer guidance on how to reduce the vulnerability and insecurity of fishing people by recognising their basic human rights, including rights to food, healthy environment, fisheries resources, capacity-building and education, livelihoods and work[39]

3.1.3   The United Nations 2030 Agenda for Sustainable Development

The 2030 Agenda for Sustainable Development presents a set of 17 interwoven global goals designed to create a blueprint to achieve a better and more sustainable future for all by the year 2030. The SDGs have made explicit the importance of conserving and fisheries resources and managing ocean resources. In particular, the Sustainable Development Goal 14 (SDG 14) which is about 'Life below Water" calls for the conservation and sustainable use of the oceans, seas and marine resources for sustainable development. Box 4 presents the targets of the SDG 14.

> **Box 4 Target of SDG 14[40]**
> Target 4.1: [Reduce] Marine Pollution
>   Target 14.2 Protect and Restore Ecosystems;
>   Target 14.3, Reduce Ocean Acidification;
>   Target 14.4 Sustainable fishing
>   Target 14, 5 Conserve Coastal and Marine Area;
>   Target 14.6 End Subsidies Contributing to Overfishing
>   Target 14.7, Increase the Economic Benefits from Sustainable Use of
> Marine Resources.

As can be seen in Box 4, these targets promote the sustainable utilization of fisheries resources, the reduction of activities that could lead to the destruction of fisheries resources and the increase in economic benefits from sustainable use of marine resources. In addition to the above are targets 14a–14c shown in Table 1.

Target 14*b* has potential to backing financial Inclusion in relation to SSF. It can be noted that the target promote support for the SSF to have access to the marine resources and to the markets. This is in contrast to the current policies of Namibian policies where the SSF or artisanal fishermen are allowed to catch only for recreational purposes and or for domestic consumption. The SFF needs to be supported to

---

[38] Pomeroy and Brooks (2019), pp. 361–370.

[39] Ibid.

[40] The United Nations Global Goals for Sustainable Development (2021).

Table 1 Target 14a–14c of the SDG 14 (Ibid)

Target	Goal	Elaboration of goal
Target 14a	[Increase] the Economic Benefits from Sustainable Use of Marine Resources	Increase scientific knowledge, develop research capacity and transfer marine technology, considering the Intergovernmental Oceanographic Commission Criteria and Guidelines on the Transfer of Marine Technology, in order to improve ocean health and to enhance the contribution of marine biodiversity to the development of developing countries, in particular small island developing States and least developed countries.
Target 14b	Support Small Scale Fishers	Provide access for small-scale artisanal fishers to marine resources and markets.
Target 14c	Implement and Enforce International Sea Law	Enhance the conservation and sustainable use of oceans and their resources by implementing international law as reflected in the United Nations Convention on the Law of the Sea, which provides the legal framework for the conservation and sustainable use of oceans and their resources, as recalled in paragraph 158 of "The future we want".

find the market for the sale of their catch. However, our view is that this realisation could materialize when the SFF have access to adequate financial resources. The UN Systems task team on post 2015 UN development agenda, (2013) explains the following: "[There] is a global consensus that achieving SD requires substantial mobilization and reallocation of financial resources which makes financing a central theme in the post-2015 development agenda".[41] This assertion seems to emphasize the role of SDG 17 as cross-cutting goal that support financial inclusion in the development process. The *UN Systems task team* further explains that global partnership for SD finance must remain a goal in itself, since it provides the vehicle to generate targets specific to finance. Box 5 presents the sources and tools for the sustained financing of SD.

Box 5 The Sources and Tools for the Sustained Financing of Sustainable Development
- [Mobilising] domestic public resources for sustainable development;
- Mobilising domestic and external private resources for sustainable development;
- Mobilising external public resources and improving development cooperation for sustainable development[42]

---

[41] UN Systems Task Team on Post 2015 UN Development Agenda (2013).
[42] Ibid.

It can be reasoned that the financial inclusion for the SSF is rooted in the SDG 14*b* and SDG 17 because there is a call for cooperation among the stakeholders to mobilise financial resources for SD. The notion of SDGs is to include all stakeholders including the SSF. The call for the mobilisation of financial resources must stem from local financial agencies, external partners and international financial agencies.

3.2 National Policies and Regulatory Frameworks That Should Govern Financial Inclusion for the SSF in Namibia

Before the independence of Namibia, the Namibian fisheries sector was actually guided by the South Africa colonial policies and regulatory frameworks. The literatures show at this time, the Namibian fisheries sector was over-fished and dominated by foreign fishing fleets.[43] This section discusses policies and regulatory frameworks that were undertaken since the independence of Namibia on 21 March 1990 and the purpose thereof is to help uncover areas or sections that could support or hinder financial inclusion for the SSF.

Since independence, the Namibian Fisheries Sector's legal framework became divided into two parts: one part governing the exploitation and management of marine resources and another governing the aquaculture sector.[44] It appears that since 1990, the Ministry of Fisheries and Marine Resources (MFMR) was charged with the responsibility to put an end to foreign legislation and established creditable financial policies and regulatory frameworks. Therefore, the following policies and regulatory frameworks will be unpacked. These include the Constitution of the Republic of Namibia, the Namibia Vision 2030, the National Development Plan 5, the Harambe Prosperity Plan II, and the White Paper on the Responsible Management of the Inland Fisheries of Namibia, Marine Resources Act no 27 of 2000 and the National Plan of Action/Strategy for Small Scale Fishermen in Namibia.

3.2.1 The Constitution of Republic of Namibia

The Constitution of Republic of Namibia is one of the key documents that govern inclusion in general. Section 95 which is titled promotion of the welfare of the people explain the following:[45]

---

[43] Manning (1998).

[44] Chiripanhura and Teweldemedhin (2016).

[45] Government of the Republic of Namibia 'Constitution of the Republic of Namibia' (1990) Republic of Namibia.

[The] State shall actively promote and maintain the welfare of the people by adopting, inter alia, policies aimed at the maintenance of ecosystems, essential ecological processes and biological diversity of Namibia and utilization of living natural resources on a sustainable basis for the benefit of all Namibians, both present and future; in particular, the Government shall provide measures against the dumping or recycling of foreign nuclear and toxic waste on Namibian territory.

The Constitution of the Republic of Namibia seems to call on the inclusion because it calls upon utilization of the natural resources on a sustainable basis for the benefit of all Namibians. The constitution is important because it obliges all players in Namibia to act according to the stipulations. The notion of inclusion alluded to here must include the commercial fishing companies and the SFF. There is also an aspect of intergenerational equity. This is the principle of sustainable development that should ensure that future generations should benefit from marine resources. The principle of equity is important because it may guide the obligation of ensuring all Namibians are included in benefiting from policies of empowerment, including financial aspects.

3.2.2   The Namibia Vision 2030

The Namibia Vision 2030 is the development plan that emphasizes the national goal of industrialisation and manufacturing, of which mining and agriculture are the core. The goal vision of the Namibia Vision 2030 is to create a 'prosperous and industrialized Namibia, developed by her human resources, enjoying peace, harmony and political stability'.[46] In terms of the fisheries, the intention of the Namibia Vision 2030 is to ensure that the Namibia's marine species and habitats significantly contribute to the economy and equitable socio-economic development, whilst maintaining biodiversity and the functioning of natural ecosystems in a dynamic external environment.[47] This mandate of ensuring that marine species and habitats significantly contribute to the economy and equitable socio-economic development was placed in the custodianship of the MFMR.

The Namibia Vision 2030 is a broader long-term national vision that does not specially address the aspect of financial inclusion of the SSF. However, the view of the authors is that notion of financial inclusion for the SSF is implicit in the national vision because it is a requirement for prosperity and industrialization, peace, harmony and political stability. Omar, Inaba (2020), explain that financial inclusion has moved up the global reform agenda and gained great interest for its potential to break the vicious cycle of poverty and lower income inequality.[48] As can be noted in the foregoing assertion financial inclusion for the SSF is essential to promote inclusive development and achieve the SDGs. However, the aspect of financial inclusion of the coastal SSF is yet to be realised in practice.

---

[46] Government of the Republic of Namibia 'Namibia Vision 2030–Policy Framework for Long-Term National Development' (2004) Republic of Namibia.

[47] Ibid.

[48] Omar and Inaba (2020), pp. 1–25.

3.2.3   The National Development Plan 5

Since independence of Namibia in 1990, the country has been developing National Development Plans (NDPS) to support the sustainable utilization of natural resources. The purpose if the NDPs is to support the realisation of national objectives elucidated in the Namibia Vision 2030. Presently, the NDP 5 is being implemented. The NDP 5 contain goals and intermediate targets that will lead to the nation to the realisation of the Namibian Vision 2030. The Government of the Republic of Namibia through NDP5 has outlined need for the 'Blue Economy', governance and management system by 2022.[49]

The NDP 5 is a broader national vision that does not specially address the SSF in specific terms. However, the NDP5 support the "institutionalization of marine spatial spanning". The concept of Marine Spatial Planning (MSP) is a practical way to create and establish a more rational and integrated approach to the human use of marine space and the interactions among these uses[50] and requires engagement of 'multiple actors and stakeholders at various governmental and societal levels'.[51] Our view is that to institutionalize marine spatial planning is to establish the practice of involving both the commercial fishermen as well as the SSF in the use of marine resources. The SSF must be explicitly catered for, as their fishing methods have been proven to be more of a sustainable nature when compared to the exploitative nature of the commercial fishing sector that catches fish on a very large marginal scale when compared to SSF. This view is also shared by the Namibian SSF who explained that those who contribute to overfishing are the commercial fishermen and not necessarily the Namibian SSF.[52]

3.2.4   The Harambe Prosperity Plan II

The Government of the Republic of Namibia has been developing the Harambe Prosperity Plan II. The Purpose of the Harambe Prosperity Plan II is to support the realisation of national objectives elucidated in the Namibia Vision 2030 and the NDPs.[53] The third pillar of the Harambe Propriety Plan II addresses the notion of economic advancement.[54] Under this pillar, there is a section titled optimizing the stewardship of natural resources as shown in Box 6.

---

[49] Government of the Republic of Namibia. 'Namibia Fifth National Development Plan *2017-2022'* (2017) Republic of Namibia.

[50] Ehler (2013).

[51] Santos et al. (2019).

[52] Kanyimba (2020).

[53] Government of the Republic of Namibia (2021).

[54] Ibid.

Box 6 Activities to Achieve the Optimizing the Stewardship of Natural Resources[55]
- [Update] a complete and accurate fixed public asset register.
- Following the approval of the establishment of the Sovereign Wealth Fund during HPP
- Support Public Enterprises Reform
- Review the existing regime for the allocation of fishing rights, quotas and mineral licenses
- Avail sufficient quantities of water for mining industry

The Harambe Propriety Plan II is a broader national policy that does not specially address the SSF in specific terms. In the view of the authors, activity 3 and 4 have potential to support the financial inclusion of the SFF. These activities respectively maintain the need to '[R]eview the existing regime for the allocation of fishing rights, quotas and mineral licenses' and 'to establish the Sovereign Wealth Fund during HPP'. The potential for these activities exist to implicitly support the aspect of financial inclusion for the coastal SFF because they may open opportunities for the review policies, allocation of rights and set up funding opportunities for wealth creation.

3.2.5 The White Paper on the Responsible Management of the Inland Fisheries of Namibia

The White Paper on the Responsible Management of the Inland Fisheries of Namibia regulates the fisheries resources from Namibian rivers such as Kavango Kunene, Kwando and Zambezi rivers systems. The White Paper was developed with three main objectives shown in Box 7.[56]

Box 7 The Main Objectives of The White Paper on the Responsible Management of the Inland Fisheries of Namibia
- [To] ensure the sustainable, optimal utilisation of the fresh water fish resource.
- To ensure that the objectives are based on sound ecological knowledge and principles.

(continued)

---

[55] Ibid.

[56] Ministry of Fisheries and Marine Resources 'The White Paper on the Responsible Management of the Inland Fisheries of Namibia' (1995).

> **Box 7** (continued)
> - To, in communal areas, favour utilisation by subsistence holds and fishers rather than commercialization of the resources,
> - To ensure that the responsibility for the management of communal resources is vested at local rather with central government through a top down system
> - To ensure that that local subsistence fishers through local community leader are consulted about the extent the communal resources can be used for competitive and recreation angling by tourists.
> - To strive toward a holistic approach of the fish, the rivers and flood plan environment
> - To regulate the exploitation of fish in Government owned dams
> - To regulate passport fishing in inland water and
> - To ensure coordination and cooperation between countries in the region, sharing inland water bodies and rivers with Namibia

The White paper mentions the word 'artisanal fishermen' but does not address the aspect of financial inclusion. However, the analysis of the objectives of the White Paper on the Responsible Management of the Inland Fisheries of Namibia seems to show that it was developed to reverse the over exploitation of inland fish, to devolve the responsibility for managing inland fisheries fish to the local leaders and promote cooperation with neighboring countries. However, the fact that the White Paper on the Responsible Management of the Inland Fisheries of Namibia does not address the subject of financial inclusion for the artisanal fishermen needs reversal in subsequent development of Policies and legislative framework for Namibia.

3.2.6 Marine Resources Act 27 of 2000 and the Regulations Relating to the Exploitation of Marine Resources

The Namibian government introduced the Sea Fisheries Act in 1992.[57] The Act set out the institutional framework for the operation and management of the fisheries sector. The authors maintain that the Act also governs the non-commercial exploitation of marine resources through recreational activities, conservation measures (e.g. control of trawling activities and measurement of meshes and determine the fishing seasons for various species. The 1992 Act was repealed in 2000 and replaced by the Marine Resources Act 27 of 2000; this new Act was supported by the 2001 Regulation No. 241, which regulated the exploitation of marine resources. The Namibian Marine Resources Act 27 of 2000 provide for the conservation of the marine ecosystem and the responsible utilization, conservation, protection and

---

[57] Chiripanhura and Teweldemedhin (2016).

promotion of marine resources on a sustainable basis; for that purpose, to provide for the exercise of control over marine resources; and to provide for matters connected therewith. The Namibian Marine Resources Act commercial harvesting of marine resources and provides the following prerequisites to harvesting as shown in Box 8.[58]

Box 8 Pre-requisites to Harvesting of Marine Resources Act Commercial Harvesting of Marine Resources[59]

- [No] person shall in Namibia or in Namibian waters harvest any marine resource for commercial purposes, except under a light, an exploratory right or a fisheries agreement.
- In the case of a marine resource which has been made subject to a quota, no person shall in Namibia or in Namibian waters harvest such a resource for commercial purposes, except in terms of a quota or of permitted by-catch under a right, an exploratory right or a fisheries agreement.
- No person shall in Namibian waters use any vessel to harvest any marine resource for commercial purposes, except in terms of a licence issued under section
- No person shall use a Namibian flag vessel to harvest any marine resource in any waters outside of Namibian waters, except in terms of a licence issued under section 40.
- Where Namibia is authorized by any international agreement to grant a right or exploratory right, or to allocate a quota, in respect of harvesting marine resources outside Namibian waters, no person shall use a Namibian flag vessel to harvest any marine resource to which the agreement applies, except in terms of a right granted under section 33, an exploratory right granted under section 34 or a quota allocated under section 39, as applicable.
- The issue and validity of a right, an exploratory right or a quota required under subsection (5), and the manner of its suspension or cancellation or limitation, shall be subject to the terms of the agreement referred to in that subsection

---

The Marine Resource Act 27 of 2000 does not refer to the SSF because its purpose was to provide for the harvesting of marine resources for commercial purposes only. This, in itself is inherently discriminatory against SFF. The Constitution of Namibia seems to call on the inclusion of all Namibians to utilise the natural resources on a sustainable basis for the benefit of all Namibians, which in turn contradicts the Marine Resources Act. Therefore, need exist to ensure that

---

[58] Government Gazette of the Republic of Namibia 'Marine Resources Act, 27 of 2000' (2000).
[59] Ibid.

subsequent fisheries acts are developed to cater for the inclusion of the SSF in commercialization and exploitation of marine resources.

3.2.7 Strategic Plan of the Ministry of Fisheries and Marine Resources

The vision of the Ministry of Fisheries and Marine Resources (MFMR) is to be a leading fishing nation with a well-developed aquaculture industry. Box 9 presents the MFMR strategic priorities and operational management and activities for the five years ending the next year 2022.[60] The 7 strategic objectives that were set out cover the period of 2017–2022.[61]

> **Box 9 Strategic Objectives of the Ministry of Fisheries and Marine Resources[62]**
> 1. [Encourage] scientific advice on the sustainable management of the marine ecosystem
> 2. Strengthen compliance with fisheries legislation
> 3. Develop blue economy policy and legal framework
> 4. Strengthen the development of aquaculture
> 5. Improve contribution of value-added exports to national economy
> 6. Increase employment creation and the contribution to the national economy
> 7. Enhance organizational performance.

The objectives provide the essential building blocks for implementing the Strategic Plan the Strategic plan of the Ministry. However, these do not address the SFF directly, this in itself is inherently discriminatory against the SFF. However, the presence of the strategic plan 2 "Strengthen compliance with fisheries legislation" has potential to support the development of the SSF but not necessarily their financial inclusion. Some international policies and regulatory frameworks to which compliance may be sought are, the FAO's Voluntary guidelines in the context of Food security and SDG 14 target 14b that "call for providing access for small-scale artisanal fishers to marine resources and markets and also SDG 17 that call for cross country collaboration in pursuit of all the SDGs by the year 2030 based on global security focused on the needs of the people.[63]

---

[60]Ministry of Fisheries and Marine Resources 'Strategic Plan – 2017/18 -2021/22' (2017).
[61]Ibid.
[62]Ibid.
[63]United Nations 'Transforming our World: The 2030 Agenda for Sustainable Development' (2015).

3.2.8 National Plan of Action/Strategy for Small Scale Fisheries in Namibia

The National Plan of Action/Strategy for small scale fisheries in Namibia is currently under development through the cooperation among agreement amongst FAO, the MFMR, National Inland and Coastal Fisheries Stakeholder, the University of Namibia (UNAM) and Namibian Office of the Benguela Current Large Marine Ecosystem (BCLME.) The National Plan of Action for the SFF in Namibian will seek to address the topics listed in Box 10.

> **Box 10 Activities of the National Plan of Action/Strategy for Small Scale Fisheries[64]**
> * Definition of the SFF
> * Governance and institutional arrangements
> * Contribution, role and importance of small-scale fisheries
> * Sustainable management approaches for the SSF
> * Post-harvest and trade
> * Information systems

It appears that the National Plan of Action/Strategy for small scale fisheries in Namibia provides for the policy and legislative framework for SSF, their role and importance to the Namibian national economy. In the view of the authors, the National Plan of Action/Strategy for small scale fisheries in Namibia has potential to support the SSF. However, the aspect financial inclusion for the SFF and their linkage to the credit and local markets is presently not clear. Presently, Namibia export high-value Seafood to developed countries, yet these exports mostly include the well-established companies with vessels and high technology.[65]

4 Barriers to Integrating Financial Inclusion for the Coastal SFF into the Namibian Fisheries Policies and Regulatory Frameworks

The authors completed an audit of the Namibian literature and conducted interviews with the SSF and the following were revealed as barriers to integrating financial inclusion for the Coastal SSF into the Namibian fisheries policies and regulatory framework.

---

[64] FAO & Ministry of Fisheries and Marine Resources '*Notes on the National Plan of Action/Strategy for Small Scale fisheries in Namibia*'. (n.d.), Unpublished, FAO & MFMR.
[65] Draper (2015).

4.1 Barriers Relating to Reasons for Financial Inclusion and Market Opportunities

Financial institutions are hesitant to run into business with the SFF because the majority of them do not have collateral and bank accounts. This becomes a barrier to financial inclusion because collateral and bank accounts are usually emphasized by Namibian banks in order to have access to credit. In Namibia, there are credit guarantees for the formerly disadvantaged people. These include the Youth Credit Scheme[66] and Agriculture Bank of Namibia Women and Youth Credit Scheme[67] to mention a few. However, the SFF in Namibia do not have such credit guarantee schemes and the Youth and Women in the fishing sector are never even encouraged to apply for these schemes to support their fishing activities. This becomes a barrier to financial inclusion because Credit Schemes could be used by Namibian banks to have access to credit. The SFF in Namibia do not access to the market for their catch. The Namibian SSF are not allowed to sell their catch but they are restricted to only to use their catch for subsistence consumption. This is a barrier to financial inclusion because access to a market may provide an opportunity for selling their catch. This may help the SFF to generate reasonable income, open bank accounts and through this channel have access to credit and banks.

4.2 Barriers Relating to Education, Training and Capacity for the SSF

There is a lack of educational, training and capacity building opportunities for the SSF. This becomes a barrier to because the SFF may not be familiar with post-harvesting, preservation, processing, and marketing of seafood products and providing relationship with the local fish markets. The majority of the SFF in Namibian do not have organisations that could advance their financial inclusion in policies and legislative frameworks. There SFF have a low uptake of fish and have limited production capacity because of their use low technology and do not have access to boats.[68] Some areas of the harbour at the coast are not accessible to the SSF due to lack of technology, hindering their chances of access to fish that may be sold for better income.

---

[66] Ministry of Sport, Youth and National Services 'Mainstreaming Youth Development into the National Agenda' (2020).

[67] Agriculture Bank of Namibia Women and Youth Credit Scheme (n.d.) Unpublished Paper, Agri Bank of Namibia.

[68] Kanyimba et al. (2020).

4.3   Barriers Relating Participation in Policies and Regulatory Frameworks

The financial inclusion for the SSF is not specifically developed in the Namibian policies and regulatory frameworks. The fact that the notion of financial inclusion for the SFF is not developed in Namibian policies and regulatory frameworks is barrier in itself. The participants argued that corrupt and connected government officials just think about themselves when capturing the gains from marine resources. This practice has adverse impacts on the sustainability and thus contributing to exclusion of the SFFs.

4.4   Barriers Relating to Ecological Sustainability of Fisheries Resources

There is fear that the recognition of the SSF might result in the over exploitation of marine resources if their capacity to catch more fish is enhanced. This becomes a barrier because access to marine resources may be restricted. This would eventually restrict access to finance and markets.

5   The Way Forward: Addressing Barriers to Financial Inclusion for the Coastal SSF into Namibian Fisheries Policies and Regulatory Frameworks

There is a call among fishing authorities in Namibia to ensure a nationally shared prosperity of fisheries resources.[69] The shared prosperity concept is related to financial inclusion because it is about inclusion by focusing on household consumption or income growth among the poorest population. However, this call will remain a pipedream if no efforts are made to address the plight of the SSF. In that regard, the following measures may be undertaken as a way forward to address the barriers to financial inclusion for the coastal SSF into Namibian fisheries policies and regulatory frameworks.

---

[69] Kawana (2021).

5.1 Recommendations That Can Be Implemented Immediately

The recognition of the SSF representatives and participation in the development of national policies and regulatory frameworks is strongly recommended. These may think of setting up policies and regulatory frameworks that should guide the access to credit and loans, market development and development of policies to convince Namibian banks to recognise the SSF. The Namibian government authorities are urged to develop the aspect of financial inclusion of the SSF by tapping guidance from FAO Voluntary Guidelines for Securing Sustainable Small-Scale Fisheries in the Context of Food Security and Poverty Eradication and also obtain guidance from the SDGs 14b and 17. In particulars, the code of conduct for the SSF should be emphasized. Financial institutions should be urged to offer credit opportunities to the SSF on condition that credit guarantees schemes are established for them. This may help the SSF to convince government to introduce credit guarantee schemes to accessing credit and consideration by Namibian banks.

5.2 Recommendations That Can Be Implemented on Medium Term Basis

Need exist for the Government to set up policies and action plans to provide the SSF with credit guarantees that could enable them obtain credit from banks and other financial institutions in Namibia. There is need for the SSF to set-up organisations to help them act collectively on matters of access to credit, access to markets and access to marine resources. The organisations may help the SSF to work collectively and on representative basis on matters of access to banks, access to credit, access to marine resources and access to markets.

5.3 Recommendations That Require Long-Term Planning

Educational institutions are urged to offer opportunities for education, training and capacity strengthening to the SFF. Education, training and capacity development is the most effective means through which the fishermen become aware of their problem and acquires skills for practical demonstration in areas of need.[70] The education, training and capacity development could focus on post-harvest handling, preservation, processing and marketing seafood products and providing an integral relationship between with locale fish markets.

---

[70]Belwala et al. (2015), p. 67.

6   Conclusion

This chapter has addressed the barriers to Integrating Aspects of Financial Inclusion for the SSF into the Namibian Fisheries Policies and Regulatory Frameworks. The key principle for the financial inclusion that were uncovered in the chapter are bank inclusion and credit for the SFF. It is shown that the concept of financial inclusion for the SFF is an alien concept in Namibia The reasons why the SSF experience financial exclusion relating to lack of physical and livelihood assets, lack of bank accounts, including land, that can be used as collateral; they lack education and literacy and do not have savings and organizational mechanisms; the SSF tend to be more individualistic and do not operate within the lenses of organisations that could vouch for their needs pertaining to financial inclusion, and do not have a credit history. The SSF are consistently politically and economically marginalized despite the fact they have been acknowledged globally as meaningful contributors to poverty alleviation and food security.

It appears that the international regulatory frameworks have directly and indirectly laid opportunities for the financial inclusion of the SFF. Among the international regulatory frameworks that have an important clause to support financial inclusion for the SSF are the United Nations 2030 Agenda for Sustainable Development. In particular, SDG 14, target 14c makes provision for the SFF to have to access to marine resources and markets while SDG 17 calls on various stakeholders to cooperate in efforts to mobilise financial resources to support the inclusive post-2015 development agenda. The link between the aforementioned goals create an opportunity for realizing the financial inclusion opportunity for the SSF. Moreover, the Voluntary Guidelines for Securing Sustainable Small-Scale Fisheries in the Context of Food Security and Poverty Eradication need to be aligned with the implementation process of the SDG 14, target 14c and SDG 17.

This chapter has reviewed the national policies and regulatory frameworks. These include the Constitution of the Republic of Namibia, the Namibian Vision 2030, the NDP5, the Harambe Prosperity Plan II, the White Paper on the Responsible Management of the Inland Fisheries of Namibia, and the Strategic Plan of the MFMR. It appears that these documents do not mention the aspect of financial inclusion of the Coastal SSF. However, the National Plan of Action/Strategy for Small Scale fishermen in Namibia is currently being developed and may have potential to support the inclusion of the SSF into policies and regulatory frameworks. However, the aspect of their financial inclusion and their linkage to the local markets is not clear in the National Plan of Action at this moment.

The barriers to integrating financial inclusion for the coastal SSF into Namibian policies and regulatory frameworks are grouped into four categories. *First,* are reasons for lack of financial inclusion and markets are about financial institutions may be hesitant to run into business with the SFF because the majority of them do not have collateral and bank accounts and lack of credit guarantee for the SFF. The fact that the SFF do not have a market for their harvest and only restricted to subsistence consumption restricts financial inclusion because they may not generate reasonable income to be recognized by financial institutions. The second category of barriers is about lack of education, training and capacity among those identified as the SSF. This barrier becomes aggravated because the SFF do not have an organisation that could vouch for the needs including financial inclusion. The capacity barrier also includes low uptake of fish and limited production capacity because of reliance of on low technology. The Next category of barriers are those relating to participation in policies and regulatory frameworks. This become real because the SSF concept is not specifically developed in the Namibian policies and regulatory frameworks and that the notion of financial inclusion is not explicit in key documents. Moreover, corrupt and connected government officials just think about themselves when capturing the gains from marine resources and this practice has adverse impacts on the sustainability and thus contributing to exclusion of the SFFs. *Finally,* there is a barrier relate to ecological sustainability of fisheries resources and there is fear that recognition of the SSF might result in the exploitation of marine resources if their capacity to catch more fish is enhanced.

Several recommendations are proposed to enhance financial inclusion for the SFF on a short term, mid-term and long-term basis. The recommendation that can implemented immediately pertain to recognition of the SSF representatives and their participation in the development of national policies and regulatory frameworks. There is also a need for financial institutions to be urged to offer credit opportunities to the SSF on condition that credit guarantees schemes are set-up. The recommendations that can implemented on mid-term basis is about the development of policies and action plans to provide the SSF with credit guarantees to enable them obtain credit from banks and other financial institutions in Namibia and helps them set-up organizations to help the SSF act on collectively on matters of access to credit, loans, access to local markets and marine infrastructure. The recommendations that can implemented on a long-term basis require educational institutions to offer opportunities for education, training and capacity strengthening to the SFF. The education, training and capacity development should focus on post-harvest handling, preservation, processing and marketing seafood products and providing an integral relationship between with local markets. Finally, the Ministry of fisheries and Marine Resources need to potentially support the implementation of national regulations to financial inclusion. This process should engage and obtain from guidance from FAO Voluntary Guidelines for Securing Sustainable Small-Scale Fisheries in the Context of Food Security and Poverty Eradication and also obtain guidance from the SDGs 14b and SGD 17.

Bibliography

Agriculture Bank of Namibia (n.d.) Women and Youth Credit Scheme. Unpublished Paper, Agriculture Bank of Namibia

Batty M, Tjipute M, Shapi M (2005) Overview and analysis of social, economic and fisheries information to promote artisanal fisheries managements in the BCLME Region-Namibia. BCLME Project

Belwala R, Belwala S, Jabri OI (2015) Training needs assessment of fishermen on Oman's Batinah Coast: using exploratory factor analysis. J Vocat Educ Train:310–331

Bronnmann J, Smith MD, Abbott J, Hay CJ, Næsje TF (2020) Integration of a local fish market in namibia with the global seafood trade: implications for fish traders and sustainability. World Development. www.elsevier.com/locate/worlddev. Accessed 10 May 2021

Chiripanhura B, Teweldemedhin M (2016) An analysis of the fishing industry in Namibia: the structure, performance, challenges, and prospects for growth and diversification. http://www.agrodep.org/sites/default/files/AGRODEPWP0021_0.pdf. Accessed 9 July 2020

Constitution of the Republic of Namibia, 1990

Conventions on Biological Diversity (2020) Key Elements of the Strategic Plan 2011-2020, Including Aichi Biodiversity Targets. https://www.cbd.int/sp/elements/#IV. Accessed 2 July 2021

Draper K (2015) Networks of capital: reframing knowledge in the Namibian Hake. www.elsevier.com/locate/marpol. Accessed 10 May 2021

Ehler CHN (2013) Coral Triangle Initiative: an introduction to marine spatial planning. Publication Supporting the Coral Triangle Initiative on Coral Reefs, Fisheries and Food Security (CTI-CFF). file:///C:/Users/AKANYI~1/AppData/Local/Temp/CTI_IntroductiontoMarineSpatialPlanning.pdf. Accessed 16 July 2021

FAO & Ministry of Fisheries and Marine Resources 'Notes on the National Plan of Action/Strategy for Small Scale fisheries in Namibia' Unpublished

FAO (2005) Technical Guidelines for Responsible Fisheries 'Increasing the Contribution of Small-Scale Fisheries to Poverty Alleviation and Food Security'. http://www.fao.org/3/a0237e/a0237e.pdf. Accessed 13 July 2021

FAO (2009) The code of conduct for responsible fisheries and indigenous peoples: an operational guide. https://www.fao.org/3/i0840e/i0840e.pdf. Accessed 3 Nov 2021

FAO (2018) Voluntary guidelines for securing sustainable small-scale fisheries in the context of food security and poverty eradication. https://www.fao.org/3/i8347en/I8347EN.pdf. Accessed 2 Nov 2021

Finkbeiner EM (2015) The role of diversification in dynamic small-scale fisheries: lessons from Baja California Sur, Mexico. Glob Environ Change:139–152

Government of the Republic of Namibia (2004) Namibia Vision 2030 – Policy Framework for Long-Term National Development. Office of the President

Government of the Republic of Namibia (2017) 5th National Development Plan (NDP5)

Government of the Republic of Namibia (2021) Harambe Prosperity Plan II: Action Plan of the Namibian Government towards Economic Recovery and Inclusive Growth. https://www.met.gov.na/files/downloads/f0b_Harambee%20Prosperity%20Plan%20II.pdf.   Accessed 13 July 2021

Government of the Republic of Namibia (2021) Harambe Prosperity Plan II: One Namibia, One Nation. Peace, Reconciliation, Security and Stability. Office of the President

https://doi.org/10.1016/B978-0-12-805052-1.0003. Accessed 16 July 2021

https://www.globalgoals.org/14-life-below-water. Accessed 2 July 2021

Isomov M (2020) The philosophy of national interests in the context of international relations. Eur J Mol Clin Med 2

Kanyimba AT, Tshiningayamwe S, Jonas M (2020) Exploratory notes collected during interview with small scale fishermen in the coastal areas of Namibia. Unpublished Notes, University of Namibia

Kawana A (2021) Speech of the Honorable Minister of Fisheries and Marine Resources on the Award of Fishing Rights to Namibian and Foreign Applicants

Langenheim J (2017) Millions of small scale fishermen facing economic exclusion. https://www.theguardian.com/environment/the-coral-triangle/2017/jul/28/millions-of-small-scale-fishers-facing-economic-exclusion. Accessed 13 July 2021

Le Roux J, Cilliers EJ (2014) The participatory planning paradigm shift: comparing disciplines and methods. In: 49th ISOCARP Congress. file:///C:/Users/AKANYI~1/AppData/Local/Temp/FINAL_LeRoux_Cilliers_Participatoryplanning.pdf. Accessed 16 July 2021

Manning PR (1998) Managing Namibia's Marine Fisheries: optimal resource use and national development objectives. Unpublished, London School of Economics

Marine Resources Act 27 of 2000

Ministry of Fisheries and Marine Resources (1995) The White Paper on the Responsible Management of the Inland Fisheries of Namibia

Ministry of Fisheries and Marine Resources (2017) Strategic Plan – 2017/18 -2021/22

Ministry of Sport, Youth and National Services (2020) Mainstreaming Youth Development into the National Agenda

Olsen E, Fluharty D, Hoel AH, Hostens K, Maes F (2014) Integration at the round table: marine spatial planning in multi-stakeholder settings

Omar MA, Inaba K (2020) Does financial inclusion reduce poverty and income inequality in developing countries? J Econ Struct:1–25

Pawson MG, Padda G (2008) The definition of marine recreational fishing in Europe. Mar Policy:339–350

Pomeroy R, Brooks SH (2019) Taking stock of the status of implementation of the voluntary guidelines for securing sustainable small-scale fisheries: a country-level assessment framework. Mar Policy:361–370

Pomeroy R, Cristopher CA, Lomboy G, Steve B (2020) Financial inclusion to build economic resilience in small-scale fisheries. Mar Policy:118

Santos CF, Charles N, Ehler CN, Agardy T, Andrade F, Orbach MK, Crowder LB (2019) Chapter 30, Marine Spatial Planning. World seas: an environmental evaluation

Shipalana P (2019) Digitising financial services: a tool for financial inclusion in South Africa? https://media.africaportal.org/documents/Occasional-Paper-301-shipalana.pdf.   Accessed 13 July 2021

Smith BL (2003) Public policy and public participation: engaging citizens and community in the development of public policy

Smith H, Basurto X (2019) Defining small-scale fisheries and examining the role of science in shaping perceptions of who and what counts: a systematic review

Soltanpour Y, Monaco C, Peri I (2017) Defining small-scale fisheries from a social perspective. Qual–Access Success:425–428

Sowman M, Cardoso P (2010) Small-scale fisheries and food security strategies in countries in the Benguela Current Large Marine Ecosystem (BCLME) region: Angola, Namibia and South Africa. www.elsevier.com/locate/marpol. Accessed 10 May 2021

Sustainable Development Solutions Network 'Indicators and a Monitoring Framework' https://indicators.report/targets/14-b/. Accessed 13 July 2023

The United Nations 'Mainstreaming the Concerns of Older Persons into the Social Development Agenda' https://www.un.org/esa/socdev/ageing/documents/mainstreaming/positionpaper.pdf. Accessed 16 July 2021

The United Nations Global Goals for Sustainable Development 'Goal 14 in Action' (2015)

UN General Assembly 'United Nations: Transforming Our World: The 2030 Agenda for Sustainable Development' (2015). https://sustainabledevelopment.un.org/content/documents/212 52030%20Agenda%20for%20Sustainable%20Development%20web.pdf.   Accessed 10 May 2021

United Nations Convention on the Law of the Sea https://www.un.org/depts/los/convention_
    agreements/texts/unclos/unclos_e.pdf. Accessed 2 July 2021
Warikandwa TV. Notes presented at the FAO and OOH workshop on legal training on the use of
    diagnostic tool for small scale fishermen. Unpublished Notes, FAO and OOH
Yin X, Xu X, Chen Q, Peng J (2020) The sustainable development of financial inclusion: how can
    monetary policy and economic fundamental interact with it effectively? Sustainability:1–14
Yuliana RD (2016) Banks strategies that lead to financial inclusion for the fishing industry. Journal
    Ekonomi Dan Pembangunana 24(2):121–135

Alex T. Kanyimba is an Associate Professor in Environmental Education and Education for Sustainable Development at the University of Namibia (UNAM). He holds a Doctorate in Environmental Education, Master of Science in Strategic Management of Sustainable Development, Master of Education in Environmental Education and Honours Bachelor of Education in Geography Education. He is currently the Country Director for One Ocean Hub, Namibia and Principal Researcher for Research Package 5 (RP5): *Transformative Governance for a Sustainable and Innovative Blue Society.* Professor Kanyimba has coordinated the following Projects over the past five years: These include but not limited to One Ocean Hub funded by UKRI through GCRF (RP5), *Environmental Education for Sustainable Development in Namibia and South Africa, funded by* NCRST/NRF; *In Search of Innovative Models for Developing Sustainable Health Policies and Practices through linking Indigenous Knowledge to Literacy, funded by NCRST; Education for Sustainable Development in Southern Africa,* funded by UNESCO's Participation Programme; *Educational Support to Develop Environmental Management in South African Primary Schools, funded by* Flemish Education Department of Belgium as a collaboration *between the Vrije Universiteit Brussels and North-West University (NWU); Educational Support to Develop Understanding of Environmental Education among South African In-service Teachers,* funded by Department of Environment Affairs of South Africa. Professor Kanyimba is Associate Editor for the Springer Nature Journal, Discover Sustainability, and has served as *Quest Editor* for the *International Journal of Sustainability in Higher Education, published by the* Emerald Publishing Group and *Editor* of the book titled *Education for Sustainable Development in Southern Africa published by the Namibia Environmental Education Network (NEEN).* Professor Kanyimba is also a Practitioner for Sustainable Development and has experience working with the Southern African Regional Universities Association (SARUA) and UNESCO on the integration of Sustainable Development Goals (SDGs) in Higher Education and Teacher Education.

Martha N. Jonas works as the Researcher Assistant at the University of Namibia under the One Ocean Hub project, funded by the United Kingdom Research and Innovation (UKRI) through the Global Challenges Research Fund (GCRF). Martha holds an Honours Degree with specialization in Sociology and Geography & Environmental studies from University of Namibia (UNAM). Currently she is enrolled for the Masters of Arts Degree in Development studies. Martha has experience in the administering community environment projects, particularly the management of natural resource management and tourism development and has experience in teaching Geography and Development studies in Namibian Secondary. Martha also offers introduction to sociology at Namibian College of Open Learning. Her interests are focused on developing the relationship between communities, their environment and natural resources to maximise beneficiation in wider environment of society.

Policy and Regulatory Frameworks for Financial Inclusion in South Africa, Botswana, Namibia and Zimbabwe

Tendai D. Svotwa, Eukeria Wealth, and Charles Makanyeza

Abstract This chapter interrogates the policy and regulatory frameworks for financial inclusion in the Southern African Development Community (SADC) region, focusing on South Africa, Botswana, Namibia and Zimbabwe. Financial inclusion plays a pivotal role in the economic development and inclusive growth of a country, as well as a critical role in the alleviation of poverty, reduction of gender inequalities and improvement in the standards of living for societies. Notwithstanding these benefits, constraints to financial inclusion in the countries under study include lack of trust in the financial services sector, financial illiteracy, high costs of setting up banks in remote rural areas and poor infrastructure. Generally, to some extent, the sampled countries have instituted country specific policies and regulations that are geared towards the enhancement of financial inclusion in their respective countries which has resulted in positive outcomes. However, in some instances, there is no coordination between financial policies and other legislation to realise countrywide financial inclusion. In view of the preceding information, it can be recommended that there should be common financial inclusion legislation that is effectively and homogeneously applied in the SADC region, that must be upheld by all member states for uniformity to realise greater financial inclusion.

T. D. Svotwa
Department of Graduate Studies, Botho University, Gaborone, Botswana
e-mail: douglas.svotwa@bothouniveristy.ac.bw

E. Wealth
School of Accounting, Faculty of Commerce, Management and Law, University of Namibia, Windhoek, Namibia
e-mail: ewealth@unam.na

C. Makanyeza (✉)
Namibia Business School, University of Namibia, Windhoek, Namibia
e-mail: cmakanyeza@unam.na

1 Introduction

Financial inclusion plays a pivotal role in economic development and inclusive growth of a country.[1] Further benefits of financial inclusion encompass the alleviation of poverty, reduction of gender inequalities and an improvement of the standards of living for societies.[2] There has been a multiplicity of definitions of financial inclusion without consensus on what it really entails. Financial inclusion has been defined as the delivery of formal financial products and services to all segments of a population irrespective of their economic situation.[3] While this definition is all encompassing in that financial inclusion includes everyone within the population, this may not be the reality since some people may be excluded from the formal financial system. The different definitions that have been proffered for financial inclusion to some extent zoom on one of several aspects which are related to: access of the population to financial services, the degree of use of these services, and their quality and cost.[4]

There has been considerable progress regarding financial inclusion globally in the last ten years. Statistics reveal that in 2018 3.8 billion people had access to formal financial services which represented about 70 percent of all adults, compared to 51% in 2011.[5] However, regardless of the considerable progress made towards financial inclusion, more than 1.7 billion adults remain financially excluded, that is unbanked. The marginalised people in society, especially the poor, account for a significant share of the unbanked. Globally, half of the unbanked adults come from the poorest 40 percent of households within their economy, the other half from the richest 60 percent.[6]

In view of the socio-economic benefits of financial inclusion to a country, policymakers have acted positively regarding financial inclusion. As highlighted by the World Bank's 2014 Global Financial Development Report about 50 countries adopted explicit policies to boost financial inclusion.[7] The adoption of policies aimed at boosting financial inclusion by various countries bears testimony to the importance of financial inclusion globally. Despite the global commitment and the increase in efforts to ameliorate more inclusive financial systems in both developed and developing countries, research in this area remains somewhat hazy and limited.[8] The aim of this chapter is therefore to add to the literature regarding the enactment of policy and regulatory frameworks to promote financial inclusion in SADC. In the SADC region, there is no common financial inclusion legislation that is effectively

---

[1]Evans (2016), p. 22.
[2]Ozilli (2020), p. 9; Oji (2015), p. 1; World Bank (2017).
[3]Wyman (2017), p. 4.
[4]Barajas et al. (2020), p. 5.
[5]G20 (2020), p. 4.
[6]Demirgüç-Kunt et al. (2020), p. 4.
[7]Barajas et al. (2020), p. 5.
[8]Sha'ban et al. (2019), p. 3.

and homogeneously applied in the region, which becomes an inhibiting factor for the growth of financial inclusion. This chapter provides a synopsis of the policy and regulatory framework for financial inclusion in the SADC region. Barriers to financial inclusion are also explored in the chapter. The chapter further explicates the policy and regulatory frameworks for financial inclusion in the selected SADC countries under study namely, South Africa, Botswana, Namibia, and Zimbabwe, employing a doctrinal methodology in understanding some of the statutes which are related to financial inclusion. Recommendations are then suggested for policy and regulatory frameworks for financial inclusion in the SADC region.

2 Financial Inclusion in the SADC Region

This part of the chapter presents an overview of and the barriers to financial inclusion in the SADC region.

2.1 Overview

The concept of financial inclusion within SADC is analysed from three intertwined dimensions, namely: access, usage, and quality. While access to finance means that businesses and individuals can gain access to financial products, it is noteworthy that since the same businesses and individuals have access to finance, they may not have access to meet all their financial needs.[9] From the perspective of SADC, it is crucial to have some delineation in terms of the classification of businesses/individuals who are financially included:[10]

a) The 'banked': refers to businesses and individuals who utilise products and services that are provided by a licenced financial services provider, based on a banking licence.
b) Other formal (non-bank) consumers: refers to businesses and individuals who are served by other regulated financial institutions such as credit providers, micro-finance banks and other institutions insurance companies.
c) The 'underbanked' consumers: refers to businesses and individuals who have needs for many products, but only have access or use a selected few.

There are also other members of society who are informally served, that is, individuals who do not rely on the formal financial sector to access finance. Rather, this group relies mostly on credit associations, group savings, and remittances within the informal sector. These credit associations will be responsible for advancing loans to

---

[9] SADC 'Financial Inclusion Strategy, 2016–2021' (2016) *SADC* 12.
[10] Ibid.

members within the association who may require such loans as and when the need arises.

Generally, the level of financial inclusion in the SADC region is very low, with statistics showing an unbanked population of 45 million people, with a variation across all the SADC countries.[11] The low rates of financial inclusion to some extent explains why despite the relatively high returns on investments in Africa, growth has remained subdued, constrained and acutely low while the levels of poverty and income inequalities are relatively high.[12] Countries such as South Africa, Mauritius, Namibia, and Lesotho have the highest number of the adult population that is financially included. On the other hand, countries which have very low rates of financial inclusion include Malawi, Democratic Republic of Congo, Mozambique, and Zambia. Statistics for the latter three countries indicate that more than 50 percent of the adult population do not have any access to financial products and services within the formal financial services sector.[13] SADC, in its 2016–2021 Financial Inclusion Strategy, confirmed the levels of financial inclusion in statistics presented above.[14] As of 2016, 66 percent of the adult population in SADC were financially included, with the remainder not having access to finance in both the formal and informal sector.

2.2   Barriers to Financial Inclusion

While it is evident that several SADC countries are geared towards financial inclusion for most people in each member state, some factors have been noted which militate against such a noble and worthy cause. This section provides a discussion of some of the barriers to financial inclusion as confirmed in the extant literature,[15] from previous research carried out in Asia and the SADC region.

There are numerous entry barriers which restrict individuals and businesses entering the financial services sector: These are demand-side constraints which inhibit individuals from signing up for formal financial services, as well as supply-side constraints that restrict suppliers from providing products and services. In addition, the demand side barriers for financial inclusion also includes low literacy levels, lack of awareness and understanding of financial products and services available, coupled with irregular income.

---

[11] For this study, the SADC countries include Angola, Botswana, Comoros, Democratic Republic of Congo, Eswatini, Lesotho, Madagascar, Malawi, Mauritius, Mozambique, Namibia, Seychelles, South Africa, Tanzania, Zambia, and Zimbabwe. See also Finmark Trust (2018), p. 1.

[12] Masiyandima et al. (2017), p. 2.

[13] SADC (2016), p. 15.

[14] Ibid, p. 16.

[15] Wyman (2017), p. 11.

In addition, other entry barriers include lack of formal identification documents such as identity cards, consumers' lack of trust in the financial services system, the rural poor who cannot afford to utilise financial services, coupled with gender inequality, and high transaction costs of financial services.[16]

On the other hand, some of the supply-side factors include exorbitant charges levied by banks in maintaining accounts as well as high costs in advancing credit to customers. Furthermore, some of the supply side factors which inhibit financial inclusion also include remoteness, weak transportation links, mostly in rural communities, and underdeveloped communication infrastructure, worsened by low population densities.[17] Consequently, many people are left out of the formal financial system, thus exacerbating the problem of financial exclusion.

Regulatory oversight also presents a barrier for excluded consumers to actively participate in the formal financial services sector: This includes constraints arising from the nature of regulatory oversight, and lack of coordination between different regulatory bodies in the financial services sector. In some countries new players in the financial services sector must comply with a multitude of licencing laws and regulations.[18]

High entry barriers: Research shows that it is generally expensive to establish a company in the financial services sector to serve the diverse needs of the population, especially the poor and low-income group.[19] Because of the competitive nature of the financial services sector, it could be very challenging to be profitable especially when operating in remote rural areas due to the limited market.

Lack of consumer data: Financial service providers lack information on potential customers due to information asymmetry which constraints them in terms of the specific products/services that can be offered to potential customers thereby inhibiting financial inclusion.[20]

The factors identified above are the main inhibitors of financial inclusion. As such, policies that should be prescribed by any nation should take cognisance of the factors discussed above if indeed the Governments are committed to the full financial inclusion of their citizens.

---

[16] Barugahara (2021), p. 261.

[17] Sykes (2016), p. 4.

[18] Wyman (2017), p. 11.

[19] SADC (2016), p. 36.

[20] Ibid.

3 Overview of Policy and Regulatory Frameworks for Financial Inclusion in SADC

This section gives an overview of the policy and regulatory frameworks as they obtain in the SADC region. As already noted in the introduction, there is no common financial inclusion legislation that is effectively and homogeneously applied in the SADC region, which becomes an inhibiting factor for the growth of financial inclusion. Member states apply policies and regulatory frameworks in the financial services sector which they deem appropriate in their respective countries. In this regard, since there is no financial inclusion legislation in the SADC region, member states are not bound to enforce laws which promote financial inclusion. As such, this becomes an inhibiting factor since not all SADC member states will pursue a financial inclusive strategy which caters for everyone to be involved in the formal financial services sector.

Countries such as the Democratic Republic of Congo, Mozambique and Malawi have high rates of financial exclusion which present opportunities for widening the scope of financial inclusion. In this regard, some of these countries instituted regulations which were meant towards the promotion of product innovation, and robust Information Communication Technology (ICT) infrastructure aimed at enhancing and deepening financial inclusion.[21] With the easing of such regulations, these positive moves are critical for reducing the seemingly high levels of financial exclusion in the identified SADC states.

Previous research carried out in the SADC region confirm the following policy and regulatory weaknesses in member states:[22]

i) Significant policy uncertainty: the current legal and regulatory frameworks within SADC member states is evolving which is a recipe for the creation of market uncertainties. The frameworks which are available are fragmented and manifests lack of cohesion in the governance of financial service players which hampers investor confidence, thus limiting the deepening of financial inclusion;

ii) Insufficient financial market structures: financial market structures within SADC which include the payment systems are not strong in terms of performance which affects the growth of transaction volumes;

iii) Inconsistent industry monitoring: there are no prudential governance structures across the financial services sectors of member countries which results in price variations for the products and services offered, for instance high lending rates;

iv) Lack of policy harmonisation: research established that policy and regulatory frameworks within the SADC region are not at par with the innovations that take place in the financial services sector which creates policy distortions and conflicts. In this instance, there is a lack of policy coherence and harmonisation on similar topics across the member states, and

---

[21] SADC (2016), p. 30.
[22] Ibid.

v) Suboptimal customer protection: the transition from the use of cash to digital platforms require that there be clear and consistent customer protection in the regulations of a country to inculcate consumer trust in the financial services sector. It is apparent that customer protection is not included in the regulatory processes of some SADC member states and some customers may not be aware of their rights and processes for redress in the event of consumer disputes.

The preceding discussion highlights gaps and loopholes in the policy and regulatory frameworks of member states within the SADC region. These policy inconsistencies need to be addressed so that uniform policies could be applied across the region which are geared towards the harmonization of laws and regulations that govern financial inclusion. In their current form of policy disintegration and disharmony, it could be challenging to achieve total financial inclusion for all in SADC. The discussion which follows focuses on the policy and regulatory frameworks for South Africa, Botswana, Namibia, and Zimbabwe to recommend a viable, harmonised SADC region in terms of the policies and regulations governing financial service providers' operations.

3.1 South Africa

In the SADC region, South Africa possesses the most complex and advanced financial system and is a very good example in terms of exhibiting high levels of financial inclusion in Africa that is stable and well-regulated. Prior to 1994, the financial services sector was mired in many inefficiencies that resulted in the exclusion of more than 60 percent of the population. With the advent of democracy in 1994, the new African National Congress led Government focused on the promotion of financial inclusion for all South Africans in terms of making the products/services available in the formal financial services sector, especially the previously disadvantaged groups.

South Africa has instituted various legal frameworks that were meant to magnify financial inclusion since 2003, with the enactment of the Black Economic Empowerment Act, 2003 in addressing some historical imbalances. In 2004, the financial services sector voluntarily undertook some reforms in implementing the Financial Service Charter in promoting the socio-economic integration and enhancement of financial inclusion, most especially to the black people. In 2012, the Government introduced the Financial Sector Code (FSC) and established the Financial Sector Transformation Council (FSTC) which oversees the operations of the FSC and the regulation of the financial services sector.[23]

---

[23] Shipalana (2019), p. 13.

Previous research[24] confirms that the FSTC set up industry standards for compliance to enhance financial inclusion and attain the Government's target of reaching a financial inclusion rate of 90 percent by 2030. Notable successes were witnessed in the financial services sector as early as 2004 with the voluntary participation of banks wherein they opened a low-cost banking account called 'Mzansi' and by 2008 more than 6 million bank accounts were opened by people who had never had the opportunity to do so in the past. Significant progress was also witnessed in the advancement of bank loans to small and medium enterprises (SMEs) by the end of 2010. On the contrary, research also shows that poverty is still rampant in South Africa with statistics indicating that more than 30 million South Africans are poor and do not have access to financial services due to financial illiteracy, high bank fees, consumer lack of trust in the banking system, and lack of the required documentation to open a bank account such as national identity cards.[25]

In advancing financial literacy and educating consumers, two pieces of legislation were enacted, namely the National Credit Act (NCA) in 2005 and Consumer Protection Act (CPA) in 2008.[26] The rationale for the introduction of the NCA was to regulate consumer credit and improve the dissemination of consumer information in South Africa, while the CPA was enacted to protect consumers regarding the trading of consumer products and services on the marketplace. Hence CPA was introduced to enhance financial education and financial literacy, thus enhance financial inclusion.[27]

Furthermore, to show its commitment to financial inclusion, the Government enacted the Financial Sector Regulation Act, 2017 (FSR Act) whose main objective was the establishment of a regulatory and supervisory framework that promotes financial inclusion. The FSR Act also established the Financial Sector Conduct Authority (FSCA), whose objectives were: the protection of the customer by ensuring that customers are treated fairly by financial institutions and providing financial customers with financial education programs.[28] Results from the enactment of Financial Sector Regulation Act have been quite commendable with current statistics indicating that the level of financial inclusion has reached 90 percent, with women being more financially included.[29] In fact, arguments are being proffered to the extent that South Africa has now reached a saturation point in terms of transactional banking.[30] Resultantly, transactional banking and account ownership has grown phenomenally because of these friendly policies and regulations.

The facts described above attest to the fact that the financial service sector's growth and improvement in terms of financial inclusion levels can be attributed to

---

[24] Ibid.

[25] Chitimira and Ncube (2020), p. 339; Allen et al. (2016), pp. 18–27.

[26] Chitimira and Ncube (2020), p. 344.

[27] Ibid.

[28] Financial Sector Conduct Authority 'Financial Inclusion Strategy' (2019).

[29] Shipalana (2019), p. 15.

[30] Ibid.

the sound financial policies instituted by the Government. To a greater extent this also highlights the commitment of the regulatory authorities in making sure that most of the population are not financially excluded. As evidenced, the goal of attaining financial inclusion of 90 percent by 2030 has been attained, which was part of the National Development Plan in 2011. In this regard, it can be concluded that South Africa has performed exceedingly well in the SADC region in instituting the necessary regulatory frameworks and realising its intended objectives. However, there could be few shortcomings, for instance, the growth of the informal sector, with indications that in 2018 there was a growth in adults using the informal sector, from 56 percent to 63 percent. This could be a challenge in trying to financially include everyone in instances where some people resort to the informal sector for financial accommodation.

3.2 Botswana

In the past fifty years, Botswana has metamorphosised from a poor country status to an upper-middle income country supported by a sound leadership in prudently managing the country's mineral resources for the benefit of most of its citizens.[31] Notwithstanding these positive developments, income disparities still exist in the country with high levels of poverty being evident in the social strata.

The Bank of Botswana came into being because of the Banking Act, 1975 and the same year saw the promulgation of the Financial Institutions Act, 8, which was meant to provide for the licensing, control and regulation of financial institutions.[32] In the early 1980s, the financial services sector was dominated by two large banks, Barclays Bank (now Absa Bank) and Standard Chartered Bank, with the market being controlled by the Bank of Botswana which set the levels of interest rates. With the liberalisation policies of the Government, by the end of 2008 there were eleven players in the financial services sector. The eleven players were: Barclays Bank Botswana, Standard Chartered Bank, Bank of Credit and Commerce Botswana, Zimbank Botswana (a subsidiary of Zimbabwe Banking Corporation Limited), First National Bank, ANZ Grindlays and Union Bank (A subsidiary of Standard Bank Group, South Africa), Botswana Cooperative Bank, Stanbic Bank, Bank of Baroda, Bank Gaborone and Capital Bank.[33] The same year also saw the establishment of the Non-Bank Financial Regulatory Authority (NBFIRA) which was meant to provide a new regulatory and institutional framework for all non-bank financial institutions.[34] Non-bank financial institutions include the Botswana Stock Exchange, pension funds, insurers, asset managers, microfinance and credit

---

[31] Mogomotsi and Madigele (2016), p. 55; Chibba (2009), p. 224.

[32] Government of Botswana 'Financial Institutions Act' (1975).

[33] Capital Resources (2009).

[34] Ibid.

institutions. Currently the banking sector has been liberalised to an extent that the Bank of Botswana no longer controls the interest rates, the allocation of credit or the pricing of products although it can still give guidelines in terms of bank charges as well as the spread between deposit and lending rates.[35] The growth in the number of banks operating in the financial services sector meant that several people have now been financially included in the formal system.

The financial sector in Botswana is relatively strong, and the Government showed a firm commitment to financial sector reforms by instituting its own financial inclusion strategy through the promulgation of the Banking Act in 1995.[36] The Act was meant to enhance access to finance in commercial banks and reduce the role of the Government in the financial services sector. Further financial inclusion efforts were shown in the legislation of the Financial Sector Development Strategy (2012–2016).[37] The premise of the strategy was to modernise the regulatory structure, which included the preparation of new legislation governing the regulation of banks, insurance companies, and pension funds. However, progress on implementation of the strategy has been slow.[38] Additional policies were also crafted, such as The Botswana Financial Inclusion Roadmap 2015–2020 which laid out the country's priorities for the enhancement of financial inclusion.

In terms of the regulatory framework in Botswana, the financial services landscape is governed by two authorities: the Bank of Botswana (BoB) and the Non-Bank Financial Institutions Regulatory Authority (NBFIRA).[39] To cater for the non-bank players, including micro financing institutions, the Government enacted the Non-Bank Financial Institutions Regulatory Board (NBFIRA) Act in 2016 to improve efficiency in the financial system and promote orderliness in the non-bank financial sector. These informal financial institutions avail small cash loans which complement the formal banking system, thus widening the scope of financial inclusion. To some degree, the non-bank financial sector plays a critical role in accommodating members of the society who may not qualify to access financial products/services from the formal financial sector, thus deepening financial inclusion. However, the situation has been different in rural Botswana, especially among the poor who largely remain unbanked, with major disparities between the urban and rural communities. Despite some of these challenges, Botswana managed to reduce the rate of those who were financially excluded, from 96 percent, five decades ago, and the country registered a financial inclusion rate of 50 percent by 2014[40] which reflects that the Government's policies on financial inclusion are bearing fruit.

---

[35] Ibid.

[36] Ibid.

[37] World Bank 'Botswana Systematic Country Diagnostic' (2015), p. 54.

[38] World Bank 'Botswana Systematic Country Diagnostic' (2015), p. 54.

[39] Making Access Possible (MAP) (2015).

[40] Chibba (2009), p. 224. See also Molefhi (2019), p. 4.

3.3 Namibia

Namibia is another upper middle-income country in the SADC region. Regarding the policies and regulatory frameworks for financial inclusion, it is imperative to have an analysis of these regulations that relate to the financial services sector in Namibia. The Namibian financial services sector is relatively profitable, mature, and stable. The Namibian financial sector regulatory system is comprised of the Central Bank, that is, The Bank of Namibia which was established through the promulgation of the Bank of Namibia Act, Act No. 15 of 1997, which regulates the operations of the banking sector.[41] In addition, non-banking financial institutions are regulated by the Namibia Financial Institutions Supervisory Authority (NAMFISA), established through the Namibia Financial Institutions Supervisory Authority Act, Act No. 3 of 2001.[42] It is noteworthy that there are other financial institutions which do not fall under the purview of The Bank of Namibia or NAMFISA, and these are governed by the statutes under which they were established or fall under specific ministries to which they report.

The introduction of the New Equitable Economic Empowerment Framework (NEEEF) of 2008 was meant to increase the levels of financial participation and inclusion of the previously disadvantaged citizens. The NEEEF required private financial institutions to participate in financing the transformation of ownership and requires commercial financial institutions to regularly report the ways and levels of assistance to businesses owned by previously disadvantaged Namibians.[43] Based on these various legislative measures, one could argue that the Namibian Government is much committed to alleviating the high level of poverty which is around 28.7 percent, coupled with youth unemployment at 43.4 percent and national unemployment at 34 percent.[44] Further commitment of the Namibian Government in broadening the scope of financial inclusion was shown in 2012 with the enactment of legislation on the Namibian Financial Sector Strategy (NFSS), 2011–2021 by the Minister of Finance. In this regard, Namibia outlined its strategy as part of its broader financial sector strategy. The rationale of the strategy was mainly to address some of the inefficiencies which were witnessed in the delivery of financial services to the population by the financial services sector, hence the need to correct these anomalies and imbalances. In the same year (2012) the Financial Literacy Strategy was also introduced to educate Namibians regarding the availability of financial services so that they could make informed choices and decisions on financial matters.

NFSS was meant to create an inclusive financial sector that was supposed to be efficient, effective and competitive by 2021, accessible to the majority of the people who were previously excluded.[45] In 2014, the Namibian Government promulgated

---

[41] Haiyambo (2016), p. 44.

[42] Ibid.

[43] Government of the Republic of Namibia (2008).

[44] World Bank (2020).

[45] Matongela (2014), p. 173; Shiimi (2013).

the Determination on the Standards for a Basic Bank Account and Cash Deposit Fee within the National Payment System, that required banking institutions to provide at least one basic account to consumers, all cash deposits were supposed to be zero rated and finally all cash deposit fees for business accounts with an annual turnover of Namibian dollar one million or less were supposed to be zero rated.[46]

Furthermore, the main goals of the National Financial Sector Strategy were financial markets deepening and development, financial safety nets, financial inclusion, localisation of the financial sector and skills development in the financial sector. Ultimately, the main goal of financial inclusion was to make sure that financial services are availed to the greater segments of the Namibian population who previously had no access to financial services.

Driven by the desire to increase the level of financial inclusion, the Bank of Namibia in 2015 embarked on a programme that was targeted at the reduction of banking fees and other related charges which resulted in the introduction of basic bank accounts and discontinuation of cash deposits by commercial banks. All these developments were a result of the concerted efforts of the Bank of Namibia which came up with a regulatory framework called the National Payments System Vision 2015.

In terms of financial inclusion, Namibia has made great strides in this regard. Current statistics as provided by the 2017 financial inclusion report for Namibia highlights that 79.8 percent of eligible women are financially included, compared to 76.1 percent of eligible men.[47] Although Namibia has made significant progress in financial inclusion, challenges remain due to lack of collateral demanded by banks in advancing credit, as well as the low-income levels among citizens, which are a result of the high poverty levels in the country. The other challenges also include lack of appropriate financial products which suit the needs of the poor, physical barriers arising from the distance that one must walk to a bank branch, and inability to provide documentation, for instance an identity card as required by financial institutions as well as financial illiteracy.[48] Conclusively, one could argue that Namibia enacted legislation and implemented policies within the financial services sector domain which have been conducive for business since the sector has remained sound, stable and profitable over the years.

3.4   Zimbabwe

Prior to the introduction of the World Bank supported Economic Structural Adjustment Programme (ESAP) in 1991, the financial services sector in Zimbabwe was mostly dominated by foreign owned banks, with three major players namely

---

[46]Matongela (2014), p. 173.

[47]Namibia Statistics Agency (2017), p. 27.

[48]Matongela (2014), p. 172.

Barclays Bank, Standard Chartered Bank and Stanbic Bank (formerly Grindlays Bank). The sector is highly regulated by the Reserve Bank of Zimbabwe (Central bank), through the Reserve Bank of Zimbabwe Act, 1999 [Chapter 22:15] which empowered the central bank to supervise all commercial banking operations in the financial services sector. The advent of ESAP in 1991 led to financial liberalisation of the financial services sector resulting in the entry of new players mainly, domestic players culminating in the competitiveness of the sector.[49]

Financial liberalisation has had a positive impact on the financial services sector as well as financial inclusion. Prior studies have shown that by 2004, the country witnessed the largest number of commercial banks in history, that is 42 banks, which was mainly driven by the entry of indigenous banks. Further research[50] indicates that the increased number of financial players improved financial inclusion as banks penetrated through to access new and traditionally unbanked areas and individuals to enhance their market shares. The result of liberalisation was improved choice for products and services especially to people who were formally marginalised and could not access financial sector products and services.

On the contrary, deregulation brought about intense competition in the financial services sector and since most of the banks were owned by indigenous people who managed the banks as Chief Executive Officers, there were several compromises to corporate governance issues which resulted in nine banks being placed under curatorship in 2004 and by 2009, only 26 banks were remaining. The results of curatorship, mergers, and acquisitions in the sector driven by the desire to consolidate market position/share meant that several people were now financially excluded.[51]

Microfinancing has been viewed as one area which may increase the levels of financial inclusion. Microfinance institutions are involved in advancing loans to small and informal sector businesses. In line with the promotion of financial inclusion, in 2008, the Government of Zimbabwe (GoZ) promulgated the National Microfinance Policy through the Microfinance Act (Chapter 24: 29.)[52] The objectives of the policy were among others to promote the development of an inclusive financial sector, to promote synergy and mainstreaming of the informal sub-sector into the national financial system, and lastly to enhance the delivery of service by microfinance institutions especially to the economically active poor and small and medium enterprises (SMEs).[53]

The use of mobile money has been viewed as a way of contributing to financial inclusion especially for the rural poor and the unbanked population. However, it has been argued that the Zimbabwean mobile money market has not positively responded to changes in technology brought about by mobile money, coupled

---

[49]Masiyandima et al. (2017), p. 5.

[50]Ibid.

[51]Ibid.

[52]Makina et al. (2014), p. 22.

[53]Ibid.

with the fact that in Zimbabwe there is no specific legislation that regulates mobile money.[54] While the Banking Act (1999) governs the operations of mobile money that is offered by commercial banks, there is no express regulation of mobile money that is offered by telecommunication companies such as Econet, Telecel and NetOne. The effective regulation of mobile money is important since mobile money combines a telecommunication service on the one hand and a financial service on the other.[55]

Motivated by the desire to broaden financial inclusion, in 2016 Zimbabwe drafted a National Financial Inclusion Strategy (NFIS) (2016–2020) that was geared towards the promotion of access to and use of financial services by the country's unbanked individuals, coupled with enhancing financial inclusion of marginalised groups, such as the rural poor and women. The NFIS revolves around four key areas namely financial capability, financial innovation, financial consumer protection and microfinance. The NFIS was crafted to align with the SADC Financial Inclusion Strategy, 2016–2021.

Although there has been commendable progress in terms of financially including most people in the financial services sector, there were some barriers which constrained people from accessing such services.[56] However, for the purposes of the theme of this chapter, focus will be placed on regulatory barriers. Policy and regulatory frameworks have limitations in making sure that most people are financially included in the formal financial system. Some of the regulatory barriers include the absence of a coordinated policy and strategy on financial inclusion in terms of the parameters that should be followed. In addition, there is lack of clarity in the regulatory framework regarding how consumers should be protected legally by the financial system if consumers seek recourse to problems arising from the sector. In mitigating some of the challenges identified above, researchers argue that the GoZ should enact legislation and implement related policies that are geared towards the marginalized groups who are financially excluded such as the elderly, rural population, low-income earners, and women.[57] Furthermore, GoZ should also legislate a strong consumer protection regulatory framework to restore confidence in the financial system to enhance the level of consumer trust in the financial services system.[58]

---

[54] Chitimira and Torerai (2021), p. 22.

[55] Ibid.

[56] Reserve Bank of Zimbabwe (2016), p. 11.

[57] Barugahara (2021), p. 269.

[58] Ibid.

3.5   Comparative Analysis of Similarities and Differences in Financial Policies and Regulatory Frameworks for South Africa, Botswana, Namibia and Zimbabwe

Table 1 summarizes the various policies that were implemented as well as the regulatory frameworks that were enacted by the governments of the four countries under study in enhancing the levels of financial inclusion in their respective countries. It is quite evident from Table 1 that the four countries under study are concerned about the issue of financial inclusion, hence the enactment of various legislations in their jurisdictions to enhance the levels of financial inclusion.

4   Recommendations for Policy and Regulatory Frameworks for Financial Inclusion in SADC

The recommendations proffered here are made considering the shortcomings of the present policies and regulatory frameworks as they obtain mostly in the four countries under study. The variations in policy prescriptions in different states call for a more unified SADC financial inclusion strategy which has a major point of convergence. Considering this it will be incumbent upon SADC to make sure that there is an alignment between national and regional financial inclusion strategies. Already, Governments within SADC have crafted national financial inclusion policies in their respective states as alluded to earlier on regarding the countries under study. As a regional body, SADC will have to work with the states at a national level to make sure that there is alignment at regional policy regarding financial inclusion. It is commendable that the SADC Council of Ministers approved in August 2016 a SADC Financial Inclusion Strategy which is aimed at reducing the barriers to financial inclusion in the region.[59] The results from the regional strategy are yet to be realised.

Regulations at the national level should be explicit in terms of specifying partnerships, especially with non-governmental organisations in the quest to increase the levels of financial inclusion. Previous research confirms that these non-government entities are often better placed to lead on specific programmes based on their institutional flexibility and access to technical expertise and resources needed for implementation of interventions,[60] for instance Finmark Trust. Currently there are existing partnerships between Finmark Trust and SADC when it comes to capacity building, technical assistance and research and development which will be driven by the desire to increase the levels of financial inclusion. SADC member states need to pronounce such synergies in their regulatory frameworks especially regarding

---

[59]Finmark Trust (2018), p. 7.
[60]SADC (2016), p. 51.

Table 1 Policies and regulatory frameworks in the four selected SADC countries

Country	Policy and regulatory framework	Focus of policy and regulatory framework
South Africa	Black Economic Empowerment Act (2003)	Address historical imbalances and financially include the black majority.
	Financial Services Charter (2004)	Promote socio-economic integration, enhancement of financial inclusion, most especially the black majority.
	National Credit Act (2004)	Regulate consumer credit and improve dissemination of consumer information.
	Consumer Protection Act (2008)	Promote financial education and financial literacy, hence financial inclusion.
	Voluntary participation of banks (2008)	Creation of more than 6 million 'Mzansi' accounts to increase financial inclusion levels to most of the population.
	National Development Plan (2011)	Attain financial inclusion of 90% by 2030.
	Financial Sector Code (FSC) and Financial Sector Transformation Council (FSTC) (2012)	FSTC oversees the operations of the FSC and regulation of the financial services sector.
	Financial Sector Regulation Act (2017)	Establishment of a regulatory and supervisory framework that promotes financial inclusion.
	Financial Sector Conduct Authority (FSCA) (2017)	Fair treatment of customers by financial institutions, provide customers with financial education programmes.
Botswana	The Banking Act (1975)	The establishment of the Bank of Botswana as a regulatory institution to the financial services sector.
	The Financial Institutions Act (1975)	Provide for the licensing, control and regulation of financial institutions.
	The Banking Act (1995)	Enhance access to finance in Banks and reduce the role of government in the financial services sector. In the early 1980s, market was dominated by Barclays Bank and Standard Chartered Bank only.
	Non-Bank Financial Institution Regulatory Authority (NBFIRA) (2008)	Provided a new regulatory and institutional framework for all non-bank financial institutions.
	National Development 10 (2009)	Access to finance as an important component of financial development that aids financial inclusion.
	Financial Sector Development Strategy (2012), (2012–2016)	Modernize the regulatory structure, preparation of new legislation governing the regulation of banks,

(continued)

Table 1 (continued)

Country	Policy and regulatory framework	Focus of policy and regulatory framework
		insurance companies and pension funds.
	Botswana Financial Inclusion Roadmap (2015–2020)	Laid out Botswana's priorities for the enhancement of financial inclusion.
Namibia	Bank of Namibia Act (1997)	Establishment of Bank of Namibia regulating the operations of the banking sector.
	Namibia Financial Institutions Supervisory Authority Act (2001)	The creation of the Namibia Financial Institutions Supervisory Authority regulating non-bank financial institutions.
	New Equitable Economic Empowerment Framework (NEEEF) (2008)	To increase the levels of financial participation and inclusion of previously disadvantaged citizens.
	Namibian Financial Sector Strategy (NFSS) (2011–2021)	Address inefficiencies in the delivery of services to the population and deepen financial inclusion.
	Financial Literacy Strategy (2012)	Educate the population on the availability of financial services to make informed choices on financial matters.
	Determination on the Standards for a Basic Bank account and Cash Deposit fee in the Payments system (2014)	Banks to provide at least one bank account to consumers and all cash deposits to be zero rated.
Zimbabwe	The Economic Structural Adjustment Programme (ESAP) (1991)	Financial liberalization of the financial services sector.
	Reserve Bank of Zimbabwe Act (1999)	Empowerment of the central bank to regulate and supervise the operations of financial service providers.
	Banking Act [Chapter 24:20] 9 of 1999	To provide for the registration, supervision and regulation of persons conducting banking business and financial activities in Zimbabwe; to establish a deposit protection scheme to protect depositors in the event of the insolvency of a contributory institution.
	Microfinance Act (Chapter 24: 29) (2008)	Promote the development of an inclusive financial sector, to promote synergy and mainstreaming of the informal sub-sector into the national financial system.
	National Financial Inclusion Strategy (NFIS) (2016–2020)	Promotion of access to and use of financial services by the country's unbanked individuals.
	Banking (Money Transmission, Mobile Banking and Mobile Money	Seeks to coordinate mobile money services from different providers in a

(continued)

Table 1 (continued)

Country	Policy and regulatory framework	Focus of policy and regulatory framework
	Interoperability) Regulations, 2020 (Banking Regulations, 2020)	way that benefits the end user in Zimbabwe.[a]

Source: Authors' own compilation
[a] Chitimira and Torerai (2021), p. 15

research with Finmark Trust to enhance financial inclusion. At the regional level SADC would then coordinate the diverse efforts of member states to have a pronounced, visible regional financial inclusion strategy which is currently missing.

Furthermore, previous research confirms that national governments have a great role to play both at the national and regional level in facilitating, convening, and coordinating various stakeholders from both the public and private sectors in boosting financial inclusion. It has been argued that Governments are also best placed to create an enabling policy and regulatory environment to facilitate the entry of new players as well as products and services to drive financial inclusion[61] in the SADC region. Arguing from the field of Economics, based on demand and supply: An increase in the number of players in the financial services sector will result in more competition, which results in the prices of products and services falling. The price could relate to the cost of servicing loans or possibly be related to the cost of maintaining a bank account which falls because of the presence of many players in the market. If services and products are cheaper, they become easily accessible to consumers, hence enhancing financial inclusion.

Based on the cases discussed in this chapter, it was established that there is an absence of a coordinated national policy and strategy on financial inclusion. Even though member states within SADC have financial inclusion strategies in place, it was observed that the financial inclusion strategies and policies do not feed into the main national policies of the country concerned. This disconnect obliterates the financial inclusion efforts of a particular country. In view of this, it is imperative that national Governments should have a holistic and well-coordinated approach to financial inclusion, which should be clearly articulated in the national policies of a country.

At the regional level, it is recommended that SADC should establish parameters with The Group of Twenty (G20), (which accounts for more than 80% of the world Gross Domestic Product (GDP)), through which they could collaborate in terms of mutual partnerships especially in policy and regulatory frameworks regarding financial inclusion.[62] In 2010, the G20 came up with the Global Partnership for Financial Inclusion (GPFI) which is a platform for G20 and non-G20 members geared towards financial inclusivity across the globe especially to the financially excluded businesses and individuals through the implementation of policies and regulations that

---

[61] SADC (2016), p. 51.
[62] Lee (2013), p. 483.

facilitate financial inclusion. The GPFI's primary focus, which is the implementation of the G20 Financial Inclusion Action Plan (FIAP), is carried forward, for the purposes of policy and regulatory frameworks by two of its four Subgroups namely: Regulation and Standard-Setting Bodies, and Financial Consumer Protection and Financial Literacy.[63]

Based on the experiences of the G20 which is implementing the financial inclusion policies in the member states considering the regulations and protection of consumers, SADC could possibly implement some of the G20 policies which are benefitting the bloc. For instance, The Regulation and Standard-Setting Bodies (SSBs) Subgroup was at some point engaged in mainstreaming financial inclusion in the work of the SSBs by encouraging the incorporation of financial inclusion in financial sector assessments of the International Monetary Fund (IMF). Resultantly between 2014 and 2017 the SSBs assisted in the production of eleven documents which are critical to financial inclusion which were adopted by member states.

Previous research recommended the creation of a Regional Financial Inclusion Forum. The Forum could be constituted by SADC Banking Association, the Committee of Insurance, Securities and Non-banking Financial Authorities (CISNA), and the Committee of Central Bank Governors (CCBG) whose aim would be to provide an effective platform for deliberations, upon which to enhance greater financial inclusion in the region.[64] The relations and interaction that Committee members often have with government policymakers also position the SADC Secretariat well to secure commitment to drive financial inclusion at the national level. Considering that the SADC Secretariat has already initiated the regional financial inclusion strategy, it is imperative that the regional body intensify all its efforts in the realisation of regional integration by making sure that all member states participate in the envisaged Forum and accede to the objectives of the Forum.

Furthermore, legislation on consumer protection that is linked to financial inclusion is lacking in some SADC states. The Subgroup on Consumer Protection and Financial Literacy in the G20 worked on various initiatives which resulted in the publication of several reports which were critical in informing policy makers on implementation approaches for Financial Consumer Protection and Financial Literacy measures. Between 2014 and 2017 eleven countries in the G20 had implemented the National Financial strategies. Considering the preceding information, one would recommend that SADC member states adopt some of these Consumer Protection laws to be applied at national and regional levels since they have worked in the G20. The implementation of these policies could possibly be adapted to the SADC environment and adjusted where needed or as required.

Previous research on digital financial inclusion(digitisation) attests to the fact that it is a major element of economic development policies globally, hence should be considered in financial inclusion since more than 60 percent of the global population has access to digital financial services. In this regard, recommendations have been

---

[63] G20 (2017), p. 5.
[64] SADC (2016), p. 56.

made to the effect that digitisation which brings about new products, interfaces providers, and delivery mechanisms present specific risks and challenges to the financial sector. Therefore, policymakers must come up with a comprehensive package to tackle market challenges and reduce consumer risk.[65] The element of consumer risk should also be tackled in the relevant Consumer protection legislation that should be enacted within SADC member states which should provide recourse to aggrieved consumers in the event of disputes arising. Related to digitisation, for people to benefit from digital financial services SADC member states should institute robust payment systems, good physical infrastructure,[66] enact the appropriate regulations, and ensure that there are sufficient consumer protection laws and regulations.

Financial inclusion is a multi-sectoral approach which does not require the efforts of one specific ministry in a country. There is need to consult and work with other departments and ministries. For instance, in Botswana financial inclusion efforts should be based on the collaborative work of the Ministry of Finance and Economic Development, Ministry of Transport and Communications (especially for digitisation), Ministry of Investment, Trade and Industry, and other related departments such as the Department of Consumer Affairs (for the protection of consumers and consumer rights), as well as Botswana Communications Regulatory Authority (BOCRA). In this instance, BOCRA would complement the Ministry of Transport and Communications on the regulation of digital financial services. The Ministry of Finance and Economic Development, through the Bank of Botswana will have to craft policies which are favourable to the financial services sector while at the same time monitoring the activities and operations of the players in the banking sector. Therefore, financial inclusion policies and regulations should not only be left entirely under the responsibilities of the Ministry of Finance and Economic Development. This envisaged holistic approach to financial inclusion may be replicated in the other SADC member states, that is, Namibia, South Africa, and Zimbabwe employing similar Ministries and departments. Ultimately, these concerted efforts will pay off in terms of the enhancement of financial inclusion in each of the countries under study in this Chapter, as well as other SADC member states.

5   Conclusion

This chapter focused on the policy and regulatory frameworks for financial inclusion in the SADC region, focusing on four-member states namely Botswana, Namibia, South Africa, and Zimbabwe. Financial inclusion plays a critical role in poverty alleviation and addressing gender inequalities. In instances where people are given the opportunity to access financial services and products, that results in consumer

---

[65] Shipalana (2019), p. 24.
[66] Demirguc-Kunt et al. (2018).

choices in savings, investments, and access to loans. Consequently, financial inclusion enhances economic growth and stability of a country in which people have equal opportunity and access to financial services and products. It is noteworthy that member states in SADC have enacted financial inclusion policies which are country specific.

However, as evidenced in the chapter, there is a lack of homogeneity in terms of the applicable policies, laws and regulations which govern financial products and services at both the national and regional (SADC) level. In fact, there are no universal financial inclusion policies at the SADC level which can be adopted by the member states for the purposes of uniformity and standardisation. SADC should play a coordinating role in the harmonisation of country specific laws and align them to the regional level. In member states where financial inclusion policies are not evident, it should be incumbent upon SADC as a regional body to lobby these Governments to come up with such beneficial legislation.

Recommendations were proffered to the effect that SADC could adopt some of the Regulations for Standard-Setting bodies coupled with Consumer Protection laws promulgated by the G20, which have yielded positive results for the G20 member states between 2014 and 2017. Financial inclusion can only be enhanced in a conducive operating environment that should be created by Governments of various states in SADC. This calls for the crafting and enactment of friendly regulations and the implementation of policies that advance the use of financial products and services, thus eliminating the negative shocks of financial exclusion.

Bibliography

<https://finmark.org.za/system/documents/files/000/000/184/original/ME_Report.18.pdf?1601 965010>. Accessed 18 July 2021

Allen F, Klapper L, Demirgüç-Kunt A, Peria MSM (2016) The foundations of financial inclusion: understanding ownership and use of formal accounts. J Financ Intermed:18–27

Barajas A, Beck T, Belhaj M, Naceur SB (2020) Financial inclusion: what have we learned so far? What do we have to learn? International Monetary Fund, pp 1–51

Barugahara S (2021) Financial inclusion in Zimbabwe: determinants, challenges and opportunities. Int J Financ Res 12(3):261–270

Capital Resources (2009) Botswana Financial Sector Review, 2009/2010. Capital Resources. <https://www.econsult.co.bw/tempex/BOTSWANA%20FINANCIAL%20SECTOR%20 OVERVIEW.pdf>. Accessed 21 Jan 2021

Chibba M (2009) Financial inclusion, poverty reduction and the millennium development goals. Eur J Dev Res 21(2):213–230

Chitimira H, Ncube M (2020) Legislative and other selected challenges affecting financial inclusion for the poor and low-income earners in South Africa. J Afr Law 64(3):337–355

Chitimira H, Torerai E (2021) The nexus between mobile money regulation, innovative technology and the promotion of financial inclusion in Zimbabwe. Potchefstroom Electron Law J:1–33

Demirgüç-Kunt A, Klapper L, Singer D, Ansar S, Hess J (2020) The Global Findex Database 2017: measuring financial inclusion and opportunities to expand access to and use of financial services. World Bank Econ Rev:S2–S8

Evans O (2016) Determinants of financial inclusion in Africa: a dynamic panel data approach. Univ Mauritius Res J:1–24

Financial Sector Conduct Authority (2019) Financial Inclusion Strategy. <www.fsca.co.za>. Accessed 5 Jan 2021

Finmark Trust (2018) Measuring Progress: Financial Inclusion in SADC

G20 (2017) Global Partnership for Financial Inclusion: 2017 Financial Inclusion Action Plan

G20 (2020) Financial Inclusion Action Plan, pp 1–23

Government of the Republic of Namibia (2008) New Equitable Economic Empowerment Framework. <https://www.ecb.org.na/images/docs/Investor_Portal/NEEEF.pdf>. Accessed 10 Jan 2021

Haiyambo E (2016) An impact assessment of the regulation of microfinance institutions in Namibia. Doctoral Thesis, Stellenbosch University

Lee JW (2013) The contribution of foreign direct investment to clean energy use, carbon emissions and economic growth. Energy Policy:483–489

Makina D, Chiwunze G, Ndari E (2014) Financial inclusion strategies for making financial markets work for the poor in Zimbabwe. Zimbabwe Economic Policy Analysis and Research Unit, pp 1–43

Making Access Possible (2015) Botswana - demand, supply, policy and regulation. Diagnostic Final Report, pp 1–247

Matongela AM (2014) Understanding the state of financial inclusion in Namibia. Res J Finance Account 5(23):171–175

Mogomotsi GE, Madigele PK (2016) Improving financial inclusion of the socially and economically disadvantaged in Botswana through the Grameen Bank Microcredit Model. Botswana J Bus 9(1):55–65

Molefhi K (2019) Financial inclusion and its impact on employment creation in Botswana. Botswana Institute for Development Policy Analysis, pp 1–28

Namibia Statistics Agency (2017) Namibia Financial Inclusion Survey. Financial Inclusion Report of Namibia <www.https://cms2.my.na/assets/documents/NFIS_2017_Report.pdf>. Accessed 20 Nov 2020

Oji CK (2015) Promoting financial inclusion for inclusive growth in Africa. South African Institute of International Affairs, pp 1–18

Ozilli PK (2020) Financial inclusion research around the world: a review. Forum for Social Economics, pp 1–9

Reserve Bank of Zimbabwe (2016) National Financial Inclusion Strategy 2016-2020. Reserve Bank of Zimbabwe, pp 1–62

SADC (2016) SADC Financial Inclusion Strategy, pp 1–63

Sha'ban M, Girardone C, Sarkisyan A (2020) Cross-country variation in financial inclusion: a global perspective. Eur J Finance:319–340

Shipalana P (2019) Digitising financial services: a tool for financial inclusion in South Africa? South African Institute of International Affairs, pp 1–38

Sykes J, Elder S, Gurbuzer Y, Principi M (2016) Exploring the linkages between youth financial inclusion and job creation. Evidence from the ILO School-To-Work Transition Surveys: International Labour Organization

World Bank (2015) Botswana systematic country diagnostic. The World Bank Group, pp 1–125

World Bank (2017) Botswana Global Financial Inclusion. <https://datacatalog.worldbank.org/dataset/botswana-global-financial-inclusion-global-findex-database-2017>. Accessed 20 Feb 2021

World Bank (2020) <https://www.worldbank.org/en/country/namibia/overview>. Accessed 12 Jan 2021

Wyman O (2017) Accelerating financial inclusion in South-East Asia with digital finance. Asian Development Bank, pp 1–86

Tendai D. Svotwa holds a Bachelor of Business Studies *(Honours)*, a Master of Business Administration (MBA) degree from the University of Zimbabwe and a PhD in Business Management from North-West University, Mafikeng, South Africa. Dr Svotwa is also a seasoned banker with more than 12 years' experience working in the Corporate sector, mainly in the Treasury Department. He is also an accomplished researcher, having published extensively in peer reviewed journals and has presented at local and international Conferences such as Botswana, Namibia, South Africa, Tanzania, Morocco, and France. Dr Svotwa is also a renowned academic, who has taught at tertiary institutions since 2009, starting off his teaching career at the University of Zimbabwe. He is a Senior Lecturer at Botho University, Graduate Studies and Research Department, Gaborone, Botswana where he teaches and supervises postgraduate students. His research interests are in the fields of strategy, leadership, general management, entrepreneurship, family businesses and marketing management. He is a member of The European Academy of Management (EURAM), Africa Academy of Management (AFAM), South African Association of Public Administration and Management (SAAPAM), and a Life-time member of the Golden Key International Honour Society. In 2017, he was one of the two African scholars selected to represent Africa in Rabat, Morocco, at the PhD Doctoral Colloquium: EURAM Early Career Colloquium (EECC), facilitated by EURAM. Currently he is part of a 10-member team engaged as a Co-Country Investigator (CCI) in Botswana for the Global Leadership and Business Effectiveness (GLOBE) survey focusing on organisational culture, trust, and leadership in more than 110 countries across the globe.

Eukeria Wealth is an established, competent and proficient lecturer with more than 11 years teaching experience at university level. Eukeria holds the following qualifications; PhD Accounting Sciences, Master of Commerce in Accounting, Bachelor of Commerce in Accounting, Post Graduate Diploma in Tertiary Education (PDTE), Post Graduate Diploma in Applied Taxation (ICTAZ), Certified Public Accountant (ICPAZ), Certified Tax Accountant (ICTAZ), Registered and Practicing Accountant (RPAccZ) with PAAB. Eukeria is currently a senior lecturer in the School of Accounting, University of Namibia. She has specialised in Accounting and taxation, and her research interests include transfer pricing, taxation, financial inclusion and diversification. Before joining the university of Namibia, she was the Head of department for the department of Accounting at Midlands State University. Her flagship projects include (i) Accounting education for fourth industrial revolution accountants in Africa, commissioned by African Accounting and Finance Association (AAFA) in collaboration with Pan-African Federation of Accountants (PAFA) (2020), (ii) Experiences in the Zimbabwe Hotel Industry during Hyperinflation sponsored by the Macro-economic and Financial Management Institute of Eastern and Southern Africa (MEFMI) (2016), (ii) Illicit Trade, Economic Growth and the Role of Customs as commissioned by the World Customs Organisation (2014).

Charles Makanyeza is a senior academic, researcher and consultant who commands respect among his peers. At the time of writing, Charles has more than eleven years of teaching experience at university level, more than five years of experience in university administration, and more than ten years of industry experience. He holds the following qualifications: PhD Marketing, Executive MBA, MSc Marketing, Postgraduate Diploma in Project Management, BCom Marketing, Diploma in Agriculture, Certificate in International Computer Driving Licence (ICDL), and Training and Resources in Research Ethics Evaluation (TRREE) Certificates in Introduction to Research Ethics; Research Ethics Evaluation; Informed Consent; Good Clinical Practice; HIV Vaccine Trials; Adolescent Involvement in HIV Prevention Trials; Public Health Research Ethics; and South Africa. Charles is currently an Associate Professor of Marketing and Strategy at the Namibia Business School, University of Namibia. His specialisation and research areas of interest include marketing, strategy, entrepreneurship and quantitative research. Before joining the University of Namibia, he served as Director of the Graduate Business School, Acting Dean, Deputy Dean, Programme Coordinator, Associate Professor, Senior Lecturer and Lecturer at Chinhoyi University of Technology. Charles has also served as a Senior Lecturer and Lecturer and various institutions both full-time and part-time. His recent key projects include (i) Causes of lack of professionalism and poor organisational performance at Apple Valley Primary School and appropriate solutions (ii) Conducted, in partnership with CeDRE International Africa, an evaluation of the project on strengthening smallholder farmer incomes and rural social infrastructure in Chimanimani district of Zimbabwe in 2016. The project was commissioned by the TSURO Trust in cooperation with BFDW – EED. The major components of the project were on transparent community planning, monitoring and governance processes, community managed social and health care, local healthy food products and market development.